Student, Parent, Teacher
Internet Resources

Science Online ca8.msscience.com

Access your Student Edition on the Internet so you don't need to bring your textbook home every night. You can link to features and get additional practice with these Online Study Tools.

Check out the following features on your **Online Learning Center:**

Study Tools

Concepts In Motion
- Interactive Tables
- Interactive Time Line
- Animated Illustrations
- Lesson Self-Check Quizzes
- Chapter Test Practice
- Standardized Test Practice

- Vocabulary PuzzleMaker
- Interactive Tutor
- Interactive Tutor
- Multilingual Science Glossary
- Study to Go
- Online Student Edition
- **Brain POP** BrainPop Movies

Extensions

- Virtual Labs
- Microscopy Links
- Periodic Table Links
- Career Links

- Prescreened Web Links
- WebQuest Project
- Science Fair Ideas
- Internet Labs

For Teachers

- Teacher Bulletin Board
- Teaching Today, and much more!

Safety Symbols

These safety symbols are used in laboratory and field investigations in this book to indicate possible hazards. Learn the meaning of each symbol and refer to this page often. *Remember to wash your hands thoroughly after completing lab procedures.*

SAFETY SYMBOLS	HAZARD	EXAMPLES	PRECAUTION	REMEDY
DISPOSAL	Special disposal procedures need to be followed.	certain chemicals, living organisms	Do not dispose of these materials in the sink or trash can.	Dispose of wastes as directed by your teacher.
BIOLOGICAL	Organisms or other biological materials that might be harmful to humans	bacteria, fungi, blood, unpreserved tissues, plant materials	Avoid skin contact with these materials. Wear mask or gloves.	Notify your teacher if you suspect contact with material. Wash hands thoroughly.
EXTREME TEMPERATURE	Objects that can burn skin by being too cold or too hot	boiling liquids, hot plates, dry ice, liquid nitrogen	Use proper protection when handling.	Go to your teacher for first aid.
SHARP OBJECT	Use of tools or glassware that can easily puncture or slice skin	razor blades, pins, scalpels, pointed tools, dissecting probes, broken glass	Practice common-sense behavior and follow guidelines for use of the tool.	Go to your teacher for first aid.
FUME	Possible danger to respiratory tract from fumes	ammonia, acetone, nail polish remover, heated sulfur, moth balls	Make sure there is good ventilation. Never smell fumes directly. Wear a mask.	Leave foul area and notify your teacher immediately.
ELECTRICAL	Possible danger from electrical shock or burn	improper grounding, liquid spills, short circuits, exposed wires	Double-check setup with teacher. Check condition of wires and apparatus. Use GFI-protected outlets.	Do not attempt to fix electrical problems. Notify your teacher immediately.
IRRITANT	Substances that can irritate the skin or mucous membranes of the respiratory tract	pollen, moth balls, steel wool, fiberglass, potassium permanganate	Wear dust mask and gloves. Practice extra care when handling these materials.	Go to your teacher for first aid.
CHEMICAL	Chemicals that can react with and destroy tissue and other materials	bleaches such as hydrogen peroxide; acids such as sulfuric acid, hydrochloric acid; bases such as ammonia, sodium hydroxide	Wear goggles, gloves, and an apron.	Immediately flush the affected area with water and notify your teacher.
TOXIC	Substance may be poisonous if touched, inhaled, or swallowed.	mercury, many metal compounds, iodine, poinsettia plant parts	Follow your teacher's instructions.	Always wash hands thoroughly after use. Go to your teacher for first aid.
FLAMMABLE	Open flame may ignite flammable chemicals, loose clothing, or hair.	alcohol, kerosene, potassium permanganate, hair, clothing	Avoid open flames and heat when using flammable chemicals.	Notify your teacher immediately. Use fire safety equipment if applicable.
OPEN FLAME	Open flame in use, may cause fire.	hair, clothing, paper, synthetic materials	Tie back hair and loose clothing. Follow teacher's instructions on lighting and extinguishing flames.	Always wash hands thoroughly after use. Go to your teacher for first aid.

 Eye Safety Proper eye protection must be worn at all times by anyone performing or observing science activities.

 Clothing Protection This symbol appears when substances could stain or burn clothing.

 Animal Safety This symbol appears when safety of animals and students must be ensured.

 Handwashing After the lab, wash hands with soap and water before removing goggles.

Focus On Physical Science

Glencoe Science

CALIFORNIA
GRADE
8

NATIONAL
GEOGRAPHIC
ca8.msscience.com

Mc Graw Hill **Glencoe**

New York, New York   Columbus, Ohio   Chicago, Illinois   Peoria, Illinois   Woodland Hills, California

Glencoe Science

Focus On Physical Science

The Palomar Observatory in north San Diego County is home to many telescopes including the Hale Telescope. The 5.1m Hale Telescope is used nightly for astronomical studies.

Science Online ca8.msscience.com

Check out the following features on your
Online Learning Center:

Study Tools

- Concepts In Motion
  - Interactive Tables
  - Interactive Time Line
  - Animated Illustrations
- Lesson Self-Check Quizzes
- Chapter Test Practice
- Standardized Test Practice
- Vocabulary PuzzleMaker
- Interactive Tutor
- Multilingual Science Glossary
- Study to Go
- Online Student Edition
- BrainPop Movies

Extensions

- Virtual Labs
- Microscopy Links
- Periodic Table Links
- Career Links
- Prescreened Web Links
- WebQuest Project
- Science Fair Ideas
- Internet Labs

For Teachers

- Teacher Bulletin Board
- Teaching Today, and much more!

 **Glencoe**

The *McGraw-Hill* Companies

Send all inquiries to:
Glencoe/McGraw-Hill
8787 Orion Place
Columbus, OH 43240-4027

ISBN-13: 978-0-07-879440-7
ISBN-10: 0-07-879440-4

Printed in the United States of America.

2 3 4 5 6 7 8 9 10 079/043 11 10 09 08 07

Contents in Brief

Introduction to Investigation and
Experimentation 2

9.a, 9.b, 9.c, 9.e, 9.f, 9.g

Unit 1
Motion and Forces **42**

1.a, 1.b, 1.c, 1.d, 1.e, 1.f, 9.b, 9.d, 9.e, 9.f

Chapter 1 Motion 44

2.a, 2.b, 2.c, 2.d, 2.e, 2.f, 9.a, 9.d, 9.g

Chapter 2 Forces 84

8.a, 8.b, 8.c, 8.d, 9.f

Chapter 3 Density and Buoyancy 126

Unit 2
Structure of Matter **168**

Chapter 4 Understanding the Atom 170

3.a, 3.f, 7.b, 9.e

Chapter 5 Combining Atoms and Molecules . 214

3.a, 3.b, 3.c, 3.f, 7.c, 9.a, 9.e

Chapter 6 States of Matter 250

3.d, 3.e, 9.e, 9.g

Chapter 7 The Periodic Table and
Physical Properties 286

3.f, 5.d, 7.a, 7.b, 7.c, 9.a, 9.e

Unit 3
Chemical Interactions **332**

Chapter 8 Chemical Reactions 334

3.b, 3.f, 5.a, 5.b, 5.c, 7.c, 9.a, 9.e

Chapter 9 Acids and Bases in Solution 376

5.e, 7.c, 9.a, 9.b, 9.e

Chapter 10 Chemistry of Living Systems 418

3.c, 6.a, 6.b, 6.c, 9.c

Unit 4
Earth in Space **456**

Chapter 11 Our Solar System 458

2.g, 4.c, 4.d, 4.e, 9.a, 9.e

Chapter 12 Stars and Galaxies 504

2.g, 4.a, 4.b, 4.c, 4.d, 9.d

Teacher Advisory Board

The California Science Teacher Advisory Board provided valuable input in the development of the 2007 edition of *Focus On Physical Science.* They helped create the scope and sequence of the Student Edition, provided content and pedagogical comments, and provided feedback for the Teacher Wraparound Edition.

Charles Beecroft
8th Grade Science
   Teacher
Columbia School District
Redding, CA

Douglas Fisher
Director of Professional
   Development
City Heights Educational
   Collaborative
San Diego, CA

Patricia Juárez
Coordinator III
Sacramento City Unified
   School District
Sacramento, CA

Tom Castro
Science Teacher
Martinez JHS/
   Martinez USD
Martinez, CA

Mindi Fisher
Leadership Team
   Administrator
Peninsula Union School
   District
Samoa, CA

Kathy Molnar
Professional
   Development Mentor
Etiwanda School District
Etiwanda, CA

Lisa L. Cordes
Science Department
   Chair
Rivera Middle School/
   El Rancho USD
Pico Rivera, CA

Frederick W. Freking
Faculty Advisor
University of California,
   Los Angeles
Los Angeles, CA

Carol Orton
Teacher
Bernardo Heights
   Middle School
San Diego, CA

**Justin Cunningham
EdD**
Coordinator, Small
   School District Services
San Diego, County Office
   of Education
San Diego, CA

Nancy Frey
Associate Professor of
   Literacy
San Diego State
   University
San Diego, CA

Joycalyn Peoples
Science Specialist
Riverside Unified School
   District
Riverside, CA

Richard Filson
Science Department
   Chair
Edison High School,
   Stockton Unified
   School District
Stockton, CA

Maria C. Grant
Teacher
Hoover High School/
   San Diego City School
   and San Diego State
   University
San Diego, CA

Wendi L. Rodriguez
Teacher
Heritage/Snowline JUSD
Phelan, CA

Bruce Fisher
Distinguished Teacher
   in Residence
Humboldt State
   University
Arcata, CA

Patrick Horton
Science Teacher
Day Creek Intermediate
   School
Etiwanda, CA

Gladys Sorensen
Science Department
   Chair
Patrick Henry Middle
   School
Grenada Hills, CA

Patty Horton
Professional
   Development Provider
Etiwanda School District
Etiwanda, CA

Granger B. Ward
California
   Superintendent and
   Former Science Teacher
San Diego, CA

Acknowledgements

Authors

 Science Online Learn more about the authors at ca8.msscience.com.

Laurel Dingrando, MAT
Secondary Science Coordinator
Garland Independent School District
Garland, TX

Douglas Fisher, PhD
Director of Professional Development and Professor
City Heights Educational Collaborative, San Diego State University
San Diego, CA

Jennifer Gonya, PhD
Science Content Consultant
The Ohio State University
Columbus, OH

David G. Haase, PhD
Professor of Physics and Director of The Science House
North Carolina State University
Raleigh, NC

Cindy Klevickis, PhD
Professor of Integrated Science and Technology
James Madison University
Harrisonburg, VA

Isaac Turiel, PhD
Retired Staff Scientist
Lawrence Berkeley National Laboratory,
Berkeley, CA

Margaret K. Zorn, MS
Science Writer
Yorktown, VA

Dinah Zike, MEd
Educational Consultant
Dinah-Might Activities, Inc.
San Antonio, TX

NATIONAL GEOGRAPHIC

National Geographic
Education Division
Washington, D.C.

Series Consultants

Content consultants reviewed the chapters in their area of expertise and provided suggestions for improving the effectiveness of the science instruction.

Science Consultants

Richard Allen, PhD
University of California, Berkeley
Berkeley, CA

Karamjeet Arya, PhD
San Jose State University
San Jose, CA

Teaster Baird, PhD
San Francisco State University
San Francisco, CA

Natalie Batalha, PhD
San Jose State University
San Jose, CA

Robin Bennett, MS
University of Washington
Seattle, WA

William B. N. Berry, PhD
University of California, Berkeley
Berkeley, CA

Diane Clayton, PhD
NASA
Santa Barbara, CA

Susan Crawford, PhD
California State University
Sacramento, CA

Stephen F. Cunha, PhD
Humboldt State University
Arcata, CA

Jennifer A. Dever, PhD
University of San Francisco
San Francisco, CA

Alejandro Garcia, PhD
San Jose State University
San Jose, CA

Alan Gishlick, PhD
National Center for Science Education
Oakland, CA

Juno Hsu, PhD
University of California, Irvine
Irvine, CA

Martha Jagucki, MS
Geologist
Columbus, OH

Lee Kats, PhD
Pepperdine University
Malibu, CA

Christopher Kim, PhD
Chapman University
Orange, CA

Monika Kress, PhD
San Jose State University
San Jose, CA

Steve Lund, PhD
University of Southern California
Los Angeles, CA

Michael Manga, PhD
University of California, Berkeley
Berkeley, CA

Kate Schafer, PhD
Aquamarine Research
Mountain View, CA

Julio G. Soto, PhD
San Jose State University
San Jose, CA

Acknowledgements

Dr. Edward Walton
California Polytechnical Institute
Pomona, CA

VivianLee Ward
National Health Museum
Washington, DC

Math Consultant

Grant Fraser, PhD
California State University
Los Angeles, CA

Reading Consultant

ReLeah Cossett Lent
Author/Educational Consultant
Alford, FL

Safety Consultant

Jeff Vogt, MEd
Federal Hocking Middle School
Stewart, OH

Series Teacher Reviewers

Each Teacher Reviewer reviewed at least two chapters, providing feedback and suggestions for improving the effectiveness of the science instruction.

Joel Austin
Roosevelt Middle School
San Francisco, CA

Nicole Belong
Coronado Middle School
Coronado, CA

Patrick Brickey
Lakeview Junior High School
Santa Maria, CA

Mary Pilles Bryant
Henry J. Kaiser High School
Fontana, CA

Edward Case
Washington Academic Middle School
Sanger, CA

Monaliza Chian
E. O. Green Junior High School
Oxnard, CA

Valesca Lopez Dwyer
Park View Middle School
Yucaipa, CA

Kathryn Froman
North Davis Elementary School
Davis, CA

Brian Gary
Margaret Landell Elementary
Cypress, CA

Jeanette George-Becker
Roosevelt Elementary School
San Gabriel, CA

Bret Harrison
Frank Ledesma Elementary
Soledad, CA

Rick Hoffman
Kastner Intermediate School
Fresno, CA

Kimberly Klein
Barstow Intermediate School
Barstow, CA

David Kulka
South Peninsula Hebrew Day School
Sunnyvale, CA

Christina Lambie
Highland Elementary School
Richmond, CA

Kathleen Magnani
Center Junior High School
Antelope, CA

Tara McGuigan
Monroe Clark Middle School
San Diego, CA

Shelia Patterson
K–12 Alliance-California
Oceano, CA

Sharon Pendola
St. Albans Country Day School
Roseville, CA

Lori Poublon-Ramirez
Herman Intermediate School
San Jose, CA

Martha Romero
E. O. Green Junior High School
Oxnard, CA

Arlene Sackman
Earlimart Middle School
Earlimart, CA

Rex Scates
Herman Intermediate School
San Jose, CA

Robert Sherriff
Winston Churchill Middle School
Carmichael, CA

Maria Mendez Simpson
School Programs Coordinator/ Birch Aquarium
La Jolla, CA

Lorre Stange
Laytonville Elementary School
Laytonville, CA

Louann Talbert
Laytonville Middle School
Laytonville, CA

Gina Marie Turcketta
St. Joan of Arc School
Los Angeles, CA

Table of Contents

Introduction to Investigation and Experimentation.................... 2   `9.a, 9.b, 9.c, 9.e, 9.f, 9.g`

What is science? 2   `9.b`

Tools of the Physical Scientist 7   `9.a, 9.b, 9.c, 9.e, 9.f, 9.g`

Case Study: Wind Turbines for the Birds 34   `9.a, 9.c, 9.f`

Unit 1 Motion and Forces...42

Chapter 1
Motion................................. 44   `California Standards`

Lesson 1 Determining Position 48   1.a

Lesson 2 Speed, Velocity, and Acceleration 56   1.b, 1.c, 1.d, 1.e, 9.b, 9.f

Lesson 3 Graphing Motion..................... 64   1.f, 9.d, 9.e

Standards Assessment 82–83

Chapter 2
Forces 84

Lesson 1 Combining Forces 88   2.a, 2.b, 2.c, 9.g

Lesson 2 Types of Forces..................... 96   2.d

Lesson 3 Unbalanced Forces and Acceleration 106   2.d, 2.e, 2.f, 9.a, 9.d

Standards Assessment 124–125

Chapter 3
Density and Buoyancy 126

Lesson 1 Density 130   8.a, 8.b, 9.f

Lesson 2 Pressure and the Buoyant Force........ 140   8.c

Lesson 3 Sinking and Floating 150   8.d, 9.f

Standards Assessment 164–165

Read on Your Own.................... 166

Unit Test 167

Spiny box fish

Table of Contents

Unit 2 Structure of Matter............................168

Chapter 4
Understanding the Atom................ 170

California Standards

Lesson 1 Atoms—Basic Units of Matter.........174   3.a

Lesson 2 Discovering Parts of the Atom.........182   3.a

Lesson 3 Elements, Isotopes, and Ions—How Atoms Differ........................195   3.f, 7.b, 9.e

Standards Assessment 212–213

Chapter 5
Combining Atoms and Molecules.........214

Lesson 1 How Atoms Form Compounds........218   3.a, 3.b, 3.f

Lesson 2 Forming Solids.....................230   3.b, 3.c, 7.c, 9.a, 9.e

Standards Assessment 248–249

Atomic force micrograph of yttrium oxide molecules

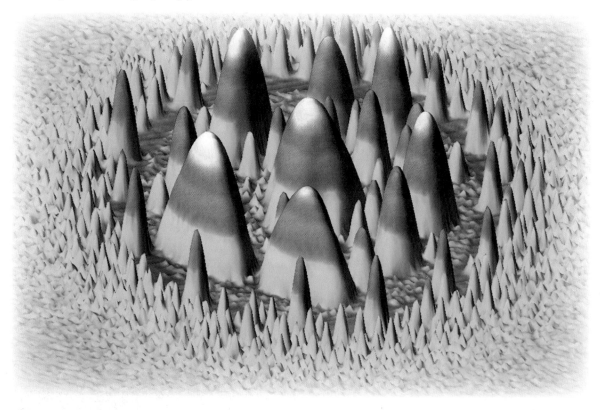

Table of Contents

Chapter 6
States of Matter 250

California Standards

Lesson 1 Solids, Liquids, and Gases.............254   3.d, 3.e

Lesson 2 Changes in States of Matter 261   3.d, 3.e, 9.e, 9.g

Standards Assessment 284–285

Chapter 7
The Periodic Table and Physical Properties 286

Lesson 1 Organization of the Periodic Table 290   3.f, 7.a

Lesson 2 Isotopes and Radioactivity 301   7.a, 7.b, 9.e

Lesson 3 Physical Properties and Changes 313   5.d, 7.c, 9.a

Standards Assessment 328–329

Read on Your Own..................... 330

Unit Test 331

Unit 3 Chemical Interactions...332

Chapter 8
Chemical Reactions 334

Lesson 1 Chemical Properties and Changes 338   3.f, 5.a, 7.c

Lesson 2 Chemical Equations..................346   3.b, 3.f, 5.b

Lesson 3 Energy and Chemical Changes.........358   5.c, 9.a, 9.e

Standards Assessment 374–375

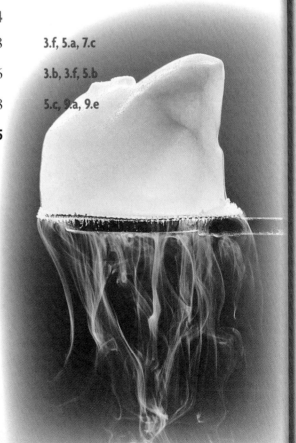

Dry ice sublimating

Table of Contents

Chapter 9
Acids and Bases in Solution **376**

California Standards

Lesson 1 Solutions 380   7.c, 9.e

Lesson 2 Acidic, Basic, and Neutral Solutions 394   5.e, 9.a, 9.b, 9.e

Standards Assessment **416–417**

Chapter 10
Chemistry of Living Systems **418**

Lesson 1 Chemistry of Life 422   6.b, 6.c

Lesson 2 Carbon Compounds 428   3.c, 6.a, 6.b

Lesson 3 Compounds of Life 438   6.c, 9.c

Standards Assessment **452–453**

Read on Your Own **454**
Unit Test **455**

Unit 4 Earth in Space **456**

Chapter 11
Our Solar System **458**

Lesson 1 Structures of the Solar System 462   2.g, 4.c, 4.d, 4.e

Lesson 2 The Sun-Earth-Moon System 472   4.d

Lesson 3 The Planets and Their Moons 478   4.d, 4.e, 9.e

Lesson 4 Asteroids, Comets, and Meteoroids 489   4.c, 4.e, 9.a

Standards Assessment **502–503**

The Sun

Table of Contents

Chapter 12
Stars and Galaxies **504**

California Standards

Lesson 1 Stars 508   4.b, 4.c, 4.d

Lesson 2 How Stars Shine .519   2.g, 4.d

Lesson 3 Galaxies 528   4.a, 4.b, 4.c, 9.d

 Standards Assessment **544–545**

Read on Your Own **546**
Unit Test **547**

At-Home Standards Practice **548**

Galaxy NGC 3310 as viewed through the Hubble telescope.

Table of Contents

Student Resources...........570

Science Safety Skill Handbook 572

Technology Skill Handbook 575

Math Skill Handbook
  Math Review........................579
  Science Applications 589

Reference Handbook
  Using a Calculator 594

Understanding Scientific Terms 595
Science Reference Guide 597
Physical Science Reference Tables 598
Periodic Table of the Elements...........600

English/Spanish Glossary 602
Index 614
Credits...........................624

The Japanese bullet train can travel at speeds up to 260 km/h.

BrainPOP Movies

To view BrainPOP Movies go to ca8.msscience.com. The features listed here correlate to their respective chapter's science content.

BrainPOP Movies

Title	Chapter-Lesson
Acceleration	1-2
Newton's Laws of Motion	2-1
Atomic Model	4-2
Isotopes	4-3
Matter Changing State	6-1
States of Matter	6-2
Property Changes	8-1
Acids and Bases	9-2
Tides	11-2
Solar System	11-3

Real World Science

The features listed here correlate to their respective chapter's science content.

Chapter/ Page	Science & Career	Science & Technology	Science & History	Science & Society
1 *76–77*	Automobile Designer	GPS Shows the Way	Galileo and Scientific Theories	Henry Ford and the Assembly Line
2 *118–119*	Rocket Scientist	Hi-Tech Roller Coasters	Isaac Newton: Bestselling Author?	What keeps a bridge from falling down?
3 *158–159*	Can ice cubes sink in water?	Biodiesel	Cannery Row	Los Angeles Smog
4 *206–207*	Chien-Shiung Wu	Nuclear Power	Three Mile Island Accident	Dropping the Atomic Bomb
5 *242–243*	CFCs and the Ozone Layer	Sweeter Than Sugar	Discovering DNA's Structure	The Human Genome Project
6 *278–279*	New and Improved	World Record Holder	Statistical Matters	A Cool Way To Go
7 *322–323*	The Chemistry of Color	Superconductors	Uses of Lead in History	Fluoridation of Drinking Water
8 *368–369*	Hazardous Materials Specialist	Green Chemistry at Work	Soft Drinks, Erasers, and More	The Nose Knows
9 *410–411*	Yuan T. Lee	Acid Rain Prevention	Gilbert N. Lewis	Acetylsalicylic Acid
10 *446–447*	Something in the Air...	Now, Spit!	What do you mean by that?	Labeling Trans Fat
11 *496–497*	Designing the New Generation of Spacecraft	The Search for Extra-Solar Planets	Johannes Kepler's Revolutionary Laws	Deadly Impact
12 *538–539*	Stephen Hawking: An Extraordinary Mind	Adaptive Optics	Kepler's Supernova	Watching the Heat

Labs

Labs

Labs

California Standards

Chapter 3 A Homemade Hydrometer 156–157   **8.d, 9.f**

Chapter 5 Growing Crystals 240–241   **3.c, 9.a**

Chapter 6 Does change of state take longer for some liquids? 276–277   **9.e**

Chapter 7 Investigating Physical Changes 320–321   **7.c, 9.a**

Chapter 10 Polarity and Living Systems 444–445   **6.c, 9.c**

Chapter 11 Model the Solar System 494–495   **4.c, 9.a**

Design Your Own Labs

Chapter 1 Graphing Motion 74–75   **1.f, 9.e**

Chapter 2 Comparing Mass and Weight 116–117   **2.d, 9.a, 9.d**

Chapter 4 Build an Atom...............................204–205   **3.a**

Chapter 8 Dirty Jewelry 366–367   **5.a, 9.a**

Chapter 9 Solubility and pH 408–409   **5.e, 9.a, 9.e**

Chapter 12 A Star is Born 536–537   **4.b, 4.d**

Labs

Launch Labs

California Standards

Chapter 1	How do you get there from here?	45	1.a, 9.b
Chapter 2	Can you feel the force?	85	2.c
Chapter 3	Can you push the beach ball under water?	127	8.c
Chapter 4	What's in the box?	171	3.a
Chapter 5	What do structures made of atoms look like?	215	3.b
Chapter 6	Model for Particle Movement	251	3.e
Chapter 7	Which element are you?	287	3.f
Chapter 8	Can you see a chemical reaction taking place?	335	5.a
Chapter 9	Where's that bubble?	377	5.e
Chapter 10	What is a life chemical?	419	6.b
Chapter 11	How do you measure distance?	459	9.b
Chapter 12	How far away are the stars and how many are there?	505	2.g, 4.a, 4.b, 4.c

MiniLabs

California Standards

Chapter 1	Negative Positions	49	1.a
	Can you measure average speed?	63	1.b, 9.b
Chapter 2	Can you measure the force of friction?	105	2.a, 2.d
	Does water exert a force?	110	2.e
Chapter 3	Can you feel the buoyant force?	149	8.c
	Do cold things float?	155	8.d
Chapter 4	How big are the particles in an atom? (Try at Home)	181	3.a
	How do electrons move?	186	3.a
Chapter 5	How can you model molecules? (Try at Home)	229	3.b
Chapter 6	Observing Fluid Motion (Try at Home)	255	3.e
	Sensing Evaporation	268	3.e
Chapter 7	Can you guess the element?	300	3.f
	Which parachute will drop first?	319	7.c, 9.a
Chapter 8	How can you tell a chemical change from a physical change?	345	5.a
	Can you model the burning of methane?	357	3.b, 5.b

MiniLabs (continued)

			California Standards
Chapter 9	How can you determine pH?	406	5.e, 9.b
Chapter 10	How much water is in celery? (Try at Home)	425	6.c
	Modeling Organic Compounds	434	6.a
Chapter 11	How do planets move?	464	4.d
	How does the Moon change its shape in the sky? (Try at Home)	477	4.d
	How do craters appear? (Try at Home)	492	4.e

DataLabs

			California Standards
Chapter 1	How can a graph show relative positions? (Try at Home)	55	1.a
	What can you learn from a graph? (Try at Home)	73	1.f, 9.d
Chapter 2	Can you add vertical forces?	95	2.c, 9.g
Chapter 3	Can you calculate the density?	139	8.b, 9.f
Chapter 4	How do atoms differ? (Try at Home)	203	3.a, 3.f, 9.e
Chapter 5	How are ionic radii and lattice energies of salts related? (Try at Home)	239	3.b, 9.e
Chapter 6	How are boiling point and atmospheric pressure related? (Try at Home)	274	3.d, 9.g
Chapter 7	How can you show a visual explanation of half-life? (Try at Home)	312	7.b, 9.e
Chapter 8	Where does the tablet go?	348	5.b
	How does temperature change as chemicals react? (Try at Home)	364	5.c, 9.e
Chapter 9	How do solubilities differ? (Try at Home)	393	7.c, 9.e
Chapter 10	Which fat is healthy for you? (Try at Home)	443	6.c, 9.e
Chapter 11	How large are the planets? (Try at Home)	485	4.e, 9.e
Chapter 12	Can you identify elements in a star?	517	4.d
	How fast is the universe expanding?	535	4.c

 This lab might be performed at home.

Math & Language Arts

The California Science, Math and Language Arts correlations for these features can be found on the referenced page.

Get Ready to Read

Chapter 1 Preview 46
Chapter 2 Identify the Main Idea 86
Chapter 3 New Vocabulary 128
Chapter 4 Monitor. 172
Chapter 5 Visualize 216
Chapter 6 Questioning 252
Chapter 7 Make Predictions 288
Chapter 8 Identify Cause and Effect. 336
Chapter 9 Make Connections. 378
Chapter 10 Summarize. 420
Chapter 11 Compare and Contrast 460
Chapter 12 Make Inferences 506

Target Your Reading

Chapter 1 47
Chapter 2 87
Chapter 3 129
Chapter 4 173
Chapter 5 217
Chapter 6 253
Chapter 7 289
Chapter 8 337
Chapter 9 379
Chapter 10 421
Chapter 11 461
Chapter 12 507

Applying Math

Chapter 1 Using the Speed Equation to Find Distance and Time 62
Chapter 2 Finding Force and Acceleration 115
Chapter 3 Solve for Volume. 135
Using the Density Equation to Find Mass and Volume 138
Solve for Pressure 142
Chapter 4 Mass of Subatomic Particles 180
Chapter 5 Formula Units 238
Chapter 6 Packing Efficiency. 275
Chapter 7 Isotope Half-Life Conversions 311
Chapter 8 Calculate Change in Heat of a Reaction 365
Chapter 9 Comparing pH Values. 407
Chapter 10 Bond Angles in Organic Chemistry . . . 437
Chapter 11 Parts of an Elliptical Orbit 471
Chapter 12 Brightness of Stars 518

A Guide to California Standards

For Students and Their Families

What is the purpose of the California Content Standards?

Content standards were designed to encourage the highest achievement of every student, by defining the knowledge, concepts, and skills that students should acquire at each grade level.

This Guide Contains:

Science Content Standards, Grade 8 and Correlations xx

Math Content Standards, Grade 8 xxvi

English-Language Arts Content Standards, Grade 8 . . . xxviii

California State Capitol Building, Sacramento

CALIFORNIA REPUBLIC

California Science Content Standards

Grade 8 Focus On Physical Science

The science curriculum in grade eight emphasizes the study of physical sciences. Students in grade eight study topics in physical sciences, such as motion, forces, and the structure of matter, by using a quantitative, mathematically based approach similar to the procedures they will use in high school. Earth, the solar system, chemical reactions, the chemistry of biological processes, the periodic table, and density and buoyancy are additional topics that will be treated with increased mathematical rigor, again in anticipation of high school courses. Students should begin to grasp four concepts that help to unify physical sciences: force and energy; the laws of conservation; atoms, molecules, and the atomic theory; and kinetic theory. Those concepts serve as important organizers that will be required as students continue to learn science. Although much of the science called for in the standards is considered "classical" physics and chemistry, it should provide a powerful basis for understanding modern science and serve students as well as adults.

Mastery of the eighth-grade physical sciences content will greatly enhance the ability of students to succeed in high school science classes. Modern molecular biology and earth sciences, as well as chemistry and physics, require that students have a good understanding of the basics of physical sciences. Items within the text that relate to a Science Content Standard will be represented like this: 2.b

California Science Content Standards

Correlated to *Focus On Physical Science*

Science Content Standards	Page Numbers
Motion	
1. The velocity of an object is the rate of change of its position. As a basis for understanding this concept:	
1.a Students know position is defined in relation to some choice of a standard reference point and a set of reference directions.	**48–49,** 51–52
1.b Students know that average speed is the total distance traveled divided by the total time elapsed and that the speed of an object along the path traveled can vary.	**56–58,** 63, 66, 68
1.c Students know how to solve problems involving distance, time, and average speed.	**56,** 61, **62,** 67, 80, 81
1.d Students know the velocity of an object must be described by specifying both the direction and the speed of the object.	**59,** 89, 107, 108, 109
1.e Students know changes in velocity may be due to changes in speed, direction, or both.	**60,** 92, 93, 107, 108, 109
1.f Students know how to interpret graphs of position versus time and graphs of speed versus time for motion in a single direction.	**64–71**

Bold page numbers indicate in-depth coverage of standard.

California Science Content Standards

Science Content Standards	Page Numbers
Forces	
2. Unbalanced forces cause changes in velocity. As a basis for understanding this concept:	
2.a Students know a force has both direction and magnitude.	**88–89**, 97, 98, 99, 100, 101, 102, 103
2.b Students know when an object is subject to two or more forces at once, the result is the cumulative effect of all the forces.	**90–91**, 99, 102, 103, 105, 106–108
2.c Students know when the forces on an object are balanced, the motion of the object does not change.	**92–93**, 95, 112, 113, 462, 468
2.d Students know how to identify separately the two or more forces that are acting on a single static object, including gravity, elastic forces due to tension or compression in matter, and friction.	**96–103**, 105, 116
2.e Students know that when the forces on an object are unbalanced, the object will change its velocity (that is, it will speed up, slow down, or change direction).	**106–108**, 110
2.f Students know the greater the mass of an object, the more force is needed to achieve the same rate of change in motion.	**109**, 112, 113
2.g Students know the role of gravity in forming and maintaining the shapes of planets, stars, and the solar system.	**96–98**, 467–470, 519–527
Structure of Matter	
3. Each of the more than 100 elements of matter has distinct properties and a distinct atomic structure. All forms of matter are composed of one or more of the elements. As a basis for understanding this concept:	
3.a Students know the structure of the atom and know it is composed of protons, neutrons, and electrons.	171, **175**, 176–178, 180, 181, **182–193, 200–201**, 203–205, 223–224
3.b Students know that compounds are formed by combining two or more different elements and that compounds have properties that are different from their constituent elements.	**215, 218–222, 225–227**, 229, 233, 235–236, 239, 350, **354**, 357
3.c Students know atoms and molecules form solids by building up repeating patterns, such as the crystal structure of NaCl or long-chain polymers.	**230–236**, 240–241, 434

Bold page numbers indicate in-depth coverage of standard.

California Science Content Standards

Science Content Standards	Page Numbers
Structure of Matter (continued)	
3.d Students know the states of matter (solid, liquid, gas) depend on molecular motion.	**255–259**, 263, **264–269**, 274
3.e Students know that in solids the atoms are closely locked in position and can only vibrate; in liquids the atoms and molecules are more loosely connected and can collide with and move past one another; and in gases the atoms and molecules are free to move independently, colliding frequently.	**255–259**, 265, 266, 267–268, 269
3.f Students know how to use the periodic table to identify elements in simple compounds.	**195–196**, 203, **221–222**, **224**, 287, **290–298**, 300, 342, 350
Earth in the Solar System (Earth Sciences)	
4. The structure and composition of the universe can be learned from studying stars and galaxies and their evolution. As a basis for understanding this concept:	
4.a Students know galaxies are clusters of billions of stars and may have different shapes.	**528–537**
4.b Students know that the Sun is one of many stars in the Milky Way galaxy and that stars may differ in size, temperature, and color.	**508–517**, 519–527, **530**
4.c Students know how to use astronomical units and light years as measures of distances between the Sun, stars, and Earth.	**466**, 479, 481, 491, 494–495, **508**, 513–514, 520, **531, 535**
4.d Students know that stars are the source of light for all bright objects in outer space and that the Moon and planets shine by reflected sunlight, not by their own light.	462, 471, **474–477**, **480–483**, 508–517, 519–527
4.e Students know the appearance, general composition, relative position and size, and motion of objects in the solar system, including planets, planetary satellites, comets, and asteroids.	**462–470**, 471, 472–473, 474, **478–488**, 489–493

Bold page numbers indicate in-depth coverage of standard.

California Science Content Standards

Science Content Standards	Page Numbers
Reactions	
5. Chemical reactions are processes in which atoms are rearranged into different combinations of molecules. As a basis for understanding this concept:	
5.a Students know reactant atoms and molecules interact to form products with different chemical properties.	335, **339, 341–342**, 345, **349, 354–355**, 366–367
5.b Students know the idea of atoms explains the conservation of matter: In chemical reactions the number of atoms stays the same no matter how they are arranged, so their total mass stays the same.	**346–347**, 348, **351–355**, 357
5.c Students know chemical reactions usually liberate heat or absorb heat.	**358–362**, 364
5.d Students know physical processes include freezing and boiling, in which a material changes form with no chemical reaction.	264–266, 266–270, 272, **314**
5.e Students know how to determine whether a solution is acidic, basic, or neutral.	377, **394–404**, 406, 408–409
Chemistry of Living Systems (Life Sciences)	
6. Principles of chemistry underlie the functioning of biological systems. As a basis for understanding this concept:	
6.a Students know that carbon, because of its ability to combine in many ways with itself and other elements, has a central role in the chemistry of living organisms.	**428–435**
6.b Students know that living organisms are made of molecules consisting largely of carbon, hydrogen, nitrogen, oxygen, phosphorus, and sulfur.	419, **422–424, 434**
6.c Students know that living organisms have many different kinds of molecules, including small ones, such as water and salt, and very large ones, such as carbohydrates, fats, proteins, and DNA.	**425–426, 438–441**, 443, 444–445

Bold page numbers indicate in-depth coverage of standard.

California Science Content Standards

Science Content Standards	Page Numbers
Periodic Table	
7. The organization of the periodic table is based on the properties of the elements and reflects the structure of atoms. As a basis for understanding this concept:	
7.a Students know how to identify regions corresponding to metals, nonmetals, and inert gases.	**290–298**, 306–309
7.b Students know each element has a specific number of protons in the nucleus (the atomic number) and each isotope of the element has a different but specific number of neutrons in the nucleus.	**195–198, 200, 301–306**, 312
7.c Students know substances can be classified by their properties, including their melting temperature, density, hardness, and thermal and electrical conductivity.	136, 231–232, **313–317**, 319–321, **338–343**, 380–385, **386**, 387–391, 393
Density and Buoyancy	
8. All objects experience a buoyant force when immersed in a fluid. As a basis for understanding this concept:	
8.a Students know density is mass per unit volume.	**130–133**, 138
8.b Students know how to calculate the density of substances (regular and irregular solids and liquids) from measurements of mass and volume.	**134–136**, 139
8.c Students know the buoyant force on an object in a fluid is an upward force equal to the weight of the fluid the object has displaced.	127, **146–147**, 149, 151
8.d Students know how to predict whether an object will float or sink.	**150–151**, 153, 155, 156–157

Bold page numbers indicate in-depth coverage of standard.

California Science Content Standards

Science Content Standards	Page Numbers
Investigation and Experimentation	
9. Scientific progress is made by asking meaningful questions and conducting careful investigations. As a basis for understanding this concept and addressing the content in the other three strands, students should develop their own questions and perform investigations. Students will:	
9.a Plan and conduct a scientific investigation to test a hypothesis.	7–33, 34–41, **105, 240–241, 319–321, 366–367, 408–409, 494–495**
9.b Evaluate the accuracy and reproducibility of data.	5, 17, 20, 21, **63, 406**
9.c Distinguish between variable and controlled parameters in a test.	29, 39–41, **444–445**
9.d Recognize the slope of the linear graph as the constant in the relationship $y = kx$ and apply this principle in interpreting graphs constructed from data.	**67, 73, 116**
9.e Construct appropriate graphs from data and develop quantitative statements about the relationships between variables.	22–27, **74–75, 203, 239, 312, 364, 393, 408–409, 443, 485**
9.f Apply simple mathematic relationships to determine a missing quantity in a mathematic expression, given the two remaining terms (including speed = distance/time, density = mass/volume, force = pressure × area, volume = area × height).	24, 37, **62, 115, 138**
9.g Distinguish between linear and nonlinear relationships on a graph of data.	23, **95, 274**

Bold page numbers indicate in-depth coverage of standard.

California Math Content Standards

Items within the text that relate to a Math Content Standard will be represented like this: **ALG: 1.1**

ALG: 1.0 Students identify and use the arithmetic properties of subsets of integers and rational, irrational, and real numbers, including closure properties for the four basic arithmetic operations where applicable:

ALG: 1.1 Students use properties of numbers to demonstrate whether assertions are true or false.

ALG: 2.0 Students understand and use such operations as taking the opposite, finding the reciprocal, taking a root, and raising to a fractional power. They understand and use the rules of exponents.

ALG: 3.0 Students solve equations and inequalities involving absolute values.

ALG: 4.0 Students simplify expressions before solving linear equations and inequalities in one variable, such as $3(2x - 5) + 4(x - 2) = 12$.

ALG: 5.0 Students solve multistep problems, including word problems, involving linear equations and linear inequalities in one variable and provide justification for each step.

ALG: 6.0 Students graph a linear equation and compute the x- and y-intercepts (e.g., graph $2x + 6y = 4$). They are also able to sketch the region defined by linear inequality (e.g., they sketch the region defined by $2x + 6y < 4$).

ALG: 7.0 Students verify that a point lies on a line, given an equation of the line. Students are able to derive linear equations by using the point-slope formula.

ALG: 8.0 Students understand the concepts of parallel lines and perpendicular lines and how those slopes are related. Students are able to find the equation of a line perpendicular to a given line that passes through a given point.

ALG: 9.0 Students solve a system of two linear equations in two variables algebraically and are able to interpret the answer graphically. Students are able to solve a system of two linear inequalities in two variables and to sketch the solution sets.

ALG: 10.0 Students add, subtract, multiply, and divide monomials and polynomials. Students solve multistep problems, including word problems, by using these techniques.

ALG: 11.0 Students apply basic factoring techniques to second- and simple third-degree polynomials. These techniques include finding a common factor for all terms in a polynomial, recognizing the difference of two squares, and recognizing perfect squares of binomials.

ALG: 12.0 Students simplify fractions with polynomials in the numerator and denominator by factoring both and reducing them to the lowest terms.

ALG: 13.0 Students add, subtract, multiply, and divide rational expressions and functions. Students solve both computationally and conceptually challenging problems by using these techniques.

ALG: 14.0 Students solve a quadratic equation by factoring or completing the square.

ALG: 15.0 Students apply algebraic techniques to solve rate problems, work problems, and percent mixture problems.

ALG: 16.0 Students understand the concepts of a relation and a function, determine whether a given relation defines a function, and give pertinent information about given relations and functions.

California Math Content Standards

ALG: 17.0 Students determine the domain of independent variables and the range of dependent variables defined by a graph, a set of ordered pairs, or a symbolic expression.

ALG: 18.0 Students determine whether a relation defined by a graph, a set of ordered pairs, or a symbolic expression is a function and justify the conclusion.

ALG: 19.0 Students know the quadratic formula and are familiar with its proof by completing the square.

ALG: 20.0 Students use the quadratic formula to find the roots of a second-degree polynomial and to solve quadratic equations.

ALG: 21.0 Students graph quadratic functions and know that their roots are the x-intercepts.

ALG: 22.0 Students use the quadratic formula or factoring techniques or both to determine whether the graph of a quadratic function will intersect the x-axis in zero, one, or two points.

ALG: 23.0 Students apply quadratic equations to physical problems, such as the motion of an object under the force of gravity.

ALG: 24.0 Students use and know simple aspects of a logical argument:

ALG: 24.1 Students explain the difference between inductive and deductive reasoning and identify and provide examples of each.

ALG: 24.2 Students identify the hypothesis and conclusion in logical deduction.

ALG: 24.3 Students use counterexamples to show that an assertion is false and recognize that a single counterexample is sufficient to refute an assertion.

ALG: 25.0 Students use properties of the number system to judge the validity of results, to justify each step of a procedure, and to prove or disprove statements:

ALG: 25.1 Students use properties of numbers to construct simple, valid arguments (direct and indirect) for, or formulate counterexamples to, claimed assertions.

ALG: 25.2 Students judge the validity of an argument according to whether the properties of the real number system and the order of operations have been applied correctly at each step.

ALG: 25.3 Given a specific algebraic statement involving linear, quadratic, or absolute value expressions or equations or inequalities, students determine whether the statement is true sometimes, always, or never.

California English-Language Arts Content Standards

Items within the text that relate to an English-Language Arts Content Standard will be represented like this: **ELA8: R 1.4**

Reading

ELA8: R 1.0   Word Analysis, Fluency, and Systematic Vocabulary Development

Vocabulary and Concept Development

ELA8: R 1.1   Analyze idioms, analogies, metaphors, and similes to infer the literal and figurative meanings of phrases.

ELA8: R 1.2   Understand the most important points in the history of English language and use common word origins to determine the historical influences on English word meanings.

ELA8: R 1.3   Use word meanings within the appropriate context and show ability to verify those meanings by definition, restatement, example, comparison, or contrast.

ELA8: R 2.0   Reading Comprehension (Focus on Informational Materials)

Structural Features of Informational Materials

ELA8: R 2.1   Compare and contrast the features and elements of consumer materials to gain meaning from documents (e.g., warranties, contracts, product information, instruction manuals).

ELA8: R 2.2   Analyze text that uses proposition and support patterns.

Comprehension and Analysis of Grade-Level-Appropriate Text

ELA8: R 2.3   Find similarities and differences between texts in the treatment, scope, or organization of ideas.

ELA8: R 2.4   Compare the original text to a summary to determine whether the summary accurately captures the main ideas, includes critical details, and conveys the underlying meaning.

ELA8: R 2.5   Understand and explain the use of a complex mechanical device by following technical directions.

ELA8: R 2.6   Use information from a variety of consumer, workplace, and public documents to explain a situation or decision and to solve a problem.

Expository Critique

ELA8: R 2.7   Evaluate the unity, coherence, logic, internal consistency, and structural patterns of text.

ELA8: R 3.0   Literary Response and Analysis

Structural Features of Literature

ELA8: R 3.1   Determine and articulate the relationship between the purposes and characteristics of different forms of poetry (e.g., ballad, lyric, couplet, epic, elegy, ode, sonnet).

Narrative Analysis of Grade-Level-Appropriate Text

ELA8: R 3.2   Evaluate the structural elements of the plot (e.g., subplots, parallel episodes, climax), the plot's development, and the way in which conflicts are (or are not) addressed and resolved.

ELA8: R 3.3   Compare and contrast motivations and reactions of literary characters from different historical eras confronting similar situations or conflicts.

ELA8: R 3.4   Analyze the relevance of the setting (e.g., place, time, customs) to the mood, tone, and meaning of the text.

ELA8: R 3.5   Identify and analyze recurring themes (e.g., good versus evil) across traditional and contemporary works.

ELA8: R 3.6   Identify significant literary devices (e.g., metaphor, symbolism, dialect, irony) that define a writer's style and use those elements to interpret the work.

Literary Criticism

ELA8: R 3.7   Analyze a work of literature, showing how it reflects the heritage, traditions, attitudes, and beliefs of its author. (Biographical approach)

Writing

ELA8: W 1.0   Writing Strategies

Organization and Focus

ELA8: W 1.1   Create compositions that establish a controlling impression, have a coherent thesis, and end with a clear and well-supported conclusion.

ELA8: W 1.2   Establish coherence within and among paragraphs through effective transitions, parallel structures, and similar writing techniques.

ELA8: W 1.3   Support theses or conclusions with analogies, paraphrases, quotations, opinions from authorities, comparisons, and similar devices.

Research and Technology

ELA8: W 1.4   Plan and conduct multiple-step information searches by using computer networks and modems.

ELA8: W 1.5   Achieve an effective balance between researched information and original ideas.

Evaluation and Revision

ELA8: W 1.6   Revise writing for word choice; appropriate organization; consistent point of view; and transitions between paragraphs, passages, and ideas.

ELA8: W 2.0   Writing Applications (Genres and Their Characteristics) Using the writing strategies of grade eight outlined in Writing Standard 1.0, students:

ELA8: W 2.1   Write biographies, autobiographies, short stories, or narratives:
   a. Relate a clear, coherent incident, event, or situation by using well-chosen details.
   b. Reveal the significance of, or the writer's attitude about, the subject.
   c. Employ narrative and descriptive strategies (e.g., relevant dialogue, specific action, physical description, background description, comparison or contrast of characters).

ELA8: W 2.2   Write responses to literature:
   a. Exhibit careful reading and insight in their interpretations.
   b. Connect the student's own responses to the writer's techniques and to specific textual references.
   c. Draw supported inferences about the effects of a literary work on its audience.
   d. Support judgments through references to the text, other works, other authors, or to personal knowledge.

ELA8: W 2.3   Write research reports:
   a. Define a thesis.
   b. Record important ideas, concepts, and direct quotations from significant information sources and paraphrase and summarize all perspectives on the topic, as appropriate.
   c. Use a variety of primary and secondary sources and distinguish the nature and value of each.
   d. Organize and display information on charts, maps, and graphs.

ELA8: W 2.4 Write persuasive compositions:
a. Include a well-defined thesis (i.e., one that makes a clear and knowledgeable judgment).
b. Present detailed evidence, examples, and reasoning to support arguments, differentiating between facts and opinion.
c. Provide details, reasons, and examples, arranging them effectively by anticipating and answering reader concerns and counterarguments.

ELA8: W 2.5 Write documents related to career development, including simple business letters and job applications:
a. Present information purposefully and succinctly and meet the needs of the intended audience.
b. Follow the conventional format for the type of document (e.g., letter of inquiry, memorandum).

ELA8: W 2.6 Write technical documents:
a. Identify the sequence of activities needed to design a system, operate a tool, or explain the bylaws of an organization.
b. Include all the factors and variables that need to be considered.
c. Use formatting techniques (e.g., headings, differing fonts) to aid comprehension.

Written and Oral English Language Conventions

ELA8: WO 1.0 Written and Oral English Language Conventions

Sentence Structure

ELA8: WO 1.1 Use correct and varied sentence types and sentence openings to present a lively and effective personal style.
ELA8: WO 1.2 Identify and use parallelism, including similar grammatical forms, in all written discourse to present items in a series and items juxtaposed for emphasis.
ELA8: WO 1.3 Use subordination, coordination, apposition, and other devices to indicate clearly the relationship between ideas.

Grammar

ELA8: WO 1.4 Edit written manuscripts to ensure that correct grammar is used.

Punctuation and Capitalization

ELA8: WO 1.5 Use correct punctuation and capitalization.

Spelling

ELA8: WO 1.6 Use correct spelling conventions.

Listening and Speaking

ELA8: LS 1.0 Listening and Speaking Strategies

Comprehension

ELA8: LS 1.1 Analyze oral interpretations of literature, including language choice and delivery, and the effect of the interpretations on the listener.
ELA8: LS 1.2 Paraphrase a speaker's purpose and point of view and ask relevant questions concerning the speaker's content, delivery, and purpose.

Organization and Delivery of Oral Communication

ELA8: LS 1.3 Organize information to achieve particular purposes by matching the message, vocabulary, voice modulation, expression, and tone to the audience and purpose.

ELA8: LS 1.4 Prepare a speech outline based upon a chosen pattern of organization, which generally includes an introduction; transitions, previews, and summaries; a logically developed body; and an effective conclusion.
ELA8: LS 1.5 Use precise language, action verbs, sensory details, appropriate and colorful modifiers, and the active rather than the passive voice in ways that enliven oral presentations.
ELA8: LS 1.6 Use appropriate grammar, word choice, enunciation, and pace during formal presentations.
ELA8: LS 1.7 Use audience feedback (e.g., verbal and nonverbal cues):
a. Reconsider and modify the organizational structure or plan.
b. Rearrange words and sentences to clarify the meaning.

Analysis and Evaluation of Oral and Media Communications

ELA8: LS 1.8 Evaluate the credibility of a speaker (e.g., hidden agendas, slanted or biased material).
ELA8: LS 1.9 Interpret and evaluate the various ways in which visual image makers (e.g., graphic artists, illustrators, news photographers) communicate information and affect impressions and opinions.

ELA8: LS 2.0 Speaking Applications (Genres and Their Characteristics) Using the speaking strategies of grade eight outlined in Listening and Speaking Standard 1.0, students:

ELA8: LS 2.1 Deliver narrative presentations (e.g., biographical, autobiographical):
a. Relate a clear, coherent incident, event, or situation by using well-chosen details.
b. Reveal the significance of, and the subject's attitude about, the incident, event, or situation.
c. Employ narrative and descriptive strategies (e.g., relevant dialogue, specific action, physical description, background description, comparison or contrast of characters).
ELA8: LS 2.2 Deliver oral responses to literature:
a. Interpret a reading and provide insight.
b. Connect the students' own responses to the writer's techniques and to specific textual references.
c. Draw supported inferences about the effects of a literary work on its audience.
d. Support judgments through references to the text, other works, other authors, or personal knowledge.
ELA8: LS 2.3 Deliver research presentations:
a. Define a thesis.
b. Record important ideas, concepts, and direct quotations from significant information sources and paraphrase and summarize all relevant perspectives on the topic, as appropriate.
c. Use a variety of primary and secondary sources and distinguish the nature and value of each.
d. Organize and record information on charts, maps, and graphs.
ELA8: LS 2.4 Deliver persuasive presentations:
a. Include a well-defined thesis (i.e., one that makes a clear and knowledgeable judgment).
b. Differentiate fact from opinion and support arguments with detailed evidence, examples, and reasoning.
c. Anticipate and answer listener concerns and counterarguments effectively through the inclusion and arrangement of details, reasons, examples, and other elements.
d. Maintain a reasonable tone.
ELA8: LS 2.5 Recite poems (of four to six stanzas), sections of speeches, or dramatic soliloquies, using voice modulation, tone, and gestures expressively to enhance the meaning.

Reading for Information

When you read *Focus On Physical Science*, you are reading for information. Science is nonfiction writing—it describes real-life events, people, ideas, and technology. Here are some tools that *Focus On Physical Science* has to help you read.

Before You Read

By reading (The BIG Idea) and (Main Idea) prior to reading the chapter or lesson, you will get a preview of the coming material.

On the first page of each chapter you will find (The BIG Idea). The Big Idea is a sentence that describes what you will learn about in the chapter.

Source: Chapter 3, p. 126

(The BIG Idea) is divided into Main Ideas. Each lesson of the chapter has a (Main Idea) that describes the focus of the lesson.

Source: Chapter 3, Lesson 1, p. 130

Other Ways to Preview

- Read the chapter title to find out what area of science you will study.

- Skim the photo, illustrations, captions, graphs, and tables.

- Look for key terms that are boldfaced and . highlighted.

Reading for Information

The Get Ready to Read section allows you to learn, practice, and apply a reading skill before you start reading the chapter's first lesson. Target Your Reading will help you keep the main idea in focus as you read the chapter.

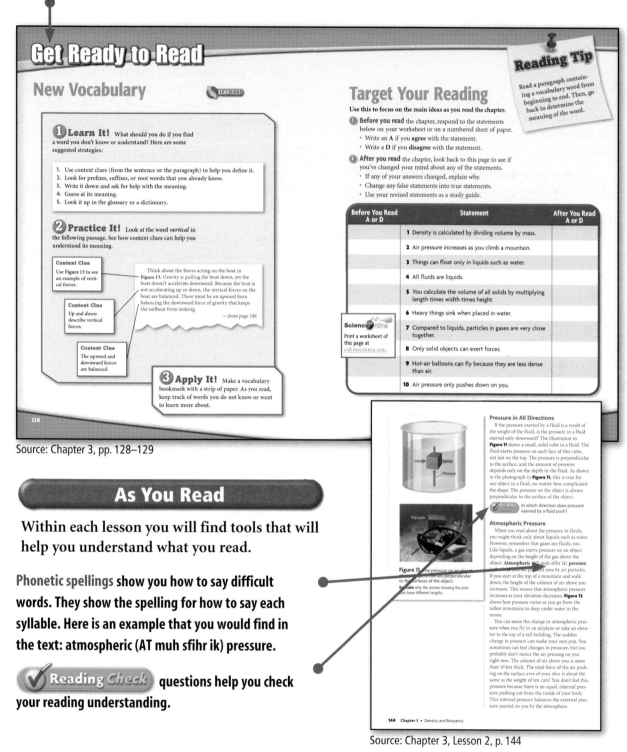

Get Ready to Read

New Vocabulary

ELAB:R.1.3

① Learn It! What should you do if you find a word you don't know or understand? Here are some suggested strategies:

1. Use context clues (from the sentence or the paragraph) to help you define it.
2. Look for prefixes, suffixes, or root words that you already know.
3. Write it down and ask for help with the meaning.
4. Guess at its meaning.
5. Look it up in the glossary or a dictionary.

② Practice It! Look at the word *vertical* in the following passage. See how context clues can help you understand its meaning.

Context Clue
Use Figure 13 to see an example of vertical forces.

Context Clue
Up and *down* describe vertical forces.

Context Clue
The upward and downward forces are balanced.

Think about the forces acting on the boat in **Figure 13**. Gravity is pulling the boat down, yet the boat doesn't accelerate downward. Because the boat is not accelerating up or down, the vertical forces on the boat are balanced. There must be an upward force balancing the downward force of gravity that keeps the sailboat from sinking.

—from page 146

③ Apply It! Make a vocabulary bookmark with a strip of paper. As you read, keep track of words you do not know or want to learn more about.

128

Target Your Reading

Use this to focus on the main ideas as you read the chapter.

① Before you read the chapter, respond to the statements below on your worksheet or on a numbered sheet of paper.
- Write an **A** if you **agree** with the statement.
- Write a **D** if you **disagree** with the statement.

② After you read the chapter, look back to this page to see if you've changed your mind about any of the statements.
- If any of your answers changed, explain why.
- Change any false statements into true statements.
- Use your revised statements as a study guide.

Science Online
Print a worksheet of this page at ca8.msscience.com.

Before You Read A or D	Statement	After You Read A or D
	1 Density is calculated by dividing volume by mass.	
	2 Air pressure increases as you climb a mountain.	
	3 Things can float only in liquids such as water.	
	4 All fluids are liquids.	
	5 You calculate the volume of all solids by multiplying length times width times height.	
	6 Heavy things sink when placed in water.	
	7 Compared to liquids, particles in gases are very close together.	
	8 Only solid objects can exert forces.	
	9 Hot-air balloons can fly because they are less dense than air.	
	10 Air pressure only pushes down on you.	

Source: Chapter 3, pp. 128–129

Reading Tip
Read a paragraph containing a vocabulary word from beginning to end. Then, go back to determine the meaning of the word.

As You Read

Within each lesson you will find tools that will help you understand what you read.

Phonetic spellings show you how to say difficult words. They show the spelling for how to say each syllable. Here is an example that you would find in the text: atmospheric (AT muh sfihr ik) pressure.

✓ Reading Check questions help you check your reading understanding.

Pressure in All Directions

If the pressure exerted by a fluid is a result of the weight of the fluid, is the pressure in a fluid exerted only downward? The illustration in **Figure 11** shows a small, solid cube in a fluid. The fluid exerts pressure on each face of this cube, not just on the top. The pressure is perpendicular to the surface, and the amount of pressure depends only on the depth in the fluid. As shown in the photograph in **Figure 11**, this is true for any object in a fluid, no matter how complicated the shape. The pressure on the object is always perpendicular to the surface of the object.

✓ Reading Check In which direction does pressure exerted by a fluid push?

Atmospheric Pressure

When you read about the pressure in fluids, you might think only about liquids such as water. However, remember that gases are fluids, too. Like liquids, a gas exerts pressure on an object depending on the height of the gas above the object. **Atmospheric (AT muh sfihr ik) pressure** is the pressure exerted per unit area by air particles. If you start at the top of a mountain and walk down, the height of the column of air above you increases. This means that atmospheric pressure increases as your elevation decreases. **Figure 12** shows how pressure varies as you go from the tallest mountains to deep under water in the ocean.

You can sense the change in atmospheric pressure when you fly in an airplane or take an elevator to the top of a tall building. The sudden change in pressure can make your ears pop. You sometimes can feel changes in pressure, but you probably don't notice the air pressing on you right now. The column of air above you is more than 10 km thick. The total force of the air pushing on the surface area of your skin is about the same as the weight of ten cars! You don't feel this pressure because there is an equal, internal pressure pushing out from the inside of your body. This internal pressure balances the external pressure exerted on you by the atmosphere.

Figure 11 The pressure on an object is always exerted perpendicular to the surfaces of the object.

Explain why the arrows showing the pressure have different lengths.

144 Chapter 3 • Density and Buoyancy

Source: Chapter 3, Lesson 2, p. 144

Reading for Information

Other Skills to Exercise as You Read

Question
- What is the **Main Idea**?
- What is **The BIG Idea**?

Connect
- As you read, think about people, places, and situations you've encountered. Are there any similarities with those in *Focus On Physical Science*?
- Can you relate the information in *Focus On Physical Science* to other areas of your life?

Predict
- Predict events or outcomes by using clues and information you already know.
- Change your prediction as you read and gather new information.

Visualize
- Create a picture in your mind about what you are reading. Picture the setting—for example, a laboratory, a roller coaster, or a mountain.
- A mental image can help you remember what you read for a longer time.

Compare and Contrast Sentences
- Look for clue words and phrases that signal comparison, such as *similar to, just as, both, in common, also,* and *too.*
- Look for clue words and phrases that signal contrast, such as *on the other hand, in contrast to, however, different, instead of, rather than, but,* and *unlike.*

Cause-and-Effect Sentences
- Look for clue words and phrases such as *because, as a result, therefore, that is why, since, so, for this reason,* and *consequently.*

Sequential Sentences
- Look for clue words and phrases such as *after, before, first, next, last, during, finally, earlier, later, since,* and *then.*

After You Read

Follow up your reading with a summary and an assessment of the material to evaluate if you understood the text.

Summarize
- Describe **The BIG Idea** and how the details support it.
- Describe the **Main Idea** and how the details support it.
- Use your own words to explain what you read.
- Complete the Summary Activity at the end of the lesson.

Assess
- What was **The BIG Idea**?
- What was the **Main Idea**?
- Did you learn anything new from the material?
- Can you use this new information in other school subjects or at home?
- What other sources could you use to find out more information about the topic?

Previewing Your Textbook

Follow the tour through the next few pages to learn about using your textbook, *Focus On Physical Science*. This tour will help you understand what you will discover as you read *Focus On Physical Science*. Before you begin reading, take the tour so that you are familiar with how this textbook works.

Unit Preview

West-Coast Events Time Line See significant events that occurred on the West Coast of the United States and compare them to events that occurred around the world.

World Events Time Line See significant events that occurred around the world and compare them to events that occurred on the West Coast.

Science Online A visual reminder to explore online tools to learn more about a scientist's career.

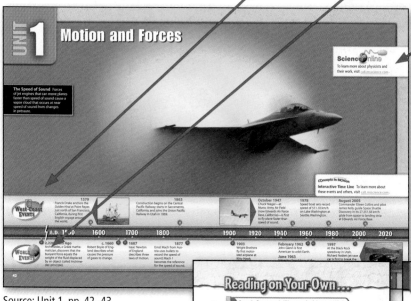

Source: Unit 1, pp. 42–43

Unit Review

Reading on Your Own a listing of books recommended by the California State Board of Education

Unit Test multiple-choice questions and written-response questions that review the unit

Source: Unit 1, pp. 166–167

Previewing Your Textbook

Chapters

The BIG Idea The Big Idea is a sentence that describes what you will learn about in the chapter.

Main Idea The Main Ideas support the Big Idea. Each lesson of the chapter has a Main Idea that describes the focus of the lesson.

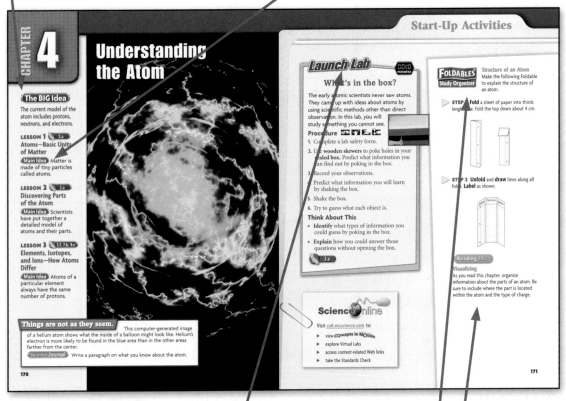

Source: Chapter 4, pp. 170–171

Launch Lab a short investigation that introduces the chapter's subject

Foldables™ Study Organizer an easy way to take notes as you read the chapter and a valuable tool for review

Reading Skill This is a reading skill that you will practice throughout the chapter.

Previewing Your Textbook

Lessons

Main Idea The Big Idea is supported by Main Ideas. Each lesson of the chapter has a Main Idea that describes the focus of the lesson.

Science Content Standards a listing of the California Science Content Standards that are covered within the lesson

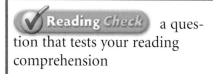 **Reading Check** a question that tests your reading comprehension

 **Visual Check** and Caption Questions questions found throughout the lesson about important graphs, photos, or illustrations

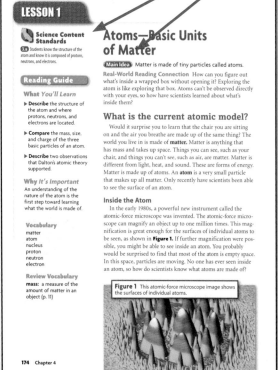

Source: Chapter 4, Lesson 1, p. 174

Summarize Use this exercise to help you create your own summary of the lesson's content.

Lesson Review

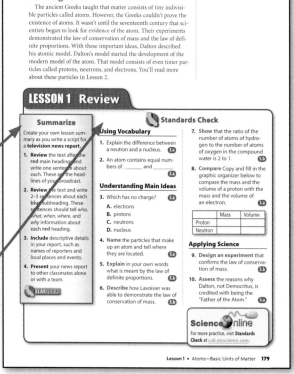

Source: Chapter 4, Lesson 1, p. 179

Self Check A series of questions to check your understanding of the lesson's material.

Previewing Your Textbook

Hands-On Science

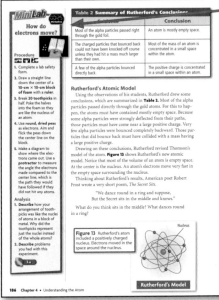

Source: Chapter 4, p. 186

MiniLab These investigations emphasize the lesson's content. MiniLabs are located in either a margin, like the one shown here, or on a full page. The California Science Content Standards that correlate to the material are listed.

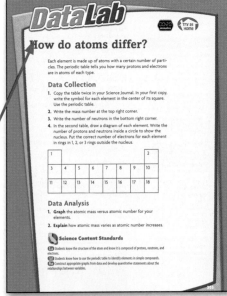

Source: Chapter 4, p. 203

DataLab These investigations emphasize the lesson's content by using mathematical analysis. DataLabs are located in either a margin or on a full page, as shown here. The California Science Content Standards and the California Mathematics Content Standards that correlate to the material are listed.

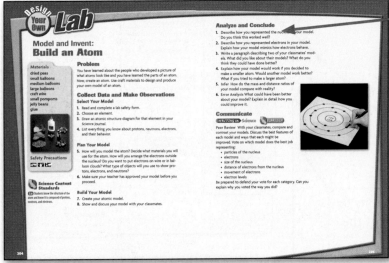

Source: Chapter 4, pp. 204–205

Lab Full-length investigations emphasize the chapter's content. Included are Labs or Design Your Own Labs. The California Science Content Standards that correlate to the material are listed.

Previewing Your Textbook

Special Features

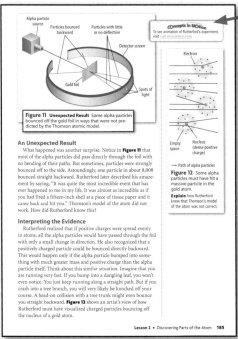

Source: Chapter 4, Lesson 2, p. 185

Concepts in Motion interactive art or diagrams that can be accessed through the Glencoe Web site to help you build understanding of concepts

Real-World Science Four connections with science are made in this feature: Science and Career, Science and Technology, Science and History, and Science and Society. These four connections will help you practice written and oral presentation skills.

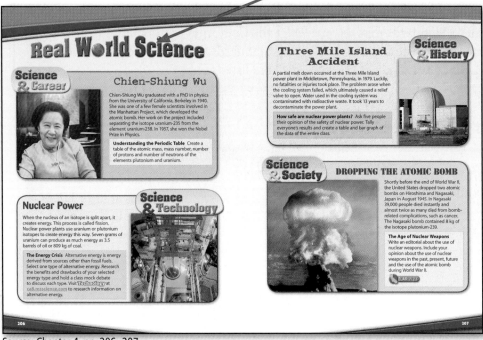

Source: Chapter 4, pp. 206–207

Previewing Your Textbook

Standards Review

Linking Vocabulary and Main Ideas a concept map to assist you in reviewing your vocabulary

Using Vocabulary a variety of questions that will check your understanding of vocabulary definitions

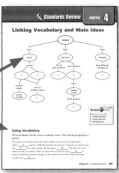

Source: Chapter 4, p. 209

Understanding Main Ideas multiple-choice questions

Applying Science short-answer and extended-response questions to practice higher-level thinking skills

Cumulative Review short-answer questions covering material from earlier in the unit

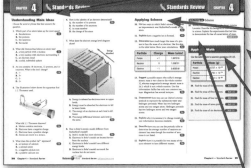

Source: Chapter 4, pp. 210–211

Applying Math a series of questions that practice math skills related to the chapter; the California Mathematics Content Standards that correlate to the material are listed

Writing in Science an exercise to practice writing skills; the California English/Language Arts Content Standards that correlate to the material are listed

Standards Assessment

Standards Assessment multiple-choice questions to review the California Science Content Standards covered in the chapter

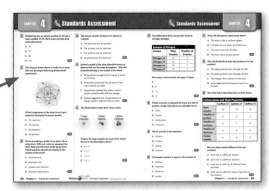

Source: Chapter 4, pp. 212–213

Scavenger Hunt

Focus On Physical Science contains a wealth of information. The secret is to know where to look to learn as much as you can.

As you complete this scavenger hunt, either on your own or with your teachers or family, you will quickly learn how the textbook is organized and how to get the most out of your reading and study time.

1. How many units are in the book? How many chapters?

2. On what page does the glossary begin? What glossary is online?

3. In which Student Resource at the back of your book can you find a listing of Laboratory Safety Symbols?

4. Suppose you want to find a list of all the Launch Labs, MiniLabs, DataLabs, and Labs, where in the front do you look?

5. How can you quickly find the pages that have information about Ernest Rutherford?

6. What is the name of the table that summarizes the key concepts and vocabulary of a chapter? On what page in Chapter 4 are these two things located?

7. In which Student Resource at the back of your book can you find information on unit conversion? What are the page numbers?

8. On what page can you find **The BIG Idea** for Chapter 1? On what page can you find the **Main Idea** for Chapter 1, Lesson 2?

9. What feature at the start of each unit provides insight into a scientist's work?

10. What study tool shown at the beginning of a chapter can you make from notebook paper?

11. **Concepts In Motion** are interactive animations. Where do you go to interact with the animation?

12. What activities at the beginning of each chapter will help improve your reading?

Introduction to
Investigation and Experimentation

What is science? Science is the process of studying nature at all levels, from the farthest reaches of space to the smallest particle of matter, and the collection of information that is learned through this process. Every day, scientists ask questions about the natural world and propose explanations based on evidence they gather. This evidence can then be used by other scientists to answer their own questions about the natural world.

What is physical science?

Physical science is that study of what things are made of—matter—and how things change—energy. Physical science is the combination of two sciences—chemistry and physics. Chemists study the structure and properties of matter and interactions of matter. Physics focuses on the energy and its ability to change matter. In this book you will investigate questions about motion, forces and the structure of matter.

Table of Contents

What is science? 4
- The Branches of Science
- Scientific Methods
- Scientific Theories
- Scientific Laws

Tools of the Physical Scientist 7

Lab and Field Study Tools 7
- Science Journal
- Rulers and Metersticks
- Thermometers
- Beakers
- Test Tubes
- pH Hydrion Paper
- Graduated Cylinder
- Triple-Beam Balance
- Spring Scale
- Calculator
- Stopwatch
- Telescope
- Computers and the Internet

Tools of Scientific Thinking 15
- The International System of Measurement
- Converting Between SI Units
- Scientific Notation
- Precision and Accuracy
- Measurement and Uncertainty
- Significant Figures
- Hypotheses and Predictions
- Evaluating Evidence and Explanations
- Avoiding Bias in Investigations
- Multiple Trials

Data Analysis Tools 22
- Making Data Tables
- Understanding Linear Relationships
- Understanding Nonlinear Relationships
- Analyzing Central Tendency in Data
- Making Line Graphs
- Making Bar Graphs
- Making Circle Graphs

Designing a Controlled Experiment 28
- Asking Scientific Questions
- Writing a Hypothesis and Prediction
- Defining Variables and Constants
- Experimental Group and Control Group
- Measuring the Dependent Variable
- Writing a Procedure
- Determining Materials
- Recording Observations
- Analyzing Results
- Drawing Conclusions
- Analyzing Error

Case Study: Wind Turbines for the Birds 34
- Wind Farms—An Alternative to Fossil Fuels
- A Problem with Wind Power
- Field Experiments at APWRA
- Controlled Studies in the Laboratory
- Field Testing Painted Blades
- A Final Note

The Branches of Science

There are an infinite number of questions to ask about the natural world. However, these questions are often organized into different fields of study. The chart below lists three areas of science that you will study in middle school.

Earth Science

Volcanologists are Earth scientists that study volcanoes. This team of student volcanologists is studying patterns in cooled volcanic lava. This team of volcanologists is studying a hot volcano lava tube in Kilauea, Hawaii.

Earth scientists ask questions such as:
- What makes the ocean salty?
- What causes an earthquake?
- Why are there more earthquakes in California than in Arizona?
- How are mountains formed?
- What causes a tsunami?

Life Science

Microbiologists are life scientists that ask questions about organisms that are too small to see with the naked eye. This microbiologist is studying the growth of bacteria in order to find out which medicine can treat a disease.

Life scientists ask questions such as:
- What causes plants to grow?
- How do diseases spread in a population?
- Why do some whales beach themselves, but others do not?

Physical Science

Electron microscopists are physical scientists that observe objects at magnifications up to 800,000 times their actual size. This electron microscopist is using a scanning electron microscope at the University of California, Berkeley to observe the structure of an ant's head.

Physical scientists ask questions such as:
- Why does the sunlight melt snow?
- Why are some buildings damaged more than others during earthquakes?
- What makes up stars?
- What causes acid rain to form?

Scientific Methods

You might think that science is only about facts and discoveries. But, science is also about the skills and thought processes required to make discoveries. There is no one scientific method used by scientists. Instead, scientific methods are based on basic assumptions about the natural world and how humans understand it.

Dr. Paul Chu studies a magnet levitating above a superconductive ceramic in his lab.

Assumptions of the Scientific Method

1. There are patterns in nature.

Science assumes that there are patterns in nature. Patterns are characteristics or interactions between things that repeat over and over. Patterns can be observed using the five human senses—sight, hearing, touch, smell, and taste.

2. People can use logic to understand an observation.

Science assumes that an individual can make an observation and then create a series of logical steps in order to find a valid explanation for the observation. This series of steps can then be communicated to others.

3. Scientific discoveries are replicable.

Something that is replicable in science means that it can be repeated over and over again. If one scientist claims to have made a discovery using a certain set of steps in their investigation, then another scientist should be able to repeat the same steps and get the same result. This ensures that when people make scientific claims they provide reliable evidence to support their claim.

Scientific methods cannot answer all questions.

Questions that deal with your feelings, values, beliefs, and personal opinions cannot be answered using scientific methods. Although people sometimes use scientific evidence to form arguments about these topics, there is no way to find answers for them using scientific methods. Good science is based on carefully crafted questions and objectively collected data.

Questions Science Cannot Answer

The following are examples of questions that cannot be answered by science.

- Which band has the best songs?
- Why do bad things happen?
- What does it mean to be a good person?

Scientific Theories

Using scientific methods to ask questions about the natural world has led to the formation of scientific theories. A **scientific theory** is explanation of things or events that is based on knowledge gained from many observations and investigations. They are independently tested by many scientists and are objectively verified. However, even the best scientific theory can be rejected if new scientific discoveries reveal new information.

How is a scientific theory different from a common theory?

Scientific Theory	Common Theory
• A scientific theory is an explanation for a observation supported by evidence from many scientific investigations.	• A common theory is a collection of related ideas that one supposes to be true.
• Strength of a scientific theory lies solely in the accuracy of its predictions.	• Strength of a theory is based on the clarity of the explanation, not necessarily objectively obtained evidence.
• A scientific theory is modified or rejected if new evidence makes the theories predictions no longer true.	• A common theory may or may not be modified or rejected when presented with new evidence.
• A scientific theory must be rejectable.	• A common theory does not have to be rejectable.

Scientific Laws

A rule that describes a pattern in nature is a **scientific law.** For an observation to become a scientific law, it must be observed repeatedly. The law then stands until someone makes observations that do not follow the law. A law helps you predict that an apple dropped from arm's length will always fall to Earth. A scientific law, unlike a scientific theory, does not attempt to explain *why* something happens. It simply describes a pattern.

9.a Plan and conduct a scientific investigation to test a hypothesis.

Lab and Field Study Tools

Lab and field study tools are physical tools that help you make better observations during scientific investigations. These tools enable you to measure the amounts of liquids, measure how much material is in an object, and observe things that are too small or too far away to be seen with the naked eye. Learning how to use them properly will help you when designing your own investigations.

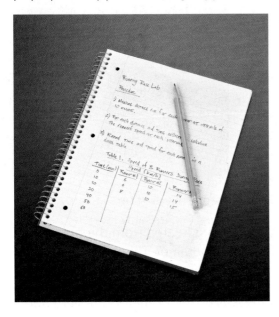

Science Journal Use a Science Journal to record questions, procedures, observations, and conclusions from your investigations.

TIP Your Science Journal can be a spiral-bound binder, a loose-leaf notebook, or anything that will help you record and save information.

TIP It is important that you keep your Science Journal organized. An organized journal will enable you to find information that you have collected in the past.

TIP Write down the date when you are recording information in your Science Journal, and leave extra space to go back to later.

Rulers and Metersticks Use metric rulers and metersticks to measure an object's length or the distance between two points.

TIP The SI base unit for measuring length is the meter (m).

TIP Metric units of measurement for length include meters (m) centimeters (cm) millimeters (mm) and kilometers (km).

TIP **Meters** (m) are a good unit of measurement to measure short distances such as the length of your classroom.

TIP Measure small objects such as the length of a leaf in **centimeters** (cm).

TIP Measure very small objects such as the length of an insect in **millimeters** (mm).

TIP Measure long distances such the distance from your home to your school in **kilometers** (km).

TIP Estimate 1 decimal place beyond the markings on the ruler. For a meterstick, measure to the nearest 0.5 mm.

Tools of the Physical Scientist:
Lab and Field Study Tools

9.a Plan and conduct a scientific investigation to test a hypothesis.

Thermometers Use a thermometer to measure the temperature of a substance.

TIP The physical property of temperature is related to how hot or cold an object is. Temperature is a measure of of the kinetic energy, or energy of motion, of particles that make up matter.

TIP The SI unit of measurement for temperature is the Kelvin (K) scale, which starts at 0. The Fahrenheit and Celsius temperature scales are the two most common scales used on thermometers and in classroom laboratories.

TIP A 1 K difference in temperature is the same as a 1°C difference in temperature.

TIP On the Celsius scale, 0°C is the freezing point of liquid water and 100°C is the boiling point of liquid water.

TIP When measuring the temperature of a liquid that is being heated from the bottom, do not let the thermometer rest on the bottom of the container. This will result in an inaccurate reading.

SAFETY Be careful when transporting a glass thermometer. Glass thermometers are very fragile and are easily broken if dropped or bumped.

Beakers Use a beaker for holding and pouring liquids.

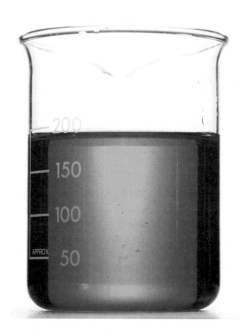

TIP Use a graduated cylinder instead of a beaker to measure the volume of a liquid. The lines on the side of a beaker are not accurate.

SAFETY Use a beaker that holds about twice as much liquid as you are measuring to avoid overflow.

TIP Use a hot plate to keep a substance warmer than room temperature.

SAFETY Use goggles to protect your eyes when working with liquids in the lab.

SAFETY Use gloves to protect your hands when working with liquids in the lab.

9.a Plan and conduct a scientific investigation to test a hypothesis.

Tools of the Physical Scientist:
Lab and Field Study Tools

Test Tubes Use a test tube to study small samples of solids, liquids, and gases.

TIP Use a test-tube rack to keep your test tubes upright and organized.

SAFETY Since liquids can spill or splash from test tubes, use small amounts of liquids and keep the mouth of the test tube pointed away from you and other people.

SAFETY Use a test-tube holder if you are heating the substance in a test tube or if the substance in the test tube is dangerous to touch.

SAFETY Do not put a stopper in a test tube if you are heating it.

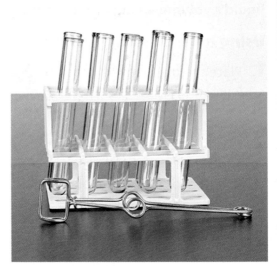

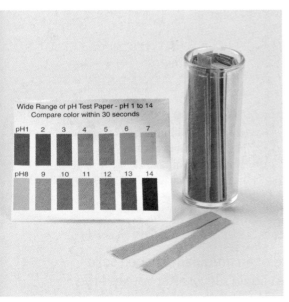

pH Hydrion Paper Use pH hydrion paper to indicate the acidity or alkalinity of a liquid substance.

Using pH Hydrion Paper

1. Place the edge of a 5-cm piece of pH Hydrion paper into the substance.

2. Observe the color change of the pH paper.

3. Remove the paper from the substance. Try to match the resulting color to the colors listed on the outside of the pH hydrion paper package.

4. The color will correlate with a pH number. This number is the pH value of the substance.

5. If the number is less than 7, the substance is acidic. If the number is more than 7, the substance is basic.

SAFETY Be sure to wear gloves, goggles, and a lab apron when testing the pH of a substance. Highly acidic and highly basic substances can irritate eyes, burn skin, and damage your clothing.

Tools of the Physical Scientist:
Lab and Field Study Tools

 9.a Plan and conduct a scientific investigation to test a hypothesis.

Graduated Cylinder Use a graduated cylinder to measure a liquid's volume, or amount of space it occupies.

Using a Graduated Cylinder

1. Place the graduated cylinder on a level surface so that your measurement will be accurate.

2. To read the scale on a graduated cylinder, make sure to have your eyes at the level of the surface of the liquid.

3. The surface of the liquid in a graduated cylinder will be curved—this curve is called a meniscus. Read the graduate or line at the bottom of the meniscus.

> **TIP** A 10 mL graduated cylinder will measure a small volume of liquid more precisely than a 100 mL graduated cylinder.

> **TIP** Estimate 1 decimal place beyond the markings on the graduated cylinder. For a 100 mL graduated cylinder, estimate to the nearest 0.1 mL.

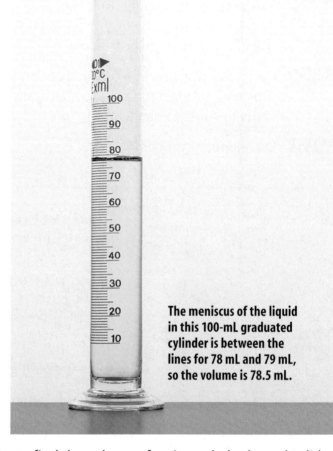

The meniscus of the liquid in this 100-mL graduated cylinder is between the lines for 78 mL and 79 mL, so the volume is 78.5 mL.

> **TIP** You can use a graduated cylinder to find the volume of an irregularly shaped solid object, such as a rock, by measuring the increase in a liquid's level after you add the object to the cylinder.

> **TIP** To find the volume of a solid, rectangular object such as your textbook, measure its length, width and height. Then, multiply them together.

9.a Plan and conduct a scientific investigation to test a hypothesis.

Tools of the Physical Scientist:
Lab and Field Study Tools

Triple-Beam Balance Use a triple-beam balance to measure the mass, or amount of material contained in an object.

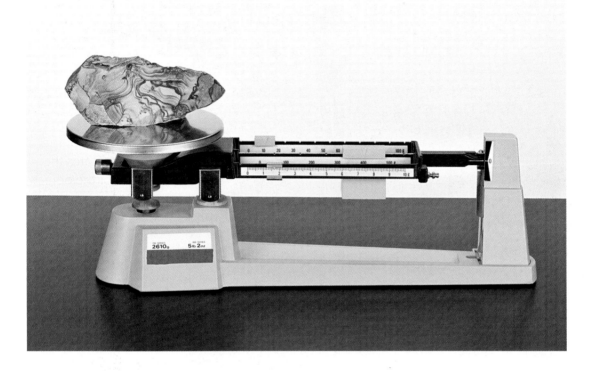

Using a Triple-Beam Balance

1. When nothing is on the pan, make sure the pointer of the balance and the riders are at zero.

2. Place the object you want to measure on the pan. The pointer will rise above the zero mark.

3. Adjust the riders to bring the pointer back down to zero. To do this, start by moving the largest rider (100 g) away from the pan one notch at a time. If moving the largest rider causes the pointer to fall below zero, set the largest rider back at the previous notch. Then, move the next smaller rider (10 g) in the same way.

4. Move the smallest rider (1 g) until the pointer rests at the zero mark. This means the object on the pan and the riders are balanced.

5. Add the measurements from the three beams together to determine the mass of the object.

Tools of the Physical Scientist:
Lab and Field Study Tools

9.a Plan and conduct a scientific investigation to test a hypothesis.

Spring Scale Use a spring scale to measure the weight, or the amount of force due to gravity, applied to an object.

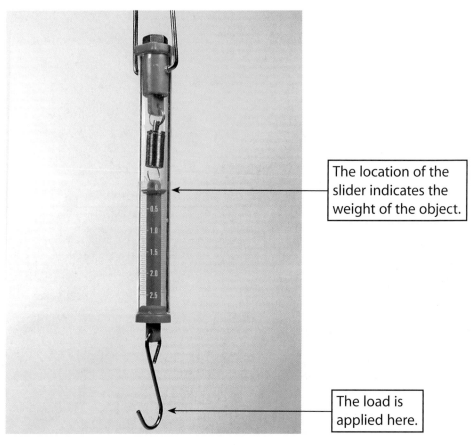

The location of the slider indicates the weight of the object.

The load is applied here.

TIP   The SI unit for weight is the Newton (N).

TIP   Gravitational force, or weight, is different on each planet in the solar system. For example, if you were to weigh an object on Earth and then weigh the same object on Mars, you would find that it weighs much less on Mars.

Calculator Use a calculator to quickly and easily perform mathematical calculations with quantitative data you have collected from scientific investigations.

TIP   Graphing calculators allow display graphs of algebraic formulas.

TIP   Most computer operating systems are equipped with a calculator program which will perform many of the same functions as a standard calculator.

9.a Plan and conduct a scientific investigation to test a hypothesis.

Tools of the Physical Scientist:
Lab and Field Study Tools

Stopwatch Use a stopwatch to measure the time it take for an event to occur.

TIP The SI unit of measurement for time is the second (s). However, for longer events, time is measured in hours (h).

TIP A **rate** is the amount of change of one measurement in a given amount of time. One rate you are probably familiar with is speed. Speed is the distance traveled in a given amount of time. Speeds are often measured in kilometers per hour (km/h).

TIP A rate can be a measure of anything that changes with time. For example, you can measure the number of cars that pass through an intersection per hour in cars/h.

Telescope Telescopes and spotting scopes allow you to observe celestial objects such as the Moon, stars and planets.

Using a Telescope

1. Set up your telescope. Make sure the tripod is stable and the lens caps are off.

2. Identify the object you want to view with your naked eye, then point the spotting scope in the general direction of your object.

3. Look through the spotting scope and slowly move the telescope until you find your object. Center it on the crosshairs in the spotting scope and tighten the scope so it doesn't move any more.

4. Look through the eyepiece and center the object in the field of view. Use the focus knob to bring the image into focus.

TIP If you do not have access to a telescope, binoculars are a good alternative. Binoculars can give you an excellent view of the moon and better views of Jupiter, Saturn and comets than you get with the naked eye.

Tools of the Physical Scientist:
Lab and Field Study Tools

9.a Plan and conduct a scientific investigation to test a hypothesis.

Computers and the Internet

Use a computer to collect, organize and store information about a topic you are researching. That information can be an article you found on the Internet or data from an experiment you performed.

Using Spreadsheet Programs

Use a spreadsheet program to create data tables and graphs.

TIP Think about how to organize your data before you begin entering data.

TIP Columns are assigned letters and rows are assigned numbers. Each point where a row and column intersect is called a cell, and is labeled according to where is located. For example: column A, row 1 is A1.

TIP To edit text in a cell, activate the cell by clicking on it.

TIP When using a spreadsheet program to create a graph, use the type of graph that best represents the data.

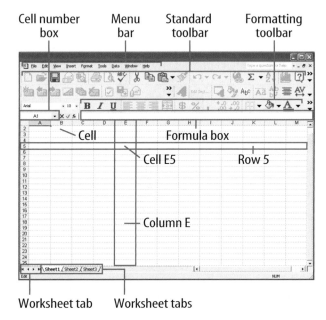

Using Search Engines

Use a web browser to search for information resources on the Internet.

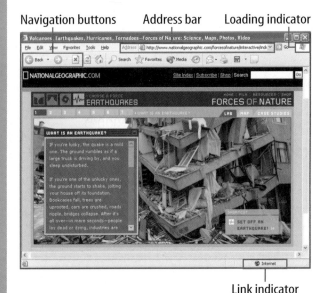

TIP Enclose phrases in quotes to narrow your search results. For example, "global warming."

TIP Use Boolean operators to further modify a search.

- **and**—narrows a search by requiring all terms to appear in document. For example, "global warming" *and* oceans.

- **or**—broadens a search by at least one of the terms joined by it to appear in the document. For example, "global warming" *or* "climate change."

- **and not**—limits a search by excluding documents whether they meet the other criteria of the search or not. For example, "global warming" *and* oceans *and not* **California.**

Tools of Scientific Thinking

Scientific thinking tools are techniques help you to refine your questions, make useful observations, and think critically about scientific information. As you work in the lab, refer to this guide to help you understand the nature of science.

The International System of Measurement

The International System of Units, or SI, is the internationally accepted system for measurement. It was created to provide a worldwide standard for measurement in science.

SI Base Units

Whenever you make quantitative observations during an experiment, you measure the physical property of an object. The International System of Units has a standard of measurement, called a base unit, that you can use to measure that property.

Table 1. SI Base Units		
Quantity Measured	**Unit**	**Symbol**
Length	meter	m
Mass	kilogram	kg
Time	second	s
Electric current	ampere	A
Temperature	kelvin	K
Amount of substance	mole	mol
Intensity of light	candela	cd

SI Units Prefixes

The SI system is easy to use because it is based on multiples of ten. Rather than having to remember rules like there are 12 inches in a foot and 5,280 feet in a mile, any SI unit is related to another by multiplying by a power of 10. The prefix in front of the unit represents a factor of 10. For example the prefix **kilo-** means 1000. So, a kilogram means 1000 grams.

Table 2. Common SI Prefixes		
Prefix	**Symbol**	**Multiplying Factor**
Kilo-	k	1,000
Deci-	d	0.1
Centi-	c	0.01
Milli-	m	0.001
Micro-	µ	0.000001
Nano-	n	0.000000001

Converting Between SI Units

To convert one unit of measurement to another, you must multiply measurement by a conversation factor. A **conversation factor** is a ratio that describes how much of one unit is in another.

EXAMPLE

The paper clip in the drawing measures 3.1 cm. Convert that measurement to mm.

1. First, determine the appropriate conversion factor. There are **10 mm** in **1 cm**. So, **10 mm/1 cm = 1.**

2. Then multiply the measurement by the conversion factor. **3.1 cm × 10 mm/1 cm = 31 mm.**

3. Check your units. The unit cm cancels in the equation, so the answer is **31 mm.**

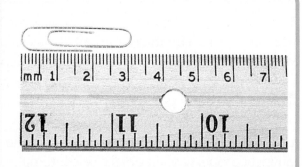

Scientific Notation

Scientific notation is a convenient way to write very small or large numbers. In scientific notation numbers are separated into two parts, a number between 1 and 10 and a power of 10. For example, the mass of Earth is 5,974,200,000,000,000,000,000,000 kg. Expressed in scientific notation, Earth's mass is 5.9742×10^{24}.

Converting Standard Numbers to Scientific Notation

Numbers can be converted between standard form and scientific notation by moving the number's decimal point to the left or right to make it a number between 1 and 10. The number of places the decimal point is moved is expressed as a power of 10. When you move the decimal to the left, the exponent is positive. When you move the decimal to the right, the exponent is negative.

Standard Form	Scientific Notation
610,000	6.1×10^5
Move decimal 5 places to the left.	Exponent is 5.
0.000078	7.8×10^{-5}
Move decimal 5 places to the right.	Exponent is −5.

Precision and Accuracy

Precision and accuracy are terms that can be used to evaluate quantitative observations, or measurement. The tools you use to make measurements have different degrees of precision and accuracy. It is important to describe how precise and accurate you think your measurements are whenever you perform scientific investigations. These descriptions help others interpret the evidence you present in your report.

Precision

Precision is a description of how similar or close measurements are to each other. For example, imagine you and your friend each measured the distance from your house to your school three times. Each time you measured 1.5 km. Your friend also measured the distance three times, but got 1.6 km, 1.4 km and 1.5 km. Because your measurement was the same every time, it is more precise than your friend's measurement.

Accuracy

Accuracy is a description of how close a measurement is to an accepted value. Even a tool that is very precise can be inaccurate. For example, a clock with a second hand is more precise than a clock that only has hour and minute hands. However, if the clock with the second hand is running an hour behind the correct time, even though it is precise, it is not accurate.

EXAMPLE

A way to visualize the difference between precision and accuracy is shown below. Imagine that the targets below show one archer's results in an archery competition. Look at positions of the arrows and then read the descriptions below them.

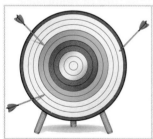			
Not Accurate, Not Precise	**Precise, Not Accurate**	**Accurate, Not Precise**	**Accurate and Precise**
This is a random pattern. The arrows are not clustered together and are not near the bull's-eye.	The arrows are clustered together but they are not near the bull's-eye.	There is only one arrow. Multiple arrows are needed to determine precision.	The arrows are tightly clustered and their average position is the center of the bull's-eye.

Tools of the Physical Scientist:
Tools of Scientific Thinking

9.a Plan and conduct a scientific investigation to test a hypothesis.

Measurement and Uncertainty

No measuring tool can provide a perfect measurement. Therefore all measurements have some degree of error, or uncertainty. Instruments with greater precision produce measurements with less uncertainty than instruments with relatively less precision.

EXAMPLE

The paper clips below are being measured with two rulers. The bottom ruler has a cm scale only. So you can say that the clip measures about 4.5 cm. By comparison, the top ruler has a mm scale. This allows you to measure the clip with greater precision. Based on the more precise scale, you can say that the clip measures 4.70 cm in length.

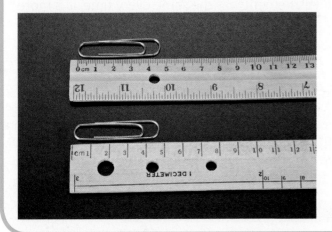

Significant Figures

One way of expressing measurement uncertainty is with significant figures. **Significant figures** are the number of digits in a measurement that you know with a certain degree of reliability. Significant figures are determined using the following rules:

• Digits other than zero are always significant.	1.234 g has 4 significant figures, 1.2 g has 2 significant figures.
• Zeroes to the right of a decimal point are significant.	0.023 mL has 2 significant figures, 0.200 g has 3 significant figures.
• Zeroes between nonzero digits are significant.	1002 kg has 4 significant figures, 3.07 mL has 3 significant figures.
• Zeroes to the left of the first nonzero digits are not significant; such zeroes merely indicate the position of the decimal point.	0.001°C has only 1 significant figure, 0.012 g has 2 significant figures.
• When a number ends in zeroes that are not to the right of a decimal point, the zeroes are not necessarily significant. To avoid confusion with this rule, use scientific notation to indicate the correct number of significant figures.	50,600 calories may be 3, 4, or 5 significant figures. 5.06×10^4 calories (3 significant figures) 5.060×10^4 calories (4 significant figures), 5.0600×10^4 calories (5 significant figures).

9.a Plan and conduct a scientific investigation to test a hypothesis.

Tools of the Physical Scientist:
Tools of Scientific Thinking

Hypotheses and Predictions

A **hypothesis** is a tentative explanation or an answer to a question that can be tested with a scientific investigation to describe *what* will happen and *why* it will happen.

A **prediction** is a forecast of what will happen next in a sequence of events, but it does not explain why something happens.

EXAMPLE

Imagine you have two daisies in your classroom. One looks healthy while the other is turning brown. You notice that the healthy-looking daisy receives a lot of sunlight, and the unhealthy daisy receives less sunlight. You know both plants are given the same amount of water every day.

What is one hypothesis that could be used to investigate why one daisy is healthy and the other is not?

1. Start by asking a **question**.	**1. Question:** Why is one daisy healthy and the other is not?
2. Document what you already know from **prior observations**.	**2. Observations:** The healthy-looking daisy receives a lot of sunlight. The unhealthy daisy receives little sunlight.
3. Write a **hypothesis** which tentatively explains your observation.	**3. Hypothesis:** The daisy is not healthy because it is not receiving enough light to grow.
4. Write a **prediction** that can be used to test your hypothesis.	**4. Prediction:** If I provide the unhealthy daisy with the same amount of sunlight as the healthy daisy, it will become healthier.

TIP The results of an experiment do not *prove* that a hypothesis is correct. Instead, the results of an experiment either *support or do not support* the hypothesis. This is because scientific inquiry is uncertain. You cannot be sure that you are aware of everything that could have affected the results of your experiment.

TIP An experiment is not a failure if the results do not support your hypothesis. In the experiment above, if the unhealthy plant does not improve after providing it with more light, you can eliminate that as the cause of the problem and revise your hypothesis.

Evaluating Evidence and Explanations

Whether you are reading science articles and lab reports or drawing conclusions from data you have collected in a lab, it is essential to think critically about the data and the scientific explanations presented to you. **Critical thinking** means comparing what you already know with the explanation you are given in order to decide if you agree with it or not.

Evaluating Scientific Evidence

Start by evaluating the quality of the evidence presented to you. Valid scientific investigations contain quantitative or qualitative evidence called **data**. Data can be descriptions, tables, graphs, or labeled drawings. Data are used to support or refute the investigation's hypothesis. When evaluating data from an investigation ask the following questions:

- **Does the journal article or lab report contain data?** A proper scientific investigation always contains data to support an explanation.

- **Are the data precise?** Data used to support an explanation should be exact. Quantitative observations or detailed descriptions and drawings of events are much better than vague descriptions of events. Imprecise phrases such as "a lot" and "a little" do not accurately describe an event because it's impossible to know to what that description is being compared. Vague descriptions lead to incorrect explanations.

- **Have the results of the experiment been repeated?** If a friend told you he could hit a home run, but he was unable to do it while you watched, would you believe him? Probably not. Likewise, scientific data are more reliable when the investigator has repeated an experiment several times and consistently produced the same results. Scientific evidence is considered to be even more reliable when multiple investigators try the same experiment and get the same results.

Think Like a Scientist

Why do you think scientific evidence is more reliable when different investigators try the same experiment rather than the same investigator performing the experiment multiple times?

Evaluating Scientific Explanations

Having good data is the first step to providing a good explanation for the data. However, it's easy to make a mistake and accidentally arrive at the wrong conclusion. When evaluating an inference or a conclusion, ask yourself the following questions:

- **Does the explanation make sense?** Be skeptical! There need to be logical connections between the investigator's question, hypothesis, predictions, data, and conclusions. Read the information carefully. Can the investigator reasonably draw his or her conclusion from the results of the experiment?

- **Are there any other possible explanations?** Since it is virtually impossible to control every variable that could affect the outcome of an experiment, it's important to think of other explanations for the results of an experiment. This is particularly true when the data are unusual or unexpected.

9.a Plan and conduct a scientific investigation to test a hypothesis.

9.b Evaluate the accuracy and reproducibility of data.

Tools of the Physical Scientist:
Tools of Scientific Thinking

Avoiding Bias in Investigations

Science produces reliable data if investigations are conducted objectively. In a scientific investigation, **bias** is an intentional or unintentional preference for one outcome over another.

Random Sampling

Sampling is a method of data collection that involves studying small amounts of something in order to learn something about the larger whole or group. Taking samples randomly prevents bias.

EXAMPLE

What percentage of jellybeans in this jar do you think are the following colors: brown, green, yellow, orange, red and black?

1. Close your eyes and take out 10 jellybeans.

2. Count how many jellybeans are each color in your pile of 10.

3. Calculate what percentage of the sample is represented by each color. Do this again for two more samples of 10.

4. Average results for each color and give an estimate of the percentages for the jar.

Blinded Study

A **blinded study** is a procedure that reduces bias by making the subject, investigator, or both unaware of which treatment they are testing.

EXAMPLE

In a taste test, people are blind-folded and asked to taste different brands of a product to determine which they prefer. Because the subject doesn't know which brand they are tasting, he or she is more likely to provide an unbiased data to the investigator.

Multiple Trials

It is easy to mislead yourself by basing your conclusions on too few data. Each trial of an experiment is likely to give you slightly different data. To avoid drawing incorrect conclusions, repeat your experiment.

EXAMPLE

Imagine you decide to test the idea that if you drop a piece of toast it will always land butter side down. You conduct three trials using three different pieces of buttered toast dropped 4 times each. After the first trial you might conclude that toast always lands butter side down. However, the data from Trials 2 and 3 indicate that toast landed butter side down 50% of the time.

Toast Dropping Data			
	Trial 1	**Trial 2**	**Trial 3**
Drop 1	down	down	up
Drop 2	down	up	down
Drop 3	down	up	up
Drop 4	down	down	down

Tools of the Physical Scientist:
Data Analysis Tools

9.e Construct appropriate graphs from data and develop quantitative state-ments about the relationships between variables.

Data Analysis Tools

Use data analysis tools to help you organize your data and display patterns in your results.

Making Data Tables

Data tables help you organize and record the measurements you make. A data table displays information in rows and columns so that it is eas-ier to read and understand.

EXAMPLE

Suppose you were competing in a 50-km bicycle race. You planned to keep a pace of 10 km/h. In order to know if you stayed on pace or not, you had a friend record your time at every 10 km.

Construct the Data Table

Step 1.	Think about the variables you plan to investigate. Then, organize the data table into columns and rows.
Step 2.	Create headings that describe the variable and the correspond-ing unit of measurement.
Step 3.	Give the data table a title and a number.

Your data can be organized like this:

Table 1 Bicycle Race Data

Distance (km)	Time (h)
0	0
10	0.75
20	2
30	3.5
40	4
50	5

Or like this:

Table 2 Bicycle Race Data

Distance (km)	0	10	20	30	40	50
Time (h)	0	0.75	2	3.5	4	5

 Think Like a Scientist

Study the types of graphs discussed in the pages ahead. Which type of graph would be appropri-ate for displaying the bicycle race data—a line graph, bar graph or circle graph? Why?

9.e Construct appropriate graphs from data and develop quantitative statements about the relationships between variables.

9.g Distinguish between linear and nonlinear relationships on a graph of data.

Tools of the Physical Scientist:
Data Analysis Tools

Understanding Linear Relationships

A **linear relationship** between variables results in a straight line on a graph.

EXAMPLE

Imagine riding a street luge down a steady slope. You and the luge increase in speed 2 m/s every second. Plotted on a graph, these data make a line.

Street Luge Speed

Time (s)	Speed (m/s)
0	0
1	2
2	4
3	6
4	8
5	10

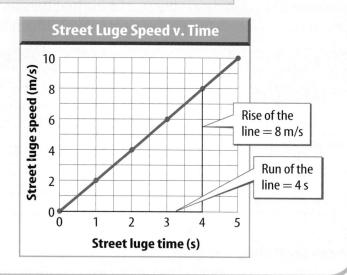

Rise of the line = 8 m/s

Run of the line = 4 s

Understanding Nonlinear Relationships

A **nonlinear relationship** between variables results in a curve on a graph.

EXAMPLE

Imagine riding down a hill that gets steeper and steeper. At the top, your speed increases 1 m/s each second. But after 4 s, your speed increases 8 m/s each second. Plotted on a graph, these data make a curve.

Street Luge Speed

Time (s)	Speed (m/s)
0	0
1	1
2	2
3	4
4	8
5	16

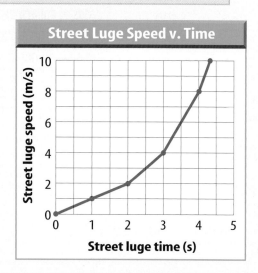

Tools of the Physical Scientist:
Data Analysis Tools

9.e Construct appropriate graphs from data and develop quantitative statements about the relationships between variables.

Analyzing Central Tendency in Data

Investigations in physical science often involve collecting large amounts of quantitative data. These data are likely to vary, making them hard to analyze at a glance. Measurements of central tendency help you summarize your data with a single middle value so that it is easier to draw conclusions about what occurred in the experiment.

Understanding Arithmetic Mean

The **mean** of a set of data is the sum of the numbers divided by the number of items in the set. It is the most commonly used measure of central tendency and is often referred to as an "average."

Table 1. Race Car Lap Times	
Lap Number	**Time (sec)**
1	101.1
2	103.7
3	97.9
4	100.8
5	102.3

EXAMPLE

Imagine you are at a car race and want to measure a typical lap time for your favorite driver. So, you record the time it takes her to drive five different laps. To find the mean, you use the following formula:

Mean = (sum of values)/(number of values)

= (sum of lap times)/(number of laps timed)

= (101.1 s + 103.7 s + 97.9 s + 100.8 s + 102.3 s)/(5)

= 101.2 s

Understanding Median

The **median** is the middle number in a data set when the data are arranged in numerical order. For example, the median of the number sequence {1,2,3,4,5} is 3. But consider the sequence, {1,2,3,4,20}. In this case, the median is still 3, even though there is a much higher number than the others in the sequence. For this reason, the median is a better choice than the mean when one extreme value does not represent the group.

Table 2. Mountain Bike Prices	
Mountain Bike	**Price**
Rockjumper	$250
Trailhound	$400
Singletrack	$500
Hipercara	$2,500

EXAMPLE

Suppose you want to know the typical price for a mountain bike. You go to the shop and write down the model name and corresponding price for each mountain bike. All of the bikes are priced in the hundreds of dollars, except for one. This bike is so expensive it doesn't represent the group. So, you calculate the median price. Since there are an even number of bikes, you average the middle two values: $\frac{\$400 + \$500}{2} = \$450$.

9.e Construct appropriate graphs from data and develop quantitative statements about the relationships between variables.

Tools of the Physical Scientist:
Data Analysis Tools

Making Line Graphs

A line graph shows a relationship between two variables that change continuously.

- Line graphs are good for showing how an independent variable affects a dependent variable or showing how a variable changes over time.
- Both variables in a line graph must be numbers.

EXAMPLE

Imagine three of your friends are running a 10-km foot race. You record their speed and time at 10 minute intervals for 60 minutes. You organize the data in a data table and plot each runner's time and speed on line graph.

Speed of 3 Runners During 10 km Race			
	Speed (km/h)		
Time (min)	Amelia	Sonja	Hiroko
0	6	10	12
10	6	10	12
20	8	10	14
30	12	10	16
40	11	10	0
50	11	10	3
60	12	10	6

Construct the Graph

Step 1.	Use the x-axis for the independent variable (time) and the y-axis for the dependent variable (speed).
Step 2.	Draw the x-axis and the y-axis using a scale that contains the smallest and largest values for each variable. Label each axis.
Step 3.	To plot the first data point, find the x-value (0) on the x-axis. Imagine a line rising vertically from that place on the scale. Then, find the corresponding y-value for Amelia (6) on the y-axis. Imagine a line moving horizontally from that place on the scale. Make a data point where the two imaginary lines intersect. Repeat this process for all the data points.
Step 4.	Choose a color for each runner and connect the data points with lines.
Step 5.	Title the graph.

Interpreting Line Graphs

- Sonja ran at a steady speed of 10 km/h for the entire 10 km race.
- Amelia's speed increased from 6 km/h to 12 km/h in the first half of the race. Her speed decreased to 11 km/h for the next 20 minutes. She then increased her speed to 12 km/h during the last 10 minutes she ran.
- Hiroko ran at a faster rate than her friends for the first 30 minutes of the race, accelerating from 12 km/h to 16 km/h. However, by minute 40 she had come to a complete stop. Hiroko then finished the remainder of the race running at a speed that varied between 3 km/h and 6 km/h.

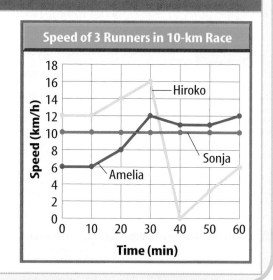

Tools of the Physical Scientist:
Data Analysis Tools

9.e Construct appropriate graphs from data and develop quantitative statements about the relationships between variables.

Making Bar Graphs

A bar graph uses rectangular blocks, or bars, of varying sizes to represent and compare quantitative data. The length of each bar is determined by the amount of the variable you are measuring.

EXAMPLE

Suppose you want to know if there is a seasonal difference in the pH of the rainwater in California. You look up the average pH measurements in several counties, record the data in a data table, and then plot the data on a graph.

Table 2. Average pH of Rainwater, Fall 2004 and Spring 2005

County	Spring pH	Fall pH
Los Angeles	4.7	5.2
Mendocino	5.3	5.4
Nevada	5.3	5.4
San Benito	5.7	5.4
San Bernardino	4.9	5.9
Montague	5.3	5.5
Davis	6	5.6
Shasta	5	5.2

Constructing the Graph

Step 1.	Use the x-axis for the category (county) and the y-axis for the measured variable (pH).
Step 2.	Draw the x-axis and the y-axis. Evenly space the category names below the x-axis. Use a scale that contains the smallest and largest values for the measured variable. Then, label each axis.
Step 3.	Draw the bars above each category name. Each bar should be as tall as the measured variable.
Step 4.	Title the graph.

Interpreting Bar Graphs

- Which county had the greatest difference in average rainfall pH between Fall 2004 and Spring 2005?

- How many counties had a lower average pH in the Spring 2005 than Fall 2004?

- Questions to ask: *How has rainfall pH in California changed over time?*

TIP Changing the scale can help you show trends when there are small differences in your data. However, be careful to avoid misinterpreting the data based on what you see.

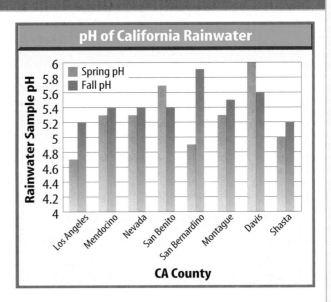

9.e Construct appropriate graphs from data and develop quantitative statements about the relationships between variables.

Tools of the Physical Scientist:
Data Analysis Tools

Making Circle Graphs

A circle graph, or pie graph, is used to show some fixed quantity is broken down into parts. The circular pie represents the total. The slices represent the parts and usually are presented as percentages.

EXAMPLE

Suppose your teacher told you how many students scored each grade on your last physical science test. You want to know how well you scored compared to other students in the class. You record the test data in a data table and draw a circle graph.

Table 3. Test Scores for Physical Science Class	
Test Score	**Number of Students**
A	3
B	7
C	6
D	3
E	1

Constructing the Graph

Step 1.	Find the total of the measured variable (number of students): $3 + 7 + 6 + 3 + 1 = 20$
Step 2.	Calculate the size of the slice for the first category's value (3). Write a fraction comparing the category's value with the total for all categories (3/20). Multiply this fraction by 360°: **(3/20) × 360° = 54°.** Repeat for the remaining categories.
Step 3.	Draw a circle. Use a protractor to draw the angle (number of degrees) for each category.
Step 4.	Color and label each section of the graph.
Step 5.	Title the graph.

Interpreting Circle Graphs

- To calculate what percent of the class scored each grade, write a fraction comparing the number of students that got each grade to the total number of students. Then multiply by 100.
  A: (3/20) × 100 = 15%
- 80% of the class scored a C or better on the test.
- <u>Questions to ask:</u> *Is this range of test scores typical for a middle school physical science class?*

Physical Science Test Scores

Tools of the Physical Scientist:
Designing a Controlled Experiment

9.a Plan and conduct a scientific investigation to test a hypothesis.

Designing a Controlled Experiment

In this section you will apply your lab skills, scientific thinking skills, and data analysis skills to the task of designing your own controlled experiment. A controlled experiment is a type of scientific investigation that tests how one thing affects another. Use this section to help you with Design Your Own Labs and science projects.

Asking Scientific Questions

Scientific investigations often begin when someone observes an event in nature and wonders why or how it occurs. To begin designing an experiment, questions need to be refined into specific questions that can be answered with the time and resources available to you.

EXAMPLE

Some professional baseball players have been known to illegally modify their bats using a process called "corking." When a bat is corked, a hole is bored into the wide end of the bat and filled with cork. These baseball players claim that using a corked bat makes it easier to hit the ball a greater distance. Being curious and skeptical, you decide to investigate the issue using a controlled experiment.

Question:

Does a "corked" bat hit a baseball a greater distance than a normal bat? If so, what causes it to do so?

Observations:

- Some baseball players claim that a corked bat enables them to hit the ball a greater distance than a regulation bat.

- The structure of the bat is changed when a bat is corked: the inside of the bat is hollowed out and wood is replaced with cork.

- Cork is less massive per unit volume than the ash-wood bats from which bats are made, so a corked bat must have less mass than a regulation bat.

- Library research indicates the more mass an object has, the more momentum when it is in motion.

Refined Question:

Does changing the mass of a regulation wooden baseball bat affect the distance a baseball is hit?

9.a Plan and conduct a scientific investigation to test a hypothesis.

9.c Distinguish between variable and controlled parameters in a test.

Tools of the Physical Scientist:
Designing a Controlled Experiment

Writing a Hypothesis and Prediction

A **hypothesis** is a tentative explanation that can be tested with a scientific investigation. It uses your prior knowledge and observations to predict what will happen and why. A **prediction** is a statement of what will happen next in a sequence of events—in this case, your experiment. If the results of the experiment match the prediction, the hypothesis is considered to be supported.

Hypothesis:
A regulation bat will hit a baseball a greater distance than a corked bat because the corked bat contains less mass than the regulation bat.

Predictions:
(1) A regulation baseball bat that has been filled with cork will hit a baseball a shorter distance than a comparable unmodified bat.

(2) A regulation baseball bat that has been filled with copper BBs will hit a baseball a greater distance than a comparable unmodified bat.

Defining Variables and Constants

To test a prediction, you need to identify variables and constants you want to use in your experiment. Variables and constants are factors you think could affect the outcome of your experiment.

Variables

A **variable** is any factor that can have more than one value. In a controlled experiment, there are two types of variables—independent variables and dependent variables.

The **independent variable** is the factor you want to test. It is manipulated or changed by the investigator to observe how it affects a dependent variable.

A **dependent variable** is the factor you measure or observe during an experiment.

Constants

To test how the independent variable affects the dependent variable, you need to keep all other factors the same for each test. The factors that remain the same are called **constants**. Without constants, two independent variables could change at the same time and you won't know which variable affected the dependent variable.

Independent Variable: baseball bat modification

Dependent Variable: distance baseball travels in the air after collision with bat

Constants: same brand and model of baseball bat, same baseball, same batting tee, same batting device

Tools of the Physical Scientist:
Designing a Controlled Experiment

9.a Plan and conduct a scientific investigation to test a hypothesis.

Experimental Group and Control Group

A controlled experiment has at least two groups—a control group and an experimental group. The **experimental group** is used to study the effect of a change in the independent variable on the dependent variable. The **control group** contains the same factors as the experimental group, but the independent variable is not changed. Without a control, it is impossible to know if your experimental observations result from the variable you are testing or some other factor.

Experimental group:
Modified regulation baseball bats

Control group:
Unmodified regulation baseball bat

Measuring the Dependent Variable

Before you write a procedure, think about what kind of data you need to gather from the dependent variable to know how it relates to the changes you make to the independent variable. Dependent variables can be measured qualitatively or quantitatively.

Qualitative Measurement

Qualitative measurements of the dependent variable use words to describe what you observe in your experiment. Qualitative measurements are easy to make. For some investigations, qualitative data might be the only kind of data you can collect.

Qualitative Measurement of Baseball Distance in Air After Collision with Bat

Independent Variable
Type of modification made to bat

Dependent Variable
Distance defined as greater or lesser than control bat from starting point at batting tee to contact with ground

Quantitative Measurement

Quantitative measurements of the dependent variable use numbers to describe what you observe in your experiment. In most experiments, quantitative measurements will provide you with greater precision in your data than qualitative measurements.

Quantitative Measurement of Baseball Distance Traveled After Collision with Bat

Independent Variable
Type of modification made to bat

Dependent Variable
Distance defined as meters (m) from starting point at batting tee to contact with ground

9.a Plan and conduct a scientific investigation to test a hypothesis.

Tools of the Physical Scientist:
Designing a Controlled Experiment

Writing a Procedure

A procedure is a set of instructions that you use to gather the data you need to answer your question. Each step in the experiment's procedure should be clear and easy to follow. Record your procedure in your Science Journal so you can execute it with precision.

Bat Preparation Procedure:

Step 1 Cut off the top 2 cm of two bats.

Step 2 Using a drill, hollow out a vertical chamber 2.5 cm in diameter and 20 cm deep.

Step 3 Fill bat 1 with cork. Fill bat 2 with BBs. Using wood glue, replace ends of bats.

Step 4 Measure and record each bat's mass.

Batting Device Construction Procedure:

Step 1 Anchor pine 2 × 4 column to plywood base.

Step 2 Attach torsion spring to top of column.

Step 3 Attach 2 × 4 swinging arm to top of torsion spring.

Step 4 Attach metal straps to arm to hold bat.

Step 5 Stack concrete blocks on plywood base for stability.

Bat Test Procedure

Step 1 Attach bat to be tested to batting device using metal straps.

Step 2 Adjust batting tee to align with bat's swing. Place baseball on tee.

Step 3 Pull bat back 180° from its resting position and release.

Step 4 Measure the linear distance from the tee to the baseball's landing spot. Record data in data table. Repeat this procedure, 10 trials per bat.

Step 5 Calculate the average distance for the modified bats and control.

Determining Materials

Carefully examine each step in your procedures. Determine what materials and tools are required to complete each step.

1. <u>To modify bats:</u> vise, saw, safety goggles, drill, cork, BBs, solid ash wood bats (3), glue

2. <u>To construct batting machine:</u> Screws, torsion spring, metal straps, plywood board, pine 2x4, concrete blocks

3. <u>To test bats:</u> Batting tee, baseball, triple-beam balance, tape measure

9.a Plan and conduct a scientific investigation to test a hypothesis.

9.b Evaluate the accuracy and reproducibility of data.

Recording Observations

Once your procedure has been approved, follow the steps in your procedure and record your data. As you make observations, note anything that differs from your intended procedure. If you change a material or have to adjust the amount of time you observe something, write that down in your Science Journal.

Figure 1 Distance (m) Ball Traveled After Contact with Bat

	Corked Bat	BB Modified Bat	Regular Bat
Trial 1	3.8	4.6	3.8
Trial 2	3.6	4.7	3.8
Trial 3	3.5	4.6	3.8
Trial 4	3.4	4.6	3.7
Trial 5	3.8	4.9	4.0
Trial 6	3.8	4.7	3.9
Trial 7	3.7	4.3	4.0
Trial 8	3.5	4.7	3.9
Trial 9	3.7	4.5	4.0
Trial 10	3.7	4.7	3.9
Average	**3.7**	**4.6**	**3.9**

Analyzing Results

To summarize your data, look at all of your observations together. Look for meaningful ways to present your observations. Presenting your data in the form of a graph is a powerful tool to communicate patterns in your data.

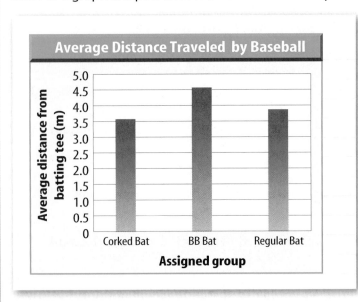

9.a Plan and conduct a scientific investigation to test a hypothesis.

9.b Evaluate the accuracy and reproducibility of data.

Tools of the Physical Scientist:
Designing a Controlled Experiment

Drawing Conclusions

To draw conclusions from your experiment, examine the data tables and graphs you have created. Describe trends you see in the data. Then, compare the results to your prediction and hypothesis. Determine if the results support or do not support your hypothesis. Use evidence in your results to support your determination.

The results show that the corked bat consistently hit the baseball less distance than the unmodified bat used as a control. Also, the bat filled with BBs consistently hit the baseball a greater distance than the control. Since the corked bat is less massive than the control and the BB bat is more massive than the control, these results support the hypothesis that a bat with greater mass should hit the ball a greater distance.

The results of this experiment cast doubt on the belief that a corked bat would help a baseball player hit the ball a greater distance. However, mass is not the only factor involved in hitting a ball a great distance in the actual game of baseball. For example, a less massive bat may help a player adjust his or her swing to hit the ball more effectively, resulting in consistently greater distance for each hit. Further investigation is required to gather data about this factor.

Analyzing Error

Error is a part of any scientific research. It's important to document anything that you changed in your procedure or could have caused uncertainty in your measurements. Be sure to include unanticipated factors or accidents that may have influenced your results and offer alternative explanations for your results.

Error for this experiment results from the following:

- Bat in batting machine may have been pulled back to slightly more or less than 180° for each trial.

- Judgment by eyesight of baseball landing spot may have been plus or minus 1 cm.

- Measurement of distance with the tape measurement may have plus or minus 1 cm.

Overall, variations in the data appear random. Multiple trials helped to insure the reliability of the conclusions drawn from these data.

Case Study: Wind Turbines for the Birds

Professor William Hodos of the University of Maryland has spent his entire career trying to understand how birds see the world. So when researchers at California's largest wind energy farm found that thousands of birds were colliding with wind turbines there, they asked Professor Hodos for advice.

Wind Farms—An Alternative to Fossil Fuels

Current interest in wind farms as a source of energy goes back thirty years. In the 1970s, a major oil shortage forced Americans to look for new energy sources. The United States had become overly dependent on fossil fuels—natural gas, coal and oil, for its energy needs. Obtaining energy from the wind was an attractive alternative. The wind did not create pollution. Its cost was competitive with fossil fuel energy. And it was inexhaustible.

Wind turbines convert wind energy into electricity. They differ from windmills, which use wind energy to pump water or grind grain. In 1892, a Danish inventor constructed the first wind turbine from a Dutch windmill. Wind turned the blades. The blades then drove a shaft connected to an electrical generator, producing electricity.

Wind turbines supplied electricity to rural areas in the United States until the 1930s. But unlike fossil-fuel plants, they could not operate around the clock. They could only produce electricity when the wind was blowing. To overcome this problem, modern wind turbines usually connect to utility power networks. When the wind is not blowing, fossil fuels produce the electricity.

A single wind turbine can produce enough electricity for 150 to 400 homes.

Wind Farms in California

California was one of the first states to develop wind power. There are now 13,000 wind turbines in the state, and wind produces about one percent of the state's electricity. A single wind turbine can produce enough electricity for 150 to 400 homes. That is equivalent to 1.5 to 4.0 million kilowatt-hours of electricity each year. One kilowatt-hour is the amount of energy required to keep a 100-watt light bulb burning for 10 hours.

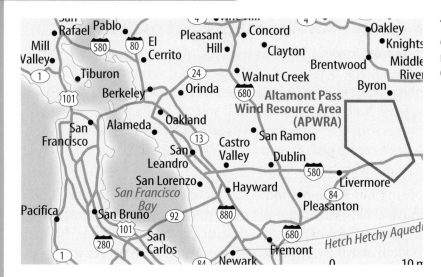

The Altamont Pass Wind Resource Area occupies 50,000 acres of land approximately 50 miles east of San Francisco, California.

The Altamont Pass Wind Resource Area

The Altamont Pass Wind Resource Area (APWRA) is the largest wind farm in California. Located about 50 miles east of San Francisco, APWRA first began producing electricity from the wind in the 1970s. There are now about 5,400 wind turbines at the site.

Because a wind turbine may require up to two acres of its own land, wind farms tend to be quite large. APWRA, for example, occupies 50,000 acres. The rolling, grass-covered hills at APWRA also provide land for farming and cattle grazing.

A Problem with Wind Power

Hawks, owls, eagles and other birds live in the hills at APWRA. In the 1980s, studies showed that the wind turbine blades were killing thousands of birds each year. The same winds that make APWRA an excellent location for wind turbines carry the birds over Altamont Pass each winter. The birds are in direct competition with the wind turbines for air space.

Federal and state laws protect many of these birds. Although APWRA has a permit to operate at a capacity of 800 megawatts (1 megawatt = 1,000,000 watts), local officials have limited APWRA's capacity to 580 megawatts until a way is found to reduce the bird deaths.

California also has large wind farms at Pacheco Pass, San Gorgonio Pass, and Tehachapi Pass, and in Solano County. Dead birds have been found at these sites too. The operators of those wind farms are closely monitoring developments at APWRA.

Field Experiments at APWRA

The first studies of bird deaths at APWRA looked at the older turbines on the site. These turbines were smaller than the ones currently in use. They had smaller blades than the newer designs, and shorter towers.

Make the blades larger?

Some investigators thought they could reduce the bird fatalities by replacing the smaller blades with larger ones that moved more slowly. They also thought the blades in the taller designs would be out of the birds' flight path. However, researchers at another wind farm in California have found that the newer turbines have killed more birds than the older ones.

Make the blades less likely to hit?

A few researchers have developed mathematical models to study the collisions. They first try to calculate the probability that a bird will collide with a spinning blade—rather like predicting whether a dart will hit a dartboard. They then propose designs that will reduce that probability. Based on their calculations, tall turbines with large blades should be safest for birds. But the field data do not appear to support this conclusion. The mathematical models do not consider how the birds see the blades.

The Altamont Pass Wind Resource Area is a migration path for birds of prey such as the golden eagle. As a result, thousands of such birds are killed each year when they collide into spinning turbine blades.

Move the blades?

Other investigators have studied the locations of the wind turbines in the hills. They believe that the way the birds see the turbines is more important than the probability of a collision. Ideally, one could place the wind turbines out of the flight paths. But there is little scientific basis for deciding how to do this.

Make the blades less attractive to birds?

Another approach has been to try to make the wind farm less attractive to the birds. Researchers have designed new towers that are more difficult for birds to sit on. They have also poisoned the ground squirrels that the birds feed on. But birds have been flying over Altamont Pass for thousands of years, and their behavior has not changed very much.

Shut down the wind farm?

Still other investigators have proposed shutting down the wind farm during part of the year. In the fall of 2005, local officials voted to shut down half of the Altamont Pass wind turbines in the winter. Most of the bird deaths occur at this time of year, and the wind turbines are least productive then. But critics doubt a partial shut down will solve the problem.

9.a Plan and conduct a scientific investigation to test a hypothesis.

Controlled Studies in the Laboratory

It has been very difficult to design controlled experiments at APWRA. Many of the variables that could influence a bird's collision with a wind turbine—for example, wind velocity, air density and flight behavior, are beyond human control.

There are other problems as well. Although many birds have died at APWRA, the chances that a bird will collide with any particular wind turbine are small. The number of wind turbines included in a field study at APWRA would have to be quite large. Under these conditions, it could take many years to test a scientific hypothesis. And the cost of the experiment could be very high.

Professor Hodos performed controlled experiments that measured the American kestrel's ability to perceive moving objects.

Professor Hodos Tries a New Approach

Unlike field researchers at APWRA, Professor William Hodos has attempted to identify the cause of the bird deaths in a laboratory. There he can control the experimental variables. Hodos has been looking at how the American kestrel (*Falco sparverius*), a small North American falcon, perceives the spinning wind turbine blades. Many kestrels have died at APWRA.

Professor Hodos is a psychophysicist. He studies the way the senses—sight, sound, scent, taste and touch, get information from the physical world. As a college student, one of his first experiments looked at how rats experience bitter tastes. The experiment taught him the usefulness of having training in several areas of science.

Later, while at the Walter Reed Army Institute of Research in Washington, D.C., Dr. Hodos met another scientist who was interested in how birds process information. Hodos realized that an understanding of bird vision would be important in these studies.

By the time the bird deaths were discovered at the California wind farm, Professor Hodos had acquired a reputation as a leading expert on bird vision. At the request of the U.S. Department of Energy, he began performing laboratory experiments to see if there was a way to prevent further deaths. The wind farm is now testing Professor Hodos' laboratory findings.

9.a Plan and conduct a scientific investigation to test a hypothesis.

9.b Evaluate the accuracy and reproducibility of data.

Physical Science Case Study:
Wind Turbines for the Birds

A First Hypothesis

Professor Hodos hoped to prevent the bird deaths based on understanding how the birds saw the spinning blades. But before he could perform any experiments, he had to develop a testable hypothesis. His first hypothesis was that the birds at APWRA were so busy searching the ground that they did not notice the turbines, and therefore flew into them. But he already knew that birds, unlike humans, can focus at the same time on objects that are far apart. So he decided to reject this hypothesis.

A Second Hypothesis

He then considered a second hypothesis—that the birds flew into the spinning blades because *they could not see them*. Hodos knew that when he travels in a car at high speeds, he can see objects that are far away clearly. But objects that are closer appear blurred. He decided to find out whether birds and people see fast moving objects the same way.

Professor Hodos hypothesized that the kestrels were unable to see the spinning turbine blades when the kestrels were close to them.

Hodos designed an experiment to measure the response of the kestrel's retina—the part of the eye where images form before they are sent to the brain, to moving turbine blades. In the experiment, he would attach electrodes to the eyelids of 15 kestrels. The electrodes would detect the electrical signals produced when light from the moving blades struck a bird's retina. The experiment called for the birds to receive a light anesthesia, so that they would be comfortable during the experiment.

Experiment 1—Painting All Three Blades

In Professor Hodos' first experiment, he tested the response of three kestrels (in seven sessions, with three measurements per session) to several blade patterns. These included blank blades, blades painted with thin stripes, and blades painted with thick stripes. The patterns on each blade were unique. For comparison, he also measured the response when the birds eyes were covered.

This experiment allowed Hodos to measure how fast the blade's image moved across the bird's retina, and how well the birds could process that information. He found that, at slow rotations, the thin-striped blades were up to four times as easy to see as the blank blades. Under similar conditions, the thick-striped blades were nearly twice as visible. But when the image was moving across the retina more rapidly, differences in visibility became smaller. At still higher velocities, all of the blades were invisible to the kestrels.

Physical Science Case Study:
Wind Turbines for the Birds

9.a Plan and conduct a scientific investigation to test a hypothesis.

9.b Evaluate the accuracy and reproducibility of data.

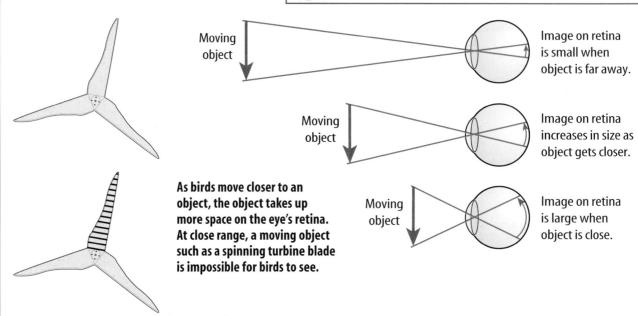

Moving object — Image on retina is small when object is far away.

Moving object — Image on retina increases in size as object gets closer.

Moving object — Image on retina is large when object is close.

As birds move closer to an object, the object takes up more space on the eye's retina. At close range, a moving object such as a spinning turbine blade is impossible for birds to see.

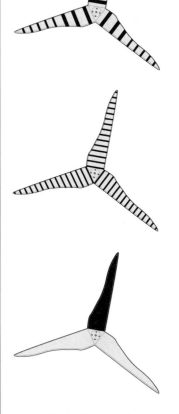

In the lab, Professor Hodos tested the ability of kestrels to perceive different turbine blade patterns while they were in motion.

Experiment 2—Painting Only One Blade

Hodos then wanted to know whether he could reduce how fast the birds' eyes received information from the spinning blades. If this information arrived slowly enough, he thought, the birds would be able to see even fast moving blades. Hodos' decided to paint only one of the three spinning blades, so that the overall pattern would be irregular.

In his second experiment, Hodos tested the kestrels' ability to see seven blade patterns. He again measured the electrical signals that were produced when the birds' eyes detected moving patterns. The table on page 41 shows his results.

Hodos found that the single black blade paired with two blank blades were most visible to the birds. However, even the painted blades appeared blurred to the kestrels when spinning very rapidly.

Hodos next calculated the distances at which the birds could just make out the rotating blades. He was surprised to discover that the birds could see fast moving, smaller blades best. They were much easier to see than slowly moving, larger blades. The kestrels could see the small, fast moving blades as close as 20 m, but the larger, slow moving blades became hard to see at 50 m.

9.a Plan and conduct a scientific investigation to test a hypothesis.
9.b Evaluate the accuracy and reproducibility of data.

Physical Science Case Study:
Wind Turbines for the Birds

	Pattern	Visibility (microVolts above noise)
1	Noise. Birds eyes covered	0.00
2	Three blank blades	1.03
3	Two blades blank, one blade with thin stripes	1.71
4	Three blades with staggered thick and thin stripes	1.75
5	Three blades, thin non-staggered stripes	1.77
6	Two blank blades, one blade with thick and thin stripes	1.77
7	Three blades, staggered thin stripes	1.98
8	Two blank blades, one solid black blade	2.37

Field Testing Painted Blades

Hodos' laboratory experiments showed that the kestrels could see painted blades better than unpainted ones. He hoped that the kestrels would be able to avoid the painted wind turbine blades at APWRA more easily than unpainted ones. But his laboratory experiments only looked at the birds' visual response to moving turbine blades. They did not consider the bird's psychology. There was no way of knowing, for example, whether birds at APWRA would be scared away by the painted blades, whether they would be attracted to them, or whether they would pay no attention to them.

In order to answer this question, Hodos designed a field test to be conducted at APWRA. In the test, some of the wind turbines would have unpainted blades. The others would have one solid black blade and two blank blades. The turbines would be placed where large numbers of birds had been killed in the past. In the first year, this field test would measure the number of birds killed at the turbines.

Wind farm operators at APWRA are now testing Professor Hodos' painted blades. If the number of birds killed by the turbines with painted blades in the first year turns out to be lower than that at the other turbines, the blade patterns will be switched. If the painted blades still show fewer bird deaths, the field test will support the conclusion that the painted blades are effective in preventing collisions with turbine blades.

A Final Note

Human beings have been trying to find better ways to harness the wind for thousands of years. Five thousand years ago, the Egyptians found they could sail down the Nile under wind power. The first windmills appeared in Persia around 950 AD. About 100 years ago, the first wind turbine was constructed. Each of these advances depended upon an improved understanding of motion and forces.

Attempts to find a solution to the bird deaths at APWRA rest on many of the same physical principles. As you will hopefully discover, the research methods and fundamental principles described in this textbook lend themselves to an extremely wide range of scientific investigations.

UNIT 1
Motion and Forces

The Speed of Sound Forces of jet engines that can move planes faster than speed of sound cause a vapor cloud that occurs at near speed of sound from changes in pressure.

West Coast Events

1579
Francis Drake anchors the *Golden Hind* at Point Reyes just north of San Francisco, California, during first English voyage around the world.

1863
Construction begins on the Central Pacific Railway; starts in Sacramento, California, and joins the Union Pacific Railway in Utah in 1869.

A.D. 1500   1600   1700   1800

World Events

2,220 Years Ago
Archimedes, a Greek mathematician, discovers that the buoyant force equals the weight of the fluid displaced by an object (called Archimedes' principle).

c. 1660
Robert Boyle of England describes what causes the pressure of gases to change.

1687
Isaac Newton of England describes three laws of motion.

1877
Ernst Mach from Austria uses bullets to record the speed of sound; Mach 1 becomes the reference for the speed of sound.

Science Online

To learn more about physicists and their work, visit ca8.msscience.com.

Concepts In Motion

Interactive Time Line To learn more about these events and others, visit ca8.msscience.com.

October 1947
Chuck Yeager—at Muroc Army Air Field (now Edwards Air Force Base, California)—is first to fly plane faster than speed of sound.

1978
Speed boat sets record speed of 511.10 km/h on Lake Washington at Seattle, Washington.

August 2005
Commander Eileen Collins and pilot James Kelly guide Space Shuttle Discovery in its 27,357.58 km/h glide from space to landing strip at Edwards Air Force Base.

1900 **1920** **1940** **1960** **1980** **2000** **2020**

1903
Wright Brothers fly first motorized airplane at Kitty Hawk, North Carolina.

February 1962
John Glenn is first American to orbit Earth.

June 1963
Valentina Tereshkova of the Soviet Union is the first woman to orbit Earth.

1997
At the Black Rock speedway in Utah, Richard Noble's jet race car is first to break the sound barrier on land (1227.93 km/h).

Motion

The BIG Idea

Motion occurs when the position of an object changes.

LESSON 1 — 1.a
Determining Position

Main Idea Position is defined relative to a reference point and reference directions.

LESSON 2
1.b, 1.c, 1.d, 1.e, 9.b, 9.f

Speed, Velocity, and Acceleration

Main Idea Speed, velocity, and acceleration describe how an object's position and motion change in time.

LESSON 3 — 1.f, 9.d, 9.e
Graphing Motion

Main Idea Graphs can show how objects change their position or speed.

No Snow Required!

The road is just a blur to these street-luge racers, who reach speeds over 88 km/h lying on specially-built boards made out of aluminum. Street-luge courses are usually about 1 km long and are downhill, although the course can have turns and parts that are uphill.

Science Journal Write a short description of how the motion of the racers might change from the start of the race to the finish line.

How do you get there from here?

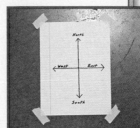

How would you give directions to a friend trying to walk from one place to another in your classroom?

Procedure

1. Place a **sheet of paper labeled** *North, East, South,* **and** *West* on the floor.

2. Walk from the paper to one of the three goals labeled in the classroom. Have a partner record the number of steps and the directions of movement.

3. Repeat steps 1 and 2 for the other goals.

Think About This

- **Explain** why having a common starting point is important when giving directions.

- **Suggest** ways to improve the distance measurements made during this lab.

 1.a, 9.b

Science Online

Visit ca8.msscience.com to:

▶ view **Concepts in Motion**

▶ explore Virtual Labs

▶ access content-related Web links

▶ take the Standards Check

 **Motion** Make the following Foldable to describe speed, velocity, and acceleration and discuss how they are related.

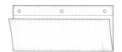 **STEP 1** **Fold** a sheet of paper in half lengthwise. Make the back edge about 3 cm longer than the front edge.

 STEP 2 **Fold** into thirds.

STEP 3 **Unfold** and **cut** along the folds of the top flap to make three flaps.

STEP 4 **Label** as shown.

 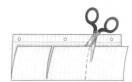

Reading Skill

Interpreting
As you read this chapter, record information about each of the types of motion. Be sure to include information about how the term is related to the other terms.

Get Ready to Read

Preview

① Learn It! If you know what to expect before reading, it will be easier to understand ideas and relationships presented in the text. Follow these steps to preview your reading assignments.

1. Look at the title and any illustrations that are included.
2. Read the headings, subheadings, and anything in bold letters.
3. Skim over the passage to see how it is organized. Is it divided into many parts?
4. Look at the graphics—pictures, maps, or diagrams. Read their titles, labels, and captions.
5. Set a purpose for your reading. Are you reading to learn something new? Are you reading to find specific information?

② Practice It! Take some time to preview this chapter. Skim all the main headings and subheadings. With a partner, discuss your answers to these questions.

- Which part of this chapter looks most interesting to you?
- Are there any words in the headings that are unfamiliar to you?
- Choose one of the lesson review questions to discuss with a partner.

③ Apply It! Now that you have skimmed the chapter, write a short paragraph describing one thing you want to learn from this chapter.

Target Your Reading

Use this to focus on the main ideas as you read the chapter.

Reading Tip

As you preview this chapter, be sure to scan the illustrations, tables, and graphs. Skim the captions.

1 **Before you read** the chapter, respond to the statements below on your worksheet or on a numbered sheet of paper.
- Write an **A** if you **agree** with the statement.
- Write a **D** if you **disagree** with the statement.

2 **After you read** the chapter, look back to this page to see if you've changed your mind about any of the statements.
- If any of your answers changed, explain why.
- Change any false statements into true statements.
- Use your revised statements as a study guide.

Before You Read A or D	Statement	After You Read A or D
	1 Giving a starting point isn't important when giving directions.	
	2 Some measurements have both size and direction.	
	3 If an object is not moving, all observers will give the same directions to the object.	
	4 Speed and velocity mean the same thing.	
	5 An object is accelerating only if its speed is changing.	
	6 Average speed is total time divided by total distance.	
	7 Speed always is measured in miles per hour.	
	8 The slope of a line on a position-time graph is the acceleration of an object.	
	9 If a line plotted on a graph is horizontal, the line's slope is zero.	
	10 A straight line on a position-time graph means the speed of the object is not changing.	

Science Online

Print a worksheet of this page at ca8.msscience.com.

Science Content Standards

1.a Students know position is defined in relation to some choice of a standard reference point and a set of reference directions.

Reading Guide

What *You'll Learn*

▶ **Explain** how position depends on the choice of a reference point and reference direction.

▶ **Determine** the position of an object in two dimensions.

▶ **Describe** the difference between distance and displacement.

Why *It's Important*

To know how to get where you want to go, you first must know where you are.

Vocabulary

reference point
vector
displacement

Review Vocabulary

distance: the length of a path from one point to another (p. 7)

Determining Position

 Position is defined relative to a reference point and reference directions.

Real-World Reading Connection How would you describe where you are right now? Maybe your description would include the name of a street or a building. Or maybe it would include directions from a familiar landmark or road. How could you describe your location so that anyone could find you?

Position and Reference Points

Suppose that **Figure 1** is an aerial view of your neighborhood. A classmate tells you that her house is two blocks west and one block south of your house. To reach your classmate's house, you start at your house and walk two blocks west and one block south. Your house is the starting place for you to find the location, or position, of your classmate's house. A **reference point** is a starting point used to describe the position of an object. A reference point is sometimes called the origin.

Reading Check What is a reference point?

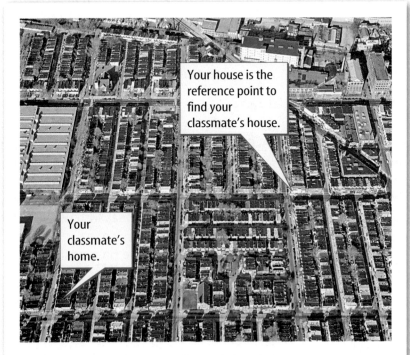

Figure 1 A reference point is needed in order to describe the location of a house in the neighborhood.

Figure 2 The flagpole can be used as a reference point for finding the bicycle.

5 m

Reference Points and Reference Directions

Your classmate told you where to start, which direction, and how far to walk to reach her house. You had to start at the grocery store, which was the reference point. The direction you had to walk was east, for a distance of three blocks. To describe an object's position, you must include three things in your description: a reference point, a direction from the reference point, and a distance from the reference point.

How would you describe the position of the bicycle in **Figure 2?** First, choose a reference point: the flagpole. Next, choose a direction from the reference point: toward the front door of the school. Finally, give the distance from the reference point: 5 m. Notice that the distance is described in units of length, in this case, meters.

Describing the Reference Direction

How can you indicate the direction from the reference point? One way is to use a plus (+) or a minus (−) sign to indicate the direction. The plus sign means the direction from the reference point is in the reference direction. A minus sign means the direction is opposite to the reference direction. For instance, + might be used to indicate *toward the school* and − to indicate *away from the school*. Or, + could mean *to the right of the flagpole*, and − could mean *to the left of the flagpole*. In this way, the position of the bicycle can be described as a distance from the origin together with a plus or minus sign that indicates the direction.

If you define *toward the school* as the reference direction, the bicycle's position in **Figure 2** is +5 m. If *away from the school* is the reference direction, then the bicycle's position is −5 m. The description of an object's motion also depends on the reference point chosen. **Figure 3** shows how the description of Earth's motion through space changes as the reference point changes.

Visualizing Earth's Motion

Figure 3

In the vastness of space, Earth's motion can be described only in relation to other objects such as stars and galaxies. This figure shows how Earth moves relative to the Sun and to the Milky Way galaxy. This galaxy is part of a cluster of galaxies called the local group.

A Imagine you are looking down on the Sun's north pole. If the Sun is the reference point, Earth moves in a nearly circular path counter-clockwise around the Sun.

B The Sun belongs to a group of several billion stars that make up the Milky Way galaxy. Viewed from above the galaxy, the Sun moves clockwise in a nearly circular orbit around the galaxy's center. If the center of the Milky Way galaxy is the reference point, Earth's motion traces out a corkscrew path as it moves with the Sun.
*Earth's corkscrew path not shown to scale.

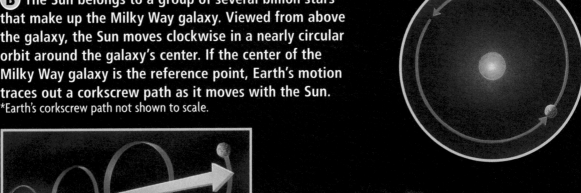

C The Milky Way galaxy is moving relative to the center of the Local Group cluster of galaxies. So you can think of Earth's motion this way: Earth orbits the Sun, which moves around the Milky Way galaxy, which is moving around the center of the Local Group.

Contributed by National Geographic

Position as a Vector

To describe the position of an object, you must specify two things. One is the distance from the reference point. The other is the direction from the reference point. One way to represent the position of an object is by an arrow. The arrow points in the direction of the object from the reference point. The length of the arrow represents the distance of the object from the reference point. **Figure 4** shows how the position of an object can be represented by an arrow.

The position of an object is an example of a vector. A **vector** (VEK tur) is a quantity that has both a size and a direction. For example, the size of a position vector is the distance of an object from the reference point. The direction of a position vector is the direction from the reference point to the object. A vector can be represented by an arrow. The length of the arrow represents the size of the vector. The arrows in **Figure 4** represent the position vectors of the two football players.

 What does the length of a position vector represent?

Position in Two Dimensions

A 100-m track sprinter runs in only one direction—toward the finish line. You could describe the sprinter's position by choosing the starting line as the reference point. You could choose the reference direction to be the direction from the starting line to the finish line. However, because the sprinter runs in a straight line, you need to choose only one reference direction.

A car driving from San Diego to Sacramento, as shown in **Figure 5,** wouldn't move in a straight line. It moves north and south, as well as east and west. To describe the motion of the car, you would need to choose two reference directions. North and east are often chosen as the positive reference directions.

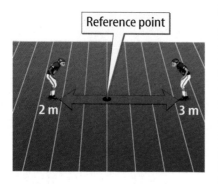

Figure 4 The position of each football player can be represented by an arrow.

WORD ORIGIN

vector
from Latin *vehere;* means
carry, convey

Figure 5 A car traveling from San Diego to Sacramento goes both north and west.

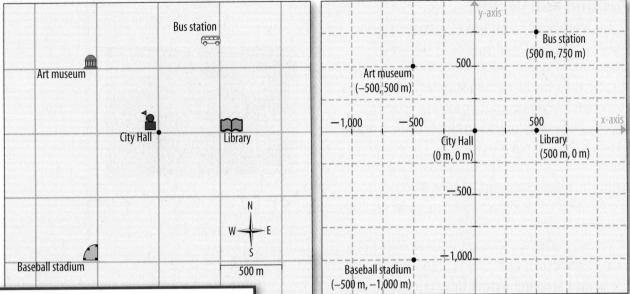

Figure 6 A city map can be represented as a two-dimensional graph.

Showing Positions with Two Directions

Visitors to a city find their way using maps such as the one shown on the left in **Figure 6.** The map has two positive reference directions: north and east. The map also has a scale to show the distances in meters.

If a tourist arriving at the bus station wants to visit the art museum, in which directions should she walk? She could walk two blocks west and one half block south. If each city block is 500 m long, then she would walk 1,000 m west and 250 m south. The bus station is the reference point, and 1,000 m west and 250 m south are distances and directions in two **dimensions**.

ACADEMIC VOCABULARY

dimension (duh MEN shun)

(noun) measure in one direction

To find the area of the rectangle, she measured both of its dimensions: length and width.

Locating a Position in Two Dimensions

The map that the visitor uses to find her way is similar to the graphs you've studied in mathematics classes. A two-dimensional map is a graph used to represent the location of an object with two reference directions. To make this graph, you can name east as the positive *x* direction. North is named the positive *y* direction. You also have to choose a location that will be the origin of the graph.

To transfer the visitor's city map into a two dimensional map, you could choose City Hall to be the origin. Its position is *x* = 0 m and *y* = 0 m. The *x*-axis goes east through City Hall. The *y*-axis goes north through City Hall. Then mark the distance units on the axes and place the locations of the buildings on the graph, as in **Figure 6.** The bus station is 500 m east and 750 m north of City Hall, so its location is *x* = 500 m and *y* = 750 m.

 Figure 6 What is the location of the art museum?

Changing Position

Suppose you walk to a friend's home from your home, and then walk back. How has your position changed? You might have walked a distance of many meters, but your final position is the same as your beginning position. So your distance traveled and your change in position are different.

Displacement

The change in your position is called the displacement. **Displacement** is the difference between the initial position and the final position of an object.

Just as position does, displacement includes a size and a direction. As a result, displacement is also a vector. The direction of a displacement vector is the direction from the initial position to the final position. The size of a displacement vector is the distance from the initial position to the final position.

 What are the size and direction of the displacement vector?

Distance and Displacement

What's the difference between the distance you travel and your displacement? Suppose you are walking in a park, as shown in **Figure 7.** Your initial position is the reference point. The positive reference directions are north and east.

You first walk a distance of 40 m to the east. The difference between your initial and final position is 40 m. The direction from your initial to your final position is east. This means your displacement is 40 m east.

Suppose you then walk 30 m north. The total distance you've traveled from the starting point is 40 m + 30 m, or 70 m. However, your final position is not 70 m from your initial position. Instead the distance between your final and initial position is 50 m. Your displacement is 50 m northeast.

Suppose you continue walking and return to your initial position. **Figure 7** shows that the total distance you travel is 140 m, but your displacement is 0 m.

Figure 7 Distance depends on the path traveled. Displacement depends on only the initial position and the final position.

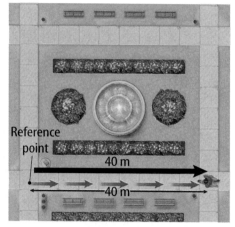

Distance: 40 m
Displacement: 40 m east

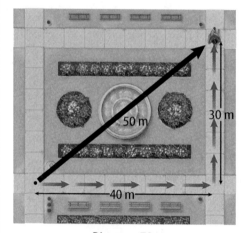

Distance: 70 m
Displacement: 50 m northeast

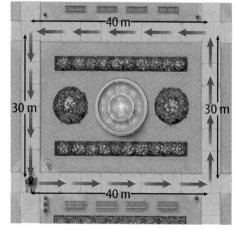

Distance: 140 m
Displacement: 0 m

What have you learned?

You first read about how the choice of a reference point and a reference direction determines an object's position. In the Launch Lab, for example, the number of steps you had to take to get from the reference point to each goal depended on where you put the reference point. In the DataLab on the next page, you will graph the data you collected in the Launch Lab.

In this lesson, you also read about displacement and why displacement is a vector. In addition to displacement, there are other quantities that have both size and direction. You will study two other vectors in Lesson 2.

LESSON 1 Review

Summarize

Create your own lesson summary as you organize an **outline**.

1. **Scan** the lesson. Find and list the first **red** main heading.

2. **Review** the text after the heading and list 2–3 details about the heading.

3. **Find** and list each **blue** subheading that follows the **red** main heading.

4. **List** 2–3 details, key terms, and definitions under each **blue** subheading.

5. **Review** additional **red** main headings and their supporting **blue** subheadings. List 2–3 details about each.

ELA8: R 2.3

Standards Check

Using Vocabulary

1. Displacement is a(n) _____ because it has both magnitude and direction. **1.a**

2. Define *reference point* in your own words. **1.a**

Understanding Main Ideas

3. Which of the following is a true statement? **1.a**

   A. Displacement always equals distance traveled.

   B. Distance traveled is the magnitude of the displacement vector.

   C. Displacement and distance traveled are the same measurements.

   D. Distance traveled sometimes equals the magnitude of the displacement vector.

4. **State** the relationship between the plus (+) and minus (–) sign when used with a reference direction. **1.a**

5. **Explain** the importance of communicating the reference point when giving a position. **1.a**

6. **Summarize** Copy and fill in the graphic organizer below to identify the two parts of a displacement vector. **1.a**

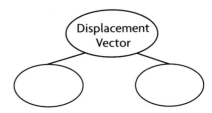

Applying Science

7. **Evaluate** these descriptions of the position of an object. Suggest ways to improve each description. **a.** The store is three blocks from my car. **b.** My house is 200 m north of the freeway. **c.** The grocery is 100 m west of here. **1.a**

Science nline
For more practice, visit **Standards Check** at ca8.msscience.com.

DataLab

How can a graph show relative positions?

In the Launch Lab, you moved around the classroom from a reference point to three different positions. Now put your movement on a graph to show your directions.

Data Collection

1. Mark the *x*- and *y*-axis clearly on your **graph paper.**

2. Label the intersecting point of the axes (0, 0). This is the origin, or reference point. Label north, south, east, and west.

3. Have each square on the graph represent one step.

4. Copy the Position of Goals table into your Science Journal.

5. Trace your path from the reference point to the three goals. Use a different **colored pencil** for each goal.

6. Label each position as *Goal 1, Goal 2,* or *Goal 3.* Include each position's *x*- and *y*-coordinates (*x*-coordinate, *y*-coordinate).

Position of Goals		
Goal	North-South Direction	East-West Direction
1		
2		
3		

Data Analysis

1. **Compare** your graph to your partner's graph. Suggest a reason for any differences.

2. **Use** your graph to state the position of one goal in relation to another goal. For example, "Goal 2 is three steps south and 9 steps west of Goal 1."

3. **Compare** your statements to the statements of a student from another group. Explain the similarities and differences.

4. **Develop** a way to convert the scale of your graph from steps to meters.

Science Content Standards

1.a Students know position is defined in relation to some choice of a standard reference point and a set of reference directions.

 ALG: 6.0

Science Content Standards

1.b Students know that average speed is the total distance traveled divided by the total time elapsed and that the speed of an object along the path traveled can vary.

1.c Students know how to solve problems involving distance, time, and average speed.

1.d Students know the velocity of an object must be described by specifying both the direction and the speed of the object.

1.e Students know changes in velocity may be due to changes in speed, direction, or both.

Also covers: 9.b, 9.f

Reading Guide

What *You'll Learn*

▶ **Explain** how speed is a rate of change.

▶ **Solve** motion problems involving average speed.

▶ **Explain** why velocity is a vector.

▶ **Determine** when acceleration occurs.

Why *It's Important*

Knowing an object's velocity can help you predict where it will be in the future.

Vocabulary

speed
constant speed
instantaneous speed
average speed
velocity
acceleration

Review Vocabulary

rate: the change in something that occurs in a unit of time

Speed, Velocity, and Acceleration

Main Idea Speed, velocity, and acceleration describe how an object's position and motion change in time.

Real-World Reading Connection Think about a train traveling through the desert, a pizza delivery van on busy city streets, and a racecar going around a track. Do these vehicles travel at the same speed? Do they travel in straight lines? Do they change the direction of their motion?

What is speed?

You are familiar with different rates. A rate measures the change in something over a particular length of time. For example, imagine a child who is 104 cm tall on her fifth birthday and 112 cm tall on her sixth birthday. The rate of change of her height is 8 cm for that year.

Look at the runner in **Figure 8.** The runner's position is changing. To describe her position, you can use the first hurdle as the reference point and use *to the right* as the positive reference direction. The distance between each hurdle is 10 m. It takes the runner 2 s to move from one hurdle to the next. This means that in one second, her position changes by 5 m. Her **speed,** or rate of change of distance with time, is 5 m per second. For every 1 s that goes by, the runner moves an additional 5 m away from the first hurdle.

 Figure 8 What is the runner's speed?

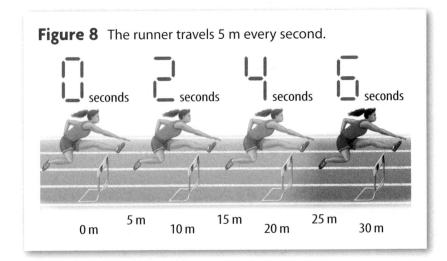

Figure 8 The runner travels 5 m every second.

| 0 seconds | 2 seconds | 4 seconds | 6 seconds |

| 5 m | 15 m | 25 m |
| 0 m | 10 m | 20 m | 30 m |

Constant Speed

For the part of the race shown in **Figure 8,** the hurdler runs at a **constant** rate. For every second that goes by, she moves an equal distance from the reference point. An object that moves at a **constant speed** travels the same distance each second. Can you think of other things that travel at a constant speed? Imagine a car on a freeway with cruise control on. Cruise control keeps the car moving with a constant speed. If a car with a constant speed travels 100 km in 1 h, then it will travel another 100 km in the next hour. If its speed stays constant, in 5 h it will travel 500 km.

Changing Speed

Unlike a car with cruise control on, most objects speed up and slow down as they move from place to place. The car shown in **Figure 9** slows down and stops at a stop sign, and then starts moving again. The car doesn't travel the same distance in every two-second interval. Its speed is not constant. Instead, it speeds up as it moves away from the stop sign.

When the speed of an object isn't constant, it is helpful to determine its **instantaneous speed** (ihn stuhn TAY nee us), or speed at a specific instant in time. A speedometer shows a car's instantaneous speed. As the car travels along the road in **Figure 9,** the speedometer above each position shows how fast the car is moving at each location and time.

Consider a car traveling on a highway at a constant speed of 80 km/h. What is the instantaneous speed of the car? For an object moving at a constant speed, its instantaneous speed doesn't change from moment to moment. Therefore, the car's instantaneous speed is unchanging, so it is the same as its constant speed, 80 km/h.

 **Reading Check** Describe the reading on a speedometer of a car that is moving at a constant speed.

Concepts In Motion
To see an animation of the car's motion, visit ca8.msscience.com.

Figure 9 The car's speed changes as it leaves the stop sign.

0 s   2 s   4 s   6 s   8 s

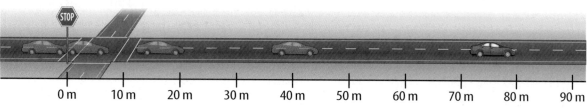

0 m   10 m   20 m   30 m   40 m   50 m   60 m   70 m   80 m   90 m

What is average speed?

How can you describe the speed of something when it is speeding up or slowing down? One way is to calculate the average speed of the object as it moves from one place to another.

Calculating Average Speed

The **average speed** is the total distance traveled divided by the total time. You can calculate the average speed from this equation:

Average Speed Equation

$$\text{average speed (in m/s)} = \frac{\text{total distance (in m)}}{\text{total time (in s)}}$$

$$v = \frac{d}{t}$$

In this equation, the letter v stands for average speed. Because speed equals distance divided by time, the unit for speed is a distance unit divided by a time unit. Suppose distance is measured in meters and time is measured in seconds. Then the unit for speed is m/s. Your average walking speed is about 1.5 m/s. In the United States speed is usually measured in miles per hour (mph).

Speed Equation

1.c, 9.f

ALG: 5.0

Solve for Average Speed It takes a swimmer 57.2 s to swim a distance of 100 m. What is the swimmer's average speed?

1 **This is what you know:**
distance: $d = 100$ m
time: $t = 57.2$ s

2 **This is what you need to find:** average speed: v

3 **Use this formula:** $v = \frac{d}{t}$

4 **Substitute:** $v = \frac{100}{57.2}$ is 1.75
the values for d and t
into the formula and divide.

5 **Determine the units:** units of $v = \frac{\text{units of } d}{\text{units of } t} = $ m/s

Answer: The swimmer's average speed is 1.75 m/s.

ScienceOnline
For more equation practice,
visit ca8.msscience.com.

Practice Problems

1. A bicycle coasting downhill travels 170.5 m in 21.0 s. What is the bicycle's average speed?

2. What is the average speed of a car that travels 870 km in 14.5 h?

Calculating Distance and Time

The average speed equation contains three variables: rate, distance, and time. If you know any two of the variables, you can use the average speed equation to figure out the third, unknown quantity. The math feature at the end of this lesson shows how to use the average speed equation to calculate distance and time.

Velocity

When you describe a walk in the woods to a friend, do you tell him in which direction you hiked? Does it matter whether you walked north to the mountain or east to the lake? To describe the motion of an object, you need to know more than its speed. You also need to know in which direction the object travels. **Velocity** (vuh LAH suh tee) is the speed and direction of motion.

Velocity as a Vector

To describe the velocity of an object, you have to specify both the object's speed and its direction of motion. This means that velocity is a vector. The size of the velocity vector is the speed. A velocity vector can be represented by an arrow that points in the direction of motion. The length of the arrow represents the speed. The length of the arrow increases as the speed increases. **Figure 10** shows how the velocity vector of a bouncing ball changes.

 **Reading Check** What is the size of a velocity vector?

Velocity and Speed

Sometimes in everyday language the words velocity and speed are used to mean the same thing. However, speed tells only how fast something is going. Velocity tells how fast something is going and in what direction.

WORD ORIGIN
velocity
from Latin *velocitatem;* means *swiftness, speed*

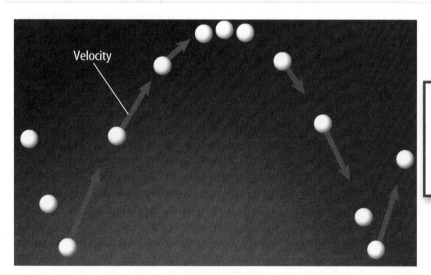

Figure 10 The velocity vector of a ball changes when the direction and speed of the ball change.

Determine where the ball's speed is increasing.

Figure 11 Acceleration occurs when an object speeds up, slows down, or changes its direction of motion.

Acceleration

Initial velocity

Final velocity

Speeding Up

Acceleration

Initial velocity

Final velocity

Slowing Down

Velocity

Changing Direction

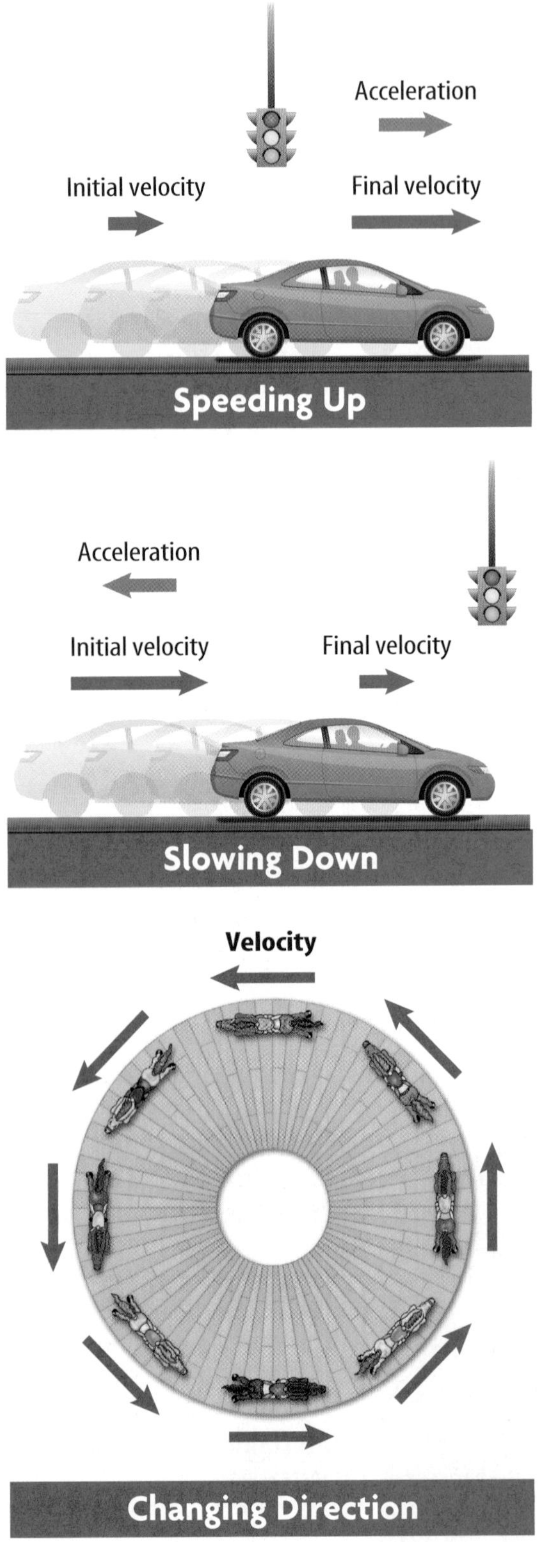

Acceleration

When you watch the first few seconds of a rocket liftoff, the rocket barely seems to move. With each passing second, however, you can see it moving faster. Because velocity includes both speed and direction, the velocity of the rocket changes as it speeds up. The rocket's velocity also changes as its direction of motion changes. An object is accelerating when its velocity changes. **Acceleration** (ak sel uh RAY shun) is the rate at which velocity changes with time. Just like velocity, acceleration is a vector. To specify an object's acceleration, both a size and a direction must be given.

Acceleration and Change in Speed

The velocity of an object changes when it speeds up or slows down. As a result, the object is accelerating. A sprinter taking off from the starting blocks and a car slowing down at an intersection are both accelerating. **Figure 11** shows how the direction of the acceleration depends on whether an object is speeding up or slowing down. If an object is speeding up, the direction of its acceleration is in the same direction that it is moving. If an object is slowing down, the acceleration is in the opposite direction that the object is moving.

Acceleration and Change in Direction of Motion

The velocity of an object can change even if its speed doesn't change. The horses on the carousel in **Figure 11** are moving with constant speed. However, as the carousel turns, their direction of motion is constantly changing. As a result, the velocity of each horse is changing and the horses are accelerating.

Have you ever been in a car that has changed speed or direction quickly? You might have felt the seat push against you as the car sped up. Or maybe you felt the door push against your side when going around a sharp curve. In Chapter 2 you will read about the connection between acceleration and forces.

What have you learned?

You first read about speed, or the rate of change of position with time. You saw an example of calculating average speed by dividing the distance traveled by the time taken to travel the distance.

In Lesson 1, you read that a vector is a quantity with both size and direction. In this Lesson, you learned about two vector quantities—velocity and acceleration. Velocity is the speed and direction of an object's motion. Acceleration is the rate of change of velocity over time. Acceleration occurs when an object's speed or direction of motion changes.

WORD ORIGIN
acceleration
from Latin *acceleratus;* means *quicken*

LESSON 2 Review

Summarize

Create your own lesson summary as you write a **newsletter.**

1. **Write** this lesson title, number, and page numbers at the top of a sheet of paper.

2. **Review** the text after the **red** main headings and write one sentence about each. These will be the headlines of your newsletter.

3. **Review** the text and write 2–3 sentences about each **blue** subheading. These sentences should tell *who, what, when, where,* and *why* information about each headline.

4. **Illustrate** your newsletter with diagrams of important structures and processes next to each headline.

ELA8: W 2.1

Standards Check

Using Vocabulary

1. Distinguish between *velocity* and *acceleration.* **1.e**

2. _____ is the rate of change of velocity. **1.e**

Understanding Main Ideas

3. **Identify** Copy and fill in the graphic organizer below to identify three vectors. **1.d**

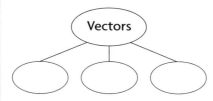

Vectors

4. Which of the following is not accelerating? **1.e**

   A. a car coming to a stop at a traffic light

   B. a sprinter starting from rest and running 100 m in 9.8 s

   C. a racecar traveling 175 km/hr on a straight track

   D. an airplane traveling at 500 km/hr and turning to the north

5. **State** the ways velocity can change. **1.e**

6. **Calculate** how far an airplane would fly in 3 h if its average speed is 800 km/h. **1.c**

7. **Give an example** of an object that is accelerating but is traveling at a constant speed. **1.e**

8. **Relate** speed, velocity, and acceleration. **1.d**

Applying Math

9. **Calculate** the average speed of a spacecraft orbiting Mars if the spacecraft takes 2.2 h to complete an orbit that is 26,500 km long. **1.b**

10. **Calculate** the average speed of an airplane flying between San Francisco and Los Angeles. The flight lasts 1.2 h, and the flight path is 650 km. **1.b**

Science Online

For more practice, visit **Standards Check** at ca8.msscience.com.

Applying Math

Using the Speed Equation to Find Distance and Time

You can use the speed equation to find distance and time, as well as speed.

Using the Speed Equation to Find Distance

If the average speed, v, and travel time, t, are known, you can find the distance, d, the object traveled. First multiply both sides of the speed equation by t:

$$v \times t = \frac{d}{t} \times t$$

The variable t cancels on the right side of the above equation:

$$v \times t = \frac{d}{\cancel{t}} \times \cancel{t}$$

So the equation for the distance traveled by an object if its average speed and travel time are known is:

$$d = v\,t$$

You can find the distance by multiplying the average speed and the travel time.

Using the Speed Equation to Find Time

If the average speed, v, and distance traveled, d, are known, you can find the travel time, t. Use the equation above, and divide both sides by v:

$$\frac{d}{v} = \frac{v \times t}{v}$$

The variable v cancels on the right side of the above equation:

$$\frac{d}{v} = \frac{\cancel{v} \times t}{\cancel{v}}$$

So the equation for the travel time if the distance traveled and average speed are known is:

$$t = \frac{d}{v}$$

You can find the travel time by dividing the distance by the average speed.

Practice Problems

1. Find the distance traveled by a car that travels with an average speed of 110 km/h for 3.5 h.

2. How long does it take a baseball moving with an average speed of 35 m/s to travel 18 m?

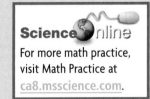

Science Online

For more math practice, visit Math Practice at ca8.msscience.com.

MiniLab

Can you measure average speed?

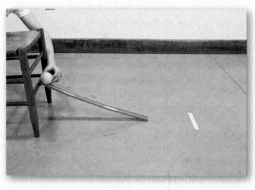

Using a stopwatch you can time a ball rolling down a ramp and across the floor. You also can measure the distance the ball rolls from one point to another. If you perform more than one trial, how similar are your results?

Procedure

1. Complete a lab safety form.
2. Use a piece of **plastic track** to make a ramp from a **chair** seat to the floor.
3. Lay a piece of **masking tape** 15 cm from the bottom of the ramp. Lay another piece of masking tape 5 m farther along the ball's path.
4. Hold a **tennis ball** at the top of the ramp.
5. Release the ball to allow it to roll down the ramp.
6. Students who are observing will start their **stopwatches** when the ball reaches the first tape and stop them when the ball reaches the second tape.
7. Repeat steps 4–6 three more times.

Analysis

1. **Calculate** the average speed of the rolling ball for each trial.
2. **Compare** the average speed of the ball in each trial. Are the results accurate and reproducible? Explain.
3. **Evaluate** the timing process by comparing your time measurements with the measurements of other group members. Suggest reasons for any differences and ways to improve the timing process.

Science Content Standards

1.b Students know that average speed is the total distance traveled divided by the total time elapsed and that the speed of an object along the path traveled can vary.
9.b Evaluate the accuracy and reproducibility of data.

ALG: 6.0

Reading Guide

What *You'll Learn*

▶ **Construct** a position-time graph.

▶ **Calculate** speed from a position-time graph.

▶ **Describe** how motion with constant speed and changing speed appears on a speed-time graph.

Why *It's Important*

Graphs display a great deal of information in a compact space.

Vocabulary

slope
rise
run

Review Vocabulary

linear: relating to or resembling a straight line (p. 23)

Graphing Motion

Main Idea Graphs can show how objects change their position or speed.

Real-World Reading Connection Have you ever used a hammer to drive a nail into a piece of wood? Would you use a screwdriver to pound a nail into wood? Although you probably could hit the nail with a screwdriver, using the right tool makes the job easier. Graphs often are the most useful tool for summarizing many kinds of information.

Position-Time Graphs

Graphs often are used to show how something changes with time. For example, the graph in **Figure 12** shows temperature versus time for a summer day in Santa Barbara, California. From this graph, you can determine the maximum and minimum temperatures. You also can tell when those temperatures occurred. What other information can you read from the graph?

A graph of temperature versus time shows how the temperature of something is changing. A graph of position versus time can show how an object's position is changing. In other words, a position-time graph can show how an object is moving.

 Visual Check **Figure 12** When did the temperature reach its minimum value?

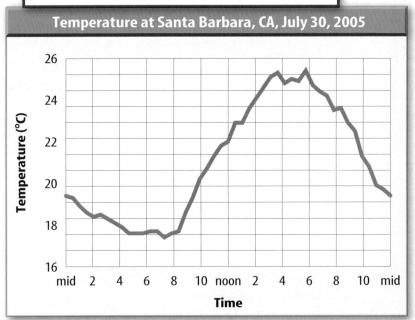

Figure 12 This graph shows temperature versus time for a summer day in Santa Barbara, California.

Temperature at Santa Barbara, CA, July 30, 2005

Figure 13 The time and position of the turtle are measured and recorded to determine the turtle's speed.

200 cm
100 cm
50 cm
10 cm

Making a Position-Time Graph

As an example of graphing position, look at the turtle as it crawls straight across the sidewalk in **Figure 13.** You can measure the position of the turtle with a meterstick and the elapsed time with a digital watch. Every 20 seconds, you write down the position and time in a table, such as **Table 1.**

Figure 14 shows the graph of the turtle's position and time data. The position of the turtle is plotted on the *y*-axis, and the elapsed time is plotted on the *x*-axis. The points appear to lie on a line, so a ruler was used to draw the best-fit line through the data points. The line that is drawn can be used to estimate the position of the turtle for times you did not measure.

 What is plotted on the *x*-axis on a position-time graph?

Table 1 Turtle's Position and Time	
Elapsed Time (s)	**Position (cm)**
0	0
20	40
40	81
60	123
80	158
100	202

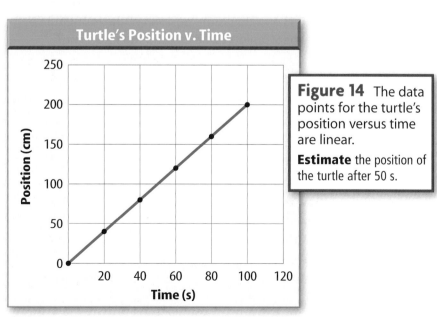

Turtle's Position v. Time

Figure 14 The data points for the turtle's position versus time are linear.

Estimate the position of the turtle after 50 s.

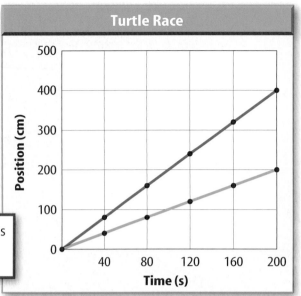

Turtle Race

Figure 15 By comparing the positions of two turtles on the same graph, you can determine which crawled faster.

Units on Position-Time Graphs

The values plotted on a position-time graph have units. Each plotted point is the position at a certain instant of time. Position always has units of length, such as centimeters, meters, or kilometers. However, all positions must be measured in the same unit. For example, in **Figure 14,** all positions are measured in the same unit—centimeters. All values for time also must have the same unit. In **Figure 14,** the unit for time is seconds.

Using Position-Time Graphs

A position-time graph can be used to compare the motion of two objects. For example, the graph in **Figure 15** shows how the position of two turtles changes in a 400-cm race. The positions of the turtles were measured every 20 seconds. The position-time data for each turtle was then plotted on the same graph. The winning turtle is the one who reaches 400 cm first.

 Figure 15 What was the position of the losing turtle when the winning turtle crossed the finish line?

SCIENCE USE V. COMMON USE
slope

Science Use the steepness of a line. *The slope of the line on the position-time graph equals the object's speed.*
Common Use a hill or mountain. *Many slopes in California are used as ski areas.*

The Slope of a Position-Time Graph

Recall that average speed equals the distance traveled divided by the time needed to travel the distance. The winning turtle travels 400 cm in 200 s. So its average speed is (400 cm)/(200 s), which equals 2 cm/s. The losing turtle travels 200 cm in 200 s, so its average speed is 1 cm/s.

The graph in **Figure 15** shows that the plotted line for the winning turtle is steeper than the plotted line for the losing turtle. The steepness of a line is the **slope** of the line. On a position-time graph, a steeper line means a greater average speed. This means that the slope of the line is greater for objects that move faster.

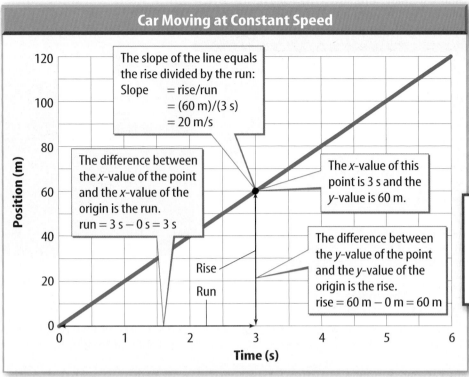

Car Moving at Constant Speed

The slope of the line equals the rise divided by the run:
Slope   = rise/run
        = (60 m)/(3 s)
        = 20 m/s

The difference between the *x*-value of the point and the *x*-value of the origin is the run.
run = 3 s − 0 s = 3 s

The *x*-value of this point is 3 s and the *y*-value is 60 m.

The difference between the *y*-value of the point and the *y*-value of the origin is the rise.
rise = 60 m − 0 m = 60 m

Rise

Run

Figure 16 To find the slope of a line, the origin and another point are used to calculate the rise and the run.

Calculating the Slope of a Position-Time Graph

Two points must be used to calculate the slope of a line plotted on a position-time graph. One point can be the origin of the graph, as shown in **Figure 16.** The other point can be any other point on the plotted line. To calculate the slope, first calculate the change in units in the vertical direction from the origin to the chosen point. This change in the vertical direction sometimes is called the **rise.** It is the number of units the line rises in the vertical direction from the origin.

Next, calculate the change in units in the horizontal direction from the origin to the chosen point. This change in the horizontal direction is sometimes called the **run.** The slope is calculated by dividing the rise by the run. **Figure 17** summarizes how to calculate the slope of a line on a graph.

 How is the slope of a line calculated?

Slope and Average Speed

Recall that the average speed of an object is equal to the distance traveled divided by the time taken to travel that distance. On a position-time graph, the slope equals the rise over the run. However, the rise is the same as the distance traveled. The run equals the time needed to travel that distance. As a result, the slope of a line on a position-time graph equals the average speed. In **Figure 16,** the rise is equal to 60 m and the run is equal to 3 s. Then the average speed is 20 m/s.

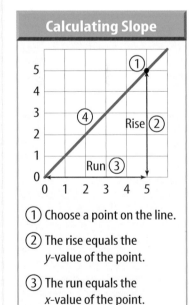

Figure 17 The slope of a line can be calculated by following these steps.

Calculating Slope

① Choose a point on the line.

② The rise equals the *y*-value of the point.

③ The run equals the *x*-value of the point.

④ Calculate the slope by dividing the rise by the run.

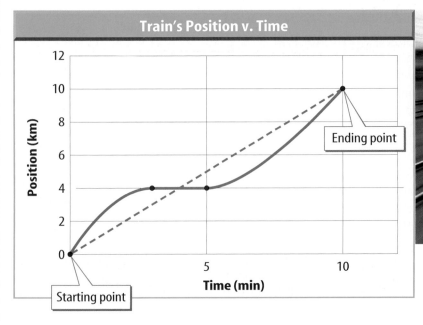

Train's Position v. Time

Position (km) vs. Time (min)

Ending point

Starting point

Figure 18 Even though the train's speed isn't constant, you can calculate the train's average speed from a position-time graph.

Average Speed When Speed is Changing

Even when the speed of an object isn't constant, you can calculate its average speed from a position-time graph. **Figure 18** is a position-time graph for a train that slows down and stops at a station for two minutes, and then starts moving again. Notice that the graph is not a straight line. Only objects that move at a constant speed will have position-time graphs that are straight lines. Because the speed of the train isn't constant, the graph of its motion on a position-time graph isn't a straight line. However, you can find its average speed by following a procedure **similar** to the one used in the constant speed case. To find the average speed of the entire trip, use the starting and ending data points. Then calculate the slope of the line that would connect those two points as shown in **Figure 18.**

 What is the average speed of the train for the trip shown in **Figure 18?**

Position-Time Graphs for Changing Speed

When an object is changing speed, its position-time graph is a curved line. The way the line curves depends on whether the object is speeding up or slowing down, For example, between 0 min and 3 min, the train is slowing down as it pulls into the station. As **Figure 18** shows, the position-time graph for an object that slows down is a line that curves downward. Between 5 min and 10 min the train is speeding up after it leaves the station. The position-time graph for an object that speeds up is a line that curves upward.

ACADEMIC VOCABULARY

similar (SIH muh luhr)
(adjective) having characteristics in common
The twins are so similar only their parents can tell them apart.

Speed-Time Graphs

Another way of graphing motion is to graph the instantaneous speed of the object on the *y*-axis and the time on the *x*-axis. This graph does not show where the object is, but how the speed of the object changes with time.

Constant Speed on a Speed-Time Graph

Suppose a car is moving with a constant speed. Then at every instant of time its speed is the same. If the speed of this car is plotted on a speed-time graph, the graph looks like the one shown at the top of **Figure 19.** Because the speed is constant, the plotted line is horizontal. A horizontal line on a speed-time graph tells you that the object moved at a constant speed. However, the faster the speed of the object, the greater the distance of the line from the *x*-axis.

 Figure 19 How does the position of the line in the top figure change if the car is moving at a faster constant speed?

Increasing Speed

If the car speeds up, its speed becomes larger as time increases. Then the change in the car's speed on a speed-time graph looks like the graph shown in the middle of **Figure 19.** The plotted line slants upward toward the right. This is true for any object whose speed is increasing. What's the difference if one object speeds up more quickly than another object? Then its plotted line on a speed-time graph slants upward more steeply and has a steeper slope.

Decreasing Speed

If a car slows down, its speed becomes smaller as time increases. Then the change in the car's speed looks like the graph shown in the bottom of **Figure 19.** The plotted line slants downward toward the right. If the car slows down more quickly, then the line slants downward more steeply. **Table 2** on the next page summarizes position-time graphs and speed-time graphs for different types of motion.

Figure 19 A speed-time graph shows if an object is speeding up, slowing down, or moving with a constant speed.

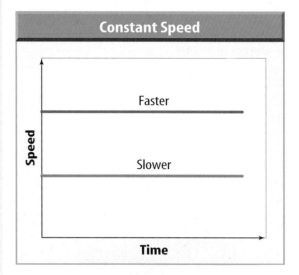

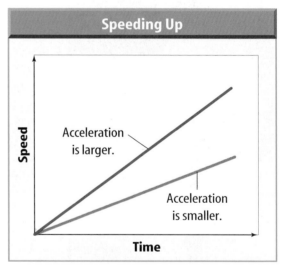

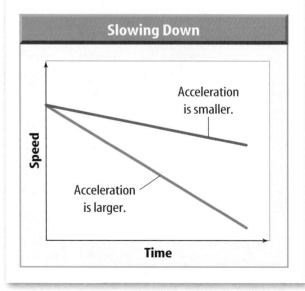

CONcepts In MOtion

Interactive Table Organize information about position-time graphs and speed-time graphs at ca8.msscience.com.

Table 2 Position-Time and Speed-Time Graphs

Description of Motion	Position-Time Graph	Speed-Time Graph
Object is at rest.		

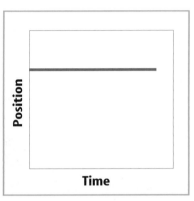

If an object is at rest, the position of the object doesn't change. The graph is a horizontal line on a position-time graph.

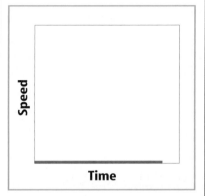

For an object at rest, the speed is zero and doesn't change. The graph is a horizontal line on a speed-time graph.

Object is moving at a constant speed in the positive reference direction.

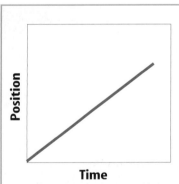

For an object with constant speed, the position increases linearly with time. The slope of the line equals the speed.

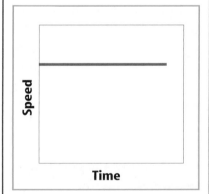

If the speed is constant, the speed doesn't change. The y-value of the horizontal line equals the speed.

Table 2 Position-Time and Speed-Time Graphs

Description of Motion	Position-Time Graph	Speed-Time Graph
Object is speeding up.		

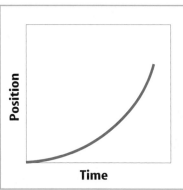

When the object is speeding up, the position increases nonlinearly with time. The line on a position-time graph curves upward.

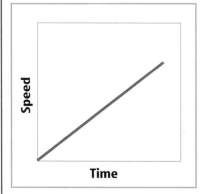

If the speed is increasing with time, the line on a speed-time graph slopes upward as time increases.

| **Object is slowing down.** | | |

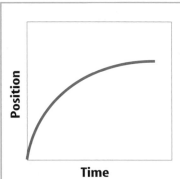

When the object is slowing upward, the position increases nonlinearly with time. The line on a position-time graph curves downward.

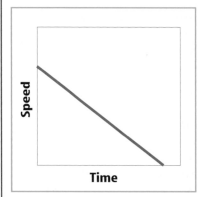

If speed is decreasing with time, the line on a speed-time graph slopes downward as time increases.

What have you learned?

In this lesson you read about how to represent the motion of an object using position-time and speed-time graphs. A position-time graph shows how the position of an object changes with time. The slope of a line on a position-time graph is the speed of the object. To calculate the slope, first choose a point on the line. Then divide the rise by the run. If the speed of the object isn't constant, the plotted position-time graph is not a straight line.

A speed-time graph shows how the speed of an object changes with time. A horizontal line means the speed is constant. A line that slopes upward means the object is speeding up. A line that slopes downward means the object is slowing down.

LESSON 3 Review

Summarize

Create your own lesson summary as you design a **visual aid.**

1. **Write** the lesson title, number, and page numbers at the top of your poster.

2. **Scan** the lesson to find the **red** main headings. Organize these headings on your poster, leaving space between each.

3. **Design** an information box beneath each **red** heading. In the box, list 2–3 details, key terms, and definitions from each **blue** subheading.

4. **Illustrate** your poster with diagrams of important structures or processes next to each information box.

 ELA8: R 2.3

Standards Check

Using Vocabulary

1. _____ describes the steepness of a line on a graph. **1.f**

2. Define *rise* and *run* in your own words. **1.f**

Understanding Main Ideas

3. **State** appropriate units for the *x*-axis and *y*-axis on a position-time graph for a turtle, a walking person, and an automobile on the highway. **1.f**

4. **Describe** the speed-time graph of an object that is not moving. **1.f**

5. **Sequence** Draw a graphic organizer like the one below to show the sequence of steps in calculating the slope of a line. **1.f**

6. Describe the motion of the object whose position-time graph is shown below. **1.f**

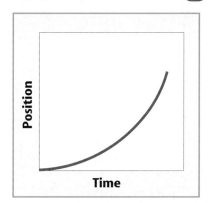

Applying Math

7. **Calculate** the slope of the line on a position-time graph for a car that starts at the origin at 0 s and moves at a constant velocity for 15 s to a position 300 m from the origin. **9.d**

Science nline

For more practice, visit **Standards Check** at ca8.msscience.com.

Data Lab

What can you learn from a graph?

The graph below represents a student's 200-m sprint on a bicycle.

Data

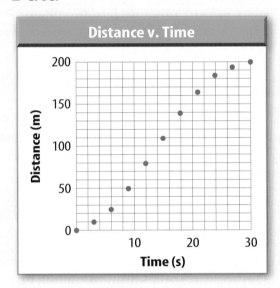

Distance v. Time

Data Analysis

1. **Construct** a data table for the points plotted on the position-time graph.

2. **Calculate** the average speed for the following three time intervals: 0–9 s, 9–18 s, and 21–30 s. Also, calculate the average speed for the entire ride.

3. **Compose** a short paragraph explaining the shape of the position-time graph. Suggest reasons why the velocity changed over time.

 Science Content Standards

1.f Students know how to interpret graphs of position versus time and graphs of speed versus time for motion in a single direction.

9.d Recognize the slope of the linear graph as the constant in the relationship $y = kx$ and apply this principle in interpreting graphs constructed from data.

Graphing Motion

Materials

masking tape
stopwatch
graph paper

Safety Precautions

Science Content Standards

1.f Students know how to interpret graphs of position versus time and graphs of speed versus time for motion in a single direction.

9.e Construct appropriate graphs from data and develop quantitative statements about the relationships between variables.

Problem

You have read that describing motion involves a point of reference and that you can move in a positive or negative direction from that point. You know how to determine average speed using the distance traveled and the time it takes to reach a given point. You can make graphs representing how objects' positions and speeds change over time. Use this knowledge to collect data and produce graphs of a student's motion.

Form a Hypothesis

➤ **Review** the results from this chapter's laboratory investigations.

➤ **Make a prediction** about the shape of the motion's position-time graph. Make a sketch of your prediction and explain why you think it will have that shape.

Collect Data and Make Observations

1. Read and complete a lab safety form.

2. Write a plan for collecting data that includes a description of the motion you will graph. The movement should include at least three different speeds. Include in your plan approximate distances students will move, how many students will record times with stopwatches, and the distance between the timers.

3. Record your observations in a table similar to the one shown below.

Position-Time Data	
Time (s)	Position (m)

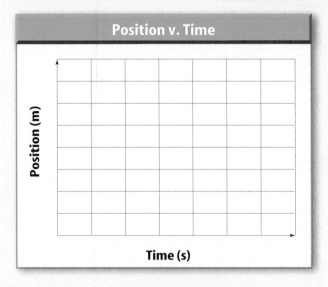

Position v. Time

Position (m)

Time (s)

Analyze and Conclude

1. **Explain** how putting measurements in a table helped you organize the data.

2. **Construct** a position-time graph of the movement. Put position on the *y*-axis and time on the *x*-axis.

3. **Calculate** the average speed of the student over the entire movement.

4. **Calculate** the speed of the student during each portion of the motion.

5. **Compare** the graphed data with your predicted graph. Explain any differences in shape.

6. **Describe** what the slope of the graph indicates about the student's motion.

7. **Evaluate** your procedure for timing the motion. Explain how having more timers would make your graph a more accurate representation of the motion. If you had more timers, where would you put them to be most useful?

Communicate

 **WRITING in** ▶ **Science**   **ELA8:** W 2.3

Write a Report Describe the procedure you followed in a written report. Include in your report why you chose the procedure you used. Also include a discussion of the sources of error in your data and how these errors could be reduced.

Real World Science

Automobile Designer

All the parts of a car that you see, including the headlights, grill, door handles, seats, and steering wheel, are designed by automobile designers. They also design the shape of the overall vehicle. To become an automobile designer, you must combine artistic creativity with technical knowledge of automobiles. Your background should include courses in art and design, as well as courses in the physical sciences.

Visit **Careers** at **ca8.msscience.com** for more information on automobile designers. Present a news broadcast describing how the design of cars might change over the next ten years.

GPS Shows the Way

One way to determine your position anywhere on Earth is to use a GPS receiver. GPS stands for Global Positioning System, which is a system of 24 operational satellites, five tracking stations, and GPS receivers. By receiving signals from four satellites at the same time, a GPS receiver can determine its position on Earth's surface with an accuracy of about 10 m. GPS receivers are used in airplanes, ships, and even in cars. Some receivers are small enough to fit in the palm of your hand.

Visit **Technology** at **ca8.msscience.com** for more information about GPS. Write a paragraph describing several different ways that GPS is used.

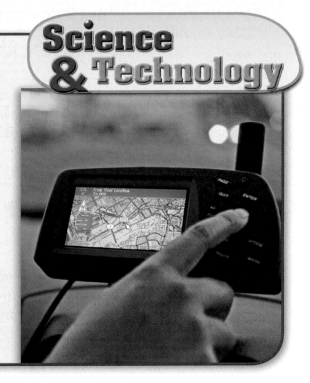

GALILEO AND SCIENTIFIC THEORIES

Galileo Galilei was an Italian scientist who lived from 1564 to 1642. He was one of the first to realize that scientific theories had to be tested by carrying out experiments. During Galileo's time, people believed that heavier objects would fall faster than lighter ones. Galileo carried out experiments that showed that all objects had the same acceleration as they fell. Galileo also made astronomical observations using a small telescope that he made. These observations helped prove that Earth and the planets moved around the Sun.

Visit **History** at ca8.msscience.com for more information about Galileo's life. Write a newspaper article describing Galileo's astronomical discoveries.

 ELA8: W 2.1

Henry Ford and the Assembly Line

Millions of cars are built and sold each year by automobile manufacturers. The methods needed to build cars and other products in large numbers were pioneered by Henry Ford during the early 1900s. Ford developed the assembly line, where a car was assembled step by step as it moved along a conveyor belt. Ford's assembly line helped lower the cost of his cars so that millions of people could buy them. Today, robots, such as those in the photo, perform some jobs on automobile assembly lines.

Visit **Society** at ca8.msscience.com for more information on Henry Ford and the assembly line. Make a graph showing the number of cars registered in California by year from 1970 to 2003.

The BIG Idea Motion occurs when the position of an object changes.

Lesson 1 Determining Position
1.a

Main Idea Position is defined relative to a reference point and reference directions.

- The position of an object includes the distance and direction from the reference point.

- The description of an object's position in two dimensions requires a reference point, called the origin, and two directions perpendicular to each other.

- A vector is quantity that has both size and direction.

- Displacement is a vector that gives the distance and direction for a change in position.

- **displacement** (p. 53)
- **reference point** (p. 48)
- **vector** (p. 51)

Lesson 2 Speed, Velocity, and Acceleration
1.b, 1.c, 1.d, 1.e, 9.b, 9.f

Main Idea Speed, velocity, and acceleration describe how an object's position and motion change in time.

- Speed is the rate of change of distance.

- The average speed of an object is the total distance traveled divided by the total time that it traveled.

- The velocity of an object is a vector that includes the speed of the object and the direction of the object's motion.

- A velocity vector can be described by an arrow. The length of the arrow represents the speed. The direction of the arrow represents the direction of motion.

- An object accelerates when it changes the speed or direction of its motion.

- **acceleration** (p. 60)
- **average speed** (p. 58)
- **constant speed** (p. 57)
- **instantaneous speed** (p. 57)
- **speed** (p. 56)
- **velocity** (p. 59)

Lesson 3 Graphing Motion
1.f, 9.d, 9.e

Main Idea Graphs can show how objects change their position or speed.

- The slope of the graph of position-time data shows the speed of the moving object.

- If the graph of an object's position versus time is a horizontal line, the object's speed is zero.

- If the graph of an object's speed versus time is a horizontal line, the object's speed is constant.

- If the graph of speed versus time is not horizontal, the object is speeding up or slowing down.

- **rise** (p. 67)
- **run** (p. 67)
- **slope** (p. 66)

Download quizzes, key terms, and flash cards from ca8.msscience.com.

Linking Vocabulary and Main Ideas

Use vocabulary terms from page 78 to complete this concept map.

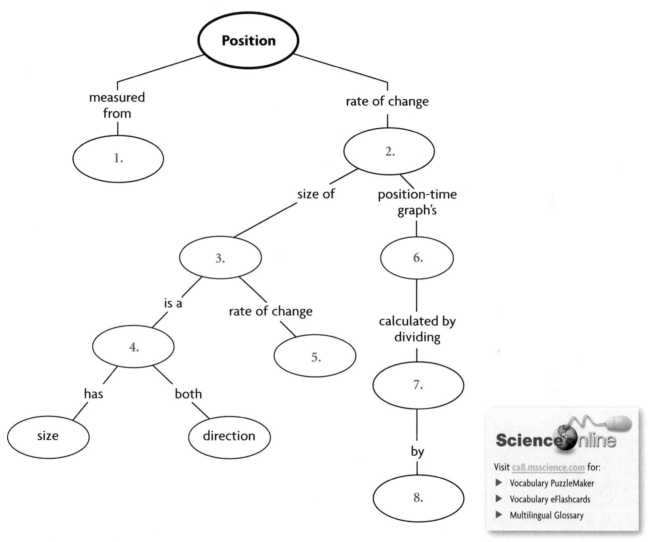

Using Vocabulary

Match a vocabulary term to each definition below.

9. total distance traveled divided by total time taken

10. a number describing how steep a plotted line on a graph is; equal to the rise divided by the run

11. speed at a specific instant in time

12. a quantity with both size and direction

13. rate of change of velocity with time

14. the change in the value of the vertical coordinate between two points on a graph

15. a starting point used to describe the position of an object

16. a vector that represents the distance and direction of an object's change in position

17. rate of change of position with time

Understanding Main Ideas

Choose the word or phrase that best answers the question.

1. Which units could you use for the *y*-axis of a graph of speed-time to display the motion of an automobile?
   A. h/s
   B. cm/km
   C. km/m
   D. km/h   **1.b**

Use the figure below to answer questions 2, 3, and 4.

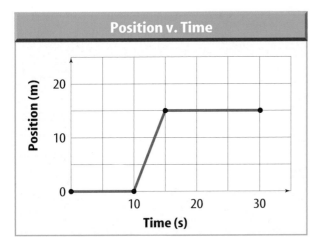

2. Which best describes the motion of the object from 10 s to 15 s?
   A. It is not moving.
   B. It is moving at a constant speed.
   C. Its speed is increasing
   D. Its speed is decreasing.   **1.f**

3. What is the average speed of the object for the 30 s shown in this graph?
   A. 0.5 m/s
   B. 2 m/s
   C. 10 m/s
   D. 100 m/s   **1.c**

4. What is the position of the object at 15 s?
   A. 0 m
   B. 7.5 m
   C. 15 m
   D. can't be determined from this graph   **1.f**

5. Which of the following equals average speed?
   A. acceleration/time
   B. (change in velocity)/time
   C. distance/time
   D. displacement/time   **1.b**

6. Which of the following is the rate of change of velocity with time?
   A. acceleration
   B. displacement
   C. speed
   D. vector   **1.e**

Use the table below to answer questions 7 and 8.

Distance and Time Data		
Runner	Distance Covered (km)	Time (min)
Andrés	11	42
Keshia	7.8	38
Matt	10.5	32
Sandra	8.9	30

7. What is Andrés's average speed?
   A. 0.26 km/min
   B. 3.8 km/min
   C. 53 km/min
   D. 462 km/min   **1.c**

8. Which runner has the fastest average speed?
   A. Andrés
   B. Keshia
   C. Matt
   D. Sandra   **1.c**

9. Which describes an object with constant velocity?
   A. It is changing direction.
   B. Its acceleration is increasing.
   C. Its acceleration is zero.
   D. Its acceleration is negative.   **1.e**

Applying Science

10. Propose three different reference points you could use to describe where you are right now. **1.a**

11. Relate displacement and distance traveled. When does distance traveled equal the magnitude of the displacement vector? **1.a**

12. Construct a two-dimensional graph showing the following locations: school is at the origin; a restaurant is 500 m north and 200 m east of the school; a bookstore is 300 m south and 300 m west of the restaurant. What is the location of the bookstore in relation to the school? **1.a**

Use the graph below to answer questions 13 and 14.

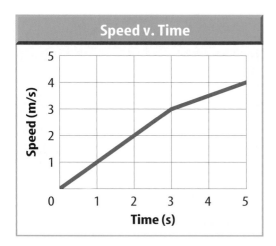

Speed v. Time

13. Determine the speed of the object at 4 s. **1.f**

14. Compare the acceleration of the object between 0 s and 3 s and the acceleration between 3 s and 5 s. **1.f**

15. Describe three ways to change the velocity of a car. **1.e**

16. Calculate the average speed of a car that travels 120 km in 2 h. **1.b**

17. Compare the information that can be learned from a position-time graph and from a speed-time graph. **1.f**

WRITING in Science

18. Write a short story that illustrates the differences between speed, velocity, and acceleration. Your story should be a few paragraphs long and should use speed, velocity, and acceleration in ways that demonstrate the relationships between the terms. **ELA8: W 2.1**

Applying Math

19. On a vacation, Linda's family traveled 790 km at an average speed of 95 km/h. How long did the trip take? **ALG: 15.0**

20. If you rode your bike for 2 h and traveled 40 km, what was your average speed? **ALG: 15.0**

21. If you rode your bike at an average speed of 15 km/h for 4 h, how many kilometers did you travel? **ALG: 15.0**

22. The table below shows the distance traveled by a car at different times.

Distance Traveled by Car	
Distance (km)	**Time (h)**
55	1
120	2
180	3

What is the car's average speed over the time period 1 h to 3 h? **ALG: 15.0**

1 What is the distance traveled divided by the time taken to travel that distance?

A acceleration   `1.b`

B velocity

C speed

D inertia

Use the figure below to answer questions 2 and 3.

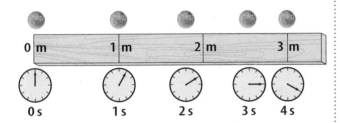

2 The illustration above shows the position of a ball at one-second time intervals. Over which time period is the ball's average speed largest?

A 0 s to 1 s   `1.b`

B 1 s to 2 s

C 2 s to 3 s

D 3 s to 4 s

3 What is the average speed of the ball over the 3-m distance in the illustration above?

A 0.75 m/s   `1.c`

B 1.0 m/s

C 1.25 m/s

D 1.5 m/s

Use the table below to answer questions 4 and 5.

| Distance v. Time ||
Distance	Time
0	0
4	2
8	4
14	6
20	8
26	10
32	12

4 What is the average speed of the object over the time interval 6 s to 12 s?

A 2.0 m/s   `1.b`

B 2.7 m/s

C 3.0 m/s

D 5.3 m/s

5 Over which time interval did the object accelerate?

A 2 s to 4 s   `1.e`

B 4 s to 6 s

C 6 s to 8 s

D 8 s to 10 s

6 What does a car's speedometer measure?

A average speed   `1.d`

B instantaneous speed

C acceleration

D velocity

7 Which can occur when an object is accelerating?

   1.e

A It speeds up.

B It slows down.

C It changes direction.

D all of the above

8 Sound travels at a speed of 330 m/s. How long does it take for the sound of thunder to travel 1,485 m?

A 45 s   **1.c**

B 4.5 s

C 4,900 s

D 0.22 s

9 The graph below shows a speed-time graph.

Speed v. Time

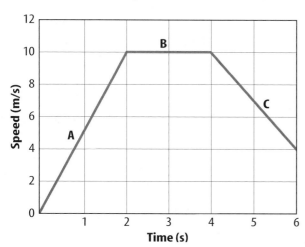

Over what time interval is the speed of the object constant in the graph above?

A 0 s to 1 s   **1.f**

B 1 s to 2 s

C 2 s to 3 s

D 4 s to 5 s

10 The graph below shows the motion of two students.

Distance v. Time

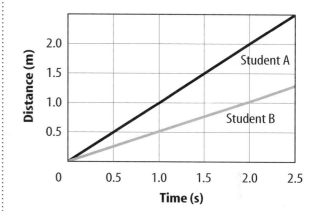

How does the speed of student A compare to the speed of student B?

A It is half as large.   **1.f**

B It is the same.

C It is twice as large.

D It is three times as large.

11 A car travels for 5.5 h at an average speed of 75 km/h. How far did the car travel?

A 0.073 km   **1.c**

B 13.6 km

C 80.5 km

D 412.5 km

12 Which of the following is a vector?

A distance   **1.d**

B mass

C speed

D velocity

Forces

The BIG Idea

An object's motion changes if the forces acting on the object are unbalanced.

LESSON 1 **2.a, 2.b, 2.c, 9.g**
Combining Forces

Main Idea When more than one force acts on an object, the combined effect is caused by the sum of all applied forces.

LESSON 2 **2.d, 2.g**
Types of Forces

Main Idea There are different types of forces that act on objects.

LESSON 3
2.e, 2.f, 9.a, 9.d
Unbalanced Forces and Acceleration

Main Idea Unbalanced forces cause accelerations.

A Long Way Down

Step by step, this climber slowly creeps up the side of a 1,000-m-tall rock face. The secret to clinging like a fly on a wall is a force called friction. This force is exerted on the climber at each place where he touches the rock. Friction balances gravity's downward pull on the climber and keeps him from sliding down the wall.

Science Journal Describe three examples of pushing or pulling on an object. In each case, how did the object move?

Launch Lab

minutes

Can you feel the force?

Imagine pushing a chair that has wheels on its legs. Now imagine pushing the chair with a friend sitting in it. Is there a difference in how hard you would have to push?

Procedure

1. Set your **textbook** on the table in front of you and push it so that it moves at a constant velocity.

2. Put at least one more **book** on top of your textbook and push the stack of books at a constant speed.

Think About This

Imagine performing the experiment on ice instead of on the table. Do you think the pushes needed to keep the books moving across ice would be different than the pushes needed to move them across the table? Explain your answer.

2.c

Forces Make the following Foldable to organize information about the different kinds of forces.

▷ **STEP 1 Fold** a sheet of paper into thirds lengthwise. Fold the top down about 3 cm.

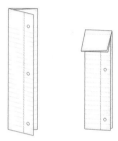

▷ **STEP 2 Unfold** and **draw** lines along all folds. **Label** as shown.

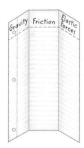

Reading *Skill*

Determining the Main Idea
As you read this chapter, identify and record the main ideas about the different kinds of forces that are discussed.

Visit ca8.msscience.com to:

▶ view **Concepts in Motion**

▶ explore Virtual Labs

▶ access content-related Web links

▶ take the Standards Check

Get Ready to Read

Identify the Main Idea

1 Learn It! Main ideas are the most important ideas in a paragraph, a lesson, or a chapter. Supporting details are facts or examples that explain the main idea. Understanding the main idea allows you to grasp the whole picture.

2 Practice It! Read the following paragraph. Draw a graphic organizer like the one below to show the main idea and supporting details.

> The unit for the size of a force is the newton (N). A force with a size of 1 N is a small force. The force needed to lift a half-stick of butter or a fast-food hamburger is about 1 N. To lift a 2-L bottle of water requires a force of about 20 N.
>
> —*from page 89*

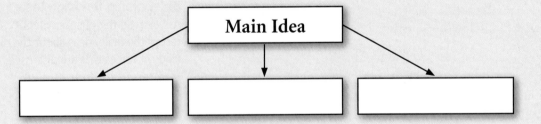

3 Apply It! Pick a paragraph from another section of this chapter and diagram the main idea as you did above.

Target Your Reading

Reading Tip

The main idea is often the first sentence in a paragraph, but not always.

Use this to focus on the main ideas as you read the chapter.

1. **Before you read** the chapter, respond to the statements below on your worksheet or on a numbered sheet of paper.
   - Write an **A** if you **agree** with the statement.
   - Write a **D** if you **disagree** with the statement.

2. **After you read** the chapter, look back to this page to see if you've changed your mind about any of the statements.
   - If any of your answers changed, explain why.
   - Change any false statements into true statements.
   - Use your revised statements as a study guide.

Before You Read A or D	Statement	After You Read A or D
	1 A force is a push or a pull.	
	2 Things must be touching each other to apply forces.	
	3 Only one force at a time can act on an object.	
	4 If the total force acting on an object is zero, the object will not move.	
	5 Gravity pulls on all objects that have mass.	
	6 If objects of different sizes apply forces on each other, the larger object applies a greater force on the smaller object.	
	7 A moving object comes to a stop because no force is acting on it.	
	8 An object at rest can have forces acting on it.	
	9 Forces cause objects to speed up.	
	10 An object moving in a circle must have forces acting on it.	

Science Online

Print a worksheet of this page at ca8.msscience.com.

Reading Guide

What *You'll Learn*

▶ **Define** force.

▶ **Explain** how forces combine.

▶ **Describe** how balanced and unbalanced forces affect motion.

Why *It's Important*

Usually, more than one force acts on you and on the objects around you.

Vocabulary

force
contact force
noncontact force
net force
unbalanced force
balanced force
Newton's first law of motion

Review Vocabulary

vector: a quantity with both size and direction (p. 51)

Combining Forces

Main Idea When more than one force acts on an object, the combined effect is caused by the sum of all applied forces.

Real-World Reading Connection Think about all the things you push or pull every day. You might push on computer keys, pull open a door, push a shopping cart, or pull a heavy backpack from the floor onto your shoulders. What happens when more than one push or pull acts on an object?

What is a force?

A push or a pull is called a **force.** Forces are always exerted by one object on another object. In **Figure 1,** a hand exerts a force on the boards and on the bow string. The hand pushes on the boards and pulls on the bow string. What other pushes or pulls do you observe around you?

Contact Forces

When you press the keys on a computer keyboard, your fingers exert a force on the keys. This force can be exerted only when your fingers are touching the keys. A force that is exerted only when two objects are touching is a **contact force.** A contact force can be small, such as the force you exert to push a pencil across a sheet of paper, or large, such as the force exerted by a tow truck as it pulls a car along a street. Both of the forces shown in **Figure 1** are contact forces.

Figure 1 The hand exerts a force on the wood and on the bow string.
Explain why both of these forces are contact forces.

Noncontact Forces

When you jump up in the air, you are pulled back to the ground, even though nothing seems to be touching you. The skydiver in **Figure 2** is also being pulled downward, even though there seems to be nothing touching him. Forces can be exerted by one object on another even though they aren't touching each other. The force pulling you and the skydiver down to Earth is the gravitational force exerted by Earth. This force is a noncontact force. A **noncontact force** is a force that one object exerts on another when they are not touching. The magnetic force that two magnets exert on each other is also an example of a noncontact force. Noncontact forces include the gravitational force, the electric force, and the magnetic force.

Force is a Vector

Recall from the previous chapter that the velocity of an object is a vector. A vector has a size and a direction. A velocity vector is represented by an arrow that points in the direction of motion. The length of the arrow represents the object's speed. A force also is a vector that can be represented by an arrow. The direction of the arrow is the direction of the push or the pull. The length of the arrow represents the size, or strength, of the force. The arrow becomes longer as the size of the force increases.

The unit for the size of a force is the newton (N). A force with a size of 1 N is a small force. The force needed to lift a half-stick of butter or a fast-food hamburger is about 1 N. To lift a 2-L bottle of water requires a force of about 20 N. **Figure 3** shows some examples of force vectors.

 Reading Check What does the length of a force vector arrow represent?

Figure 2 The skydiver is pulled downward by a noncontact gravitational force.

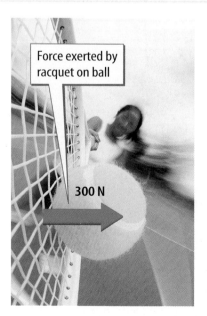

Force exerted by racquet on ball

300 N

Force exerted by foot on ball

200 N

Figure 3 A force is a vector that has a size and a direction.

Combining Forces

Suppose you are trying to move a heavy piece of furniture, such as the dresser shown in **Figure 4.** You don't have to push as hard if a friend helps and you both push together in the same direction. When more than one force acts on an object, the forces combine. The combination of all the forces acting on an object is called the **net force.** How forces combine depends on the direction of the forces applied to an object.

 What is the net force acting on an object?

Combining Forces in the Same Direction

If you and a friend both push on the same side of the dresser, the forces that you both exert are in the same direction. When the forces acting on an object are in the same direction, they add together, as shown in **Figure 4,** to form the net force. When you both push on the dresser in the same direction, the net force is in the same direction in which both of you push.

Because forces are vectors, it is necessary to **specify** a reference direction to be able to combine forces. For example, you could choose "to the right" as the positive reference direction in **Figure 4.** Then, both forces would be positive. For example, suppose you push with a force of 200 N to the right and your friend pushes with a force of 100 N to the right. Then the net force is 200 N + 100 N = 300 N. Because the net force is a positive number, its direction is to the right. The dresser will slide as if it were being pushed by one person exerting a force of 300 N to the right.

 Figure 4 Describe the net force acting on the dresser.

ACADEMIC VOCABULARY
specify
(verb) to name or state in detail
The store clerk asked the customer to specify the size and color of the shirt he wanted.

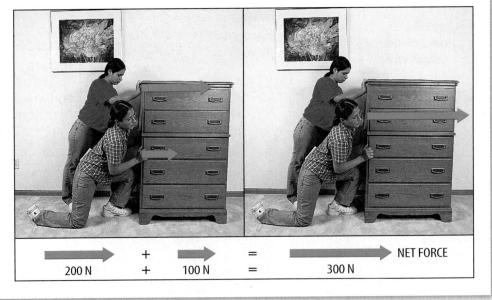

Figure 4 When forces in the same direction combine, the net force is also in the same direction. The size of the net force is the sum of the two forces.

200 N + 100 N = 300 N NET FORCE

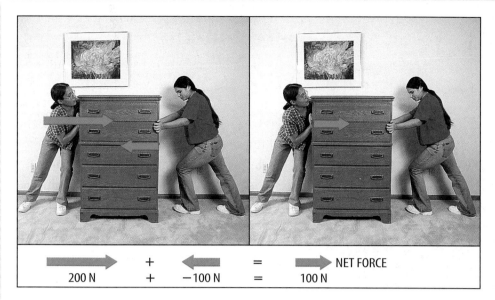

Figure 5 When two forces in opposite directions combine, the net force is in the same direction as the larger force. The size of the net force is the difference in the sizes of the two forces.

200 N	+	−100 N	=	100 N NET FORCE

Combining Forces in Opposite Directions

Suppose you and a friend push on the dresser, as shown in **Figure 5.** Then the two forces are in opposite directions. If "to the right" is the positive reference direction, then one force is positive and the other is negative. For example, a force of 200 N is exerted to the right and a force of 100 N is exerted to the left. Then the force exerted to the left is a negative number. The net force equals 200 N − 100 N = 100 N. Because the net force is a positive number, it is being exerted to the right.

Unbalanced and Balanced Forces

In the two examples just discussed, the net force on the dresser was not zero. When the net force on an object is not zero, the forces are **unbalanced forces. Figure 6** shows an example in which the net force on the dresser is zero. When the net force on an object is zero, the forces on the object are called **balanced forces.**

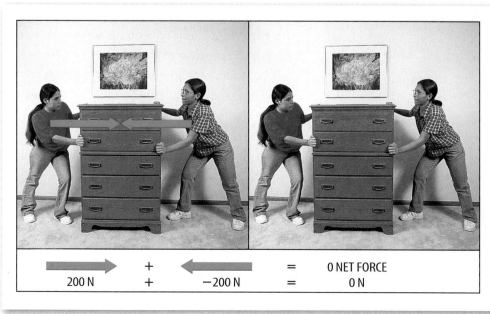

Figure 6 The net force on the dresser is zero, so the two forces on the dresser are balanced forces.

200 N	+	−200 N	=	0 NET FORCE / 0 N

Figure 7 The net force on the ball is unbalanced, causing the velocity of the ball to change.

Figure 8 The forces on the skydiver are balanced, so the velocity of the skydiver doesn't change.

Infer the net force on the skydiver.

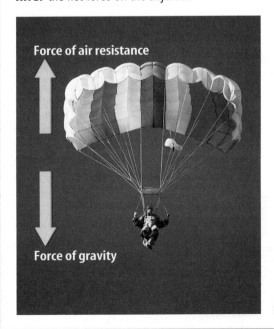

How do forces affect motion?

What happens when you push or pull on an object? When you pull your backpack upward, its motion changes as it moves upward. However, when you push against a brick wall, the wall doesn't move. The motion of an object changes when it changes speed or changes direction. Whether the motion of an object changes depends on whether the forces acting on it are balanced or unbalanced.

Unbalanced Forces and Motion

If you kick a soccer ball, you apply a contact force to the ball. You exert a force when your foot is in contact with the ball. The force you exert causes the ball to change speed and direction. When you kick the ball, the force exerted by your foot combines with other forces on the ball to form the net force on the ball. **Figure 7** shows the net force on the soccer ball as you kick it. Because the net force on the ball is not zero, the forces on the ball are unbalanced. The unbalanced forces on the ball caused its velocity to change. This is true for any object. The velocity of an object changes if the forces acting on it are unbalanced.

Balanced Forces and Motion

Imagine two people push on a dresser in opposite directions with forces of the same size. You probably know what happens—the dresser doesn't move. In this case the net force is zero and the forces on the dresser are balanced. When the forces on an object are balanced, the motion of the object doesn't change.

Even when the forces acting on an object are balanced, the object can be moving. **Figure 8** shows the forces acting on a skydiver after the parachute opens. The downward force of gravity on the skydiver is balanced by the upward force exerted by the parachute. Because the forces are balanced, the velocity of the skydiver doesn't change. The skydiver floats downward at a constant speed.

Figure 9 Because of inertia, the crash-test dummies without seat belts keep moving forward after the car has stopped.

Newton's First Law of Motion

Isaac Newton, a scientist who lived from 1642 to 1727, explained how forces cause motion to change. He developed three rules that are now called Newton's laws of motion. Newton's first law of motion describes how an object moves when the forces acting on it are balanced. According to **Newton's first law of motion,** if the net force on an object is zero, an object at rest remains at rest, or, if the object is moving, it continues to move in a straight line with constant speed. In other words, if the net force on an object is zero, the velocity of the object doesn't change.

 What is Newton's first law of motion?

Inertia

According to the first law of motion, the motion of an object changes only when unbalanced forces act on it. The tendency of an object to resist a change in its motion is called inertia. Inertia explains the motion of the crash-test dummies in **Figure 9.** When the car hits the barrier, the barrier exerts an unbalanced force on the car. This unbalanced force changes the motion of the car and makes it stop. However, without a safety belt that exerts an unbalanced force on the dummies, their motion doesn't change. Each dummy keeps moving until it hits the steering wheel, the dashboard, or the windshield.

Mass and Change in Motion

The size of the net force needed to cause a certain change in motion depends on the object's mass. Imagine trying to stop a bicycle or a car both traveling at the same speed. You wouldn't have to push very hard to stop the bicycle. However, the car might have 100 times more mass than the bicycle. A much larger net force is needed to cause the same change in motion as the bicycle.

What have you learned?

In this lesson you read that forces acting on an object can be added together to determine the net force acting the object. Since forces are vectors, it is important to include the size and direction of the force when adding them together. If the forces add to a zero net force, the forces are balanced and the motion of the object does not change. Newton's first law of motion states that the motion of an object will not change if the net force is zero. If the net force is not zero, the motion of the object will change.

LESSON 1 Review

Summarize

Create your own lesson summary as you design a **study web.**

1. **Write** the lesson title, number, and page numbers at the top of a sheet of paper.

2. **Scan** the lesson to find the **red** main headings.

3. **Organize** these headings clockwise on branches around the lesson title.

4. **Review** the information under each **red** heading to design a branch for each **blue** subheading.

5. **List** 2–3 details, key terms, and definitions from each **blue** subheading on branches extending from the main heading branches.

 ELA8: R 2.3

Standards Check

Using Vocabulary

1. _____ is the combination of all the forces acting on an object. **2.a**

2. Restate Newton's first law of motion in your own words. **2.c**

Understanding Main Ideas

3. **State** what you know about the forces acting on an object that is moving at a constant velocity. Are the forces balanced or unbalanced? **2.c**

4. **Describe** how a 300-N force can combine with a 100-N force to produce a net force of 200 N on a sled. **2.b**

5. **Take Notes** Copy the graphic organizer below, and describe the effect balanced and unbalanced forces have on objects' motion. **2.c**

	Effect on Objects' Motion
Balanced forces	
Unbalanced forces	

6. Which statement is true?

   A. An object in motion always has an unbalanced force acting on it.

   B. An object in motion cannot be acted on by more than one force.

   C. An object at rest will remain at rest unless an unbalanced force acts on it.

   D. The net force on an object in motion can't be zero. **2.c**

Applying Science

7. **Imagine** a car being acted on by unbalanced forces. What do you know about the motion of the car? **2.c**

8. **Assess** the differences between an object that has no force acting on it and an object that has a zero net force acting on it. Can you determine which is which? **2.c**

Science Online

For more practice, visit **Standards Check** at ca8.msscience.com.

00:30 minutes

Can you add vertical forces?

How do forces add in the vertical direction? How can you tell when vertical forces are balanced?

Data Collection

1. Read and complete a lab safety form.

2. Set up a **ring stand** and clamp an **extension rod** near the top. Attach a **spring scale** to the extension. Hook a **rubber band** and a **large paper clip** on the other end of the scale.

3. Add **mass** to the rubber band by hooking it onto the paper clip. Record the measurement of the force on the spring scale and the length of the rubber band.

4. Continue to add mass until you have five data points. Record the force and length of rubber band.

Force and Length of Rubber Band		
Trial Number	Force (N)	Length of rubber band (cm)
1		
2		

Data Analysis

1. **Explain** how you know the forces acting on the mass are balanced. Draw a diagram of the forces acting on the mass.

2. **Create** a graph of force versus length with force on the *y*-axis and length on the *x*-axis. Is the relationship between the two variables linear or nonlinear? How do you know?

3. **Use** the graph to estimate the length of the rubber band when a 1.5-N force acts on the rubber band.

 Science Content Standards ALG: 6.0

2.c Students know when the forces on an object are balanced, the motion of the object does not change.
9.8 Distinguish between linear and nonlinear relationships on a graph of data.

Reading Guide

What *You'll Learn*

▶ **Explain** how the force due to gravity depends on mass and distance.

▶ **Analyze** static and sliding frictional forces.

▶ **Describe** elastic forces due to tension and compression in matter.

▶ **Identify** forces acting on common objects.

Why *It's Important*

Identifying the forces acting on objects helps explain why things move as they do.

Vocabulary

gravity
law of universal gravitation
weight
friction
elastic force
tension force
compression force
normal force

Review Vocabulary

velocity: the speed and direction in which an object is traveling (p. 59)

Types of Forces

Main Idea There are different types of forces that act on objects.

Real-World Reading Connection Have you ever kicked a soccer ball up into the air? You apply an unbalanced force to the ball with your foot, and it lifts off the ground into the air. It eventually falls back to the ground and rolls to a stop. What forces act on the ball as it follows this path?

What is gravity?

In **Figure 10,** the basketball is at rest until the player applies an unbalanced force. After the ball is shot into the air, the player no longer applies a force to the ball. According to Newton's first law of motion, the ball should travel in a straight line at a constant speed unless an unbalanced force acts on it. The basketball does not travel at a constant speed or in a straight line, so there must be an unbalanced force acting on it. The unbalanced force that acts on the ball while it's in the air is gravity. **Gravity** is an attractive force that exists between all objects that have mass. Earth exerts the gravitational force that causes the ball to follow the path shown in **Figure 10.**

Figure 10 The basketball follows a curved path through the air.

Identify the force that causes the ball's path to be curved.

The Law of Universal Gravitation

In the seventeenth century, Isaac Newton was thinking about gravity. He wondered if the motion of falling objects and the motion of the Moon around Earth are caused by the same type of force. Newton found that it was gravity that pulled objects downward and caused the Moon to orbit Earth. In 1687, he published the law of universal gravitation (yew nuh VER sul • gra vuh TAY shun) that showed how to calculate this force. According to the **law of universal gravitation,** all objects are attracted to each other with a force that depends on the masses of the objects and the distance between them.

Gravity, Mass, and Distance

Figure 11 shows how the size of the force of gravity depends on the mass of the objects and the distance between them. The gravitational force becomes stronger as the mass of one or both of the objects increases. The force becomes weaker as the distance between the objects increases.

 How does the force of gravity between two objects change as they move closer together?

Table 1 compares the force of gravity exerted on a 70-kg person by a textbook, the Sun, and Earth. The force exerted by the textbook is extremely small because its mass is small. The force exerted by the Sun is also small because it is so far away. **Table 1** shows that only Earth is close enough and massive enough to exert a noticeable gravitational force on the person.

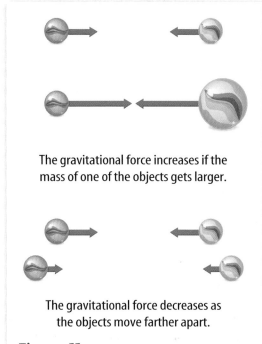

The gravitational force increases if the mass of one of the objects gets larger.

The gravitational force decreases as the objects move farther apart.

Figure 11 Gravitational force depends on the masses of the objects and the distance between them.

Table 1 Gravitational Forces on 70-kg Person			
Object	**Mass of Object (kg)**	**Distance to Object (m)**	**Size of Force (N)**
Book	2.0	1.0	9.3×10^{-9}
Sun	1.99×10^{30}	1.5×10^{11}	0.41
Earth	5.98×10^{24}	6.4×10^6	690

Weight and Mass

When you stand on a bathroom scale, what are you measuring? You are measuring the pull of Earth's gravity—a force. The **weight** of an object is the gravitational force exerted on an object. Recall that mass is the amount of matter in an object and does not change with location. Mass is not a vector because there is no direction **involved.** Weight, however, is a force vector; it has a size and direction. Your weight is a force that always points toward the center of Earth.

ACADEMIC VOCABULARY

involve

(verb) to have within or as part of itself
The test involves multiple-choice and essay questions.

Relationship Between Weight and Mass The size of an object's weight at the surface of Earth is proportional to the object's mass. For example, if the mass of an object doubles, the weight of the object doubles. If the mass is reduced by half, the object's weight is reduced by half.

 What is the relationship between mass and weight?

Weight and Mass High Above Earth In addition to mass, the distance between objects also affects weight. **Figure 12** shows how weight changes with height above Earth. An astronaut on the surface of Earth may have a mass of 55 kg and a weight of 540 N directed toward the center of Earth. While in orbit, the astronaut's mass doesn't change. However, the gravitational force on her would be smaller because she is farther from Earth. As a result, her weight would be reduced to about 500 N.

Figure 12 The astronaut's mass does not change as she travels from Earth to the Space Station.

Compare the astronaut's weight at the two locations. Why are they different?

Mass: 55 kg
Weight: 500 N

Mass: 55 kg
Weight: 540 N

350 km

Friction

Imagine pushing a book away from you across a table. As the book slides, it slows down and then stops. The force causing the book to slow down is a type of friction. **Friction** (FRIHK shun) is a force that opposes the movement between two surfaces in contact. The size of the friction force depends on the types of surfaces in contact. The frictional force usually becomes smaller as the surfaces become smoother.

Static Friction

Suppose you push on a heavy box, as in **Figure 13,** and the box doesn't move. Then the forces on the box are balanced. The force you exert on the box is balanced by a force acting on the box in the opposite direction. This force is called static friction. Static friction is the force between two surfaces in contact that keeps them from sliding when a force is applied. The static friction force is exerted on the bottom of the box where it touches the floor.

As you push harder, the box still doesn't move. This means that the force of static friction has increased to balance the force you apply, as shown in **Figure 13.** The force due to static friction increases as you increase the force you apply. However, there is a limit to the size of the static friction force between two surfaces. If you push hard enough, your applied force will be greater than the maximum static friction force. Then the forces on the box are no longer balanced and the box begins to move.

WORD ORIGIN············

friction
from Latin *fricare;* means
to rub

SCIENCE USE v. COMMON USE·

static
Science Use at rest or having no motion. *The fluid in the pipe was static.*
Common Use noise produced in a radio or a television. *After the radio was dropped, all we could hear was static.*

Figure 13 Static friction keeps the box from moving.

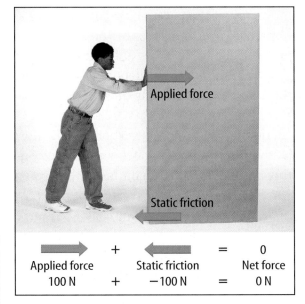

Applied force

Static friction

				Net force
Applied force	+	Static friction	=	Net force
100 N	+	−100 N	=	0 N

Static friction balances the force applied to the box.

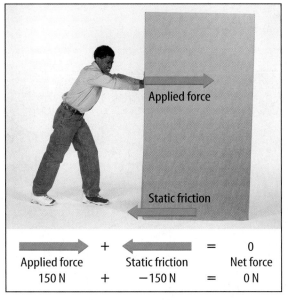

Applied force

Static friction

				Net force
Applied force	+	Static friction	=	Net force
150 N	+	−150 N	=	0 N

Static friction increases to balance the larger force applied to the box.

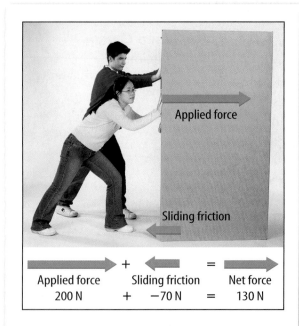

Applied force

Sliding friction

Applied force	+	Sliding friction	=	Net force	
200 N	+	−70 N	=	130 N	

Figure 14 The force of sliding friction is always opposite to the motion of the sliding box.

Sliding Friction

When the force pushing on the box is larger than the maximum static friction force, the box begins to slide. When the box is sliding, a different frictional force acts on the box. This force is sliding friction. The size of sliding friction is usually smaller than static friction. The direction of sliding friction is always opposite to the velocity of the sliding object, as shown in **Figure 14.**

 Visual Check **Figure 14** Compare the size of the applied force and sliding friction.

Unlike static friction, the size of sliding friction does not change if you push on the box harder. As long as the object is sliding, the force of sliding friction is the same. If the force you apply is greater than sliding friction, the box speeds up as it slides. If the force you apply is equal to sliding friction, the box slides with a constant velocity.

Reading Check How would the velocity of the book change if the applied force were equal to the sliding friction force?

Motion Without Friction

At one time, people thought that forces caused motion. In other words, a object would move only if there were unbalanced forces acting on it. For example, once you stop pushing on a skateboard, it slows down and stops. You might think that the skateboard stops because there are no forces acting on it. However, it stops because friction acts on it. On Earth, friction is present whenever something moves. Without friction, the skateboard would continue to move in a straight line with constant speed. According to the first law of motion, instead of causing motion, unbalanced forces cause changes in motion. When friction is greatly reduced, as in **Figure 15,** objects move with a nearly constant velocity.

Figure 15 In an air-hockey game, the puck floats on a layer of air so that friction is almost eliminated. As a result, the puck moves in a straight line with nearly constant speed after it's been hit.

Elastic Forces

In **Figure 16,** a diver standing on the end of the diving board bends the board downward. Because he is not moving, the forces acting on him must be balanced. One of the forces acting on him is the downward pull of Earth's gravity. This means there must be an upward force acting on him that balances the downward force of gravity. This force is exerted on the diver by the diving board and is called an elastic (ih LAS tik) force. An **elastic force** is the force exerted by a material when it is stretched or compressed. The diving board exerts an upward elastic force on the diver when it is bent downward.

Figure 16 The diving board exerts an upward elastic force on the diver.

Tension

Think about stretching a rubber band, as shown in **Figure 17.** You apply a force to the rubber band, and you can feel the rubber band pulling back as it is stretched. The force exerted by the rubber band is an elastic force caused by the stretching of the rubber band. The force you apply to the rubber band that stretches it is a tension (TEN shun) force. A **tension force** is a pulling force applied to an object that can make the object stretch. A tension force applied to an object causes the object to exert an elastic force that pulls back in the opposite direction. The size of this elastic force equals the size of the tension force.

Compression

When you squeeze a rubber ball, the ball changes shape. You can feel the ball push back on your hand as you squeeze. The rubber ball exerts an elastic force on your hand when you squeeze it. The force you exert on the ball is a compression force. A **compression force** is a squeezing force applied to an object that can make an object shrink. The elastic force exerted by the ball is equal to the compression force you exert on the ball.

WORD ORIGIN

tension
from Latin *tensionem*; means *stretching*

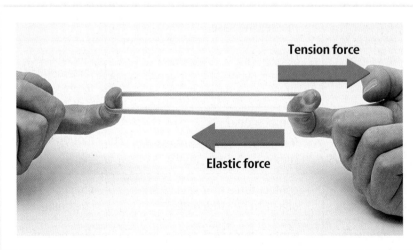

Tension force

Elastic force

Figure 17 The force applied to the rubber band by the fingers is a tension force that causes the rubber band to exert an elastic force.

Weight of glass

Normal force

Figure 18
The forces on the glass are balanced because the table exerts an upward normal force on the glass.

Normal Forces

The glass sitting on the table in **Figure 18** is not moving, so the forces acting on it are balanced. The table exerts an upward force on the glass, called the normal force, that balances the downward pull of gravity. A **normal force** is a force exerted by an object that is perpendicular to the surface of the object. The upward normal force exerted by the table balances the downward force of gravity on the glass.

The normal force exerted by the table is an elastic force. The weight of the glass pushing down on the table is a compression force. This causes the material in the table to be squeezed together. As a result, the table pushes back upward on the glass. **Table 2** summarizes the forces discussed in this lesson.

Table 2 Types of Forces		
Force	**Properties**	**Direction**
Gravity	• noncontact force • strength increases as masses get closer together • strength increases if one or both masses increase	force on one mass is toward the other mass
Static friction	• contact force • force prevents the surfaces from sliding past each other	opposite to force applied to object
Sliding friction	• contact force • force exists when surfaces are sliding past each other	opposite to motion of object
Tension force	• contact force that causes an object to be stretched	direction of stretching
Compression force	• contact force that causes an object to be squeezed	direction of squeezing

Identifying Forces on an Object

More than one force can act on an object at the same time. These forces can also be acting in different directions. For example, the force of gravity acting on a box sliding on a floor is downward. The sliding friction force is horizontal, parallel to the floor. The forces acting in the vertical direction can cause an object's vertical motion. Horizontal forces can change an object's horizontal motion.

Forces in the Horizontal Direction

Suppose you push a book at a constant speed across a flat table, as shown in **Figure 19.** The book is moving in a horizontal direction with a constant velocity as you push it. According to the first law of motion, this means that the forces on the book must be balanced.

You apply a force on the book in the horizontal direction. Because the book is sliding, a sliding friction force is acting on the book. The direction of this force is horizontal, in the opposite direction to the force you apply. The size of this force must be equal to the size of your push. Then the horizontal forces on the book are balanced. As a result, the horizontal motion of the book doesn't change. The book moves in a straight line with constant speed.

 Why are the horizontal forces acting on the book balanced?

Forces in the Vertical Direction

As the book slides across the table, it doesn't move up or down. This means that the forces in the vertical direction must be balanced, as shown in **Figure 19.** The force of gravity pulls the book downward. The table exerts an upward normal force on the book. For these forces to be balanced, the upward normal force must have the same size as the downward force of gravity. Because the vertical forces are balanced, the vertical motion of the book doesn't change. In this case, the book doesn't move in the vertical direction.

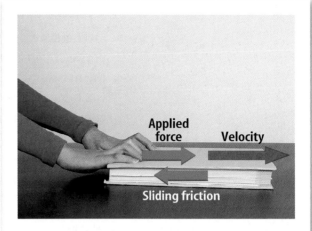

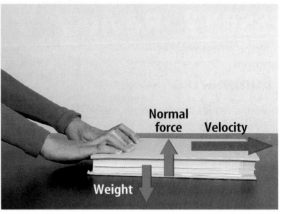

Figure 19 Horizontal and vertical forces act on the notebook at the same time.

Identify the horizontal and vertical forces acting on the notebook.

What have you learned?

There are different types of forces. Gravity is an attractive force between two objects. The size of the gravitational force depends on the masses of the objects and the distance between them. Friction is a force that always opposes the sliding motion of two surfaces in contact. An elastic force results when an object is stretched or compressed. These forces can act on an object at the same time. It is often useful to further group the forces into horizontal and vertical forces so you can predict how the motion of the object will change in the horizontal and vertical directions.

LESSON 2 Review

Summarize

Create your own lesson summary as you write a script for a **television news report.**

1. **Review** the text after the **red** main headings and write one sentence about each. These are the headlines of your broadcast.

2. **Review** the text and write 2–3 sentences about each **blue** subheading. These sentences should tell *who, what, when, where,* and *why* information about each **red** heading.

3. **Include** descriptive details in your report, such as names of reporters and local places and events.

4. **Present** your news report to other classmates alone or with a team.

ELA8: LS 2.1

Standards Check

Using Vocabulary

1. Define *normal force* in your own words. **2.d**

2. _____ is the gravitational force acting on an object. **2.g**

Understanding Main Ideas

3. **Identify** all of the types of forces acting on you as you sit in your chair. **2.d**

4. **State** the universal law of gravitation. **2.g**

5. **Organize Information** Copy the graphic organizer below and list forces and brief descriptions of forces mentioned in this lesson. **2.d**

Force	Description

6. **Give an example** of a moving object that has balanced horizontal forces and balanced vertical forces acting on it. **2.d**

7. Why do you notice the pull of Earth's gravity but not the pull of the Sun's gravity?

   A. Gravity only pulls on objects that are touching each other. **2.g**

   B. Earth is much heavier than the Sun.

   C. The Sun is very far away.

   D. The Sun's gravity only pulls on you during the day.

Applying Science

8. **Evaluate** the following statement: "An object is acted on by either horizontal or vertical forces." Give an example not discussed in the text that shows this statement is false. **2.d**

9. **Construct** a diagram of a mass hanging from a spring scale. What are the forces acting on the mass? **2.d**

Science nline
For more practice, visit **Standards Check** at ca8.msscience.com.

MiniLab

Can you measure the force of friction?

When two surfaces slide against each other, friction acts to oppose the sliding motion. How can you measure this force of sliding friction?

Procedure

1. Read and complete a lab safety form.

2. Divide a large piece of **poster board** into three sections lengthwise. Tape **rough sandpaper** on the first section and **fine sandpaper** on the middle section.

3. Attach a **spring scale** to a **block of wood.** Pull the block across the first section with constant speed. Record the reading on the spring scale. Repeat two more times and average your results.

4. Repeat Step 3 for the other two sections.

Force of Friction	Force (N)			
	Trial 1	**Trial 2**	**Trial 3**	**Average**
Rough sandpaper				
Fine sandpaper				
Posterboard				

Analysis

1. **Draw** a diagram of the horizontal forces acting on the block.

2. **Infer** whether the forces acting on the block are balanced or unbalanced.

3. **Rank** the surfaces in order of increasing force of friction.

 Science Content Standards

2.a Students know a force has both direction and magnitude.

2.d Students know how to identify separately the two or more forces that are acting on a single static object, including gravity, elastic forces due to tension or compression in matter, and friction.

LESSON 3

Science Content Standards

2.e Students know that when the forces on an object are unbalanced, the object will change its velocity (that is, it will speed up, slow down, or change direction).

2.f Students know the greater the mass of an object, the more force is needed to achieve the same rate of change in motion.

9.d Recognize the slope of the linear graph as the constant in the relationship $y = kx$ and apply this principle in interpreting graphs constructed from data.

Also covers: 9.a

Reading Guide

What *You'll Learn*

▶ **Describe** how unbalanced forces cause velocity to change.

▶ **Explain** how the acceleration of an object depends on the net force acting on the object.

▶ **Explain** how the acceleration of an object depends on the object's mass.

Why *It's Important*

If an object's velocity changes, an unbalanced force is acting on it.

Vocabulary

centripetal force
Newton's second law of motion
Newton's third law of motion

Review Vocabulary

acceleration: the rate of change of velocity with time (p. 60)

Unbalanced Forces and Acceleration

Main Idea Unbalanced forces cause accelerations.

Real-World Reading Connection When a tennis player hits a ball, the racket exerts an unbalanced force on the ball. The ball's speed and direction of motion changes. What other examples of changes in objects' velocities do you observe every day?

Unbalanced Forces and Velocity

When an object's speed or direction of motion changes, you know that there is an unbalanced force acting on the object. How do unbalanced forces affect objects at rest and in motion?

Unbalanced Forces on an Object at Rest

The ball on the left side of **Figure 20** is at rest. What two forces act on the ball to result in a zero net force? The downward force resulting from gravity is balanced by the upward normal force exerted by the hand. However, when the normal force is removed, the forces on the ball are unbalanced. Then the velocity of the ball increases in the downward direction as it falls. In other words, the ball accelerates in the downward direction. This is the same direction as the unbalanced force on the ball. When an unbalanced force acts on an object at rest, the object accelerates in the direction of the unbalanced force.

 Figure 20 Identify the unbalanced force acting on the ball.

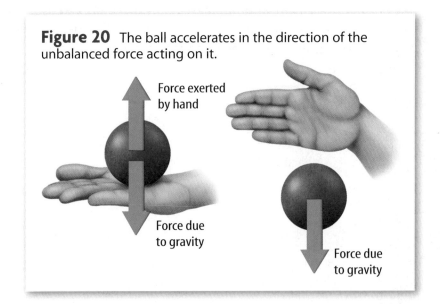

Figure 20 The ball accelerates in the direction of the unbalanced force acting on it.

Force exerted by hand

Force due to gravity

Force due to gravity

Figure 21 An unbalanced force can cause an object in motion to speed up or slow down.

Net force

Velocity

Speeding Up

Net force

Velocity

Slowing Down

Unbalanced Forces on an Object in Motion

Unbalanced forces can also change the motion of objects that are already moving. Whether the unbalanced force causes the object to speed up or slow down depends on the direction of the unbalanced force in relation to the direction of motion.

Speeding Up When does an unbalanced force cause an object to speed up? If an object is moving, a net force applied in the same direction the object is moving causes the object to speed up. For example, in **Figure 21,** the net force is in the same direction as the sled's velocity. This makes the sled speed up and its velocity increase.

The net force on a ball falling to the ground is downward. This force is in the same direction the ball is moving. Because the net force on the ball is in the same direction as the ball's velocity, the ball speeds up as it falls.

Slowing Down If the net force on an object is in the direction opposite to the object's velocity, the object slows down. In **Figure 21,** the force of sliding friction becomes larger when the boy puts his feet in the snow. The net force on the sled is the combination of gravity and sliding friction. When the sliding friction force becomes large enough, the net force is opposite to the sled's velocity. This causes the sled to slow down.

If an object is slowing down, what is the relationship between the object's velocity and the net force acting on the object?

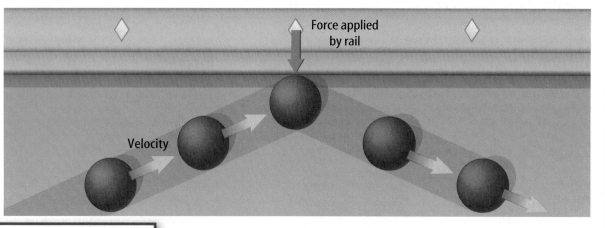

Figure 22 The rail exerts an unbalanced force on the ball, changing the ball's motion.

ACADEMIC VOCABULARY

affect

(verb) to cause a change in
The injury to Maria's knee
affected her ability to play
basketball.

WORD ORIGIN

centripetal

from Latin *centripetus;* means
toward the center

Unbalanced Forces and Direction of Motion

The direction of motion can also change when the forces on an object are unbalanced. The ball in **Figure 22** is moving in a straight line before it hits the rail. The rail then exerts an unbalanced force on the ball, causing its direction of motion to change. The rail affects the ball's motion only when it is in contact with the ball.

Figure 23 shows a ball that is tied to a string and swung in a horizontal circle. This type of motion is called circular motion. The velocity of the ball is changing as it moves because the direction of its motion is changing. The unbalanced force acting on the ball is the tension force exerted by the string. This force is called the centripetal (sen TRIH put ul) force. In circular motion, the **centripetal force** is the force that is perpendicular to the velocity and toward the center of the circle. The force exerted by the string is the centripetal force that keeps the ball moving in a circle.

 In what direction is the centripetal force?

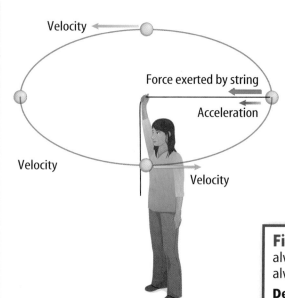

Figure 23 The force exerted by the string is always perpendicular to the ball's velocity. It also always points to the center of the circle.

Describe how the ball's velocity is changing.

Newton's Second Law of Motion

Unbalanced forces can cause an object to speed up, slow down, or change direction. When an object changes speed or direction, its velocity changes and the object is accelerating. In other words, unbalanced forces cause an object to accelerate. According to **Newton's second law of motion,** the acceleration of an object equals the net force divided by the object's mass. The acceleration is in the same direction as the net force. Newton's second law of motion can be written as this equation:

Newton's Second Law Equation

$$\text{acceleration (in m/s}^2) = \frac{\text{net force (in N)}}{\text{mass (in kg)}}$$

$$a = \frac{F}{m}$$

In this equation, force is measured in newtons and mass is measured in kilograms. When force is measured in newtons and mass in kilograms, the unit for acceleration is meter/second^2. This unit is the same as meter/(seconds × seconds).

Second Law Equation

2.e, 2.f

Solve for Acceleration You throw a 0.5-kg basketball with a force of 10 N. What is the ball's acceleration?

1 **This is what you know:**
mass: $m = 0.5$ kg
force: $F = 10$ N

2 **This is what you need to find:** acceleration: a

3 **Use this formula:** $a = F/m$

4 **Substitute:**
the values for F and m
into the formula and divide.
$a = \frac{10 \text{ N}}{0.5 \text{ kg}}$ is 20 m/s^2

5 **Determine the units:** units of $a = \frac{\text{units of } F}{\text{units of } m} = \frac{\text{N}}{\text{kg}} = \frac{\text{m}}{\text{s}^2} = \text{m/s}^2$

Answer: The ball's acceleration is 20 m/s^2.

Sciencenline
For more equation practice,
visit ca8.msscience.com.

Practice Problems

1. You push a 20-kg crate with a force of 10 N. What is the crate's acceleration?

2. Calculate the acceleration of an 80-kg sprinter if the force on the sprinter is 80 N.

MiniLab

Does water exert a force?

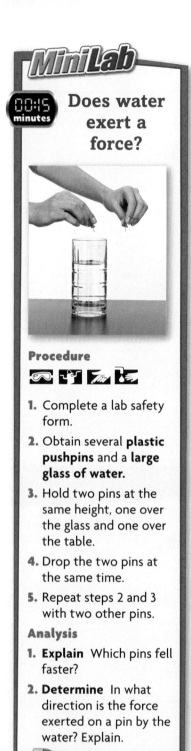

Procedure

1. Complete a lab safety form.
2. Obtain several **plastic pushpins** and a **large glass of water.**
3. Hold two pins at the same height, one over the glass and one over the table.
4. Drop the two pins at the same time.
5. Repeat steps 2 and 3 with two other pins.

Analysis

1. **Explain** Which pins fell faster?
2. **Determine** In what direction is the force exerted on a pin by the water? Explain.

2.e

Newton's Second Law and the Net Force

Newton's second law of motion explains how balanced and unbalanced forces affect an object's motion. When the forces are balanced, the net force is zero. According to the second law of motion, this means that the object's acceleration is zero. Then the velocity is constant and the object's motion doesn't change.

If the forces on the object are unbalanced, then the net force is not zero. According to the second law of motion, the acceleration is not zero, and the velocity of the object changes. In other words, only unbalanced forces cause the motion of objects to change.

Reading Check If the acceleration is not zero, are the forces on the object balanced or unbalanced?

Newton's Second Law and Planetary Motion

The planets, including Earth, move around the Sun in nearly circular paths. This means that the planets are accelerating because their direction of motion is always changing. According to the second law of motion, there must be an unbalanced force acting on Earth and the other planets. Isaac Newton realized that this force was the gravitational force exerted by the Sun. **Figure 24** shows how the gravitational force exerted by the Sun keeps Earth moving in a circular path.

Recall that a centripetal force keeps an object moving in a circle. The gravitational force exerted by the Sun is the centripetal force that keeps the planets moving around the Sun. You will read more about gravity and the motion of the planets in Chapter 11.

Figure 24 The Sun's gravity is the centripetal force that keeps Earth moving in a circular path around the Sun.

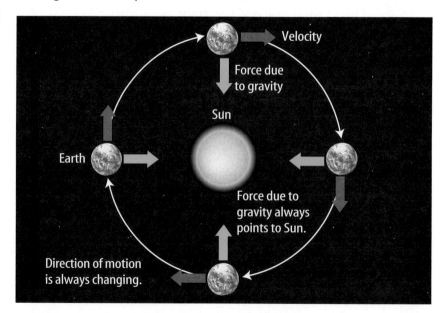

Newton's Third Law of Motion

How high can you jump? Think about the forces acting on you when you jump. Because you are accelerating, there must be an unbalanced force acting on you. What causes this force? You might think it's your legs and feet that push you upward. You're partly right.

According to the **Newton's third law of motion,** when one object exerts a force on a second object, the second object exerts an equal force in the opposite direction on the first object. In the case of jumping, as in **Figure 25,** the feet exert a force on the ground. The ground then pushes upward on the feet, causing the jumper to accelerate upward.

Force Pairs

The forces two objects exert on each other are called force pairs. The forces in a force pair act in opposite directions and are always equal in size.

If force pairs are equal in size and act in opposite directions, why don't they cancel each other out? Remember that the forces in force pairs act on different objects. When you jump, you exert a force on Earth, and Earth exerts a force on you. One force in the force pair acts on Earth, and the other force acts on you. These forces do not result in a zero net force because they act on different objects. Equal and opposite forces cancel out only if they act on the same object. **Figure 26** shows an example of a force pair. One force acts on the boat and the other force acts on the person.

 Figure 26 Explain why the force pair does not result in a zero net force.

Action and Reaction

In force pairs, one force of the force pair is sometimes called the action force, and the other force is the reaction force. When you push on a wall, the action force is the force you exert on the wall. The reaction force is the force exerted by the wall on you. For every action force, there is a reaction force that is equal in size, but opposite in direction.

Figure 25 According to the third law of motion, the ground exerts the upward force that pushes the jumper into the air.

Figure 26 The force pair is the force exerted by the person on the boat and the force the boat exerts on the person.

Applying Newton's Laws

Newton's laws of motion describe how forces affect the motion of any object. For example, the motion of the jumping basketball player in **Figure 27** can be explained by the laws of motion.

When you push down on the ground, the third law of motion says that the ground pushes up on you. This force combines with the downward force of gravity to form the net force acting on you. If you push down hard enough, the direction of the net force becomes upward. According to the second law of motion, you accelerate upward.

When you are in the air, the downward force due to gravity is in the direction opposite to your motion. This causes you to slow down until you reach the top of your jump. Then as you start moving downward, gravity is in the same direction as you are moving, so you speed up as you fall.

 Why do you speed up when you fall?

When you hit the ground, the upward force exerted on you by the ground brings you to a stop. Then the forces on you are balanced, and you remain at rest. **Table 3** and **Figure 28** provide more examples of how Newton's laws of motion explain objects' motion.

Figure 27 Newton's laws of motion describe how the forces acting on this basketball player affect his motion.

Table 3 Newton's Laws of Motion		
Law	**Statement of Law**	**Example**
Newton's first law of motion	An object at rest will remain at rest unless acted on by an unbalanced force. An object in motion will continue moving at a constant velocity unless acted on by an unbalanced force.	The forces acting on a book at rest on a table are balanced, so the book's motion does not change. The forces acting on a skydiver with an open parachute are balanced, so the skydiver falls in a straight line at a constant speed.
Newton's second law of motion	The size of the acceleration of an object is equal to the net force on the object divided by its mass. The acceleration is in the same direction as the net force.	A skydiver jumping out of a plane accelerates toward the ground as gravity pulls her down.
Newton's third law of motion	When one object exerts a force on another object, the second object exerts a force on the first object that is equal in size but opposite in direction.	When you push on a wall with a force of 100 N, the wall pushes back on you with a force of 100 N.

Concepts In Motion
Interactive Table Organize information about Newton's laws of motion at ca8.msscience.com.

Newton's Laws in Sports

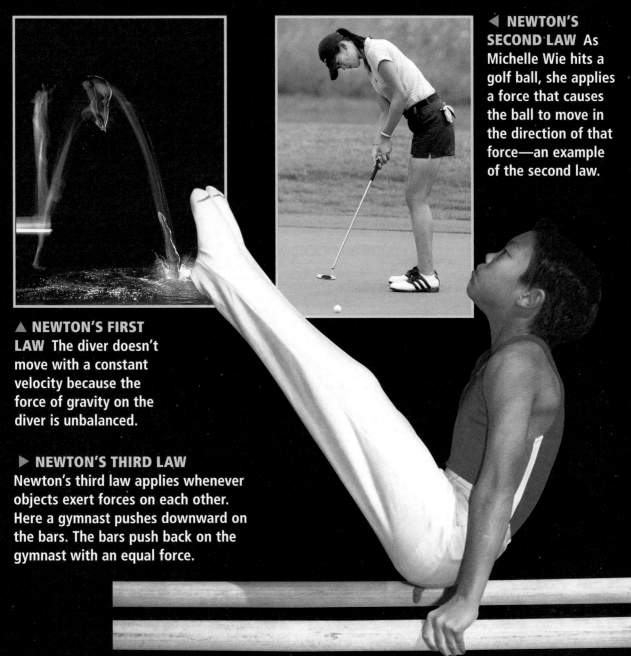

Figure 28

The motion of people, balls, and other objects during sports activities can be explained by Newton's laws of motion. According to the first law, an object in motion moves with a constant speed in a straight line unless acted upon by an unbalanced force. If an object is at rest, it stays at rest unless acted upon by an unbalanced force. According to the second law, an object accelerates in the direction of the net force. The third law can be stated this way—for every action force, there is an equal and opposite reaction force.

◄ **NEWTON'S SECOND LAW** As Michelle Wie hits a golf ball, she applies a force that causes the ball to move in the direction of that force—an example of the second law.

▲ **NEWTON'S FIRST LAW** The diver doesn't move with a constant velocity because the force of gravity on the diver is unbalanced.

► **NEWTON'S THIRD LAW** Newton's third law applies whenever objects exert forces on each other. Here a gymnast pushes downward on the bars. The bars push back on the gymnast with an equal force.

What have you learned?

In Lesson 1 you read that unbalanced forces cause the motion of an object to change. In this lesson you read about how forces cause motion to change. An object accelerates when it changes speed or direction. According to Newton's second law of motion, the acceleration of an object equals the net force divided by the object's mass. The acceleration is in the same direction as the net force. The third law of motion says that forces are always exerted in pairs. This means that when you push on a door, the door pushes on you with a force of the same size in the opposite direction.

LESSON 3 Review

Summarize

Create your own lesson summary as you organize an **outline.**

1. **Scan** the lesson. Find and list the first **red** main heading.

2. **Review** the text after the heading and list 2–3 details about the heading.

3. **Find** and list each **blue** subheading that follows the **red** main heading.

4. **List** 2–3 details, key terms, and definitions under each **blue** subheading.

5. **Review** additional **red** main headings and their supporting **blue** subheadings. List 2–3 details about each.

 ELA8: R 2.3

Standards Check

Using Vocabulary

1. _____ states that an object's acceleration is the ratio of net force to the object's mass. **2.f**

2. Define *centripetal force* in your own words. **2.e**

Understanding Main Ideas

3. **Explain** how you know the forces acting on an object at rest are balanced. **2.e**

4. **Determine Cause and Effect** Copy and fill in the graphic organizer below to describe two ways to increase the magnitude of an object's acceleration. **2.f**

5. **Compare** how your weight, mass, and the normal force exerted by the floor change when you are in an elevator that starts from rest and accelerates upward. **2.e**

6. How does the velocity of an object traveling in a straight line change if a nonzero net force acts in the same direction as the object's velocity?

   A. It will not change. **2.e**

   B. The speed increases.

   C. The direction of motion changes.

   D. The speed decreases.

Applying Math

7. **Calculate** The net force on a rock with a mass of 2.0 kg is 19.6 N. What is the acceleration of the rock? **2.f**

8. **Calculate** At the start of a race, the net force on a sprinter is 640 N. If the mass of the sprinter is 80.0 kg, find the sprinter's acceleration. **2.f**

For more practice, visit **Standards Check** at ca8.msscience.com.

Applying Math

Finding Force and Acceleration

Newton's second law of motion can be used to find an unknown force or acceleration if the other two variables are known.

Example 1

Solve for Force A car has a mass of 1,500 kg and an acceleration of 2.0 m/s². What is the net force acting on the car?

1 **This is what you know:**
    mass: $m = 1,500$ kg
    acceleration: $a = 2.0$ m/s²

2 **This is what you need to find:** force: F

3 **Use this formula:**
    $F = ma$

4 **Substitute:**
the values for m and a
into the formula and multiply.
    $F = (1,500 \text{ kg})(2.0 \text{ m/s}^2) = 3,000$ N

Answer: The net force is 3,000 N.

Example 2

Solve for Mass A softball hit by a bat has an acceleration of 1,500 m/s². If the net force on the softball is 300 N, what is the softball's mass?

1 **This is what you know:**
    Force: $F = 300$ N
    acceleration: $a = 1,500$ m/s²

2 **This is what you need to find:** mass: m

3 **Use this formula:**
    $m = \frac{F}{a}$

4 **Substitute:**
    $m = \frac{(300 \text{ N})}{(1,500 \text{ m/s}^2)} = 0.2$ kg

the values for F and a
into the formula and divide.

Answer: The mass is 0.2 kg.

Practice Problems

1. What is the net force on a backpack with a mass of 12.0 kg and an acceleration of 0.5 m/s²?

2. Find the mass of a dragster if the net force is 27,000 N and the acceleration is 30.0 m/s².

Sciencenline
For more math practice, visit **Math Practice** at ca8.msscience.com.

Comparing Mass and Weight

Materials

objects with various masses
string
balance
2,000-g spring scale
graph paper

Safety Precautions

Science Content Standards

2.d Students know how to identify separately the two or more forces that are acting on a single static object, including gravity, elastic forces due to tension or compression in matter, and friction.
9.a Plan and conduct a scientific investigation to test a hypothesis.
9.d Recognize the slope of the linear graph as the constant in the relationship $y = kx$ and apply this principle in interpreting graphs constructed from data.

Problem

What is the difference between mass and weight? Weight is a measure of the gravitational force on an object. Earth's gravitational pull on an object decreases as the object gets farther from Earth. When astronauts orbit Earth, their weight is less than when they are standing on the ground. However, the mass of an astronaut doesn't change when the astronaut gets farther from Earth. The mass of an object is the amount of matter that makes up the object. Unlike weight, the mass of an object does not depend on where the object is located.

Form a Hypothesis

➤ **Review** the results from this chapter's laboratory investigations.

➤ **Form a hypothesis** about the relationship between the mass and the weight of an object. As mass increases or decreases, how does the weight of an object change?

Collect Data and Make Observations

Make a Plan

1. Read and complete a lab safety form.
2. As a group, decide upon the materials you will need to test your hypothesis. Include any safety equipment you need to collect or safety procedures you need follow to ensure the safety of your group members.
3. Devise an experiment to test your hypothesis. Be specific. List the steps of your experiment in logical order. State exactly how you will use your equipment and what you will do during each step.
4. Copy the data table on the next page into your Science Journal. Be certain your table contains enough rows to record the results of all your planned trials.
5. Have one group member read your entire experiment aloud to the group to make certain you have all the necessary materials and that your experimental steps are in logical order and can be easily followed.

Mass and Weight Data		
Object	Mass (kg)	Weight (N)

Follow Your Plan

1. Show your materials list, experiment steps, and data table to your teacher. Include any changes in your plan that your teacher suggests.
2. Carry out your experiment as approved, taking all the necessary safety precautions.
3. Record your results in your data table as you complete each measurement.

Analyze and Conclude

1. **Graph** your data. Plot the measured weight on the *y*-axis and the mass on the *x*-axis. Draw a straight line on your graph that comes closest to all the data points. The line should include the zero point on both axes.
2. **Determine** the slope of your line.
3. **Use** your graph to determine the weights of objects with 0.10 kg, 0.20 kg, and 0.30 kg. Calculate the ratio of weight to mass for each of these objects.
4. **Infer** how the ratio of weight to mass depends on the mass.
5. **Explain** how the weight of any mass can be calculated using the slope of your line.

Communicate

WRITING in Science  ELA8: W 1.2

Write a newspaper article describing the results of your experiment. The article should be at least three paragraphs long and should include information about who performed the experiment, how the experiment was performed, and what was learned about the relationship between mass and weight.

Real World Science

Science & Career

ROCKET SCIENTIST

At NASA's Jet Propulsion Laboratory in Pasadena, California, aerospace engineers are responsible for propelling spacecraft into outer space. They also help develop the computer systems on board these spacecraft that will guide them millions of miles and then slow them down as they near their destination. Besides designing spacecraft and their systems, aerospace engineers also design aircraft and their related systems.

Visit **Career** at **ca8.msscience.com** to learn more about what aerospace engineers do and what they are required to know. Then write a fictitious want ad for a aerospace engineer at NASA.

Hi-Tech Roller Coasters

Science & Technology

Modern roller coaster rides can reach heights of over 450 feet. These rides use launch systems that enable the roller-coaster cars to climb to these dizzying heights. New technologies can accelerate roller coaster cars to speeds over 190 km/h in just 3–4 seconds. The fastest rides use specially designed hydraulic systems to power a cable that propels the cars down the first part of the track. Other designs use special motors called linear induction motors to accelerate the cars to high speeds.

Visit **Technology** at **ca8.msscience.com** to learn more at roller coasters. Make a table showing the five fastest roller coaster rides and the five highest roller coasters.

Isaac Newton: Bestselling Author?

Newton's three laws of motion were first published in 1687 in a book called *The Mathematical Principals of Natural Philosophy*. Originally the book was in Latin and today it is known as the *Principia*, the shortened form of its Latin title. It is one of the most influential scientific books ever published. The *Principia* also included Newton's discussion of the law of universal gravitation and how gravity caused the observed motions of the planets and their moons.

Visit **History** at *ca8.msscience.com* to learn more about the life of Isaac Newton. Hold a mock interview with Newton. Imagine that the *Principia* has just been published and Newton is on a book-promotion tour.

What keeps a bridge from falling down?

Without tension and compression, traveling in and out of San Francisco would be a lot harder. Tension and compression are the forces that keep suspension bridges like the Golden Gate Bridge standing. The thick, horizontal cables strung over the tops of the orange towers are under tension because they are anchored into the ground. The towers are put under compression because most of the weight is transferred to the towers through the vertical suspender cables.

Visit **Society** at *ca8.msscience.com* to learn more about suspension bridges. Draw a picture of the Golden Gate Bridge, labeling the main elements and drawing arrows showing the direction of tension and compression forces.

The BIG Idea An object's motion changes if the forces acting on the object are unbalanced.

Lesson 1 Combining Forces
2.a, 2.b, 2.c, 9.g

Main Idea When more than one force acts on an object, the combined effect is caused by the sum of all applied forces.

- A force is a push or a pull. Forces are described by vectors that show the force's magnitude and direction.

- The net force is the sum of all forces acting on an object.

- If the net force is zero, the forces are balanced. If the net force is not zero, the forces are unbalanced.

- If the forces on an object are balanced, the motion of the object does not change.

- Unbalanced forces change the object's speed or direction of motion.

- Newton's first law of motion states that if the net force on an object is zero, the motion of the object will not change.

- **balanced force** (p. 91)
- **contact force** (p. 88)
- **force** (p. 88)
- **net force** (p. 90)
- **Newton's first law of motion** (p. 93)
- **noncontact force** (p. 89)
- **unbalanced force** (p. 91)

Lesson 2 Types of Forces
2.d, 2.g

Main Idea There are different types of forces that act on objects.

- Gravity is an attractive force between all objects that have mass.

- Friction forces push parallel to sliding surfaces, opposing the motion of the surfaces.

- Compression and tension forces cause an object to be compressed or stretched.

- **compression force** (p. 101)
- **elastic force** (p. 101)
- **friction** (p. 99)
- **gravity** (p. 96)
- **law of universal gravitation** (p. 97)
- **normal force** (p. 102)
- **tension force** (p. 101)
- **weight** (p. 98)

Lesson 3 Unbalanced Forces and Acceleration
2.e, 2.f, 9.a, 9.d

Main Idea Unbalanced forces cause accelerations.

- Unbalanced forces cause objects to accelerate.

- An unbalanced force will cause an object to speed up, slow down, or change direction.

- Newton's second law states that the acceleration of an object equals the net force on the object divided by the object's mass. The acceleration is in the direction of the net force.

- Newton's third law of motion states that all forces come in pairs. When an object exerts a force on a second object, the second object exerts a force equal in size but opposite in direction on the first object.

- **centripetal force** (p. 108)
- **Newton's second law of motion** (p. 109)
- **Newton's third law of motion** (p. 111)

STUDY TO GO Download quizzes, key terms, and flash cards from ca8.msscience.com.

Linking Vocabulary and Main Ideas

Use vocabulary terms from page 120 to complete this concept map.

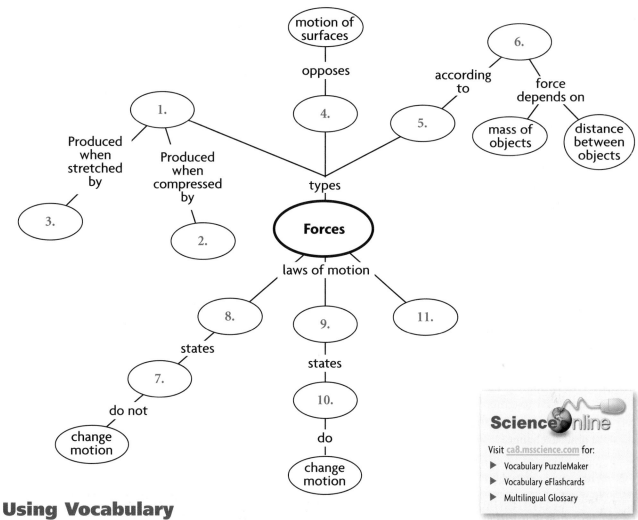

Using Vocabulary

Fill in each blank with the correct vocabulary term.

12. The astronaut's _____ decreased as her rocket took her farther away from Earth.

13. Gravity is a(n) _____ because it is exerted on objects even when they are not touching each other.

14. If the _____ acting on an object is not zero, the object accelerates.

15. The weight of a book at rest on a horizontal table is balanced by the _____ exerted by the table on the book.

16. Gravity is the _____ that pulls the Moon in its orbit around Earth.

17. A(n) _____ is a push or a pull.

18. Friction is a(n) _____ because the objects exerting the force are touching each other.

Science nline

Visit ca8.msscience.com for:
► Vocabulary PuzzleMaker
► Vocabulary eFlashcards
► Multilingual Glossary

Understanding Main Ideas

Choose the word or phrase that best answers the question.

1. What changes when unbalanced forces act on an object?
   A. mass
   B. motion
   C. inertia
   D. weight   `2.e`

2. The figure below shows the gravitational forces between two objects.

 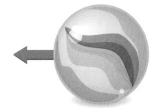

What would be the effect of decreasing the distance between the objects?
   A. The force would remain the same.
   B. The force would increase because the objects are closer together.
   C. The force would decrease because the objects are closer together.
   D. The force only changes if the masses of the objects change.   `2.g`

3. What force slows a book sliding on a table?
   A. inertia
   B. gravity
   C. reaction force
   D. sliding friction   `2.d`

4. What does the length of a force vector represent?
   A. the object's velocity
   B. the force's direction
   C. the force's magnitude
   D. the direction of acceleration   `2.a`

5. What would cause an object to have a smaller acceleration?
   A. increasing the net force on the object
   B. decreasing the mass of the object, keeping the net force constant
   C. increasing the mass of the object, keeping the net force constant
   D. decreasing the mass of the object and increasing the net force on the object   `2.f`

6. The graph shows the speed of a car moving in a straight line.

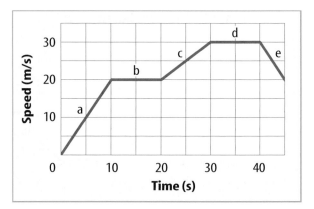

Over which segments are the forces on the car balanced?
   A. a and c
   B. b and d
   C. c and e
   D. d only   `2.c`

7. A car is driving at a constant velocity. Which is *not* true?
   A. All the forces acting on the car are balanced.
   B. A net force keeps it moving.
   C. The car is moving in a straight line at a constant speed.
   D. The car is not accelerating.   `2.c`

8. If a student pushes a book across a table with a force of 6 N and the force of friction is 4 N, what is the net force on the book?
   A. 0 N
   B. 2 N
   C. 10 N
   D. 24 N   `2.b`

Science Online   Standards Review ca8.msscience.com

Applying Science

9. **Compare** the motion of an object acted on by balanced forces with the motion of an object acted on by unbalanced forces. **2.c**

10. **Explain** how the gravitational force between Earth and the Moon would change if the distance between them increased. **2.g**

11. **Create** a diagram showing the following forces acting on an object. What is the net force acting on the object? **2.d**

Forces on an Object	
Direction	**Magnitude(N)**
Up	4
Down	4
Left	2
Right	6

12. **Compare** an astronaut's weight in orbit with the astronaut's weight on Earth, assuming the mass of the astronaut does not change. **2.g**

13. **Imagine** a book moving to the right across a table. As it slides across the table, it slows down and comes to a stop. In what direction is the net force acting on the book as it slows down? **2.f**

14. **Determine** whether the forces acting on a car are balanced or unbalanced if the car is turning while moving at a constant speed. Explain your answer. **2.e**

15. **Infer** the net force acting on a rope in a tug-of-war if the rope is moving with a constant speed in a straight line. **2.c**

16. **Give an example** in which gravity speeds up a moving object and example in which gravity slows down a moving object. **2.f**

17. **Explain** how an arrow is used to represent a force vector. **2.a**

WRITING in Science

18. **Write** an essay describing an example of how one of Newton's laws of motion is demonstrated in your favorite sport or activity. **ELA8: W 1.1**

Cumulative Review

19. **Determine** your displacement and distance traveled if you walked 20 m, took a book from a table, turned around and walked straight back to your seat. **1.d**

20. **Calculate** the average speed of a train that travels 160 km in 2.5 h. **1.c**

Applying Math

21. If the net force on a 2-kg object is 8.0 N, what is the object's acceleration? **MA8: ALG: 5.0**

22. The net force on an object is 10.0 N and its acceleration is 2.0 m/s^2. What is its mass? **MA8: ALG: 5.0**

23. Find the net force on an object that has a mass of 20.0 kg if its acceleration is 2.3 m/s^2. **MA8: ALG: 5.0**

24. The figure shows the forces on a box.

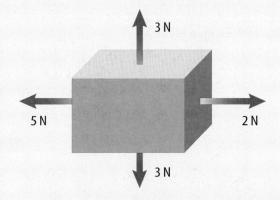

If the mass of the box is 10 kg, what is the size and direction of the acceleration of the box? **MA8: ALG: 5.0**

1 **Which indicates that the forces acting on an object are balanced?**

  A The object speeds up.

  B The object slows down.

  C The velocity of the object doesn't change.

  D The mass of the object doesn't change. **2.c**

2 **The figure shows the path of a ball tossed into the air.**

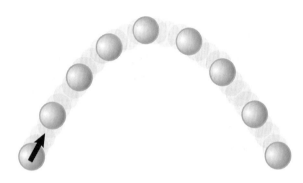

Which causes the velocity of the ball to change?

  A compression force

  B gravity

  C inertia

  D tension force **2.d**

3 **Which is not a vector?**

  A acceleration

  B force

  C mass

  D velocity **2.a**

Use the figure below to answer question 4 and 5.

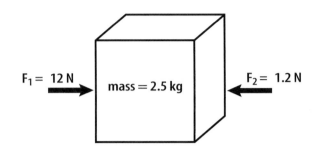

4 **If the vertical forces acting on the box are balanced, what is the net force on the box?**

  A 13.2 N to the left

  B 13.2 N to the right

  C 10.8 N to the left

  D 10.8 N to the right **2.b**

5 **What is the acceleration of the box?**

  A 5.3 m/s^2 to the left

  B 5.3 m/s^2 to the right

  C 4.3 m/s^2 to the left

  D 4.3 m/s^2 to the right **2.f**

6 **Which is a true statement?**

  A Your mass increases as you get closer to Earth.

  B Your mass decreases as you get closer to Earth.

  C The weight of an object is the frictional force on the object.

  D The weight of an object is the gravitational force on the object. **2.d**

7 Which would cause the gravitational force between object A and object B to increase?

A The mass of object A decreases.

B The mass of object B decreases.

C The objects move closer together.

D The objects move farther apart.   `2.g`

8 A ball is moving in a circular horizontal path. The net force on the ball is in which direction?

A downward

B upward

C parallel to the ball's path

D perpendicular to the ball's path   `2.e`

9 A box is sitting on a floor. Maria and Sam push on the box as shown in the figure below.

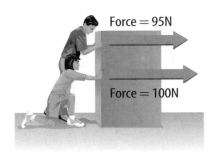

Force = 95N

Force = 100N

If the box doesn't move, what is the force of static friction exerted on the box?

A 5 N to the left

B 5 N to the right

C 195 N to the left

D 195 N to the right   `2.c`

10 The graph below shows how the speed of a book changes as it slides across a table.

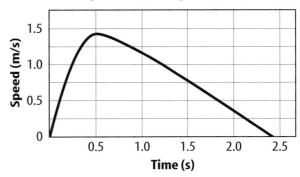

Speed of Sliding Book

Over what time interval is the net force on the book in the same direction as the book's velocity?

A 0 s to 0.5 s

B 0.5 s to 1.0 s

C 0 s to 1.5 s

D 1.0 s to 2.0 s   `2.e`

11 The speed of a soccer ball is decreasing as it rolls along the ground. Which best describes the net force on the soccer ball?

A The net force is zero.

B The net force is at a right angle to the ball's motion.

C The net force is in the same direction as the ball's motion.

D The net force is the direction opposite to the ball's motion.   `2.e`

12 You stretch a spring by pulling one end of it to the right. Which best describes the force exerted on the spring?

A compressional force to the left

B compressional force to the right

C tension force to the left

D tension force to the right   `2.d`

Density and Buoyancy

The BIG Idea

A fluid exerts an upward force on an object that is placed in the fluid.

LESSON 1 8.a, 8.b, 9.f
Density

Main Idea The density of a material is a measure of how much matter is packed into a unit volume of the material.

LESSON 2 8.c
Pressure and the Buoyant Force

Main Idea Objects in a fluid experience a buoyant force resulting from the pressure exerted by the fluid.

LESSON 3 8.d, 9.f
Sinking and Floating

Main Idea An object will float in a fluid if the density of the object is less than the density of the fluid.

Floating on Air

These hot-air balloons weigh hundreds of pounds, but still are able to rise through the air. A hot-air balloon has three main parts—the balloon envelope, the burner, and the basket. When the burner heats the air inside the envelope, the envelope expands and the balloon rises. What forces push the balloon upward?

Science Journal Compare and contrast three objects that float with three objects that sink.

Launch Lab

00:10 minutes

Can you push the beach ball under water?

A beach ball is made of lightweight material and is filled with air. It is easy to lift and throw into the air. Is it difficult to hold the ball under water?

Procedure

1. Complete a lab safety form.

2. Put the **beach ball** into a **large bucket** filled with **tap water**.

3. Slowly push the ball downward.

4. Draw a diagram of the forces acting on the ball.

Think About This

- **Name** other objects you have observed floating. How are they similar to the ball? How are they different?

- **Propose** a reason why the ball does not stay underwater when you push it down into the water.

8.c

Science Online

Visit ca8.msscience.com to:

▶ view **Concepts in Motion**

▶ explore Virtual Labs

▶ access content-related Web links

▶ take the Standards Check

FOLDABLES™ Study Organizer

Floating and Sinking

Make the following Foldable to increase your understanding of what causes floating and sinking.

▷ **STEP 1 Fold** a sheet of paper into thirds lengthwise and fold the top down about 3 cm from the top.

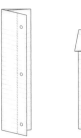

▷ **STEP 2 Unfold** and **draw** lines along the folds. **Label** as shown.

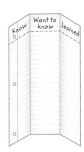

Know | Want to know | Learned

Reading Skill

Using What You Know

In the first column, list everything you already know about floating and sinking. In the second column, write the things that you would like to know more about. As you read this chapter, check your Foldable to make sure that your understanding of floating and sinking is correct. Record explanations and new information in the last column.

Get Ready to Read

New Vocabulary

ELA8: R 1.3

① Learn It! What should you do if you find a word you don't know or understand? Here are some suggested strategies:

1. Use context clues (from the sentence or the paragraph) to help you define it.
2. Look for prefixes, suffixes, or root words that you already know.
3. Write it down and ask for help with the meaning.
4. Guess at its meaning.
5. Look it up in the glossary or a dictionary.

② Practice It! Look at the word *vertical* in the following passage. See how context clues can help you understand its meaning.

Context Clue

Use **Figure 13** to see an example of vertical forces.

Context Clue

Up and *down* describe vertical forces.

Context Clue

The upward and downward forces are balanced.

Think about the forces acting on the boat in **Figure 13.** Gravity is pulling the boat down, yet the boat doesn't accelerate downward. Because the boat is not accelerating up or down, the vertical forces on the boat are balanced. There must be an upward force balancing the downward force of gravity that keeps the sailboat from sinking.

—*from page 146*

③ Apply It! Make a vocabulary bookmark with a strip of paper. As you read, keep track of words you do not know or want to learn more about.

Target Your Reading

Use this to focus on the main ideas as you read the chapter.

1 **Before you read** the chapter, respond to the statements below on your worksheet or on a numbered sheet of paper.

- Write an **A** if you **agree** with the statement.
- Write a **D** if you **disagree** with the statement.

2 **After you read** the chapter, look back to this page to see if you've changed your mind about any of the statements.

- If any of your answers changed, explain why.
- Change any false statements into true statements.
- Use your revised statements as a study guide.

Reading Tip

Read a paragraph containing a vocabulary word from beginning to end. Then, go back to determine the meaning of the word.

Science Online

Print a worksheet of this page at ca8.msscience.com.

Before You Read A or D	Statement	After You Read A or D
	1 Density is calculated by dividing volume by mass.	
	2 Air pressure increases as you climb a mountain.	
	3 Things can float only in liquids such as water.	
	4 All fluids are liquids.	
	5 You calculate the volume of all solids by multiplying length times width times height.	
	6 Heavy things sink when placed in water.	
	7 Compared to liquids, particles in gases are very close together.	
	8 Only solid objects can exert forces.	
	9 Hot-air balloons can fly because they are less dense than air.	
	10 Air pressure only pushes down on you.	

LESSON 1

Science Content Standards

8.a Students know density is mass per unit volume.

8.b Students know how to calculate the density of substances (regular and irregular solids and liquids) from measurements of mass and volume.

9.f Apply simple mathematic relationships to determine a missing quantity in a mathematic expression, given the two remaining terms (including speed = distance/time, density = mass/volume, force = pressure × area, volume = area × height).

Reading Guide

What *You'll Learn*

- **Explain** how the density of a material is independent of the amount of the material.
- **Calculate** the density of an object given its mass and volume.
- **Describe** how to measure the density of a liquid and a solid.

Why *It's Important*

Density can be used to determine the identity of unknown materials.

Vocabulary

density
rectangular solid

Review Vocabulary

volume: the amount of space taken up by an object (p. 10)

Density

Main Idea The density of a material is a measure of how much matter is packed into a unit volume of the material.

Real-World Reading Connection Can you imagine trying to lift a rock that is as big as a basketball? The rock and the basketball are the same size, but the rock is much heavier because it has more matter packed into the same volume of space.

What is density?

Which would have more mass, the balloon filled with air or the bottle of water shown in **Figure 1?** The mass of an object depends not only on the size of the object, but also on the material the object contains. All materials, such as the air in the balloon and the water in the bottle, have a property called density. **Density** (DEN suh tee) is the amount of mass per unit volume of a material.

Matter is made of particles, such as atoms or molecules, that have mass. The density of a material depends on the masses and the number of particles packed into a given volume. **Figure 1** shows that the volume of air has fewer particles and less mass than the same volume of water. As a result, the density of air is less than the density of water.

Figure 1 The balloon has less mass because it contains fewer particles of matter than the water in the bottle does.
Compare the density of air to the density of water.

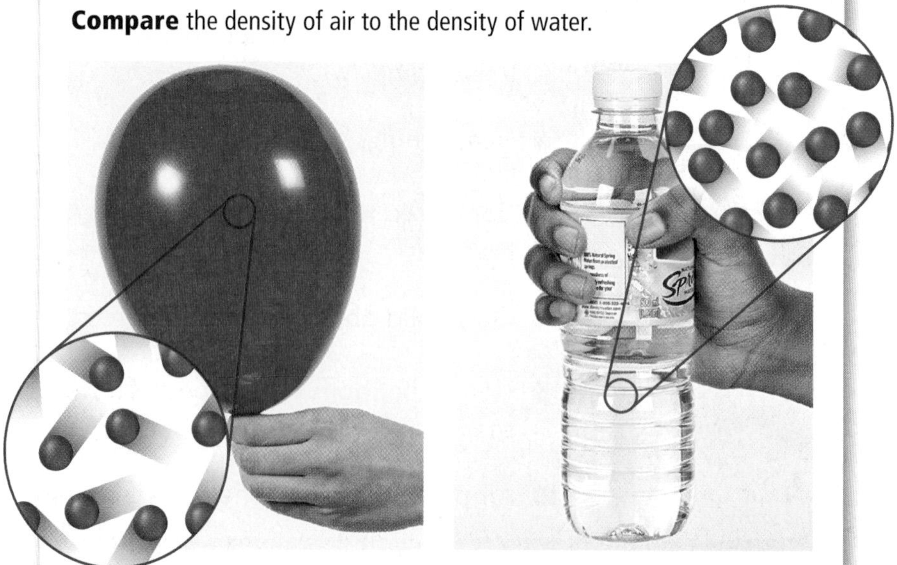

Calculating Density

The density of an object is the mass of an object divided by its volume. Density can be calculated using the following equation:

Density Equation

$$\text{density (in g/cm}^3) = \frac{\text{mass (in g)}}{\text{volume (in cm}^3)}$$

$$D = \frac{m}{V}$$

In this equation, D is density, m is the mass of the material, and V is the volume of the material. Because density equals mass divided by volume, the units for density always are a mass unit divided by a volume unit. If mass is measured in grams (g) and volume is measured in cubic centimeters (cm³), density has units of g/cm³. Density is the mass in grams of 1 cubic centimeter of the material. For example, silver has a density of 10.5 g/cm³. This means that 1 cm³ of silver has a mass of 10.5 g.

 Reading Check What are the units of density?

WORD ORIGIN·············
density
from Latin *densus*; means *thick, crowded*

Density Equation

8.a, 8.b

ALG: 5.0

Solve for Density
A piece of metal has a mass of 90.51 g and its volume is 11.5 cm³. What is the density of the metal?

1 This is what you know:
mass: $m = 90.51$ g
volume: $V = 11.5$ cm³

2 This is what you need to find: density: D

3 Use this formula: $D = \frac{m}{V}$

4 Substitute:
the values for m and V
into the formula and divide.
$D = \frac{90.51}{11.5} = 7.87$

5 Determine the units:
units of D = $\frac{\text{units of } m}{\text{units of } V}$ = $\frac{\text{g}}{\text{cm}^3}$ = g/cm³

Answer: The density is 7.87 g/cm³.

 Science nline
For more equation practice,
visit ca8.msscience.com.

Practice Problems

1. Find the density of a gold bar that has a mass of 1,930 g and a volume of 100 cm³.

2. What is the density of a bar of soap that has a volume of 80 cm³ and a mass of 90 g?

preceding (pree SEE ding)
(*adjective*) coming just before
*Good test-takers often look for
clues in preceding questions.*

Calculating Mass and Volume

The density equation on the **preceding** page is the relationship among the mass, volume, and density of an object. You can use the density equation to calculate either the mass or the volume of an object. For example, if you know the volume and the density of the object, you can use the density equation to find the object's mass. If you know the mass and the density, the density equation can be solved for the volume. The math feature at the end of this lesson shows how to use the density equation to solve for the mass and the volume.

Density and Materials

Imagine you have a chocolate bar, such as the one shown in **Figure 2,** that has a density of 1.2 g/cm³. Suppose you break the bar into two pieces. The two pieces of chocolate now are smaller than the whole chocolate bar. Does the density of the chocolate change when the pieces become smaller?

However, as **Figure 2** shows, the density of each of the two pieces is the same as the whole bar. The density of an object, such as a piece of chocolate, depends only on the material the object is made from. It does not depend on the object's size. If you break the chocolate bar into smaller pieces, each piece will have the same density. The density of each piece will be 1.2 g/cm³, the same as the density of the whole bar. The density of each piece is the same because each piece is made from the same material—chocolate.

Figure 2 The density of a piece of chocolate does not depend of the size of the piece.

Identify the variables of the density equation that do change as the chocolate bar is broken into smaller pieces.

mass of chocolate bar = 226 g, volume = 190 cm³
density = mass/volume
      = (226 g)/(190 cm³)
      = 1.2 g/ cm³

m = 113 g, V = 95 cm³
$D = m/V$
      = (113 g)/(95 cm³)
      = 1.2 g/cm³

m = 113 g, V = 95 cm³
$D = m/V$
      = (113 g)/(95 cm³)
      = 1.2 g/cm³

Concepts In Motion

Interactive Table Organize information about density at ca8.msscience.com.

Table 1 Densities of Some Common Materials

Solids		Liquids		Gases	
Material	**Density (g/cm³)**	**Material**	**Density (g/cm³)**	**Material**	**Density (g/cm³)**
Butter	0.86	Gasoline	0.74	Hydrogen	0.00009
Ice	0.92	Sunflower oil	0.92	Helium	0.00018
Aluminum	2.70	Water	1.00	Air	0.00129
Copper	8.96	Milk	1.03	Oxygen	0.00143
Gold	19.28	Mercury	13.55	Carbon dioxide	0.00198

What does density depend on?

The densities of some solids, liquids, and gases are listed in **Table 1.** The table shows that the density of gold, for example, is more than 19 times greater than the density of water. Also, the density of some solids and liquids, such as mercury, can be more than 10,000 times greater than the density of some gases, such as helium. Why do different materials have different densities?

Mass of Particles The density of a material depends on the mass of the particles, such as atoms or molecules, that make up the material. The more mass these particles have, the greater the density of the material. For example, the mass of a gold atom is more than seven times the mass of an aluminum atom. As a result, the density of gold is much greater than the density of aluminum.

Distance Between Particles The density of a material also depends on the distance between the particles in the material. The greater the distance between the atoms or molecules, the smaller the density. **Table 1** shows that in gases, particles are much farther apart than in solids or liquids. As a result, the density of a gas is usually much less than the density of a solid or a liquid.

Table 1 Which solids listed are less dense than water?

Mass of beaker = 144 g.

Mass of beaker and liquid = 331 g.

Figure 3 Two measurements are needed to measure the mass of a liquid.

Mass of beaker = 144 g
Mass of beaker and liquid = 331 g
Mass of liquid = (Mass of beaker
                    and liquid)
                  − (Mass of beaker)
Mass of liquid = 331 g − 144 g
                  = 187 g

1 Measure the mass of the empty container.

2 Measure the total mass of the container and the liquid.

3 Subtract the mass of the container from the total mass to find the mass of the liquid.

Measuring Density

To measure the density of a material or an object, you first need to measure both its mass and its volume. The volume of a liquid is usually measured using a graduated cylinder. The method for measuring the volume of a solid depends on whether it has a rectangular or an irregular shape.

Measuring Mass

A balance can be used to determine the mass of an object or a material. You can place most solids directly on the pan of the balance and read the result. If the solid is a powder, or if you want to find the mass of a liquid, you use a container and follow the steps shown in **Figure 3.** First, measure the mass of the empty container. Then, find the total mass of the container and sample. Finally, subtract the mass of the container from the total mass.

Visual Check **Figure 3** What are the three steps in measuring the mass of a sample?

Measuring the Volume of a Liquid

The method for measuring volume is different for liquids and solids. For a liquid, you can use a graduated cylinder to measure volume, as shown in **Figure 4.** Then, the volume will be measured in units of milliliters. The density of a liquid can be determined by using a balance to measure the mass of the liquid and a graduated cylinder to measure its volume. Then, these values for mass and volume are substituted into the density equation to calculate the liquid's density. Suppose that you measure a volume of 73 mL for a liquid. If the mass of the liquid is 80.3 g, then its density is 80.3 g divided by 73 mL, or 1.1 g/mL. Because 1 mL is equal to 1 cm^3, this density value can also be written as 1.1 g/cm^3.

Figure 4 A graduated cylinder can be used to find the volume of a liquid.

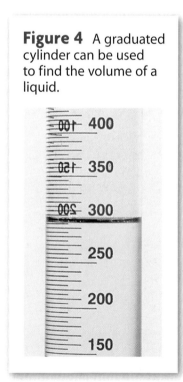

Measuring the Volume of a Rectangular Solid

You can use a graduated cylinder to measure a liquid's volume. How can you measure the volume of a solid? The method for measuring a solid's volume depends on the solid's shape. A **rectangular** (rehk TAN gyoo lar) **solid** is a six-sided block in which all sides are rectangles, as shown in **Figure 5.** To determine the volume of a rectangular solid, first measure its length, width, and height, and then use the following equation to find the volume:

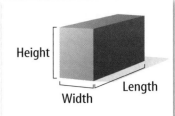

Figure 5 The volume of a rectangular solid depends on its length, width, and height.

Volume of a Rectangular Solid

$$\text{volume (cm}^3) = \text{length (cm)} \times \text{width (cm)} \times \text{height (cm)}$$
$$V = l \times w \times h$$

 Can the formula shown above be used to find the volume of any solid object? Explain.

Volume Equation

8.b

ALG: 5.0

Solve for Volume
A rectangular block of stone has a length of 12.3 cm, a width of 7.6 cm, and a height of 4.7 cm. What is the volume of the stone block?

1. **This is what you know:**
   - length: $l = 12.3$ cm
   - width: $w = 7.6$ cm
   - height: $h = 4.7$ cm

2. **This is what you need to find:** volume: V

3. **Use this formula:** $V = l \times w \times h$

4. **Substitute:** $V = (12.3) \times (7.6) \times (4.7) = 439.4$
   the values for l, w, and h into the formula and multiply.

5. **Determine the units:** units of V = (units of l) $\times$ (units of w) $\times$ (units of h) = cm $\times$ cm $\times$ cm = cm^3

Answer: The volume is 439.4 cm^3.

Science nline
For more equation practice, visit ca8.msscience.com.

Practice Problems

1. What is the volume of a brick that is 20.3 cm long, 8.9 cm wide, and 5.7 cm high?
2. Find the volume of a box with a height of 15 cm, a width of 18 cm, and a length of 30 cm.

Figure 6 The volume of an irregular solid can be measured using the displacement method.

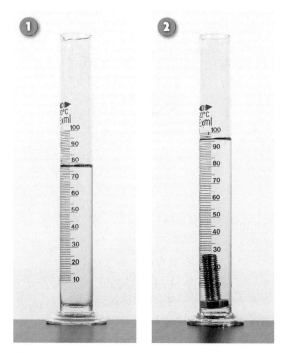

① Record the volume of the water:

volume of water = 78 mL

② Place the object in the water and record the combined volume of the object and water:

volume of water and bolt = 96 mL

③ Calculate the volume of the object by subtracting the volume of the water from the combined volume of the object and water:

volume of bolt = 96 mL – 78 mL
= 18 mL
= 18 cm³

Measuring the Volume of an Irregular Solid

There isn't a simple formula to find the volume of a solid if the object has an irregular shape. For example, how would you measure the volume of a football or a fork? **Figure 6** shows how to find the volume of a solid with an irregular shape using the displacement method. Displacement occurs when an object is placed in a liquid. The object pushes aside, or displaces, some of the liquid.

Using the Displacement Method

When you place an object in the graduated cylinder shown in **Figure 6,** the level of the liquid moves upward. However, the volume of the liquid hasn't changed. Instead, the liquid level moves upward because the solid has displaced some of the liquid. The volume at the new level of liquid is the combined volume of the liquid and the object. You can find the volume of the object by subtracting the liquid volume from the combined volume of the liquid and the object, as shown in **Figure 6.** After you find the volume, you can calculate the density of the object by dividing its mass by its volume.

 Figure 6 What are the three steps used to measure volume with the displacement method?

Density as a Physical Property

A physical property is a property of a material that you can measure without changing the composition of the material. The composition of a material changes when the material changes into a different substance. When you measure the density of a material, you measure the material's mass and volume. However, measuring the mass or the volume doesn't cause the material to change into a different substance. This means that density is a physical property of a material. You will read more about density and physical properties of materials in Chapter 7.

 What is a physical property?

What have you learned?

In this lesson you read that the density of a material depends on the kinds of particles that make up the material as well as the spacing of the particles in the material. You also read that density does not change as the size of the sample changes. Finally, you read about how to measure an object's mass and volume to be able to calculate the density of the object. You will use your knowledge of density in the next lessons as you study sinking and floating.

LESSON 1 Review

Summarize

Create your own lesson summary as you write a **newsletter.**

1. **Write** this lesson title, number, and page numbers at the top of a sheet of paper.

2. **Review** the text after the **red** main headings and write one sentence about each. These will be the headlines of your newsletter.

3. **Review** the text and write 2–3 sentences about each **blue** subheading. These sentences should tell *who, what, when, where,* and *why* information about each headline.

4. **Illustrate** your newsletter with diagrams of important structures and processes next to each headline.

ELA8: W 2.1

Standards Check

Using Vocabulary

1. _____ is the mass per unit volume of a material. **8.a**

2. Write a sentence using the term *rectangular solid.* **8.b**

Understanding Main Ideas

3. **State** the density of a 25-g sample of silver if a 5-g sample of silver has a density of 10.5 g/cm³. How do you know? **8.a**

4. **Organize Information** Copy and fill in the graphic organizer below to show the three steps of measuring volume using the displacement method. **8.b**

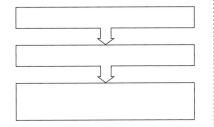

5. **Convert** 1.3 g/mL to g/cm³. **8.b**

6. **Compare** the densities of two objects that have the same volume, but one feels heavier than the other. **8.a**

7. **Identify** a situation in which it is important to use density instead of mass when comparing how heavy two materials are. **8.a**

8. **Calculate** the volume of the rectangular solid shown below. **8.b**

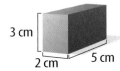

3 cm
2 cm
5 cm

Applying Math

9. **Calculate** the density of a limestone rock that has a mass of 175 g and a volume of 65 cm³. **8.b**

10. **Calculate** the volume of a diamond that has a density of 3.5 g/cm³ and a mass of 9.1 g. **8.b**

Science nline

For more practice, visit **Standards Check** at ca8.msscience.com.

Applying Math

Using the Density Equation to Find Mass and Volume

The density equation is a relationship between the mass of an object, its volume, and the density of the object. If you know any two of the variables in the density equation, you can calculate the unknown variable.

Using the Density Equation to Find Mass

If the density, *D*, and volume, *V*, of an object are known, you can find the mass, *m*, of the object.

First multiply both sides of the density equation by *V*:
$$V \times D = V \times \frac{m}{V}$$

The variable *V* cancels on the right side of the above equation:
$$V \times D = \cancel{V} \times \frac{m}{\cancel{V}} = m$$

So the equation for the mass of an object if its density and volume are known is:
$$m = V \times D$$

You can find the mass by multiplying the volume and the density.

Using the Density Equation to Find Volume

If the density, *D*, and mass, *m*, of an object are known, you can find the volume, *V*, of the object.

Use the equation above, and divide both sides by *D*:
$$\frac{m}{D} = \frac{V \times D}{D}$$

The variable *D* cancels on the right side of the above equation:
$$\frac{m}{D} = \frac{V \times \cancel{D}}{\cancel{D}} = V$$

So the equation for the volume of an object if its density and mass are known is:
$$V = \frac{m}{D}$$

You can find the volume by dividing the mass by the density.

Practice Problems

1. Lead has a density of 11.3 g/cm³. If a piece of lead has a volume of 4 cm³, what is its mass?

2. A stainless steel rod has a mass of 59.2 g and a density of 7.9 g/cm³. What is the volume of the rod?

Science nline
For more math practice, visit **Math Practice** at ca8.msscience.com.

DataLab

Can you calculate the density?

Regardless of a sample's form, it has mass, volume, and density. If you can measure the mass and volume, you can calculate the sample's density.

Data Collection

1. Read and complete a lab safety form.

2. Make a data table as shown below.

Density				
Sample	Description	Mass (g)	Volume (cm³)	Density (g/cm³)
1				
2				

3. Write a brief description of the sample in the table.

4. Use a **balance** to measure the mass of the material. For a liquid, follow the steps shown in **Figure 3**.

5. Find the volume of the sample. Use a **graduated cylinder** to find the volume of a liquid or an irregular solid. For an irregular solid, follow the steps in **Figure 6**.

6. Repeat steps 3, 4, and 5 for the remaining sample.

Data Analysis

1. **Calculate** the density for each sample.

2. **Explain** how the density you calculated would change if the size of the sample doubled.

3. **Compare** your results to those of other groups.

 Science Content Standards

8.b Students know how to calculate the density of substances (regular and irregular solids and liquids) from measurements of mass and volume.
9.f Apply simple mathematic relationships to determine a missing quantity in a mathematic expression, given the two remaining terms (including speed = distance/time, density = mass/volume, force = pressure × area, volume = area × height).

LESSON 2

Science Content Standards

8.c Students know the buoyant force on an object in a fluid is an upward force equal to the weight of the fluid the object has displaced.

Reading Guide

What *You'll Learn*

▶ **Describe** how a fluid exerts pressure on objects submerged in the fluid.

▶ **Compare** the pressure on an object at different depths in a fluid.

▶ **Explain** Archimedes' principle.

Why *It's Important*

The buoyant force explains how huge ships made of metal are able to float.

Vocabulary
fluid
pressure
atmospheric pressure
buoyant force
Archimedes' principle

Review Vocabulary
force: a push or a pull (p. 88)

Pressure and the Buoyant Force

(**Main Idea**) Objects in a fluid experience a buoyant force resulting from the pressure exerted by the fluid.

Real-World Reading Connection A beach ball filled with air floats on the surface of a swimming pool. Pushing the beach ball under water can be hard to do. If you hold the ball under water, why does the ball pop out of the water when you let go?

Pressure in a Fluid

You probably can think of many examples in which the force exerted by an object pushes or pulls on another object. A bat exerts a force on a baseball. Your hand pulls on a handle to open a door. It might seem that only solid objects can exert forces on each other. However, liquids and gases also can exert forces. Think about the waves crashing against you at the seashore or the air pushing against you on a windy day. Liquids and gases are **fluids,** which are materials that can flow and have no definite shape. Like solid objects, fluids can exert forces.

For example, when the swimmer in **Figure 7** tries to push the beach ball under the water, the water exerts an upward force on the ball. This force becomes greater as more of the ball is pushed into the water. When the swimmer lets go, the upward force exerted by the water can cause the ball to pop up.

Figure 7 Pushing an inflated ball under water is hard because of the upward force that the water exerts on the ball.

Downward force on ball

Upward force on ball

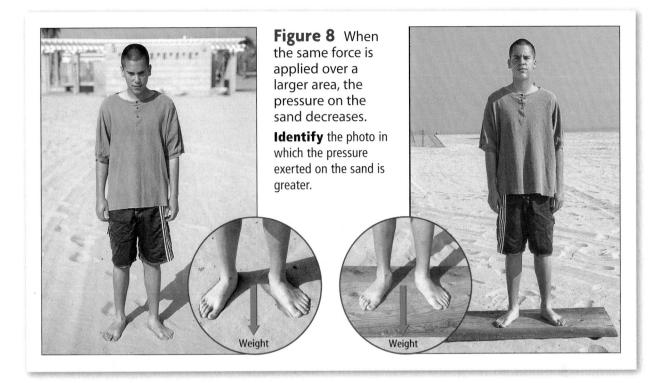

Figure 8 When the same force is applied over a larger area, the pressure on the sand decreases.

Identify the photo in which the pressure exerted on the sand is greater.

Weight

Weight

What is pressure?

What happens when you walk in deep, soft snow or dry sand? Your feet sink into the snow or sand, and walking can be difficult. If you ride a bicycle with narrow tires over the sand or the snow, the tires would sink even deeper than your feet.

How deep you sink depends on two things. One is the force you apply to the surface of the sand or the snow. This force is equal to your weight. How deep you sink also depends on the area over which the force is applied. Like the person in **Figure 8,** when you stand on two feet, the force you exert is spread out over the area covered by your two feet. However, suppose you stand on a large board, as in **Figure 8.** Then the force you exert on the sand is spread out over the area covered by the board. Because this area is larger than the area covered by your feet, the force you apply is more spread out when you stand on the board.

 What happens when the area over which a force is applied increases?

Why don't you sink as deep when you stand on the board? In both cases, you exerted a downward force on the sand. What changed was the area over which the force was exerted on the sand. By changing this area, you changed the pressure you exerted on the sand. **Pressure** is the force per unit of area applied on the surface of an object. Pressure decreases when a force is spread out over a larger area. When you stood on the board, the pressure you exerted on the sand decreased. As a result, you didn't sink as deep.

ACADEMIC VOCABULARY
area (AIR ee uh)
(noun) the number of unit squares that fit onto a surface
The area of an average adult human's skin is about 2.0 m².

WORD ORIGIN
fluid
from Latin *fluere;* means *to flow*

Calculating Pressure

Pressure depends on the force applied and the area of contact over which the force is applied. Pressure can be calculated from the following equation:

Pressure Equation

$$\text{pressure (in pascals)} = \frac{\text{force (in newtons)}}{\text{area (in meters squared)}}$$

$$P = \frac{F}{A}$$

The unit of pressure is the pascal, abbreviated Pa. Recall from Chapter 2 that the unit for force is the newton (N). A pressure of 1 Pa is equal to a force of 1 N applied over an area of 1 m², or 1 Pa = 1 N/m². The weight of a dollar bill resting completely flat on a table exerts a pressure of about 1 Pa on the table. Because 1 Pa is a small pressure, larger pressures are often expressed in units of a kilopascal (kPa), which is 1,000 Pa.

Pressure Equation

8.c

ALG: 5.0

Solve for Pressure A box exerts a force of 420 N on a floor. The bottom of the box has an area of 0.7 m². What is the pressure exerted by the box on the floor?

1 **This is what you know:**
force: $F = 420$ N
area: $A = 0.7$ m²

2 **This is what you need to find:** pressure: P

3 **Use this formula:** $P = \frac{F}{A}$

4 **Substitute:** $P = \frac{420}{0.7} = 600$
the values for F and A into the formula and divide.

5 **Determine the units:** units of $P = \frac{\text{units of } F}{\text{units of } A} = \frac{\text{N}}{\text{m}^2} = \text{N/m}^2 = \text{Pa}$

Answer: The pressure is 600 Pa.

Practice Problems

1. A person lying on a floor exerts a force of 750 N over a floor area of 1.1 m². Find the pressure exerted by the person on the floor.

2. A car makes contact with the ground over an area of 0.85 m². What is the pressure exerted by the car on the ground if the car exerts a force of 9,350 N on the ground?

Sciencenline

For more equation practice, visit ca8.msscience.com.

Pressure and Fluid Height

Suppose you pour the same amount of water into wide and narrow graduated cylinders, as shown in the left photo of **Figure 9.** Notice that the height of the water in the narrow cylinder is greater than in the wide cylinder. Is the pressure caused by the weight of the water the same at the bottom of each cylinder? The weight of the water in each cylinder is the same, but the contact area at the bottom of the narrow cylinder is smaller. Therefore, the pressure is greater at the bottom of the small cylinder.

 **Reading Check** Why is the pressure greater at the bottom of the narrow cylinder than at the bottom of the wide cylinder?

How could you increase the pressure at the bottom of the wide cylinder? If you added water to the cylinder, the weight of the water would increase. This would increase the force on the bottom of the cylinder, thereby increasing the pressure. In the right photo, the pressure at the bottom of both cylinders is the same. What do you notice about the height of the column of water in each cylinder? It is the same, too! This is not just a coincidence resulting from the shapes of the containers. It is true for any fluid: the pressure depends only on the height of the column of fluid above the surface where you measure the pressure. The greater the height of the column of fluid above a surface, the greater the pressure exerted by the fluid on the surface.

Pressure and Depth

Figure 10 shows how pressure changes with depth. At the top of the glass, the water pressure is zero because there is no column of water above that level. Pressure in the middle of the glass depends on the column of water from the top of the glass to the middle of the glass. Pressure at the bottom depends on the entire height of the water. Pressure increases with depth because the column of water pushing down becomes taller and heavier. You can feel how pressure changes with depth if you dive under water. As you swim deeper, the water pressure on you increases.

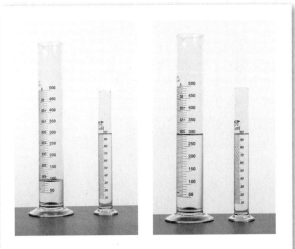

Figure 9 The pressure exerted by a column of fluid depends only on the height of the fluid column.

Figure 10 The pressure exerted by a fluid increases as the depth in the fluid increases.

Increasing Pressure

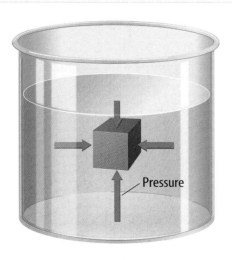

Figure 11 The pressure on an object of any shape is exerted perpendicular to the surfaces of the object.

Explain why the arrows showing the pressure have different lengths.

Pressure in All Directions

If the pressure exerted by a fluid is a result of the weight of the fluid, is the pressure in a fluid exerted only downward? The illustration in **Figure 11** shows a small, solid cube in a fluid. The fluid exerts pressure on each face of this cube, not just on the top. The pressure is perpendicular to the surface, and the amount of pressure depends only on the depth in the fluid. As shown in the photograph in **Figure 11,** this is true for any object in a fluid, no matter how complicated the shape. The pressure on the object is always perpendicular to the surface of the object.

 In which direction does pressure exerted by a fluid push?

Atmospheric Pressure

When you read about the pressure in fluids, you might think only about liquids such as water. However, remember that gases are fluids, too. Like liquids, a gas exerts pressure on an object depending on the height of the gas above the object. **Atmospheric** (AT muh sfihr ik) **pressure** is the force exerted per unit area by air particles. If you start at the top of a mountain and walk down, the height of the column of air above you increases. This means that atmospheric pressure increases as your elevation decreases. **Figure 12** shows how pressure varies as you go from the tallest mountains to deep under water in the ocean.

You can sense the change in atmospheric pressure when you fly in an airplane or take an elevator to the top of a tall building. The sudden change in pressure can make your ears pop. You sometimes can feel changes in pressure, but you probably don't notice the air pressing on you right now. The column of air above you is more than 10 km thick. The total force of the air pushing on the surface area of your skin is about the same as the weight of ten cars! You don't feel this pressure because there is an equal, internal pressure pushing out from the inside of your body. This internal pressure balances the external pressure exerted on you by the atmosphere.

Visualizing Pressure at Varying Elevations

Figure 12 No matter where you are on Earth, you're under pressure. Air and water are fluids that exert pressure on your body. The pressure exerted on you depends on your elevation in Earth's atmosphere. If you are underwater, the pressure on you also depends on your depth below the water surface.

▲ **High Elevation** With increasing elevation, the amount of air above you decreases, and so does the air pressure. At the 8,850-m summit of Mt. Everest, air pressure is a mere 33 kPa—about one third of the pressure at sea level.

▲ **Sea Level** Air pressure is the pressure exerted by the weight of the atmosphere above you. At sea level the atmosphere exerts a force of about 100,000 N on every square meter of area. This pressure is also called one atmosphere (atm) and is equal to 100 kPa.

▶ **Reef Level** When you descend below the sea surface, pressure increases by about 1 atm every 10 m. At 20 m depth, you'd experience 2 atm of water pressure and 1 atm of air pressure, a total of 3 atm of pressure on your body.

▶ **Deep in the Ocean** The deeper you dive, the greater the pressure. The water pressure on a submersible at a depth of 2,200 m is about 220 times greater than the atmospheric pressure at sea level.

Contributed by National Geographic

What causes the buoyant force?

Think about the forces acting on the boat in **Figure 13.** Gravity is pulling the boat down, yet the boat doesn't accelerate downward. Because the boat is not accelerating up or down, the vertical forces on the boat are balanced. There must be an upward force balancing the downward force of gravity that keeps the sailboat from sinking.

Buoyant Force and Pressure

Recall that the pressure exerted by a fluid has two properties. One is that the direction of the pressure on a surface is always perpendicular to the surface of the object. The other is that the pressure exerted by a fluid increases as you go deeper into the fluid. **Figure 14** shows these two properties of pressure exerted by a fluid. The forces acting in the horizontal direction cancel because there are equal forces pushing to the left and to the right. For objects of any shape submerged in a liquid, there is no net horizontal force caused by water pressure.

However, water pressure at the top surface of the fish is less than water pressure at the bottom surface. The force pushing up on the fish is therefore greater than the force pushing down on the fish. The vertical forces do not balance each other. There is an upward force on the fish resulting from differences in water pressure. The **buoyant** (BOY unt) **force** is the upward force on an object in a fluid exerted by the surrounding fluid. The buoyant force is a result of increasing pressure at increasing depth.

Figure 13 A boat floats because of a buoyant force pushing up on it.

WORD ORIGIN · · · · · · · · · · · ·
buoyant
from Spanish *boyante;* means *to float*

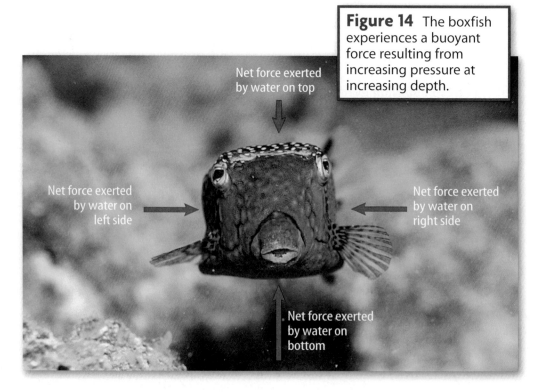

Figure 14 The boxfish experiences a buoyant force resulting from increasing pressure at increasing depth.

Net force exerted by water on top

Net force exerted by water on left side

Net force exerted by water on right side

Net force exerted by water on bottom

Buoyant Force and Depth

The pressure exerted by a fluid increases with depth. However, the buoyant force on the fish in **Figure 14** doesn't change as the fish swims deeper. The reason is that the buoyant force is the difference in the forces exerted on the upper and lower surfaces of the fish. As the fish swims deeper, the pressure on these surfaces increases by the same amount. The difference in the forces doesn't change and the buoyant force on the fish stays the same.

 **Reading Check** How does the buoyant force change as the depth of the object changes?

Archimedes' Principle

A beach ball floating in water displaces some of the water. The volume of the water displaced by the ball is equal to the volume of the ball that is in the water. Archimedes, a Greek mathematician who lived more than 2,200 years ago, found that the buoyant force on an object depends on the displaced fluid. According to **Archimedes' principle,** the buoyant force on an object is equal to the weight of the fluid the object displaces. The weight of the fluid displaced depends only on the density and the volume of the fluid displaced. As **Figure 15** shows, the buoyant force on an object does not depend on the object's density or its weight.

Archimedes' principle explains why the upward buoyant force on a beach ball increases as the ball is pushed underwater. The volume of the water displaced by the ball is much greater when it is underwater than when it is floating. So the weight of the water displaced, and the buoyant force, also is much greater when the ball is underwater than when it is floating.

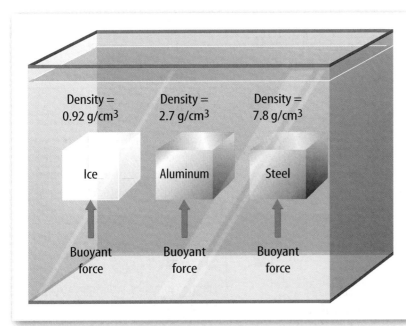

Figure 15 The buoyant force on each cube is the same, because each cube has the same volume and displaces the same amount of water.

Determine which cube has the greatest weight.

What have you learned?

A fluid exerts an upward buoyant force on an object in the fluid. The buoyant force acting on an object submerged in a fluid is caused by the difference in pressure on the top and bottom of the object. This difference in pressure does not change as the object moves deeper into the fluid. This means that the buoyant force does not change as the depth of the object changes. According to Archimedes' principle, this buoyant force also equals the weight of the fluid displaced by the object. This means that the buoyant force on an object does not depend on the weight of the object. Instead, it depends on the volume and the density of the displaced fluid.

LESSON 2 Review

Summarize

Create your own lesson summary as you design a **visual aid.**

1. **Write** the lesson title, number, and page numbers at the top of your poster.

2. **Scan** the lesson to find the **red** main headings. Organize these headings on your poster, leaving space between each.

3. **Design** an information box beneath each **red** heading. In the box, list 2–3 details, key terms, and definitions from each **blue** subheading.

4. **Illustrate** your poster with diagrams of important structures or processes next to each information box.

 ELA8: R 2.3

Standards Check

Using Vocabulary

1. _____ is force per unit area. **8.c**

2. Restate Archimedes' principle in your own words. **8.c**

Understanding Main Ideas

3. **Determine Cause and Effect** Copy and fill in the graphic organizer below to describe two ways to increase the pressure exerted on an object. **8.c**

Increase pressure

4. **Compare** the pressure at a depth of 10 m to a depth of 2,000 m below the surface of the ocean. Explain the cause of the difference in pressure. **8.c**

5. **Identify** the vertical forces acting on the boat in the figure below. **8.c**

6. **Explain** why you feel that you weigh less than normal when you are in a swimming pool. **8.c**

Applying Science

7. **Evaluate** the statement, "Heavy things sink and light things float." Is the statement true or false? If false, rewrite a true statement about floating and sinking objects. **8.c**

For more practice, visit **Standards Check** at ca8.msscience.com.

MiniLab

Can you feel the buoyant force?

A fluid exerts an upward buoyant force on all objects placed in the fluid. Can you detect the buoyant force that acts on a heavy rock?

Procedure

1. Read and complete a lab safety form.

2. *Station A:* Fill a **clear plastic bowl** or **pitcher** with clean **tap water.** Put a **sandwich bag** under water and fill it so no air gets into the bag. Seal the bag while it is underwater. Remove the bag from the water. Place the bag into the bowl of water and observe how far it sinks. Write your observations in your Science Journal.

3. *Station B:* Observe the **heavy rock** with the **rope** tied around it at the bottom of the **large plastic storage container** filled with clear **tap water.** Lift the rock halfway up in the container, but keep it under the water. Think about how difficult or easy it was to lift. Lift the rock all the way out of the water and hold it above the water. Think about how difficult or easy it was to lift and to hold in this position. Write your observations in your Science Journal.

Analysis

1. **Compare** the behavior of the bag of water and the rock to the beach ball you studied in the Launch Lab. How do the densities of the bag of water, the rock, and the ball compare to the density of water?

2. **Diagram** the forces acting on the rock when it is sitting at the bottom of the container, when you held it above the bottom but still underwater, and when you held it out of the water.

 Science Content Standards

8.c Students know the buoyant force on an object in a fluid is an upward force equal to the weight of the fluid the object has displaced.

Reading Guide

What *You'll Learn*

▶ **Explain** how the buoyant force is related to floating and sinking.

▶ **Describe** how to use densities to predict whether an object will float.

▶ **Explain** how a hydrometer measures the density of a fluid.

Why *It's Important*

Knowing the density of a material can help predict if the material will sink or float.

Vocabulary

hydrometer

Review Vocabulary

gravity: an attractive force between all objects that have mass (p. 96)

Sinking and Floating

Main Idea An object will float in a fluid if the density of the object is less than the density of the fluid.

Real-World Reading Connection If you've visited a lake or an ocean, you've probably seen boats of all sizes and shapes. A small fishing boat might be just big enough for two or three people. A larger group of people can fit on a large sailing boat. A cruise ship can carry thousands of people! Think about the weight of all the people and equipment on a cruise ship. What keeps this heavy ship from sinking?

Why do objects sink or float?

A fluid exerts pressure on any object that is in the fluid. This pressure exerts an upward buoyant force on the object. However, the buoyant force isn't the only force acting on the object. The force due to Earth's gravity pulls down on an object. This downward force is the object's weight. Whether an object sinks or floats depends on the sizes of the upward buoyant force on the object and object's weight. Why do some objects sink and some objects float?

Sinking and Buoyant Force

If the upward buoyant force on an object is less than the object's weight, then the net force on the object is downward. The object accelerates downward because the unbalanced force is downward. The stone in **Figure 16** moves downward, or sinks, because its weight is greater than the buoyant force acting on it.

Figure 16 The stone sinks because the net force on the stone is downward.

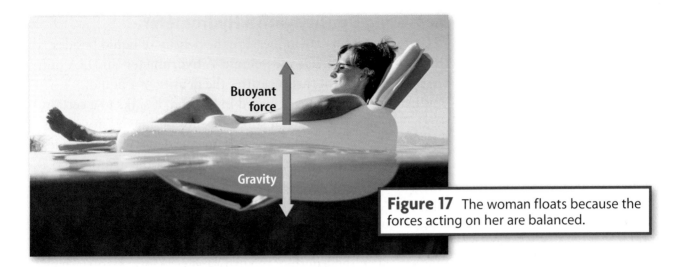

Figure 17 The woman floats because the forces acting on her are balanced.

Floating and Buoyant Force

The woman floating on the water in **Figure 17** isn't accelerating in the vertical direction. When an object isn't accelerating, the forces acting on the object are balanced. The downward weight of the woman is balanced by the buoyant force pushing upward on the woman. If an object is floating, the buoyant force equals the object's weight.

 If an object is floating, what are the relative sizes of the weight and the buoyant force?

The Buoyant Force and Density

According to Archimedes' principle, the buoyant force equals the weight of the displaced fluid. Therefore, if an object is floating, the weight of the displaced fluid equals the weight of the object. For example, the weight of the water displaced by the woman in **Figure 17** equals the weight of the woman.

How can metal boats float?

Almost all metals have a density greater than the density of water. According to Archimedes' principle, you might predict that a piece of metal will sink in water. Why, then, do metal boats such as the ship in **Figure 18** float? Remember that the mass of an object doesn't determine whether or not it floats. For an object to float, the overall density of the object must be less than the density of the fluid it is in. The overall density of a metal boat is made smaller by making the volume of the boat larger. The ship in **Figure 18** has a large volume that is filled with air. By making the air-filled volume large enough, the overall density of the boat can be made smaller than the density of water. As a result, the boat floats, even though it is made from metal.

 Figure 18 How does changing the shape of the metal affect the density of the boat?

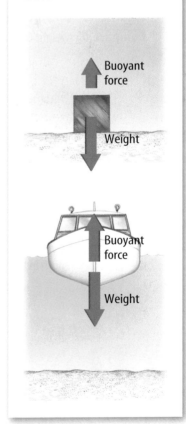

Figure 18 The boat and the cube have the same weight. The boat floats because its large volume causes its overall density to be less than the density of water.

There is another way to measure the density of liquid besides first measuring its mass and volume. A **hydrometer** (hi DRA mih ter) is an instrument that measures the density of a liquid.

When the hydrometer is placed in a liquid, it sinks to a certain depth. The depth to which it sinks depends on the density of the liquid, as shown in **Figure 19.** The lower the density of the liquid, the deeper the hydrometer sinks. The length of the hydrometer tube below the liquid, or submerged, is related to the density of the liquid. The lower the density of the liquid, the longer the length of the hydrometer tube submerged below the liquid.

To measure the density of a liquid, the hydrometer is first placed in water. Then the length of the hydrometer below the surface of the water is measured. Next, the hydrometer is placed in the liquid and the length of the hydrometer below the surface of the liquid is measured. The **ratio** of the submerged lengths of the hydrometer in the water and in the liquid is related to the ratio of the densities of the water and the liquid. For example, suppose the ratio of the length submerged in water divided by the length submerged in the liquid is 2.0. Then the density of the unknown liquid is 2.0 times the density of water. Water has a density of 1.0 g/cm^3, so the density of the liquid is 2.0 g/cm^3.

WORD ORIGIN············

hydrometer
hydro– from Greek *hydro;*
means *water*
–meter from Latin *metreum;*
means *measure*

ACADEMIC VOCABULARY···

ratio (RAY she oh)
(noun) the relation between
two numbers expressed by
dividing one by the other
*The ratio of 19 to 11 is equal
to 19/11.*

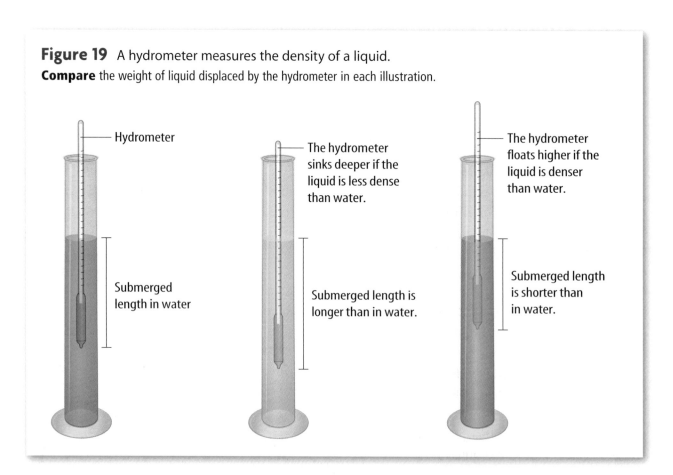

Figure 19   A hydrometer measures the density of a liquid.
Compare the weight of liquid displaced by the hydrometer in each illustration.

Hydrometer

Submerged length in water

The hydrometer sinks deeper if the liquid is less dense than water.

Submerged length is longer than in water.

The hydrometer floats higher if the liquid is denser than water.

Submerged length is shorter than in water.

Floating and Sinking in the Atmosphere

Objects float in all fluids, including gases. Air is a fluid made of gases. Objects can float or rise in air because of the buoyant force produced by air pressure.

Helium Balloons

The balloons in **Figure 20** can float in air because they contain helium gas. Air is made of mostly nitrogen gas and oxygen gas, which are much denser than helium. When a balloon is filled with helium, its density is less than the density of the surrounding air. The balloon rises if the buoyant force on the balloon is greater than the weight of the balloon.

 Why does a helium balloon float in air?

If you've ever had a helium balloon, you know that it eventually stops floating. The helium atoms are so small that they can seep out through tiny holes in the rubber balloon. This causes the balloon to shrink. As a result, the density of the balloon increases. When the density of the balloon becomes greater than the density of the surrounding air, the balloon sinks.

Hot-Air Balloons

A hot-air balloon, such as the one shown in **Figure 21,** floats because its density is less than the density of the surrounding air. The overall density of the hot-air balloon is controlled by changing the temperature of the air inside the balloon. A pilot controls the air temperature using burners below the opening of the balloon.

When the flame of the burner heats the air in the balloon, the air particles move farther apart. The density of the balloon decreases and becomes less dense than the air outside the balloon. This causes the balloon to rise. When the burner is turned off, the air in the balloon cools and its density increases. If the air in the balloon cools enough, the balloon will sink. The rising and sinking of the balloon is determined by the densities of the air inside and outside the balloon.

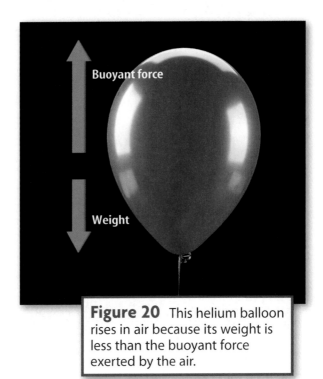

Figure 20 This helium balloon rises in air because its weight is less than the buoyant force exerted by the air.

Figure 21 A hot-air balloon rises when the air in the balloon is heated. This makes the balloon's overall density less than the density of the surrounding air.

Explain how heating the air in the balloon affects the density of the balloon.

What have you learned?

In this lesson you read about sinking and floating. You used the things you learned about forces in the previous chapter to explain why things sink or float. When placed in a fluid, an object sinks if the buoyant force and the object's weight are unbalanced. If the object floats, the forces are balanced.

You also combined your understanding of forces with facts you learned about density to explain how even heavy metal boats can float. You read that boats that weigh thousands of tons can float because the overall density of the boat is less than the density of water.

LESSON 3 Review

Summarize

Create your own lesson summary as you design a **study web.**

1. **Write** the lesson title, number, and page numbers at the top of a sheet of paper.

2. **Scan** the lesson to find the **red** main headings.

3. **Organize** these headings clockwise on branches around the lesson title.

4. **Review** the information under each **red** heading to design a branch for each **blue** subheading.

5. **List** 2–3 details, key terms, and definitions from each **blue** subheading on branches extending from the main heading branches.

 **ELA8: R 2.3**

Standards Check

Using Vocabulary

1. Define *hydrometer* in your own words. **8.d**

Understanding Main Ideas

2. **Explain** how it is possible for an object to sink even though a buoyant force is pushing up on it. **8.d**

3. **Describe** how you could make modeling clay float in water even though it has a density greater than the density of water. **8.d**

4. **Compare and Contrast** Copy and fill in the graphic organizer below to compare and contrast how helium balloons and hot air balloons float in the atmosphere. **8.d**

Floating in the Atmosphere	Similarities	Differences
Helium balloon		
Hot-air balloon		

5. More of a ship is underwater when it is in a river than when it is in the ocean. What can you infer about the density of the ocean water compared to the density of the river water?

   A. The river water is colder than the ocean water. **8.d**

   B. The ocean water is warmer than the river water.

   C. The ocean water is denser than the river water.

   D. The ocean water is less dense than the river water.

Applying Science

6. **Evaluate** the usefulness of a hydrometer, and explain why determining density is better done in different situations with a hydrometer or by measuring mass and volume. **8.d**

 **Science Online**

For more practice, visit **Standards Check** at <u>ca8.msscience.com</u>.

MiniLab

Do cold things float?

On a hot day, you might put a few ice cubes into a glass of water to cool off. The ice cubes float near the top of the liquid. Do ice cubes float because they are cold? What does temperature have to do with sinking and floating?

Procedure

1. Read and complete a lab safety form.

2. Get a container of **room-temperature water** from your teacher.

3. Fill a **sandwich bag** with some **hot water** and seal the bag. Be sure to remove any air bubbles from the bag.

4. Write a prediction in your Science Journal. Will the bag filled with hot water sink or float in the room-temperature water? Observe the bag in the water and record the observation.

5. Get another container of room-temperature water from your teacher and another sandwich bag. Fill the bag with **cold tap water** and place **several ice cubes** into the bag before sealing it. Let the bag sit for a few minutes while the ice cools the water.

6. Write a prediction. Do you think the cold water will sink or float? Place the bag in the room-temperature water and observe. Record the observation.

Analysis

1. **Describe** what happened when you put the hot water into the room-temperature water. What happened when you put the cold water into the room temperature water?

2. **Compare** the behavior of the hot and cold bags of water to the bag of water you observed in the MiniLab at the end of Lesson 2.

3. **Explain** what effect temperature has on the density of the water. How did this affect the floating of the bags?

 Science Content Standards

8.d Students know how to predict whether an object will float or sink.

Investigation Lab:
A Homemade Hydrometer

Materials

pencil with an eraser
thumbtack
permanent marker
graduated cylinder
two liquids in addition
  to water
paper towels

Safety Precautions

WARNING: Keep surfaces and equipment dry so they do not become slippery.

Science Content Standards

8.d Students know how to predict whether an object will float or sink.
9.f Apply simple mathematic relationships to determine a missing quantity in a mathematic expression, given the two remaining terms (including speed = distance/time, density = mass/volume, force = pressure × area, volume = area × height).

Problem

A hydrometer is a device used to compare the densities of liquids. You can make a hydrometer by using a pencil with a thumbtack in the eraser. With your pencil hydrometer, you can compare the densities of several liquids to the density of water. You can even make a scale on your pencil to have a quantitative comparison for the liquids that you test.

Form a Hypothesis

➤ **Review** the results from this chapter's laboratory investigations.

➤ **Make a prediction** about the densities of the unknown liquids. Are they more or less dense than water? Why do you think so?

Collect Data and Make Observations

1. Read and complete a lab safety form.
2. Make a data table like the one on the next page.
3. Add clean tap water to the graduated cylinder until it is three-fourths full.
4. Measuring from the tip of the eraser, mark on the pencil in half-centimeter steps.
5. Push the thumbtack into the eraser of the pencil. Drop the pencil into the graduated cylinder so that the pencil floats upright with the eraser end down.
6. Measure the length of the part of the pencil that was submerged in the water. This length represents a density of 1.0 g/cm^3. Record this value in your data table.
7. Wipe the pencil dry and then place it in one of the unknown liquids. Measure the length of the pencil that was submerged in the liquid. Record this value in your data table.
8. Repeat step 7 for the other unknown liquid.

Analyze and Conclude

1. **Explain** why it was important to clean the hydrometer before each test of a new liquid.

2. **Calculate** the ratio, W/U, of the submerged length of the pencil in water (W) to the submerged length of the pencil in the first unknown liquid (U). Record this ratio in your data table.

3. **Infer** from your calculation whether the density of the first liquid is greater or less than the density of water. Explain.

4. **Calculate** the ratio, W/U, of the submerged length of the pencil in water (W) to the submerged length of the pencil in the second unknown liquid (U). Record this ratio in your data table.

5. **Infer** from your calculation whether the density of the second liquid is greater or less than the density of water. Explain.

6. **Calculate** the density of each unknown liquid by multiplying the ratio W/U for each liquid by the density of water, 1.0 g/cm³. Record the calculated values in your data table.

7. **Compare** the weight of the displaced fluid when the pencil is placed in each of the three liquids.

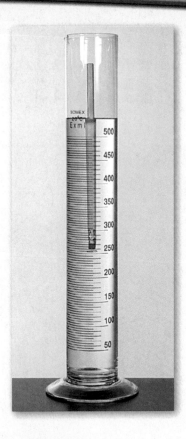

Comparison of Density of Water to Unknown Liquids			
W Submerged Length of Hydrometer in Water (cm)	U Submerged Length of Hydrometer in Unknown Liquid (cm)	Ratio W/U	Density of Unknown Liquid (g/cm³)

Communicate

 Science  ELA8: W 2.3

Research how hydrometers are used in different industries, such as the food industry, and how they are used by auto mechanics. Write a one-page report on one application for hydrometers. Explain why the measurement of density is important.

Real World Science

Can ice cubes sink in water?

You are probably familiar with the ice that is in your freezer or ice that forms outside on cold days. However, there are over a dozen different kinds of ice that can form depending on temperature and pressure. Some even sink in water instead of floating. Physicists and chemists research properties such as density of water and ice. To prepare for this type of research, take chemistry, physics, and math classes in high school and college.

Visit **Careers** at <u>ca8.msscience.com</u> to find out more about scientific reasearch. **List** five questions you have about ice. Suggest two things you could do to answer these questions.

Biodiesel

Density is very important in separations of liquids and gases. Biodiesel, a vegetable-based fuel, is made by mixing methanol and cooking oil. The reaction forms glycerin, an ingredient used to make soap, and biodiesel. Because biodiesel is less dense than glycerin, it rises to the top of the reaction chamber. The glycerin is drained and the biodeisel that remains is used as a fuel.

Create a layered sugar solution. Make the water green, the low-sugar solution colorless, and the high-sugar solution red. Carefully layer the less dense fluid on the denser fluid using a plastic syringe.

CANNERY ROW

Cold water from the bottom of the Pacific Ocean rises upward off the California coast. This nutrient-rich water nourishes an enormous number of fish. At one time, large numbers of these fish were caught by the California sardine industry. But a failure to impose sustainable limits on the catch and natural cycles led to the end of the trade.

Visit **History** at ca8.msscience.com to read more about the California sardine industry. Imagine you are a fisherman in 1933. **Write** a journal entry discussing your business and your outlook for each year until 1943.

ELA8: W 1.1

Science & Society

LOS ANGELES Smog

The San Fernando Valley traps the pollution created in Los Angeles. A warm layer of air is trapped between dense, cooler layers above and below, and between the sea and the mountains. It holds chemicals that sunlight turns to smog, which can irritate the lungs and eyes.

Visit **Society** at ca8.msscience.com to find out more about the history and future of air pollution control. **List** five things you can do now to reduce air pollution, and list five things you will be able to do when you are 25 years old.

The BIG Idea A fluid exerts an upward force on an object that is placed in the fluid.

Lesson 1 Density

8.a, 8.b, 9.f

Main Idea The density of a material is a measure of how much matter is packed into a unit volume of the material.

- Density is the mass of a material divided by its volume.
- Mass can be measured with a balance.
- The volume of a liquid is measured with a graduated cylinder.
- The volume of a solid can be found by using the displacement method.

- **density** (p. 130)
- **rectangular solid** (p. 135)

Lesson 2 Pressure and the Buoyant Force

8.c

Main Idea Objects in a fluid experience a buoyant force resulting from the pressure exerted by the fluid.

- Pressure is force divided by unit area.
- The pressure in a fluid increases with depth.
- Fluid pressure causes a buoyant force on an object in the fluid.
- Pressure is exerted on all surfaces of an object in a fluid.
- Forces due to fluid pressure act perpendicular to any surface in a fluid.
- The buoyant force on an object is equal to the weight of the fluid the object displaces.

- **Archimedes' principle** (p. 147)
- **atmospheric pressure** (p. 144)
- **buoyant force** (p. 146)
- **fluid** (p. 140)
- **pressure** (p. 141)

Lesson 3 Sinking and Floating

8.d, 9.f

Main Idea An object will float in a fluid if the density of the object is less than the density of the fluid.

- An object sinks if the buoyant force is less than the weight of the object.
- An object floats if the buoyant force equals the weight of the object.
- An object will float if the density of the object is less than the density of the fluid.
- A hydrometer measures the density of a fluid.

- **hydrometer** (p. 152)

 Download quizzes, key terms, and flash cards from ca8.msscience.com.

Linking Vocabulary and Main Ideas

Use vocabulary terms from page 160 to complete this concept map.

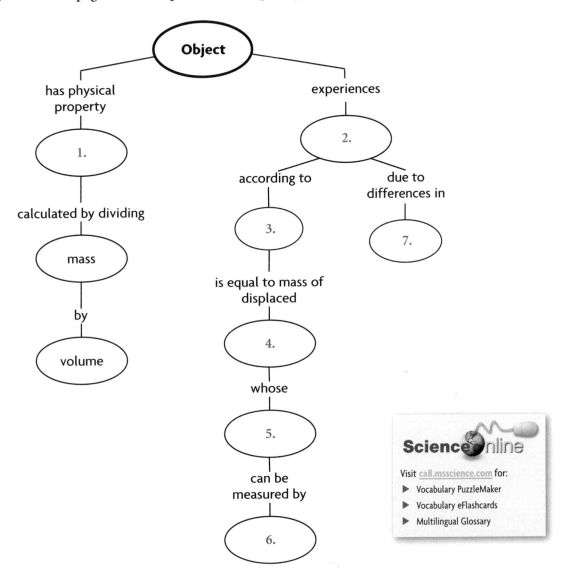

Object

has physical property

1.

calculated by dividing

mass

by

volume

experiences

2.

according to

3.

is equal to mass of displaced

4.

whose

5.

can be measured by

6.

due to differences in

7.

Science Online

Visit ca8.msscience.com for:
- ▶ Vocabulary PuzzleMaker
- ▶ Vocabulary eFlashcards
- ▶ Multilingual Glossary

Using Vocabulary

Match a vocabulary term to each definition below.

8. the force per unit area exerted by air particles

9. any material that can flow, including liquids and gases

10. force per unit area

11. upward force on an object submerged in a fluid

12. the mass per unit volume of a material

13. an instrument that measures the density of a fluid

14. the buoyant force exerted by a fluid on an object equals the weight of the fluid displaced by the object

Understanding Main Ideas

Choose the word or phrase that best answers the question.

1. Gold has a density of 19.3 g/cm³. Silver has a density of 10.5 g/cm³. Which is a true statement?
   A. A 2-cm³ block of gold has less mass than a 2-cm³ block of silver. **8.a**
   B. 50 g of gold has a lower volume than 50 g of silver.
   C. The weight of a 10.5-g block of gold equals the weight of a 19.3-g block of silver.
   D. The volume of a 15-g block of gold is greater than the volume of a 35-g block of silver.

2. A student measured the densities of four different materials. The table below shows the results of the measurements.

Material	Density (g/cm³)
1	0.93
2	1.05
3	1.13
4	0.87

   Which of the materials would you expect to float if they were placed in water?
   A. materials 2 and 3 **8.b**
   B. materials 1 and 4
   C. materials 2 and 4
   D. materials 1 and 3

3. If you toss a rock into a lake, what happens to the rock as it sinks?
   A. Pressure increases; buoyant force changes very little.
   B. Buoyant force increases; pressure changes very little. **8.c**
   C. Pressure decreases; buoyant force changes very little.
   D. Buoyant force decreases; pressure changes very little.

4. Which is true about an inflatable beach ball as it is pushed under water?

   A. When the ball is under water, the pressure on the ball is the same at all places on the surface of the ball. **8.c**
   B. The buoyant force on the ball increases the farther below the surface of the water you push the ball.
   C. The buoyant force on the ball increases until the entire ball is underwater.
   D. The ball experiences pressure from the water only in the vertical direction.

5. What does the buoyant force on an object submerged in a fluid equal?
   A. weight of the object that the buoyant force acts on **8.c**
   B. weight of the fluid displaced by the object
   C. weight of the column of fluid above the object
   D. weight of the object minus the weight of the displaced fluid

6. Which of the four objects listed below would you expect to float? **8.d**

Object	Weight (N)	Buoyant Force (N)
A	17	12
B	116	86
C	325	325
D	53	35

Science Online Standards Review ca8.msscience.com

Applying Science

7. Suggest a way that you could determine whether a silver spoon is made of pure silver or a mixture of metals. **8.b**

8. Give an example of how you know an object in a liquid experiences a buoyant force. **8.c**

9. Compare the buoyant force on a fish as it swims from the water's surface into deep water. **8.c**

10. Suggest two ways to determine the volume of a baseball. **8.b**

11. Imagine you attach a lead block to a spring scale and observe its weight. You then lower the lead block, still attached to the spring scale, into water. Explain how the weight measured by the scale will change as you lower the block into the water. **8.c**

12. Predict what you would observe if you mixed the liquids shown in the table below. **8.d**

Liquid	Density (g/mL)
Olive oil	0.918
Corn oil	0.922
Water	1.00

13. Suggest why it is important to use a strong material when making an air tank used by scuba divers for swimming deep below the ocean surface. **8.c**

14. Infer the relative densities of ice and water if you see ice floating in water. **8.d**

15. Compare the buoyant force on two objects submerged in water that have the same volume but different densities. **8.d**

WRITING in Science

16. Write a news article about the sinking of a fictional ship. The article should be at least two paragraphs long. It should explain to the reader why the ship was unable to float. **ELA8: W 1.1**

Cumulative Review

17. Imagine a rock at rest on the bottom of a lake. What three vertical forces are acting on the rock? Are the forces acting on the rock balanced? Explain how you know. **2.d**

18. Suppose a rock that weighs 57 N experiences a buoyant force of 35 N when it is submerged in water. What is the sum of these two forces acting on the rock as it sinks through the water? **2.b**

Applying Math

19. What is the density of a metal bolt that has a volume of 5.2 cm^3 and a mass of 41.0 g? **ALG: 1.0**

20. Platinum has a density of 21.45 g/cm^3. If a piece of platinum has a volume of 1.2 cm^3, what is its mass? **ALG: 1.0**

21. The density of sodium is 0.97 g/cm^3. Find the volume of a sample that has a mass of 6.7 g. **ALG: 1.0**

22. The palm of Sheila's hand has an area of 0.0017 m^2. If the atmospheric pressure on the palm is 100,000 Pa, what force is being exerted on Sheila's palm by the atmosphere? **ALG: 1.0**

23. The table shows the pressure in a pond at different depths.

Pressure in a Pond	
Depth (m)	Pressure (Pa)
0.1	980
0.5	4,900
1.0	9,800

What would be the pressure in the pond at a depth of 1.5 m? **ALG: 1.0**

Use the figure below to answer questions 1 and 2.

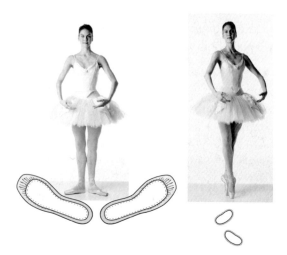

1 The figure on the left shows the dancer's footprints while standing with her feet flat on the floor. The figure on the right shows her footprints when standing on her toes. How does the pressure exerted on the floor in the left figure compare with the pressure exerted in the right figure?

A The pressure is greater in the left figure. **9.f**

B The pressure is greater in the right figure.

C The pressure is the same in both figures.

D The pressure is smaller in the right figure.

2 The area of the floor in contact with the dancer's feet is 300 cm² in the left photo and 30 cm² in the right photo. How does the force exerted on the floor change from the left photo to the right photo?

A The force decreases by 270 N. **9.f**

B The force becomes 10 times larger.

C The force becomes 10 times smaller.

D The force acting on the floor does not change.

3 A force of 25 N is exerted on a surface with an area of 0.1 m². What is the pressure exerted on the surface?

A 0.04 Pa **9.f**

B 2.5 Pa

C 25 Pa

D 250 Pa

4 Use the figure below to answer question 4.

Which statement is true about the volume of the water displaced by the golf ball?

A It is equal to the volume of the golf ball. **8.c**

B It is greater than the volume of the golf ball.

C It is less than the volume of the golf ball.

D The volume depends on the density of the golf ball.

5 A 15-g block of aluminum has a volume of 5.5 cm³. What is the block's density?

A 0.37 g/cm³ **8.b**

B 2.7 g/cm³

C 20.5 g/cm³

D 82.5 g/cm³

Science Online Standards Assessment ca8.msscience.com

Use the figure below to answer questions 6–8.

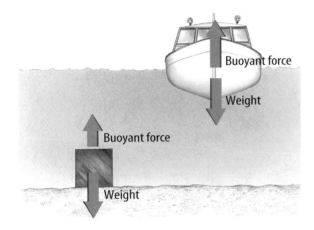

6 **The boat and the cube have the same mass. Which statement is correct?**

A The boat displaces less water than the cube.

B The densities of the boat and the cube are equal.

C The density of the boat is less than the density of the cube.

D The density of the boat is greater than the density of the water.   `8.d`

7 **A student measures the density of an unknown liquid. She finds the density is 1.42 g/cm³. She then pours half of the liquid into another container and measures the density again. What should be the result of her second measurement?**

A 0.71 g/cm^3 `8.a`

B 1.42 g/cm^3

C 2.00 g/cm^3

D 2.84 g/cm^3

8 **The density of gold is 19.3 g/cm³. What is the volume of a 100-g gold necklace?**

A 0.193 cm^3 `8.b`

B 5.18 cm^3

C 119.3 cm^3

D 1930 cm^3

9 **As you drive down a high mountain, what happens to the atmospheric pressure?**

A It decreases.   `8.d`

B It increases.

C It increases, then decreases.

D It stays the same.

10 **The photograph below shows a large boat floating in the ocean.**

How does the buoyant force acting on the boat change if the boat is loaded so that more of the boat is below the water?

A The buoyant force increases.   `8.c`

B The buoyant force decreases.

C The buoyant force stays the same.

D The buoyant force decreases, then returns to the original value.

Reading on Your Own...

Are you interested in learning more about motion, forces, buoyancy, and density? If so, check out these great books.

Science Fiction

Project Pendulum, by Robert Silverberg, is the story of Earth's first time travelers in 2016. One brother is carried back 95 million years in time and the other forward 95 million years in time. The book records each brother's observations in alternating chapters. ***The content of this book is related to*** *Science Standard 8.1.*

Nonfiction

The Cartoon Guide to Physics, by Larry Gonick, provides concise explanations of physical principles with the help of amusing cartoons. Topics include motion, Newton's laws, momentum, energy, electricity, and magnetism. ***The content of this book is related to*** *Science Standard 8.1.*

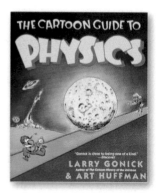

Nonfiction

Objects in Motion: Principles of Classical Mechanics, by Paul Fleisher, uses real-life examples to make natural laws easy to understand. The topics covered in this book include planetary motion, pendulums and falling objects, Newton's three laws of motion, the law of universal gravitation, and conservation of momentum. ***The content of this book is related to*** *Science Standard 8.2.*

Narrative Nonfiction

Dive! My Adventures in the Deep Frontier, by Sylvia Earle, is the author's story of her investigation and exploration of the marine ecosystem. Her experiences include tracking whales, living in an underwater laboratory, and helping design a deep-water submarine. ***The content of this book is related to*** *Science Standard 8.8.*

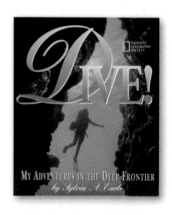

Choose the word or phrase that best answers the question.

1. Which of these is not a vector?
   A. force
   B. distance
   C. position
   D. velocity `1.d`

2. Which type of force causes a sliding box to slow down and stop?
   A. buoyant
   B. compression
   C. friction
   D. gravity `2.e`

3. The forces applied to an object are 8 N to the left and 5 N to the right. What is the net force on the object?
   A. 3 N to the right
   B. 3 N to the left
   C. 13 N to the right
   D. 13 N to the left `2.b`

4. In which situation are the forces acting on a bicycle balanced?
   A. The bicycle speeds up as you pedal.
   B. The speed of the bicycle is constant as it turns.
   C. The bicycle slows down as it coasts.
   D. The bicycle moves in a straight line with constant speed as you pedal. `2.c`

5. What is the density of a ring that has a mass of 11.5 g and a volume of 0.8 cm³?
   A. 0.07 g/cm³
   B. 9.2 g/cm³
   C. 12.3 g/cm³
   D. 14.4 g/cm³ `8.a`

Write your responses on a sheet of paper.

6. The graph below shows how Paul's position changed as he walked to school.

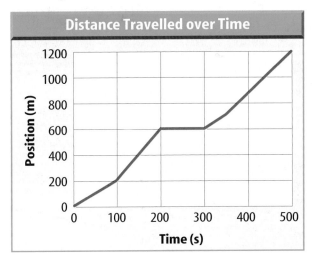

   Calculate Paul's average speed over his entire trip. `1.b`

7. **Predict** A baseball is traveling 40 km/h east toward a batter. After the batter hits the ball, the ball is moving west at 40 km/h. Did the ball accelerate? Support your reasoning. `1.e`

8. **Describe** A rocket coasting toward Earth fires one of its rocket engines. The force exerted on the ship is in the direction opposite to the rocket's velocity. How does the motion of the rocket change? `2.e`

9. **Predict** An object weighing 30 N is floating in water. What is the weight of the water displaced by the object? Support your reasoning. `8.c`

10. **Analyze** why it is easier to lift an object that is under water than it is to lift the object when it is out of the water. `8.c`

11. **Evaluate** how the gravitational force between Earth and the space shuttle changes as the shuttle moves farther from Earth. `2.g`

12. **Explain** how a balloon filled with helium floats in the air. `8.c`

Structure of Matter

Paying Honor with Gold
The innermost coffin of King Tutankhamen is made of solid gold.

West Coast Events

January 1848
James Marshall discovers gold at John Sutter's sawmill near Sacramento, California; a rush for gold begins.

1848–1852
People come from around the world to find gold; California's population grows from 14,000 to 223,000.

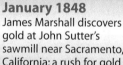

A.D. 1800   1820   1840   1860   188

World Events

3,500 Years Ago
Gold from Nubia makes Egypt a wealthy nation because many cultures prize it and exchange goods for it.

1800s
John Dalton from England offers proof that atoms exist and changes views held since Aristotle; his model shows atom as a small solid sphere.

1869
Dmitri Mendeleev of Russia discovers a pattern in properties of elements and arranges that information in a periodic table; he left room for elements not yet discovered.

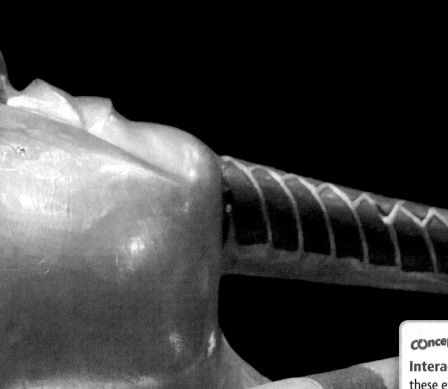

Science Online

To learn more about chemists and their work, visit ca8.msscience.com.

Concepts In Motion

Interactive Time Line To learn more about these events and others, visit ca8.msscience.com.

1941
Glenn T. Seaborg and other scientists at UC Berkeley prepare the element plutonium (94) in the laboratory.

1950
Stanley G. Thompson and other scientists at UC Berkeley prepare the element californium (98).

2004
Scientists in Russia and Lawrence Livermore National Laboratory in California prepare the elements ununtrium (113) and ununpentium (115).

| 1900 | 1920 | 1940 | 1960 | 1980 | 2000 | 2020 |

1911
Ernest Rutherford proposes model of atom with a positive nucleus surrounded by orbiting negative electrons.

1926
Scientists develop electron cloud model used today.

1939
Lise Meitner of Austria is first to explain how nuclear fission occurs.

1998
Scientists in Dubna, Russia, are first to prepare element ununquadium (114).

Understanding the Atom

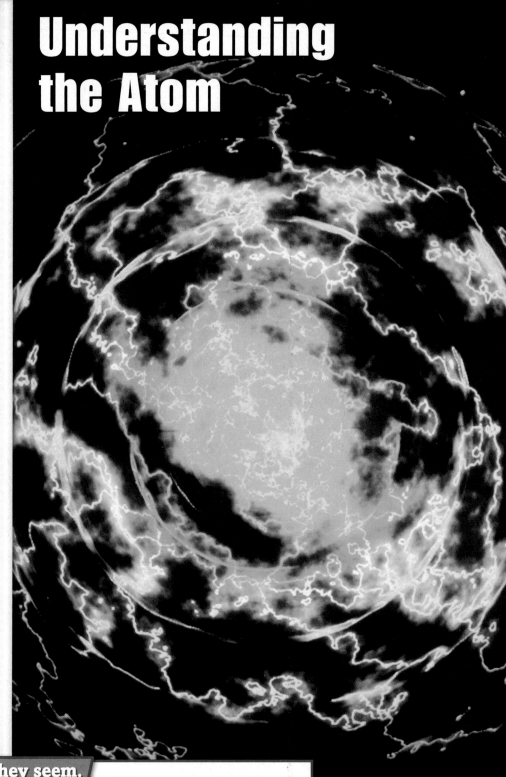

The BIG Idea

The current model of the atom includes protons, neutrons, and electrons.

LESSON 1 `3.a`

Atoms—Basic Units of Matter

Main Idea Matter is made of tiny particles called atoms.

LESSON 2 `3.a`

Discovering Parts of the Atom

Main Idea Scientists have put together a detailed model of atoms and their parts.

LESSON 3 `3.f, 7.b, 9.e`

Elements, Isotopes, and Ions—How Atoms Differ

Main Idea Atoms of a particular element always have the same number of protons.

Things are not as they seem.

This computer-generated image of a helium atom shows what the inside of a balloon might look like. Helium's electron is more likely to be found in the blue area than in the other areas farther from the center.

Science Journal Write a paragraph on what you know about the atom.

Launch Lab

00:10 minutes

What's in the box?

The early atomic scientists never saw atoms. They came up with ideas about atoms by using scientific methods other than direct observation. In this lab, you will study something you cannot see.

Procedure

1. Complete a lab safety form.

2. Use **wooden skewers** to poke holes in your **sealed box.** Predict what information you can find out by poking in the box.

3. Record your observations.

4. Predict what information you will learn by shaking the box.

5. Shake the box.

6. Try to guess what each object is.

Think About This

- **Identify** what types of information you could guess by poking in the box.

- **Explain** how you could answer those questions without opening the box.

3.a

Science Online

Visit ca8.msscience.com to:

► view **Concepts in Motion**

► explore Virtual Labs

► access content-related Web links

► take the Standards Check

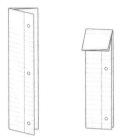

FOLDABLES
Study Organizer

Structure of an Atom
Make the following Foldable to explain the structure of an atom.

> **STEP 1** **Fold** a sheet of paper into thirds lengthwise. Fold the top down about 4 cm.

> **STEP 2** **Unfold** and **draw** lines along all folds. **Label** as shown.

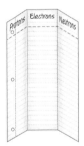

Protons   Electrons   Neutrons

Reading *Skill*

Visualizing

As you read this chapter, organize information about the parts of an atom. Be sure to include where the part is located within the atom and the type of charge.

Get Ready to Read

Monitor

①Learn It! An important strategy to help you improve your reading is monitoring, or finding your reading strengths and weaknesses. As you read, monitor yourself to make sure the text makes sense. Discover different monitoring techniques you can use at different times, depending on the type of test and situation.

②Practice It! The paragraph below appears in Lesson 2. Read the passage and answer the questions that follow. Discuss your answers with other students to see how they monitor their reading.

In Bohr's model of the atom, each energy level can hold a given number of electrons. The way the electrons are placed in energy levels is similar to the way students might fill the rows of seats in an auditorium.

—from page 191

- What questions do you still have after reading?
- Do you understand all of the words in the passage?
- Did you have to stop reading often? Is the reading level appropriate for you?

③Apply It! Identify one paragraph that is difficult to understand. Discuss it with a partner to improve your understanding.

Target Your Reading

Reading Tip

Monitor your reading by slowing down or speeding up depending on your understanding of the text.

Use this to focus on the main ideas as you read the chapter.

1 **Before you read** the chapter, respond to the statements below on your worksheet or on a numbered sheet of paper.

- Write an **A** if you **agree** with the statement.
- Write a **D** if you **disagree** with the statement.

2 **After you read** the chapter, look back to this page to see if you've changed your mind about any of the statements.

- If any of your answers changed, explain why.
- Change any false statements into true statements.
- Use your revised statements as a study guide.

Before You Read A or D	Statement	After You Read A or D
	1 An atom is the smallest particle of matter.	
	2 The idea of an atom was already being discussed by the Greeks in 400 B.C.	
	3 Dalton's atom is a uniform sphere of matter.	
	4 Thomson discovered a positively charged particle called an electron.	
	5 Rutherford demonstrated that the atom was mostly empty space.	
	6 In the current model of the atom, the nucleus of the atom is at the center of an electron cloud.	
	7 A filled outer energy level means that an atom will combine with other atoms.	
	8 You can determine the number of protons, neutrons, and electrons from the mass number.	
	9 Isotopes of the same element have the same number of protons but different numbers of electrons.	

Science Online

Print a worksheet of this page at ca8.msscience.com.

Science Content Standards

3.a Students know the structure of the atom and know it is composed of protons, neutrons, and electrons.

Reading Guide

What *You'll Learn*

▶ **Describe** the structure of the atom and where protons, neutrons, and electrons are located.

▶ **Compare** the mass, size, and charge of the three basic particles of an atom.

▶ **Describe** two observations that Dalton's atomic theory supported.

Why *It's Important*

An understanding of the nature of the atom is the first step toward learning what the world is made of.

Vocabulary

matter
atom
nucleus
proton
neutron
electron

Review Vocabulary

mass: a measure of the amount of matter in an object (p. 11)

Atoms—Basic Units of Matter

Main Idea Matter is made of tiny particles called atoms.

Real-World Reading Connection How can you figure out what's inside a wrapped box without opening it? Exploring the atom is like exploring that box. Atoms can't be observed directly with your eyes, so how have scientists learned about what's inside them?

What is the current atomic model?

Would it surprise you to learn that the chair you are sitting on and the air you breathe are made up of the same thing? The world you live in is made of **matter.** Matter is anything that has mass and takes up space. Things you can see, such as your chair, and things you can't see, such as air, are matter. Matter is different from light, heat, and sound. These are forms of energy. Matter is made up of atoms. An **atom** is a very small particle that makes up all matter. Only recently have scientists been able to see the surface of an atom.

Inside the Atom

In the early 1980s, a powerful new instrument called the atomic-force microscope was invented. The atomic-force microscope can magnify an object up to one million times. This magnification is great enough for the surfaces of individual atoms to be seen, as shown in **Figure 1.** If further magnification were possible, you might be able to see inside an atom. You probably would be surprised to find that most of the atom is empty space. In this space, particles are moving. No one has ever seen inside an atom, so how do scientists know what atoms are made of?

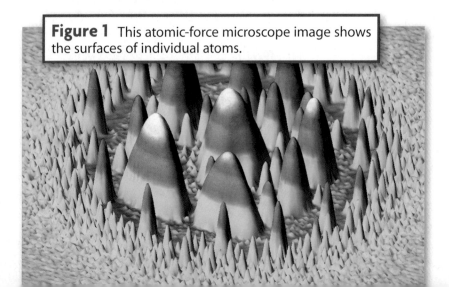

Figure 1 This atomic-force microscope image shows the surfaces of individual atoms.

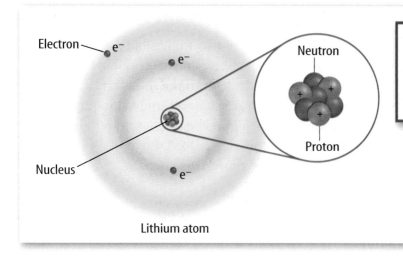

Figure 2 An atom of lithium has three electrons, three protons, and four neutrons.

Describe the locations of the protons, the neutrons, and the electrons.

Electron — e⁻

Neutron

Nucleus

Proton

e⁻

e⁻

Lithium atom

Parts of Atoms—Protons, Neutrons, and Electrons

Many experiments performed by scientists during the last 200 years have established what is inside an atom. An atom is mostly empty space surrounding a tiny nucleus. The **nucleus** is a region that is located at the center of an atom and contains most of the atom's mass. **Figure 2** shows that the nucleus contains positively charged particles and neutral particles. A positively charged particle located in the nucleus is a **proton.** A neutral particle, which has no charge, located in the nucleus is a **neutron.** Atoms also contain particles called electrons. An **electron** is a negatively charged particle that moves in the space surrounding the nucleus.

The Size of Atoms

As tiny as atoms are, electrons, protons, and neutrons are even smaller. The data in **Table 1** show that protons and neutrons have about the same mass. Electrons have only about 1/2,000 the mass of a proton or a neutron. If you held a textbook and placed a paper clip on it, you wouldn't notice the added mass because the mass of a paper clip is small compared to the mass of the book. In a similar way, the masses of an atom's electrons are negligible compared to an atom's mass. An atom's protons and neutrons are packed tightly into a tiny nucleus. Visualize the nucleus as the size of an ant. How large would the atom be? Amazingly, the atom would be the size of a football stadium.

WORD ORIGIN · · · · · · · · · · · · ·

nucleus
from Latin *nucula*; means *little nut*

Table 1 Properities of Atomic Particles			
Particle	**Charge**	**Mass (g)**	**Mass (amu)**
Proton	+1	1.6727×10^{-24}	1.007316
Neutron	0	1.6750×10^{-24}	1.008701
Electron	−1	9.110×10^{-28}	0.000549

Is there historical evidence of atoms?

The idea that matter is made of tiny indivisible particles was proposed as early as 400 B.C. But experimental evidence to support the idea of atoms was not available until the seventeenth and eigthteenth centuries. Actually, the current understanding of atomic structure has developed over the last several hundred years. Each time new evidence becomes available, the model of atomic structure becomes clearer and more **accurate.**

ACADEMIC VOCABULARY
accurate
(adjective) free from error or mistake
The scale at the doctor's office is accurate.

Democritus and the Atom

Greek philosopher Democritus (c. 460–370 B.C.) was the first person to use the word *atom*. *Atom* comes from the Greek word *atoma*, which means "indivisible." *Indivisible* describes something that cannot be divided into smaller pieces. Democritus provided a much more detailed idea of the atom than any that ever had been proposed. He thought that atoms were very small, solid spheres with no holes and no empty space inside.

Democritus argued that atoms were indivisible. He imagined cutting a piece of matter into smaller and smaller pieces. He hypothesized that eventually he would come to a point at which he could not cut any more pieces. He would have come to a piece consisting of one atom that could not be divided.

The student in **Figure 3** is illustrating Democritus's experiment. She is cutting a piece of aluminum in half, and again in half, over and over again. The pieces become smaller and smaller, but each is still aluminum. Suppose she could continue to cut beyond the point where the pieces are too small to see. She would eventually reach a point where the final piece is just one indivisible aluminum atom. An atom is the smallest piece that still is aluminum.

 What was Democritus's idea of the atom?

Figure 3 Democritus's ideas were based on reasoning rather than experiments. This picture is recreating Democritus's concept of the indivisible atom.

The Law of Conservation of Mass

What happens to the atoms in substances during a chemical reaction? A chemical reaction is a process in which the atoms in the starting materials rearrange to form products with different properties. French scientist Antoine Lavoisier (AN twan • luh VWAH see ay) (1743–1797) conducted experiments that helped answer this question. Lavoisier placed a carefully measured mass of solid mercury(II) oxide into a sealed container. When he heated the container, he saw something different. The red powder of mercury(II) oxide had changed into a silvery liquid and a gas. The silvery liquid was mercury. Lavoisier established that the gas produced was a component of air. This component is oxygen. In his experiments, Lavoisier recorded the masses of the starting materials and of the products. He found that the total mass of the starting materials was always the same as the total mass of the products. Experiments such as this led to the recognition of the law of conservation of mass. This law states that the mass of the products always is the same as the mass of the starting materials.

 Reading Check What data did Lavoisier record in his experiments?

The Law of Definite Proportions

By 1799, J. L. Proust had completed a different series of experiments. Proust analyzed a variety of pure compounds to determine their compositions. He found that any pure compound always contains the same elements in the same **proportion** by mass. This principle is called the law of definite proportions. The law applies to any compound no matter where the sample comes from or how large or small it might be. **Figure 4** illustrates that water's composition is the same whether the sample comes from your kitchen sink or from an ice cap on Mars. Water always contains two hydrogen atoms and one oxygen atom. The law of definite proportions provided evidence to support the work of John Dalton as he developed his atomic model.

ACADEMIC VOCABULARY
proportion
(*noun*) the relation of one part to another or to the whole
A large proportion of the people present were students.

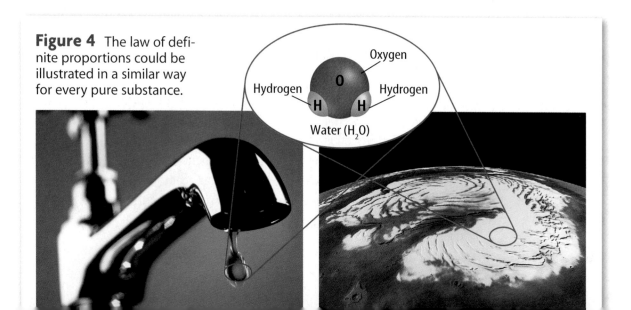

Figure 4 The law of definite proportions could be illustrated in a similar way for every pure substance.

Oxygen

Hydrogen

Hydrogen

Water (H$_2$O)

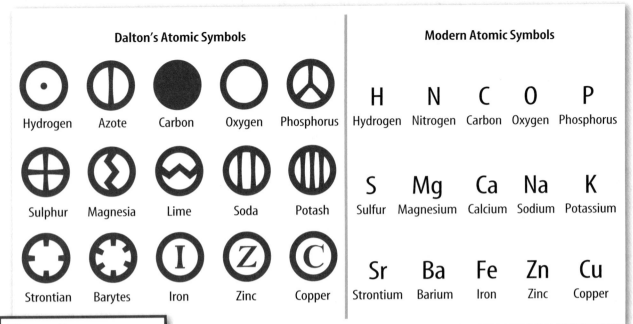

Dalton's Atomic Symbols					Modern Atomic Symbols				
Hydrogen	Azote	Carbon	Oxygen	Phosphorus	H Hydrogen	N Nitrogen	C Carbon	O Oxygen	P Phosphorus
Sulphur	Magnesia	Lime	Soda	Potash	S Sulfur	Mg Magnesium	Ca Calcium	Na Sodium	K Potassium
Strontian	Barytes	Iron	Zinc	Copper	Sr Strontium	Ba Barium	Fe Iron	Zn Zinc	Cu Copper

Figure 5 Dalton created pictures for each of the elements. These were helpful for writing down his results, just as our modern symbols are.

Dalton's Atomic Model

English schoolteacher and scientist John Dalton (1766–1844) was interested in the physical properties of gases. Like Lavoisier and Proust, Dalton made careful measurements of starting materials and products in a number of chemical reactions. To record his results accurately, he invented symbols for the known elements. As **Figure 5** shows, these are more complex than modern symbols, but they helped scientists communicate better.

Dalton gathered information from his own observations and from the findings of other scientists. He put these results together. Dalton then proposed a new atomic theory. His atomic theory consists of five principles. Notice that the second principle is another way of stating the law of conservation of mass.

1. All matter is made up of atoms.
2. Atoms are neither created nor destroyed in chemical reactions.
3. Atoms of different elements combine in whole-number ratios.
4. Each element is made of a different kind of atom.
5. The atoms of different elements have different masses and properties.

 Which principle states the law of conservation of mass?

Dalton brought all that was known about the atom into a reasonable theory. Other scientists then could continue his work. They could improve Dalton's theory or prove that it was wrong. Over time, Dalton's theory was modified as new evidence became available. Scientists now know that nuclear reactions can convert atoms of one element into atoms of a different element. We also know that atoms are made of smaller particles.

Looking Back at the Lesson

The ancient Greeks taught that matter consists of tiny indivisible particles called atoms. However, the Greeks couldn't prove the existence of atoms. It wasn't until the seventeenth century that scientists began to look for evidence of the atom. Their experiments demonstrated the law of conservation of mass and the law of definite proportions. With these important ideas, Dalton described his atomic model. Dalton's model started the development of the modern model of the atom. That model consists of even tinier particles called protons, neutrons, and electrons. You'll read more about these particles in Lesson 2.

LESSON 1 Review

Summarize

Create your own lesson summary as you write a script for a **television news report.**

1. **Review** the text after the **red** main headings and write one sentence about each. These are the headlines of your broadcast.

2. **Review** the text and write 2–3 sentences about each **blue** subheading. These sentences should tell *who, what, when, where,* and *why* information about each **red** heading.

3. **Include** descriptive details in your report, such as names of reporters and local places and events.

4. **Present** your news report to other classmates alone or with a team.

 ELA8: LS 2.1

Standards Check

Using Vocabulary

1. Explain the difference between a neutron and a nucleus. **3.a**

2. An atom contains equal numbers of _____ and _____. **3.a**

Understanding Main Ideas

3. Which has no charge? **3.a**

   A. electrons
   B. protons
   C. neutrons
   D. nucleus

4. **Name** the particles that make up an atom and tell where they are located. **3.a**

5. **Explain** in your own words what is meant by the law of definite proportions. **5.b**

6. **Describe** how Lavoisier was able to demonstrate the law of conservation of mass. **5.b**

7. **Show** that the ratio of the number of atoms of hydrogen to the number of atoms of oxygen in the compound water is 2 to 1. **5.b**

8. **Compare** Copy and fill in the graphic organizer below to compare the mass and the volume of a proton with the mass and the volume of an electron. **3.a**

	Mass	Volume
Proton		
Electron		

Applying Science

9. **Design an experiment** that confirms the law of conservation of mass. **5.b**

10. **Assess** the reasons why Dalton, not Democritus, is credited with being the "Father of the Atom." **3.a**

 Science Online

For more practice, visit **Standards Check** at ca8.msscience.com.

Applying Math

Mass of Subatomic Particles

The subatomic particles of protons, neutrons, and electrons have very small masses, as shown in the table.

Example

Find the mass of nine protons.

Particle	Mass (g)
Proton	1.6727×10^{-24}
Neutron	1.6750×10^{-24}
Electron	9.110×10^{-28}

What you know: mass of one proton: 1.6727×10^{-24} g

What you want to know: mass of 9 protons

Use this equation: mass of 9 protons = 9 × mass of one proton
mass of 9 protons = $9 \times (1.6727 \times 10^{-24}$ g$)$
which can be written as $(9 \times 1.6727$ g$) \times 10^{-24}$

1 **Multiply the base numbers:** $(9 \times 1.6727$ g$) \times 10^{-24} = 15.0543 \times 10^{-24}$ g

2 **Write the solution in scientific notation:** Write 15.0543 in scientific notation, with one number to the left of the decimal point. So, 15.0543 is written as 1.50543×10^{1}. The product is $1.50543 \times 10^{1} \times 10^{-24}$ g

3 **Find the exponent of the product:** To multiply powers of ten, add their exponents. $1 + (-24) = -23$. The new exponent is -23. So, $1.50543 \times 10^{1} \times 10^{-24}$ g $= 1.50543 \times 10^{-23}$ g

Answer: The mass of 9 protons is 1.50543×10^{-23} g.

Practice Problems

1. Find the mass of eight neutrons.
2. Find the mass of two electrons.

Science nline
For more math practice, visit **Math Practice** at ca8.msscience.com.

MiniLab

Try at Home

How big are the particles in an atom?

Protons and neutrons are about 1,836 times heavier than an electron. How can you model the proportions?

Procedure

1. Read and complete a lab safety form.

2. To represent a proton, measure 1,836 mL of **water** into a **large container.** Label the container *proton.*

3. To represent a neutron, label **another large container** *neutron.* Fill it with 1,836 mL of water.

4. Measure 1 mL of water into a **teaspoon.** This represents the electron.

5. Record what you see in your Science Journal.

Analysis

1. **Assess** whether this model is a good comparison of protons and neutrons. What is good about it? What is negative about it? How would you improve it?

2. **Calculate** the mass of water that should be used for an atom of lithium. Lithium has 3 protons, 4 neutrons, and 3 electrons. Show your work.

Science Content Standards

3.a Students know the structure of the atom and know it is composed of protons, neutrons, and electrons.

Science Content Standards

3.a Students know the structure of the atom and know it is composed of protons, neutrons, and electrons.

Reading Guide

What *You'll Learn*

▶ **Describe** the arrangement of electrons, protons, and neutrons within an atom.

▶ **Explain** how Rutherford developed his model of the atom.

▶ **List** the evidence that showed the existence of electrons, protons, and neutrons.

▶ **Compare** Thomson's, Rutherford's, and Bohr's models of the atom.

Why *It's Important*

The structure of the atom is the key to understanding chemistry.

Vocabulary

spectral line
energy level
electron cloud

Review Vocabulary

electromagnetic spectrum: the entire range of electromagnetic waves of different wavelengths (p. 428)

Discovering Parts of the Atom

Main Idea Scientists have put together a detailed model of atoms and their parts.

Real-World Reading Connection Imagine you are a detective. You go to a crime scene. You can only make observations and analyze clues because there are no witnesses to the crime. Similarly, scientists make observations and gather clues that help them build a model of the atom even though they cannot see inside one.

How were electrons discovered?

Since the time of the ancient Greeks, around 400 B.C., scientists thought atoms were the smallest units of matter. But more than 2,000 years later, in the late 1800s, a series of experiments led scientists to a better understanding of atoms. They learned that atoms are made of even smaller particles. Many of these experiments used a cathode-ray tube similar to the one in **Figure 6.** Cathode rays are given off at the cathode, which is a negatively charged disk. A cathode ray is a stream of particles that can be seen when an electric current is passed through a vacuum tube. The cathode rays travel to the positively charged disk at the other end of the tube.

 Figure 6 What is the positively charged disk called?

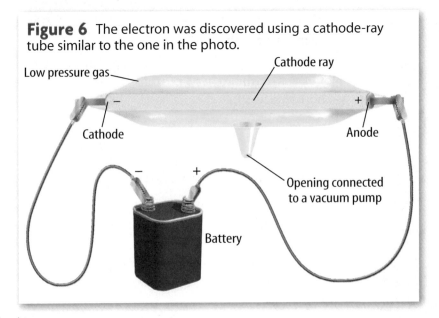

Figure 6 The electron was discovered using a cathode-ray tube similar to the one in the photo.

Low pressure gas

Cathode ray

Cathode

Anode

Opening connected to a vacuum pump

Battery

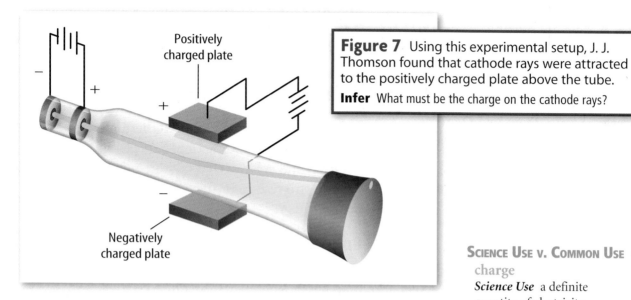

Positively charged plate

Negatively charged plate

Figure 7 Using this experimental setup, J. J. Thomson found that cathode rays were attracted to the positively charged plate above the tube.

Infer What must be the charge on the cathode rays?

Thomson's Experiments

In 1897, English scientist J. J. Thomson wanted to find out how electric currents affect cathode rays. He changed the cathode-ray tube by putting charged metal plates above and below the tube, as shown in **Figure 7.** One plate was positively charged. The other plate was negatively charged. Thomson found that the cathode rays did not follow a straight path down the tube. Instead, they bent in the direction of the positive plate. Recall that opposite charges attract one another and like charges repel one another. Thomson concluded that the particles in a cathode ray must have a negative charge. He named the newly discovered particles *electrons.*

Thomson also was able to use the cathode-ray tube to measure the mass of the charged particles. To his surprise, he found that the mass of an electron is much smaller than the mass of an atom. He concluded that atoms are not indivisible, as Dalton had proposed. Thomson also realized that atoms must contain positive charges to balance the negative charges of the electrons. His findings must have been true because atoms are neutral.

 **Reading Check** What did Thomson learn from his experiment about the mass of electrons?

Thomson's Atomic Model

With this new information, Thomson proposed a new model for the atom. Instead of a solid, neutral sphere that had the same matter all the way through, Thomson's model of the atom contained both positive and negative charges. He proposed that an atom was a positively charged sphere. The electrons were mixed evenly through the sphere, similar to how raisins are mixed in cookie dough. **Figure 8** shows a cutaway view of an atom in which the small spheres represent the electrons.

Figure 8 Thomson suggested that electrons mixed evenly into the positively charged spherical atom.

Positively charged sphere

Negatively charged electrons

Thomson's Model

Rutherford—Discovering the Nucleus

ACADEMIC VOCABULARY ····
research
(noun) the collecting of information about a particular subject
She did research on atoms at the library.

The discovery of electrons stunned scientists and made them want to find out more about the atom. Ernest Rutherford was a **research** student of J. J. Thomson at the Cavendish Laboratory in England. Rutherford was interested in understanding the structure of Thomson's model of the atom. By 1911, Rutherford had a laboratory and students of his own. Rutherford expected his students to find that electrons and positive charges were mixed together in an atom. But as you will read in the next section, what they found was another surprise.

The Gold Foil Experiment

Two of Rutherford's students set up a series of experiments to see if Thomson's model was correct. Particles with a positive charge, called alpha particles, were shot through a sheet of thin gold foil. The apparatus is shown in **Figure 9.** A detector beyond the gold foil glowed with a spot of light wherever the particles hit. Rutherford thought the positive charge of the gold atom was spread evenly throughout the atom. At no place would the speeding alpha particles come upon a charge large enough to strongly repel them. **Figure 10** shows a close-up view of what Rutherford might have expected. The alpha particles would speed through the foil with only slight changes in their paths. This was the result predicted by the Thomson model.

Reading Check Why did Rutherford think the alpha particles would move straight through the gold foil?

Electron

Evenly
distributed
positive charge

→ Path of alpha particles

Figure 10 Rutherford expected most particles to crash through the gold foil with little change in direction.

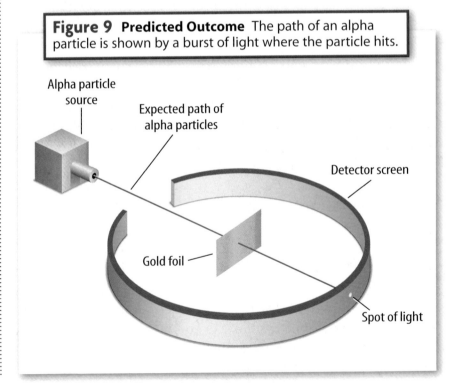

Figure 9 Predicted Outcome The path of an alpha particle is shown by a burst of light where the particle hits.

Alpha particle source

Expected path of alpha particles

Detector screen

Gold foil

Spot of light

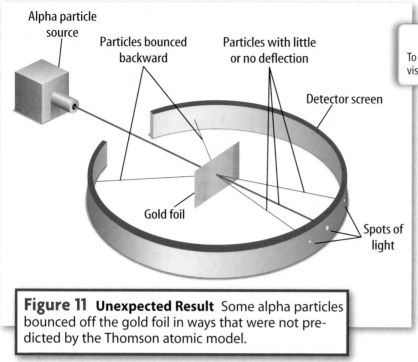

Alpha particle source

Particles bounced backward

Particles with little or no deflection

Detector screen

Gold foil

Spots of light

Concepts In Motion
To see animation of Rutherford's experiment, visit ca8.msscience.com.

Figure 11 **Unexpected Result** Some alpha particles bounced off the gold foil in ways that were not predicted by the Thomson atomic model.

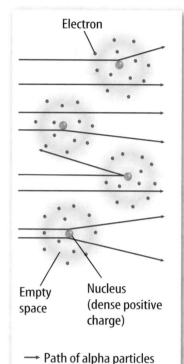

Electron

Empty space

Nucleus (dense positive charge)

⟶ Path of alpha particles

Figure 12 Some alpha particles must have hit a massive particle in the gold atom.

Explain how Rutherford knew that Thomson's model of the atom was not correct.

An Unexpected Result

What happened was another surprise. Notice in **Figure 11** that most of the alpha particles did pass directly through the foil with no bending of their paths. But sometimes, particles were strongly bounced off to the side. Astoundingly, one particle in about 8,000 bounced straight backward. Rutherford later described his amazement by saying, "It was quite the most incredible event that has ever happened to me in my life. It was almost as incredible as if you had fired a fifteen-inch shell at a piece of tissue paper and it came back and hit you." Thomson's model of the atom did not work. How did Rutherford know this?

Interpreting the Evidence

Rutherford realized that if positive charges were spread evenly in atoms, all the alpha particles would have passed through the foil with only a small change in direction. He also recognized that a positively charged particle could be bounced directly backward. This would happen only if the alpha particle bumped into something with much greater mass and positive charge than the alpha particle itself. Think about this similar situation. Imagine that you are running very fast. If you bump into a dangling leaf, you won't even notice. You just keep running along a straight path. But if you crash into a tree branch, you will very likely be knocked off your course. A head-on collision with a tree trunk might even bounce you straight backward. **Figure 12** shows an artist's view of how Rutherford must have visualized charged particles bouncing off the nucleus of a gold atom.

MiniLab

00:25 minutes

How do electrons move?

Procedure

1. Complete a lab safety form.
2. Draw a straight line down the center of a **10-cm × 10-cm block of foam** with a **ruler**.
3. Break **20 toothpicks** in half. Poke the halves into the foam so they are like the nucleus of an atom.
4. Use **round, dried peas** as electrons. Aim and flick the peas down the center line on the block.
5. Make a diagram to show where the electrons came out. Use a **protractor** to measure the angle the electrons made compared to the center line, which is the path they would have followed if they did not hit any atoms.

Analysis

1. **Describe** how your arrangement of toothpicks was like the nuclei of atoms in a block of metal. Why did the toothpicks represent just the nuclei instead of the whole atoms?
2. **Describe** problems you had with this experiment.

 3.a

Table 2 Summary of Rutherford's Conclusions	
Evidence	**Conclusion**
Most of the alpha particles passed right through the gold foil.	An atom is mostly empty space.
The charged particles that bounced back could not have been knocked off course unless they had hit a mass much larger than their own.	Most of the mass of an atom is concentrated in a small space within the atom.
A few of the alpha particles bounced directly back.	The positive charge is concentrated in a small space within an atom.

Rutherford's Atomic Model

Using the observations of his students, Rutherford drew some conclusions, which are summarized in **Table 2.** Most of the alpha particles passed directly through the gold atoms. For this to happen, the atoms must have contained mostly empty space. Because some alpha particles were strongly deflected from their paths, those particles must have come near a large positive charge. Very few alpha particles were bounced completely backward. Those particles that did bounce back must have collided with a mass having a large positive charge.

Drawing on these conclusions, Rutherford revised Thomson's model of the atom. **Figure 13** shows Rutherford's new atomic model. Notice that most of the volume of an atom is empty space. At the center is the nucleus. An atom's electrons move very fast in the empty space surrounding the nucleus.

Thinking about Rutherford's results, American poet Robert Frost wrote a very short poem, *The Secret Sits.*

"We dance round in a ring and suppose,
But the Secret sits in the middle and knows."

What do you think sits in the middle? What dances round in a ring?

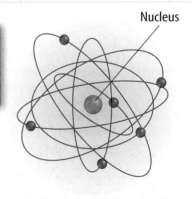

Figure 13 Rutherford's atom included a positively charged nucleus. Electrons moved in the space around the nucleus.

Nucleus

Rutherford's Model

Completing Rutherford's Model

Rutherford used cathode-ray tubes for other experiments. He wanted to find out about the positive charge in an atom's nucleus. The result of these experiments was the discovery of another particle, called the proton. A proton is an atomic particle with a +1 charge. Rutherford and his students knew the approximate mass of a proton. They could determine how many protons were in atoms. However, they couldn't account for all of the mass of an atom. Rutherford predicted that an atom contains another undiscovered particle. But, it wasn't until 1932 that the existence of the neutron was proved by English physicist James Chadwick. A neutron is a neutral atomic particle with a mass similar to a proton but has no charge. An atom's neutrons occupy the nucleus along with its protons. Neutrons were difficult to find because they have no charge, unlike protons and electrons. Both protons and electrons are deflected by a magnetic field.

Reading Check Compare and contrast protons and neutrons.

WORD ORIGIN
proton
from Greek *protos*; means *first*

Weakness in the Rutherford Model

Rutherford's model explained much of the experimental evidence, but it also brought up new questions. How are electrons arranged in atoms? How can differences in the chemical behavior of different elements be explained? For example, why does oxygen react easily with metals? Why is argon not very reactive? One clue came from the observation that elements give off colored light when heated in a flame. **Figure 14** shows the bright colors of the elements barium, sodium, strontium, and potassium when they are placed in a flame. Each element creates its own flame color. Some elements are used in fireworks to produce the brilliant colors of a display. Rutherford's model could not explain where this light comes from.

Figure 14 Scientists wanted to know what causes the colored light when elements are heated.

Identify the color produced when barium is placed in a flame.

Barium   Sodium   Strontium   Potassium

Figure 15 By gradually letting out more string and twirling faster, the ball will travel in increasingly large circles.

Short String and Low Energy

Longer String and Greater Energy

Bohr and the Hydrogen Atom

In 1918, Danish scientist Niels Bohr began to answer some of the questions about Rutherford's model. Rutherford had proposed that electrons could move around the nucleus at any distance from the nucleus. He thought electrons might move like the ball on a string, shown in the top illustration of **Figure 15.** In the figure, a boy has tied a soft sponge ball to a long string and is slowly twirling it above his head. The ball doesn't have much energy and moves in a small circle. Suppose the boy releases more string and twirls more energetically. The bottom illustration of **Figure 15** shows that the ball moves in a larger circle farther from his head. Depending on the energy the boy provides and the length of the string he releases, the ball could circle his head at any distance up to the length of the string. Bohr showed that Rutherford's idea that electrons could circle the nucleus at any distance was incorrect. His experiments convinced him that electrons did not behave like a twirling ball that could travel in circles of any diameter. Electrons could only move in circles with certain diameters, like the planets that circle the Sun. Like the planets, an electron's path around the nucleus had a definite radius.

 **Reading Check** What did Bohr compare the path of an electron to?

Bohr came to this conclusion by studying the hydrogen atom. He chose hydrogen because it is the simplest element, with only one electron. Bohr was interested in the light given off by hydrogen gas when it is excited. Atoms become excited when they absorb energy by being heated in a flame or by electricity. **Figure 16** shows the element neon in an advertising sign. The red light is produced when neon is excited by electricity.

Bohr wanted to know what was happening inside an atom to cause it to release energy in the form of colored light. Was there a connection between the light and the structure of the atom?

Figure 16 Neon gas is excited by electricity and glows red.

The Spectrum of Hydrogen

To understand the light given off by excited atoms, think about the rainbow of colors you see when ordinary light moves through a prism. The colors red, orange, yellow, green, blue, and violet blend into each other in a continuous spectrum of colors. Recall that colors at the red end of the spectrum have longer wavelengths and lower energies. Colors at the violet end have shorter wavelengths and higher energies. **Visible** light is just a small section of all the possible wavelengths in the electromagnetic spectrum. Ultraviolet rays have shorter wavelengths and higher energies than does visible light. Infrared rays have longer wavelengths and lower energies than does visible light. You cannot see ultraviolet rays or infrared rays. The electromagnetic spectrum is the whole range of electromagnetic waves with different energies and wavelengths.

ACADEMIC VOCABULARY
visible
(*adjective*) capable of being seen with the eye
On a clear night, the stars are visible in the night sky.

 Arrange visible light, infrared rays, and ultraviolet rays in order of their energies, from lowest to highest.

How is the energy of electrons related to the electromagnetic spectrum? The light given off by excited hydrogen atoms doesn't have a continuous spectrum of colors. Instead, hydrogen gives off light of specific colors, as shown in **Figure 17.** The narrow bands of red, green, blue, and violet light given off by an excited hydrogen atom are called its spectral lines.

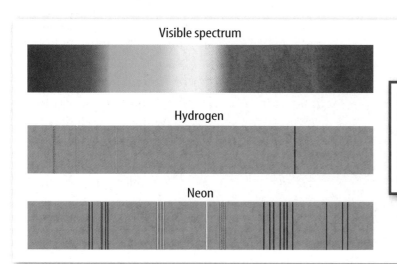

Visible spectrum

Hydrogen

Neon

Figure 17 The light given off by hydrogen and neon is not continuous like the rainbow of color produced by white light. Each element has its own specific spectral lines with specific energies.

Spectral Lines and Energy Levels

A **spectral line** is a single wavelength of light that can be seen when the light from an excited element is passed through a prism. If you compare the spectrum of hydrogen to the spectrum of light in **Figure 17,** you'll notice that hydrogen has a red line and then a green line. Between those lines, all the colors you see in the spectrum of sunlight are missing. The same is true for the colors between hydrogen's green line and its blue line. Each color is a different wavelength and energy. Bohr knew that if the electrons in an excited atom could have every possible energy, they would give off light just like the spectrum of sunlight. But hydrogen gives off only specific wavelengths of light. That means that an excited hydrogen atom releases only certain amounts of energy. Because electrons only can have certain amounts of energy, they can move around the nucleus only at distances that correspond to those amounts of energy. These regions of space in which electrons can move about the nucleus of an atom are called **energy levels.**

 Reading Check What is the difference between the spectrum of hydrogen and the spectrum of sunlight?

Energy levels can be compared to the ladder shown in **Figure 18.** You can stand on the ladder only at the level of each step, not between levels. Similarly, electrons can be only at certain energy levels, not between levels. If an electron absorbs energy from a flame or from an electric current, it can jump from a lower energy level to a higher energy level. When the electron falls back down from a higher energy level to a lower one, it releases energy. In **Figure 19,** energy levels are compared to a staircase in which the steps are not evenly spaced.

Figure 18 A person can move on a ladder only by standing on the steps. An electron can move in an atom only by jumping from energy level to energy level.

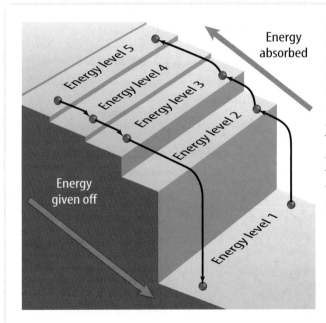

Figure 19 Electrons climb an energy staircase as they move to upper energy levels. They give off energy in the form of light when they fall back down.

Energy absorbed

Energy given off

Energy level 5
Energy level 4
Energy level 3
Energy level 2
Energy level 1

Bohr's Atomic Model

Bohr proposed that what he had learned from studying the hydrogen atom applied to all atoms. Like Rutherford's model, Bohr's atomic model contains a nucleus. Electrons move in circles around the nucleus. But, as shown in **Figure 20,** the electrons can move only in circles with certain diameters. Each of these circles, called energy levels, has its own energy. The energy levels are at set distances from the nucleus and have specific energies.

Electrons in the Bohr Atom

In Bohr's model of the atom, each energy level can hold a given number of electrons. The way that electrons are placed in energy levels is similar to the way students might fill the rows of seats in an auditorium. Students fill the front row closest to the stage first. Then they fill the second row. When the second row is filled, they continue to the third row and beyond until all students are seated. Maybe the last occupied row is full of students. Or, maybe it is only partly filled.

Similarly, electrons fill the lowest energy level first. The lowest energy level is closest to the nucleus and can hold two electrons. When this first energy level is full, electrons begin to fill the second level. The second energy level can hold eight electrons. When the second energy level is filled, electrons go to the next higher level. The last occupied energy level may or may not be completely filled. **Figure 21** shows how electrons are placed in the elements with atomic numbers 1–10.

Figure 20 In Bohr's atom, electrons orbit the nucleus at set distances.

Bohr's Model

 Figure 21 Which two atoms have filled energy levels? Which atom has four electrons in its outer energy level?

Figure 21 As the number of electrons increases from one to ten, two electrons fill the lowest energy level. Then, eight electrons fill the second energy level.

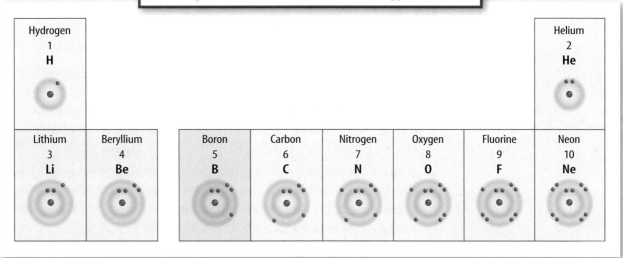

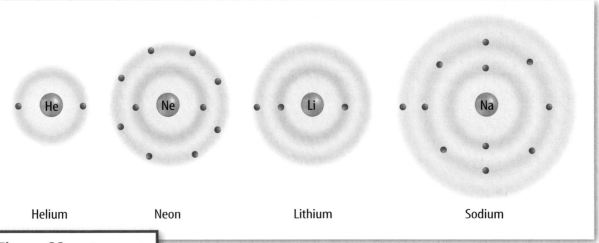

Helium Neon Lithium Sodium

Figure 22 Helium and neon, with filled outer energy levels, are unreactive. Lithium and sodium, with one electron each in their outer energy levels, are very reactive.

Bohr's Model and Chemical Properties

Why do elements have different chemical properties? Bohr's model provided an answer. The clue to the chemical properties of an element is in the number of electrons in its outer energy level. Elements with the exact number of electrons to fill their outermost energy level are unreactive. **Figure 22** shows that helium and neon have filled outer energy levels. This means these elements do not combine with other atoms to form compounds, or new substances. As you might guess, elements with partially filled outer energy levels are likely to form compounds. **Figure 22** shows that lithium and sodium have one electron in their outermost energy levels. Both are very reactive metals.

Limitations of Bohr's Atomic Model

Bohr's model explained much about chemical behavior. He proposed that energy levels were like circular orbits. That idea seemed to work for the simple hydrogen atom, but it did not work for more complex elements. If electrons don't travel in circular orbits, how do they move in the space around the nucleus?

The Electron Cloud

Today, scientists think of an electron in an atom as being in an electron cloud. An **electron cloud** is a region surrounding an atomic nucleus where an electron is most likely to be found. Electrons move rapidly from one place to another. They can be anywhere. But they are more likely to be closer to the nucleus than farther away because of the attraction of the negatively charged electrons for the positively charged nucleus. **Figure 23** shows a diagram of an electron cloud. The electron cloud is much larger than the diameter of the nucleus. If the nucleus were the size of a period, the atom would have a diameter of about 5 m. **Figure 24** summarizes how knowledge about the atom has increased through experiments.

Figure 23 An electron can be anywhere, even outside the edges of this illustration. The electron cloud shows only where the electrons are most likely to be found.

Nucleus

Electron Cloud Model

Figure 24 Development of Atomic Models The history of the development of the current model of the atom is an example for how science works. Models are proposed and tested. As more is learned, models are revised to fit the new observations.

Dalton

John Dalton's picture of the atom was a simple, neutral sphere of indivisible matter that was the same throughout. Atoms of different elements, however, were different from one another.

Thomson

J. J. Thomson's amazing discovery of the electron showed that atoms were not indivisible. They contained negative electrons and positive charges to make them neutral.

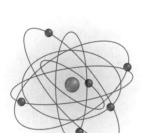

Rutherford

Ernest Rutherford's experiments showed that most of an atom's mass is squeezed into a tiny nucleus. In the remaining space, electrons move in orbits of all possible diameters.

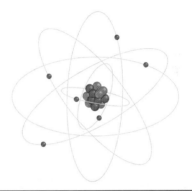

Bohr

Neils Bohr used information from line spectra to define the orbits of electrons as having certain definite diameters.

Electron Cloud

In the current model, electrons occupy a space around the nucleus, but it is impossible to tell where an electron is at any particular time.

How has the atomic model changed?

For Dalton, atoms were simple spheres of matter. Now the model of the atom is an electron cloud. How did this change take place? J. J. Thomson showed that the atom contains even smaller particles, called electrons. Rutherford proved that the atom has a nucleus packed with protons. Chadwick found out that neutrons also share space in the nucleus. Neils Bohr hypothesized that electrons move in energy levels. Today, scientists know that the motions of electrons can't be known. The electron cloud model shows only where electrons are most likely to be. Nevertheless, this model has been useful to chemists.

LESSON 2 Review

Summarize

Create your own lesson summary as you organize an **outline**.

1. **Scan** the lesson. Find and list the first **red** main heading.

2. **Review** the text after the heading and list 2–3 details about the heading.

3. **Find** and list each **blue** subheading that follows the **red** main heading.

4. **List** 2–3 details, key terms, and definitions under each **blue** subheading.

5. **Review** additional **red** main headings and their supporting **blue** subheadings. List 2–3 details about each.

Standards Check

Using Vocabulary

1. Define *electron cloud* in your own words. **3.a**

2. Use the phrase *energy level* in a sentence. **3.a**

Understanding Main Ideas

3. What did the gold-foil experiment show? **3.a**

   A. Electrons exist.

   B. Protons exist.

   C. An atom has a nucleus.

   D. Electrons move in circles.

4. **List** the experimental evidence that led to the development of these atomic models: Thomson's, Rutherford's, and Bohr's. **3.a**

5. **Explain** why Rutherford's model is sometimes called the nuclear atom. **3.a**

6. **Describe** the way electrons, protons, and neutrons are arranged in an atom. **3.a**

7. **Compare** Copy and fill in the graphic organizer below. Compare Thomson's, Rutherford's, and Bohr's atomic models to identify principles that are common to all. **3.a**

Applying Science

8. **Construct diagrams** to illustrate Thomson's, Rutherford's and Bohr's models of the atom. **3.a**

9. **Decide** whether research on particles such as quarks is likely to have an important effect on the principles of chemistry. **3.a**

For more practice, visit **Standards Check** at ca8.msscience.com.

Atomic Model ca8.msscience.com

Science Content Standards

3.f Students know how to use the periodic table to identify elements in simple compounds.

7.b Students know each element has a specific number of protons in the nucleus (the atomic number) and each isotope of the element has a different but specific number of neutrons in the nucleus.

9.e Construct appropriate graphs from data and develop quantitative statements about the relationship between variables.

Reading Guide

What *You'll Learn*

▶ **Explain** how elements differ.

▶ **Identify** elements and atomic masses on the periodic table.

▶ **Explain** how two isotopes differ.

▶ **Explain** how two ions differ.

Why *It's Important*

To understand their chemical behavior, it's important to know how the atoms of an element can differ.

Vocabulary

element
atomic number
mass number
isotope
average atomic mass
ion

Review Vocabulary

periodic table: table of the elements arranged according to repeated changes in properties (Grade 5)

Elements, Isotopes, and Ions—How Atoms Differ

Main Idea Atoms of a particular element always have the same number of protons.

Real-World Reading Connection You touch a doorknob and get a shock. Electrons are moving between the doorknob and your hand. Electrons can move from one atom to another atom. Why does this happen?

Different Elements—Different Numbers of Protons

Early Greek philosophers thought of matter as combinations of four basic elements. These elements were earth, water, fire, and air. Today, an element is defined differently. An **element** is a pure substance made from atoms that all have the same number of protons. All atoms of the same element have the same number of protons. For example, all aluminum atoms have 13 protons. That means that all atoms that have 13 protons are aluminum atoms. The number of protons in the atom of an element is the element's **atomic number**. **Figure 25** shows some elements with their atomic numbers.

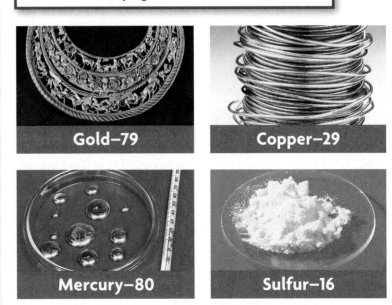

Figure 25 Atoms of each of these elements have their own identifying atomic numbers.

Gold–79

Copper–29

Mercury–80

Sulfur–16

Figure 26 Periodic Table of Elements

The periodic table is a way of organizing the elements and understanding the relationships among their chemical properties.

1	2	3	4	5	6	7	8	9	10	11	12	13	14	15	16	17	18
Hydrogen 1 H																	Helium 2 He
Lithium 3 Li	Beryllium 4 Be											Boron 5 B	Carbon 6 C	Nitrogen 7 N	Oxygen 8 O	Fluorine 9 F	Neon 10 Ne
Sodium 11 Na	Magnesium 12 Mg											Aluminum 13 Al	Silicon 14 Si	Phosphorus 15 P	Sulfur 16 S	Chlorine 17 Cl	Argon 18 Ar
Potassium 19 K	Calcium 20 Ca	Scandium 21 Sc	Titanium 22 Ti	Vanadium 23 V	Chromium 24 Cr	Manganese 25 Mn	Iron 26 Fe	Cobalt 27 Co	Nickel 28 Ni	Copper 29 Cu	Zinc 30 Zn	Gallium 31 Ga	Germanium 32 Ge	Arsenic 33 As	Selenium 34 Se	Bromine 35 Br	Krypton 36 Kr
Rubidium 37 Rb	Strontium 38 Sr	Yttrium 39 Y	Zirconium 40 Zr	Niobium 41 Nb	Molybdenum 42 Mo	Technetium 43 Tc	Ruthenium 44 Ru	Rhodium 45 Rh	Palladium 46 Pd	Silver 47 Ag	Cadmium 48 Cd	Indium 49 In	Tin 50 Sn	Antimony 51 Sb	Tellurium 52 Te	Iodine 53 I	Xenon 54 Xe
Cesium 55 Cs	Barium 56 Ba	Lanthanum 57 La	Hafnium 72 Hf	Tantalum 73 Ta	Tungsten 74 W	Rhenium 75 Re	Osmium 76 Os	Iridium 77 Ir	Platinum 78 Pt	Gold 79 Au	Mercury 80 Hg	Thallium 81 Tl	Lead 82 Pb	Bismuth 83 Bi	Polonium 84 Po	Astatine 85 At	Radon 86 Rn
Francium 87 Fr	Radium 88 Ra	Actinium 89 Ac	Rutherfordium 104 Rf	Dubnium 105 Db	Seaborgium 106 Sg	Bohrium 107 Bh	Hassium 108 Hs	Meitnerium 109 Mt	Darmstadtium * 110 Ds	Roentgenium 111 Rg	Ununbium 112 Uub		Ununquadium 114 Uuq				

Cerium 58 Ce	Praseodymium 59 Pr	Neodymium 60 Nd	Promethium 61 Pm	Samarium 62 Sm	Europium 63 Eu	Gadolinium 64 Gd	Terbium 65 Tb	Dysprosium 66 Dy	Holmium 67 Ho	Erbium 68 Er	Thulium 69 Tm	Ytterbium 70 Yb	Lutetium 71 Lu
Thorium 90 Th	Protactinium 91 Pa	Uranium 92 U	Neptunium 93 Np	Plutonium 94 Pu	Americium 95 Am	Curium 96 Cm	Berkelium 97 Bk	Californium 98 Cf	Einsteinium 99 Es	Fermium 100 Fm	Mendelevium 101 Md	Nobelium 102 No	Lawrencium 103 Lr

Atomic Number and the Periodic Table

How can you find out how many protons an element has if you don't know its atomic number? You can use the periodic table of elements, shown in **Figure 26.** Elements in the periodic table are arranged horizontally in order of increasing atomic numbers. The elements are also arranged vertically in groups with similar chemical properties. In almost all periodic tables, the block for each element gives the element's atomic number, name, and symbol. Often, the atomic mass also is included.

 Figure 26 How many elements are in the first row of the periodic table? How many are in the second and third rows?

In the periodic table shown in **Figure 26,** the blocks for most of the elements are colored light blue. These elements are metals. Notice that most of the elements are classified as metals. The blocks for nonmetals are yellow. These blocks are located at the right side of the table. Between the metals and nonmetals are the semimetals. These elements are represented by the green blocks. Semimetals are elements that have properties similar to those of both metals and nonmetals.

Isotopes—Different Numbers of Neutrons

In Lesson 2, you read that an atom's nucleus contains neutrons in addition to protons. Unlike protons, neutrons have no charge. Atoms of the same element always have the same number of protons. However, atoms of the same element sometimes have different numbers of neutrons.

Protons, Neutrons, and Mass Number

The atomic number of an element tells you the number of protons in its atoms. But, how can you know the number of neutrons an atom has? To find out, you need to know the atom's mass number. An atom's **mass number** is the sum of the number of protons and neutrons the atom has. Subtract the number of protons (the atomic number) from the mass number to calculate the number of neutrons.

Number of neutrons = mass number − number of protons

Figure 27 shows the nuclei of two different atoms of neon. The atomic number of both atoms is 10, so each atom should have 10 protons (+). But one atom has a mass number of 20. The other's mass number is 22. A third type of neon atom also occurs naturally, but in very small amounts.

 Figure 27 Count the number of neutrons in each model. Check your results using the equation above.

You may have read previously that an element is a substance composed of one kind of atom. Now you are learning that atoms of an element can have different numbers of neutrons in their nuclei. But, as you will read in Chapters 7 and 8, the chemical behavior of an element doesn't depend on the contents of its nucleus. All atoms of the same element act the same chemically because they have the same number of electrons.

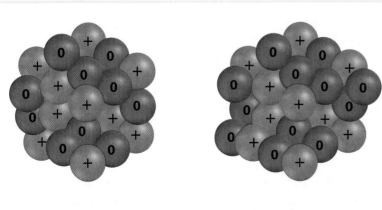

Neon-20 nucleus   Neon-22 nucleus

Figure 27 Count the protons and neutrons in each nucleus. Show that the mass number equals the number of protons plus the number of neutrons.

Table 3 Comparison of Three Carbon Isotopes

Isotope	Symbol	Atomic Number	Number of Neutrons	Mass Number	Radioactive?
Carbon-12	C-12	6	6	12	No
Carbon-13	C-13	6	7	13	No
Carbon-14	C-14	6	8	14	Yes

ACADEMIC VOCABULARY

contrast (kahn TRAST)
(verb) to show differences when compared *The student wrote a poem that contrasted winter and summer.*

WORD ORIGIN

isotope
from Greek *isos* (means *equal*) and *topos* (means *place*)

Isotopes

Recall that all the atoms of a particular element have the same atomic number. Having the same atomic number means that these atoms contain the same number of protons. In **contrast,** you have read that not all atoms of an element have the same mass number. This means that atoms of the same element can have different numbers of neutrons. Neon was the example shown in **Figure 27.** Atoms of the same element that contain different numbers of neutrons are called **isotopes.**

Because most elements have more than one isotope, each element has an average atomic mass. The **average atomic mass** of an element is the weighted average mass of the mixture of an element's isotopes. The most common of carbon's isotopes has six protons and six neutrons. If you add the number of protons and neutrons (6 + 6), you find that this isotope has a mass number of 12. Another of carbon's isotopes has seven neutrons. Add to the number its 6 protons and you have its mass number of 13. Can you see why carbon's third isotope has a mass number of 14? The symbols for these three isotopes are C-12, C-13, and C-14. What other property, shown in **Table 3,** is different for one of the three carbon isotopes besides the number of neutrons?

 What are the atomic number and mass number of the most common isotope of carbon?

Using Isotopes

Carbon-14 is radioactive. Radioactive isotopes have unstable nuclei that break down and release particles, radiation, and energy. This property makes an isotope useful for a variety of purposes. Carbon-14 is useful for dating bones, wood, and charcoal up to 50,000 years old. Geologists use uranium-238 to determine the age of rocks. In hospitals and clinics, radioactive isotopes help diagnose and treat many medical conditions. In **Figure 28,** you can find out what a tracer element is and how tracers are used in a variety of ways.

Visualizing Tracer Elements

Figure 28

Radiation from radioactive isotopes, often called radioisotopes, can penetrate matter and harm living cells. But many radioisotopes with short half-lives can be used in tiny amounts without harming people. Radioisotopes are called tracers because when a small amount of the isotope is introduced into a system, its flow through the system can be followed by a device that detects radiation. A variety of radioactive tracers, such as iodine-131, gadolinium-153 (atomic number 64), and technetium-99 have many uses in industry, medicine, and research.

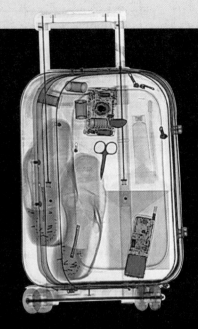

▲ Californium-252 (atomic number 98) is used to inspect airline luggage for hidden explosives and weapons.

▲ Nuclear medicine is a growing field of medicine for both diagnosis and treatment of disease. Tumors often are treated with radiation by implanting a tiny capsule or "seed" containing a radioisotope directly at the site of the cancer. Radiation from a cobalt-60 source can also be focused on the cancer.

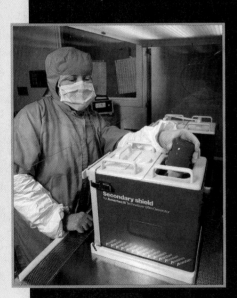

▲ Because of its short half-life, technetium-99 is produced as needed in small generators at the hospital where it is to be used.

▶ Scans of brain activity help scientists understand what parts of the brain are involved in different mental activity. These photos show the brain's response to different stimulation.

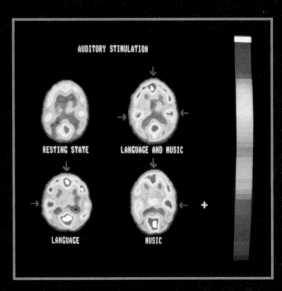

AUDITORY STIMULATION

RESTING STATE   LANGUAGE AND MUSIC

LANGUAGE   MUSIC

Concepts In Motion

Interactive Table Organize information about the hydrogen isotopes at ca8.msscience.com.

Table 4 Isotopes of Hydrogen

Name	Protium	Deuterium	Tritium
Symbol	H–1	H–2	H–3
Atomic number	1	1	1
Mass number	1	2	3
Radioactive?	No	No	Yes
Atomic structure	——1 Proton 0 Neutrons	——1 Proton 1 Neutron	——1 Proton 2 Neutrons

Isotopes of Hydrogen

The atomic number of hydrogen is l. This element is in the first block of the periodic table. All hydrogen atoms have one proton. The most common isotope of hydrogen sometimes is called protium. Protium (PROH tee um) has no neutrons. Its mass number is the same as its atomic number—one. Two other hydrogen isotopes are called deuterium (doo TEER ee um) and tritium (TRIH tee um). These isotopes do have neutrons. Deuterium has one proton and one neutron. Its mass number is 2. Tritium has one proton and two neutrons. Its mass number is 3. **Table 4** illustrates how the three isotopes differ. How many electrons are in the atoms of each of the hydrogen isotopes?

Protium, deuterium, and tritium are the only isotopes of any element that have special names. They have the same chemical properties. However, they have different physical properties. Of the three isotopes, tritium is the only one that is radioactive. Tritium is useful in scientific research because its radioactivity makes it easy to detect. Scientists also use deuterium to study chemical reactions.

 Table 4 What is the name of the isotope of hydrogen that has two neutrons?

Ions—Gaining or Losing Electrons

Because the number of protons and the number of electrons are equal, an atom is neutral. The positive and negative charges of the two types of particles balance. However, atoms can lose or gain electrons. An atom that has lost or gained electrons doesn't have the same number of electrons as protons. This means the atom is no longer neutral. It has become an ion. An **ion** is an atom that is no longer neutral because it has gained or lost electrons. Ions form substances called ionic compounds.

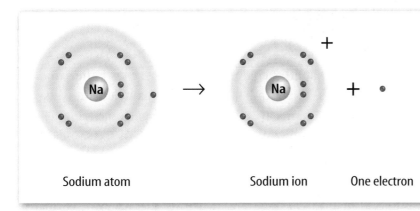

Figure 29 The sodium atom has eleven protons and eleven electrons. The sodium ion has eleven protons and only ten electrons.

Determine what neutral atom has ten electrons.

Sodium atom   Sodium ion   One electron

Positive Ions—Losing Electrons

When an atom loses an electron, it has more protons than electrons. As a result, it has a positive charge. An atom with a positive charge is called a positive ion. A positive ion is represented by the element's symbol with a superscript plus sign (+). A positively charged hydrogen ion is written H^+. If an atom loses two electrons, the symbol for the ion has the superscript $2+$. For example, calcium loses two electrons and forms the positive ion Ca^{2+}. **Figure 29** shows a diagram of sodium becoming an ion. When you look at the figure, remember that electrons do not move in circular orbits. Diagrams are drawn in this way for ease of use.

As you read, refer to the periodic table in **Figure 26.** Note the positions of the elements being discussed. Elements on the left side of the periodic table are most likely to lose electrons to form positive ions. For example, elements in Group 1, such as lithium and potassium, easily lose one electron to form ions. These ions have $+1$ charge, Li^+, and K^+. Elements in Group 2, such as magnesium and calcium, easily lose two electrons. These elements form ions with $+2$ charges, Mg^{2+} and Ca^{2+}. Some members of Group 13 can lose three electrons and form ions with $+3$ charges. Aluminum, for example, forms the ion Al^{3+}.

Negative Ions—Gaining Electrons

When an atom gains an electron, it forms an ion with a negative charge. A negative ion has more electrons than protons. Elements on the right side of the periodic table are most likely to form negative ions. Elements in Group 17 easily gain one electron. For example, fluorine and chlorine can form ions with a -1 charge. A single negative charge is shown as a superscript minus sign. The ions of fluorine and chlorine are represented as F^- and Cl^-. Oxygen and sulfur are in Group 16. These atoms can gain two electrons to form ions with -2 charges, O^{2-} and S^{2-}. Positive and negative ions attract each other because of their opposite charges. In this way, compounds are formed.

Reviewing Elements, Isotopes, and Ions

You have read that all the atoms of an element have the same number of protons. The number of protons in an element is its atomic number. Elements are arranged in the periodic table according to their atomic numbers. Some atoms of the same element may have different numbers of neutrons in their nuclei. These different types of atoms are called isotopes. The total number of protons and neutrons in an atom is its mass number. Some atoms can lose electrons to become positive ions. Other atoms can gain electrons to become negative ions. In the next chapter, you will see how ions can combine to form ionic compounds.

LESSON 3 Review

Summarize

Create your own lesson summary as you write a **newsletter.**

1. **Write** this lesson title, number, and page numbers at the top of a sheet of paper.

2. **Review** the text after the **red** main headings and write one sentence about each. These will be the headlines of your newsletter.

3. **Review** the text and write 2–3 sentences about each **blue** subheading. These sentences should tell *who, what, when, where,* and *why* information about each headline.

4. **Illustrate** your newsletter with diagrams of important structures and processes next to each headline.

 ELA8: W 2.1

Standards Check

Using Vocabulary

1. **Distinguish** between atomic number and mass number.

2. **Define** *average atomic mass* in your own words. **7.b**

Understanding Main Ideas

3. **What** is the number of neutrons in an atom called? **7.b**

   A. mass number
   B. atomic number
   C. the mass number plus the atomic number
   D. the mass number minus the atomic number

4. **Explain** the difference between oxygen-16 and oxygen-17. **7.b**

5. **Describe** the way in which a neutral atom becomes a positive ion of the same element.

6. **Determine** the number of neutrons in an isotope of argon that has a mass number of 40 and an atomic number of 18. **7.b**

7. **Compare** Copy and fill in the graphic organizer below to compare the two isotopes of lithium that have three and four neutrons. Use the periodic table.

Applying Science

8. **Draw a conclusion** about whether the periodic table could be arranged according to atomic mass rather than atomic number. **3.f**

Science Online

For more practice, visit **Standards Check** at ca8.msscience.com.

Isotopes ca8.msscience.com Brain POP

Data Lab

How do atoms differ?

Each element is made up of atoms with a certain number of particles. The periodic table tells you how many protons and electrons are in atoms of each type.

Data Collection

1. Copy the table twice in your Science Journal. In your first copy, write the symbol for each element in the center of its square. Use the periodic table.

2. Write the mass number at the top right corner.

3. Write the number of neutrons in the bottom right corner.

4. In the second table, draw a diagram of each element. Write the number of protons and neutrons inside a circle to show the nucleus. Put the correct number of electrons for each element in rings in 1, 2, or 3 rings outside the nucleus.

1							2
3	4	5	6	7	8	9	10
11	12	13	14	15	16	17	18

Data Analysis

1. **Graph** the atomic mass versus atomic number for your elements.

2. **Explain** how atomic mass varies as atomic number increases.

 Science Content Standards

3.a Students know the structure of the atom and know it is composed of protons, neutrons, and electrons.

3.f Students know how to use the periodic table to identify elements in simple compounds.

9.e Construct appropriate graphs from data and develop quantitative statements about the relationships between variables.

Model and Invent:
Build an Atom

Materials

dried peas
small balloons
medium balloons
large balloons
craft wire
small pompoms
jelly beans
glue

Safety Precautions

Science Content Standards

3.a Students know the structure of the atom and know it is composed of protons, neutrons, and electrons.

Problem

You have learned about the people who developed a picture of what atoms look like and you have learned the parts of an atom. Now, create an atom. Use craft materials to design and produce your own model of an atom.

Collect Data and Make Observations

Select Your Model

1. Read and complete a lab safety form.
2. Choose an element.
3. Draw an atomic structure diagram for that element in your Science Journal.
4. List everything you know about protons, neutrons, electrons, and their behavior.

Plan Your Model

5. How will you model the atom? Decide what materials you will use for the atom. How will you arrange the electrons outside the nucleus? Do you want to put electrons on wire or in balloon clouds? What type of objects will you use to show protons, electrons, and neutrons?
6. Make sure your teacher has approved your model before you proceed.

Build Your Model

7. Create your atomic model.
8. Show and discuss your model with your classmates.

Analyze and Conclude

1. **Describe** how you represented the nucleus in your model. Do you think this worked well?

2. **Describe** how you represented electrons in your model. Explain how your model mimics how electrons behave.

3. **Write** a paragraph describing two of your classmates' models. What did you like about their models? What do you think they could have done better?

4. **Explain** how your model would work if you decided to make a smaller atom. Would another model work better? What if you tried to make a larger atom?

5. **Infer** How do the mass and distance ratios of your model compare with reality?

6. **Error Analysis** What could have been better about your model? Explain in detail how you could improve it.

Communicate

Peer Review With your classmates, compare and contrast your models. Discuss the best features of each model and ways that each might be improved. Vote on which model does the best job representing:

- particles of the nucleus
- electrons
- size of the nucleus
- distance of electrons from the nucleus
- movement of electrons
- electron levels

Be prepared to defend your vote for each category. Can you explain why you voted the way you did?

Real World Science

Science & Career

Chien-Shiung Wu

Chien-Shiung Wu graduated with a PhD in physics from the University of California, Berkeley in 1940. She was one of a few female scientists involved in the Manhattan Project, which developed the atomic bomb. Her work on the project included separating the isotope uranium-235 from the element uranium-238. In 1957, she won the Nobel Prize in Physics.

Understanding the Periodic Table Create a table of the atomic mass, mass number, number of protons and number of neutrons of the elements plutonium and uranium.

Nuclear Power

When the nucleus of an isotope is split apart, it creates energy. This process is called fission. Nuclear power plants use uranium or plutonium isotopes to create energy this way. Seven grams of uranium can produce as much energy as 3.5 barrels of oil or 809 kg of coal.

The Energy Crisis Alternative energy is energy derived from sources other than fossil fuels. Select one type of alternative energy. Research the benefits and drawbacks of your selected energy type and hold a class mock debate to discuss each type. Visit **Technology** at ca8.msscience.com to research information on alternative energy.

Science & Technology

Three Mile Island Accident

A partial melt down occurred at the Three Mile Island power plant in Middletown, Pennsylvania, in 1979. Luckily, no fatalities or injuries took place. The problem arose when the cooling system failed, which ultimately caused a relief valve to open. Water used in the cooling system was contaminated with radioactive waste. It took 13 years to decontaminate the power plant.

How safe are nuclear power plants? Ask five people their opinion of the safety of nuclear power. Tally everyone's results and create a table and bar graph of the data of the entire class.

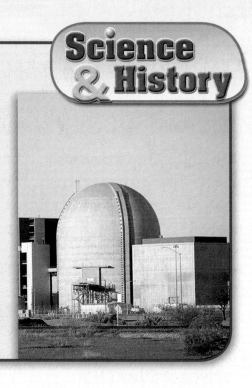

DROPPING THE ATOMIC BOMB

Shortly before the end of World War II, the United States dropped two atomic bombs on Hiroshima and Nagasaki, Japan in August 1945. In Nagasaki 39,000 people died instantly and almost twice as many died from bomb-related complications, such as cancer. The Nagasaki bomb contained 8 kg of the isotope plutonium-239.

The Age of Nuclear Weapons
Write an editorial about the use of nuclear weapons. Include your opinion about the use of nuclear weapons in the past, present, future and the use of the atomic bomb during World War II.

 **ELA8:** W 2.4

The BIG Idea
The current model of the atom includes protons, neutrons, and electrons.

Lesson 1 Atoms—Basic Units of Matter
3.a

Main Idea **Matter is made of tiny particles called atoms.**

- All matter is composed of tiny particles called atoms.
- Atoms contain electrons, protons, and neutrons.
- Protons and neutrons are located in the nucleus of an atom and make up most of the mass of an atom.
- Electrons move around the outside of the nucleus and take up most of the space in an atom.

- **atom** (p. 174)
- **electron** (p. 175)
- **matter** (p. 174)
- **neutron** (p. 175)
- **nucleus** (p. 175)
- **proton** (p. 175)

Lesson 2 Discovering Parts of the Atoms
3.a

Main Idea **Scientists have put together a detailed model of atoms and their parts.**

- Rutherford showed that an atom has a tiny nucleus surrounded by a large space in which electrons move.
- Rutherford's atomic model was an improvement over Thomson's model but could not describe the motion of the electrons.
- Bohr's model included different energy levels for the atom's electrons.
- Bohr's model explained the spectrum of hydrogen and why elements have different chemical properties.
- In today's atomic model, electrons move in electron clouds at different energy levels.

- **electron cloud** (p. 190)
- **energy level** (p. 190)
- **spectral line** (p. 191)

Lesson 3 Elements, Isotopes, and Ions—How Atoms Differ
3.f, 7.b, 9.e

Main Idea **Atoms of a particular element always have the same number of protons.**

- The number of protons in the atoms of an element is called the atomic number.
- The atomic number is the same for all atoms of the same element.
- Elements are arranged on the periodic table according to their atomic numbers.
- Atoms with the same number of protons but different numbers of neutrons are called isotopes.
- Atoms can lose or gain electrons to form positive or negative ions.
- Elements in the same group of the periodic table form ions with the same charge.

- **atomic number** (p. 195)
- **average atomic mass** (p. 198)
- **element** (p. 195)
- **ion** (p. 200)
- **isotope** (p. 198)
- **mass number** (p. 197)

STUDY TO GO Download quizzes, key terms, and flash cards from ca8.msscience.com.

Linking Vocabulary and Main Ideas

Use vocabulary terms from page 208 to complete this map.

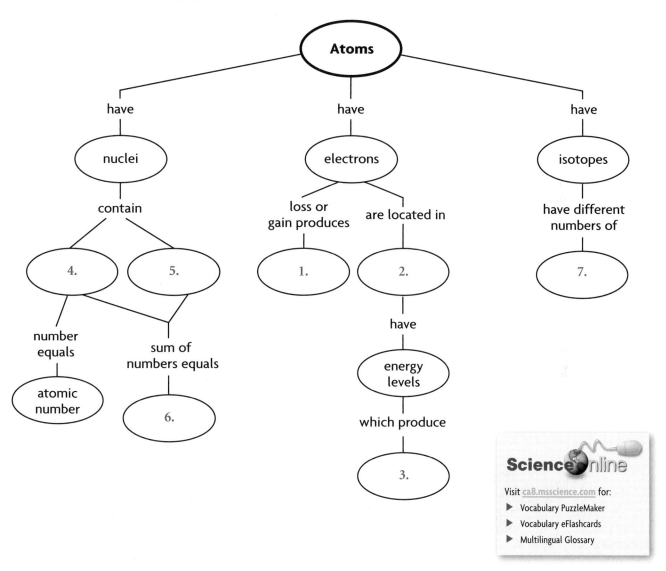

Using Vocabulary

Fill in the blanks with the correct vocabulary terms. Then read the paragraph to a partner.

The atoms of an element have the same number of protons, but some atoms called _____8._____ can have different numbers of neutrons. Neutrons are packed into the _____9._____ of an atom along with the atom's _____10._____. The electron is another particle in an atom. When an atom loses an electron, a(n) _____11._____ is formed which has a positive charge. In the current model of the atom, electrons occupy a(n) _____12._____.

Understanding Main Ideas

Choose the word or phrase that best answers the question.

1. Which part of an atom takes up the most space?
   A. the electrons   **3.a**
   B. the protons
   C. the neutrons
   D. the nuclei

2. What did Democritus believe an atom was?
   A. a tiny particle with a nucleus   **3.a**
   B. a tiny nucleus with electrons surrounding it
   C. an electron cloud
   D. a solid, indivisible sphere

3. An ion contains 10 electrons, 12 protons, and 13 neutrons. What is the ion's charge?
   A. 1−   **7.b**
   B. 3+
   C. 2−
   D. 2+

4. The illustration below shows the apparatus that J. J. Thomson used.

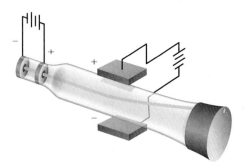

   What did J. J. Thomson discover?
   A. Matter contains neutrons.   **3.a**
   B. Electrons have a negative charge.
   C. Electrons have a positive charge.
   D. Atoms can move in a stream.

5. What does the symbol Ca^{2+} represent?
   A. an isotope of calcium   **7.b**
   B. a calcium atom
   C. a negative calcium ion
   D. a positive calcium ion

6. How is the identity of an element determined?
   A. the number of its protons   **7.b**
   B. the number of its neutrons
   C. its mass number
   D. the charge of the atom

7. What does the electron energy level diagram show?

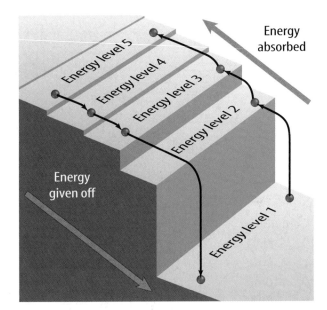

   A. Energy is released as electrons move to upper levels.
   B. Energy must be absorbed for electrons to fall to lower levels.
   C. The energy of an electron at each level is different.
   D. The energy difference between each level is the same.   **3.a**

8. How is Bohr's atomic model different from Rutherford's model?
   A. Bohr's model has more electrons.   **3.a**
   B. Electrons in Bohr's model are located farther from the nucleus.
   C. Electrons in Bohr's model have different energy levels.
   D. Electrons in Bohr's model surround the nucleus but do not move.

 Science Online   Standards Review ca8.msscience.com

Applying Science

9. **List** two ways in which Bohr's atomic model was an improvement over Rutherford's model of the atom. **3.a**

10. **Explain** how a negative ion is formed. **7.b**

11. **Determine** how much larger the mass of a proton is than the mass of an electron. Use the data in the table below. Show your calculations. **3.a**

Particle	Charge	Mass (amu)
Proton	+1	1.007316
Neutron	0	1.008701
Electron	−1	0.000549

12. **Suggest** a possible reason why sulfur's average atomic mass is very close to the whole number 32, whereas magnesium's average atomic mass is 24.3, which is not a whole number. Use this information: Sulfur has only one common isotope. Magnesium has several isotopes. **7.b**

13. **Demonstrate** how you can use Dalton's atomic symbols to represent the substances water and hydrogen perioxide. Water has two hydrogen atoms and one oxygen atom. Hydrogen peroxide has two hydrogen atoms and two oxygen atoms. **3.a**

14. **Explain** why it is necessary to change models as new information becomes available. **3.a**

15. **Describe** how you can use the periodic table to determine the average number of neutrons an element has, even though the number of neutrons is not listed. **3.f**

16. **Explain** how it is possible for two atoms of the same element to have different masses. **7.b**

WRITING in Science

17. **Write** a 500–700-word biography about Antoine Lavoisier. Describe his background and schooling in science. Explain the experiments that led him to demonstrate the law of conservation of mass. **ELA8:** W 2.1

Applying Math

Use the table below to answer questions 18–22.

Particle	Mass (g)
Proton	1.6727×10^{-24}
Neutron	1.6750×10^{-24}
Electron	9.110×10^{-28}

18. Find the mass of three protons. **ALG: 2.0**

19. Find the mass of five electrons. **ALG: 2.0**

20. Find the mass of four neutrons. **ALG: 2.0**

21. Find the mass of seven protons. **ALG: 2.0**

22. Find the mass of six electrons. **ALG: 2.0**

1 Ruthenium has an atomic number of 44 and a mass number of 101. How many protons does ruthenium have?

A 44

B 57

C 88

D 101   **7.b**

2 The diagram below shows a model of an atom that was developed following Rutherford's experiment.

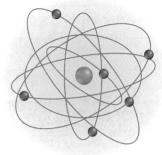

Which component of the atom is not represented in Rutherford's atomic model?

A the neutrons

B the nucleus

C the electrons

D the protons   **3.a**

3 Gloria is making a model of an atom. She is using three different colors to represent the three basic particles that make up an atom. Which particles should she display in the nucleus of the atom?

A neutrons only

B electrons only

C protons and neutrons

D electrons and protons   **3.a**

4 The atomic number of boron is 5. Boron-11 contains

A five electrons and six protons.

B five protons and six electrons.

C five protons and six neutrons.

D six protons and five neutrons.   **7.b**

5 Dalton's model of the atom described atoms as spheres that are the same throughout. Why did scientists develop a new model of the atom?

A Philosophers thought that all matter is made up of atoms.

B Researchers proposed that all atoms of the same element are alike.

C Experiments showed that atoms contain smaller particles with different charges.

D Studies suggested that a large amount of energy could be released from an atom.   **3.a**

6 The illustrations below show three nuclei.

| 1 Proton 0 Neutrons | 1 Proton 1 Neutron | 1 Proton 2 Neutrons |

What is the mass number for each of the nuclei shown in the illustration above?

A 0, 1, 2

B 1, 1, 1

C 1, 2, 2

D 1, 2, 3   **7.b**

Science online Standards Assessment ca8.msscience.com

7 The table below shows properties of four nitrogen isotopes.

Isotopes of Nitrogen		
Isotope	**Mass Number**	**Number of Protons**
Nitrogen-12	12	7
Nitrogen-13	13	7
Nitrogen-14	14	7
Nitrogen-15	15	7

How many neutrons does nitrogen-15 have?

A 7

B 8

C 15

D 21 **7.b**

8 Which scientist envisioned the atom as a ball of positive charge with electrons embedded in it?

A Bohr

B Dalton

C Rutherford

D Thomson **3.a**

9 Which particle is the smallest?

A electron

B nucleus

C proton

D neutron **3.a**

10 The atomic number is equal to the number of

A protons.

B neutrons.

C electrons.

D quarks. **3.a**

11 What did Thomson's experiment show?

A The atom is like a uniform sphere.

B Cathode rays are made up of electrons.

C The atom cannot be divided.

D The atom was a neutral sphere **3.a**

12 Why did Rutherford infer the presence of a tiny nucleus?

A The alpha particle went through the foil.

B No alpha particles went through the foil.

C The charges were uniform in the atom.

D Some alpha particles bounced back from the foil. **3.a**

13 The table below describes three carbon atoms.

Carbon Atoms and Their Properties			
	Carbon-12	**Carbon-13**	**Carbon-14**
Mass number	12	13	14
Number of protons	6	6	6
Number of neutrons	6	7	8
Number of electrons	6	6	6
Atomic number	6	6	6

How are these atoms different from one another?

A Each one is a different isotope.

B Each one is a different element.

C Each one is made up of different types particles.

D Each one has different types of particles in the nucleus. **7.b**

Combining Atoms and Molecules

The BIG Idea

Atoms of two or more elements can combine to form compounds that have different properties from those of the elements that formed them.

LESSON 1 3.a, 3.b, 3.f
How Atoms Form Compounds

Main Idea Compounds are chemical combinations of elements that have properties different from the elements that formed them.

LESSON 2
3.b, 3.c, 7.c, 9.a, 9.e
Forming Solids

Main Idea Atoms, ions, and molecules can link together to form large, repeating structures such as solid metals, ionic and molecular crystals, and polymers.

The Hardest Known Natural Substance

This is a computer-generated image of the molecular structure of diamonds. The blue spheres are carbon atoms. The carbon atoms are joined to other carbon atoms. Diamonds are made from carbon atoms that have been subjected to extreme heat and pressure. They are the hardest known natural substance.

Science Journal Write three questions you have about solids.

Launch Lab

00:20 minutes

What do structures made of atoms look like?

Atoms make up everything in your world. What makes plastic different from cotton or steel?

Procedure

1. Complete a lab safety form.

2. Build a model of a two-atom molecule using two **gumdrops** and one **toothpick**.

3. Build a model of a chain.

4. Build a model of connected cubes using 16 **gumdrops** and 28 **toothpicks**.

5. Build a model of three hexagons connected along two sides.

Think About This

- **Evaluate** How rigid is the structure? Is the model rigid in one direction, but less rigid in another direction?

- **Consider** Are your models able to flow or slide easily past one another? Is the model able to bend easily?

 3.b

Science Online

Visit ca8.msscience.com to:

▶ view **Concepts in Motion**

▶ explore Virtual Labs

▶ access content-related Web links

▶ take the Standards Check

 **Compounds and Bonds** Make the following Foldable to explain the ways compounds form.

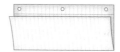

STEP 1 **Fold** a sheet of paper in half lengthwise. Make the back edge about 2 cm longer than the front edge.

STEP 2 **Fold** into thirds.

STEP 3 **Unfold** and **cut** along the folds of the top flap to make three flaps.

STEP 4 **Label** the flaps as shown.

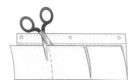

Compounds and Bonds

| Ionic Bonds | Covalent Bonds | Metallic Bonds |

Reading Skill

Visualizing As you read this chapter, describe how each type of bond forms, list the properties of the compounds formed, and give examples of each.

Get Ready to Read

Visualize

① Learn It! Visualize by forming mental images of the text as you read. Imagine how the text descriptions look, sound, feel, smell, or taste. Look for any pictures or diagrams on the page that may help you add to your understanding.

② Practice It! Read the following paragraph. As you read, use the underlined details to form a picture in your mind.

> Sodium chloride, NaCl, is an ionic crystal. Even a tiny grain of sodium chloride contains billions of sodium ions and chloride ions. Crystals of sodium chloride have a regular, cubic structure. The patterns in the sodium chloride crystal are simple. Sodium ions (Na^+) alternate with chloride ions (Cl^-) in a three-dimensional pattern.
>
> —*from page 233*

Based on the description above, try to visualize a sodium chloride crystal. Now look at the photo on page 233.

- How closely does it match your mental picture?
- Reread the passage and look at the picture again. Did your ideas change?
- Compare your image with what others in your class visualized.

③ Apply It! Read the chapter and list three subjects you were able to visualize. Make a rough sketch showing what you visualized.

Target Your Reading

Reading Tip

Forming your own mental images will help you remember what you read.

Use this to focus on the main ideas as you read the chapter.

1 Before you read the chapter, respond to the statements below on your worksheet or on a numbered sheet of paper.
- Write an **A** if you **agree** with the statement.
- Write a **D** if you **disagree** with the statement.

2 After you read the chapter, look back to this page to see if you've changed your mind about any of the statements.
- If any of your answers changed, explain why.
- Change any false statements into true statements.
- Use your revised statements as a study guide.

Before You Read A or D	Statement	After You Read A or D
	1 Compounds have properties very similar to the properties of the elements they contain.	
	2 A given compound always has the same formula showing the same elements in the same ratios.	
	3 All elements can form both covalent and ionic bonds.	
	4 An atom that loses an electron becomes a negative ion.	
	5 Covalent bonds can be single, double, or triple.	
	6 Some of the electrons in metals are free to move from atom to atom.	
	7 All crystals are held together with ionic bonds.	
	8 In a sodium chloride crystal, sodium ions surround chloride ions.	
	9 A polymer is a stringlike compound made of repeating units.	

Science Online

Print a worksheet of this page at ca8.msscience.com.

Reading Guide

What *You'll Learn*

▶ **Describe** how a compound differs from its component elements.

▶ **Explain** the differences between ionic and covalent bonding.

▶ **Explain** how atoms can become stable by forming chemical bonds.

Why *It's Important*

Learning how atoms combine helps explain how new compounds are made.

Vocabulary

compound
chemical formula
molecule
chemical bond
ionic bond
valence
covalent bond

Review Vocabulary

ion: a charged particle that forms from an atom that has gained or lost electrons (p. 200)

How Atoms Form Compounds

Main Idea Compounds are chemical combinations of elements with properties that are different from the elements that formed them.

Real-World Reading Connection To make corn tortillas, you mix together water, salt, and masa harina (a type of cornmeal) to make dough. Then, you roll or press pieces of the dough into thin circles and cook them on a griddle. The cooked tortillas are not at all like the ingredients you mixed. Like tortillas, compounds are combinations of elements that have chemical and physical properties different from the elements that make them up.

What is a compound?

Think about all the different kinds of materials you see and use every day. The world is made up of far more substances than the approximately 100 known elements. This wide variety of materials exists because atoms of different elements combine to form compounds. A **compound** is a pure substance that contains two or more elements. Most of the matter around you is made of compounds. **Figure 1** shows examples of elements and compounds that you may recognize.

Figure 1 Elements, such as helium, gold, and carbon (diamond) are less common than compounds such as water, sucrose (table sugar), and sodium chloride (table salt).

Elements　　　**Compounds**

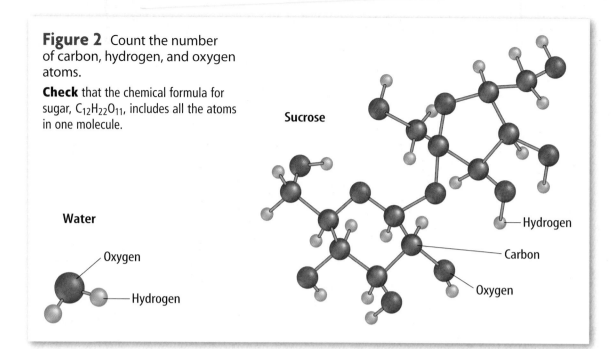

Figure 2 Count the number of carbon, hydrogen, and oxygen atoms.

Check that the chemical formula for sugar, $C_{12}H_{22}O_{11}$, includes all the atoms in one molecule.

Sucrose

Water

Oxygen

Hydrogen

Hydrogen

Carbon

Oxygen

Chemical Formulas for Compounds

Gold is an element, so it contains only gold atoms. Water and sugar are compounds. How can you tell what elements make up a compound? An ingredient list would help. Such a list would name all the elements contained in a compound. It also would tell how much of each element is present. An ingredient list for a compound is called its chemical formula. A **chemical formula** contains atomic symbols and subscripts to show the elements and the number of atoms of each element that combine to form a compound.

Describing Compounds Maybe you have referred to water as "H two O." That's how you would read the chemical formula for water, which is H_2O. The subscript 2 after the hydrogen symbol means that a molecule of water contains two hydrogen atoms. A **molecule** is a neutral particle that forms as a result of electron sharing. The element oxygen (O) has no subscript, which means that a molecule of water contains only one oxygen atom. The chemical formula for table sugar is $C_{12}H_{22}O_{11}$. Carbon's subscript, 12, shows that one molecule of sugar contains 12 carbon atoms. How many hydrogen atoms are in one sugar molecule?

Formulas and the Law of Definite Proportions Table sugar always contains 12 carbon atoms, 22 hydrogen atoms, and 11 oxygen atoms. Water always contains two hydrogen atoms and one oxygen atom. Recall that the law of definite proportions states that a pure compound will always contain the same elements in the same proportion by mass. **Figure 2** shows models of how the atoms in water and sugar are arranged.

WORD ORIGIN
molecule
from Latin *moles*; means *mass*

Reading Check What is the law of definite proportions?

Compounds and Their Elements

Compounds have different properties than those of the elements that make them up. Sodium chloride is an example. Sodium is a soft, shiny metal. Chlorine is a greenish-yellow gas at room temperature. When sodium and chlorine combine to form a compound, the product is the familiar white table salt, sodium chloride. What holds sodium chloride together?

Ionic Bonds and Ionic Compounds

Suppose you blow up two balloons. You rub one with wool and the other with plastic wrap. You find that the balloons stick together. The balloon rubbed with wool becomes negatively charged. The balloon rubbed with plastic wrap becomes positively charged. Opposite charges attract, so the balloons are attracted to each other. The force that holds the balloons together is similar to the force that holds atoms together in a compound. A **chemical bond** is a force that holds atoms together in a compound. Each of the connections between the atoms in **Figure 2** represents a chemical bond.

Ionic Bonds—Transferring Electrons

Just as the balloons became charged by rubbing, an atom of an element can become charged by transferring one or more electrons to a different atom. Both atoms become charged particles, or ions. A positive ion has fewer electrons than protons. A negative ion has more electrons than protons. The atom that gives up the electron becomes positively charged. The atom that receives the electron becomes negatively charged. In **Figure 3,** a lithium (LIH thee um) atom transfers an electron to a fluorine (FLOOR een) atom. Lithium becomes a positively charged ion. Fluorine becomes a negatively charged ion. Like the balloons, the two ions attract each other and stick together. They form a chemical bond. A bond between oppositely charged ions is called an ionic bond. An **ionic bond** is an electrical attraction between positively and negatively charged ions in an ionic compound.

SCIENCE USE v. COMMON USE
bond

Science Use a force that holds atoms together in a compound. *Two types of chemical bonds are ionic and covalent.*

Common Use a close personal relationship between people. *A strong bond of friendship developed between the two girls.*

Figure 3 Lithium and fluorine attract each other like two charged balloons.

Explain how lithium becomes positively charged and fluorine becomes negatively charged.

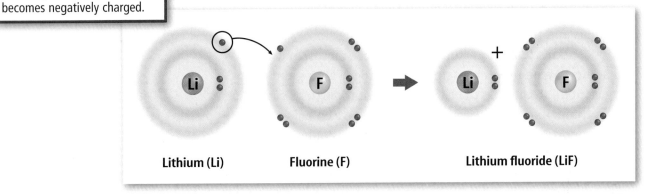

Lithium (Li)   Fluorine (F)   Lithium fluoride (LiF)

Ionic compounds

In **Figure 3,** you saw how a lithium ion and a flouride ion attract one another and form an ionic bond. The compound lithium flouride is formed. Lithium flouride is an example of the simplest ionic compound—one that contains ions of two elements. Usually, the positive ion is a metal. The negative ion is a nonmetal. An ionic compound with only two different ions is called a binary compound. *Binary* describes anything that consists of two parts. The charges of the ions in a compound always balance. When the charges are balanced, the overall charge of the compound is zero and the compound is neutral.

Positive Ions How can you tell whether the ions that an atom forms will be positive or negative? The periodic table can help. Elements in the same column of the periodic table are a group. The groups are identified by a number at the top of the column. A metal in Group 1, such as sodium, can transfer one electron. In doing so, it becomes an ion with a +1 charge. The **symbol** for the sodium ion is Na^+.

 Potassium is in Group 1. What is the symbol for the potassium ion?

Negative Ions The Group 17 elements are nonmetals. A Group 17 element can gain an electron to form an ion with a –1 charge. The symbol for the chloride ion is Cl^-. When a positive ion from Group 1 combines with a negative ion from Group 17, the result is a salt such as sodium chloride (NaCl). **Figure 4** highlights the elements in Groups 1 and 17 and the important role that some of these elements play in your life. What about neighboring Groups 2 and 16? Can the elements from these groups form binary ionic compounds?

Figure 4 Potatoes and bananas are rich in sodium and potassium. Table salt contains chlorine. These elements from Groups 1 and 17 are essential in your diet.

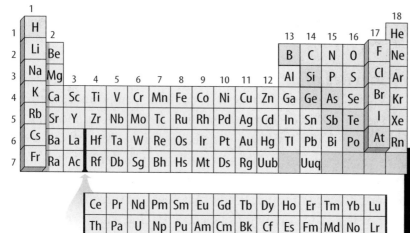

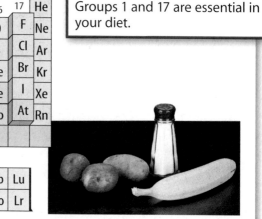

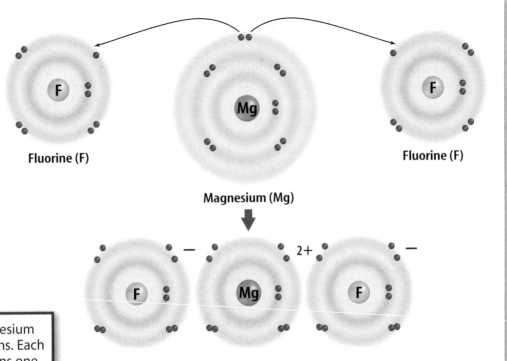

Figure 5 Magnesium loses two electrons. Each fluorine atom gains one electron as magnesium fluoride is formed.

Fluorine (F)

Magnesium (Mg)

Fluorine (F)

Other Binary Ionic Compounds

Salts formed from Group 1 and Group 17 elements are not the only common ionic compounds. Group 2 elements, such as magnesium and calcium, are also metals. They often lose two electrons and form ions with +2 charges (Mg^{2+} and Ca^{2+}). Elements in Group 16, such as oxygen and sulfur, are nonmetals. These elements can gain electrons to form ions with –2 charges (O^{2-} and S^{2-}). Ionic compounds can form when elements in Group 2 transfer electrons to elements in either Group 16 or Group 17. Magnesium transfers two electrons to oxygen to form magnesium oxide, MgO. Magnesium can also transfer electrons to fluorine atoms to form magnesium fluoride, MgF_2. **Figure 5** illustrates how a magnesium atom transfers one electron to each of two fluorine atoms. The new compound that forms has different properties from either magnesium or fluorine.

 Figure 5 Why are there two fluoride ions in magnesium fluoride but only one fluoride ion in lithium fluoride?

Properties of Ionic Compounds

What are some of the properties of ionic compounds, such as magnesium fluoride and sodium chloride? These compounds are usually solids at room temperature. They are brittle, which means they easily break apart. They have relatively high melting points and high boiling points. Like sodium chloride, many ionic compounds dissolve in water. Water that contains dissolved ionic compounds is a good conductor of electricity. The charges of the ions and the forces that hold them together in the compound are responsible for the properties of ionic compounds.

Table 1 Valence and Lewis Dot Diagrams

Concepts In Motion
Interactive Table To organize elements and their Lewis dot diagrams, visit ca8.msscience.com.

Group Number	Typical Element	Valence Electrons	Lewis Dot Diagram
1	Lithium	1	Li·
2	Beryllium	2	·Be
13	Boron	3	·B·
14	Carbon	4	·C·
15	Nitrogen	5	·N·
16	Oxygen	6	:O·
17	Fluorine	7	:F·
18	Neon	8*	:Ne:

*except helium, which has only 2 electrons

Diagramming Electrons—Lewis Dot Diagrams

American chemist Gilbert Lewis developed Lewis dot diagrams in 1923 to represent atoms and their electrons. To construct a Lewis dot diagram for an atom, you need to know the number of valence electrons an atom has. An atom's **valence** is the number of electrons in its outermost energy level. Only valence electrons are shown in a Lewis dot diagram. **Table 1** lists the valence and Lewis dot diagrams for typical elements of eight of the groups in the periodic table. All members of a group have the same number of valence electrons. A maximum of eight electrons fits around the atomic symbol, in four pairs.

One method to make a Lewis dot diagram is to first write the element's atomic symbol. Use a dot for each valence electron. Place dots one by one on the top, right, bottom, and left. If an atom has more than four electrons, continue adding dots, making pairs of electrons. Follow in the same direction as the first four electrons until you have placed a dot for each valence electron.

WORD ORIGIN
valence
from Latin *valentia;* means *strength, capacity*

Reading Check Phosphorus is a Group 15 element with five valence electrons. Draw its electron dot diagram.

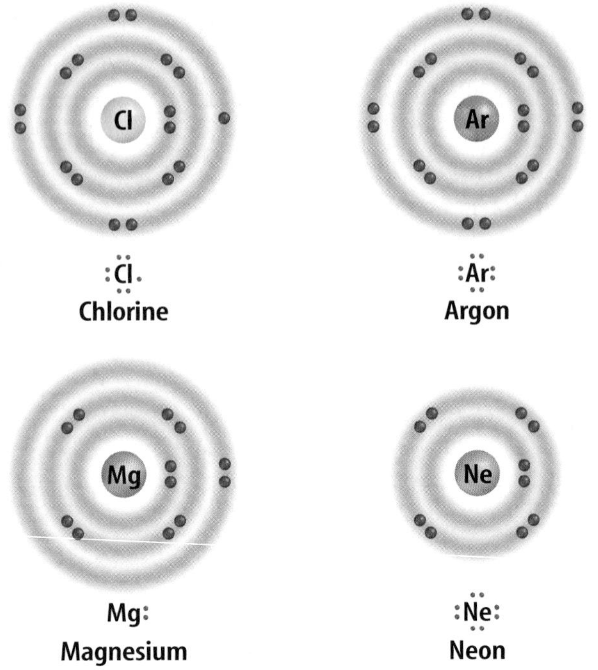

Figure 6 If chlorine gains an electron, its electron structure becomes the same as argon's. Magnesium's electron structure is the same as neon's when magnesium loses two electrons.

:C̈l·
Chlorine

:Ar:
Argon

Mg:
Magnesium

:Ne:
Neon

Ions and Noble Gases

Table 1 excludes Groups 3–12 of the periodic table. These elements are metals and have valences that can vary. Notice that for the remaining groups, the number of valence electrons increases from one to eight across the table. Elements in Group 18, called the noble gases, each have eight valence electrons. Group 18 elements are stable because their outer energy levels are filled. Elements that are stable rarely react to form compounds.

Noble Gas Structure by Gaining Electrons Some atoms can achieve the same filled outer energy levels of the noble gases if they gain or lose electrons. **Figure 6** shows the electron structures and Lewis dot diagrams for chlorine and argon. Argon is the noble gas nearest to chlorine. Compare the diagrams of the two elements. Notice that chlorine can become more stable by gaining one electron to form a negative chloride ion (Cl^-). Both argon and the chloride ion have the same electron structure.

Noble Gas Structure by Losing Electrons Magnesium is another element that can achieve the electron structure of a noble gas. The nearest noble gas to magnesium is neon. In **Figure 6,** compare the Lewis dot diagrams for magnesium and neon. Magnesium has 12 electrons; neon has 10. Magnesium can have the same stable electron structure as neon if it loses two electrons to form the magnesium ion (Mg^{2+}).

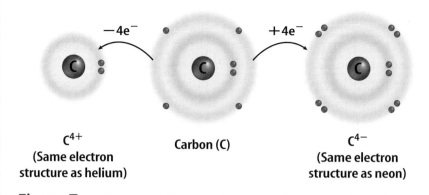

C^{4+}
(Same electron structure as helium)

Carbon (C)

C^{4-}
(Same electron structure as neon)

Figure 7 Carbon would have to lose four electrons to have the same number of electrons as helium. Or, it would have to gain four electrons to have the same number of electrons as neon.

Covalent Bonds—Sharing Electrons

You have read that ionic bonds form when electrons are transferred from a metal atom to a nonmetal atom. Atoms lose or gain the number of electrons that will give them the atomic structure of a noble gas. Ionic compounds, called salts, are formed when positive and negative ions attract each other. However, to form ions, some atoms would have to gain or lose too many electrons. As you can see in **Figure 7,** carbon has four valence electrons. It is equally close to two noble gases, helium and neon. To become an ion with the noble gas structure of neon or helium, carbon would have to either gain or lose four electrons. Too much energy is needed for this to happen easily. Nevertheless, carbon forms millions of compounds, not by transferring electrons, but by sharing electrons.

 Figure 7 Explain how C^{4-} has the same electron structure as neon.

Covalent Compounds

Atoms that do not transfer electrons often can form compounds by sharing electrons in a covalent bond. A **covalent bond** is a chemical bond formed when atoms share electrons. Elements that are close together on the periodic table are more likely to share electrons in a covalent bond than to transfer electrons. Recall that molecules are neutral particles formed when atoms share electrons. Covalent compounds are made from molecules. Covalent carbon compounds are especially important in living organisms because they include cell molecules such as DNA, proteins, and sugars. These molecules are examples of an enormous number of organic compounds that make up the materials of the living world. Organic compounds are covalent compounds containing carbon atoms.

 What is a covalent bond?

Properties of Covalent Compounds

Recall that ionic compounds usually are solids at room temperature. In contrast, covalent compounds can be solids, liquids, or gases at room temperature. Covalent compounds usually have lower melting points and boiling points than do ionic compounds. The atoms in covalent compounds do not separate in water, as the atoms in ionic compounds do. Solutions of most covalent compounds do not conduct electricity. For example, a solution of the ionic compound sodium chloride conducts electricity. A similar solution of the covalent compound sugar does not.

Single Covalent Bonds

To help you understand the sharing of electrons, think about this situation. You and a friend decide to go to the movies. The price of a ticket is $5.00, or two tickets for $8.00. You each have $4.00. You can't buy your tickets individually, but if you and your friend put your money together, you can buy tickets for both of you. Similarly, atoms that have unpaired electrons can form compounds if they share electrons. A compound held together by one or more covalent bonds is called a covalent compound.

How does electron sharing happen? Follow **Figure 8** as you read. Hydrogen, H, has one unpaired electron. Two hydrogen atoms can share their single electrons to form one pair of shared electrons. A shared pair of electrons is a covalent bond. In this case, the covalent bond holds the molecule H_2 together. Carbon has four unpaired electrons. By combining its four electrons with the electrons of four hydrogen atoms, carbon can form four covalent bonds. The compound methane, CH_4, is formed. Nitrogen has three unpaired electrons. How many covalent bonds can a nitrogen atom form with hydrogen atoms?

 Why can carbon bond with four other elements?

Figure 8 The hydrogen molecule has one single covalent bond. **Determine** how many single bonds methane has.

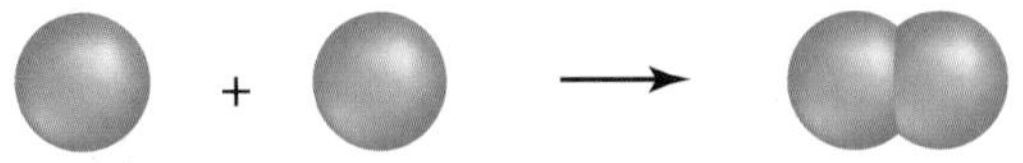

H• + H•	→	H:H
H + H	→	H_2
Hydrogen atom	Hydrogen atom	Hydrogen molecule

H : H

Single Bond

Figure 9 It's harder to pull two friends apart when they are holding on to each other with two hands. In a similar way, double bonds are stronger than single bonds.

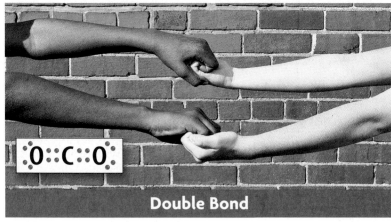

:O :: C :: O:

Double Bond

Double and Triple Bonds

Sometimes two atoms may form a stronger bond by sharing more than one pair of electrons. In **Figure 9,** a single bond is represented by two friends, each joining one of their hands. One pair of electrons is being shared. A double bond is represented by the two friends joining both of their hands. A double bond consists of two shared pairs of electrons. Double bonds are stronger than single bonds. It takes more energy to pull the two friends apart when both of their hands are joined.

 Reading Check What is the difference between a single bond and a double bond?

A triple covalent bond is three shared pairs of electrons. As you might predict, triple bonds are stronger than double or single bonds. Acetylene (uh SEE tul een), a gas that welders use, is a covalent compound with a triple bond. The atoms in the nitrogen molecule, N_2, are also held together by a triple bond. A nitrogen molecule forms when two nitrogen atoms share their three unpaired electrons in a triple bond. The strength of the triple bond makes the nitrogen molecule unreactive. Nitrogen gas, N_2, makes up almost 80 percent of the air you breathe.

What do you know about compounds?

An enormous number of substances exist in the world because atoms form compounds. Compounds can be either ionic or covalent. Ionic compounds are formed when atoms transfer electrons. Covalent compounds result from the sharing of electrons. Chemical bonds hold atoms together in molecules and compounds. Chemical formulas show the number and type of each atom in a molecule or compound. The number of bonds an atom can form is equal to the number of unpaired valence electrons the atom has.

LESSON 1 Review

Summarize

Create your own lesson summary as you design a **visual aid.**

1. **Write** the lesson title, number, and page numbers at the top of your poster.

2. **Scan** the lesson to find the **red** main headings. Organize these headings on your poster, leaving space between each.

3. **Design** an information box beneath each **red** heading. In the box, list 2–3 details, key terms, and definitions from each **blue** subheading.

4. **Illustrate** your poster with diagrams of important structures or processes next to each information box.

 ELA8: R 2.3

Standards Check

Using Vocabulary

1. **Explain** the difference between an ionic bond and a covalent bond. **3.b**

2. **Define** *valence* in your own words. **3.a**

Understanding Main Ideas

3. What element can form a positive ion? **3.a**

    A. magnesium

    B. carbon

    C. oxygen

    D. bromine

4. **Explain** why chlorine forms a –1 ion, but sulfur forms a –2 ion. **3.a**

5. **Compare** Copy and fill in the graphic organizer below to describe the properties of sodium, chlorine, and sodium chloride. **3.c**

Sodium	
Chlorine	
Sodium chloride	

6. **Predict** the number of covalent bonds an oxygen atom can make with other atoms. **3.a**

Applying Science

7. **Construct** a model to show what type of bond silicon is most likely to form with oxygen. Silicon and oxygen are in the same group of the periodic table. **3.b**

8. **Decide** whether the bond joining two chlorine atoms together in the chlorine molecule, Cl_2, is an ionic or covalent bond. Justify your answer. **3.b**

Science nline

For more practice, visit **Standards Check** at ca8.msscience.com.

MiniLab

Try at Home

00:25 minutes

How can you model molecules?

Many atoms bond to one, two, three, or four other atoms. Use your hands and feet as bonds to act like an atom.

Procedure

1. Read and complete a lab safety form.

2. Clear a space in which to move around. Make sure there are no objects anyone can trip over or bump into.

3. In your Science Journal, create a chart in which to draw Lewis dot diagrams for the first 18 elements. Determine the number of bonds each atom can form.

4. Sort the first 18 elements into a Venn diagram similar to the one below. Write elements that do not form compounds below the diagram.

Form covalent bonds   Form both   Form ionic bonds

5. Make a chart that lists the elements that form one, two, three, four and zero bonds.

6. Brainstorm how to model covalent bonds and ionic bonds. Choose the best way to model both types of bonds.

7. Choose one element. As an atom of that element, form bonds with students representing other atoms.

Analysis

1. **Describe** how the ionic bonds behaved differently from the covalent bonds.

2. **Describe** any problems you had with this modeling activity.

Science Content Standards

3.b Students know that compounds are formed by combining two or more different elements and that compounds have properties that are different from their constituent elements.

229

Science Content Standards

3.c Students know atoms and molecules form solids by building up repeating patterns, such as the crystal structure of NaCl or long-chain polymers.
Also Covers: 3.b, 7.c, 9.a, 9.e

Reading Guide

What You'll Learn

▶ **Explain** the bonding in metals.

▶ **Describe** how solids form in repeating patterns of atoms, ions, or molecules.

▶ **Describe** the crystal structure of sodium chloride.

Why It's Important

Knowing how atoms and molecules are arranged in solids will help you understand how particles undergo change.

Vocabulary

metal
metallic bond
malleability
ductility
crystal
unit cell
polymer
monomer

Review Vocabulary

element: a pure substance that can be identified by the number of protons in the nucleus of its atoms. (p. 195)

Forming Solids

 Atoms, ions, and molecules can link together to form large, repeating structures such as solid metals, ionic and molecular crystals, and polymers.

Real-World Reading Connection Imagine you pour a sack of identical round beads into a box. Each bead touches as many other beads as possible. The pattern of the beads in the box is similar to the way metal atoms pack together in a solid. Now think of a different pattern. The beads are strung together into a chain. The chain pattern is a lot like a polymer.

Metals

What do coins, beverage cans, bridges, and airplanes have in common? They are all made from metals. **Metals** are elements that are usually shiny, good conductors of heat and electricity, and solid at room temperature. They are located on the left and in the center of the periodic table. About two-thirds of all the elements are metals. Examples of common metals are gold, copper, aluminum, zinc, and iron. Metals are used to make jewelry, electrical wiring, and the skeletons of tall buildings, as shown in **Figure 10.** The properties of metals make them ideal for all of these uses and thousands more.

Reading Check Where are metals located on the periodic table?

Gold

Copper

Steel

Figure 10 Gold is malleable. Copper is ductile and conducts electricity. Steel, which is mostly iron, is strong.

Metallic Bonds

How are the atoms in a metal bonded? Metals have some features in common with ionic compounds. Like the atoms in ionic compounds, individual metal atoms lose electrons to become positive ions. Metals also have some features that resemble covalent compounds. Like covalent compounds, the atoms in metals share electrons. A **metallic bond** is a bond formed when many metal atoms share their pooled electrons. Metal atoms can bond to atoms of the same element, or they can bond with other metals. However, in metals, the electrons are not transferred directly to another atom. Instead, they move freely throughout the piece of metal. The electrons are not attached to any particular atom. They are a "sea of electrons." You can see in **Figure 11** how a sea of electrons surrounds an array of positive ions in a solid metal.

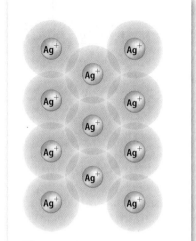

Figure 11 Electrons are free to move among all the metal ions, but the overall charge of the metal is zero.

Bonding and Properties Metallic bonding explains many of the properties of metals. Metals are good conductors of heat and electricity because their electrons are free to move. When a metal is hammered into a sheet or pulled into a wire, it does not break because the ions are in layers. The layers can slide past one another without losing their attraction to their pooled electrons.

Metal Atoms and Patterns Metal atoms combine in regular patterns in which some electrons are free to move from atom to atom. Each layer of metal atoms is arranged in a definite pattern. Recall the beads in the box. Like the beads, metal atoms in solids pack together as closely as possible in a regular, three-dimensional pattern. In **Figure 12,** you can see the pattern in which gold atoms pack together to make solid gold.

Figure 12 The atoms in this naturally crystallized gold are arranged in a regular cubic pattern.

Describe the arrangement of the gold atoms on a surface of the cube.

Figure 13 The six-sided shape of a snowflake reflects the pattern in which water molecules are arranged in the solid.

WORD ORIGIN
ductile
from Latin *ductilis;* means *that may be led or drawn*

Physical Properties of Metals

Think of the metal in a shiny new cooking pot. Like most metals, it has good electrical conductivity and thermal conductivity. The metal in the pot has a high melting point and a high boiling point. It is tough and strong. These properties are important in a material used for cooking pots.

The physical properties of metals make them valuable for many uses. Gold's color and shine make it a good material for jewelry. Gold also is one of the most malleable metals. **Malleability** is the ability of a material to be hammered or rolled into sheets. Another property of metals is ductility. **Ductility** is the ability of a substance to be pulled into wires. Metals also are good conductors of heat and electricity. Copper wire often is used as a conductor of electricity. Aluminum is used for aircraft bodies because it is tough and strong, and also light.

Crystals

The particles of different substances arrange themselves into different patterns when they solidify into crystals. A **crystal** is a regular, repeating arrangement of atoms, ions, or molecules. A snowflake, such as the one in **Figure 13,** is one of nature's most beautiful crystals. In a snowflake, water molecules freeze to form a six-sided pattern. A snowflake is an example of a molecular crystal.

In another type of crystal, the solid is held together by ionic bonds. Sodium chloride is an example of this type of crystal, which is called an ionic crystal. Diamond and quartz are examples of a third type of crystal in which particles are held together by covalent bonds. A crystal's structure is important because it helps scientists understand the crystal's physical properties. **Figure 14** shows examples of ionic crystals.

 Identify one molecular crystal, one ionic crystal, and one crystal held together with covalent bonds.

Figure 14 Aragonite, barite, and beryl are examples of minerals that are ionic compounds.

Figure 15 Sodium and chlorine ions alternate in the unit cell.

Infer how the arrangement of the ions in the cubic unit cell is reflected in the shape of the magnified crystal.

Concepts In Motion
To see a 3-D animation of the cubic arrangement of sodium chloride, visit ca8.msscience.com.

Crystal Patterns

Think of a page of stamps. The stamps are arranged next to each other in a pattern. The pattern might be five stamps across and four down. Except for the stamps along the edges, each stamp has four neighboring stamps, to the right, left, top, and bottom. Now think of a book of stamps. Every page has the same pattern. But now, each stamp also has one stamp above it and one below it. Like the pages and books of stamps, crystals are formed from repeating patterns of smaller parts. A **unit cell** is the smallest repeating pattern that shows how the atoms, ions, or molecules are arranged in a crystal. The unit cell for sodium chloride is shown in **Figure 15,** with a microscopic view of the crystalline surface. **Figure 16** shows photos of crystals created by atoms, ions, and molecules, and the regular patterns that form their crystal structures.

Sodium Chloride

Sodium chloride, NaCl, is an ionic crystal. Even a tiny grain of sodium chloride contains billions of sodium ions and chloride ions. Crystals of sodium chloride have a regular, cubic structure. The pattern in the sodium chloride crystal is simple. Sodium ions (Na^+) **alternate** with chloride ions (Cl^-) in a three-dimensional pattern. Ionic bonds hold the ions together. You can see this pattern in **Figure 15.** Unlike solid metals, ionic crystals are brittle. Only a small amount of pressure is needed to make a sodium chloride crystal crumble.

ACADEMIC VOCABULARY
alternate (ALL tuhr nayte)
(verb) to perform by turns or in succession
The students alternate reading from the text and answering the questions.

 Figure 15 In the sodium chloride unit cell, which ion, sodium or chloride, is at each corner?

Visualizing Crystal Structure

Figure 16 Many solids exist as crystals. Whether it is a tiny grain of table salt or a big block of quartz, a crystal's shape often is a reflection of the arrangement of its particles. Knowing a solid's crystal structure helps scientists understand its physical properties.

HEXAGONAL Quartz crystals are six-sided, just as a snowflake is. This is because the molecules that make up both quartz and snowflakes arrange themselves into hexagonal patterns.

CUBIC Fluorite, above, and sodium chloride form cube-shaped crystals. This shape is a reflection of the cube-shaped arrangement of the ions in the crystal.

Contributed by National Geographic

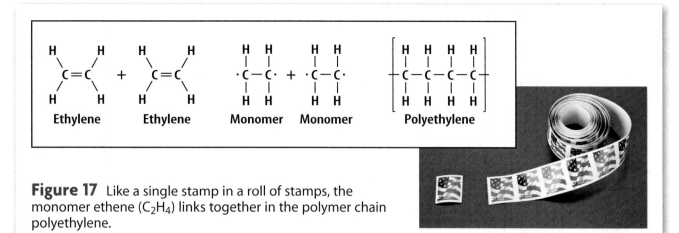

Figure 17 Like a single stamp in a roll of stamps, the monomer ethene (C_2H_4) links together in the polymer chain polyethylene.

What is a polymer?

Just as a crystal can be compared to the pattern of stamps in a book of stamps, a polymer can be compared to the pattern in a roll of stamps. In a roll of stamps, individual stamps are joined together to form a long chain. A **polymer** is a covalent compound made up of many small, repeating units linked together in a chain. The word *polymer* means "many parts." DNA is a polymer. So are plastics, synthetic fibers, many paints, and synthetic elastic compounds.

Stringlike Molecules

If a polymer is similar to a roll of stamps, a monomer is like a single stamp. A **monomer** is a small molecule that forms a link in a polymer chain. Often, the monomer is a gas at room temperature. Many hundreds of these small molecules link up by means of covalent bonds to form a solid polymer.

Synthetic Polymers

In **Figure 17,** you can see how the monomer ethene (EH theen), links together to form polyethylene (pah lee EH thuh leen). Each line connecting the atoms in the monomer and polymer represents one pair of shared electrons. Polyethylene is a synthetic, or manufactured, polymer. It is used for grocery bags and food wrap because it is lightweight and flexible. Many different synthetic polymers are made from monomers that are variations of the ethene monomer. For example, if fluorine atoms are substituted for each of the hydrogen atoms in ethene, an entirely different polymer is formed. This polymer has properties that make it useful as a nonstick coating for pots and pans.

 **Reading Check** What kind of chemical bond holds polymers together?

ACADEMIC VOCABULARY

consist (kuhn SIHST)
(verb) to be composed or
made up
*Some lunches consist of sand-
wiches and fruit.*

Natural Polymers

Did you notice in **Figure 17** that the polyethylene chain **consists** of carbon atoms? Recall that compounds based on carbon are called organic compounds. Organic compounds are the materials of life. Cells must contain three important kinds of natural organic polymers. These are proteins, carbohydrates, and nucleic acids, such as DNA. DNA is present in every living cell, and contains all the information needed for building and maintaining a living creature.

 Reading Check What element is found in all organic compounds?

Proteins and carbohydrates, which are made or used by your body, are also natural organic polymers. Proteins make up your hair, your skin, and your muscles. A protein's monomer is an amino acid, which includes carbon, nitrogen, and oxygen atoms. In carbohydrates, the monomer is a sugar molecule called a monosaccharide. Monosaccharides link up to form starches and cellulose. These long chains, called polysaccharides, include carbon, hydrogen, and oxygen atoms. **Figure 18** shows protein and carbohydrate polymers with their monomers.

Natural polymers are giant molecules. Nevertheless, the same kind of chemical bond holds these giant molecules together as binds together even a small molecule such as water. Both synthetic and natural organic polymers play important roles in your life.

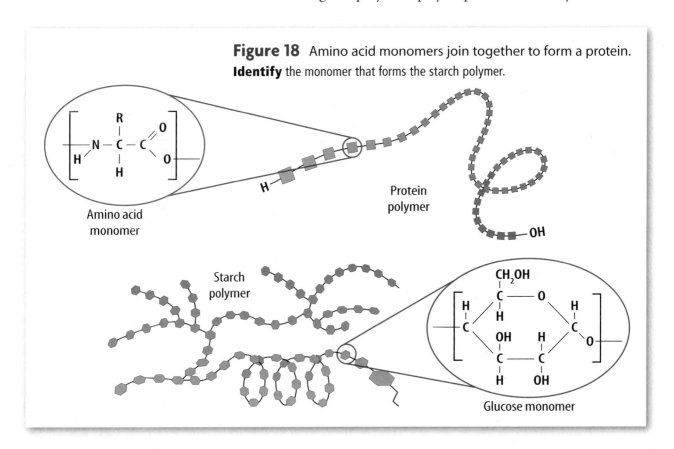

Figure 18 Amino acid monomers join together to form a protein. **Identify** the monomer that forms the starch polymer.

Amino acid monomer

Protein polymer

Starch polymer

Glucose monomer

What do you know about metals, crystals, and polymers?

Metal atoms are bound together in a solid by a sea of shared electrons. These electrons are free to move throughout the solid. They are responsible for the properties of metals, such as malleability, ductility, and conductivity. Crystals are solid substances in which atoms, ions, or molecules are arranged in a regular pattern called a unit cell. In sodium chloride, sodium ions and chloride ions alternate in rows and layers. Natural and synthetic polymers are stringlike molecules made up of repeating units of small molecules called monomers. In the next chapter, you will read more about solids, as well as the liquid and gas states of matter.

LESSON 2 Review

Summarize

Create your own lesson summary as you design a **study web**.

1. **Write** the lesson title, number, and page numbers at the top of a sheet of paper.

2. **Scan** the lesson to find the **red** main headings.

3. **Organize** these headings clockwise on branches around the lesson title.

4. **Review** the information under each **red** heading to design a branch for each **blue** subheading.

5. **List** 2–3 details, key terms, and definitions from each **blue** subheading on branches extending from the main heading branches.

 **ELA8: R 2.3**

Standards Check

Using Vocabulary

1. A(n) _____ is made up of repeating unit cells. **3.c**

2. Two properties of metals are _____ and _____. **7.c**

Understanding Main Ideas

3. What holds sodium chloride crystals together? **3.b**

   A. covalent bonds
   B. ionic bonds
   C. a sea of electrons
   D. metallic bonds

4. **Identify** each material as a metal, crystal, or polymer.

   A. a brittle solid with a high melting point
   B. a shiny, thin sheet that conducts heat
   C. a thin, clear, lightweight, and flexible wrap **3.c**

5. **Explain** what is meant by a sea of electrons. **3.b**

6. **Describe** how a monomer is related to a polymer. **3.c**

7. **Compare and Contrast** Copy and fill in the graphic organizer below to compare and contrast ionic crystals and solid metals, including the chemical bonds they form. **3.c**

[topic]	Similarities	Differences

Applying Science

8. **Create** a drawing showing how eight chloride ions and seven sodium ions might be arranged in a single layer of a crystal. **3.c**

9. **Design an experiment** to determine whether an unknown substance is a metal or an ionic crystal. **3.c**

 **Science**nline

For more practice, visit **Standards Check** at ca8.msscience.com.

Applying Math

Formula Units

3.b, 3.f

MA8: ALG 1.0

A formula unit is the base molecule that is used to build a compound. Use multiplication to find how many atoms are in a molecule.

Example

How many hydrogen (H) atoms, sulfur (S) atoms, and oxygen (O) atoms are in 3 molecules of sulfuric acid (H_2SO_4)?

1 Find the number of hydrogen atoms in one molecule of H_2SO_4. H_2SO_4 is made of:

2 hydrogen atoms–H_2
1 sulfur atom–S
4 oxygen atoms–O_4

One molecule of H_2SO_4 contains 2 hydrogen atoms, 1 sulfur atom, and 4 oxygen atoms.

Elements in Formula Unit	Number of Atoms
Sulfur (S)	1
Hydrogen (H)	2
Oxygen (O)	4

2 Now find the number of sulfur, hydrogen, and oxygen atoms in 3 molecules of H_2SO_4. Multiply each number of atoms by 3.

3 molecules $\times$ 2 hydrogen atoms each = 6 hydrogen atoms
3 molecules $\times$ 1 sulfur atom each = 3 sulfur atoms
3 molecules $\times$ 4 oxygen atoms each = 12 oxygen atoms

Answer: Three molecules of sulfuric acid contain 6 hydrogen atoms, 3 sulfur atoms, and 12 oxygen atoms.

Practice Problems

Use the following formula to answer questions 1 and 2.

$$Ca(OH)_2$$

1. How many atoms of hydrogen are in this compound?

2. How many atoms of calcium and oxygen are in 2 formula units of this compound?

Science nline

For more math practice, visit Math Practice at ca8.msscience.com.

DataLab

How are ionic radii and lattice energies of salts related?

The lattice energy of a crystal tells how strong the bonds in the crystal are. How do you think lattice energy is related to the distance between the atoms in the crystal?

Data

Atomic Radii (pm)						
Li	Na	K	F	Cl	Br	I
152	186	227	72	100	114	133

Data Analysis

1. **Calculate** For each ionic compound in the table, add the radii of its two elements. This is the distance between the atoms in each crystal.

2. **Create** a graph with "Distance between atoms" on the x-axis and "Lattice energy" on the y-axis.

3. **Determine** the relationship between distance and lattice energy.

4. **Predict** the approximate lattice energy for NaBr.

 Science Content Standards

3.b Students know that compounds are formed by combining two or more different elements and that compounds have properties that are different from their constituent elements.

9.e Construct appropriate graphs from data and develop quantitative statements about the relationships between variables.

 **MA8:** ALG 6.0

Lattice Energies	
Salt	Energy (kJ/mol)
LiF	1,036
NaF	923
KF	821
LiCl	853
NaCl	786
KCl	715
LiBr	807
NaBr	
KBr	682
LiI	757
NaI	704
KI	649

Growing Crystals

Materials

alum
distilled water
salt
sugar
filter paper
string
hot plate
beaker
spatula
hand lens

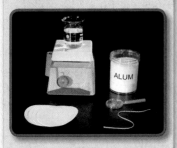

Safety Precautions

Problem

Crystals of ionic compounds can be made to grow from super-saturated solutions.

Form a Hypothesis

Read the procedure. What conditions do you think will produce the best crystals? Write a hypothesis to explain your prediction.

Collect Data and Make Observations

1. Read and complete a safety form.
2. Thoroughly clean and rinse all equipment with distilled water before starting. Impurities from dirty equipment might prevent the crystals from growing.
3. Use a pencil with a 7-cm string attached as the framework for growing crystals. Dangle the framework into the supersaturated solution. You may want to put a seed crystal, a small crystal of the same chemical, on the string. Make sure that you do not use metal, which could react with the crystal compound. Make sure the framework is very clean.
4. A supersaturated solution can be made by stirring as much solute, or dissolving substance as possible into boiling water. Add solute spoonful by spoonful to 100 mL of boiling water until it no longer dissolves. If undissolved solute settles on the bottom, carefully pour your solution into a clean beaker.

5. When growing the crystals, it is best to leave them undisturbed in an area with no vibrations. Cover the beaker to protect the growing crystals from dust. You may choose to grow your crystals at room temperature or in a refrigerator or freezer.

6. Leave your crystal setup for several hours or overnight. When you return to the lab, record observations about your own crystals and those of other lab groups.

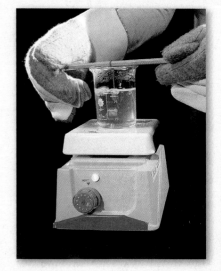

Analyze and Conclude

1. **Identify** the compound that grew the best crystals.

2. **Describe** which condition grew the best crystals.

3. **Describe** your experiment and those of your classmates. Make note of similarities and differences in procedures and results. Explain how you think that each of the changes in procedure affected the product.

4. **Infer** Do you think there is a difference in the way crystals in the sugar (molecular compound) and the salts (ionic compounds) grew? Explain, using your observations.

5. **Draw a diagram** on how you think the crystals grow on a molecular level.

6. **Describe** the errors that were made. How could the procedures have been improved?

Communicate

Write a procedure for growing crystals of rock candy at home. Imagine that your procedure would be part of a book of fun experiments to be done in the kitchen.

 Science Content Standards

3.c Students know atoms and molecules form solids by building up repeating patterns, such as the crystal structure of NaCl or long-chain polymers.
9.a Plan and conduct a scientific investigation to test a hypothesis.

Real World Science

Science & Career

CFCs and the Ozone Layer

Mario J. Molina was born in Mexico. He conducted research on chlorofluorocarbon at the University of California–Berkeley in the 1970s. Molina, along with two colleagues, discovered that CFCs were depleting the ozone layer. In 1995, he was awarded the Nobel Prize in Chemistry for his work on the formation and decomposition of ozone in the atmosphere.

Mario J. Molina Visit **Careers** at ca8.msscience.com to reasearch Molina's accomplishments. Write a 400–500-word biography of Mario J. Molina's life. Include facts about his childhood, education, and research background.

ELA8: W 2.1

Science & Technology

Sweeter Than Sugar

Sucralose is a molecule made by combining sucrose (sugar) and chlorine atoms. This molecule, which was first synthesized in 1976, is approximately 500–600 times sweeter than sugar.
Aspartame is another sugar substitute; it is made from the amino acid phenylalanine. This molecule was discovered in 1965 by accident. It is approximately 180 times sweeter than sugar.

Sugar Substitutes Go to **Technology** at ca8.msscience.com to gather information about sucralose and aspartame. Create a table on the uses, properties, and side effects of each molecule.

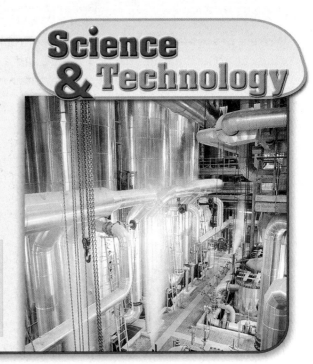

Discovering DNA's Structure

In the early 1950s, Rosalind Franklin, Francis Crick, and James Watson were trying to discover the shape of the DNA molecule. Using X-ray crystallography Rosalind Franklin determined that DNA had a double-helix structure, meaning that it contains two strands that are intertwined. James Watson and Francis Crick used this information to construct the first model of DNA.

The History of DNA Create a time line of the important DNA discoveries in the past 200 years. Visit **History** at ca8.msscience.com to find information about important DNA advancements.

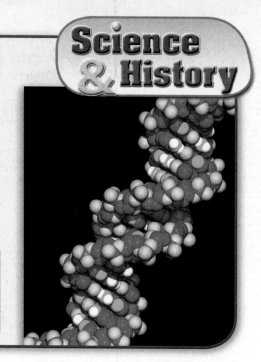

THE HUMAN GENOME PROJECT

A genome is all the genetic information of an organism. The human genome project set out to identify the nucleotide sequences of every gene on every human chromosome. The project was started in 1986 and completed in 2003.

The Future of Medicine How do you think the human genome project will be used to diagnose and treat diseases in the future? Write a futuristic newspaper article about the potential benefits of the human genome project.

ELA8: W 2.1

The BIG Idea Atoms of two or more elements can combine to form compounds that have different properties from those of the elements that formed them.

Lesson 1 How Atoms Form Compounds
3.a, 3.b, 3.f

Main Idea Compounds are chemical combinations of elements that have properties different from the elements that formed them.

- Atoms of different elements can combine to form compounds.
- The properties of a compound usually are different from the properties of the elements that make it up.
- Ionic bonds usually involve the transfer of electrons from a metal atom to a nonmetal atom.
- Ionic compounds are usually solid at room temperature. They have relatively high melting and boiling points. They are soluble in water and their solutions conduct electricity.
- A pair of electrons is shared in a covalent bond.
- Two pairs of electrons are shared in a double covalent bond. In a triple covalent bond, three pairs of electrons are shared.

- **chemical bond** (p. 220)
- **chemical formula** (p. 219)
- **compound** (p. 218)
- **covalent bond** (p. 225)
- **ionic bond** (p. 220)
- **molecule** (p. 219)
- **valence** (p. 223)

Lesson 2 Forming Solids
3.b, 3.c, 7.c, 9.a, 9.e

Main Idea Atoms, ions, and molecules can link together to form large, repeating structures such as solid metals, ionic and molecular crystals, and polymers.

- Solid metals are held together by metallic bonds.
- Metallic bonds account for many of the properties of solid metals.
- A single crystal has billions of atoms, ions, or molecules held together in a regular pattern.
- Crystals can be held together by either ionic bonds or covalent bonds.
- Polymers are long, stringlike molecules made up of small monomers linked together in a chain.
- Natural polymers such as proteins and carbohydrates contain the element carbon.

- **crystal** (p. 232)
- **ductility** (p. 232)
- **malleability** (p.232)
- **metal** (p. 230)
- **metallic bond** (p. 231)
- **monomer** (p. 235)
- **polymer** (p. 235)
- **unit cell** (p. 233)

Download quizzes, key terms, and flash cards from ca8.msscience.com.

 Interactive Tutor ca8.msscience.com

Linking Vocabulary and Main Ideas

Use vocabulary terms from page 244 to complete this concept map.

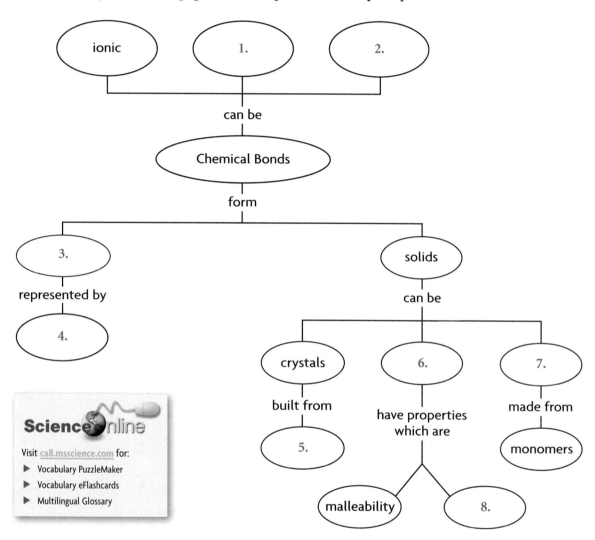

Using Vocabulary

Describe the relationship between each pair of terms.

9. monomer and polymer

10. covalent bond and valence

11. ductility and maleability

12. chemical bond and ionic bond

Match a vocabulary term to each definition below.

13. a bond formed when many metal atoms share their pooled electrons

14. a regular, repeating arrangement of atoms, ions, or molecules

15. uses atomic symbols and subscripts to show the elements and the number of atoms of each element that combine to form a compound

Understanding Main Ideas

Choose the word or phrase that best completes the statement.

1. What does an ionic compound usually contain besides a positively charged metal ion?
   A. a negatively charged nonmetal ion
   B. a positively charged nonmetal ion
   C. a negatively charged metal ion
   D. a positively charged metal ion   3.b

2. What is most of the matter around you made of?
   A. pure elements
   B. mixture of pure elements
   C. compounds
   D. crystals   3.b

3. The illustration below shows the electronic structure for carbon.

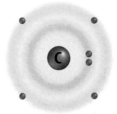

Carbon (C)

   Determine the number of valence electrons carbon has.
   A. zero
   B. two
   C. four
   D. six   3.a

4. State the number of dots in a Lewis dot diagram for the Group 17 element fluorine.
   A. 2 dots
   B. 3 dots
   C. 7 dots
   D. 8 dots   3.a

5. Name the type of bond that carbon will NOT form.
   A. single bond
   B. ionic bond
   C. double bond
   D. triple bond   3.b

6. What is an example of a synthetic polymer?
   A. polyethylene
   B. polysaccharide
   C. carbohydrate
   D. protein   3.b

7. Which does the illustration represent?

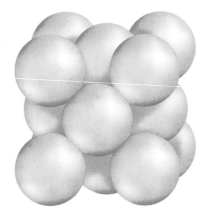

   A. an ionic crystal
   B. a covalent crystal
   C. a metallic solid
   D. a synthetic polymer   3.c

8. When an atom is chemically stable, how many electrons are in its outer energy level?
   A. 8
   B. 7
   C. 4
   D. 1   3.a

9. On the periodic table, which groups of elements tend to form positive ions?
   A. Group 1 and Group 2
   B. Group 16 and Group 17
   C. Group13 and Group 14
   D. Group 16 and Group18   3.b

10. What structure will atoms have after losing or gaining electrons?
    A. a crystal
    B. a polymer
    C. a binary compound
    D. a noble gas   3.a

Applying Science

11. **Compare** the ways in which the elements sodium and carbon form chemical bonds.   **3.b**

12. **Predict** whether an element with a valence of 8 is most likely form ionic bonds, covalent bonds, or no chemical bonds with other atoms. Explain.   **3.b**

13. **Propose an explanation** for why the element carbon, rather than sodium, is important in forming natural polymers.   **3.c**

14. **Classify** the unknown substance described in the table of properties as a solid metal, ionic crystal, covalent crystal, or polymer.   **3.c**

Properties of an Unknown Solid	
Hardness	brittle
Melting point	very high
Water solubilty	very soluble
Electrical conductivity in a water solution	yes

15. **Design** an experiment to compare the properties of sodium chloride and sand.   **3.c**

16. **Propose an explanation** for why chlorine does not form double bonds.   **3.b**

17. **Explain** why Groups 1 and 2 form many compounds with Groups 16 and 17.   **3.f**

18. **Think Critically** Silicon has four electrons in its outer energy level. What type of bond is silicon most likely to form with other elements? Explain.   **3.b**

WRITING in Science

19. **Write** rules for a new game that you and your classmates could play to increase your understanding of chemical bonds.   **ELA8: W 2.6**

Cumulative Review

20. **Describe** the location of the neutrons and protons in an atom.   **3.a**

21. **Explain** why Rutherford's model of the atom is called the nuclear atom.   **3.a**

22. **Explain** what is meant by the electron cloud atom.   **3.a**

Applying Math

Use the following formulas to answer questions 23–27.

Formula Table			
Chemical Formula	C_6H_6	H_2O	NaCl
Chemical Name	Benzene	Water	Sodium chloride

23. How many atoms of hydrogen are in 2 molecules of benzene?   **MA8: ALG 1.0**

24. How many atoms of carbon are in 3 molecules of benzene?   **MA8: ALG 1.0**

25. How many atoms of oxygen are in 3 molecules of water?   **MA8: ALG 1.0**

26. How many atoms of chloride are in 6 molecules of sodium chloride?   **MA8: ALG 1.0**

1 Sodium combines with fluorine to produce sodium fluoride (NaF), an active ingredient in toothpaste. In this form, sodium has the electron configuration of which other element?

A neon

B magnesium

C lithium

D chlorine `3.b`

2 The illustration below shows the electron configuration for potassium.

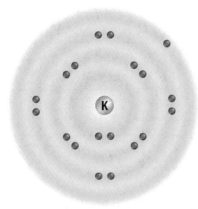

How many electrons does potassium need to gain or lose to become stable?

A gain 1

B gain 2

C lose 1

D lose 2 `3.a`

3 What are the small units that make up polymers?

A monomers

B crystal

C unit cell

D chain `3.c`

4 Which elements are least likely to react with other elements?

A metals

B noble gases

C nonmetals

D semimetals `3.b`

5 What type of bond connects the atoms in a molecule of nitrogen gas (N_2)?

A ionic

B single

C double

D triple `3.b`

Use the illustration below to answer questions 6 and 7.

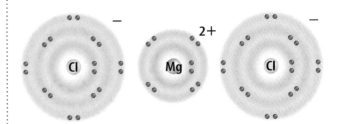

6 Which term best describes the type of bonding in magnesium chloride?

A ionic

B pooling

C metallic

D covalent `3.b`

7 How many electrons did magnesium give to each chlorine atom?

A 0

B 1

C 2

D 3 `3.a`

8 What is the number of the group in which the elements have a stable outer energy level?

A 1

B 13

C 16

D 18   3.a

9 Why are metals good conductors of heat and electricity?

A They have loosely bound electrons within the atom.

B They have luster and malleability.

C They are composed of mixtures

D They have a shiny appearance.   7.c

10 The illustration below shows a sodium chloride crystal.

Na⁺
Cl⁻

What type of crystal is sodium chloride?

A ionic

B covalent

C metallic

D molecular   3.c

11 What property allows metals to be shaped into a musical instrument?

A conductivity

B ductility

C luster

D malleability   7.c

12 Which molecule is a synthetic polymer?

A DNA

B polyethylene

C carbohydrates

D proteins   3.c

13 What is the electron diagram for the ionic compound sodium fluoride (NaF)?

A $\left[Na \right]^+ \left[F \right]^-$

B $\left[Na \right]^+ \left[:\ddot{F}: \right]^-$

C $\left[Na: \right]^+ \left[\ddot{F}: \right]^-$

D $\left[Na: \right]^+ \left[\dot{\ddot{F}}: \right]^-$ 3.b

14 Which describes what is represented by the symbol Cl⁻?

A an ionic compound

B a polar molecule

C a negative ion

D a positive ion   3.b

15 When magnesium loses its valence electrons, it has the atomic structure of what element?

A neon

B fluorine

C argon

D sodium   3.a

States of Matter

The BIG Idea

Matter can undergo a physical change from one state to another as an increase or decrease in thermal energy changes the motion of its particles.

LESSON 1 3.d, 3.e
Solids, Liquids, and Gases
Main Idea The state of matter depends on the motion of its particles.

LESSON 2 3.d, 3.e, 9.e, 9.g
Changes in States of Matter
Main Idea Changes in energy can cause matter to change from one state to another.

Moving Up a Slippery Slope

This climber is actually slowly moving up a waterfall. In the winter this waterfall in the Swiss Alps mountains has turned into solid ice. Even though ice and water contain the same atoms and molecules, they have different properties. Why are the properties of ice and water so different?

Science Journal List three differences between ice and water.

Model for Particle Movement

Matter can exist as a solid, a liquid, or a gas. How do particles move in each state of matter?

Procedure

1. Complete a lab safety form.

2. Using **masking tape** and a **meterstick,** mark off a 4-m square area in your classroom. Have four people move about the marked-off area.

3. Divide the space in half and mark with masking tape. Have the same four people move about the marked-off area.

4. Repeat step 3.

Think About This

- **Describe** how the movement of people changed as they got closer together.

3.e

Properties of Matter
Make the following Foldable to organize the properties of the three states of matter.

▷ **STEP 1 Fold** a sheet of paper into thirds lengthwise and fold the top down about 3 cm.

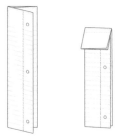

▷ **STEP 2 Unfold** and **draw** lines along all folds. Label as shown.

Reading *Skill*

Reviewing As you read this chapter, record the properties of each state of matter in the appropriate column. Include information about shape, volume, attractive forces, and particle movement. Include an illustration of the particles in each type of matter.

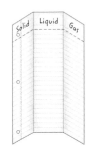

Science Online

Visit ca8.msscience.com to:

▶ view **Concepts in Motion**

▶ explore Virtual Labs

▶ access content-related Web links

▶ take the Standards Check

Get Ready to Read

Questioning

①Learn It! Asking questions helps you to understand what you read. As you read, think about the questions you'd like answered. Often you can find the answer in the next paragraph or lesson. Learn to ask good questions by asking *who, what, when, where, why, and how.*

②Practice It! Read the following passage from Lesson 2.

> One way to measure temperature is to use a liquid thermometer. Some thermometers have a red liquid inside a glass tube. When the liquid gets warmer, the particles in the liquid begin to move faster. The particles then get farther apart and take up more space. This causes the liquid to expand and rise in the tube.
>
> —*from page 262*

Here are some questions you might ask about this paragraph:

- Where is the liquid being discussed located?
- When do the particles in the liquid move faster?
- Why does the liquid expand?

③Apply It! As you read the chapter, look for answers to lesson headings that are in the form of questions.

Target Your Reading

Reading Tip

Test yourself. Create questions and then read to find answers to your own questions.

Use this to focus on the main ideas as you read the chapter.

1 **Before you read** the chapter, respond to the statements below on your worksheet or on a numbered sheet of paper.

- Write an **A** if you **agree** with the statement.
- Write a **D** if you **disagree** with the statement.

2 **After you read** the chapter, look back to this page to see if you've changed your mind about any of the statements.

- If any of your answers changed, explain why.
- Change any false statements into true statements.
- Use your revised statements as a study guide.

Science Online

Print a worksheet of this page at ca8.msscience.com.

Before You Read A or D	Statement	After You Read A or D
	1 All matter is made of particles that are moving at the same speed.	
	2 The particles in a solid are free to move and flow past each other.	
	3 Particles are closer together in a gas than they are in a solid.	
	4 Particles in matter are moving in different directions.	
	5 A thermometer measures the thermal energy in a substance.	
	6 Particles of matter have both potential energy and kinetic energy.	
	7 The freezing point of a substance is the temperature at which the substance changes from a gas to a liquid.	
	8 The temperature of a substance increases when the particles in the substance move faster.	

Science Content Standards

3.d Students know the states of matter (solid, liquid, gas) depend on molecular motion.

3.e Students know that in solids the atoms are closely locked in position and can only vibrate; in liquids the atoms and molecules are more loosely connected and can collide with and move past one another; and in gases the atoms and molecules are free to move independently, colliding frequently.

Reading Guide

What *You'll Learn*

▶ **Recognize** that matter is made of particles that always are moving.

▶ **Compare** the motion of particles in solids, liquids, and gases.

▶ **Compare** the arrangement of particles in solids, liquids, and gases.

Why *It's Important*

All matter that surrounds you is composed of particles that are in constant motion.

Vocabulary
random motion
solid
liquid
gas

Review Vocabulary

matter: anything that takes up space and has mass (Chapter 4)

Solids, Liquids, and Gases

Main Idea The state of matter depends on the motion of its particles.

Real-World Reading Connection A glass of ice-cold lemonade may be just the thing to cool you off after a hard game of soccer. This drink also contains two states of matter. Lemonade is a liquid that easily flows from a glass when you tip it. Solid ice keeps its shape until it melts. The air in a soccer ball is a third state of matter. Air is a gas that expands to fill the ball.

What are states of matter?

The ice, soft drink, and bubbles in **Figure 1** are examples of the three familiar states of matter: solids, liquids, and gases. The ice is a solid, the soft drink is a liquid, and the bubbles are filled with a gas. These are the three states of matter that usually occur on Earth.

Stars, such as the Sun, are made of another state of matter called plasma. The plasma state is similar to the gas state and usually occurs at high temperatures. A plasma is made of atoms that have been broken apart and contains electrically charged particles. Although plasmas can be found in lightning and in fluorescent lights, the plasma state is not common on Earth.

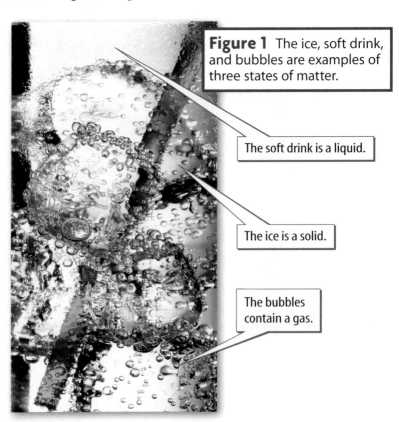

Figure 1 The ice, soft drink, and bubbles are examples of three states of matter.

The soft drink is a liquid.

The ice is a solid.

The bubbles contain a gas.

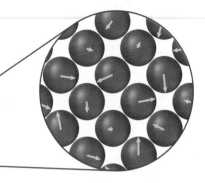

Figure 2 The particles in all matter are moving in random motion. They move in different directions and at different speeds.

Explain why an object does not move when its particles are in random motion.

Particles in Matter

Recall from Chapter 4 that all matter is made of very small particles called atoms. In Chapter 5 you read that atoms can combine to form molecules, which are also very small particles of matter. All objects, such as the flower shown in **Figure 2,** are made of these particles.

In all objects and materials, these tiny particles of matter are always in motion. Even though the flower in **Figure 2** is not moving, the atoms and molecules in the flower are always moving. Some particles move to the left or the right, some move up and down, and some move in other directions.

Particles in matter move in a type of motion called random motion. In **random motion,** particles can move in any direction and can have different speeds. In any object, the number of particles moving in one direction is always equal to the number of particles moving in the opposite direction. As particles move, they also collide with other particles. These collisions can change a particle's direction of motion and its speed.

 In random motion, how are particles moving?

Particles Attract

As they are moving, atoms and molecules usually exert a pull, or an attractive force, on each other. These forces tend to pull particles closer together. Recall from Chapter 4 that atoms contain positively charged protons and negatively charged electrons. These electric charges can cause attractions between the atoms and molecules in matter. If particles move closer together, the attractive forces between them become stronger. As they move farther apart, the attraction between them becomes weaker.

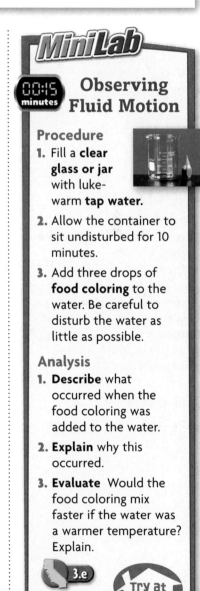

MiniLab

00:15 minutes

Observing Fluid Motion

Procedure

1. Fill a **clear glass or jar** with luke- warm **tap water.**

2. Allow the container to sit undisturbed for 10 minutes.

3. Add three drops of **food coloring** to the water. Be careful to disturb the water as little as possible.

Analysis

1. **Describe** what occurred when the food coloring was added to the water.

2. **Explain** why this occurred.

3. **Evaluate** Would the food coloring mix faster if the water was a warmer temperature? Explain.

3.e

Try at Home

Figure 3 The particles that make up a solid vibrate in fixed locations. A solid has a fixed shape and a fixed volume.

Solids

Why is the dumbbell in **Figure 3** a solid? If you hold the dumbbell in your hand, it doesn't flow or make a puddle like water does. If you place the dumbbell in a box, its shape doesn't change to match the shape of the box. Like all solids, the volume and shape of a dumbell do not change. A **solid** is matter with a fixed shape and a fixed volume.

SCIENCE USE v. COMMON USE

state

Science Use a condition of matter. *Three common states of matter are solid, liquid, and gas.*
Common Use a condition of mind or being. *Before the big test, the students were in a nervous state.*

The Forces Between Particles in a Solid

The motion of the particles and the strength of the attractive forces between them determine whether a substance is a solid, a liquid, or a gas. As in all matter, the particles in a solid always are in motion. However, the particles in a solid are so close together that the attractive forces between them are strong.

 In a solid, why are the attractive forces between particles strong?

The Motion of Particles in a Solid

The particles in a solid are attracted to each other by strong forces that keep the particles close together. Because the forces between particles are strong, particles in a solid cannot move very far from each other. The motion of the particles in a solid is shown in **Figure 3.** Each particle moves only a short distance back and forth between neighboring particles. As a result, the particles in a solid stay in nearly the same position, vibrating back and forth in all directions. Because the particles in a solid don't move from one place to another, the shape and volume of the solid remain fixed.

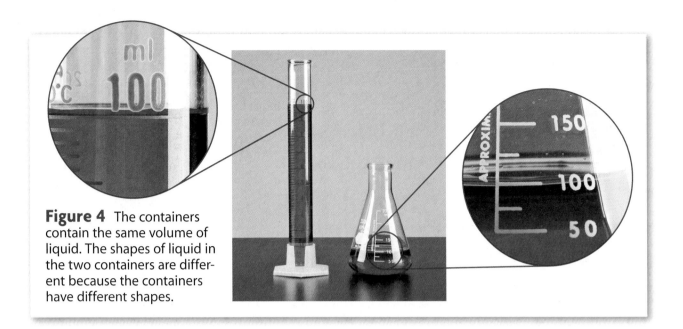

Figure 4 The containers contain the same volume of liquid. The shapes of liquid in the two containers are different because the containers have different shapes.

Liquids

Unlike a solid, a liquid can flow and does not have a fixed shape. As shown in **Figure 4,** a liquid has the shape of the container in which it is placed. A **liquid** is matter with a fixed volume but not a fixed shape.

The Forces Between Particles in a Liquid

The attractive forces between particles in a liquid are weaker than they are in a solid. These forces are not strong enough to keep the particles in fixed positions. As a result, the particles in a liquid move more freely than they do in a solid.

Motion of Particles in a Liquid

Figure 5 shows how the particles in a liquid move. In a solid, a particle stays in one place and moves a short distance back and forth. In a liquid, particles can move past neighboring particles. Because the particles in a liquid can move from one place to another, a liquid can flow and change shape. However, the forces between particles in a liquid are strong enough to keep the particles close to each other. This causes the volume of the liquid to remain fixed.

Figure 5 Particles in a liquid are close together, but can slide past each other.

Compare the motion of particles in a solid and in a liquid.

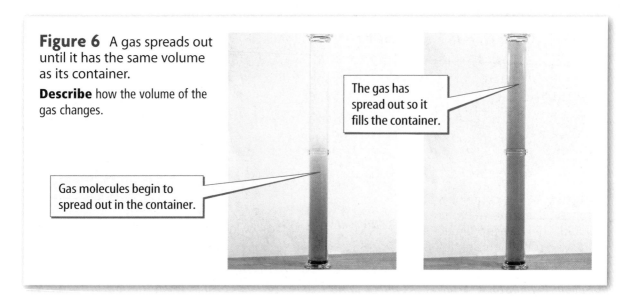

Figure 6 A gas spreads out until it has the same volume as its container.

Describe how the volume of the gas changes.

The gas has spread out so it fills the container.

Gas molecules begin to spread out in the container.

WORD ORIGIN ·············

gas
from Greek *khaos;* means *empty space*

·············

Gases

Every second you are surrounded by a gas—the air around you. When you breathe, you force this gas to flow into and out of your lungs. Even though a gas can flow, it is different from a liquid. A **gas** is matter that has no fixed volume and no fixed shape.

Changes in Shape and Volume

Gases and liquids do not have a fixed shape. Unlike solids or liquids, a gas also does not have a fixed volume. If any amount of gas is put in a container, the gas expands until it fills the container, as shown in **Figure 6.** This means that the shape and the volume of the gas depend on the shape and volume of the container the gas is in.

Forces Between Particles in a Gas

The particles in a gas are much farther apart than the particles in a solid or a liquid, as shown in **Figure 7.** Because the particles in a gas are so far apart, the forces between these particles are weak. As a result, the particles in a gas are not held together and move freely past each other.

Figure 7 Particles in a gas are far apart and move freely.

Motion of Particles in a Gas

Inside a container, gas particles move in random motion from place to place. As gas particles move, they collide with each other and with the sides of the container. Between collisions, a gas particle moves in a straight line. However, a collision can make the particle move in a different direction and can also change its speed. Because the particles in a gas can move freely from place to place, a gas does not have a fixed shape.

 What can cause the direction and speed of a particle in a gas to change?

Unlike particles in solids and liquids, gas particles are not held together by attractive forces. As a result, gas particles spread out until they are evenly **distributed** throughout a container. No matter how large the container, the volume of a gas is always the same as the volume of the container the gas is in. **Table 1** summarizes some of the differences between solids, liquids, and gases.

ACADEMIC VOCABULARY ····
distribute (dih STRIH byewt)
(verb) to spread out to cover something
Sandra distributed the seeds throughout the garden.

Concepts In Motion
Interactive Table Organize information about solids, liquids, and gases at ca8.msscience.com.

Table 1 Familiar States of Matter	
State of Matter	**Example**
Solid • fixed shape • fixed volume • particles are close together • strong attractive forces between particles • particles vibrate in all directions	
Liquid • no fixed shape, a liquid takes the shape of container • fixed volume • particles are close together • attractive forces between particles are weaker in liquids than in solids • particles are free to move past neighboring particles	
Gas • no fixed shape • no fixed volume, a gas expands to fill volume of container • particles are very far apart • extremely weak attractive forces between particles • particles move freely	

What have you learned?

All matter is made of particles, such as atoms or molecules, that are in random motion. In solids, the particles are close together and they can only vibrate in place. The attractive force between the particles in a solid is strong. Because of these strong forces, the shape and volume of a solid remain fixed.

The attraction between the particles in liquids is weaker than the attraction between the particles in solids. Because of the weaker attractive forces between particles, particles in liquids can move past each other. As a result, liquids are able to flow and to take the shape of their container.

In gases, the particles are very far apart and the attractive forces between them are weak. The particles of a gas move freely and collide with the walls of its container and other gas particles. Because the particles move freely, gases have no fixed shape or volume.

LESSON 1 Review

Summarize

Create your own lesson summary as you write a script for a **television news report.**

1. **Review** the text after the **red** main headings and write one sentence about each. These are the headlines of your broadcast.

2. **Review** the text and write 2–3 sentences about each **blue** subheading. These sentences should tell *who, what, when, where,* and *why* information about each **red** heading.

3. **Include** descriptive details in your report, such as names of reporters and local places and events.

4. **Present** your news report to other classmates alone or with a team.

ELA8: LS 2.1

Standards Check

Using Vocabulary

1. Write the definitions of *solid, liquid,* and *gas* in your own words. **3.d**

2. In _____, particles can move in any direction. **3.d**

Understanding Main Ideas

3. Which state of matter is found in fluorescent lights and lightning strikes, but is relatively uncommon on Earth? **3.d**

   A. gas
   B. liquid
   C. plasma
   D. solid

4. **Summarize** the motion of particles in solids, liquids, and gases. **3.e**

5. **Compare** Copy and fill in the graphic organizer below and compare the distance between particles in solids, liquids, and gases. **3.e**

Solids	
Liquids	
Gases	

6. **Compare** the attractive forces between particles in a solid and in a gas. **3.e**

Applying Science

7. **Determine** how the volume of air in a room would change if the volume of the room were doubled. **3.e**

Science Online
For more practice, visit **Standards Check** at ca8.msscience.com.

Science Content Standards

3.d Students know the states of matter (solid, liquid, gas) depend on molecular motion.

3.e Students know that in solids the atoms are closely locked in position and can only vibrate; in liquids the atoms and molecules are more loosely connected and can collide with and move past one another; and in gases the atoms and molecules are free to move independently, colliding frequently.
Also covers: 9.e, 9.g

Reading Guide

What *You'll Learn*

▶ **Compare** melting and freezing.

▶ **Compare** vaporization and condensation.

Why *It's Important*

The energy released when water changes from a gas to a liquid helps produce storms.

Vocabulary

temperature
thermal energy
melting point
freezing point
vaporization
boiling
boiling point
evaporation
condensation
sublimation
deposition

Review Vocabulary

potential energy: the energy an object has due to its position (Grade 6)

Changes in States of Matter

Main Idea Changes in energy can cause matter to change from one state to another.

Real-World Reading Connection Changes in the weather can cause changes in states of matter. In early spring, snow melts into liquid water. A summer rain leaves puddles of water on the sidewalk, but the warm Sun makes the puddles evaporate into a gas.

Temperature, Thermal Energy, and Heat

Ice and liquid water are different states of the same substance. They both are made from particles that are water molecules. But how can an ice cube change into liquid water? A change from one state of matter to another is a result of two things. One is changes in the motion of the particles. The other is the strength of the forces among particles.

Moving Particles and Kinetic Energy

Recall that moving objects, such as a car or a train, have kinetic energy. The kinetic energy of an object increases as its speed increases. Even when an object is not moving, the particles in the object are in random motion. As a result, these particles also have kinetic energy. For example, the particles in the balloon shown in **Figure 8** have kinetic energy even though the balloon is not moving.

Figure 8 The gas particles inside the balloon have energy because they are moving.

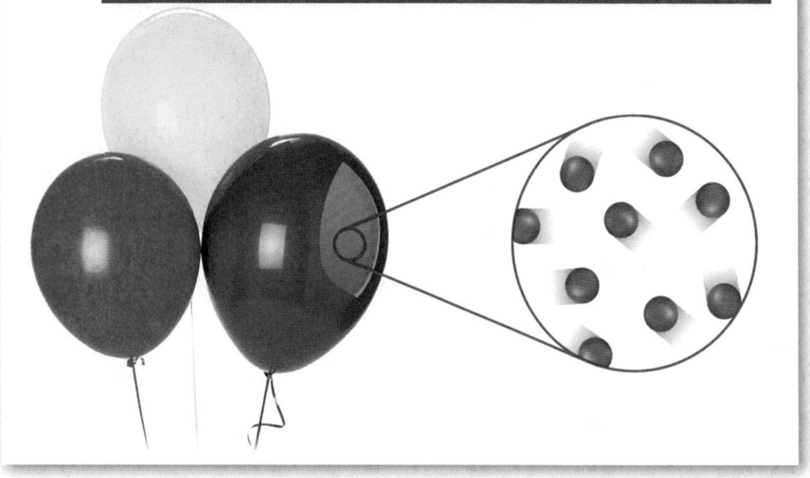

Figure 9 The temperature of a substance increases as the particles move faster and have more kinetic energy.

Compare the motion of air particles inside and outside the balloon.

Temperature and Average Kinetic Energy

The air inside the hot-air balloon in **Figure 9** has a higher temperature than the air outside. **Temperature** is a measure of the average kinetic energy of the particles in a material. This means that the average kinetic energy of particles inside the balloon is greater than the average kinetic energy of particles outside. As a result, particles inside the balloon are moving faster on average than particles outside the balloon. Particles in matter move faster as the temperature increases.

Measuring Temperature

One way to measure temperature is to use a liquid thermometer. Some thermometers have a red liquid inside a glass tube. When the liquid gets warmer, the particles in the liquid begin to move faster. The particles then get farther apart and take up more space. This causes the liquid to expand and the liquid rises in the tube.

The marks on a thermometer tell you the temperature in degrees. **Figure 10** shows three common temperature scales. The range between the temperatures at which water freezes and boils on the different scales is shown. This range is divided into 180 degrees on the Fahrenheit scale. It is divided into 100 degrees on the Celsius and Kelvin scales. The Fahrenheit scale is widely used in the United States, but the Celsius scale is usually used in other countries. The Celsius and Kelvin scales are used in science.

Figure 10 The boiling and freezing points of water are different on the Fahrenheit, Celsius, and Kelvin temperature scales.

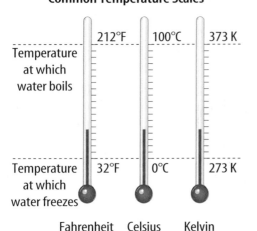

Common Temperature Scales

Temperature at which water boils — 212°F · 100°C · 373 K

Temperature at which water freezes — 32°F · 0°C · 273 K

Fahrenheit · Celsius · Kelvin

The ball has more potential energy.

The ball has less potential energy.

Particles of matter have more potential energy.

Particles of matter have less potential energy.

Higher Potential Energy

Lower Potential Energy

Particles of Matter and Potential Energy

In addition to having kinetic energy, the particles in a substance have potential energy as a result of the forces that they exert on each other. Potential energy decreases as particles get closer together and increases as particles get farther apart. A ball held above the ground has potential energy, as shown in **Figure 11.** The amount of potential energy depends on the distance between the ball and Earth. If you let the ball go, its potential energy decreases as it gets closer to the ground. In the same way, the potential energy of particles in matter decreases when the particles are closer together.

 What can cause the potential energy of particles in matter to increase?

Thermal Energy

A substance also has thermal energy. **Thermal energy** includes both the kinetic energy and potential energy of the particles. Different states of matter have different amounts of thermal energy. Compared to the solid state, the particles of a substance in the gas state move faster and are farther apart. These particles have more kinetic and potential energy than the particles in the solid state. This means that the thermal energy of the substance in the gas state is greater than the thermal energy in the solid state. For any given substance, the particles have the most thermal energy in the gas state and the least thermal energy in the solid state.

Figure 11 The potential energy of the ball depends on the distance between the ball and Earth. The potential energy of particles in matter depends on the distance between them.

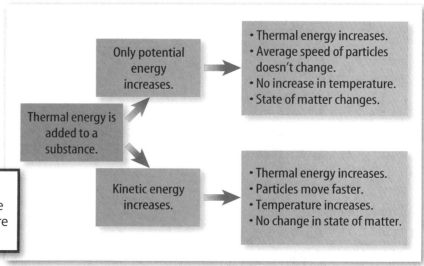

Figure 12 Adding thermal energy to a substance can cause either an increase in temperature or a change of state.

The diagram shows:

Thermal energy is added to a substance.

→ Only potential energy increases.
→ • Thermal energy increases.
• Average speed of particles doesn't change.
• No increase in temperature.
• State of matter changes.

→ Kinetic energy increases.
→ • Thermal energy increases.
• Particles move faster.
• Temperature increases.
• No change in state of matter.

ACADEMIC VOCABULARY
remove (ree MOOV)
(verb) to get rid of
Maria removed the seeds from the orange before she ate it.

Adding and Removing Thermal Energy

Thermal energy can be added to a material or **removed** from a material. When you heat a pot of water on a stove, thermal energy is added to the water. Thermal energy flows into a material when it is heated. When a warm bottle of water cools in a refrigerator, thermal energy is removed from the water. Thermal energy flows out of a material when it is cooled.

 How is thermal energy added to a material?

Thermal Energy and Changes in State

When thermal energy is added to a material, the thermal energy of the material increases. **Figure 12** shows that adding thermal energy can cause the potential energy and the kinetic energy of the particles in a material to increase. If the kinetic energy increases, then the temperature of the material increases. However, when only the potential energy increases, the temperature of the material doesn't change. Instead, the material changes from one state of matter to another. To change a material from one state of matter to another, thermal energy must flow into or out of the material.

Changes Between the Solid and Liquid States

The particles that make up the liquid steel and the solid steel in **Figure 13** are exactly the same. The difference between the liquid and the solid depends on the movement of the particles and the thermal energy they contain. Particles in the liquid steel move faster and have more thermal energy. Particles in the solid steel move more slowly and have less thermal energy. Thermal energy must be added to a material or taken away to change it from one state of matter to another.

Figure 13 Steel must be heated to about 1,400°C before it will melt.

Melting

Melting occurs when a solid changes into a liquid. When you heat a solid, thermal energy flows into the solid. Then the temperature of the solid increases until the temperature reaches the melting point. The **melting point** of a material is the temperature at which the material changes from a solid to a liquid.

Figure 14 shows how the temperature of a solid material changes as it is heated and thermal energy is added. At first, the temperature of the solid increases. But when the temperature reaches the melting point, the temperature of the material stops increasing. As the material changes from a solid to a liquid, the temperature stays constant at the melting point.

 Figure 14 Why is the line on the graph horizontal when melting is occurring?

Energy Changes During Melting

Thermal energy still is being added to the material as it melts. Because the temperature is not changing, the average kinetic energy of the particles doesn't change. Instead, the added thermal energy causes only the potential energy of the particles to increase.

When the potential energy of the particles increases, the arrangement of the particles in the material changes. In most materials, particles move farther apart. The new arrangement causes the attractive forces between particles to become weaker. When melting occurs, these forces have become weak enough that the particles can move past each other. After the solid has changed completely into a liquid, adding thermal energy causes the temperature of the liquid to increase, as shown in **Figure 14.**

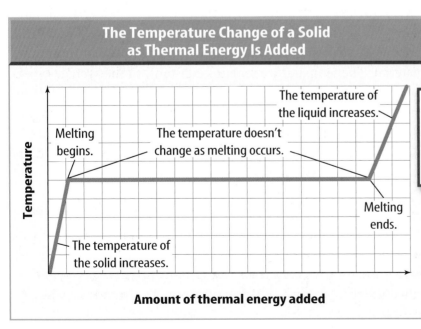

The Temperature Change of a Solid as Thermal Energy Is Added

Melting begins.

The temperature doesn't change as melting occurs.

The temperature of the liquid increases.

Melting ends.

The temperature of the solid increases.

Temperature

Amount of thermal energy added

Figure 14 The thermal energy of the liquid is greater than the thermal energy of the solid. Energy must be added to the solid to change it to a liquid.

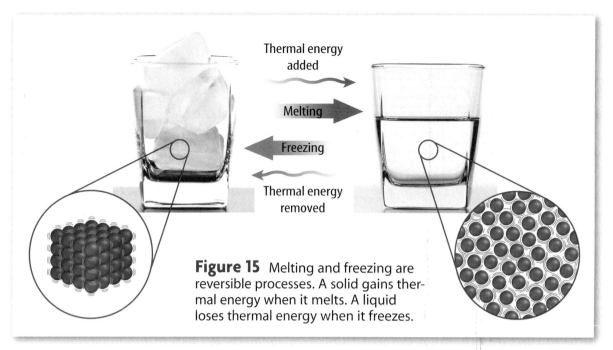

Figure 15 Melting and freezing are reversible processes. A solid gains thermal energy when it melts. A liquid loses thermal energy when it freezes.

Freezing

Freezing occurs when a liquid changes into a solid. When a material cools, thermal energy flows out of the material. The temperature of the material decreases until the freezing point is reached. The **freezing point** is the temperature at which the liquid changes to a solid. As thermal energy continues to flow out of the material, the temperature remains constant at the freezing point. After all the liquid has changed to a solid, the temperature decreases once again as thermal energy is removed.

 How does the thermal energy of a material change as it freezes?

Freezing—The Opposite of Melting

As **Figure 15** shows, freezing is the opposite of melting. For any material, the freezing point is the same as the melting point. While freezing is occurring, thermal energy is being removed from the material. The temperature remains constant, so the average kinetic energy of the particles doesn't change. Instead, the potential energy of the particles decreases. In most materials this means that the particles move closer together. Then the forces between the particles become strong enough for the particles to be held in fixed positions. The liquid becomes a solid.

Changes Between Liquids and Gases

If you heat a pot of water on the stove, as in **Figure 16,** you will notice bubbles forming in the water. Tiny water droplets in the form of steam rise into the air. Water in its invisible gas form, called *water vapor,* also rises from the pot. The liquid is changing to a gas.

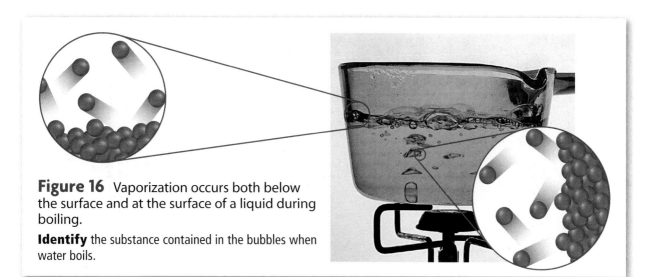

Figure 16 Vaporization occurs both below the surface and at the surface of a liquid during boiling.

Identify the substance contained in the bubbles when water boils.

Vaporization and Boiling

When liquid water is heated, its temperature rises until it reaches 100°C. At this temperature, liquid water changes into water vapor. The change from a liquid to a gas is called **vaporization.** When vaporization occurs, the attractive forces between particles are too weak to keep particles close to each other. Particles spread out and move independently.

Vaporization can occur within a liquid and at the surface of a liquid, as shown in **Figure 16.** Vaporization that occurs within a liquid is called **boiling.** When a liquid boils, bubbles form within the liquid. These bubbles contain particles of the material in the gas state.

The **boiling point** is the temperature at which boiling occurs in a liquid. As **Figure 17** shows, the temperature doesn't change while a liquid is boiling. Boiling ends after the liquid has changed to a gas. If thermal energy continues to be added, then the temperature of the gas will continue to rise.

WORD ORIGIN
vaporization
from Latin *vaporem;* means *exhalation, steam, heat*

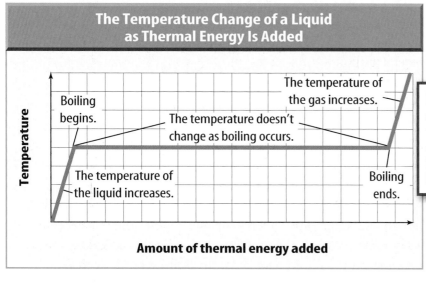

The Temperature Change of a Liquid as Thermal Energy Is Added

Boiling begins.

The temperature doesn't change as boiling occurs.

The temperature of the gas increases.

The temperature of the liquid increases.

Boiling ends.

Temperature

Amount of thermal energy added

Figure 17 The thermal energy of a gas is greater than the thermal energy of a liquid. Energy must be added to change a liquid to a gas.

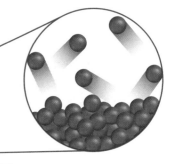

Figure 18 Evaporation occurs only at the surface of a liquid.

Compare the energy of the particles that leave the surface with those in the liquid.

MiniLab

Sensing Evaporation

Procedure

1. Complete a **lab safety form.**

2. Obtain a **bottle of rubbing alcohol** from your teacher.

3. Dip a **cotton swab** into the bottle and close the bottle.

4. Rub the alcohol-dipped swab on the back of your hand.

Analysis

1. **Describe** how the alcohol feels on your skin.

2. **Explain** why alcohol feels this way on your skin.

Evaporation

Vaporization that occurs at the surface of a liquid is called **evaporation.** Evaporation occurs during boiling and at temperatures below the boiling point. Recall that particles in a material move at different speeds. Some particles at the liquid's surface are moving much faster than other particles. Some of these particles are moving so fast that the attractive forces aren't strong enough to keep them at the surface of the liquid. As shown in **Figure 18,** these fast-moving particles escape into the space above the liquid. Above the liquid, the particles are far apart and the attractive forces between them are weak. These particles move independently and are in the gas state.

During evaporation, the fastest particles leave the surface of the liquid. The particles that remain have less kinetic energy. This means that the average kinetic energy of the liquid decreases. As a result, the liquid cools as evaporation occurs. You experience this cooling effect when perspiration evaporates from your skin.

 Reading Check Why does a liquid cool when evaporation occurs?

Pressure and the Boiling Point

The boiling point of a liquid depends on the types of atoms and molecules that make up the liquid. The boiling point also depends on the pressure exerted on the liquid. Recall the air around you exerts pressure. This pressure is exerted on a pot of water heating on a stove. For the water to boil, bubbles containing water vapor must form in water. The pressure exerted on the water by the air makes it harder for these bubbles to form. As air pressure increases, the water must be heated to a higher temperature before bubbles of water vapor form. This means that the boiling point of a liquid increases as the pressure on the liquid increases. As the pressure on the liquid decreases, the boiling point decreases.

Condensation

On a hot day, you might see drops of water on the outside of a glass of ice-cold water. These drops of water come from the air surrounding the glass. The air contains water vapor—a gas. The cold glass cools the air next to it. When the water vapor in the air next to the glass becomes cool enough, it changes from a gas to a liquid. The change from a gas to a liquid is called **condensation.** Early in the morning, you might have noticed dew on the grass, as in **Figure 19.** During the night, blades of grass cool more quickly than the air. When their temperature becomes low enough, condensation occurs and water droplets form.

Condensation—The Reverse of Vaporization

Figure 20 shows how condensation and vaporization are reversible processes. For condensation to occur, thermal energy must be removed from a gas. This causes the gas particles to move more slowly and the temperature of the gas to decrease. The gas continues to cool as thermal energy continues to be removed. Finally its temperature becomes low enough for condensation to occur. Then particles move slowly enough so that the attractive forces are able to keep the particles close together. As a result, a liquid forms.

Figure 19 Water droplets that form on blades of grass overnight are due to condensation.

Figure 20 Vaporization and condensation are reversible processes. Thermal energy must be added to a liquid to vaporize the liquid. Thermal energy must be removed from a gas to make it condense.

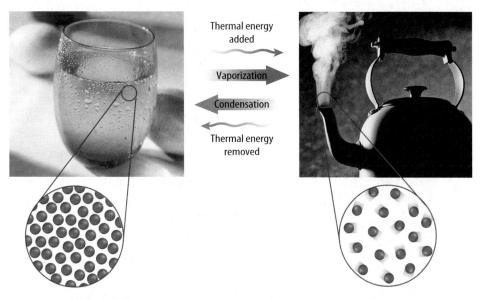

Thermal energy added

Vaporization

Condensation

Thermal energy removed

Visualizing the Heating Curve of Water

Figure 21

Water can exist as a solid—ice; as liquid water; or as a gas—water vapor. To change water from one state of matter to another, thermal energy must be added or removed.

Thermal energy is added when water is heated. The heating curve of water shows how the temperature of ice, liquid water, and water vapor changes as thermal energy is added. Melting occurs as solid ice changes to liquid water. Vaporization occurs as liquid water changes to the gas water vapor. The temperature remains constant as melting or vaporization occurs.

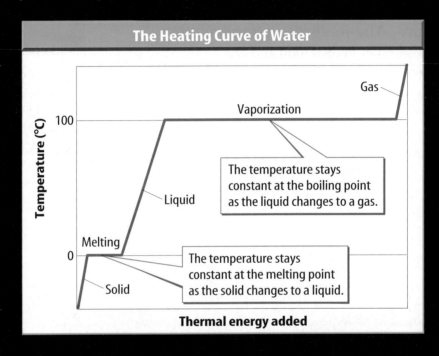

The Heating Curve of Water

The temperature stays constant at the boiling point as the liquid changes to a gas.

The temperature stays constant at the melting point as the solid changes to a liquid.

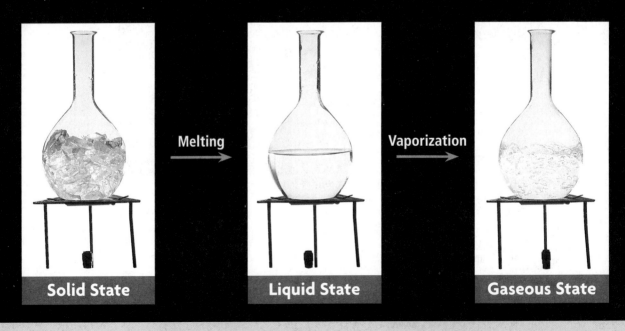

Solid State → Melting → **Liquid State** → Vaporization → **Gaseous State**

Contributed by National Geographic

Changing the States of Water

Imagine that you heat a container in which there is a piece of ice. **Figure 21** shows how the temperature of the ice changes as thermal energy is added to it.

Adding Thermal Energy

As the container is heated, the temperature of the ice increases. The temperature of the ice continues to rise until the melting point of ice is reached. **Figure 21** shows that the temperature stays constant as the ice begins to melt and change from a solid to a liquid. Even though the temperature isn't changing, thermal energy must be added to the ice to change all the solid ice to liquid water.

 As ice melts, how does its temperature change?

After all the ice has melted, the temperature of the water begins to increase as the container is heated. When the water temperature reaches the boiling point of water, the temperature stops increasing, as shown in **Figure 21.** As the container continues to be heated, liquid water changes to water vapor. Finally, all the liquid water changes to water vapor. Adding more thermal energy then causes the temperature of the water vapor to increase.

Removing Thermal Energy

Ice can be melted to form water by heating the ice. The water that is formed can be changed back into ice by removing thermal energy and cooling the water. This means that the changes between states of matter are reversible. **Figure 22** shows how water vapor can be changed back into ice by cooling.

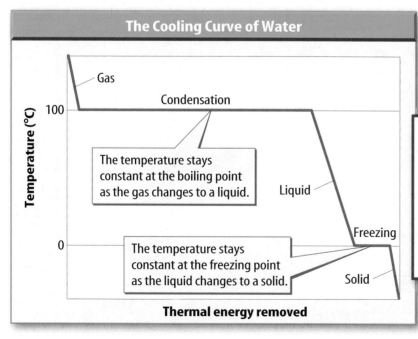

Figure 22 As thermal energy is removed, water vapor changes to liquid water, which then changes to solid ice.

Infer from the graph which change of state requires the largest change in thermal energy.

Figure 23 Sublimation causes the dry ice to change to a gas. Deposition causes frost to form on the leaf.

Sublimation

Deposition

Changes Between Solids and Gases

The dry ice in **Figure 23** produces a thick fog. Dry ice is solid carbon dioxide. At room temperature, dry ice absorbs thermal energy and changes directly into a colorless gas. **Sublimation** is the change of a solid to a gas without going through the liquid state. The thick fog around the dry ice is caused by the cold carbon dioxide gas that causes water vapor in the air to condense into small droplets. For sublimation to occur, thermal energy must be added to a solid.

The opposite of sublimation is **deposition,** the change of a gas to a solid without going through the liquid state. The frost that forms on the leaf shown in **Figure 23** is caused by deposition. For deposition to occur, thermal energy must be removed from a gas. When the leaf becomes cold enough, water vapor in the air surrounding the leaf loses enough thermal energy to change into a solid.

Changes in Energy Among States of Matter

The state of matter of a substance depends on the amount of thermal energy a substance contains. For a material to change from one state of matter to another, thermal energy must be added to the material or removed. **Figure 24** shows the energy changes that occur when a material changes from one state to another.

Figure 24 For a change in state to occur, thermal energy must move into or out of the material.

List the changes in state that can occur when thermal energy is added to a material.

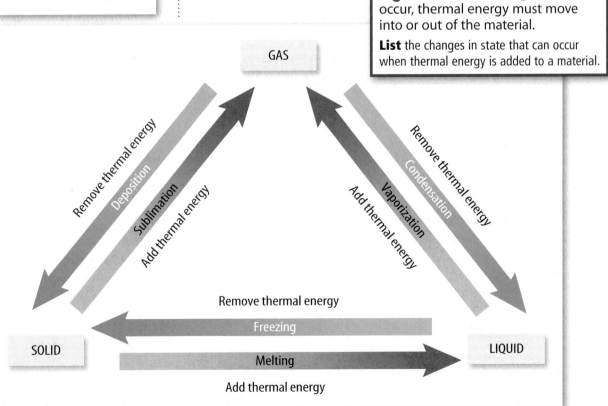

What have you learned?

The temperature of a material depends on the average kinetic energy of the particles in a material. The faster these particles move, the higher the temperature. Thermal energy is added to a material when it is heated. Thermal energy is removed when a material cools. When a material changes from one state of matter to another, thermal energy must be added or removed.

Melting occurs when a material changes from a solid to a liquid. Freezing is the reverse of melting. Vaporization occurs when a material changes from a liquid to a gas. Vaporization can occur inside a liquid by boiling or at the surface by evaporation. Condensation is the reverse of vaporization. As a material changes from one state to another, its temperature doesn't change.

LESSON 2 Review

Summarize

Create your own lesson summary as you organize an **outline.**

1. **Scan** the lesson. Find and list the first **red** main heading.

2. **Review** the text after the heading and list 2–3 details about the heading.

3. **Find** and list each **blue** subheading that follows the **red** main heading.

4. **List** 2–3 details, key terms, and definitions under each **blue** subheading.

5. **Review** additional **red** main headings and their supporting **blue** subheadings. List 2–3 details about each.

 **ELA8: R 2.3**

Standards Check

Using Vocabulary

1. Write the definitions of *freezing point* and *boiling point* in your own words. **3.d**

2. Use each term in a separate sentence: *evaporation, condensation, sublimation,* and *deposition.* **3.d**

Understanding Main Ideas

3. During which change of state do the particles in a material become farther apart? **3.e**
   - **A.** vaporization
   - **B.** freezing
   - **C.** deposition
   - **D.** condensation

4. **Compare** temperature, thermal energy, and heat. **3.d**

5. **Explain** how changes in thermal energy and changes in state of matter are related. **3.d**

6. **Compare and contrast** sublimation and deposition. **3.d**

Applying Science

7. **Summarize** Copy and fill in the graphic organizer below to identify the changes in states of matter that can occur when thermal energy is removed from a material. **3.d**

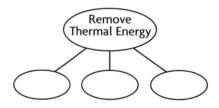
Remove Thermal Energy

8. **Explain** why a bathroom mirror becomes fogged when you take a shower. **3.d**

9. **Describe** how the potential energy of water molecules changes as water changes from a solid to a liquid and then from a liquid to a gas. **3.d**

Science Online

For more practice, visit **Standards Check** at ca8.msscience.com.

DataLab

How are boiling point and atmospheric pressure related?

The temperature at which water boils depends on the pressure above the liquid. When the liquid is in an open container, the pressure above the liquid is atmospheric pressure.

Atmospheric Pressure and Boiling Point of Water	
Pressure (kPa)	Boiling Point (°C)
98.7	99.2
100.0	99.6
101.3	100.0
102.7	100.4
105.3	101.1
106.7	101.4

Data

Graph the data in the table. Plot pressure on the *x*-axis and the boiling point on the *y*-axis. Label each axis, including the proper units. Choose an appropriate scale for each axis.

Data Analysis

1. **Determine** if atmospheric pressure and boiling point have a linear or nonlinear relationship at this pressure range.

2. **Determine** the boiling point of water at 102 kPa.

3. **Estimate** the boiling point of water at 108 kPa.

 Science Content Standards

3.d Students know the states of matter (solid, liquid, gas) depend on molecular motion.

9.g Distinguish between linear and nonlinear relationships on a graph of data.

Applying Math

Packing Efficiency

Even when atoms are packed together in a solid, there is empty space between the atoms. Packing efficiency is a measure of how much space in a solid is actually taken up by atoms. Different arrangements of atoms can result in different packing efficiencies. Find the packing efficiency by dividing the volume of atoms in the solid by the total volume of the solid. The atoms in most crystalline solids are arranged in one of the four ways listed in the table below.

Atom Arrangement	Packing Efficiency
Body-centered cubic	0.68
Face-centered cubic	0.74
Hexagonal close pack	0.74
Simple cube	0.52

Example

If the total volume of a solid is 20 cm³, what is the volume of atoms in a body-centered cubic solid?

What you know:	• packing efficiency of a body-centered cubic: 0.68 • total volume: 20 cm³
Use this equation:	$\dfrac{\text{volume of atoms}}{\text{total volume}} = \text{packing efficiency}$
Substitute:	$\dfrac{\text{volume of atoms}}{\text{total volume}} = \text{packing efficiency}$ $\dfrac{X}{20 \text{ cm}^3} = 0.68$
Multiply:	volume of atoms $= 0.68 \times 20 \text{ cm}^3 = 13.6 \text{ cm}^3$
Answer: The volume of atoms is 13.6 cm³.	

Practice Problems

1. If the volume of atoms in a body-centered cubic is 4.2 cm³, find the total volume.

2. Find the volume of atoms in a simple cube if the total volume is 12 cm³.

Science Online

For more math practice, visit Math Practice at ca8.msscience.com.

Does change of state take longer for some liquids?

Materials

electric hot plate
ring stand and clamp
thermometer
glass stirring rod
tap-water ice cubes
10% sugar solution
  cubes
grapefruit-juice cubes
cranberry-juice cubes
hot pads
stop watch
graph paper

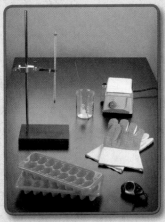

Safety Precautions

Science Content Standards

9.e Construct appropriate graphs from data and develop quantitative statements about the relationships between variables.

Problem

Not all liquids look the same. Water is clear. Even some juices, such as cranberry and white grape, are transparent. Other juices, such as tomato and grapefruit juice, are thick and pulpy. You cannot see through them. If a liquid contains materials, such as fruit or vegetable pulp, will the time it takes to change from one state to another be the same as for clear liquids?

Form a Hypothesis

Develop a hypothesis about the differences in time it takes for various liquids to change from a solid to a liquid state.

Collect Data and Make Observations

1. Read and complete a safety form.

2. Prepare a data table to record your data for each trial.

3. Set up ring stand, clamp, and thermometer as shown in the photo on the next page.

4. Pour 100 mL of tap water into the beaker and add five tap water ice cubes. Read and record the temperature every minute until the temperature stops dropping and stabilizes. Stir occasionally to ensure the temperature is the same throughout the mixture.

5. When the temperature begins to rise, move the beaker onto the burner and turn the burner to high. **DO NOT TURN THE BURNER ON AHEAD OF TIME. Caution: The beaker could break because it is very cold.**

6. Clamp the thermometer so the bulb goes into the liquid fully but does not touch the bottom of the beaker. Continue to read and record the temperature every minute. It will begin to change rapidly. When the water boils, do not stop recording. When the temperature is exactly the same for 4 min, turn off the hot plate and take the thermometer out to cool.

7. Dispose of the contents of the beaker as instructed by your teacher.

Test Additional Cubes

8. Start with a new beaker for each test or wash the beaker before each test. Rinse and dry the thermometer between each test.
9. Repeat steps 4–7 for each of the additional cubes. Record your data in your data table.
10. Graph the data with time on the x-axis and the temperature on the y-axis. Label each axis and place a title on your graph.

Analyze and Conclude

1. **Describe** the differences in the graphs for each of the different mixtures.
2. **Determine** from your graphs which mixture took the longest amount of time and which mixture took the shortest amount of time to completely change from a solid to a liquid.
3. **Describe** how the temperature changed as the ice cubes for each material were melting.
4. **Describe** the differences you observed in the boiling points and melting points of the different mixtures.
5. **Identify** the material that required the most thermal energy and the material that required the least amount of thermal energy to completely melt the ice cubes.
6. **Describe** the differences in the two materials you identified in the preceding question.
7. **Explain** whether or not your data supported your hypothesis.

Communicate

 **Science** **ELA8: W 2.1**

Write a short report describing an experiment that would measure the freezing point and boiling point of a material. Include in your report a description of how to reduce the errors in your measurements.

Real World Science

New and Improved

Sometimes physicists aren't satisfied with studying matter as it exists in the physical world. Sometimes they try to make up new matter in the laboratory. That is just what award-winning physicist Dr. Deborah Jin did when she discovered something called a "fermionic condensate." It's not exactly a gas, a liquid, *or* a solid. One of its unusual properties is that it is an extremely good conductor of electricity—it might just be the "superconductor" that helps reduce the usage of electrical energy!

Physicists can help solve some big problems. Learn more about superconductors by visiting **Careers** at <u>ca8.msscience.com</u>. **Write** a 500- to 700-word report about the ways in which they might be used.

World Record Holder

Sometimes solids aren't very dense at all. According to *The Guinness Book of World Records,* the least dense solid is Aerogel, a material developed at NASA's Pasadena, California, laboratory. Even though it is made of the same materials as glass, Aerogel is 99.8 per cent air. It looks like blue smoke, but it is strong enough to be used on spacecraft.

Why is Aerogel still a solid even though it is mostly air? **Write** an explanation for why it is still considered a solid.

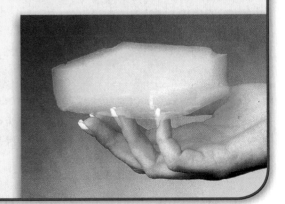

Statistical Matters

A teaspoon of water contains an unimaginable number of water molecules. How do the properties of water depend on the motions and properties of these water molecules? The answer was found by Ludwig Boltzmann, an Austrian scientist who lived from 1844 to 1906. Boltzmann helped develop a branch of physics called statistical mechanics. This approach uses statistical methods to connect the properties of materials, such as temperature, with the properties of atoms and molecules, such as their kinetic energy.

Calculate the average height of five of your classmates. How do you think this average height would compare to the average height of all the students at your school?

A COOL WAY TO GO

It's likely that every day, especially in summer, you benefit from a change in a state of matter: the change of a refrigerant from a liquid to a gas. This change in state makes air conditioning work, and it has had a huge impact on population distribution in the United States. The introduction of air conditioning around 1950 enabled large growths in populations in the states with hotter climates.

Visit **Society** at ca8.msscience.com and **make a graph** comparing population change from 1950 to 2000 in California, Florida, Arizona, Illinois, Wisconsin, and New York. Do you detect a pattern? **Explain.**

CHAPTER **6** | **Standards Study Guide**

The BIG Idea Matter can undergo a physical change from one state to another as an increase or decrease in thermal energy changes the motion of the particles.

Lesson 1 Solids, Liquids, and Gases 〔3.d, 3.e〕

(Main Idea) **The state of matter depends on the motion of its particles.**

- All particles in matter are moving in random motion.
- Particles in matter can exert attractive forces on each other.
- Solids have a fixed shape and volume.
- Particles in a solid vibrate about a fixed location.
- Liquids have a fixed volume but no fixed shape.
- Particles in a liquid can slide past each other.
- Gases have no fixed shape or volume.
- The particles in a gas move independently of each other.

- **gas** (p. 258)
- **liquid** (p. 257)
- **random motion** (p. 255)
- **solid** (p. 256)

Lesson 2 Changes in States of Matter 〔3.d, 3.e, 9.e, 9.g〕

(Main Idea) **Changes in energy can cause matter to change from one state to another.**

- Temperature is a measure of the average kinetic energy of all the particles in a material.
- Heating a material adds thermal energy, and cooling it removes thermal energy.
- Adding thermal energy can change either the state of matter or its temperature.
- A substance changes from a solid to a liquid at its melting point.
- A substance changes from a liquid to a solid at its freezing point.
- Vaporization can occur as boiling or evaporation.
- A change from a liquid to a gas occurs within a liquid at its boiling point.
- Condensation is the change from a gas to a liquid.
- Sublimation is the direct change of a solid to a gas.
- Deposition is the direct change from a gas to a solid.

- **boiling** (p. 267)
- **boiling point** (p. 267)
- **condensation** (p. 269)
- **deposition** (p. 272)
- **evaporation** (p. 268)
- **freezing point** (p. 266)
- **melting point** (p. 265)
- **sublimation** (p. 272)
- **temperature** (p. 262)
- **thermal energy** (p. 263)
- **vaporization** (p. 267)

 Download quizzes, key terms, and flash cards from ca8.msscience.com.

  Interactive Tutor ca8.msscience.com

Linking Vocabulary and Main Ideas

Use vocabulary terms from page 280 to complete this concept map.

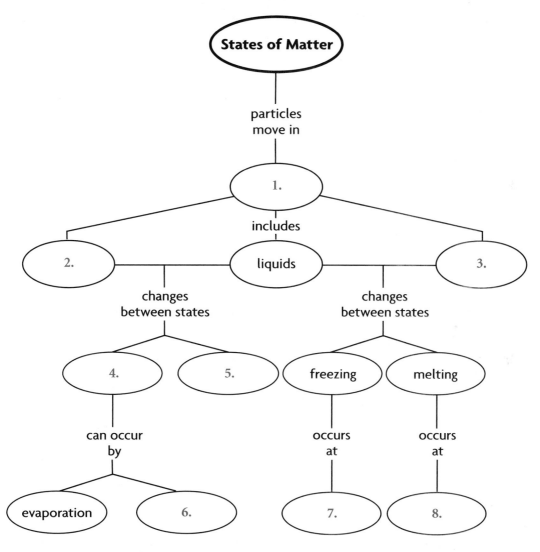

States of Matter

particles move in

1.

includes

2.   liquids   3.

changes between states   changes between states

4.   5.   freezing   melting

can occur by   occurs at   occurs at

evaporation   6.   7.   8.

Using Vocabulary

Match each phrase with the correct vocabulary term from the Study Guide.

9. includes the kinetic and potential energy of particles in a material

10. matter with a fixed volume but not a fixed shape

11. average kinetic energy of particles

12. temperature at which liquid changes to a gas within the liquid

13. a change in state directly from a solid to a gas

14. a change from a liquid to a gas at the surface of a liquid

Science nline

Visit ca8.msscience.com for:
▶ Vocabulary PuzzleMaker
▶ Vocabulary eFlashcards
▶ Multilingual Glossary

Understanding Main Ideas

Choose the word or phrase that best answers the question.

1. What would happen if you tried to squeeze a gas into a smaller container?
   A. The particles would have fewer collisions with the container.
   B. The force of the particles would prevent you from doing it.
   C. The attractive forces among the particles would increase.
   D. Repulsive forces of the particles would pull on the container.   **3.e**

Use the figures below to answer questions 2 and 3.

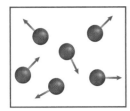

Motion 1   Motion 2

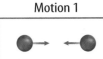

Motion 3   Motion 4

2. Which type of motion causes a pencil to remain still even though the particles that make up the pencil are always moving?
   A. motion 1
   B. motion 2
   C. motion 3
   D. motion 4   **3.d**

3. Which type of motion best represents the movement of gas particles?
   A. motion 1
   B. motion 2
   C. motion 3
   D. motion 4   **3.d**

4. A pile of snow slowly disappears into the air, even though the temperature remains below freezing. Which process explains this?
   A. condensation
   B. deposition
   C. evaporation
   D. sublimation   **3.e**

5. Which explains why liquids can flow but solids cannot?
   A. The attractive forces between particles are weaker in liquids than in solids.
   B. Solids have no repulsive forces between the particles.
   C. The distance between particles is much greater in a liquid than in a solid.
   D. Gravity pulls more strongly on the particles of a liquid than those of a solid.   **3.e**

6. Which is a form of vaporization?
   A. condensation
   B. evaporation
   C. freezing
   D. melting   **3.e**

7. The figure below shows the temperature of two beakers of water.

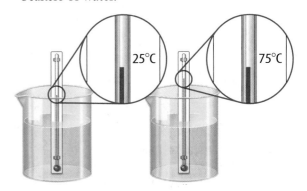

Which property of the liquid particles increased?
   A. average kinetic energy
   B. average potential energy
   C. total kinetic energy
   D. total potential energy   **3.d**

Science Online Standards Review ca8.msscience.com

Applying Science

Use the graph below to answer questions 8 and 9.

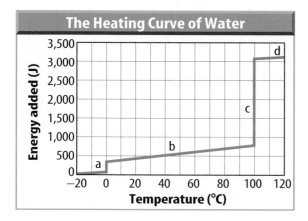

The Heating Curve of Water

8. **Estimate** the amount of thermal energy that must be added to change 1 g of ice at the melting point completely into water. **3.d**

9. **Identify** the regions on the graph where only the potential energy of the water molecules is changing. **3.d**

10. **Summarize** the differences between freedom of movement of particles in solids, liquids, and gases. **3.e**

11. **Compare** the pressure inside a pressure cooker to the air pressure outside if the boiling point of water is higher inside the pressure cooker than outside. **3.d**

12. **Explain** why evaporation of water from your skin makes you feel cooler. **3.d**

13. **Describe** how the forces between water molecules in an ice cube change as the ice cube melts. **3.d**

14. **Explain** why it is incorrect to say that air bubbles form in boiling water. **3.d**

15. **Evaluate** Your friend claims that she can cook spaghetti noodles in a pot of boiling water faster by increasing the heat on the stove. Is she correct? Explain your answer. **3.d**

16. **Predict** whether the size of an inflated balloon would change or remain the same if you placed it in a freezer. Explain your prediction. **3.e**

17. **Write** a paragraph describing how you could determine the melting point of a substance from its heating curve or cooling curve.

Cumulative Review

18. **Compare** When a solid melts, the densities of the solid and the liquid are usually nearly the same. Infer from this how the distance between particles in a solid compare with the distance between particles in a liquid. Explain. **3.e, 8.a**

19. **Compare** Adding thermal energy to water causes the water to boil, but doesn't break the chemical bonds in water molecules. Which are stronger: the attractive forces between water molecules or the chemical bonds in water molecules? Explain. **3.e**

20. **Infer** When gold melts, the density of the liquid is slightly less than the density of the solid. Will solid gold float in the melted gold? **3.e, 8.d**

Applying Math

Use the table below to answer questions 21 and 22.

Packing of Atoms	
Atom Arrangement	**Packing Efficiency**
Face-centered cubic	0.74
Hexagonal close pack	0.74
Simple cube	0.52

21. If the volume of atoms in a face-centered cubic is 5 cm^3, find the total volume. **MA8: ALG 5.0**

22. Find the volume of atoms in a simple cube if the total volume is 9.3 cm^3. **MA8: ALG 5.0**

1 Which of the following best describes the particles in matter?

  A They are larger in solids than in liquids or gases.

  B They are larger in gases than in solids or liquids.

  C They do not move in solids.

  D They are always moving. **3.d**

2 The table below shows the density of four different materials.

Density of Materials	
Material	**Density (g/cm³)**
F	7.63
G	0.78
H	0.0008
I	2.17

Which material is a gas?

  A material F

  B material G

  C material H

  D material I **3.e**

3 Which is the process of a gas cooling to form a liquid?

  A deposition

  B condensation

  C vaporization

  D sublimation **3.d**

4 The illustration below shows models of particles in four different containers.

P   Q   R   S

Which container most likely contains a gas?

  A container P

  B container Q

  C container R

  D container S **3.e**

5 During which processes must thermal energy be added to a material?

  A freezing and boiling

  B condensation and melting

  C melting and vaporization

  D sublimation and freezing **3.d**

6 The temperatures of one glass of water is 30°C and the temperature of another glass of water is 0°C. Both glasses contain the same amount of water. Which is a correct statement about the two glasses of water?

  A The molecules of the cold water are larger.

  B The molecules of the warm water are larger.

  C The molecules of the warm water have a higher average kinetic energy.

  D The molecules of the cold water have a higher average kinetic energy. **3.d**

7 **Which description best describes a liquid?**

A It has a definite shape and volume.

B It has a definite volume but no definite shape.

C It expands to fill the shape and volume of its container.

D It cannot flow. **3.e**

8 **In which state of matter are particles close together, yet are able to move past one another?**

A solid

B gas

C liquid

D plasma **3.e**

9 **The illustration below shows a gas in a closed cylinder.**

What happens to the gas as the piston moves downward?

A The volume of the gas increases.

B The attractive forces between gas particles increase.

C The distance between gas particles increases.

D The gas undergoes sublimation. **3.d**

10 **The illustration below shows the motion of particles in a material.**

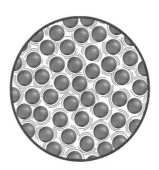

In which state of matter is the material?

A gas

B liquid

C plasma

D solid **3.e**

11 **Which statement best describes a solid?**

A Its particles vibrate in place.

B Its particles do not move at all.

C It particles can flow past each other.

D Its particles are very far apart. **3.e**

12 **Which are the two ways that vaporization can occur?**

A sublimation and deposition

B evaporation and boiling

C melting and freezing

D melting and boiling **3.d**

The Periodic Table and Physical Properties

The BIG Idea

Elements on the periodic table are grouped together based on their properties.

LESSON 1 | 3.f, 7.a
Organization of the Periodic Table

Main Idea The periodic table contains information about the structures and characteristics of elements.

LESSON 2 | 7.a, 7.b, 9.e
Isotopes and Radioactivity

Main Idea Over time, radioactive isotopes decay at varying rates.

LESSON 3 | 5.d, 7.c, 9.a
Physical Properties and Changes

Main Idea Substances have physical properties that can be described and physical changes that can be observed.

Taking It for Granite

Barre quarry in Vermont is America's oldest granite quarry. This quarry contains granite, which is composed of feldspar, quartz, and mica. These minerals are composed of elements, such as silicon, oxygen, calcium, and potassium.

Science Journal Write a paragraph explaining why you think it's helpful to keep your books, notebooks, and papers organized.

Launch Lab

00:15 minutes

Which element are you?

How can you organize your class into a periodic table?

Procedure

1. Find your assigned element on the periodic table. Color the **poster board** the same color as your element's block.

2. Use a **dark marker** to print your element's atomic number, symbol, name, and atomic mass on your poster board.

3. Find the classmates whose elements are to the left, to the right, above, and below your element on the periodic table.

4. Arrange yourselves so that you are in the correct positions.

Think About This

- **Explain** why you and your classmates arranged yourselves as you did.

- **Assess** What limitations did you find in making the table?

3.f

Science Online

Visit ca8.msscience.com to:

▶ view **Concepts in Motion**

▶ explore Virtual Labs

▶ access content-related Web links

▶ take the Standards Check

FOLDABLES™
Study Organizer

Regions of the Periodic Table Make the following Foldable to identify the regions of the periodic table.

▷ **STEP 1 Fold** a sheet of paper into thirds lengthwise.

▷ **STEP 2 Unfold** and **draw** lines along the folds. **Draw** three vertical lines to divide the paper into four columns, as shown.

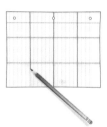

Reading *Skill*

Clarifying

Label the top row of your Foldable with the names of the regions. In the boxes below, describe the location, the properties, and some examples of elements in that region.

Get Ready to Read

Make Predictions

1 Learn It! A prediction is an educated guess based on what you already know. One way to predict while reading is to guess what you believe the author will tell you next. As you are reading, each new topic should make sense because it is related to the previous paragraph or passage.

2 Practice It! Read the excerpt below from Lesson 3. Based on what you have read, make predictions about what you will read in the rest of the lesson. After you read Lesson 3, go back to your predictions to see if they were correct.

Predict whether a solution could be formed from salt and water.

What would you predict would be a characteristic of all solutions?

Dissolving is mixing a substance into another substance to **form a solution.** As sugar dissolves in water, it disappears and seems to become part of the water. But if you boil the water away, the **sugar becomes visible again.** Dissolving is a **physical change** because the sugar is unchanged.

—from page 317

Can you predict another kind of change that matter could undergo?

3 Apply It! Before you read, skim the questions in the Standards Review. Choose three questions and predict the answers.

Target Your Reading

Reading Tip

As you read, check the predictions you made to see if they were correct.

Use this to focus on the main ideas as you read the chapter.

1 **Before you read** the chapter, respond to the statements below on your worksheet or on a numbered sheet of paper.

- Write an **A** if you **agree** with the statement.
- Write a **D** if you **disagree** with the statement.

2 **After you read** the chapter, look back to this page to see if you've changed your mind about any of the statements.

- If any of your answers changed, explain why.
- Change any false statements into true statements.
- Use your revised statements as a study guide.

Before You Read A or D	Statement	After You Read A or D
	1 The elements are arranged on the periodic table according to their atomic numbers and mass numbers.	
	2 The elements in a group have similar properties.	
	3 Metals are located on the right side of the periodic table.	
	4 Not all isotopes are radioactive.	
	5 Radioactive elements have unstable nuclei.	
	6 An element's mass number is the number of neutrons in its nucleus.	
	7 *Transmutation* is another word for *half-life*.	
	8 Melting and boiling points change with pressure.	
	9 Thermal conductivity occurs because particles collide with one another.	
	10 Density is a physical property that depends on the size of a sample.	

Science nline

Print a worksheet of this page at ca8.msscience.com.

Science Content Standards

3.f Students know how to use the periodic table to identify elements in simple compounds.
7.a Students know how to identify regions corresponding to metals, nonmetals, and inert gases.

Reading Guide

What *You'll Learn*

▶ **Describe** the arrangement of the elements in the periodic table.

▶ **Identify** metals, nonmetals, and semimetals by their positions in the periodic table.

▶ **Identify** and **describe** the noble gases.

Why *It's Important*

The periodic table will provide you with a lot of information once you know how to use it.

Vocabulary

period
group
metallic
luster
conductivity
halogen
noble gas

Review Vocabulary

element: pure substance made from atoms that all have the same number of protons (p. 195)

Organization of the Periodic Table

Main Idea The periodic table contains information about the structures and characteristics of elements.

Real-World Reading Connection A map is a source of much information. You can find streets, cities, lakes, and rivers on a map. But you must first know how to read the map. The periodic table is similar to a map. You can learn a lot about the elements once you learn how to read the periodic table.

How are the elements arranged?

Imagine what a library would be like if books weren't organized on the shelves. You wouldn't be able to find the information you needed. Like a library, the periodic table is a system for organizing information. Recall that each element has a different atomic number. The atomic number is the number of protons in an atom of an element. The elements are arranged in the periodic table according to their atomic numbers. Each element block contains the same type of information. The block for carbon is shown in **Figure 1.** A key at the top of the table shows that each block contains the element's name, atomic number, symbol, and atomic mass. Each block also has an icon, or a picture. The icon indicates whether the element is normally a gas, a liquid, or a solid. Another icon shows whether the element is found in nature or is made by humans.

 What do the icons in the element blocks show?

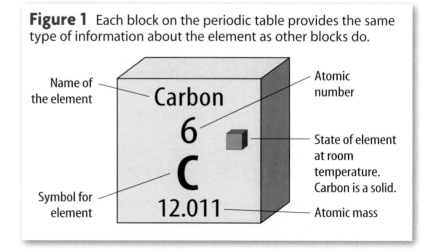

Figure 1 Each block on the periodic table provides the same type of information about the element as other blocks do.

Name of the element

Atomic number

Carbon

6

C

12.011

State of element at room temperature. Carbon is a solid.

Symbol for element

Atomic mass

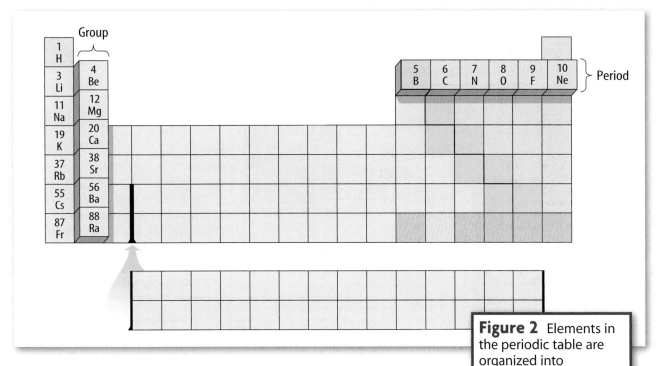

Figure 2 Elements in the periodic table are organized into horizontal periods and vertical groups.

Periods

Learning to read an individual block is the first step in understanding the periodic table. You also need to be able to read the periodic table as a whole. Notice in **Figure 2** that the elements are arranged in horizontal rows. These rows are numbered from 1 to 7 down the left side of the table. A horizontal row of elements is called a **period.** Period 2 starts with the element lithium (Li), which has the atomic number 3. Notice as you go across period 2 that the atomic numbers increase by 1.

Groups

A vertical column of elements on the periodic table is called a **group.** Groups are numbered from 1 to 18 across the top of the periodic table. **Figure 2** shows that Group 2 starts with beryllium (Be) and ends with radium (Ra). Other members of this group are calcium, magnesium, strontium (STRON tee um), and barium. Generally, groups of elements have similar chemical and physical properties. Recall from Chapter 5 that Group 2 elements are reactive. They easily form ionic compounds with elements in Groups 16 and 17. Group 2 elements share some similar physical properties. Calcium, strontium, and barium are shiny, silvery, and solid. They have the same crystal structure and similar melting and boiling points. If you know the properties of one element in a group, you can predict that the properties of the other members of the group are likely to be similar. In this way, the group number of an element can provide you with additional information.

 Figure 2 What element is in both period 2 and Group 2?

PERIODIC TABLE OF THE ELEMENTS

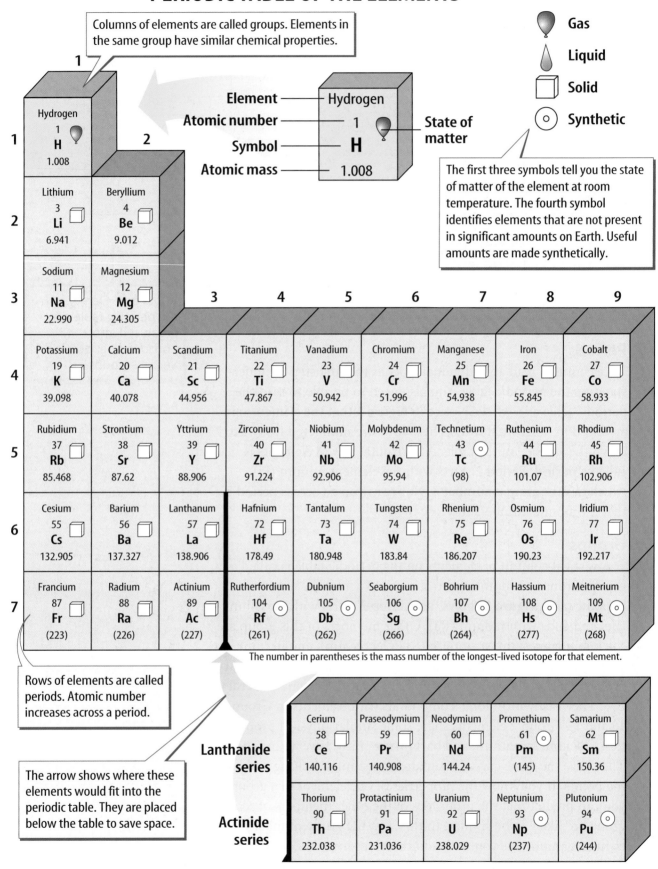

Columns of elements are called groups. Elements in the same group have similar chemical properties.

Gas

Liquid

Solid

Synthetic

Element — Hydrogen
Atomic number — 1
Symbol — H
Atomic mass — 1.008

State of matter

The first three symbols tell you the state of matter of the element at room temperature. The fourth symbol identifies elements that are not present in significant amounts on Earth. Useful amounts are made synthetically.

1
Hydrogen
1
H
1.008

2

Lithium
3
Li
6.941

Beryllium
4
Be
9.012

Sodium
11
Na
22.990

Magnesium
12
Mg
24.305

3

4

5

6

7

8

9

Potassium
19
K
39.098

Calcium
20
Ca
40.078

Scandium
21
Sc
44.956

Titanium
22
Ti
47.867

Vanadium
23
V
50.942

Chromium
24
Cr
51.996

Manganese
25
Mn
54.938

Iron
26
Fe
55.845

Cobalt
27
Co
58.933

Rubidium
37
Rb
85.468

Strontium
38
Sr
87.62

Yttrium
39
Y
88.906

Zirconium
40
Zr
91.224

Niobium
41
Nb
92.906

Molybdenum
42
Mo
95.94

Technetium
43
Tc
(98)

Ruthenium
44
Ru
101.07

Rhodium
45
Rh
102.906

Cesium
55
Cs
132.905

Barium
56
Ba
137.327

Lanthanum
57
La
138.906

Hafnium
72
Hf
178.49

Tantalum
73
Ta
180.948

Tungsten
74
W
183.84

Rhenium
75
Re
186.207

Osmium
76
Os
190.23

Iridium
77
Ir
192.217

Francium
87
Fr
(223)

Radium
88
Ra
(226)

Actinium
89
Ac
(227)

Rutherfordium
104
Rf
(261)

Dubnium
105
Db
(262)

Seaborgium
106
Sg
(266)

Bohrium
107
Bh
(264)

Hassium
108
Hs
(277)

Meitnerium
109
Mt
(268)

The number in parentheses is the mass number of the longest-lived isotope for that element.

Rows of elements are called periods. Atomic number increases across a period.

The arrow shows where these elements would fit into the periodic table. They are placed below the table to save space.

Lanthanide series

Cerium
58
Ce
140.116

Praseodymium
59
Pr
140.908

Neodymium
60
Nd
144.24

Promethium
61
Pm
(145)

Samarium
62
Sm
150.36

Actinide series

Thorium
90
Th
232.038

Protactinium
91
Pa
231.036

Uranium
92
U
238.029

Neptunium
93
Np
(237)

Plutonium
94
Pu
(244)

Metal

Metalloid

Nonmetal

The color of an element's block tells you if the element is a metal, nonmetal, or metalloid.

Concepts In MOtion
To organize infomation about the periodic table, visit ca8.msscience.com.

				13	14	15	16	17	18
									Helium 2 He 4.003
				Boron 5 B 10.811	Carbon 6 C 12.011	Nitrogen 7 N 14.007	Oxygen 8 O 15.999	Fluorine 9 F 18.998	Neon 10 Ne 20.180

	10	11	12	Aluminum 13 Al 26.982	Silicon 14 Si 28.086	Phosphorus 15 P 30.974	Sulfur 16 S 32.065	Chlorine 17 Cl 35.453	Argon 18 Ar 39.948
	Nickel 28 Ni 58.693	Copper 29 Cu 63.546	Zinc 30 Zn 65.409	Gallium 31 Ga 69.723	Germanium 32 Ge 72.64	Arsenic 33 As 74.922	Selenium 34 Se 78.96	Bromine 35 Br 79.904	Krypton 36 Kr 83.798
	Palladium 46 Pd 106.42	Silver 47 Ag 107.868	Cadmium 48 Cd 112.411	Indium 49 In 114.818	Tin 50 Sn 118.710	Antimony 51 Sb 121.760	Tellurium 52 Te 127.60	Iodine 53 I 126.904	Xenon 54 Xe 131.293
	Platinum 78 Pt 195.078	Gold 79 Au 196.967	Mercury 80 Hg 200.59	Thallium 81 Tl 204.383	Lead 82 Pb 207.2	Bismuth 83 Bi 208.980	Polonium 84 Po (209)	Astatine 85 At (210)	Radon 86 Rn (222)
	Darmstadtium 110 Ds (281)	Roentgenium 111 Rg (272)	Ununbium * 112 Uub (285)		Ununquadium * 114 Uuq (289)				

✳ The names and symbols for elements 112–114 are temporary. Final names will be selected when the elements' discoveries are verified.

Europium 63 Eu 151.964	Gadolinium 64 Gd 157.25	Terbium 65 Tb 158.925	Dysprosium 66 Dy 162.500	Holmium 67 Ho 164.930	Erbium 68 Er 167.259	Thulium 69 Tm 168.934	Ytterbium 70 Yb 173.04	Lutetium 71 Lu 174.967
Americium 95 Am (243)	Curium 96 Cm (247)	Berkelium 97 Bk (247)	Californium 98 Cf (251)	Einsteinium 99 Es (252)	Fermium 100 Fm (257)	Mendelevium 101 Md (258)	Nobelium 102 No (259)	Lawrencium 103 Lr (262)

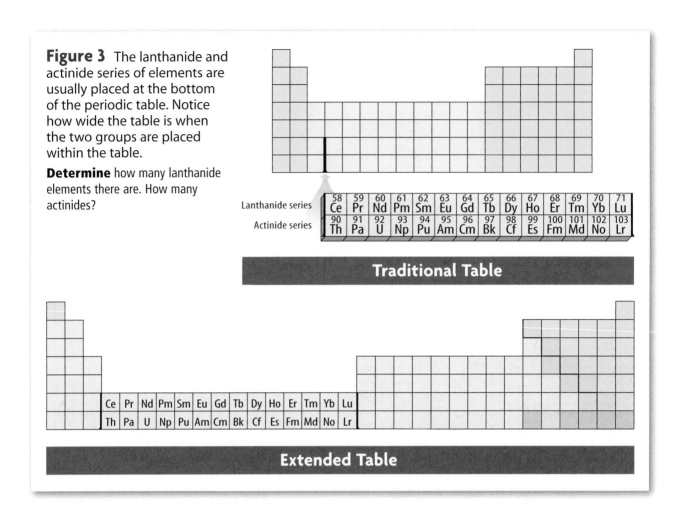

Figure 3 The lanthanide and actinide series of elements are usually placed at the bottom of the periodic table. Notice how wide the table is when the two groups are placed within the table.

Determine how many lanthanide elements there are. How many actinides?

Lanthanide series

58	59	60	61	62	63	64	65	66	67	68	69	70	71
Ce	Pr	Nd	Pm	Sm	Eu	Gd	Tb	Dy	Ho	Er	Tm	Yb	Lu

Actinide series

90	91	92	93	94	95	96	97	98	99	100	101	102	103
Th	Pa	U	Np	Pu	Am	Cm	Bk	Cf	Es	Fm	Md	No	Lr

Traditional Table

| Ce | Pr | Nd | Pm | Sm | Eu | Gd | Tb | Dy | Ho | Er | Tm | Yb | Lu |
| Th | Pa | U | Np | Pu | Am | Cm | Bk | Cf | Es | Fm | Md | No | Lr |

Extended Table

The Lanthanide and Actinide Series

By now, you have probably noticed the two rows of elements at the bottom of the periodic table. These are the lanthanide (LAN thuh nide) series and the actinide (AK tuh nide) series of elements. The lanthinide elements are also known as the rare earth elements. These elements are placed at the bottom of the table to save space. You can see in **Figure 3** how wide the periodic table becomes when they are placed inside the table. When reading across rows 6 and 7 in the traditional table, insert these elements back into the periodic table. Notice that the first member of the lanthanide series is cerium, with atomic number 58. The actinide element thorium (THOR ee um) follows actinium (AK tin ee um).

What are the regions of the periodic table?

You have seen that the elements in a group share some physical and chemical properties. The periodic table has three regions in which elements with particular properties are arranged. These regions are the metals, the nonmetals, and the semimetals.

WORD ORIGIN

luster

from Latin *lustrare;* means *spread light over, brighten*

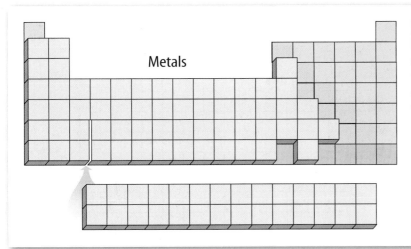

Metals

Figure 4 Notice that the blue color of the metallic elements covers most of the periodic table. Only a triangle of other element blocks is in the right corner.

Metals

All kinds of things are made of metals. The rings on a binder, aluminum foil, cars, machinery, and jewelry are all made of metals. The elements that are metals are on the left side and in the middle of the periodic table. Notice in **Figure 4** that the metal blocks are colored blue.

An element is classified as metallic if it has certain properties. **Metallic** refers to the collective properties of common metals. One property of metals is luster. **Luster** is shine. Gold and silver jewelry, copper fixtures, and stainless-steel cooking pots all exhibit luster. Metals are also malleable. Malleability is the ability of metals to be hammered into sheets. Malleable metals can also be molded into cooking pans or rolled into sheets to make car bodies. Metals are ductile. A ductile metal can be stretched or pulled into wires for conducting electricity.

 Reading Check What are two properties of metals?

Conductivity (kahn duk TIH vuh tee) is the ability of a material to transfer electricity or thermal energy (heat). Metals are good conductors of electricity. The wires that bring electricity to your home are made of metal. Metals also conduct heat well. An aluminum chair that has been standing in the Sun can be uncomfortably hot to sit on. You notice the heat because the metal conducts heat rapidly to your skin. Some metals of the lanthanide series, such as neodymium (nee oh DIH mee um), are magnetic. Strong magnets are made by combining neodymium, iron, and boron. **Figure 5** shows some of the ways that the properties of metals make them useful in everyday life.

The most reactive metals are in Group 1 and Group 2. A reactive metal combines readily with other substances to form compounds. The metals of Groups 1 and 2 are so reactive that they are never found in nature by themselves. They react with water and the oxygen in the air to form compounds.

Figure 5 The conductivity of metals makes it possible to bring electricity to your home. The properties of ductility and malleability make metals suitable for making many objects.

Figure 6 The number of nonmetals is small compared to the number of metals.

Identify the group of elements whose members are all nonmetals.

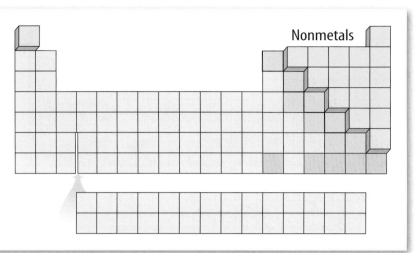

Nonmetals

Nonmetals

The elements on the right side of the periodic table are called nonmetals. They are colored yellow, as shown in **Figure 6.** Nonmetals exhibit properties that are opposite those of metals. Nonmetals are brittle, which means they break easily. They do not have luster and cannot be easily shaped. Nonmetals are not good conductors of heat and electricity. Nonmetals are found in lasers, plastics, and many other products. They are in the air you breathe and the nutrients that plants and animals need. Recall the important role that the nonmetal carbon plays in the millions of compounds that make up the living world. Other important nonmetals are hydrogen, oxygen, nitrogen, sulfur, and phosphorus. These elements combine with carbon in many compounds. Most of the elements contained in plants and animals, such as those in **Figure 7,** are made of nonmetals.

 What are four properties of nonmetals?

The most reactive nonmetals are located in Group 17. Elements in Group 17 are known as **halogens.** Like the Group 1 and Group 2 elements, halogens are highly reactive. For this reason, they are not found by themselves in nature.

Figure 7 Nonmetals make up most of the matter in the living world. Water is 100 percent nonmetallic. Rocks contain a significant amount of oxygen and carbon.

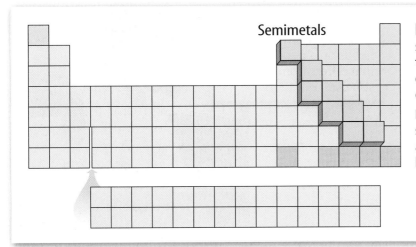

Semimetals

Figure 8 The properties of semimetals are a blend of the properties of the metals on the left to the nonmetals on the right.

Predict whether some semimetals might have a shiny appearance like a metal or be brittle like a nonmetal.

Semimetals

The blue representing metals and the yellow representing nonmetals cover most of the periodic table. But a small number of elements have green blocks. These are the semimetals, also known as metalloids. **Figure 8** shows that the semimetals are located between the metals and nonmetals. They follow a kind of stairstep pattern. Semimetals have properties of both metals and nonmetals. This makes them excellent semiconductors. A semiconductor is an element that does not **conduct** electricity as well as a metal but conducts better than a nonmetal. Silicon is an important semiconductor. It is found in computer chips used in electronics and global communication satellites, such as the one in **Figure 9.**

Noble Gases

One group of elements is unique among the nonmetals. These are the Group 18 elements, known as the **noble gases.** Noble gases are extremely stable by themselves, so they are not found naturally in compounds. In nature, they exist as individual atoms. In the past, the noble gases were known as the inert gases. *Inert* means "unreactive." Recently, however, chemists have been able to form compounds from some of the heavier Group 18 elements. This is why these gases are no longer considered inert.

ACADEMIC VOCABULARY

conduct (kun DUKT)

(verb) to lead from a position of command

The chairperson of the committee will conduct the meeting.

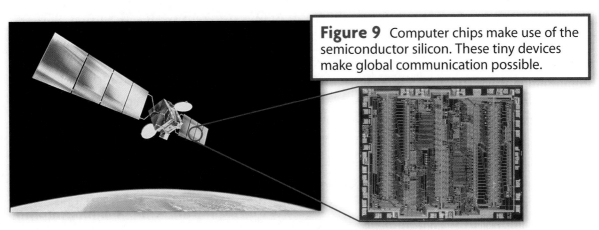

Figure 9 Computer chips make use of the semiconductor silicon. These tiny devices make global communication possible.

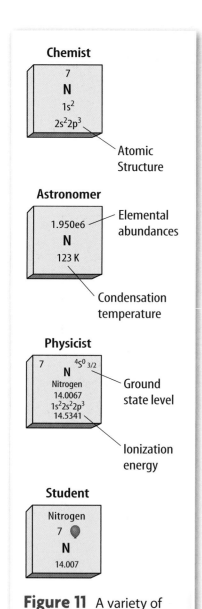

Chemist

7
N
$1s^2$
$2s^2 2p^3$

— Atomic Structure

Astronomer

1.950e6	— Elemental abundances
N	
123 K	

— Condensation temperature

Physicist

7	$^4S^0_{3/2}$
N	
Nitrogen	
14.0067	
$1s^2 2s^2 2p^3$	
14.5341	

— Ground state level

— Ionization energy

Student

Nitrogen	
7	⬤
N	
14.007	

Figure 11 A variety of periodic tables are designed to provide the information needed by different groups of people.

Deduce Are the two values for nitrogen's atomic mass on the student's and the physicist's element blocks the same number, or are they different? Explain.

Figure 10 This chemist finds the information she needs on a periodic table that differs from the one you use.

Are there other periodic tables?

Now you know how to find information about the elements by using the periodic table in this book. However, did you know that the periodic table you are studying is not the only periodic table being used today?

Periodic Tables—Meeting Different Needs

When you think of a periodic table as a road map, it makes sense that different types of scientists might need different information on their periodic tables. Your choice of a map depends on what information you need. You wouldn't use a city map to plan a cross-country trip. For a hiking trip in the Sierra Nevada, you would need to take along a map of the trails. Just as there are different kinds of maps, there are different periodic tables that provide a variety of information.

Chemists, physicists, and astronomers each do different work. They choose a periodic table just as you might choose a map. For example, the chemist shown in **Figure 10** needs information about atomic structures. Astronomers need information on how much of each element is found in the solar system. To meet these needs, the information in the blocks in each type of periodic table is unique.

Figure 11 shows four different blocks for the element nitrogen designed for the needs of four different types of scientists. All blocks show the element symbol. Almost all show the atomic number. Some give the element name. What are the differences? The element blocks for chemists and physicists have information about atomic structure. The element blocks for physicists and students show atomic masses. Notice the special information in the physicist's blocks. In spite of their differences, you can learn to use any periodic table by making use of its key.

Figure 11 What information is on the student's periodic table that is not on the chemist's periodic table?

What do you know about the periodic table?

The periodic table starts at the left with the element having the smallest atomic number, hydrogen. Elements that follow hydrogen are listed according to increasing atomic number across the table in columns numbered from 1 to 18. A column of elements is called a group. Members of a group have similar properties. A horizontal row is called a period. Metals occupy the left and middle portions of the table. Nonmetals are on the right. A few semimetals fall between the metals and nonmetals. Metals, nonmetals, and semimetals have distinctive properties. You'll learn more about the physical properties of elements in Lesson 3.

LESSON 1 Review

Summarize

Create your own lesson summary as you write a **newsletter.**

1. **Write** this lesson title, number, and page numbers at the top of a sheet of paper.

2. **Review** the text after the **red** main headings and write one sentence about each. These will be the headlines of your newsletter.

3. **Review** the text and write 2–3 sentences about each **blue** subheading. These sentences should tell *who, what, when, where,* and *why* information about each headline.

4. **Illustrate** your newsletter with diagrams of important structures and processes next to each headline.

Standards Check

Using Vocabulary

1. Distinguish between a group and a period on the periodic table. **3.f**

2. In your own words, write a definition of *conductivity.* **7.c**

Understanding Main Ideas

3. What region of the periodic table has the most elements?
   A. inert gases **7.a**
   B. metals
   C. nonmetals
   D. semimetals

4. **Identify** the group on the periodic table that contains only nonmetals. **7.a**

5. **Explain** why the noble gases are sometimes called inert gases. **7.a**

6. **Decide** which of the following elements would be best suited for electrical wiring: gold, sulfur, or neon. **7.a**

7. **Use** the periodic table to discover two characteristics of potassium besides its name. **3.f**

8. **Contrast** Copy and fill in the graphic organizer below to contrast the properties of metals and nonmetals. **7.a**

Applying Science

9. **Write instructions** to tell someone how to use the periodic table and what information can be obtained. **3.f**

10. **Give an example** of a metal, a nonmetal, and a semimetal. **7.a**

For more practice, visit **Standards Check** at ca8.msscience.com.

MiniLab

Can you guess the element?

Elements are organized in the periodic table according to their atomic numbers. An element can be a solid, a liquid, or a gas; a metal, a semi-metal, or a nonmetal. How well do you think you know some of the elements?

Calcium
20
Ca
40.078

Procedure

1. Organize the **element cards** from the Launch Lab into groups. Identify some of the physical properties of the groups.

2. Group some of the metals according to a specific property, such as luster or malleability.

3. Choose other groupings that you will remember easily. Group these with the properties that are most important.

4. Identify other elements with additional physical or chemical properties.

5. Your teacher will hold up an element card without showing its face and give one clue to the identity of the element.

6. Someone might say, "I can guess that element with just five clues!" Someone else might challenge and say, "I can guess that element with only four clues."

7. Your teacher will give the number of clues that ended the challenge. The student who won the challenge will name the element.

Analysis

1. **Identify** which properties you found easiest to become familiar with when you were organizing your notes.

2. **Give an example** of groups you found difficult to learn about.

3. **Explain** how the challenge helped you understand the organization of the periodic table.

 Science Content Standards

3.f Students know how to use the periodic table to identify elements in simple compounds.

Science Content Standards

7.b Students know each element has a specific number of protons in the nucleus (the atomic number) and each isotope of the element has a different but specific number of neutrons in the nucleus.

9.e Construct appropriate graphs from data and develop quantitative statements about the relationships between variables.

Also covers: 7.a

Reading Guide

What *You'll Learn*

▶ **Compare and contrast** the isotopes of an element.

▶ **Define** *radioactive decay.*

▶ **Contrast** varying rates of decay.

▶ **Research** how elements are named.

Why *It's Important*

Learning about isotopes will help you understand the benefits and dangers of radioactivity.

Vocabulary

radioactive decay
radioactive
transmutation
radioactive element
half-life
synthetic element
particle accelerator

Review Vocabulary

isotope: one of two or more atoms of an element having the same number of protons in their nuclei, but a different number of neutrons (p. 198)

Isotopes and Radioactivity

Main Idea Over time, radioactive isotopes decay at varying rates.

Real-World Reading Connection Some of the electricity you use in your home was probably generated by means of nuclear energy. Nuclear energy comes from spontaneous reactions of the nuclei of unstable isotopes. These reactions produce large amounts of energy and change one element into a different one.

Isotopes—Different Numbers of Neutrons

What's the difference between the two atoms in **Figure 12?** Both have the same atomic number, 8. Both have the same number of protons and electrons, eight. But notice that the atom on the right has an extra neutron. Because both atoms have the same atomic number, they are the same element, oxygen. However, these are two different versions of oxygen atoms because they have different numbers of neutrons. To distinguish between them, the symbols oxygen-16 and oxygen-17 are used. Oxygen-16 atoms, with eight neutrons, are far more common than oxygen-17, atoms with nine neutrons. These different versions are called isotopes. Isotopes are atoms of an element having the same number of protons in their nuclei, but different numbers of neutrons.

 How many neutrons does the most common form of the oxygen atom have?

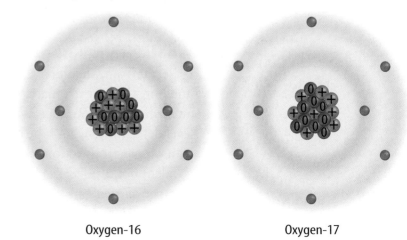

Figure 12 These isotopes of oxygen have the same properties, even though they have different numbers of neutrons.

Oxygen-16   Oxygen-17

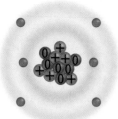
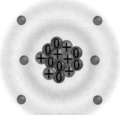
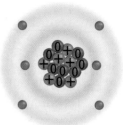

Carbon-12
Mass number 12
Atomic number 6

Carbon-13
Mass number 13
Atomic number 6

Carbon-14
Mass number 14
Atomic number 6

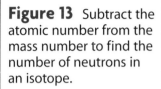

Figure 13 Subtract the atomic number from the mass number to find the number of neutrons in an isotope.

Compare and Contrast
What is the same about the three isotopes? What is different?

How Many Neutrons?

Isotopes with more neutrons are heavier than isotopes with fewer neutrons. For example, carbon occurs naturally in three isotopes: carbon-12, carbon-13, and carbon-14. Diagrams of these three isotopes are shown in **Figure 13.** The numbers 12, 13, and 14 are the mass numbers of the isotopes. An atom's mass number is the sum of the number of protons and neutrons the atom has. Starting with this information, it's easy to determine the number of neutrons in each carbon isotope. First, find the number of protons in carbon. Remember that the atomic number is the number of protons an atom has. Carbon's atomic number is 6. Therefore, carbon has six protons. Next, subtract the atomic number from the mass number of the isotope to determine the number of neutrons.

mass number	– atomic number	= number of neutrons
(neutrons plus protons) –	(protons) =	neutrons
14	– 6	= 8

Carbon-14 has eight neutrons. You can determine the number of neutrons in carbon-13 and carbon-12 in the same way. Carbon-13 has seven neutrons. Carbon-12 has six neutrons. Check these results by counting the numbers of neutrons in **Figure 13.** All of carbon's isotopes have the same number of protons and electrons but different numbers of neutrons.

What determines properties?

Recall from Chapter 4 that the number of electrons an atom has and how they are arranged determines the chemical properties of an element. The number of electrons in an element's outer energy level determines what type of bond it will form. Some elements transfer electrons to form ionic bonds. Others share electrons in covalent bonds. Because the three carbon isotopes have the same number of electrons, they have almost-identical chemical properties. This is true for all isotopes.

What is radioactive decay?

You have read that the three isotopes of carbon have the same chemical properties. But something is different about one isotope. Carbon-14 nuclei are unstable. Many atomic nuclei are stable when they have the same number of protons and neutrons. Carbon-14 has six protons and eight neutrons. To become stable, carbon-14 nuclei release particles and energy and change into other nuclei. **Radioactive decay** occurs when an unstable atomic nucleus changes into another nucleus by emitting one or more particles and energy. A nucleus that is unstable and undergoes radioactive decay is called **radioactive.** Thus, carbon-14 nuclei are radioactive.

Radioactive nuclei have found many uses in science and medicine. **Figure 14** shows an image produced when a small amount of the isotope iron-59 was injected into a patient's bloodstream. The image allows doctors to study the circulation of the patient's blood.

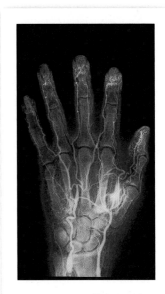

Figure 14 The radiation released by a small amount of iron-59 is detected by an instrument, which produced this photo.

Gold-Foil Experiment and Radioactive Decay

Recall from Chapter 4 that in the gold-foil experiments of Ernest Rutherford, a speeding alpha particle was used to bombard the gold foil. An alpha particle consists of two protons and two neutrons. These four nuclear particles were blasted out of an isotope as a single particle. Because of their release, the isotope gained stability. **Figure 15** shows that when an isotope of americium releases an alpha particle, two protons are lost. Because the isotope now has a different number of protons, the atomic number of the isotope is no longer that of americium. Americium has become the element neptunium. In radioactive decay processes such as this one, stability increases and a different element is formed.

Figure 15 The release of four nuclear particles as an alpha particle increases stability. A new element, neptunium, is formed.

Determine whether the numbers of particles on both sides of the equation are equal.

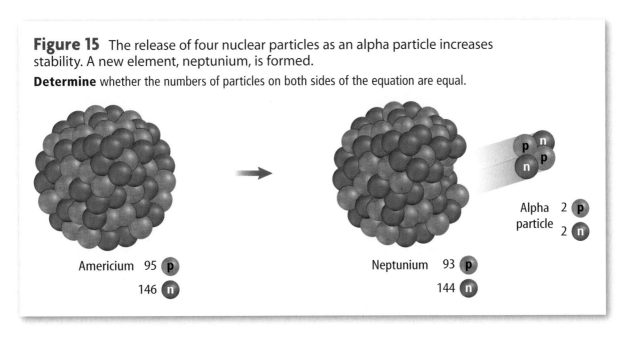

Americium 95 (p)
146 (n)

Neptunium 93 (p)
144 (n)

Alpha particle 2 (p)
2 (n)

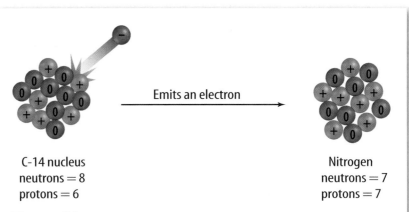

C-14 nucleus
neutrons = 8
protons = 6

Nitrogen
neutrons = 7
protons = 7

Figure 16 Carbon-14 undergoes radioactive decay by gaining a proton and emitting an electron.

WORD ORIGIN

transmutation
from Latin *trans–* (means *thoroughly*) and *mutare* (means *to change*)

Radioactive Decay and Transmutation

An isotope can increase its stability in ways other than by releasing an alpha particle. Some radioactive isotopes decay by changing their neutrons into different particles. Others trap one of their own electrons and put it in the nucleus. Each type of decay involves the release of nuclear particles and energy. The carbon-14 isotope emits an electron from its nucleus and gains a proton. An electron released from the nucleus of an atom is called a beta particle. When an isotope releases a beta particle, it gains a proton. The isotope then becomes the element with the next higher atomic number. This process is called transmutation. In **transmutation** (trans myew TAY shun), an atom of one element is changed into an atom of another element.

Transmutation occurs in most types of radioactive decay. **Figure 16** shows how carbon-14 undergoes transmutation when it emits an electron, or a beta particle. The atomic number of carbon-14 is 6. When a beta particle is emitted, a neutron is converted to a proton. The extra proton increases the isotope's atomic number to 7. However, 7 is the atomic number of nitrogen. After radioactive decay, carbon-14 is no longer carbon. It has become nitrogen.

 What happens when a radioactive isotope releases a beta particle?

Uses of Radioactive Decay

You have seen how the radioactive isotope iron-59 can provide doctors with an image of a patient's bloodstream. This is just one of many medical uses of radioactivity. These include both the detection of cancer and the killing of cancer cells. For example, cobalt-60 has been used to stop the growth of brain tumors. Radioactive isotopes are also used to preserve food. The radiation, or energy produced by the radioactive decay process, kills bacteria, fungi, insects, and other pests that cause food to spoil.

Radioactive Elements and the Periodic Table

Recall that carbon has two stable and one radioactive isotopes. Similarly, hydrogen has two stable isotopes—protium and deuterium. The third isotope, tritium, is radioactive. Some heavier elements, however, have no stable isotopes. All of their isotopes are radioactive. Elements having only radioactive isotopes are classified as **radioactive elements.**

The Discovery of Radioactive Elements In 1896, French scientist Antoine-Henri Bequerel had stored a mineral containing uranium on top of a piece of wrapped film. When the film was developed, Bequerel found that it had been exposed to radiation. Bequerel hypothesized that the radiation had come from radioactive elements in the uranium rock. Another French scientist, Marie Curie, shown in **Figure 17,** separated the radioactive elements in a uranium mineral. With her husband Pierre, she discovered two new radioactive elements, polonium and radium.

Radioactive Elements **Figure 18** shows that technetium (tehk NEE she um), promethium (proh MEE thee um), polonium (puh LOH nee um), and all elements with atomic numbers higher than 84 are radioactive. Elements with the largest numbers of protons in their nuclei tend to be unstable. For that reason, it might be puzzling that the radioactive element uranium can still be found in nature. Don't isotopes decay into different stable elements? Earth is billions of years old. It would seem reasonable that all of Earth's supply of uranium would have already been converted into some other element. How can the presence of uranium in Earth's crust be explained?

Figure 17 Marie Curie (1867–1934) won the Nobel Prize in Chemistry in 1911 for her discovery of polonium and radium.

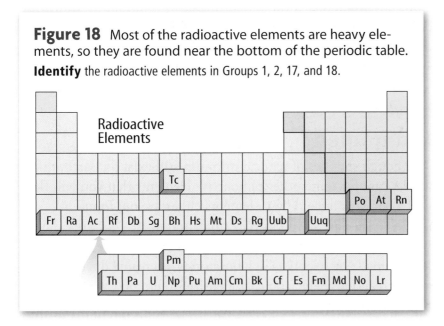

Figure 18 Most of the radioactive elements are heavy elements, so they are found near the bottom of the periodic table.

Identify the radioactive elements in Groups 1, 2, 17, and 18.

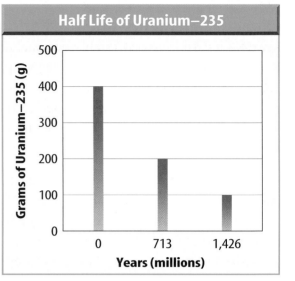

Half Life of Uranium–235

Figure 19 A nuclear submarine can operate for a long time on just 400 g of uranium-235.

Half-Life

The presence of uranium on Earth can be explained by how isotopes decay. Isotopes decay at very different rates. Some decay in a matter of days, minutes, seconds, and even milliseconds. Others take millions of years. The uranium-235 isotope has a half-life of 713 million years. **Half-life** is the time it takes for a sample of a radioactive isotope to decay to half its original mass. It would take 713 million years for a 1-g sample of uranium-235 to decay to half its mass, or 0.5 g. In another 713 million years, the sample would have decreased again by half and a mass of 0.25 g would remain. The rest of the 1-g sample would have turned into another element. With uranium's long half-life, it's not surprising that the element still exists on Earth. Uranium is mined for use in generating electricity. One nuclear submarine, like the one shown in **Figure 19,** uses more than 400 g of uranium-235 for fuel in its nuclear power plant. But it will take a very long time for the 400 g of uranium to decay.

 Figure 19 Determine what mass of uranium-235 would remain after another 713 million years.

How are elements discovered and named?

Although supplies of natural uranium still exist on Earth, this is not the case for some other radioactive elements that you will find on the periodic table. These elements either are not found in nature, or they are found in very small amounts. They are called synthetic elements. **Synthetic elements** are radioactive elements that are made by scientists in laboratories or created during nuclear reactions. The icon that identifies them on the periodic table is a small circle within a larger circle.

Synthetic Elements

Scientists have searched for technetium (atomic number 43) on Earth without success. They knew that the element must exist because of the patterns of properties in the periodic table. The element molybdenum (mah LIB duh num) belongs in Group 6. Similarly, the properties of ruthenium (roo THEE nee um) place it in Group 8. Scientists knew there must be an element between them, in Group 7. They could predict the element's properties from the periodic table. Because it was not found naturally, technetium became the first synthetic element. Scientists made it in a laboratory. Promethium (atomic number 61) is another synthetic element.

Heavy Synthetic Elements All elements with atomic numbers greater than 92 are synthetic elements. These elements exist only because scientists make them by artificial transmutation. The **process** involves crashing rapidly moving particles into target atoms. The speeding particles could be, for example, neutrons, protons, or alpha particles.

 How are synthetic elements made?

Particle Accelerators Picture yourself bowling. If you roll the ball very fast and it hits the pins, the pins will be knocked all over the place. If you roll the ball more slowly, the pins will fall differently. Suppose you use a baseball or a basketball. The results will be different for each ball. In a similar way, scientists bombard target atoms with different types of particles traveling at different speeds. To obtain the speeds needed for transmutation, scientists use a particle accelerator like the one shown in **Figure 20.** A **particle accelerator** is a giant machine that is capable of making particles move very fast. Depending on the conditions of the experiment, the speeding particles might meld together with the target atoms. The result could be a new element with a higher atomic number. You can read more about particle accelerators and how they work in **Figure 21.**

ACADEMIC VOCABULARY

process (PRAH ses)

(noun) a series of actions or operations taken to achieve an end

Students are in the process of getting an education.

Figure 20 This view of the particle accelerator at Fermilab in Batavia, Illinois shows the enormous size of the tunnel needed to accelerate particles to the speeds needed for successful collisions.

Visualizing Synthetic Elements

Figure 21

The element uranium, with 92 protons and 146 neutrons, is the heaviest element found naturally in Earth's crust. But scientists have been able to make elements with larger atomic numbers by using giant machines called particle accelerators. These machines force atomic particles to move at extremely high speeds, often close to the speed of light. The speeding particles are smashed into other particles in the hope that the particles will fuse together into new and heavier elements. Elements formed by successful collisions are usually unstable and decay into other elements in only a fraction of a second.

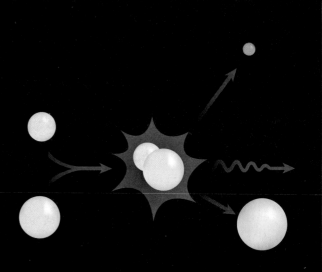

▲ Particles in an accelerator might collide with such force that they meld or fuse together into one larger particle. In the fusion process, energy and a subatomic particle are released. The new, heavier element usually has a very short half-life.

▲ Particles are moved at enormous speed down the long passage shown in this exterior view of the Stanford Linear Accelerator at Stanford University in California.

▶ Recently, the IUPAC (International Union of Pure and Applied Chemistry) General Assembly confirmed the official name and symbol of element 111. Element 111, previously known as unununium, is now called Roentgenium in honor of Wilhelm Roentgen, the discoverer of X rays.

Contributed by National Geographic

Naming New Elements

When scientists have evidence that they have made a new synthetic element, its existence must be officially confirmed. The confirmation is done by a team of scientists from the International Union of Pure and Applied Chemistry (IUPAC) and the International Union of Pure and Applied Physics (IUPAP). The scientists who made the new element write a paper describing their discovery. They ask the expert team to review their work. The team must decide whether there is enough evidence to support the scientists' claims. To make their decision, they use a set of rules. First, the experiment must be successfully repeated in another laboratory. This is important because a true scientific discovery must have dependable results. Second, the methods for making the element must be scientifically sound. That means the procedures used must follow known scientific principles. Third, the element must show distinct chemical and/or physical properties.

Figure 22 Glenn Seaborg was a Nobel Laureate who had an enormous impact on the research for synthetic elements.

 What three rules are used to determine if a new element has been made?

Once the rules are met, the scientists who discovered the element have earned the privilege of giving the element a name and a symbol. If more than one team of scientists claims to have discovered a particular element, the expert team decides who has the right to name it.

Element Names

Some names that scientists have chosen for elements are shown in **Table 1.** Notice that element names often honor the scientists who created them or the places where the scientists worked. For example, Seaborgium (see BOHR gee um) was named to honor Glenn Seaborg, shown in **Figure 22.** Seaborg was a researcher at the Lawrence Berkeley National Laboratory in Berkeley, California. Seaborg discovered 10 elements, atomic numbers 93–102. When scientists who worked with Seaborg discovered element 106, they named it in his honor.

Table 1 Origins of Element Names		
Atomic Number	**Element Name**	**Element's Namesake**
96	Curium	French scientist, Marie Curie
97	Berkelium	Place where berkelium was synthesized, Berkeley, California
99	Einsteinium	Famous scientist, Albert Einstein
106	Seaborgium	Scientist, Glenn Seaborg

What have you learned?

You have read that isotopes are atoms of an element that have the same number of protons and electrons but different numbers of neutrons. Some isotopes are radioactive and undergo radioactive decay. Radioactive decay is the spontaneous release of particles and energy from the nucleus of an atom. The process of radioactive decay is called transmutation when it results in the formation of a different element. Rates of radioactive decay vary greatly and are measured in half-lives. Many of the heavier elements exist for a short period of time. However, some elements have been made in laboratories using particle accelerators that smash nuclei together to create elements with greater mass.

LESSON 2 Review

Summarize

Create your own lesson summary as you design a **visual aid.**

1. **Write** the lesson title, number, and page numbers at the top of your poster.

2. **Scan** the lesson to find the **red** main headings. Organize these headings on your poster, leaving space between each.

3. **Design** an information box beneath each **red** heading. In the box, list 2–3 details, key terms, and definitions from each **blue** subheading.

4. **Illustrate** your poster with diagrams of important structures or processes next to each information box.

 ELA8: R 2.3

Standards Check

Using Vocabulary

1. Use the term *radioactive decay* in a sentence. **7.b**

2. Write a definition of *transmutation* in your own words. **7.b**

Understanding Main Ideas

3. **Identify** the region of the periodic table where most radioactive elements are found. **7.b**

4. **Construct a diagram** that shows how much of a 10-g sample of barium-131 would remain after 36 days. The half-life of this isotope is 12 days. **7.b**

5. **Compare and Contrast** Copy and fill in the graphic organizer below to compare and contrast synthetic and naturally occurring elements. **7.b**

6. **Calculate** how many more neutrons U-238 has than U-235. **7.b**

7.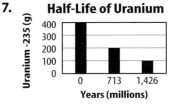

Calculate how much uranium-235 would remain after a fourth half-life. **7.b**

Applying Science

8. **Formulate a plan** for how scientists might go about trying to make an element with atomic number 115. **7.b**

9. **Judge the fairness** of the process for confirming and naming new elements. **7.a**

Science Online

For more practice, visit **Standards Check** at ca8.msscience.com.

Applying Math

Isotope Half-Life Conversions

Isotopes of an element can have varying half-lives ranging from seconds to years. In order to see the magnitude of difference between these half-lives, they need to be converted to the same units. A table of half-life values for several isotopes of erbium is shown below.

Half-Lives of Erbium	
Isotope	Half-Life
^{145}Er	0.9 s
^{147}Er	2.5 s
^{154}Er	3.73 min
^{156}Er	19.5 min
^{158}Er	2.29 h
^{169}Er	9.40 days

Example

How many seconds is the half-life for ^{154}Er?

What you know:

- Half-life for ^{154}Er: 3.73 min

- There are 60 seconds in 1 minute.

What you need to find:
- How many seconds are in 3.73 minutes?

Follow these steps:

1. Find how many seconds are in 1 minute: 60 s.

2. Multiply 60 s × 3.73 min to find how many seconds are in 1 minute.
   60 × 3.73 = 223.8 s

Practice Problems

1. How many minutes is the half-life for ^{158}Er?
2. How many seconds is the half-life for ^{158}Er?

Science Online
For more math practice, visit Math Practice at ca8.msscience.com.

DataLab

00:30 minutes Try at Home

How can you show a visual explanation of half-life?

Naturally occurring radioactive isotopes break down at known rates. Each radioactive isotope has its own half-life. A half-life may be a fraction of a second or thousands of years. You can simulate radioactive decay using pennies.

Data Collection

1. Read and complete a lab safety form.

2. Create a data table in your Science Journal.

3. Place the **pennies** in a container. Shake and gently pour the pennies onto the table.

4. Separate the pennies into two piles, those with tails showing and those with heads showing.

5. Count the pennies with tails showing, record the number, and put the pennies back into the container.

6. Repeat steps 3–5 until no more pennies remain.

Data Analysis

1. **Plot a graph** of the total number of pennies on the *x*-axis versus the number of pennies with tails showing on the *y*-axis.

2. **Plot a graph** of all students' data on the same graph and **compare** the graphs.

3. **Infer** Does the larger sample come closer to the ideal outcome, in which half of the atoms decay during each trial?

4. **State** how many atoms were represented by your original number of pennies.

5. **State** how many shakes represented one half-life.

 Science Content Standards

7.b Students know each element has a specific number of protons in the nucleus (the atomic number) and each isotope of the element has a different but specific number of neutrons in the nucleus.

9.e Students will construct appropriate graphs from data and develop quantitative statements about the relationships between variables.

 MA8: ALG 6.0

Science Content Standards

5.d Students know physical processes include freezing and boiling, in which a material changes form with no chemical reaction.

7.c Students know substances can be classified by their properties, including their melting temperature, density, hardness, and thermal and electrical conductivity.

9.a Plan and conduct a scientific investigation to test a hypothesis.

Reading Guide

What *You'll Learn*

▶ **Identify** physical properties.

▶ **Explain** why melting and boiling temperatures are physical properties.

▶ **Define** a physical change.

Why *It's Important*

The physical properties of a substance are keys to how the substance can be useful.

Vocabulary

physical property
melting point
boiling point
thermal conductivity
electrical conductivity
physical change

Review Vocabulary

density: the mass of an object divided by its volume (Grade 6)

Physical Properties and Changes

Main Idea Substances have physical properties that can be described and physical changes that can be observed.

Real-World Reading Connection Almost everybody likes frozen yogurt, but how would you describe it? You might use words such as *delicious, flavorful,* or *tasty.* But these words describe how you feel about the frozen yogurt. Other people might feel differently. A better way to describe frozen yogurt would be to state its properties.

What is a physical property?

How can you describe the frozen yogurt in **Figure 23** in a way everyone would agree upon? You could list its physical properties. A **physical property** is any characteristic of a material that can be observed without changing the identity of the material itself. Physical properties include details about a material's appearance, such as color, length, and shape. Some physical properties of chocolate frozen yogurt are brown color, smooth texture, and cold temperature. The bowl is hard, white, and round. Some physical properties, such as mass and volume, depend on the amount of matter. Other physical properties, such as density, melting point, and boiling point, do not depend on the amount of matter.

 Reading Check What are three physical properties of chocolate frozen yogurt?

Figure 23 You can observe the physical properties of frozen yogurt without changing the frozen yogurt.

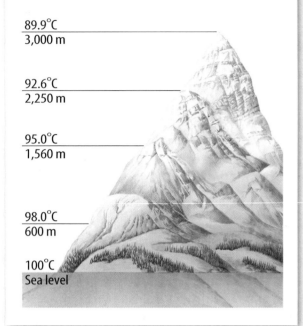

Figure 24 Water boils at lower temperatures at higher elevations because atmospheric pressure is lower than at sea level.

89.9°C
3,000 m

92.6°C
2,250 m

95.0°C
1,560 m

98.0°C
600 m

100°C
Sea level

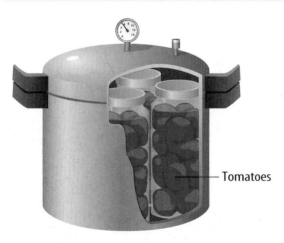

Tomatoes

Figure 25 A pressure cooker cooks food faster than an ordinary cooking pot because the temperature of the boiling water inside is hotter.

Infer why it would be important to use special care when using a pressure cooker.

Melting and Boiling Points

You have seen ice melt and water boil. In these processes, water changes its state. When ice melts, water changes from the solid to the liquid state. The temperature at which a solid changes to a liquid is its **melting point.** When water boils or evaporates, water changes from the liquid state to the gaseous state. The temperature at which a liquid changes to a gas is its **boiling point.** The temperature at which a substance changes its state is a physical property of the substance. Melting and boiling points are characteristics of a substance and can be used to identify the substance.

Attractive Forces The melting and boiling points of a substance are determined partly by the attractive forces among its particles. Molecules with greater attraction for one another are likely to have higher boiling points and melting points. Molecules with weaker attractions have lower melting and boiling points. For example, water has a much higher boiling point than molecules of similar or larger sizes. The higher boiling point occurs because water molecules are strongly attracted to one another. For water to melt or evaporate, more energy must be absorbed to break loose the molecules from one another.

 Why does water have a higher boiling point than other molecules?

Pressure The pressure of the air around a substance also affects its melting point and boiling points. The pressure of the air is called atmospheric pressure. Normal atmospheric pressure at sea level is 1 atmosphere (atm). Water has a boiling point of 100°C when the pressure is 1 atm. At elevations higher than sea level, atmospheric pressure is lower. As **Figure 24** shows, less energy is needed to change liquid water into a gas, and the boiling point decreases below 100°C. Similarly, boiling points increase as pressure increases. **Figure 25** shows a pressure cooker used for canning vegetables. Inside, the pressure can be increased enough to raise the temperature of boiling water to 140°C. This temperature ensures that microbes are killed and the food is preserved.

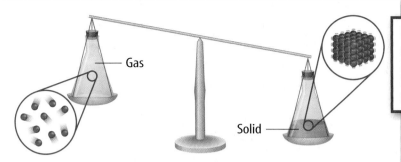

Figure 26 The volumes are the same, but the density of the gas is less than the density of the solid because there are fewer gas particles in the container.

Gas

Solid

Density

Another physical property of matter is density. Density is the mass per unit volume of a substance. The density of a substance is greater if its particles are packed tightly together. **Figure 26** shows two containers that have the same volume but different masses. One container holds a gaseous substance. The gas particles are spread far apart. The other container holds the same substance, but in the solid state. The particles in a solid and a liquid are packed close together. The mass of the gas is much lower than the mass of the liquid or the solid. Because the gas has the same volume but a smaller mass, the gas has a lower density than that of the solid or the liquid.

Hardness

Hardness is a physical property that shows how strongly the particles of a substance are held together. Diamonds, a form of carbon, are the hardest substance found in nature. **Table 2** shows that each carbon atom in a diamond is attached to four other carbon atoms. In graphite, only three covalent bonds join the carbon atoms together. The atoms form sheets of hexagons that can slip past one another. Graphite is soft compared to diamond.

Table 2 Atomic Structures of Diamond and Graphite	
	Atomic Structure
Diamond	
Graphite	

ACADEMIC VOCABULARY
transfer (TRANS fur)
(verb) to pass from one to
another
*The teacher will transfer the
book to a student.*

Thermal Conductivity

Some materials have the physical property of conducting heat well. **Thermal conductivity** is the ability of a material to **transfer** heat by collisions between its particles. Cooking pans are usually made of metal because metals have high thermal conductivity. If one part of the metal is heated, its particles move quickly and collide with nearby particles. Heat is transferred by means of these collisions.

Thermal Conductivity of Gases Gases have low thermal conductivity compared to solids and liquids. The particles in a gas are spread farther apart, so the particles collide less frequently and transfer heat more slowly. For this reason, gases are used as insulating materials, or materials that lessen heat loss.

Using Gases as Insulators For example, gases such as air and argon are sometimes sealed between two or three layers of window glass, as shown in **Figure 27.** Because the gas does not conduct heat well, less heat is lost through the windows of a building during the winter. Similarly, less heat can enter the building by means of the windows during the summer.

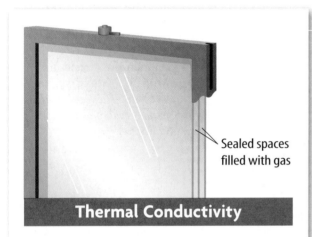

Sealed spaces filled with gas

Thermal Conductivity

Figure 27 Less heat will flow through the window because the gas that fills the space between the layers of glass has low thermal conductivity.

 Reading Check Why do some windows have air or another gas sealed between layers of glass?

Electrical Conductivity

Similar to thermal conductivity, **electrical conductivity** is the ability of a material to transfer electric charges through a material. Recall that the valence electrons in metals are able to move among the metal's atoms and can carry the charge. An electrical cord like the one in **Figure 28** consists of three copper wires covered with plastic.

Copper is used for this purpose because of its high electrical conductivity. The plastic surrounding the copper has low electrical conductivity. Its purpose is to prevent the transfer of an electric charge to your body when you touch the wire, causing you to be shocked.

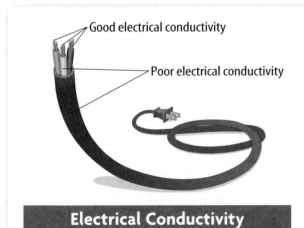

Good electrical conductivity

Poor electrical conductivity

Electrical Conductivity

Figure 28 The metal parts of this electrical cord are good conductors. The nonmetal parts are poor conductors, or insulators.

What is a physical change?

Frozen yogurt melts into a liquid. Bubble gum is blown into a sphere. A piece of modeling clay is shaped into a statue. These are physical changes. A **physical change** is any change in the size, the shape, or the state of matter in which the identity of the substance is unchanged.

Dissolving

Dissolving is mixing a substance into another substance to form a solution. As sugar dissolves in water, it disappears from view and seems to become part of the water. But if you boil the water away, the sugar becomes visible again. Dissolving is a physical change because the dissolved substance is unchanged.

Mixing

When you mix two substances, sometimes neither one dissolves in the other. In a mixture of iron filings and sand, you can identify individual particles of both substances. **Figure 29** shows that if you pass a magnet through the mixture, it attracts the iron filings and separates them from the sand. Mixing is a physical change because the substances are unchanged.

Changes in State

Changes in state are also physical changes. The ice cubes in a drink gradually melt and become liquid water. The physical properties of a substance change during a change in state, but the identity of the substance remains the same. A melted ice cube is the same substance as the original ice cube. **Figure 30** shows the element gallium changing from a solid to a liquid. The atoms that make up gallium are the same before and after the change.

Changes in state are reversible. The solid gallium that melts at normal body temperature will harden back to a solid when it is put in a cooler place. This is a physical change. A physical change does not change the particles that make up the substance.

 **Reading Check** Why are changes in state also classified as physical changes?

Figure 29 Mixtures, like this one of iron filings and sand, can be easily separated.

Infer Would this method of separation work if the mixture consisted of salt and sand?

Figure 30 Gallium melts at the temperature of your hand. The identity of the liquid gallium remains the same, so melting is a physical change.

What do you know about physical properties and changes?

You can observe and describe the physical properties of an object without changing it. Some physical properties, such as density, melting point, and boiling point, do not depend on the amount of matter. But melting and boiling points do depend on the attractive forces between particles and on atmospheric pressure. Hardness, thermal conductivity, and electrical conductivity are other physical properties. A physical change is any change in the appearance of an object that doesn't change its identity. Dissolving and mixing are examples of physical changes. Changes of state are also physical changes. Remember that a substance does not change its identity when it changes its state.

LESSON 3 Review

Summarize

Create your own lesson summary as you design a **study web.**

1. **Write** the lesson title, number, and page numbers at the top of a sheet of paper.

2. **Scan** the lesson to find the **red** main headings.

3. **Organize** these headings clockwise on branches around the lesson title.

4. **Review** the information under each **red** heading to design a branch for each **blue** subheading.

5. **List** 2–3 details, key terms, and definitions from each **blue** subheading on branches extending from the main heading branches.

 ELA8: R 2.3

Using Vocabulary

1. When ice changes to water, water undergoes a _____. **5.d**

2. Use the term *physical property* in a sentence. **7.c**

Understanding Main Ideas

3. Which is NOT a physical change? **5.d**

   A. burning
   B. dissolving
   C. melting
   D. mixing

4. **Identify** three physical properties of water and two physical changes it can undergo. **5.d**

5. **Describe** what would happen to the boiling point of a substance if the elevation were to rise. **5.d**

6. **Explain** why the rusting of an iron pole is not a physical change. **5.d**

Standards Check

7. **Compare** Copy and fill in the graphic organizer below and compare the physical properties of air and gold. **5.d**

8. **Deduce** why two objects with the same mass can have different densities. **7.c**

Applying Science

9. **Design** an experiment for comparing the thermal conductivity of glass and wood. **7.c**

10. **Assess** the importance of the physical properties of glass when it is used for windows. **7.c**

Science Online
For more practice, visit **Standards Check** at ca8.msscience.com.

MiniLab

Which parachute will drop first?

One physical property of metals is that they conduct heat. The ability of a material to transfer heat is thermal conductivity. Some metals conduct heat faster than others do. Which metals do you think conduct heat more rapidly than other metals?

Procedure

1. Read and complete a lab safety form.
2. Choose **three foil cupcake forms** and **three toy people**.
3. Use **three short pieces of thread** to attach a person to a foil form so the form becomes a parachute.
4. Choose **three rods** about 10 cm long, each made of a different metal.
5. Light a **candle** and carefully allow wax to drip on the center of the outside of a cupcake form. While the wax is melted, attach a rod horizontally to the parachute. Allow the wax to harden.
6. Repeat step 5 for the other two rods.
7. Loosely secure the **ring** on a **ring stand** to be positioned later.
8. Place the ends of the three rods as close together as possible on the ring. Use **metal clamps** to keep them secure.
9. Place a candle in a **holder** under the ring. Secure the rod ends and ring directly above the candle.
10. Light the candle and observe.

Analysis

1. **Identify** the parachute that dropped first.
2. **Explain** what property of metals caused the parachutes to drop at different times.
3. **Hypothesize** the results if three different metals had been used in this experiment.

Science Content Standards

7.c Students know substances can be classified by their properties, including their melting temperature, density, hardness, and thermal and electrical conductivity.
9.a Plan and conduct a scientific investigation to test a hypothesis.

Investigating Physical Changes

Materials

substances that are made up of some of the elements used in the Launch Lab or other elements or compounds: carbon, iron filings, sand, copper penny, copper wire, salt, ice cube, balloon, a mineral sample, milk

Safety Precautions

Problem

Matter makes up all the substances you find in your world. Matter can go through changes in size, shape or color, or even changes of state, but it still is the same matter. Matter accomplishes tasks, such as moving heat or electricity or cooling your drinks, but it still is the same matter. It is made up of the same atoms and has the same properties.

The changes in matter mentioned above are physical changes. How can you show that physical changes do not actually change matter?

Form a Hypothesis

Think about the elements you organized into a periodic table in the Launch Lab. If you change these elements in some way, or use them, can you show that they are still the same matter? Write a hypothesis for an experiment that explains why the composition of matter remains the same even though it undergoes a physical change.

Collect Data and Make Observations

1. Read and complete a lab safety form.
2. Choose five items or substances that can be put through a physical change.
3. Make a table that lists the substances and at least one element in the substance. Make a physical change to each substance and observe.
4. In your data table, record the physical change. Give a brief explanation of how the substance can be changed back.

Data Table			
Substance	Element in Substance	Physical Change to Substance	How to Change Substance Back

Analyze and Conclude

1. **Explain** why you chose certain substances for your investigation.
2. **Explain** why you chose the physical changes you made.
3. **Evaluate** how difficult it was to recover the original substance following some physical changes.
4. **Apply** Are there some physical changes that would be very difficult to reverse? Explain.
5. **Infer** You may have seen tanks marked "Liquid Nitrogen." Has the gas form of nitrogen undergone a physical change? Does the nitrogen in the tank have the same properties as the nitrogen in the air you breathe?
6. **Draw Conclusions** Matter can go through changes that make it look different and feel different, but it is still the same matter. Why is this so? Give some examples.

Error Analysis

Did you make any changes in which the original substance could not be observed or returned to its original state? For example, did you cook an egg or bake a cupcake? Check to be certain all the changes you made were physical. How can you be sure?

Communicate

 **Science**  ELA8: W 1.3

Write a Paragraph Explain how you can determine that a change in matter is a physical change. Use your observations in this experiment to provide examples.

Science Content Standards

7.c Students know substances can be classified by their properties, including their melting temperature, density, hardness, and thermal and electrical conductivity.

9.a Plan and conduct a scientific investigation to test a hypothesis.

Real World Science

The Chemistry of Color

A ceramic artist creates pieces of pottery using clay and glazes with specific properties. Glazes change color when fired in a kiln, a brick-lined oven. The artist must choose materials and heating conditions very carefully to produce the desired result. How can you become a ceramic artist? In high school, you will need to take chemistry and art classes.

Visit **Careers** at ca8.msscience.com to research how ceramic artists use chemistry. Pretend you are a ceramic artist applying for work. **Write** a letter to an art studio. Explain your credentials and your interest in their program. Mention at least three elements in your letter.

Superconductors

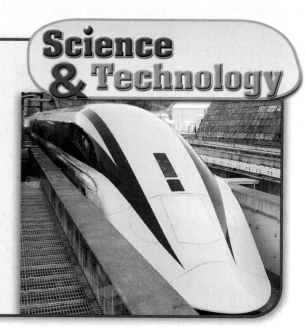

This train does not run on a normal track—it glides on a magnetic cushion created by a superconductor. A superconductor is usually a ceramic substance with specific metals added to the mix. This allows an electric current to flow without resistance. The drawback is that the susperconductor must operate at a very low temperature.

Visit **Technology** at ca8.msscience.com to research how superconductors work. **Make a bar graph** of the critical temperature of ten superconducting substances.

USES OF LEAD IN HISTORY

Although incredibly flexible and versatile, lead is also quite toxic. The Romans called lead *plumbum*, giving the element the symbol *Pb*. The Roman name of *plumbum* gives us the term plumber. The architect Vitruvius condemned the widespread use of lead in 14 B.C. His warnings went unheeded until the European League of Nations banned white-lead paint in 1922. The United States did not follow suit until 1992.

Visit **History** at ca8.msscience.com to read more about the symptoms and probable causes of lead poisoning. **Write** a public health magazine article citing the dangers and ways to avoid them.

 ELA8: W 1.3

Fluoridation of Drinking Water

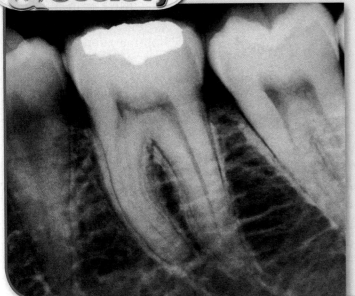

In 1945, Grand Rapids, Michigan became the first city in the world to fluoridate its drinking water. By 1956, the rate of cavities in children had dropped more than 60 percent. Many other American cities also began to fluoridate their water. Not everyone agreed with this. Many citizens and professionals continue the debate today.

Visit **Society** at ca8.msscience.com to find out more about the controversy over water fluoridation. **Evaluate** arguments and evidence presented by each side.

The BIG Idea Elements on the periodic table are grouped together based on their properties.

Lesson 1 Organization of the Periodic Table

3.f, 7.a

Main Idea **The periodic table contains information about the structure and characteristics of elements.**

- Elements on the periodic table are arranged horizontally in periods by increasing atomic number.
- Each element has a specific number of protons in its nucleus.
- Elements on the periodic table are arranged vertically in groups.
- Elements in groups share similar physical and chemical properties.
- Elements on the periodic table fall into one of three main types: metals, nonmetals, and semimetals.
- Different types of periodic tables provide different information.

- **conductivity** (p. 295)
- **group** (p. 291)
- **halogen** (p. 296)
- **luster** (p. 295)
- **metallic** (p. 295)
- **noble gas** (p. 297)
- **period** (p. 291)

Lesson 2 Isotopes and Radioactivity

7.a, 7.b, 9.e

Main Idea **Over time, radioactive isotopes decay at varying rates.**

- Isotopes have the same number of protons and electrons, but a different number of neutrons.
- The number of neutrons in an isotope can be found by subtracting the atomic number from the mass number.
- Isotopes that are radioactive have unstable nuclei.
- Elements that have atomic numbers 43, 61, and 84 and higher are radioactive.
- Radioactive isotopes undergo decay at different rates.
- Scientists who discover elements have the right to name their elements.

- **half-life** (p. 306)
- **particle accelerator** (p. 307)
- **radioactive** (p. 303)
- **radioactive decay** (p. 303)
- **radioactive element** (p. 305)
- **synthetic element** (p. 306)
- **transmutation** (p. 304)

Lesson 3 Physical Properties and Changes

5.d, 7.c, 9.a

Main Idea **Substances have physical properties that can be described and physical changes that can be observed.**

- Melting and boiling points depend on the attractions between particles and the pressure of the air.
- Density is the mass per unit volume of a substance.
- Hardness, thermal conductivity, and electrical conductivity are physical properties.
- Dissolving and mixing are physical changes.
- Changes in state are physical changes.

- **boiling point** (p. 314)
- **electrical conductivity** (p. 316)
- **melting point** (p. 314)
- **physical change** (p. 317)
- **physical property** (p. 313)
- **thermal conductivity** (p. 316)

Download quizzes, key terms, and flash cards from ca8.msscience.com.

Linking Vocabulary and Main Ideas

Use the vocabulary terms from page 324 to complete this concept map.

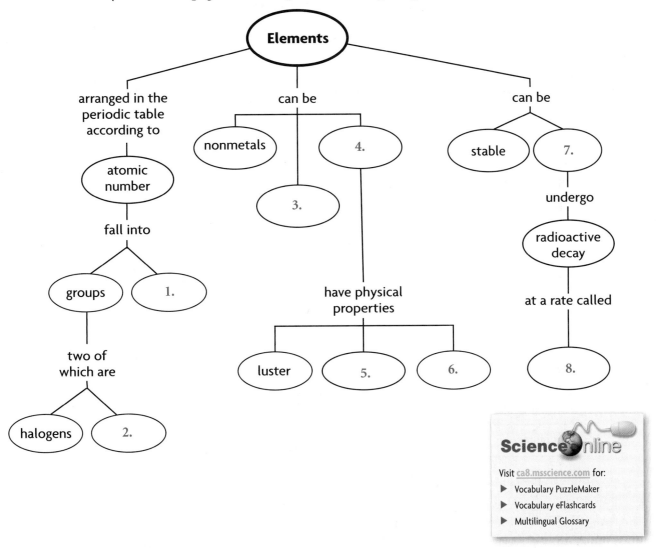

Using Vocabulary

Describe the relationship between each pair of terms.

9. *group* and *period*

10. *electrical conductivity* and *physical property*

11. *halogen* and *noble gas*

12. *particle accelerator* and *transmutation*

13. *boiling point* and *melting point*

14. *electrical conductivity* and *thermal conductivity*

Fill in the blanks with the correct vocabulary term.

15. Each radioactive isotope decays at a rate defined by its _____. **7.b**

16. Synthetic elements are made in large machines called _____. **7.b**

17. A(n) _____ occurs when a piece of clay is molded into a statue. **7.c**

Understanding Main Ideas

Choose the word or phrase that best answers the question.

1. In what way are the elements in a group similar?
   A. atomic numbers
   B. atomic masses
   C. chemical properties
   D. symbols   **7.a**

2. Which physical properties of copper wire are independent of the amount of matter?
   A. density
   B. length
   C. mass
   D. shape   **7.c**

3. The table below lists half-lives for different isotopes.

Isotope	Half-Life
Fermium-249	3 minutes
Californium-245	44 minutes
Einsteinium-250	8.6 hours
Europium-147	24.4 days

   According to the table, which isotope decays fastest?
   A. fermium-249
   B. californium-245
   C. einsteinium-250
   D. europium-147   **7.b**

4. Which is NOT a semimetal?
   A. nitrogen   C. silicon
   B. boron   D. germanium   **7.a**

5. Which is an example of a physical change?
   A. tarnishing   C. burning
   B. rusting   D. melting   **7.c**

6. Which statement is true about all synthetic elements?
   A. They are found in nature.
   B. They are radioactive.
   C. They have atomic numbers greater than 92.
   D. They have all been discovered.   **7.b**

7. Which is a property of nonmetals?
   A. malleability
   B. luster
   C. good conductor of electricity
   D. poor conductor of electricity   **7.c**

8. Which is NOT found on the element blocks of the periodic table?
   A. atomic symbol
   B. atomic number
   C. date of discovery
   D. atomic mass   **7.a**

9. The table lists the melting and boiling points for different substances.

	Melting Point (°C)	Boiling Point (°C)
Substance 1	67	215
Substance 2	−105	−26
Substance 3	−30	58
Substance 4	86	142

   Which substance is a liquid at room temperature (25°C)?
   A. substance 1
   B. substance 2
   C. substance 3
   D. substance 4   **7.c**

10. How many neutrons does the isotope molybdenum-98 have?
    A. 98   C. 56
    B. 42   D. 140   **7.b**

Applying Science

11. **Relate** three properties of metals to a cooking pan and **show** how they are important for the way the pan is used. **7.c**

12. **Suggest a reason** why the Group 1 elements would be more likely to react with halogens than with the noble gases. **7.a**

13. **Classify** the following elements as metals, non-metals, or semimetals: germanium, phosphorus, oxygen, beryllium. **7.a**

14. **Interpret** the diagram. Describe what is taking place and name the process. Are the same numbers of protons and neutrons present on both sides of the equation? What is the atomic number of radon? **7.b**

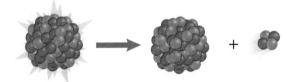

Radium-226   Radon-222   Alpha particle

15. **Suggest reasons** why it is important that the international organizations IUPAP and IUPAC are involved in approving and naming elements. **7.a**

16. **Identify** the element that is a gas among the following: boron, argon, sodium, sulfur. Use the periodic table. **7.a**

17. **Suggest a way** that you could decrease the thermal conductivity of oven mitts to better protect your hands from being burned. The mitts are made from thick squares of cloth sewn together. **7.c**

WRITING in ▶ Science

18. **Write a paragraph** describing the preparation of a meal and identify steps in the process in which physical changes occur. **ELA8: W 1.1**

Cumulative Review

19. **Identify** three types of chemical bonds. **3.b**

20. **Describe** the difference between the way carbon forms the crystal called diamond and sodium and chlorine form solid sodium chloride. **3.c**

21. **Explain** how positive and negative ions form. **3.c**

Applying Math

Use the table below to answer questions 22–26.

Half-Lives of Erbium	
Isotope	Half-Life
^{145}Er	0.9 s
^{147}Er	2.5 s
^{154}Er	3.73 min
^{156}Er	19.5 min
^{158}Er	2.29 h
^{169}Er	9.40 days

22. How many minutes is the half-life for ^{147}Er? **MA6: ALG 2.0**

23. How many seconds is the half-life for ^{156}Er? **MA6: ALG 2.0**

24. How many hours is the half-life for ^{154}Er? **MA6: ALG 2.0**

25. How many minutes is the half-life for ^{145}Er? **MA6: ALG 2.0**

26. How many seconds is the half-life for ^{169}Er? **MA6: ALG 2.0**

1 Which elements are found close to the right side of the periodic table?

A nonmetals

B metals

C metalloids

D lanthanides **7.a**

2 The illustration below shows the element block for chlorine.

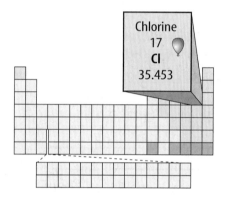

How many electrons does an uncharged atom of chlorine have?

A 17

B 18

C 35

D 36 **3.f**

3 Which property does NOT describe a metal?

A brittle

B conductive

C ductile

D malleable **7.c**

4 Many elements that are essential for life, including nitrogen, oxygen, and carbon, are part of what classification?

A semimetals

B metals

C noble gases

D nonmetals **7.a**

Use the figure below to answer questions 5 and 6.

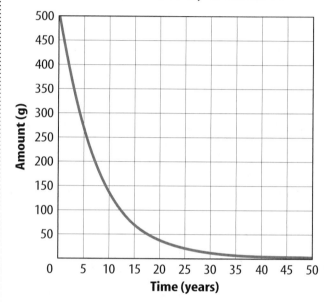

Radioactive Decay of Cobalt-60

5 What is the half-life of cobalt-60?

A 5.27 years

B 10.54 years

C 21.08 years

D 60.0 years **7.b**

6 About how much of the original 500 g of cobalt-60 will be left after 20 years?

A 30 g

B 60 g

C 90 g

D 120 g **7.b**

7　Molecules with weaker attractive forces have

A　lower melting and boiling points.

B　lower melting points and higher boiling points.

C　higher melting and boiling points.

D　higher melting points and lower boiling points.

5.d

8　What is the state of matter of semimetals at room temperature?

A　gas

B　liquid

C　plasma

D　solid

7.a

9　The illustration below shows elements in four groups in the periodic table.

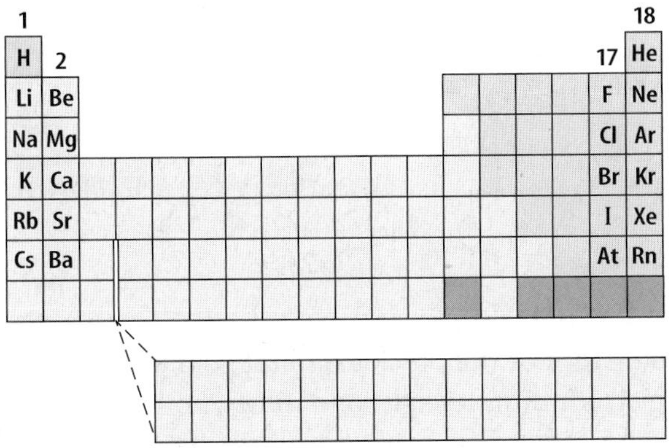

Which group of elements most readily combines with Group 17 elements?

A　Group 1

B　Group 2

C　Group 17

D　Group 18

7.a

10　How many stable isotopes does hydrogen have?

A　0

B　1

C　2

D　3

7.b

11　A nucleus that is unstable and undergoes decay is called

A　transmutation.

B　synthetic.

C　radioactive.

D　isotopes.

7.b

12　The table below describes some physical properties of bromine.

Physical Properties of Bromine	
Density	3.12 g/cm^3
Boiling Point	59°C
Melting Point	−7°C

At what temperature is bromine a solid?

A　−10°C

B　10°C

C　40°C

D　80°C

7.c

13　Which characteristic is typical of a solid non-metal element?

A　brittle

B　good electrical conductor

C　good heat conductor

D　shiny

7.c

Reading on Your Own...

From the Recommended Literature for Science and Math

Are you interested in learning more about the structure of matter, atoms, and the periodic table? If so, check out these great books.

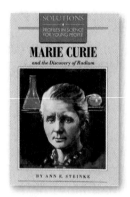

Biography

Marie Curie and the Discovery of Radium, by Ann Steinke, is a biography of Marie Curie, winner of Nobel Prizes in Physics and Mathematics. This book discusses her childhood, the obstacles she faced as a young woman, her dedication to science, and her interest in mathematics. **The content of this book is related to** Science Standard 8.3.

Nonfiction

Q Is for Quark: A Science Alphabet Book, by David Swartz, is an informational book about a wide variety of science topics. Comical illustrations help explain astronomy, mass, quarks, forces, and acid-bases. **The content of this book is related to** Science Standard 8.3.

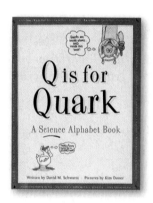

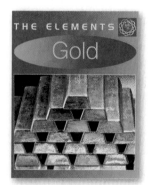

Nonfiction

Gold, by Sarah Angliss, explores the history of the precious metal gold and includes an explanation of its chemistry (atomic weight and mass), how it reacts, its uses, where it is found, and its importance. This book introduces the periodic table of elements. **The content of this book is related to** Science Standard 8.5.

Nonfiction

The Periodic Kingdom, by P. W. Atkins, tells the history of the periodic table as if it were a "periodic kingdom." Just like a kingdom, there are subjects, called elements, and regions, called families. The relationships between elements and families are discussed. **The content of this book is related to** Science Standard 8.7.

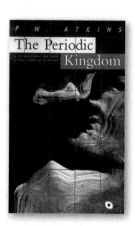

Choose the word or phrase that best answers the question.

1. In Rutherford's gold foil experiment, why did Rutherford infer the presence of a tiny, dense nucleus?

   A. The alpha particles went through the foil.

   B. No alpha particles went through the foil.

   C. The charges were uniformly distributed in the atom.

   D. Some alpha particles bounced back from the foil. `3.a`

2. Which term describes all nuclei with more than 83 protons?

   A. stable

   B. synthetic

   C. radioactive

   D. isotopes `7.c`

3. How many electrons are in the outer energy level of the Group 17 elements?

   A. 1

   B. 2

   C. 7

   D. 8 `3.a`

4. Which is the process of a gas cooling to form a liquid?

   A. boiling

   B. condensation

   C. freezing

   D. sublimation `5.d`

Write your responses on a sheet of paper.

5. The illustration below shows Rutherford's gold foil experiment.

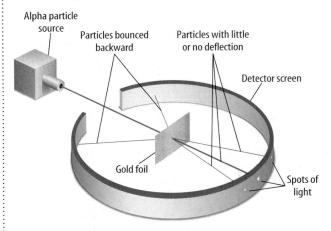

   Conclude What is the significance of the particles that reflected back from the gold foil? How did Rutherford explain his results? `3.a`

6. **Explain** why metal hammered into sheets does not break. Why do metals conduct electricity? `7.c`

7. **Define** What is an ionic bond? Describe how sodium chloride forms an ionic bond. `3.d`

8. **Explain** the difference between evaporation and boiling. `5.d`

9. **Make a Graph** Manganese-54 has a half-life of about 312 days. Draw a graph of the radioactive decay of a 600-g sample of manganese-54. `9.e`

10. **Describe** the composition of the atom. `3.a`

11. **Compare** the arrangement and movement of particles in a solid, a liquid, and a gas. `5.d`

UNIT 3

Chemical Interactions

Take a Look Inside This is an image of a chemical that is inside the body, liquid crystalline DNA. Some chemists have to understand both the living world and the chemical world to be the best at their jobs.

West Coast Events

1840
Mercury is discovered in the Santa Cruz Mountains of California; makes an amalgam with gold that makes gold easier to find and recover; later found dangerous to environment.

1868
The University of California, the oldest public university in California, is founded in Oakland; moves to Berkeley in 1873.

1880
The University of Southern California is founded.

A.D. 1700   1750   1800   1850   190

World Events

3,000 Years Ago
People in Africa are known for their iron products made by smelting iron ore and charcoal at high heat.

1777
Antoine-Laurent Lavoisier confirms law of conservation of mass.

c. 1880
Hilaire de Chardonnet accidentally discovers artificial silk fibers.

Science Online

To learn more about chemists and their work, visit ca8.msscience.com.

Concepts In Motion

Interactive Time Line To learn more about these events and others, visit ca8.msscience.com.

1930s
Linus Pauling at the California Institute of Technology determines how atoms link up to form molecules in both living and nonliving systems.

November 2005
California scientists at Lawrence Livermore National Laboratory and the University of California at Los Angeles show how new optical tools can be used to study the protein folding that can lead to nerve diseases.

| 1920 | 1940 | 1960 | 1980 | 2000 | 2020 |

1940
Peter Debye develops a light-scattering method to measure the molecular weight of large polymers.

1996
The U.S. Food and Drug Administration approves use of polymer wafer implants in the treatment of brain cancer.

2002
John B. Fenn, Koichi Tanaka, and Kurt Wüthrich share the Nobel Prize for Chemistry for developing ways to identify and analyze the structure of macromolecules.

Chemical Reactions

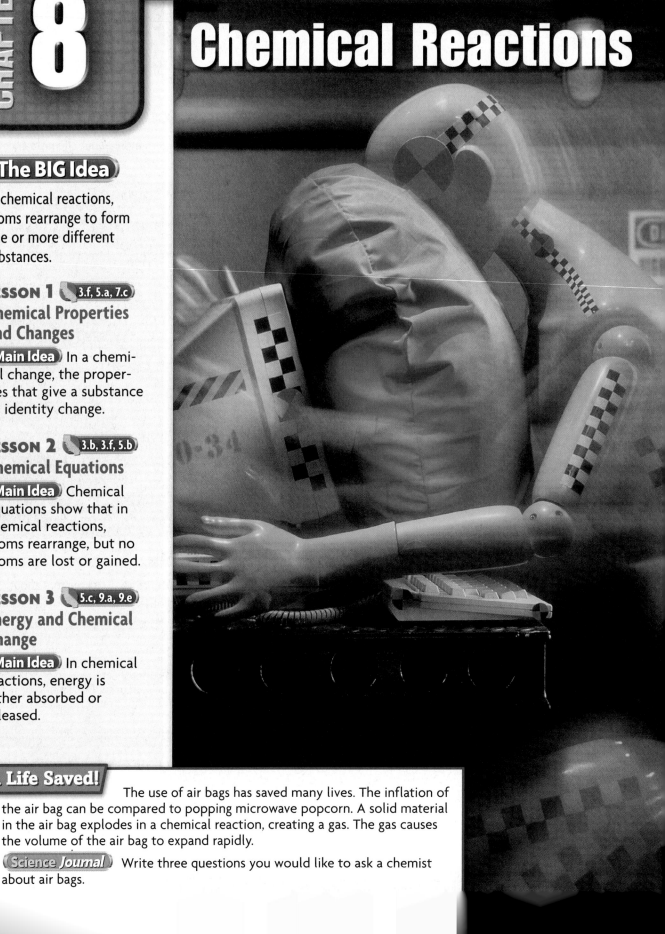

The BIG Idea

In chemical reactions, atoms rearrange to form one or more different substances.

LESSON 1 〔 3.f, 5.a, 7.c 〕
Chemical Properties and Changes

Main Idea In a chemical change, the properties that give a substance its identity change.

LESSON 2 〔 3.b, 3.f, 5.b 〕
Chemical Equations

Main Idea Chemical equations show that in chemical reactions, atoms rearrange, but no atoms are lost or gained.

LESSON 3 〔 5.c, 9.a, 9.e 〕
Energy and Chemical Change

Main Idea In chemical reactions, energy is either absorbed or released.

A Life Saved!

The use of air bags has saved many lives. The inflation of the air bag can be compared to popping microwave popcorn. A solid material in the air bag explodes in a chemical reaction, creating a gas. The gas causes the volume of the air bag to expand rapidly.

Science Journal Write three questions you would like to ask a chemist about air bags.

Launch Lab

00:15 minutes

Can you see a chemical reaction taking place?

In chemical reactions, substances combine to make new products with different properties. What changes can you observe in this reaction?

Procedure

1. Complete a lab safety form.
2. Put 50 mL of **water** into a **beaker or glass.**
3. Add 2 g of **alum.**
4. Add 10 mL of **ammonia.**
5. Observe for 5 min without moving the glass.

Think About This

- **Describe** what the starting materials looked like.
- **Compare** the material after the reaction to the starting materials.
- **List** evidence that a chemical reaction occurred.

5.a

Science Online

Visit ca8.msscience.com to:

▶ view **Concepts in Motion**
▶ explore Virtual Labs
▶ access content-related Web links
▶ take the Standards Check

FOLDABLES™
Study Organizer

Chemical Reactions
Make the following Foldable to organize the similarities and differences of chemical reactions.

▷ **STEP 1** **Fold** a sheet of paper in half lengthwise. Make the back edge about 2 cm longer than the front edge.

▷ **STEP 2** **Fold** in half again.

▷ **STEP 3** **Unfold** the paper once. **Cut** along the fold of the top flap to make two flaps.

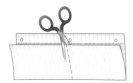

▷ **STEP 4** **Label** the flaps as shown.

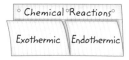

Chemical Reactions
Exothermic | Endothermic

Reading Skill

Comparing and Contrasting
As you read this chapter, record similarities and differences between exothermic and endothermic reactions.

Get Ready to Read

Identify Cause and Effect

1 Learn It! A *cause* is the reason something happens. The result of what happens is called an *effect*. Learning to identify causes and effects helps you understand why things happen. By using graphic organizers, you can sort and analyze causes and effects as you read.

2 Practice It! Read the following paragraph. Then use the graphic organizer below to show what happened when a chemical change occurs.

> A chemical change is the change of one or more substances into other substances. In a chemical change, atoms rearrange and form one or more new substances. They do this by breaking bonds and forming new ones. When paper burns, the new substances that are produced—ash, carbon dioxide, and water—can't be turned back into paper. The burning of paper is a chemical change.
>
> —*from page 341*

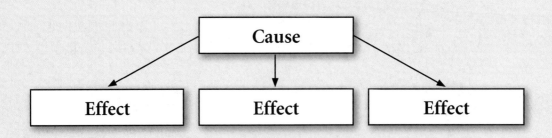

```
                    Cause
        ┌─────────────┼─────────────┐
        ▼             ▼             ▼
     Effect        Effect        Effect
```

3 Apply It! As you read the chapter, be aware of causes and effects of chemical changes. Find five causes and their effects.

Target Your Reading

Use this to focus on the main ideas as you read the chapter.

1 **Before you read** the chapter, respond to the statements below on your worksheet or on a numbered sheet of paper.

- Write an **A** if you **agree** with the statement.
- Write a **D** if you **disagree** with the statement.

2 **After you read** the chapter, look back to this page to see if you've changed your mind about any of the statements.

- If any of your answers changed, explain why.
- Change any false statements into true statements.
- Use your revised statements as a study guide.

Reading Tip

Graphic organizers such as the cause-effect organizer help you organize what you are reading so you can remember it later.

Before You Read A or D	Statement	After You Read A or D
	1 In physical and chemical changes, the identity of a substance changes.	
	2 The boiling of water is a physical change.	
	3 Physical and chemical changes are not reversible.	
	4 A molecule contains two or more atoms bonded together.	
	5 In chemical reactions, atoms rearrange to form one or more new substances.	
	6 To balance a chemical equation, it might be necessary to add coefficients and subscripts.	
	7 A chemical equation must have the same number and kinds of atoms in the reactants and products.	
	8 Energy is always released in a chemical reaction.	
	9 In an exothermic reaction, the products have less energy than the reactants.	

Science Online

Print a worksheet of this page at ca8.msscience.com.

Science Content Standards

3.f Students know how to use the periodic table to identify elements in simple compounds.

5.a Students know reactant atoms and molecules interact to form products with different chemical properties.

7.c Students know substances can be classified by their properties, including their melting temperature, density, hardness, and thermal and electrical conductivity.

Reading Guide

What *You'll Learn*

▶ **Define** chemical change.

▶ **Distinguish** between chemical and physical change.

▶ **Identify** examples of chemical and physical change.

Why *It's Important*

You can recognize a chemical reaction if you can distinguish between chemical and physical changes.

Vocabulary

chemical property
chemical change
dissolving

Review Vocabulary

physical property: any characteristic of a material that can be observed without changing the identity of the material itself (p. 313)

Chemical Properties and Changes

Main Idea In a chemical change, the properties that give a substance its identity change.

Real-World Reading Connection You take the first drink from your glass of milk. It tastes bad—the milk is sour. What kind of change occurred in the milk?

Ability to Change

You use the properties of matter to identify objects and substances. For example, you can determine whether a white substance in your kitchen is salt or sugar by tasting it. Gold and silver are different colors. Paper burns readily. Iron does not burn.

The properties of substances are either physical or chemical. Recall that a physical property is any characteristic of a substance that can be observed without changing the identity of the substance. Taste and color are physical properties. A **chemical property** is the ability or inability of a substance to combine with or change into one or more new substances. Flammability, or the ability to burn, is a chemical property. **Figure 1** shows a chemical property of potassium—it reacts with water.

Figure 1 A spectacular reaction occurs when potassium metal is dropped into water.

Describe any evidence you observe that a chemical change is occurring.

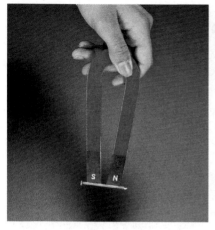

Figure 2 Iron is magnetic, but the red-brown iron oxide that forms when iron rusts is not.

Chemical Properties

You may be surprised at how often you observe chemical properties. For example, paper burns. A sliced apple turns brown in air. A car, abandoned outside, slowly rusts. These are chemical properties. To observe a chemical property, the substance undergoing the change must be converted into one or more different substances. After burning, the paper no longer exists. It has changed into ash and gases. When the iron in an abandoned car rusts, a new substance, iron oxide, is formed. **Figure 2** shows that iron oxide is a different substance with properties different from iron. Notice that the iron nail is attracted to a magnet. Iron has the physical property of magnetism. When the nail rusts, red-brown iron oxide forms on its surface. Iron oxide is not attracted to the magnet because it does not have iron's magnetic property.

 Identify a physical property and a chemical property of iron.

A chemical property also can describe the conditions under which a substance will not change identity. For example, a chemical property of helium gas is that it does not burn. Gold and platinum, if left outdoors, will not corrode. Copper and silver do not react with water. **Table 1** lists several chemical properties.

Table 1 Chemical Properties of Common Substances	
Substance	**Chemical Property**
Silver	tarnishes from sulfur in foods
Hydrogen	flammable; burns in air
Carbon dioxide	nonflammable
Aluminum	reacts with acid

Figure 3 The reddish color of copper distinguishes it from silver-colored aluminum. Both metals are malleable.

Physical Properties

If you were asked to describe yourself, you might include your hair and eye color. You also might mention your height and the length of your hair. These characteristics are some of your physical properties. They can be observed without changing you. In **Figure 3,** you can tell by their color which objects are made of copper and which are made of aluminum. Color is a physical property you can use to distinguish copper from aluminum.

 What is a physical property?

Notice that both metals are formed into various shapes. Malleability (mal yuh BIH luh tee) is the ability of a metal to be hammered or rolled into shapes. Copper and aluminum are used in cookware because of two other physical properties. Both metals conduct heat well and have high melting points. **Conductivity** (kahn duk TIH vuh tee) allows the transfer of heat from the burner to the food. A high melting point of the metal means the pans will not melt from the heat of the stove. **Table 2** lists physical properties of common substances.

Table 2 Physical Properties of Familiar Substances	
Substance	**Physical Property**
Water	boils at 100°C
Silver	good electrical conductor
Table salt, NaCl	melts at 801°C
Diamond	extremely hard
Baking soda, $NaHCO_3$	white crystalline powder
Mercury	liquid at room temperature

Chemical and Physical Changes

When a substance changes, its properties change. When ice melts, the solid water becomes liquid. When iron rusts, the metal becomes a powdery red **compound.** You grow taller; the food you eat is digested and becomes part of your body. In these changes, physical properties change. With some substances, chemical properties also change. For example, iron that has rusted is no longer iron. It is a new substance, iron oxide, which has properties that are different from iron. The food you eat is changed in the digestion process. It becomes part of the substances that make up your body tissues. These changes are different from physical changes, such as the melting of ice. Solid water and liquid water are the same substance before and after melting—both are water. Iron and iron oxide are not the same substances.

ACADEMIC VOCABULARY
compound (KAHM pownd)
(*noun*) something that is formed by a union of elements, ingredients, or parts
Salt is a compound made from sodium and chlorine.

Chemical Changes—Not Easily Reversed

How can you distinguish between physical and chemical changes? Many physical changes, such as the melting of ice, can be reversed. Ice can melt and then refreeze. Chemical changes generally are not easily reversed. A **chemical change** is the change of one or more substances into other substances. In a chemical change, atoms rearrange and form one or more new substances. They do this by breaking bonds and forming new ones. When paper burns, the new substances that are produced—ash, carbon dioxide, and water—can't be turned back into paper. The burning of paper is a chemical change. **Figure 4** shows another chemical change. Vinegar is added to baking soda. The mixture foams as carbon dioxide gas bubbles out. This change can't be reversed. You will read more about this chemical change later in the chapter.

 Figure 4 What evidence can you observe that shows that a chemical change is occurring?

Materials

Chemical Change

Figure 4 Vinegar and baking soda combine to form new substances. One is carbon dioxide gas.

Figure 5 Electrical energy is needed to decompose water into hydrogen gas and oxygen gas.

Infer from the volumes of the two product gases whether water contains equal numbers of hydrgen and oxygen atoms.

Forming New Substances

In one type of chemical change, a compound is decomposed into its elements. In **Figure 5,** electricity is used to break the chemical bonds that join hydrogen and oxygen in water molecules. Hydrogen gas and oxygen gas are produced and captured in the test tubes.

In another type of chemical change, two elements join to form a compound. Recall that sodium chloride is composed of sodium and chlorine. **Figure 6** shows that sodium is a soft, silvery metal. Sodium and potassium are in the same group on the periodic table. Elements in the same group have similar properties, so the reactivity of sodium is similar to that of potassium. Recall the vigorous reaction of potassium and water shown in **Figure 1.** Sodium metal and chlorine gas also react vigorously when they are mixed together. The result is white crystals of sodium chloride, as shown in **Figure 6.** The toxic elements, sodium and chlorine, combine to form a compound that we eat on our food. All chemical changes produce substances that are different from the starting substances.

Figure 6 The properties of sodium chloride are completely different from the properties of the elements it contains.

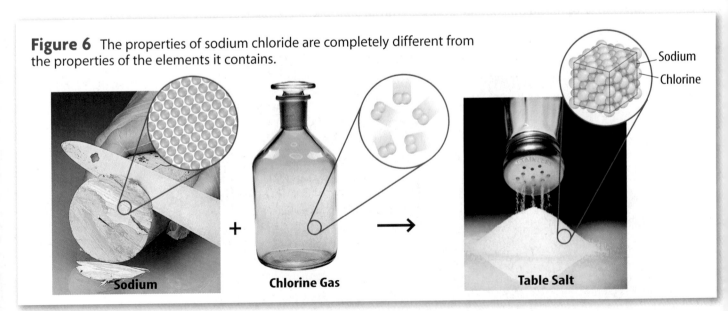

Sodium

Chlorine

Sodium + **Chlorine Gas** → **Table Salt**

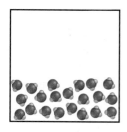

Figure 7 Matter can change from one state to another when thermal energy is released or absorbed.

$H_2O(\text{liquid}) + \text{heat} \longrightarrow H_2O(\text{gas})$

Physical Changes

You have read how chemical changes differ from physical changes. Recall that a physical change is a change in which the properties of a substance change but the identity of the substance remains the same. For example, when water boils, liquid water turns into water vapor. The water molecules do not break apart into hydrogen atoms and oxygen atoms, as they do in a chemical change. Instead, the water molecules remain intact, but they move farther apart, forming a gas.

When water in the gas phase cools, liquid water forms again. Changes of state are reversible. Recall that physical changes, but not chemical changes, usually are reversible. Therefore, changes of state are physical changes. Other substances also undergo reversible changes of state. Solder (SAH dur) is a mixture of metals used to connect wires on circuit boards, as shown in **Figure 8.** Solder is heated to change it from a solid to a liquid. After the liquid is dropped onto the wires, it cools and changes back to a solid. There is no change in the composition of the solder.

 What evidence can you give that a change of state is a physical change?

Dissolving

Dissolving sugar in water is another example of a physical change. **Dissolving** is a process in which substances mix evenly with one another. If sugar is dissolved in water, can you get the sugar back? Yes, when you evaporate the water, the sugar is unchanged, so dissolving is a physical process. The ionic salt, sodium chloride, breaks up into ions when it dissolves in water. But when the water is evaporated, the solid salt is recovered unchanged. You will read more about dissolving substances in Chapter 9.

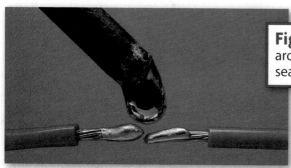

Figure 8 The liquid solder flows around and between the wires and seals them together when it hardens.

Chemical Properties and Changes

If a substance undergoes a change but can be recovered with its properties unchanged, the process is a physical change. A further clue to physical changes is that they are reversible. Melting, boiling, and dissolving are physical changes.

In a chemical change, atoms are rearranged. Clues, such as formation of bubbles and formation of solids in liquids, are helpful signs that a chemical change has taken place. The substances you have at the beginning of the change have different physical and chemical properties from those substances you have at the end.

LESSON 1 Review

Summarize

Create your own lesson summary as you write a script for a **television news report.**

1. **Review** the text after the **red** main headings and write one sentence about each. These are the headlines of your broadcast.

2. **Review** the text and write 2–3 sentences about each **blue** subheading. These sentences should tell *who, what, when, where,* and *why* information about each **red** heading.

3. **Include** descriptive details in your report, such as names of reporters and local places and events.

4. **Present** your news report to other classmates alone or with a team.

 **ELA8: LS 2.1**

Standards Check

Using Vocabulary

1. Distinguish between a chemical property and a chemical change. **5.a**

2. _____ occurs when salt is evenly mixed with water. **5.d**

Understanding Main Ideas

3. Which is a chemical change?
   A. dissolving sugar in water
   B. breaking a bone
   C. heating a copper pan in the oven
   D. frying an egg **5.a**

4. **List** two physical changes and two chemical changes. **5.a**

5. **Explain** how you know that gasoline burning in a car engine is a chemical change. **5.a**

6. **Apply** Two clear, colorless liquids are poured together. A bright yellow solid forms. What physical properties have changed? **7.c**

7. **Compare** Copy and fill in the graphic organizer below and compare physical change and chemical change. **5.a, 5.d**

Applying Science

8. **Hypothesize** Why might a bright-yellow solid form when two clear, colorless liquids are mixed? **5.a**

9. **Assess** the following evidence to decide whether a chemical change has occurred. A student heated a yellow solid. The solid melted and turned red. When the solid cooled, it returned to its original yellow color. **5.d**

Science nline

For more practice, visit **Standards Check** at ca8.msscience.com.

MiniLab

How can you tell a chemical change from a physical change?

00:20
minutes

What is the difference between a chemical and a physical change? In this activity you will observe a variety of changes and record your observations and thoughts about the changes.

Procedure

1. Copy the table into your Science Journal.
2. Complete the table as your teacher performs the changes.

Analysis

1. **List** any pieces of evidence that a chemical reaction occurred.

2. **Identify** some key words that let you know a change is chemical. Are there key words that let you know a change is physical?

Data Table	
Change or Reaction	**Chemical or Physical Change? How do you know?**
Burning wood or paper	
Breaking a match	
Striking a match	
Burning magnesium	
Shaving magnesium	
Making foil into a ball	
Placing zinc metal in copper nitrate solution	
Melting ice	
Burning a candle	
Hammering copper metal	

 Science Content Standards

5.a Students know reactant atoms and molecules interact to form products with different chemical properties.

Science Content Standards

3.b Students know that compounds are formed by combining two or more different elements and that compounds have properties that are different from their constituent elements.

3.f Students know how to use the periodic table to identify elements in simple compounds.

5.b Students know the idea of atoms explains the conservation of matter: In chemical reactions the number of atoms stays the same no matter how they are arranged, so their total mass stays the same.

Reading Guide

What *You'll Learn*

▶ **Distinguish** among elements, compounds, and molecules.

▶ **Determine** how a chemical reaction satisfies the law of conservation of mass.

▶ **Write** a balanced chemical equation.

▶ **Identify** common chemical reactions.

Why *It's Important*

Chemical equations are the language of chemistry.

Vocabulary

law of conservation of mass
reactant
product
diatomic molecule
coefficient

Review Vocabulary

molecule: a neutral particle in which atoms share electrons (p. 219)

Chemical Equations

Main Idea Chemical equations show that in chemical reactions, atoms rearrange, but no atoms are lost or gained.

Real-World Reading Connection Magicians can make a rabbit appear out of a hat and a person disappear from a box. You might be amazed, but you know that the rabbit has not come from nowhere, and the person is not gone. In chemical reactions, substances might seem to appear or disappear. But careful observations show that the same amount of matter is present after the reaction as before.

Is matter conserved in chemical reactions?

Chemical reaction is another name for chemical change. Recall that a chemical change is a change of one or more substances into other substances. In all chemical reactions, the amount of matter is the same before and after the change takes place. Another way to say this is that mass is conserved. In a chemical reaction, bonds between atoms break and new bonds form. The atoms rearrange. The illustration in **Figure 9** represents atoms as boxes linked together. The two types of atoms have different masses. The figure shows that after the reaction, the atoms are linked in different ways. But no atoms are lost, and no atoms are gained. Use the key to determine the total mass of the boxes before the reaction. Then find the total mass of the boxes after the reaction.

 Visual Check **Figure 9** Is the total mass the same after the rearrangement as it was before?

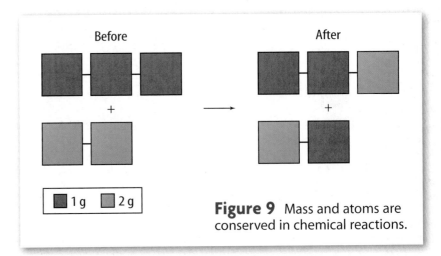

Figure 9 Mass and atoms are conserved in chemical reactions.

Figure 10 Antoine Lavoisier is known as the father of modern chemistry. He used a precise balance to measure the masses of the reactants and products in his experiments.

Antoine Lavoisier

Chemist Antoine Lavoisier (AN twan • luh VWAH see ay) (1743–1794) is given credit for showing that mass is conserved in chemical reactions. **Figure 10** shows Lavoisier's laboratory and a balance similar to the one he invented. The balance allowed him to make more **precise** measurements than had been possible before. In a series of experiments, he measured the mass of materials before and after a chemical reaction. In one experiment, Lavoisier put tin into a closed container. He measured the mass of the container and its contents. Using a large lens to focus sunlight, he heated the tin. The tin changed in color and texture. Lavoisier knew this meant that a new substance, tin oxide, had formed. He measured the mass of the container and its contents a second time. The mass before the reaction was the same as the mass after the reaction.

 What important data did Lavoisier obtain from his experiment?

Conservation of Mass

Lavoisier repeated his experiment using other materials. In all cases, the mass at the start of the reaction was the same as the mass at the end. His results supported the law of conservation of mass. The **law of conservation of mass** states that the total mass before a chemical reaction is the same as the total mass after the reaction.

Recall that atoms have definite masses. Thus, it is not surprising that there is no mass change in a chemical reaction. Atoms simply rearrange. No atoms are lost or gained.

DataLab

Where does the tablet go?

What are the bubbles you see when you open a can of soda? Are they made of anything, or are they made of nothing at all?

Data Collection

1. Read and complete a lab safety form.

2. Copy the table into your Science Journal.

3. Put 100 mL of **water** in a **plastic soda bottle** that has a screw-on cap.

4. Measure and record the mass of the bottle, cap, and water.

5. Measure and record the mass of an **effervescent tablet.**

Data Table	
Measurement	**Mass (g)**
Mass of water, bottle, and cap	
Mass of tablet	
Mass of water, bottle, cap, and tablet	
Mass of bottle, cap, and contents after tablet dissolves, before opening cap	
Mass of bottle, cap, and contents after opening the cap	

6. Drop the tablet into the bottle and quickly screw the cap on tightly. Shake the bottle until the tablet dissolves.

7. Measure and record the mass of the capped bottle and its contents.

8. Remove the cap from the bottle and agitate the contents until all the bubbles are gone. Measure and record the mass of the bottle, its contents, and the cap.

Data Analysis

1. **Compare** the mass of the bottle before and after opening the cap. Do the bubbles have mass? How much?

2. **Identify** what you think makes up the bubbles.

3. **Explain** how this reaction follows the law of conservation of mass.

 Science Content Standards

5.b Students know the idea of atoms explains the conservation of matter: In chemical reactions the number of atoms stays the same no matter how they are arranged, so their total mass stays the same.

How do you write a chemical equation?

A chemical equation is a convenient way to describe what happens in a chemical reaction. In chemical equations, the reactants are written on the left side of an arrow pointing to the right. **Reactants** are the starting materials in a chemical reaction. If there is more than one, they are separated by plus signs. The arrow is read as "produces." The products are written on the right side of the arrow. **Products** are the new substances that are formed. Plus signs are also used to separate the products if there are more than one. In the Lavoisier experiment, tin and oxygen are the reactants. Tin oxide is the product. The reaction is written as:

$$\underset{\text{reactants}}{\text{tin} \quad + \quad \text{oxygen gas}} \quad \underset{\text{produce}}{\longrightarrow} \quad \underset{\text{product}}{\text{tin oxide}}$$

The equation reads "tin plus oxygen gas produces tin oxide."

Word Equations

The equation for the reaction of tin with oxygen is an example of a word equation. Another example is the burning of charcoal on a grill, as shown in **Figure 11.** The carbon in the charcoal reacts with oxygen from the air to produce carbon dioxide gas. The word equation for the reaction is:

$$\text{carbon} + \text{oxygen} \longrightarrow \text{carbon dioxide}$$

Later in this section you will learn how to write this as a chemical equation.

Recall the reaction of baking soda and vinegar. Baking soda is the compound sodium hydrogen carbonate. Acetic acid is the part of vinegar that reacts with the baking soda. The products of this reaction are water, carbon dioxide, and sodium acetate. The reaction is described by this word equation:

$$\text{sodium hydrogen carbonate} + \text{acetic acid} \longrightarrow$$
$$\text{water} + \text{carbon dioxide} + \text{sodium acetate}$$

 **Reading Check** What are the products of the reaction of sodium hydrogen carbonate and acetic acid?

Word equations have limitations. They can be long and they do not show that mass is conserved. As you will see later in this lesson, chemical equations, written with chemical symbols, are shorter. They also provide more information.

Figure 11 In addition to the product, carbon dioxide, the burning of charcoal produces energy to cook food.

Table 3 Diatomic Elements							
Element	Hydrogen	Nitrogen	Oxygen	Fluorine	Chlorine	Bromine	Iodine
Formula	H_2	N_2	O_2	F_2	Cl_2	Br_2	I_2

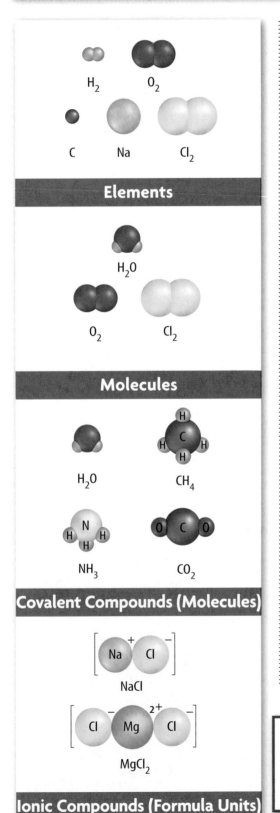

Elements

H_2 O_2

C   Na Cl_2

Molecules

H_2O

O_2 Cl_2

Covalent Compounds (Molecules)

H_2O CH_4

NH_3 CO_2

NaCl

$MgCl_2$

Ionic Compounds (Formula Units)

Elements, Compounds, and Molecules

Instead of writing long word equations, chemists use symbols to represent elements. Elements consist of one kind of atom. Remember that you can find the symbols for the elements on the periodic table. For example, iron is Fe, hydrogen is H, and helium is He.

Formulas Formulas are used to represent molecules and ionic compounds. A molecule is a neutral particle in which atoms share electrons. Molecules may be elements or compounds. If the atoms in a molecule are the same, the molecule is an element. Both oxygen gas and hydrogen gas are molecules. Hydrogen gas has the symbol H_2. Oxygen gas is represented by O_2. These molecules are diatomic. The prefix *di–* means "two." A **diatomic molecule** is a molecule that contains two atoms. **Table 3** lists the elements that normally exist as diatomic molecules. You should use these formulas when you write chemical equations.

 When is a molecule also an element?

Compounds Molecules composed of two or more different atoms are compounds. Water, H_2O, is both a molecule and a covalent compound. The atoms in water share electrons. Sodium chloride, NaCl, is an ionic compound. The formula, NaCl, represents one formula unit of sodium chloride. A formula unit is defined as the smallest whole-number ratio of the elements in an ionic compound. **Figure 12** shows examples of elements, compounds, and molecules. It is important to know the meanings of these terms. When you write chemical equations, you must use the correct formulas and symbols.

Figure 12 Some elements exist as molecules. Molecules with two or more different elements are also called compounds. Ionic compounds are called formula units.

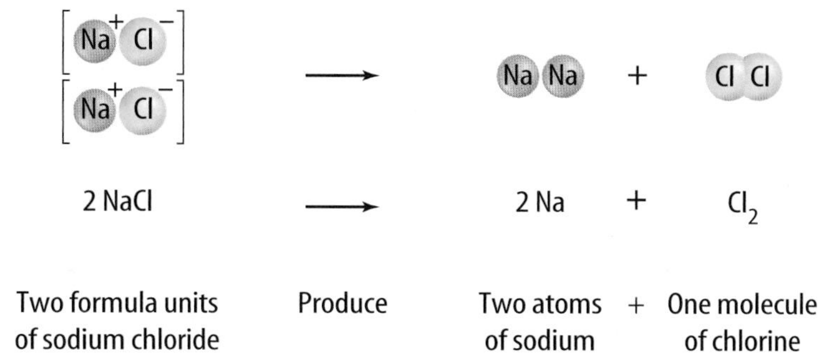

Figure 13 The illustration, the word equation, and the chemical equation show that mass is neither gained nor lost.

Categorize each substance in the equation as element, compound, molecule, or formula unit.

2 NaCl $\longrightarrow$ 2 Na + Cl_2

Two formula units of sodium chloride — Produce — Two atoms of sodium + One molecule of chlorine

Chemical Equations

You now can put together what you know and write the chemical equation for the burning of charcoal. Carbon and oxygen react to form carbon dioxide. Carbon (charcoal) and oxygen are the reactants. The product is carbon dioxide. Using the periodic table, find the symbol for carbon, which is C. In **Table 3,** note that oxygen has the diatomic formula, O_2. The formula for carbon dioxide is CO_2. Now, write the symbol and formula for the reactants. Place a plus sign between them. After the reactants, place an arrow pointing to the right. Write the formula for carbon dioxide to the right of the arrow. Your equation should look like this:

$$C + O_2 \longrightarrow CO_2$$

Read the plus sign as "reacts with." Read the arrow as "produces." The equation states that one atom of carbon reacts with one molecule of oxygen and produces one molecule of carbon dioxide.

Figure 13 shows another equation in which the reactant, sodium chloride, decomposes. Notice that the reaction produces the elements sodium and chlorine. Continue to read to find out why the number 2 is placed in front of NaCl and Na.

How do you balance a chemical equation?

Lavoisier showed experimentally that in chemical reactions, mass is neither lost nor gained. The same is true for chemical equations. Balancing an equation means showing the same number of the same kind of atom on both sides of the equation.

First, write the symbols and formulas for the reactants and products on the correct sides of the arrow. Make sure all are written correctly. Second, check for balance by counting the number of each kind of atom. Compare the number of each kind of atom in the reactants with the number of that kind of atom in the products.

Figure 14 Formulas show how many of each kind of atom are in a molecule or compound.

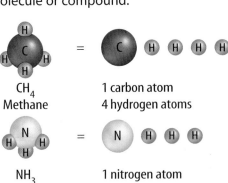

CH$_4$
Methane

1 carbon atom
4 hydrogen atoms

NH$_3$
Ammonia

1 nitrogen atom
3 hydrogen atoms

Table 4 Comparison of Coefficients and Subscripts

Formula	Meaning	Number of Atoms
H$_2$O		Two hydrogen atoms and one oxygen atom
2H$_2$O		Four hydrogen atoms and two oxygen atoms
H$_2$O$_2$		Two hydrogen atoms and two oxygen atoms

Concepts In Motion
Interactive Table Organize information about coefficients and subscripts at ca8.msscience.com.

Counting Atoms

When counting atoms, it's important to know the difference between subscripts and coefficients.

Subscripts Recall that the small number below and to the right of a symbol in a chemical formula is a subscript. A subscript tells how many atoms of an element are contained in one molecule or formula unit. In the molecule methane, CH$_4$, hydrogen's subscript is four. Carbon has no subscript. When an element has no subscript, the subscript is assumed to be one. A molecule of methane has one carbon atom and four hydrogen atoms. **Figure 14** shows the formulas and compositions of methane and ammonia. In counting atoms, it's important to write the correct formulas and know the meaning of subscripts.

Coefficients Recall the number 2 that is placed before NaCl and Na in the equation in **Figure 13.** Numbers that are written in front of a symbol or a formula in a chemical equation are called coefficients. A **coefficient** tells how many atoms, molecules, or formula units take part in the reaction. In **Figure 13,** two formula units of NaCl (2NaCl) decomposed, and two atoms of Na (2Na) were formed along with one molecule of Cl$_2$.

The expression 3H$_2$ means that three molecules of hydrogen take part in a chemical reaction. To find out how many hydrogen atoms are in 3H$_2$, multiply the subscript 2 by the coefficient 3. There are six hydrogen atoms in 3H$_2$. The difference between a subscript and a coefficient is shown in **Table 4.**

Water and hydrogen peroxide differ by a subscript. If you add the subscript 2 to oxygen in the formula for water, the new formula represents a completely different substance. Changing subscripts changes the identity of the compound.

Reading Check Explain the difference between a subscript and a coefficient.

Writing Balanced Equations

Is the equation for the burning of charcoal balanced?

$$C + O_2 \longrightarrow CO_2$$

Count the atoms. It's easy to see that one carbon atom and two oxygen atoms are on each side of the equation. The equation is balanced. Sometimes it is not as easy to tell whether an equation is balanced.

Recall the illustration in **Figure 5** that shows water decomposing when an electric current passes through it.

$$H_2O \longrightarrow H_2 + O_2$$

reactant, H_2O	products, $H_2 + O_2$
2 hydrogen atoms	2 hydrogen atoms
1 oxygen atom	2 oxygen atoms

Notice that more oxygen atoms are on the right. To balance the equation, two oxygen atoms are needed on the left. Place the coefficient 2 in front of H_2O. Now there are two molecules of H_2O.

$$2H_2O \longrightarrow H_2 + O_2$$

reactant, $2H_2O$	products, $H_2 + O_2$
4 hydrogen atoms	2 hydrogen atoms
2 oxygen atoms	2 oxygen atoms

The reaction still is not balanced. Four hydrogen atoms are on the left and only two on the right. Put the coefficient 2 in front of H_2 on the product side. Does that balance the equation?

$$2H_2O \longrightarrow 2H_2 + O_2$$

reactant, $2H_2O$	products, $2H_2 + O_2$
4 hydrogen atoms	4 hydrogen atoms
2 oxygen atoms	2 oxygen atoms

The equation is now balanced.

WORD ORIGIN

hydrogen
hydr– from Greek *hydros;* means *water*
–gene from French; means *producing*

Equations for Common Chemical Reactions

What are the steps in balancing an equation? First, write the correct symbols and formulas. Second, count atoms on both sides of the equation. Third, place coefficients in front of the symbols and formulas to balance the numbers of atoms. Remember that subscripts cannot be changed. Doing so would change the identity of the substance.

Reaction of Methane

Natural gas, the fuel used in many home furnaces and kitchen stoves, is mostly methane, CH_4. Methane reacts with oxygen in the air to form carbon dioxide and water.

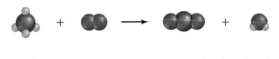

$$CH_4 + O_2 \longrightarrow CO_2 + H_2O$$

Is this equation balanced? You need to count the atoms to find out. It is a good idea to count the oxygen atoms last, because oxygen occurs in both products. Begin with carbon. The number of carbon atoms is the same on both sides of the arrow. Now, count the hydrogen atoms. There are four hydrogen atoms on the left, but only two on the right. Put the coefficient 2 in front of H_2O. This makes 2×2, or 4 hydrogen atoms, so the number of hydrogen atoms is the same on both sides.

$$CH_4 + O_2 \longrightarrow CO_2 + 2H_2O$$

Four oxygen atoms are on the right. Two are in the CO_2 molecule and two are in the H_2O molecules. Only two oxygen atoms are on the left. To balance the oxygen atoms, put the coefficient 2 in front of O_2.

$$CH_4 + 2O_2 \longrightarrow CO_2 + 2H_2O$$

reactants, $CH_4 + 2O_2$	products, $CO_2 + 2H_2O$
1 carbon atom	1 carbon atom
4 hydrogen atoms	4 hydrogen atoms
4 oxygen atoms	4 oxygen atoms

The count shows that the equation is balanced.

Baking Soda and Vinegar

Remember the reaction of vinegar with baking soda? The word equation is: baking soda, or sodium hydrogen carbonate, reacts with acetic acid in vinegar to produce carbon dioxide, water, and sodium acetate. The chemical equation is written this way:

$$NaHCO_3 + HC_2H_3O_2 \longrightarrow CO_2 + H_2O + NaC_2H_3O_2$$

The formulas for reactants and products are written correctly. Now check for atom balance.

Reactants	Products
1 atom of sodium	1 atom of sodium
5 atoms of hydrogen	5 atoms of hydrogen
3 atoms of carbon	3 atoms of carbon
5 atoms of oxygen	5 atoms of oxygen

Atoms of each element are present in equal numbers on both sides of the arrow. The equation is balanced as written.

Using Parentheses with Formulas

Calcium, Ca, plays an important role in building strong bones and teeth. **Figure 15** shows some of the foods that are a source of calcium in your diet. This Group 2 element reacts with water to produce calcium hydroxide, $Ca(OH)_2$, and hydrogen gas, H_2.

$$Ca + H_2O \longrightarrow Ca(OH)_2 + H_2$$

When you count atoms inside parentheses, the subscript following the parentheses multiplies all atoms inside. A total of two oxygen atoms and two hydrogen atoms are in $Ca(OH)_2$. A total of four atoms of hydrogen are on the right side of the equation. To balance the hydrogen atoms on the left, put the coefficient 2 in front of H_2O.

$$Ca + 2H_2O \longrightarrow Ca(OH)_2 + H_2$$

Now the equation is balanced.

Figure 15 These foods are rich in the element calcium, which your body needs for growing bones and sound teeth.

Summarizing Balancing Equations

As you write and balance your own equations, use the following steps as a guide.

Step 1 Determine the correct symbols and formulas for the reactants and products.

Step 2 Write reactant symbols and formulas to the left of an arrow and product symbols and formulas to the right.

Step 3 Count the number of each kind of atom on both sides.

Step 4 Use coefficients to make the number of each kind of atom the same on both sides of the arrow.

Step 5 Check to see that each kind of atom balances.

LESSON 2 Review

Summarize

Create your own lesson summary as you organize an **outline.**

1. **Scan** the lesson. Find and list the first **red** main heading.

2. **Review** the text after the heading and list 2–3 details about the heading.

3. **Find** and list each **blue** subheading that follows the **red** main heading.

4. **List** 2–3 details, key terms, and definitions under each **blue** subheading.

5. **Review** additional **red** main headings and their supporting **blue** subheadings. List 2–3 details about each.

 ELA8: R 2.3

Standards Check

Using Vocabulary

1. In your own words, write a **3.b** definition of *diatomic molecule*.

2. Use the word *coefficient* in a sentence. **5.b**

Understanding Main Ideas

3. How is the substance sodium chloride, NaCl, defined?

   A. an element   **3.b**
   B. a compound
   C. a molecule and a compound
   D. a diatomic molecule

4. **Identify** which substances are reactants and which are products in this equation: **5.b**
   $NaOH + HCl \longrightarrow NaCl + H_2O$.

5. **Explain** how mass is conserved when a candle burns.   **5.b**

6. **Relate** balancing an equation to the law of conservation of mass.   **5.b**

7. **Determine** the number of each kind of atom in $2P_2O_3$.   **3.b**

Applying Science

8. **Organize Information** Copy and fill in the graphic organizer below to show all the steps in balancing a chemical equation.   **5.b**

Step 1	
Step 2	
Step 3	

9. **Formulate a hypothesis** about whether every balanced equation you could write would describe a reaction that could be carried out in the laboratory.   **5.b**

10. **Solve** Balance the following chemical equations.   **5.b**

    A. $Ag + H_2S \longrightarrow Ag_2S + H_2$
    B. $Fe + O_2 \longrightarrow Fe_3O_4$
    C. $H_2 + N_2 \longrightarrow NH_3$
    D. $Al_2O_3 \longrightarrow Al + O_2$

 Science Online

For more practice, visit **Standards Check** at ca8.msscience.com.

MiniLab

Can you model the burning of methane?

00:20 minutes

When materials burn, they are reactants in a chemical reaction. In order for materials to burn, oxygen is needed. What are the products? How are they related to the reactants?

Procedure

1. Read and complete a lab safety form.
2. Observe the flame as your teacher lights the Bunsen burner.
3. Write your observations in your Science Journal.
4. The equation below is for the burning of methane. Copy it into your Science Journal.
   $$CH_4 + 2O_2 \longrightarrow CO_2 + 2H_2O$$
5. Write the names for the reactants and products under the formulas.
6. Use a **molecular model kit** to build models of the reactants and products in the equation. Draw the models in your Science Journal.

Analysis

1. **Copy and complete** the table. **Decide** whether the equation is balanced.

Number of Atoms	
Reactants	**Products**
C:	C:
H:	H:
O:	O:

2. **Identify** the physical properties of each product and reactant.
3. **Plan a way** to test whether water vapor is produced by the reaction.

Science Content Standards

3.b Students know that compounds are formed by combining two or more different elements and that compounds have properties that are different from their constituent elements.

5.b Students know the idea of atoms explains the conservation of matter: In chemical reactions the number of atoms stays the same no matter how they are arranged, so their total mass stays the same.

Science Content Standards

5.c Students know chemical reactions usually liberate heat or absorb heat.
9.a Plan and conduct a scientific investigation to test a hypothesis.
9.e Construct appropriate graphs from data and develop quantitative statements about the relationships between variables.

Reading Guide

What *You'll Learn*

▶ **Compare** and **contrast** endothermic and exothermic reactions.

▶ **Identify** forms of energy produced in a reaction.

Why *It's Important*

Energy-producing reactions are important in heating or cooling your home, cooking your food, and moving you from place to place.

Vocabulary

law of conservation of energy
exothermic process
endothermic process

Review Vocabulary

chemical bond: a force that holds atoms together in a compound (p. 220)

Energy and Chemical Change

Main Idea In chemical reactions, energy is either absorbed or released.

Real-World Reading Connection When you run fast, you get warm and perspire. This is a sign of a chemical reaction going on in your body. In your cells, molecules are being broken down to provide the energy you need. How does a chemical reaction generate energy?

Energy and Chemical Reactions

You have read that in chemical reactions, atoms rearrange to form products. The rearrangement of atoms involves some form of energy. In most cases, the energy is heat. Recall **Figure 5,** which shows the decomposition of water into hydrogen and oxygen. Electrical energy was used to break apart the water molecules. In explosive chemical reactions, such as those shown in **Figure 16,** other forms of energy are obvious. The fireworks display and the rocket launch produce energy in the form of sound, light, heat, and the movement of matter.

Figure 16 The light and sound of fireworks are two forms of released energy.

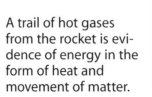

A trail of hot gases from the rocket is evidence of energy in the form of heat and movement of matter.

Figure 17 Light sticks and many organisms, such as this fire beetle, use chemical reactions to give off cold light.

Light from Chemical Reactions

Some reactions give off light with almost no **thermal** energy, or heat. The light stick shown in **Figure 17** is a plastic tube with a glass vial inside. When the plastic tube is bent, the glass vial breaks. This causes chemicals contained inside the tube and the vial to mix and react. When they react, the stick glows with cold light. Cold light occurs at room temperature. It is called cold light because its temperature is lower than the temperature of an incandescent light. You may have seen fireflies flash their beacons of cold light on summer nights. Many ocean-dwelling organisms, such as bacteria, jellies, and squid, also produce cold light. **Figure 17** shows the colorful glow of a fire beetle. Some species use their light to find food or prey. Others use it for defense or communication.

Conservation of Energy

Where does the energy of explosive reactions and cold light come from? Energy is stored in the reacting molecules. The energy changes into other forms, such as light, heat, and sound. Just as mass is conserved in chemical reactions, so is energy. The **law of conservation of energy** states that energy is neither created nor destroyed in chemical reactions. The energy simply changes its form. The energy stored in gasoline is released when the gasoline is burned in a car engine. Part of the energy powers the engine. The rest of the energy heats the surroundings. Chemical reactions in batteries provide light energy in a flashlight, sound energy in a radio, and energy of motion in remote-controlled cars. Energy is conserved in all these examples.

 Identify four types of energy.

Word Origin
thermal
from Greek *therme;* means *heat*

ACADEMIC VOCABULARY

function (FUNK shun)

(verb) to be in action, to serve or operate *He was to function as the official guide for our guest.*

Chemical Bonds

Your body needs energy to **function.** This energy comes from foods containing protein, fat, and carbohydrate molecules. These molecules have energy stored in their chemical bonds. Recall that chemical bonds hold atoms together in molecules and compounds. When you eat and digest proteins, fats, and carbohydrates, some of the energy stored in their chemical bonds is transferred to your cells. It keeps you warm. It provides the energy you need to grow, move, and think. The energy in all chemical reactions relates to chemical bonds.

Net Release of Energy

When atoms rearrange in chemical reactions, bonds are broken and new bonds form. Breaking bonds requires energy. Forming bonds releases energy. There usually is a net change in energy in any chemical reaction. The net change in energy can be either a release of energy or the absorption of energy. If less energy is required to break the original bonds than is given off when new bonds form, there is a net release of energy. An **exothermic process** releases energy. The released energy can be in forms such as light, sound, and heat. The products of an exothermic process have less energy than the reactants. Notice in the diagram in **Figure 18** that the reactants have a higher energy than the products. Did you know that an exothermic process occurs in athletic hot packs? When a hot pack is activated, the process that occurs releases heat to sooth sore muscles. **Figure 19** on the next page describes some other ways in which energy is produced.

WORD ORIGIN

exothermic

from Greek *exo–* (means *outside*) and *therme* (means *heat*)

Visual Check **Figure 18** Describe how energy changes as you go up the *y*-axis.

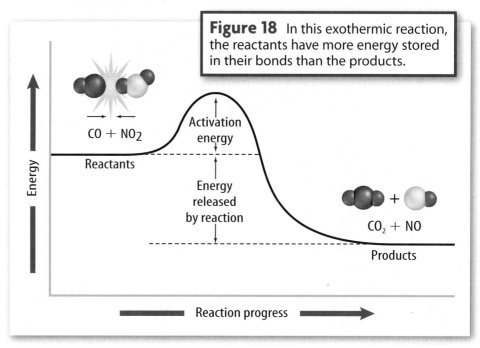

Figure 18 In this exothermic reaction, the reactants have more energy stored in their bonds than the products.

Visualizing Chemical Energy

Figure 19

Whatever the mode of transportation—car, truck, train, or plane—it's likely that gasoline or diesel fuel from oil is the source of the energy that makes it go. Millions of barrels of oil are used in the world each day. Oil was once an abundant resource, but supplies soon will begin to decline. To keep the world moving, it's important not only to conserve oil, but to research and develop other sources of fuel.

▶ Biomass is plant and animal material that can be processed into fuel. Crops, such as corn, can be grown specifically for the production of ethanol, a fuel that can be mixed with gasoline. But ordinary waste materials—garbage—can be turned into fuel to run a car and heat or cool your home. Outside Sacramento, methane gas, a product of the decomposition of vegetable matter, is pumped from mounds of decomposing trash.

◀ Fuel cells are devices that typically use hydrogen or methane to produce energy. Vehicles powered by hydrogen fuel cells are quiet and release only water into the environment.

▶ Hybrid cars conserve gasoline by dividing the energy needs of an automobile between a gasoline engine and an electric motor powered by batteries. The batteries are charged by the engine while the gasoline engine is operating.

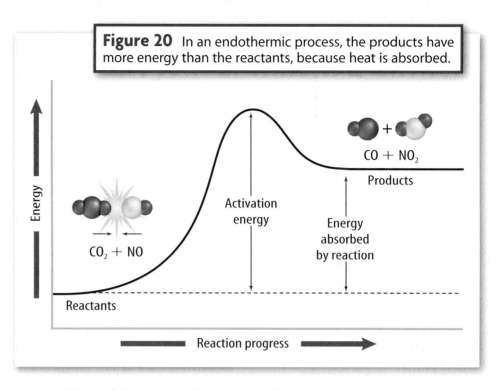

Figure 20 In an endothermic process, the products have more energy than the reactants, because heat is absorbed.

Energy

Activation energy

Energy absorbed by reaction

$CO + NO_2$

Products

$CO_2 + NO$

Reactants

Reaction progress

Net Absorption of Energy

Sometimes, the energy required to break bonds is greater than the energy released when new bonds form. In these processes, there is a net absorption of energy. An **endothermic process** absorbs energy. If you hold an ice cube in your hand, it melts. The ice absorbs energy from your hand. This is not a chemical reaction. The product, liquid water, has more energy than the reactant, ice. The energy diagram in **Figure 20** describes an endothermic chemical reaction. Notice that the reactants are lower in energy than the products. That means that the reactants are more stable than the products.

The dissolving of the ionic salt, ammonium nitrate, in water is an endothermic process. If the salt is added to water in a beaker, the beaker of liquid becomes cold. This endothermic process is used in athletic cold packs, such as the one shown in **Figure 21.**

WORD ORIGIN

endothermic

from Greek *endon–* (means *within*) and *therme* (means *heat*)

Figure 21 The energy required for the cold-pack process is drawn from the user.

 Figure 21 Explain why it's necessary to squeeze the cold pack.

The decomposition of water is another endothermic reaction. Recall from **Figure 5** that electrical energy must be supplied to cause the reaction to occur. The products hydrogen and oxygen are at a higher energy than the reactant water molecules. More energy is stored in their bonds than in the bonds of water molecules. What happens when hydrogen and oxygen combine to form water? The same amount of energy is released in the formation of water as was absorbed in its decomposition.

 Compare the energy needed to decompose water with the energy released when water forms.

What role does energy play in chemical reactions?

Bonds must break and new bonds must form if atoms are to rearrange in a chemical reaction. Sometimes it takes more energy to break bonds in the reactants than is given back when new bonds form. In this case, the reaction is endothermic. Other times, less energy is needed to break bonds in the reactants than is given back when new bonds form. These reactions release energy, so they are exothermic. The released energy can appear in forms such as heat, light, sound, and movement of matter. In the next chapter, you will read about the reactions of substances called acids and bases.

LESSON 3 Review

Summarize

Create your own lesson summary as you write a **newsletter.**

1. **Write** this lesson title, number, and page numbers at the top of a sheet of paper.

2. **Review** the text after the **red** main headings and write one sentence about each. These will be the headlines of your newsletter.

3. **Review** the text and write 2–3 sentences about each **blue** subheading. These sentences should tell *who, what, when, where,* and *why* information about each headline.

4. **Illustrate** your newsletter with diagrams of important structures and processes next to each headline.

 ELA8: W 2.1

Standards Check

Using Vocabulary

1. Distinguish between exothermic and endothermic processes. **5.c**

2. State, in your own words, the meaning of the law of conservation of energy. **5.c**

Understanding Main Ideas

3. **Identify** the reaction represented by the diagram as exothermic or endothermic. **5.c**

4. What term is used to describe the "4" in the expression $4H_2O$?

   A. coefficient

   B. formula

   C. subscript

   D. symbol **5.c**

5. **Relate** the net release of energy in a chemical reaction to bonds between atoms. **5.c**

6. **Construct** an energy diagram for the burning of charcoal: $C + O_2 \longrightarrow CO_2$. Include C, O_2, and CO_2 in your diagram. **5.c**

7. **Organize** Copy and fill in the graphic organizer below. In each oval, list different types of energy. **5.c**

Applying Science

8. **Evaluate** this statement: A reaction that produces cold light is endothermic. **5.c**

9. **Decide** what type of energy change is occurring when crystals dissolve in water and the container gets hot. **5.c**

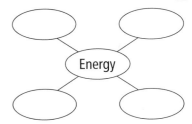

Science Online

For more practice, visit **Standards Check** at ca8.msscience.com.

DataLab

00:30 minutes

How does temperature change as chemicals react?

Some chemical reactions create heat. Others draw heat from their surroundings. Hot packs and cold packs are examples of the two kinds of reactions.

Data Table		
Time	**Temperature (°C)**	
	Calcium Chloride Reaction	Ammonium Nitrate Reaction

Data Collection

WARNING: Never stir with the thermometer.

1. Read and complete a lab safety form.

2. Create a data table like the one shown.

3. Pour 50 mL of **water** in each of two **beakers.** Measure the temperature of the water in each beaker with a **thermometer.**

4. Add 25 g of **calcium chloride** to one beaker. Begin measuring the temperature immediately and record the temperature every 15 s for 3 min. If you want to stir the mixture, use a **stirring rod.**

5. Add 25 g of **ammonium nitrate** to the other beaker. Begin measuring the temperature immediately and record the temperature every 15 s for 3 min.

6. Continue to measure the temperature of the contents of each beaker every 3 min for 24 min.

Data Analysis

1. **Create** a graph of temperature versus time for each reaction.

2. **Identify** which reaction is the hot pack reaction. Which reaction is the cold pack reaction?

3. **Analyze** your graphs to decide which reaction is exothermic and which is endothermic.

 Science Content Standards

5.c Students know chemical reactions usually liberate heat or absorb heat.
9.e Construct appropriate graphs from data and develop quantitative statements about the relationships between variables.

 MA8: ALG 6.0

Applying Math

Calculate Change in Heat of a Reaction

Energy released or absorbed during a chemical reaction is equal to the difference between the potential energy of the products and the potential energy of the reactants. Scientists call this difference ΔH, or the change in the heat of the reaction. If ΔH is positive, the reaction is endothermic and absorbs heat. If ΔH is negative, the reaction is exothermic and gives off heat.

Example

If a reaction of $CH_4(g) + 2O_2(g) \longrightarrow CO_2(g) + 2H_2O(l)$ has a potential energy of reactants of 122 kJ and potential energy of products of 1,012 kJ, find ΔH. Is this an exothermic or endothermic reaction?

What you know: Potential energy of reactants: 122 kJ
Potential energy of products: 1,012 kJ

What you need to find: The difference between the potential energy of the products and the potential energy of the reactants, ΔH

Subtract: ΔH = potential energy of products − potential energy of reactants
$\Delta H = 1{,}012 \text{ kJ} - 122 \text{ kJ}$
$\Delta H = 890 \text{ kJ}$

Answer: ΔH for this reaction is 890 kJ. Because ΔH is positive, the reaction is endothermic.

Practice Problems

1. Is the reaction of $CH_4(g) + 2O_2(g) \longrightarrow CO_2(g) + 2H_2O(l)$ exothermic or endothermic?

2. What is ΔH for the reverse reaction of $CH_4(g) + 2O_2(g) \longrightarrow CO_2(g) + 2H_2O(l)$?

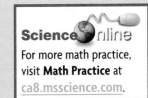

Sciencenline
For more math practice, visit **Math Practice** at ca8.msscience.com.

Forensics: Dirty Jewelry

Materials

salt
lemon juice, lime juice, vinegar
water
dirty pennies
beaker
graduated cylinder
scoop

Safety Precautions

WARNING: *Copper in solution can be poisonous. Dispose of your solutions as your teacher tells you.*

Science Content Standards

5.a Students know reactant atoms and molecules interact to form products with different chemical properties.
9.a Students will plan and conduct a scientific investigation to test a hypothesis.

Problem

Rafir was cleaning the copper jewelry in his shop when suddenly a passerby had a heart attack on the sidewalk. Rafir rushed out to help the victim. When he returned to his shop, the jewelry had turned green.

Rafir thought he must have done something incorrectly in the cleaning procedure. But in the excitement of the emergency, he couldn't remember which step he might have left out. Rafir wrote down what he thought he did.

1. I washed the jewelry with soap and water.
2. I mixed an acid (I'm not sure whether it was lemon juice or vinegar) and some salt in water.
3. I put the jewelry into the mixture to soak.
4. I took the jewelry out of the mixture and rinsed it in clean water.

Form a Hypothesis

After reviewing Rafir's procedure, where do you think Rafir might have made a mistake?

Collect Data and Make Observations

1. Read and complete a lab safety form.
2. Use copper pennies as a jewelry substitute.
3. Make a plan for tests that you will do to find out what Rafir's mistake was.
4. Write your procedure. Have your teacher approve your procedure.
5. Prepare a data table to record your observations.
6. Make sure your teacher approves your experiment before you begin.

Analyze and Conclude

1. **Describe** how well soap and water cleans the dirty pennies.
2. **Explain** how well lemon juice in water cleans pennies.
3. **Describe** how well salt water cleans pennies.
4. **Identify** what you think the dirt on the pennies was.
5. **Identify** the combination of chemicals that cleaned the pennies best.
6. **Explain** Rafir's mistake.
7. **Evaluate** any parts of your procedure that you feel did not go well. What could you do to improve the lab?
8. **Critique** What problem might arise with jewelry or money that was cleaned frequently by this method?

Communicate

Write a Pamphlet How do you think the knowledge you have gained in this lab applies to jewelry cleaning? Could you use your knowledge of household chemicals to clean old pieces of jewelry bought at flea markets? Write a short pamphlet to give to flea-market sellers describing how to clean jewelry.

Real World Science

Hazardous Materials Specialist

Hazardous materials specialists are trained to manage dangerous materials and predict how these materials interact with air, fire, water, and other substances. During an emergency, they work with the fire department and other emergency response groups to contain chemical spills that threaten people or the environment. Personal protective equipment limits their exposure to dangerous chemicals.

Visit **Careers** at ca8.msscience.com to research the properties of chemicals found in household products. Create a table to record and compare the data.

Green Chemistry at Work

When coal is burned to produce electricity, sulfur dioxide and nitrous oxide gases form. When these gases react with water and oxygen in the atmosphere, sulfuric and nitric acid forms. Today, some coal plants are using a new technology that limits sulfur and nitrogen production. By producing less nitrogen and sulfur when burning coal, the amount of particulates in the atmosphere is less, reducing the amount of pollution.

Visit **Technology** at ca8.msscience.com to research the Environmental Protection Agency's Green Chemistry program. Write a paper describing the history and principles behind this program.

 ELA8: W 1.1

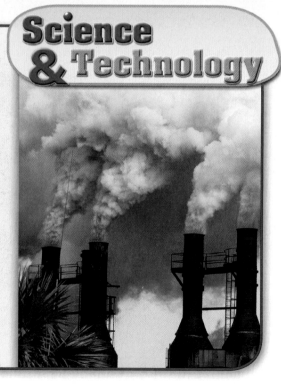

Soft Drinks, Erasers, and More

Scientists and inventors like Joseph Priestley have used physical and chemical properties of substances to create useful materials. His peers of Benjamin Franklin and Antoine Lavoisier influenced Priestley. Priestley's invention of "soda water" laid the foundation for soft drinks. He also discovered that the properties of a flexible solid called India gum. The gum rubs out pencil marks. Priestly's eraser remains a commonly used tool today.

Visit **History** at ca8.msscience.com to learn about other scientific discoveries and inventions of Joseph Priestley. Create a timeline illustrating his work and world events.

The Nose Knows

A physical property of materials is helping an elite group of animals called "chem dogs" protect our country's borders and airports. With noses highly sensitive to detecting odor, chem dogs are trained to sniff out concealed chemical weapons. These dogs learn to recognize gaseous molecules that come from chemicals such as hydrogen cyanide. When they detect an odor, the dogs alert their handlers, trace the odor to its source, and sit down in front of it.

Visit **Society** at ca8.msscience.com to research the type of dog personality, characteristics, and training of detector dogs. Prepare and share a brief oral report describing what you learned.

The BIG Idea In chemical reactions, atoms rearrange to form one or more different substances.

Lesson 1 Chemical Properties and Changes
`3.f, 5.a, 7.c`

Main Idea In a chemical change, the properties that give a substance its identity change.

- A chemical property describes the way a substance can or cannot change into another substance.

- A physical property is one that can be observed without changing the identity of the substance.

- A chemical change results in one or more substances that are different in composition from the original substance.

- A physical change is one in which the same substance is present before and after the change.

- **chemical change** (p. 341)
- **chemical property** (p. 338)
- **dissolving** (p. 343)

Lesson 2 Chemical Equations
`3.b, 3.f, 5.b`

Main Idea Chemical equations show that in chemical reactions, atoms rearrange, but no atoms are lost or gained.

- In all chemical reactions, the mass of the reactants is the same as the mass of the products.

- The number of atoms of each element is the same before and after the reaction.

- Symbols and formulas represent substances in chemical equations.

- A balanced chemical equation shows that no atoms are lost or gained in a chemical reaction.

- **coefficient** (p. 352)
- **diatomic molecule** (p. 350)
- **law of conservation of mass** (p. 347)
- **product** (p. 349)
- **reactant** (p. 349)

Lesson 3 Energy and Chemical Change
`5.c, 9.a, 9.e`

Main Idea In chemical reactions, energy is either absorbed or released.

- Energy changes occur in chemical reactions, but no energy is lost or gained.

- There is a net release of energy in exothermic reactions.

- There is a net absorption of energy in endothermic reactions.

- **endothermic process** (p. 362)
- **exothermic process** (p. 360)
- **law of conservation of energy** (p. 359)

STUDY TO GO Download quizzes, key terms, and flash cards from ca8.msscience.com.

Linking Vocabulary and Main Ideas

Use vocabulary terms from page 370 to complete this concept map.

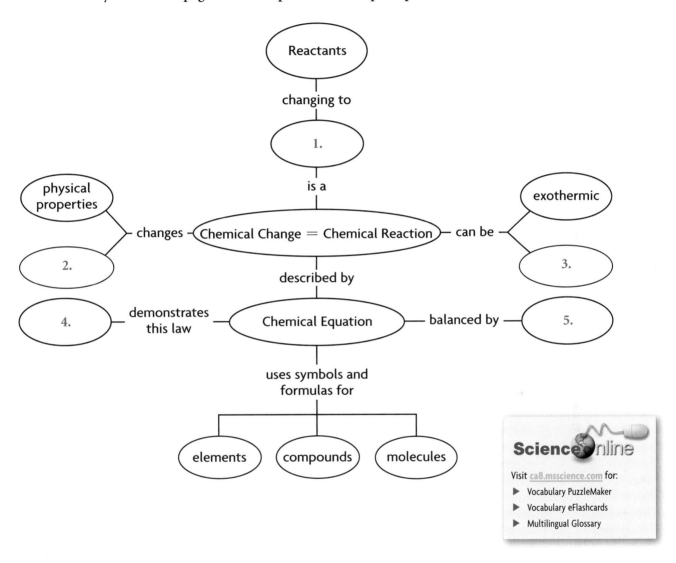

Using Vocabulary

Fill in the blanks with the correct vocabulary terms. Then read the paragraph to a partner.

A chemical reaction is described by a chemical equation in which ____6.____ are shown on the left side of an arrow and ____7.____ are shown on the right. Energy changes occur in most chemical reactions. A process in which energy is released is called a(n) ____8.____. A process in which energy is absorbed is called a(n) ____9.____. In chemical processes, no energy is lost or gained so the ____10.____ is obeyed.

Understanding Main Ideas

Choose the word or phrase that best answers the question.

1. Which description is a chemical property?
    A. burns in air
    B. has a blue color
    C. melts at room temperature
    D. is 10 cm long   **5.a**

2. Which is NOT a chemical change?
    A. copper turning green in air
    B. baking a cake
    C. drying clothes
    D. exploding dynamite   **5.a**

3. The photo below shows a demonstration of electrolysis, in which water is broken down into hydrogen and oxygen.

    Which is the best way to write the chemical equation for this process?
    A. $H_2O + energy \longrightarrow H_2 + O_2$
    B. $H_2O + energy \longrightarrow 2H_2 + O_2$
    C. $2H_2O + energy \longrightarrow 2H_2 + O_2$
    D. $2H_2O + energy \longrightarrow 2H_2 + 2O_2$ **5.b**

4. Which phrase describes an endothermic reaction?
    A. There is a net release of energy.
    B. The products are lower in energy than the reactants.
    C. The products are higher in energy than the reactants.
    D. The products are more stable than the reactants.   **5.c**

Use the following chemical equation to answer questions 5 and 6.

$$2SO_2 + O_2 \longrightarrow 2SO_3$$

5. What is the coefficient of SO_3?
    A. 1
    B. 2
    C. 4
    D. 6   **5.b**

6. How many oxygen atoms are on the reactants side?
    A. two
    B. four
    C. six
    D. eight   **5.b**

7. How many atoms of each kind are represented by $2Ca(NO_3)_2$?
    A. 1 atom Ca, 1 atom N, 3 atoms O
    B. 2 atoms Ca, 1 atom N, 3 atoms O
    C. 2 atoms Ca, 2 atoms N, 6 atoms O
    D. 2 atoms Ca, 4 atoms N, 12 atoms O   **3.b**

8. Which is a balanced chemical equation?
    A. $Na + Cl_2 \longrightarrow NaCl$
    B. $H_2O_2 \longrightarrow 2H_2O + O_2$
    C. $O_2 + 2PCl_3 \longrightarrow 2POCl_3$
    D. $Ca + H_2O \longrightarrow Ca(OH)_2 + H_2$ **5.b**

9. Which is NOT a physical property?
    A. color
    B. conducts electricity
    C. magnetism
    D. tarnishes   **7.c**

10. Preparing a meal involves both physical and chemical changes. Which is a chemical change?
    A. boiling water
    B. making ice cubes
    C. slicing a carrot
    D. toasting bread   **7.c**

Science Online Standards Review ca8.msscience.com

11. **Decide** whether a chemical change can occur without a physical change. Explain your answer. **5.a**

12. **Write** a balanced chemical equation for the reaction of propane, C_3H_8, burning in oxygen to form carbon dioxide, CO_2, and water vapor. **5.a**

13. **State** the following equation in words: $N_2 + 3H_2 \longrightarrow 2NH_3$. N_2 is nitrogen, NH_3 is ammonia. **5.a**

14. **List** two advantages that chemical equations written with symbols and formulas have over word equations. **5.b**

15. **Demonstate** how to write the balanced equation for the burning of ethene (C_2H_4) in air. The products of the reaction are carbon dioxide and water. **5.b**

The energy changes in the reaction of A + B $\longrightarrow$ C are shown in the diagram. Use the diagram to answer questions 16 and 17.

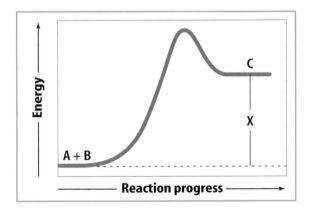

16. **Analyze** Is the formation of substance C an endothermic or exothermic reaction? Explain. **5.c**

17. **Apply** your knowledge of energy changes in chemical reactions to identify what is represented by the line labeled X. **5.c**

18. **Assess** Atoms may be rearranged in physical changes. How is this possible if no new substances form? **5.d**

WRITING in ▶ Science

19. **Write a letter** to a friend explaining the difference between an exothermic reaction and an endothermic reaction. Give two examples of exothermic chemical reactions in your daily life. **ELA8: W 1.1**

Cumulative Review

20. **Categorize** these physical changes as exothermic or endothermic: melting, freezing, subliming, condensing, boiling. **5.c**

21. **Analyze** Can an isotope become an ion? Explain your answer. **3.a, 7.b**

22. **Relate** Groups 1, 2, 14, 15, 16, and 17 on the periodic table to whether they are likely to form covalent or ionic bonds. **7.a**

Applying Math

23. If a reaction of $H_2 + \frac{1}{2}O_2 \longrightarrow H_2O$ has a potential energy of reactants of 0 kJ and potential energy of products of -68.3 kJ, find ΔH. **MA8: ALG 2.0**

24. Is the reaction of $H_2 + \frac{1}{2}O_2 \longrightarrow H_2O$ exothermic or endothermic? **MA8: ALG 2.0**

25. What is ΔH for the reverse reaction of $H_2 + \frac{1}{2}O_2 \longrightarrow H_2O$? **MA8: ALG 2.0**

26. If a reaction of $CH_4 + 2O_2 \longrightarrow CO_2 + 2H_2O$ has a potential energy of reactants of 634 kJ and potential energy of products of 828 kJ, find ΔH. **MA8: ALG 2.0**

27. Is the reaction of $CH_4 + 2O_2 \longrightarrow CO_2 + 2H_2O$ exothermic or endothermic? **MA8: ALG 2.0**

1 **Which is a chemical change?**

   A Paper is shredded.   `7.c`

   B Liquid wax turns solid.

   C A raw egg is broken.

   D Soap scum forms.

2 **Which reaction is endothermic?**

   A burning wood   `5.c`

   B iron rusting

   C using an athletic cold pack

   D using an athletic hot pack

3 **When mercury (II) oxide, HgO, is heated, liquid mercury (Hg) and oxygen (O2) are produced.**

$2HgO \rightarrow 2Hg + O_2$	
Beginning mass of HgO	216 g
Mass of Hg after heating	200 g
Mass of O_2 after heating	? g

According to the law of conservation of mass, what mass of O_2 is generated?

   A 8 g   `5.b`

   B 16 g

   C 200 g

   D 216 g

4 **Oxygen gas is always written as O_2 in chemical equations. What term is used to describe the 2 in this formula?**

   A product   `5.b`

   B coefficient

   C reactant

   D subscript

5 **The chemical reaction below is the reaction of copper (Cu) with silver nitrate ($AgNO_3$) to produce copper nitrate $Cu(NO_3)_2$ and silver (Ag).**

$$AgNO_3 + Cu \longrightarrow Cu(NO_3)_2 + 2Ag$$

Is this reaction balanced?

   A Yes, because there is one solid on each side of the equation.   `5.b`

   B Yes, because the number of copper atoms is the same on each side of the equation.

   C No, because there are two reactants and three products.

   D No, because the number of silver atoms is not equal on both sides of the equation.

6 **The photo shows bubbles created from vinegar and baking soda in water.**

What is the balanced chemical equation for this reaction?

   A $2NaHCO_3 + HC_2H_3O_2 \longrightarrow CO_2 + H_2O + 2NaC_2H_3O_2$ `5.a`

   B $NaHCO_3 + HC_2H_3O_2 \longrightarrow CO_2 + H_2O + NaC_2H_3O_2$

   C $2NaHCO_3 + 2HC_2H_3O_2 \longrightarrow 2CO_2 + H_2O + NaC_2H_3O_2$

   D $NaHCO_3 + HC_2H_3O_2 \longrightarrow 2CO_2 + 2H_2O + NaC_2H_3O_2$

Science online Standards Assessment ca8.msscience.com

7 Each procedure results in the formation of bubbles. Which is a physical change?   **7.c**

A pouring an acid onto calcium carbonate

B dropping an antacid tablet into water

C heating water to its boiling point

D pouring vinegar onto baking soda

8 Which chemical equation is balanced?   **5.b**

A $HgO \longrightarrow Hg + O_2$

B $Mg + O_2 \longrightarrow 2MgO$

C $2Li + 2H_2O \longrightarrow 2LiOH + H_2$

D $Cu + AgNO_3 \longrightarrow Cu(NO_3)_2 + 2Ag$

9 What term is used to describe the 4 in the expression $4Ca(NO_3)_2$?   **5.b**

A coefficient

B formula

C subscript

D symbol

10 In chemical reactions, the atoms in the reactants rearrange to form products. There is usually a net change in   **5.c**

A atoms.

B energy.

C mass.

D molecules.

11 What should be balanced in a chemical equation?   **3.b**

A compounds

B atoms

C molecules

D subscripts

12 What word would you use to describe tin oxide in the reaction that Lavoisier used to show conservation of mass?   **5.b**

A subscript

B product

C coefficient

D reactant

13 The illustration below shows a chemical reaction.

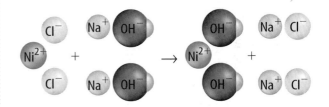

Identify the products in the reaction.

A $NiCl_2$ and $NaOH$ **5.a**

B $NaOH$ and $NaCl$

C $Ni(OH)_2$ and $NaCl$

D $Ni(OH)_2$ and $NiCl_2$

14 Which element has the physical property of magnetism?   **7.c**

A sodium

B iron

C oxygen

D calcium

15 Which warning refers to a chemical property of the material?   **7.c**

A fragile

B flammable

C handle with care

D shake well

Acids and Bases in Solution

The BIG Idea

Aqueous solutions of acids and bases have characteristic properties and can be identified by their pH values.

LESSON 1 7.c, 9.e
Solutions

Main Idea Most of the substances you encounter daily are solutions.

LESSON 2 5.e, 9.a, 9.b, 9.e
Acidic, Basic, and Neutral Solutions

Main Idea The pH scale measures the acidity of a solution.

Now how did *that* happen?

It took hundreds of years to form these strange rock towers that surround Mono Lake in California. The knobs and spires of rock "grew" year by year as water from the landlocked lake evaporated. This left behind the masses of rock that had been dissolved in its waters.

Science *Journal* Write a brief paragraph on what you think these rocks are made from.

Where's that bubble?

You encounter acids and bases every day. Do acids and bases react with one another?

Procedure

1. Read and complete a lab safety form.

2. Measure 125 mL of **distilled water** into each of two **beakers.**

3. Add 10 g of **baking powder** to one beaker and 10 g of **baking soda** to the other.

4. Stir until dissolved. Record your observations in your Science Journal.

5. Add 15 mL of **vinegar** to each beaker and record your observations.

Think About This

• **Describe** what you expected and what you observed.

• **Check** the ingredient list on the box of baking powder. Is one ingredient common to both products? How does this explain your observations?

Visit ca8.msscience.com to:

▶ view **Concepts in Motion**

▶ explore Virtual Labs

▶ access content-related Web links

▶ take the Standards Check

Determining pH Make the following Foldable to show how to determine whether a solution is acidic, basic, or neutral.

STEP 1 Fold a sheet of paper in half lengthwise. Make the back edge about 2 cm longer than the front edge.

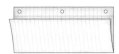

STEP 2 Fold into thirds.

STEP 3 Unfold and **cut** along the folds of the top flap to make three flaps.

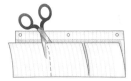

STEP 4 Label the flaps as shown.

Reading *Skill*

Interpreting
As you read Lesson 2, record important information about acidic, basic, and neutral solutions. Be sure to include examples.

Get Ready to Read

Make Connections

 ELA8: R 2.3

1 Learn It! Make connections between what you read and what you already know. Connections can be based on personal experiences (text-to-self), what you have read before (text-to-text), or events in other places (text-to-world).

As you read, ask connecting questions. Are you reminded of a personal experience? Have you read about the topic before? Did you think of a person, a place, or an event in another part of the world?

2 Practice It! Read the excerpt below and make connections to your own knowledge and experience.

> Have you ever removed all the onions from your salad before eating it?

> In addition to magnetism, what are other properties of iron?

> How can you use the property of magnetism to sort recycling materials?

Have you ever picked out your favorite nut from a bowl of mixed nuts? If so, you separated a component from a mixture. Components of mixtures can be separated by taking advantage of the differences in their physical properties. Iron has the property of magnetism, but sand does not. A mixture of iron and sand can be separated by moving a magnet through the mixture. The magnet picks up the iron from the mixture. The sand remains behind.

—*from page 386*

3 Apply It! As you read this chapter, choose five words or phrases that make a connection to something you already know.

Target Your Reading

Use this to focus on the main ideas as you read the chapter.

1 Before you read the chapter, respond to the statements below on your worksheet or on a numbered sheet of paper.

- Write an **A** if you **agree** with the statement.
- Write a **D** if you **disagree** with the statement.

2 After you read the chapter, look back to this page to see if you've changed your mind about any of the statements.

- If any of your answers changed, explain why.
- Change any false statements into true statements.
- Use your revised statements as a study guide.

Reading Tip

Make connections with memorable events, places, or people in your life. The better the connection, the more likely you will remember.

Before You Read A or D	Statement	After You Read A or D
	1 A substance can be an element or a mixture.	
	2 In a mixture, you can always see the different parts that make it up.	
	3 An alloy is a homogeneous mixture.	
	4 Water is an excellent solvent because its electrons are shared equally.	
	5 If a solution is unsaturated, you can dissolve more solute in it.	
	6 A neutral solution has a pH of 7.	
	7 Water is a product of a neutralization reaction.	
	8 You can determine the exact pH of a solution by using litmus paper.	
	9 Acids have pH values between 7 and 14.	
	10 pH can be measured accurately with a pH meter.	

Science Online

Print a worksheet of this page at ca8.msscience.com.

Reading Guide

What *You'll Learn*

▶ **Compare** two types of mixtures.

▶ **Relate** the solvent properties of water to its molecular structure.

Why *It's Important*

You will better understand acids and bases if you know how solutions differ from other types of mixtures.

Vocabulary

substance
mixture
homogeneous mixture
heterogeneous mixture
solution
solute
solvent

Review Vocabulary

liquid: matter with a definite volume but no definite shape that can flow from one place to another (p. 257)

Solutions

Main Idea Most of the substances you encounter daily are solutions.

Real-World Reading Connection When you walk down the aisles in a supermarket, you can't help but notice the variety of liquid products for sale. These include household cleaners, shampoos, fruit drinks, soft drinks, vinegar, and rubbing alcohol. What might these products have in common?

What are the types of matter?

Mono Lake is a salt lake located high in the Sierra Nevada, a mountain range in California. What's special about this lake is that its water is more than twice as salty as the ocean. Mono Lake is an ancient lake with no outlet. Streams flow into the lake, bringing with them dissolved salts and minerals. Over the centuries, the amount of this dissolved matter has increased. **Figure 1** shows some interesting formations called tufas (TOO faws) that line the lakeshore. These are composed of limestone, or calcium carbonate, that was originally dissolved in the water and then settled out.

Figure 1 These rock formations around Mono Lake in California form when the lake water can no longer contain all the salts and minerals that are dissolved in it.

Substances

The waters of Mono Lake contain only a small fraction of the different kinds of matter that exist on Earth. Recall that matter has mass and takes up space. **Figure 2** shows that matter can be separated into two categories—pure substances and mixtures. A **substance** is matter that has the same composition and properties throughout. Elements and compounds are substances. Recall from Chapter 5 that an element consists of only one kind of atom. You are probably familiar with the elements calcium, carbon, and oxygen. Compounds are composed of elements that are bound together by ionic or covalent bonds. Some compounds you probably know of are water, sodium chloride, and calcium carbonate.

WORD ORIGIN ··········
substance
from Latin *substantia;* means *being, essence, material*

Figure 2 A substance can be a compound, such as sodium chloride, or an element, such as gold.

Name two types of mixtures.

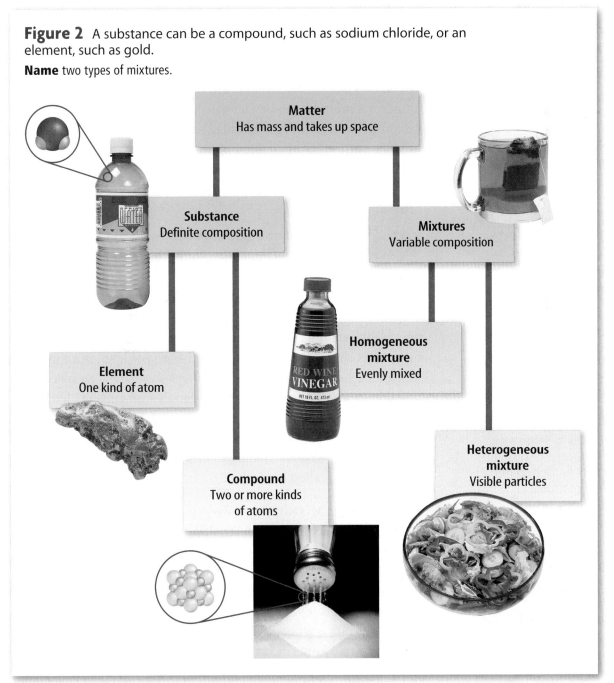

Figure 3 The doorknob is a homogenous mixture of two elements.

Zn
Cu

Brass through a magnifier

Brass at the atomic layer

Mixtures

What happens when you combine two or more substances? A **mixture** is a combination of two or more substances that can be separated by physical means. Mixtures can contain elements, compounds, or a combination of both. Each compound or element found in a mixture can be identified by its properties. Your favorite soft drink is a mixture of water, sugar or another sweetener, flavorings, and carbon dioxide. The sweet taste comes from the sugar, and the tartness comes from the carbon dioxide. Compounds have definite compositions, but the composition of a mixture can vary.

 What is the difference between a compound and a mixture?

Homogeneous Mixtures Sometimes, you can tell that a sample of matter is a mixture because you can identify more than one substance. Other times, it's impossible to decide whether or not the sample is a mixture. A **homogeneous mixture** is two or more substances that are evenly mixed on the atomic level, but the substances are not bonded together. **Figure 3** shows how an object, such as a brass doorknob, appears through a magnifying lens to be made of one substance. If you could see the atoms on the atomic level, however, you would notice that zinc and copper atoms are evenly mixed. Brass is a homogeneous mixture. A homogeneous mixture is also called a solution.

Heterogeneous Mixtures It is easy to tell that some things are mixtures by looking at them. A salad is a mixture of lettuce, tomatoes, and other ingredients. A mixture in which the substances are not evenly mixed is a **heterogeneous mixture.** Notice the regions of different colors in the sample of granite in **Figure 4.** The colors indicate that granite is made of more than one substance. Granite is a heterogeneous mixture. A bowl of vegetable soup and mixed nuts are examples of heterogeneous mixtures.

WORD ORIGIN

homogeneous
from Greek *homos* (means *same*) and *genos* (means *kind*)

heterogeneous
from Greek *heteros* (means *different*) and *genos* (means *kind*)

Figure 4 When this granite rock formed, substances of different colors hardened into a solid mixture.

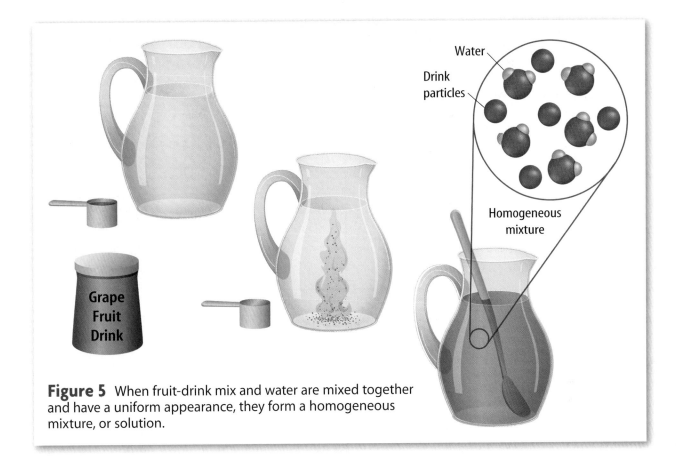

Figure 5 When fruit-drink mix and water are mixed together and have a uniform appearance, they form a homogeneous mixture, or solution.

Solutions—Homogeneous Mixtures

When table salt dissolves in water, the salt and water form a solution. A **solution** is a homogeneous mixture. You make a solution when you stir fruit-drink mix into a volume of water, as shown in **Figure 5.** In the center, the mix has just been added to the water. You can see both the solid fruit-drink mix and the liquid water. This is a heterogeneous mixture. When you stir the mixture, the solid material dissolves. Now, the solution looks the same throughout. The fruit drink on the right is ready to drink. In the formation of a solution, two or more substances are evenly mixed, but they each retain their identities. The water molecules are unchanged, and the ingredients of the fruit-drink mix remain the substances they were before dissolving.

 Figure 5 Identify evidence that the drink is a homogeneous mixture.

Imagine that you add a spoonful of salt to water and stir until the mixture is homogeneous. You have made a saltwater solution. The salt and the water are still present in the solution. Both substances retain their **individual** physical properties. The solution is clear and colorless like pure water and has a salty taste like pure salt. You can vary the amounts of salt and water by adding more salt or more water and stirring until the solution is clear again.

ACADEMIC VOCABULARY
individual
(*adjective*) distinctly associated with a person or thing
Each person had his or her own individual thoughts on the subject.

Table 1 Common Types of Solutions

State of Solution	State of Solute	State of Solvent	Example
Gas	Gas	Gas	
Liquid	Gas	Liquid	
Liquid	Liquid	Liquid	
Liquid	Solid	Liquid	
Solid	Solid	Solid	

CONcepts In MOtion
Interactive Table Organize information about types of solutions at ca8.msscience.com.

SCIENCE USE V. COMMON USE
solution

Science Use a homogeneous mixture
In a solution, you cannot see individual substances because they are evenly mixed.
Common Use an answer to a problem
He couldn't relax until he found the solution to the puzzle.

Components of Solutions Solutions are formed when one substance dissolves in another. Consider a solution of salt in water. Salt is called the solute in this solution. The **solute** in any solution is the dissolved substance. The substance that is used to dissolve the solute is the **solvent.** Water is the solvent in a saltwater solution. The solvent is the component of the solution that is present in the larger amount. Many solutions contain two or more solutes dissolved in a solvent.

Types of Solutions Substances in each of the three states of matter—solid, liquid, and gas—may act as a solute or a solvent. Solutions are usually classified by the state of the solvent: solid solutions, liquid solutions, and gaseous solutions. **Table 1** gives examples of some common types of solutions. Notice that alloys are solutions of a solid in a solid.

 How can you tell which component in a solution is the solvent?

Alloys—Solid Solutions Most metallic objects, such as a steel cooking pan, are solid solutions called alloys. An alloy is a mixture of a metal and one or more additional elements. Alloys have metallic properties even though they may contain small amounts of a nonmetal, such as carbon. A solid solution of copper and silver dissolved in gold is the alloy known as 14-karat gold (14K).

Alloys are used in making a variety of products. You may have jewelry made of sterling silver, which is an alloy of copper and silver. Many statues are made of bronze, an alloy of zinc and tin in copper. *Steel* is the name given to a wide variety of alloys of iron. Most steels contain a certain amount of carbon plus one or more metallic elements. Forks, knives, pots, and pans are often made from stainless steel. Stainless steel contains chromium and nickel dissolved in iron.

Figure 6 shows some of the alloys that are used to make an automobile. The composition of the alloy determines its properties and uses. Automobile bodies require strong, corrosion-resistant, lightweight alloys that can carry heavy loads. The engine must be made of lightweight, heat-resistant alloys.

Figure 6 Manufacturers can create different alloys to meet specific needs such as strength, durability, lightness, and appeal.
Infer why lightweight alloys are used in cars whenever possible.

Steel is an alloy of iron and carbon

Aluminum, copper, and zinc alloys in the engine

Magnesium alloy

Separating Mixtures by Physical Means

ACADEMIC VOCABULARY

component
(kum PO nent)
(*noun*) one of a number of
parts that make up a whole.
*Wheels and pedals are two
components of a bicycle.*

Have you ever picked out your favorite nut from a bowl of mixed nuts? If so, you separated a component from a mixture. **Components** of mixtures can be separated by taking advantage of the differences in their physical properties. Iron has the property of magnetism, but sand does not. A mixture of iron and sand can be separated by moving a magnet through the mixture. The magnet picks up the iron from the mixture. The sand remains behind.

Boiling, melting, dissolving, freezing, and evaporating are some physical changes that can also be used to separate mixtures. **Figure 7** illustrates how dissolving and evaporating can separate an iron-and-salt mixture. Follow the steps in the recovery of both the iron and the salt.

Figure 7 Follow the process below to see how iron can be separated from salt.
Predict whether this procedure would work for a mixture of salt and sand.

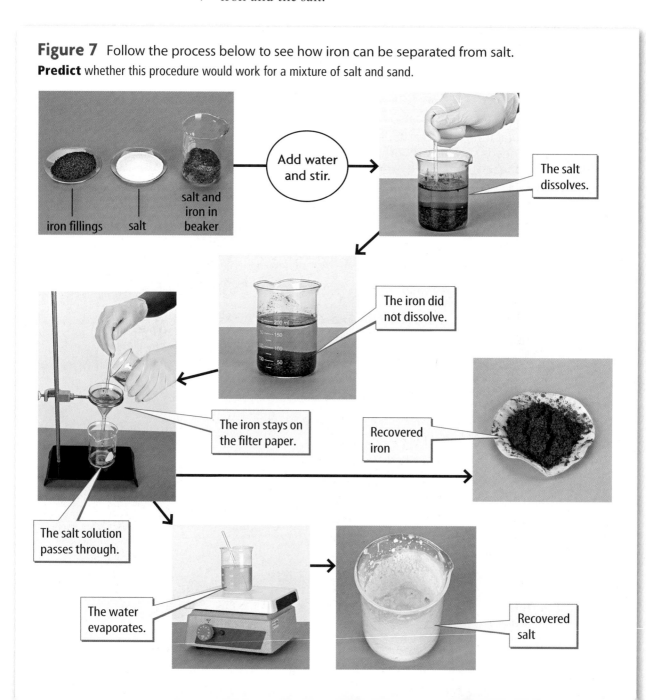

Solubility—How much can dissolve?

Is there a limit to the amount of salt that will dissolve in water? The water of Mono Lake contains more dissolved salt than the waters of the ocean. That means that in a given volume of Mono Lake's water, there is more salt than there is in the same volume of ocean water. As you read, you will learn that there are limits, and that these limits depend on temperature.

Solubility

If you add spoonful after spoonful of salt to a glass of water, at some point no more salt will dissolve. Excess salt crystals will remain on the bottom of the glass. The water contains the maximum amount of salt it can hold. Solubility is a measure of how much solute can be dissolved in a given volume or mass of solvent.

Effect of Temperature

Each substance has a unique solubility, which changes with temperature. **Figure 8** shows the solubilities of four substances at temperatures ranging from 0°C to 100°C. Notice that in the graph, solubility is measured as the number of grams of solute that will dissolve in 100 g of solvent. Using **Figure 8,** you can determine that 40 g of potassium chloride, KCl, dissolves in 100 g of water at 40°C.

Saturated and Unsaturated Solutions

When you added the first spoonful of salt to the glass of water, it dissolved, and you added a second spoonful. When the second spoonful dissolved, you could conclude that the first solution had been unsaturated. An unsaturated solution is any solution that can dissolve more solute at a given temperature. You continued adding salt until no more salt would dissolve. At that point, the solution was saturated. A saturated solution is any solution that contains all the solute it can hold at a given temperature. The water of Mono Lake is saturated with salts. When some of the water evaporates, the remaining water is not enough to hold all the salts. The salts drop out of the water and form the solid formations called tufas.

 **Reading Check** How can you tell when a solution is saturated?

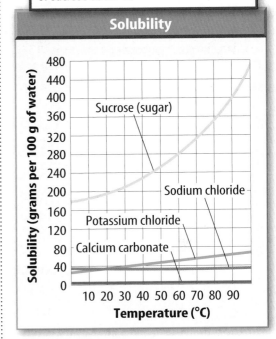

Figure 8 At each temperature, you can find the solubility for each substance. In this graph, the solubility is the mass of a substance that will dissolve in 100 g of water.

Determine from the graph the solubility of sucrose at 20°C.

Figure 9 Twice as much powder was added to the drink on the left.

Infer which is the dilute solution. Which is concentrated?

Concentration—How much is dissolved?

Whether a solution is saturated or unsaturated, it's often important to know the concentration of the solution. The concentration of a solution is the amount of solute present in a solution compared to the amount of solvent.

Concentrated and Dilute Solutions

You can always add more sugar to your lemonade if it's too sour. Adding sugar changes the concentration of the sugar in the lemonade. The concentration of sugar in the sour lemonade is low. It is a dilute solution. Sweeter lemonade is a more concentrated solution. The words *concentrated* and *dilute* are ways of describing solutions. Examples of concentrated and dilute solutions are shown in **Figure 9.**

Concentration in Grams per Liter (g/L)

The terms *concentrated* or *dilute* and *saturated* and *unsaturated* do not tell you exactly what the concentration of a solution is. A more precise way of expressing the concentration of a solution is to give the number of grams of solute that is dissolved in 1 L of solution. For example, if you dissolve 10 g of sodium chloride in enough water to make a total volume of 1 L, the concentration of your solution is 10 g/L.

Percent by Volume

Percent by volume is another way of describing a solution's concentration. Percent by volume is the volume of solute in a specified volume of solution. **Figure 10** shows the label on a bottle of hydrogen peroxide. The label states that this solution is three percent hydrogen peroxide. That means that 3 mL of hydrogen peroxide is present in every 100 mL of the solution.

 **Reading Check** What does *15 percent juice* indicate about a solution?

Figure 10 Three percent hydrogen peroxide is used as a disinfectant for minor wounds.

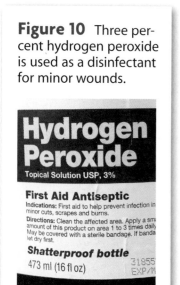

Hydrogen Peroxide
Topical Solution USP, 3%

First Aid Antiseptic
Indications: First aid to help prevent infection in minor cuts, scrapes and burns.
Directions: Clean the affected area. Apply a small amount of this product on area 1 to 3 times daily. May be covered with a sterile bandage. If banda let dry first.

Shatterproof bottle
473 ml (16 fl oz)
31855
EXP/M

Water as a Solvent

In other science classes, you might have learned that water is essential to all living organisms. Water makes up about 70 percent of your total body mass. More than 75 percent of Earth is covered with water. However, the water found in your body and in lakes, streams, and wells is not pure water. Other substances are dissolved in it. For example, you might have noticed that ocean water tastes salty. This is because salt is dissolved in it. In fact, most water that exists on Earth is in the form of a solution. Why is this?

The Polarity of Water

In nature, water nearly always exists as a solution because many different types of substances are soluble in water. For this reason, water is often referred to as "the universal solvent." What property of water allows it to dissolve so many different things? Recall that water, shown in **Figure 11,** is a covalent compound with a bent shape. One oxygen atom shares two pairs of electrons with two hydrogen atoms. However, the electrons are not shared equally. Notice that the electrons in the oxygen-hydrogen (O–H) bonds are closer to the oxygen atom than they are to the hydrogen atoms. This unequal sharing of electrons makes the oxygen atom slightly negative and both hydrogen atoms slightly positive. A molecule with a slightly negative end and a slightly positive end is called a polar molecule. Many other covalent compounds, such as sugar and alcohol, are also polar.

 Visual Check **Figure 11** Is the water molecule itself charged? Explain your answer.

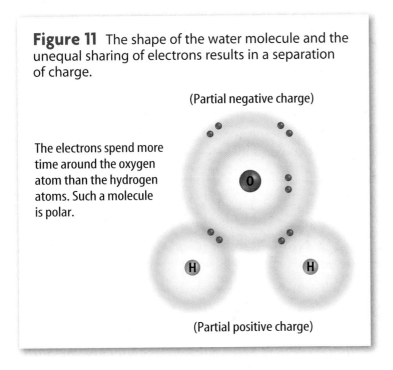

Figure 11 The shape of the water molecule and the unequal sharing of electrons results in a separation of charge.

(Partial negative charge)

The electrons spend more time around the oxygen atom than the hydrogen atoms. Such a molecule is polar.

O

H   H

(Partial positive charge)

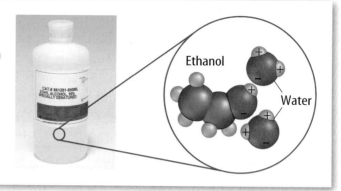

Figure 12 You can infer from the label that ethanol is the solvent in this solution because it is present in the greater amount.

Polar Solvents and Polar Molecules

Scientists often use this simple rule for solubility: "Like dissolves like." This expression suggests that polar solvent molecules, such as water, are likely to dissolve other polar molecules. **Figure 12** shows that the alcohol molecule, ethanol has one O–H bond. Like the bonds in the water molecule, electrons are unequally shared between the oxygen atom and the attached hydrogen atom, so the ethanol molecule is polar. When mixed with water, the positive ends of water molecules are attracted to the negative parts of ethanol molecules. Similarly, the negative ends of water molecules are attracted to the positive parts of ethanol molecules. In this way, ethanol molecules are pulled into solution. Ethanol and water are very soluble in each other.

Polar Solvents and Ionic Compounds

Many ionic compounds are also soluble in water. Recall that ionic compounds are composed of positive and negative ions that alternate in the solid crystal lattice. When the ionic compound sodium chloride is placed in water, as shown in **Figure 13,** water molecules attach themselves to ions in the crystal and pull them away. Notice that the positive end of the water molecule attracts the negative chloride ion. The negative end of the water molecule attracts the positive sodium ion. Thus, water molecules surround the ions and prevent them from reforming as a solid.

 Why is water a good solvent for polar molecules and ionic compounds?

Figure 13 Water molecules surround both the positive and the negative ions.

Explain the difference in the way water molecules surround the sodium ion compared to the way they surround the chloride ion.

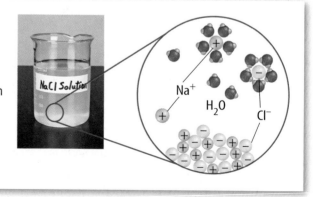

Conductivity of Aqueous Solutions

Ions in solution are responsible for the ability of an aqueous solution to conduct electricity. In order for electricity, or electric charges, to flow, there must be a continuous path along which charges can move. In the apparatus shown in **Figure 14,** the beaker contains a solution of sodium chloride. Electric charges are carried from the battery and through the wires to the lightbulb. Notice that they must also move through the water solution in the beaker. When the beaker holds a solution containing ions, the ions carry the charge, so the lightbulb lights. The light shows that sodium chloride is an electrolyte. An electrolyte is any compound that produces ions when it dissolves in water. Compounds that do not form ions in water solutions are unable to conduct electricity and are called nonelectrolytes. Many nonelectrolytes are covalent compounds such as sugar. **Figure 14** shows that when the beaker contains a solution of sugar, the lightbulb does not light.

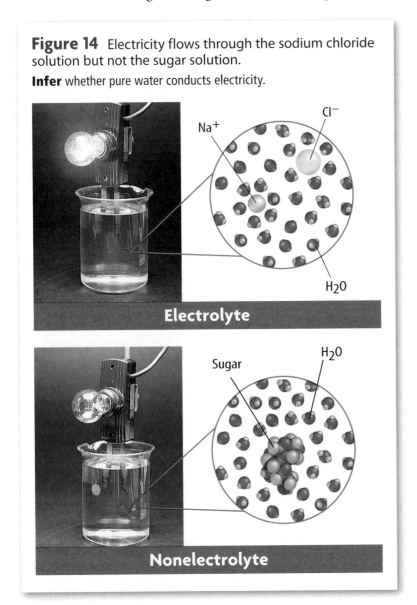

Figure 14 Electricity flows through the sodium chloride solution but not the sugar solution.

Infer whether pure water conducts electricity.

Na$^+$ Cl$^-$

H$_2$O

Electrolyte

Sugar   H$_2$O

Nonelectrolyte

How can you sum up matter?

Heterogeneous and homogeneous mixtures are the most common forms of matter. Mixtures can be separated by making use of differences in the physical properties of the components and the physical changes they undergo. Many homogeneous mixtures are aqueous solutions because water dissolves many substances. Water's excellent solvent properties are a result of its polarity and the bent shape of its molecules. Water dissolves both ionic compounds and polar covalent compounds. In aqueous solutions, ionic compounds break up into ions. Because of the dissolved ions, these solutions conduct electricity and are called electrolytes.

LESSON 1 Review

Summarize

Create your own lesson summary as you design a **visual aid.**

1. **Write** the lesson title, number, and page numbers at the top of your poster.

2. **Scan** the lesson to find the **red** main headings. Organize these headings on your poster, leaving space between each.

3. **Design** an information box beneath each **red** heading. In the box, list 2–3 details, key terms, and definitions from each **blue** subheading.

4. **Illustrate** your poster with diagrams of important structures or processes next to each information box.

 ELA8: R 2.3

Standards Check

Using Vocabulary

1. **Distinguish** between a homogeneous and a heterogeneous solution. **7.c**

2. **Describe** a solution using the words *solute* and *solvent*. **7.c**

Understanding Main Ideas

3. Which solution contains the largest volume of solvent in 100 mL? **7.c**

   A. 3 percent alcohol
   B. 30 percent alcohol
   C. 70 percent alcohol
   D. 95 percent alcohol

4. **List** four forms of matter. **7.c**

5. **Explain** why water is called the "universal solvent." **7.c**

6. **Give an example,** not found in this chapter, of a mixture that is not a solution. **7.c**

7. **Show,** by means of drawings, the difference between a saturated and an unsaturated solution. **7.c**

8. **Organize Information** Copy and fill in the graphic organizer below with details about homogeneous and heterogeneous mixtures. **7.c**

9. **Predict** whether ammonia is soluble in water. Ammonia is a polar molecule. **7.c**

Applying Science

10. **Formulate a hypothesis** about whether a substance that contains an O–H group will dissolve in water. Support your hypothesis. **7.c**

11. **Design an experiment** to determine whether alcohol is an electrolyte. **7.c**

Science Online

For more practice, visit **Standards Check** at ca8.msscience.com.

DataLab

00:20 minutes

Try at Home

How do solubilities differ?

Have you noticed that sugar dissolves more readily in hot tea than in iced tea? How do the solubilities of substances change with temperature?

Data

These data show the masses of potassium nitrate and sodium nitrate that will dissolve in 100 g of water.

Solubility Data		
Temperature (°C)	Potassium Nitrate (KNO_3) (grams)	Sodium Nitrate ($NaNO_3$) (grams)
0	14	73
20	32	87
40	63	104
60	109	124
80	170	147
100	242	176

CRC Handbook of Chemistry and Physics, 80th Edition, 1999–2000, CRC Press LLC, pp. 8–105, 8–108

Data Analysis

1. **Graph** the data on a single sheet of graph paper.

2. **Determine** the temperature at which the solubilities of both solutes are the same.

3. **Determine** the temperatures at which 100 g of each solute dissolves. How much of each solute dissolves at 55°C?

Science Content Standards

7.c Students know substances can be classified by their properties, including their melting temperature, density, hardness, and thermal and electrical conductivity.

9.e Construct appropriate graphs from data and develop quantitative statements about the relationships between variables.

ALG: 6.0

Science Content Standards

5.e Students know how to determine whether a solution is acidic, basic, or neutral.
9.a Plan and conduct a scientific investigation to test a hypothesis.
9.b Evaluate the accuracy and reproducibility of data.
9.e Construct appropriate graphs from data and develop quantitative statements about the relationships between variables.

Reading Guide

What *You'll Learn*

▶ **Distinguish** acids from bases by their properties.

▶ **Understand** the pH scale.

▶ **Identify** different ways of measuring pH.

Why *It's Important*

Many chemical reactions take place in an aqueous solution, and these reactions are affected by the presence of hydronium and hydroxide ions.

Vocabulary
acid
hydronium ion
base
pH
indicator
pH meter

Review Vocabulary
atom: very small particle that makes up all matter (p. 174)

Acidic, Basic, and Neutral Solutions

Main Idea The pH scale measures the acidity of a solution.

Real-World Reading Connection If your stomach is upset because of excess acid, you might take an antacid. You can think of an antacid as the opposite of an acid. Antacids are bases. They work in opposition to the way that acids work.

What are acids and bases?

You may have heard that acids eat through clothing and even destroy things made of metal. You may also know of products containing bases that are used for the tough jobs of cleaning clogged drains and ovens. These acids and bases are strong products. You should protect your hands and eyes with gloves and goggles when you use them. Many other products that you buy at the supermarket are also acids or bases. For example, vinegar and lemon juice are acids. Soap and baking soda are bases. **Figure 15** shows additional acids and bases that you might know about.

Figure 15 These foods contain acids, such as citric acid and folic acid, that are important in your diet. Several different bases, including sodium hydroxide and ammonia, are found in cleaning products.

Acids

What makes orange juice, dill pickles, and grapefruit juice have a sour taste? Acids cause the sour taste of these and other foods. An **acid** is a substance that releases a positively charged hydrogen ion, H^+, in water. When an acid mixes with water, the acid dissolves, releasing a hydrogen ion.

Properties of Acids

Acids are easily recognized by their sour taste. Citric acid makes lemons and limes taste sour. Vinegar is sour because it contains acetic acid. However, you should never test any material in the laboratory by tasting it. A way to test for acids is to use litmus paper. Litmus paper contains a compound that changes color in acids and bases. Acids turn blue litmus paper red.

 How does litmus paper change when dipped in an acid?

Acids also react with metals and release hydrogen gas, H_2. **Figure 16** shows that if you place a piece of zinc in an acidic solution, bubbles of hydrogen gas form. **Figure 17** shows that bubbles form when an acid reacts with limestone, or calcium carbonate. In this case, the bubbles are carbon dioxide gas. Geologists use this reaction to test and classify rocks. The ability to neutralize a base is another important chemical property of an acid. Neutralization is a chemical reaction between an acid and a base in which a salt and water are formed. A neutral solution or substance is one that is neither acidic nor basic.

What is a hydronium ion?

You have just read that an acid contains a hydrogen atom. When an acid dissolves in water, the hydrogen ion, H^+, separates from the rest of the acid molecule and combines with a water molecule. The combination of a water molecule and a hydrogen ion produces a hydronium ion. A **hydronium ion** is positively charged and has the formula H_3O^+. This formula, not H^+, accurately represents how the hydrogen ion exists in an aqueous solution.

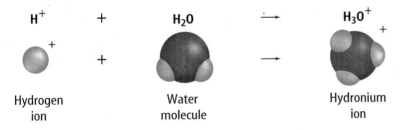

Hydrogen ion   Water molecule   Hydronium ion

All acidic solutions contain positive hydronium ions. Because they contain ions, acid solutions conduct electric currents and are called electrolytes.

Figure 16 When an acid reacts with a metal, such as zinc, hydrogen bubbles form.

Figure 17 When an acid reacts with limestone, which is calcium carbonate, carbon dioxide gas is formed.

State whether the ability to neutralize is a physical or chemical property.

Uses of Acids

You might be surprised to find out how important acids are in your life. Your stomach contains an acid that helps break down the food you eat. Amino acids are the monomers in the protein polymers that make up your body tissues. Carbonic acid and phosphoric acid maintain a delicate balance in your blood. Acids are also important in your diet. For example, vitamin C, which is found in orange juice and other foods, is ascorbic acid. Serious health problems can result from a lack of vitamin C.

Acids are also used in making many products. Manufacturers use sulfuric acid in a wide variety of products, including fertilizers, detergents, plastics, and pesticides. Hydrochloric acid, commonly called muriatic acid, is used as a strong cleaner for bricks and concrete. Like sulfuric acid, hydrochloric acid is used in manufacturing products ranging from rubber to medicine. **Figure 18** describes how acids can dissolve in water vapor in the atmosphere and fall to Earth as acid precipitation—rain, snow, and sleet.

 Explain why acids are important to your body.

Bases

Now you know something about acids. You might not be as familiar with bases as you are with acids. A **base** is a substance that produces hydroxide ions when dissolved in water. The formula for a hydroxide ion is OH^-. Every time you wash your hands, you are using a base.

Sodium hydroxide, NaOH, and magnesium hydroxide, $Mg(OH)_2$, are common bases. Sodium hydroxide is the main ingredient in some drain cleaners. Magnesium hydroxide is used in antacids.

Ammonia, NH_3, is also a base, but notice that its formula does not contain a hydroxide ion. Ammonia acts as a base by accepting a hydrogen ion from water.

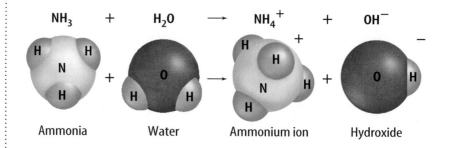

| Ammonia | Water | Ammonium ion | Hydroxide |

 What are the products of the reaction between ammonia and water?

Visualizing Acid Precipitation

Figure 18
When fossil fuels such as coal and oil are burned, a variety of chemical compounds are produced and released into the air. In the atmosphere, some of these compounds form acids that mix with water vapor and fall back to Earth as acid precipitation: rain, sleet, snow, or fog. The effects of acid precipitation on the environment can be devastating. Winds carry these acids hundreds of miles from their sources, damaging forests, corroding statues, and endangering human health.

B Sulfur dioxide and nitrogen oxides react with water vapor in the air to form highly acidic solutions of nitric acid (HNO_3) and sulfuric acid (H_2SO_4). These solutions eventually return to Earth as acid precipitation.

C Some acid rain in the United States has a pH as low as 2.3. This is close to the acidity of stomach acid.

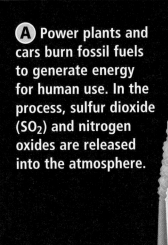

A Power plants and cars burn fossil fuels to generate energy for human use. In the process, sulfur dioxide (SO_2) and nitrogen oxides are released into the atmosphere.

Properties of Bases

Like acids, bases have a common set of properties. In aqueous solutions, they feel slippery on your skin. You experience this when you use soap, which contains a base. If you have ever gotten soap in your mouth, you know how bitter it tastes. A bitter taste is another physical property of bases. Solutions of bases cause red litmus paper to turn blue. Like solutions of acids, solutions of bases contain ions, so they are electrolytes. Bases neutralize acids by forming salts and water.

What is a hydroxide ion?

You may be wondering where the ions in a solution of a base come from. Most bases are ionic compounds. When a base dissolves in water, it separates into a positive ion and a negative hydroxide ion, as shown in **Figure 19.** All the properties of bases are a result of the presence of hydroxide ions that form when the base is dissolved in water.

Figure 19 Sodium hydroxide is a base because it produces hydroxide ions when it dissolves in water.

Identify the two ions produced in a solution of sodium hydroxide.

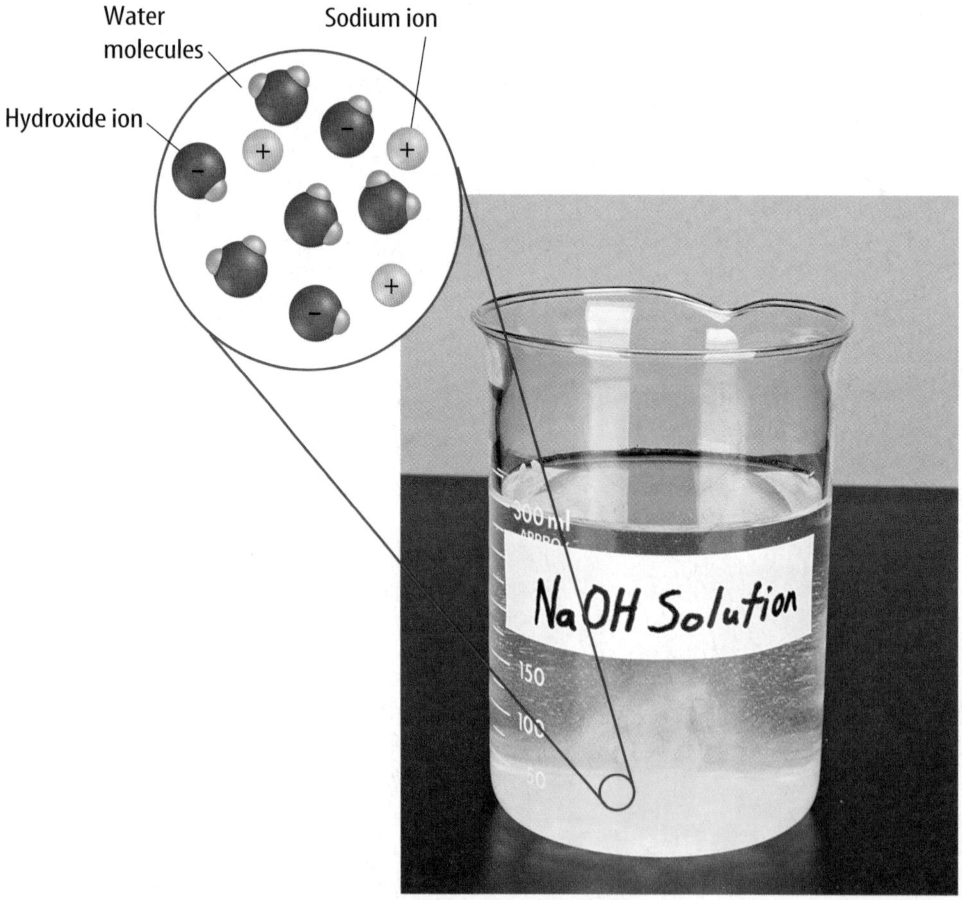

Uses of Bases

You may already know how handy a base such as magnesium hydroxide can be if you have indigestion. Magnesium hydroxide is found in milk of magnesia, a medicine used to soothe stomach distress. Another base, baking soda, is used to make biscuits and other breads. Gardeners use bases to make acidic soil neutral. Strong bases, such as sodium hydroxide, are used for cleaning because they are able to eliminate grease. Bases are also used to produce new products. For example, sodium hydroxide is used to manufacture soap, rayon, and paper. Calcium hydroxide is used to make plaster and mortar.

Not all bases are equally strong. The same is true of acids. Scientists have developed a way of measuring the acidity or basicity of solutions. Why is this important?

What is pH?

Biologists at the Monterey Bay Aquarium in California must monitor the acidity of water to ensure the survival of the animals sheltered there. Jellies, shown in **Figure 20,** are sensitive to changes in acidity. Aquarium biologists must be able to measure and control the acidity of the water. How do they measure acidity using numbers?

WORD ORIGIN

pH
from *P* (German *Potenz*; means *potency, power*) and *H* (the symbol for hydrogen); coined by S. P. L. Sörensen

The pH Scale

pH is a numerical scale used to indicate how acidic or basic a solution is. The scale runs from below 0 to above 14. Acidic solutions have a pH below 7. Highly acidic solutions have pH values near 0. Basic solutions have a pH above 7. Highly basic solutions have pH values near 14. Neutral solutions have a pH of 7.

 Reading Check If a solution has a pH of 10, is the solution acidic or basic?

Figure 20 The water in the tank that is home to these jellies at the Monterey Bay Aquarium must be kept at a pH between 8.1 and 8.4.

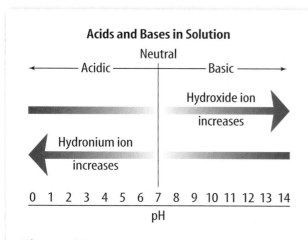

Acids and Bases in Solution

Figure 21 Hydronium ions and hydroxide ions are present in any water solution. As one ion increases, the other decreases.

Infer At what pH are the two concentrations equal?

Figure 22 The pH scale is related to the concentration of hydronium ions. As the numbers on the scale increase, the concentration of H_3O^+ decreases.

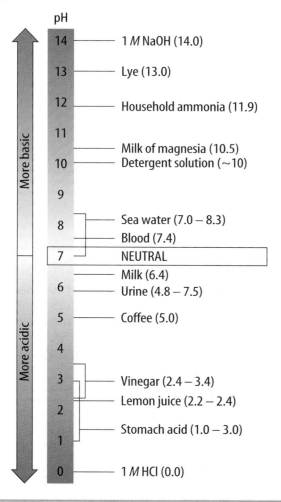

pH and Hydronium Ion Concentration

pH is a measure of the concentration of hydronium ions, H_3O^+, in a solution. The higher the concentration of hydronium ions, the more acidic the solution is. The lower the concentration of hydronium ions, the more basic the solution is. It's helpful to notice that the hydronium ion concentrations and pH values go in opposite directions. At low pH values, the concentration of hydronium ions is high. As the pH values increase, the hydronium ion concentration gradually decreases. At high pH values, the concentration of hydronium ions is low.

Hydronium Ions, Hydroxide Ions, and pH

All acid and base solutions contain both hydronium ions and hydroxide ions. What distinguishes an acid from a base is which of the two ions is present in the greater concentration. **Figure 21** shows that in an acid solution (pH less than 7), hydronium ions are present in greater concentration than hydroxide ions, OH^-. In basic solutions (pH greater than 7), the concentration of hydroxide ions is greater than the concentration of hydronium ions. In neutral solutions (pH = 7), the hydronium ion and hydroxide ion concentrations are equal.

 Which ion—hydroxide or hydronium—is present in the greater amount in an acid solution?

Milk has a pH of 6.4. What does this pH value mean? **Figure 22** shows that pH 6.4 is close to pH 7, which is neutral. At pH 7, the hydronium and hydroxide ion concentrations are equal. A pH of 6.4 means that milk is a slightly acidic mixture. The concentration of hydronium ions in milk must be slightly higher than in a neutral solution. Similarly, blood, with a pH of 7.4, is a slightly basic solution. The hydroxide ion concentration in blood must be slightly greater than it is at pH 7.

Comparing pH Values

Maybe you're wondering what the numbers on the pH scale mean. How is the concentration of hydronium ions different at pH 1 from what it is at pH 2? A change in one pH unit represents a tenfold change in the acidity or basicity of a solution. For example, if one solution has a pH of 1 and a second solution has a pH of 2, the first solution is not twice as acidic as the first. It is ten times more acidic. To determine the difference in acidity or basicity, use the following calculations. Each pH unit represents a power of 10. pH 1 is represented by 10^1, and pH 2 is represented by 10^2. The difference in acidity or basicity between two solutions is represented by 10^n, where n is the difference between two pH values. For example, how much more acidic is a solution with a pH of 1 than a solution with a pH of 2? pH 2 − pH 1 = 1; $10^n = 10^1 =$ 10 times more acidic.

 **Reading Check** How much more acidic is a solution with a pH of 1 than a solution with a pH of 3?

Figure 23 compares the pH values of orange juice and vinegar. Orange juice has a pH of 5, and vinegar has a pH of about 3. The difference between the two values is two pH units. How many times more acidic is vinegar compared to orange juice? $10^n = 10^2$ = 100. Vinegar is 100 times more acidic than orange juice. **Figure 23** shows that NaOH and detergent differ by four pH units. Sodium hydroxide is 10^4, or 10,000, times more basic than detergent.

Figure 23 Vinegar and orange juice differ by two units, so vinegar is 100 times more acidic than orange juice. Sodium hydroxide is 10,000 times more basic than detergent.

pH difference = 2

pH difference = 4

Neutralization and pH

How do antacids, such as milk of magnesia, relieve indigestion? Indigestion is caused by excess stomach acid, which is hydrochloric acid, HCl. Hydrochloric acid helps break down the food you eat, but too much of it can irritate your stomach or digestive tract. Milk of magnesia contains the base magnesium hydroxide, $Mg(OH)_2$. Stomach acid reacts with magnesium hydroxide according to the following equation:

$$2HCl + Mg(OH)_2 \rightarrow MgCl_2 + 2H_2O$$

This is a neutralization reaction. Recall that neutralization is a chemical reaction between an acid and a base that produces water and a salt. In the equation above, the salt is magnesium chloride, $MgCl_2$. Neither of the products, magnesium chloride nor water, is acidic or basic. The resulting solution has a pH of 7, and so it is neutral.

 **Reading Check** What are the products of the reaction between magnesium hydroxide and hydrochloric acid?

Sometimes you need to know the amount of acids or bases in a solution. For example, you may want to determine the amount of acetic acid in vinegar. This can be done by using a process called titration (ti TRAY shun), in which a solution of known concentration is used to determine the concentration of another solution. Neutralization is used to find out how much acid is contained in an unknown solution. Slowly add a base with a known concentration to the unknown acid while measuring the mixture's pH. When the pH equals 7, the acid is neutralized. The amount of base that was added is equal to the amount of acid originally present. Read on and find out how to measure pH.

How is pH measured?

Providing a suitable environment for jellies is only one reason why knowing the pH of a solution is important. The pH of shampoo is balanced so that it does not damage hair. Acid levels in food are controlled for people with sensitive stomachs. Farmers and gardeners must measure and adjust the pH of the soil to grow certain plants. In **Figure 24** a gardener is adding lime, $Ca(OH)_2$ to raise the pH of acidic soil. The pH of swimming pools must be carefully controlled to prevent the growth of bacteria and algae. In all of these instances, indicators, pH strips, or pH meters are used to keep track of pH.

 **Reading Check** **Explain** why knowing the pH of solutions is important to humans and animals.

Figure 24 The hydroxide ion in lime, $Ca(OH)_2$, neutralizes excess hydrogen ion in acidic or "sour" soil.

Figure 25 Using indicators is one way to monitor the pH of this swimming pool. If the pH is too high or too low, the water could damage your skin or bacteria could grow.

Indicators

You may have seen someone use indicators to test the pH of swimming pool water, as shown in **Figure 25.** An **indicator** is a compound that changes from one color to another within a particular pH range. **Figure 26** shows the color changes for some common indicators. Notice that the pH ranges for the color change are different for each indicator. If you choose the correct indicator, you can determine the **approximate** pH of any solution. The universal indicator at the bottom of **Figure 26** is a mixture of a number of indicators. The universal indicator changes color across most of the pH range. When the indicator is added to an acidic or a basic solution, the solution changes color. The color can be matched to standard colors. **Figure 26** shows that a yellow color means that the solution has a pH of about 6.

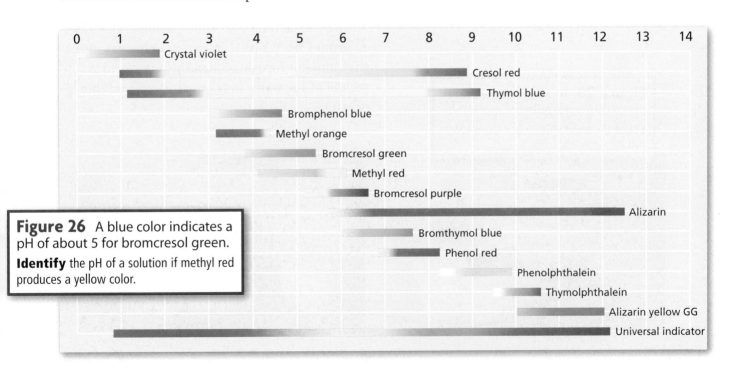

Figure 26 A blue color indicates a pH of about 5 for bromcresol green.

Identify the pH of a solution if methyl red produces a yellow color.

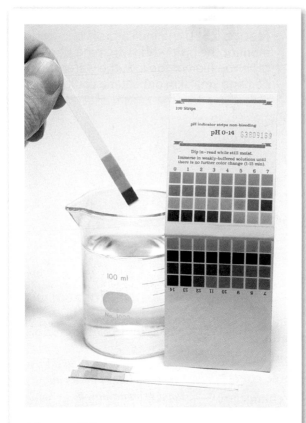

Figure 27 pH testing strips are a quick way of determining the approximate pH of a solution.

pH Strips

You have probably used litmus paper to test for acids and bases. Litmus is one of the simplest indicator test papers, but provides the least information. Recall that blue litmus paper turns red in acid solutions. Red litmus paper turns blue in basic solutions. No change in color occurs if the solution is neutral. Other pH test strips provide the approximate pH of the solution. These strips contain a universal indicator that can change to a variety of colors across the pH range. When you dip the strip into a solution, the strip changes color. You then match the new color of the strip to one of the standard colors. Notice in **Figure 27** that each standard color corresponds to a different pH value.

pH Meters

pH strips are quick and convenient to use. However, if you want an accurate measure of pH, you need a pH meter. A **pH meter** is an electronic instrument with an electrode that is sensitive to the hydronium ions in a solution. **Figure 28** shows that you can measure the exact pH of a solution quickly and accurately.

Because it is an electronic instrument, a pH meter requires a power supply. Handheld pH meters have been developed with portable power supplies such as batteries. These can be taken outside the laboratory for measuring pH in the environment. People can monitor changes in the environment by using a handheld meter to study the pH of the water in lakes, streams, and the ocean.

Figure 28 A pH meter measures pH to the hundredths of a pH unit.
State the pH of vinegar and the pH of milk of magnesia.

What do you know about acids and bases?

Acids and bases are identified by the ions that form in their aqueous solutions. Acids form hydronium ions, H_3O^+, and bases produce hydroxide ions, OH^-. The reaction that occurs between any acid and any base is called neutralization. In neutralization reactions, an acid and a base react to form a neutral solution of salt and water. The pH of a solution is a measure of the hydronium ion concentration. pH 7 is at the center of the pH scale, neither acidic nor basic. If a solution has a pH less than 7, the solution is acidic. Any solution with a pH greater than 7 is basic.

LESSON 2   Review

Summarize

Create your own lesson summary as you design a **study web**.

1. **Write** the lesson title, number, and page numbers at the top of a sheet of paper.

2. **Scan** the lesson to find the **red** main headings.

3. **Organize** these headings clockwise on branches around the lesson title.

4. **Review** the information under each **red** heading to design a branch for each **blue** subheading.

5. **List** 2–3 details, key terms, and definitions from each **blue** subheading on branches extending from the main heading branches.

 ELA8: R 2.3

Using Vocabulary

1. How does a hydronium ion differ from a hydroxide ion? **5.e**

2. Write a definition of pH using your own words. **5.e**

Understanding Main Ideas

3. **Identify** the pH ranges of acidic solutions and basic solutions. **5.e**

4. **Describe** how an indicator works. **5.e**

5. **Compare** the concentrations of hydronium ions and hydroxide ions in a neutral solution. **5.e**

6. **Summarize Information** Copy the graphic organizer below and fill in the properties of acids and bases. **5.e**

Standards Check

7. **Draw a diagram** that shows how the concentration of hydronium ions in a solution changes as pH increases from 0 to 14. **5.e**

Applying Science

8. **Hypothesize** how the pH of white vinegar would change if an ammonia solution was added to it a drop at a time. White vinegar has a pH of 3.1. **5.e**

9. **Identify** which is a property of an acid.

   A. turns litmus red
   B. has a bitter taste
   C. has a pH of 10
   D. reacts with acids **5.e**

 Science Online

For more practice, visit **Standards Check** at ca8.msscience.com.

MiniLab

How can you determine pH?

Scientists use different methods to measure pH. Some methods are more accurate than others.

Procedure

1. Read and complete a lab safety form.
2. Choose three **common household solutions.**
3. Create a table such as the one below to record the following data: acid or base, predicted pH, measured pH.
4. Use **litmus paper** to determine whether each solution is an acid or a base. Predict the pH.
5. Use one of the methods demonstrated by your teacher to determine the pH of your solutions.
6. Create a class data table.

Data Table				
Solution	Litmus Paper Acid or Base	Predicted pH	Measured pH	Method Used
1				
2				
3				

Analysis

1. **Compare** your predicted pH values to your measured pH values. How well did you predict the pH values? Were you surprised by any of your results?

2. **Evaluate** the different methods used to measure pH. Which do you think is most accurate? Which is most readily available?

 Science Content Standards

5.e Students know how to determine whether a solution is acidic, basic, or neutral.
9.b Evaluate the accuracy and reproducibility of data.

Applying Math

Comparing pH Values

Recall that each pH unit represents a power of 10 change in the acidity of a solution. Recall also that as the pH of a solution decreases, the solution becomes more acidic. To compare the acidity of two solutions, find the difference between their pH values, *n,* and then use *n* as the exponent of 10. Use the table below to determine the decimal forms for powers of 10.

Difference in pH	Power of 10	Decimal Form
1	10^1	10
2	10^2	100
3	10^3	1000
4	10^4	10,000
5	10^5	100,000
6	10^6	1,000,000

Example

If a solution of acid has a pH of 1 and a solution of coffee has a pH of 5, find the difference in acidity.

To solve, first find the difference between the pH values of the two solutions. $n = 5 - 1$ *or* 4

Let *n* = difference of the pH values of the two solutions.

Then use *n* as the exponent of 10. $10^n = 10^4 = 10,000$

Answer: The acid is 10,000 times more acidic than the coffee.

Practice Problems

1. Find the difference in acidity between a solution of rainwater that has a pH of 6 and seawater that has a pH of 8.

2. If tomato juice is 1,000,000 times more acidic than a solution of household bleach, what is the difference in pH?

Science nline

For more math practice, visit **Math Practice** at ca8.msscience.com.

Solubility and pH

Problem

How does the amount of sugar you can dissolve in lemonade compare with the amount that will dissolve in pure water? Does pH have any effect on how sweet you can make lemonade?

Form a Hypothesis

➤ **Review** the results from this chapter's laboratory investigations. What effect do you think changing the pH has on the solubility of a solute at room temperature? Will the effect be the same on any solute?

➤ **Predict** how pH will affect the dissolving of substances.

Collect Data and Make Observations

Create a Standard for Comparison

1. Read and complete a lab safety form.
2. Measure 5-g samples of your solute.
3. Begin your exploration using distilled water as your solvent. Measure and record the pH of distilled water.
4. Add your solute 5 g at a time, stirring constantly, until the solute begins to collect on bottom of the container. Record the amount of solute added.

Test Other Solvents

5. Decide whether to investigate basic or acidic solutions. Choose three of the solvents provided by your teacher. Measure and record the pH of each solvent.
6. Repeat step 4 for each solvent.

Materials

table salt, sugar, cornstarch
solvents of varying pH
distilled water
beaker
balance
pH paper

Safety Precautions

WARNING: *Do not drink, taste, or eat materials used in the lab.*

 Science Content Standards

5.e Students know how to determine whether a solution is acidic, basic, or neutral.
9.a Plan and conduct a scientific investigation to test a hypothesis.
9.e Construct appropriate graphs from data and develop quantitative statements about the relationships between variables.

Analyze and Conclude

Interpret Your Data

1. **Make a table** to organize your data.
2. **Graph** the results of your experiment.
3. **Describe** how altering the pH changed the amount of solute that could be dissolved.

Draw Conclusions

4. **Infer** from your results what would have happened if you had used solutions with different pH values.
5. **Assess** the prediction you made earlier. Were you correct?
6. **Error Assessment** Was any part of your experimental procedure subjective? How could it have affected your outcome? How accurate do you think the masses of dissolved solute in your table are?

Communicate

Write a Report Write a 100–300-word report on your results to share with your class. Did other students choose the same solute? What were their results? How do these compare with yours?

Real World Science

Yuan T. Lee

Yuan T. Lee was born in Taiwan. He graduated from the University of California–Berkeley and later became a professor there. In 1986, he, along with Dudley R. Herschbach and John C. Polanyi, won the Nobel Prize in Chemistry. Their work involved studying molecules at low pressures to see how they reacted with each other. It helped people to understand how chemical reactions occurred.

Visit **Careers** at **ca8.msscience.com** to research the requirements to become a chemist. Write a 500–700-word essay about a career as a chemist. Include educational background, job description, and other interesting facts.

ELA8: 2.3

Acid Rain Prevention

Acid rain occurs when gases such as sulfur dioxide and nitrogen oxide react with water and oxygen in the atmosphere. Sulfur dioxide and nitrogen oxide usually come from power plant pollution and can be harmful to plants and animals. Today, many power plants use new technology to remove sulfur from their gas emissions, including using limestone to convert sulfur dioxide to carbon dioxide.

Visit **Technology** at **ca8.msscience.com** for more information about air pollutants. Create a graph about air pollutants that includes the amount of air pollutants in the atmosphere over the past five years.

Gilbert N. Lewis

Gilbert N. Lewis, a famous American physical chemist, was born in 1875. Lewis was the dean of the College of Chemistry at the University of California–Berkeley. In 1923, he came up with the electron-pair theory, a way of describing acids and bases. A Lewis acid is called an electron-pair acceptor and a Lewis base is called an electron-pair donator.

Visit **History** at <u>ca8.msscience.com</u> to research more information about this American scientist. Write a 500–700-word biography about the life and scientific achievements of Gilbert N. Lewis.

ELA8: W 2.1

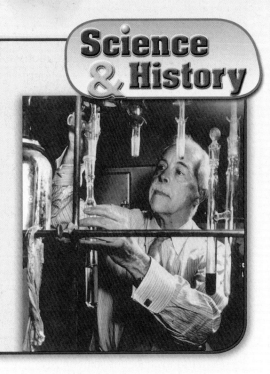

ACETYLSALICYLIC ACID

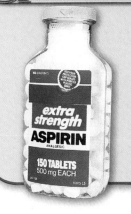

Acetylsalicylic acid is a drug known to relieve many symptoms including pain, fever, arthritis, headaches, and migraines. It is an anti-coagulant/blood thinner and, in high doses, can be used to stop heart attacks. As its name suggests, acetylsalicylic acid is very acidic and has a very low pH. This drug is widely used in the United States and most people have it in their homes.

Visit **Society** at <u>ca8.msscience.com</u> to research the physical properties of acetylsalicylic acid. Write 200–300 words on the side effects of acetylsalicylic acid.

The BIG Idea Aqueous solutions of acids and bases have characteristic properties and can be identified by their pH values.

Lesson 1 Solutions

Main Idea **Most of the substances you encounter daily are solutions.**

- Matter is composed of substances and mixtures.

- Mixtures have variable compositions and can be separated by means of physical properties or physical changes.

- Solutions are homogeneous mixtures.

- Water is found on Earth in all three states of matter and is essential to all living organisms.

- The polar nature of the water molecule and its bent shape are responsible for water's unique properties.

- Water forms aqueous solutions by dissolving ionic compounds and polar molecules.

- Solutions that contain ions can conduct an electric current.

- **heterogeneous mixture** (p. 382)
- **homogeneous mixture** (p. 382)
- **mixture** (p. 382)
- **solute** (p. 384)
- **solution** (p. 383)
- **solvent** (p. 384)
- **substance** (p. 381)

Lesson 2 Acidic, Basic, and Neutral Solutions

Main Idea **The pH scale measures the acidity of a solution.**

- Acidic solutions taste sour, neutralize bases, react with metals and calcium carbonate, and turn blue litmus paper red.

- Basic solutions taste bitter, feel slippery, neutralize acids, and turn red litmus paper blue.

- Acids release hydrogen ions in aqueous solutions, forming hydronium ions, H_3O^+.

- Bases form hydroxide ions, OH^-, in aqueous solutions.

- The pH scale ranges from below 0 to above 14 and is used to measure the acidity of a solution.

- The pH of a neutral solution is 7.

- Acidic solutions have pH values less than 7. Basic solutions have pH values greater than 7.

- The approximate pH of a solution can be determined using indicators and pH test strips.

- pH meters can measure the exact pH of a solution.

- **acid** (p. 395)
- **base** (p. 395)
- **hydronium ion** (p. 395)
- **indicator** (p. 403)
- **pH** (p. 399)
- **pH meter** (p. 404)

STUDY TO GO ▸ Download quizzes, key terms, and flash cards from ca8.msscience.com.

 Science Online Interactive Tutor ca8.msscience.com

Linking Vocabulary and Main Ideas

Use vocabulary terms from page 412 to complete this concept map.

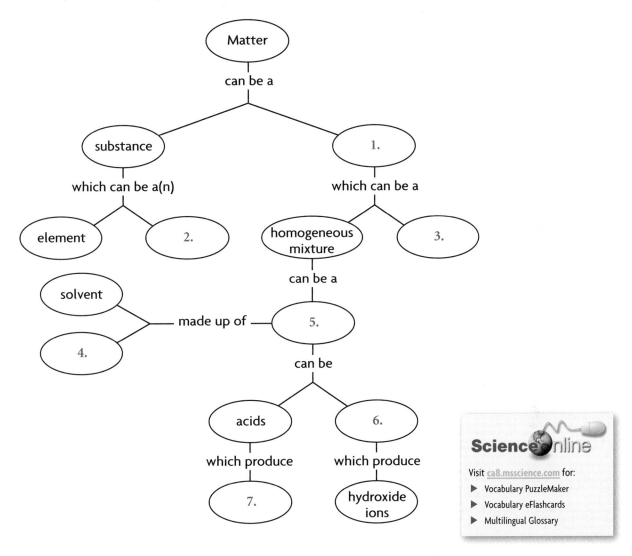

Matter

can be a

substance

which can be a(n)

element

2.

solvent

made up of

4.

1.

which can be a

homogeneous mixture

3.

can be a

5.

can be

acids

which produce

7.

6.

which produce

hydroxide ions

Science Online

Visit ca8.msscience.com for:
- ▶ Vocabulary PuzzleMaker
- ▶ Vocabulary eFlashcards
- ▶ Multilingual Glossary

Using Vocabulary

Describe the relationship between each pair of terms.

8. solute and solvent

9. mixture and solution

10. heterogeneous mixture and homogeneous mixture

11. acid and base

12. hydronium ion and pH

Match the correct vocabulary term to each definition below.

13. a form of matter that has the same composition and properties throughout the sample

14. a compound that changes from one color to another within a particular pH range

15. an electronic instrument with an electrode that is sensitive to the hydronium ions in a solution

Understanding Main Ideas

Choose the word or phrase that best answers the question.

1. Which is a solution?
   A. pure water
   B. raisin cookie dough
   C. copper
   D. vinegar　　**7.c**

2. The graph below is a solubility curve for sodium chloride, NaCl.

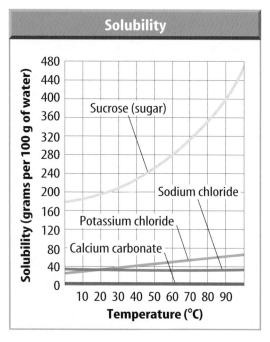

   What mass of NaCl is needed to form a saturated solution at 80°C?
   A. 30 g
   B. 35 g
   C. 40 g
   D. 80 g　　**7.c**

3. The pH of apricots is 4.5. What color would litmus paper turn if a drop of apricot juice were placed on it?
   A. red
   B. blue
   C. purple
   D. yellow　　**5.e**

4. What substance could you use to neutralize a solution with a pH of 1.5?
   A. milk
   B. vinegar
   C. ammonia
   D. water　　**5.e**

5. The figure below illustrates reaction of water molecules.

   What process is shown in the diagram?
   A. the formation of a hydroxide ion
   B. the formation of a hydronium ion
   C. neutralization
   D. saturation　　**5.e**

6. What ions must be present in the greatest amount in a solution with a pH of 8.5?
   A. hydrogen ions
   B. oxygen ions
   C. hydronium ions
   D. hydroxide ions　　**5.e**

7. Which best describes a solution that has dissolved all the solute it can hold?
   A. It is a saturated solution.
   B. It is an unsaturated solution.
   C. It is a concentrated solution.
   D. It is a dilute solution.　　**7.c**

8. Which is NOT a property of a base?
   A. turns red litmus blue
   B. is slippery to feel and bitter to taste
   C. reacts with metals to produce hydrogen
   D. is an electrolyte　　**5.e**

9. Which chemical formula describes a hydronium ion?
   A. H_3O^+
   B. OH^-
   C. H_3O^-
   D. $OH+$　　**5.e**

Applying Science

10. Make use of what you know about the concentrations of hydronium ions and hydroxide ions in a solution having a pH of 7 and explain why the solution is neutral. `5.e`

11. Explain why an indicator might not change color when it is placed in an acidic or a basic solution. `5.e`

12. Design an experiment that will allow you to separate a mixture of sugar and sand. `7.c`

13. Draw a conclusion from the graph below about why soft drinks, which contain dissolved carbon dioxide, quickly go flat as they warm up to room temperature. `7.c`

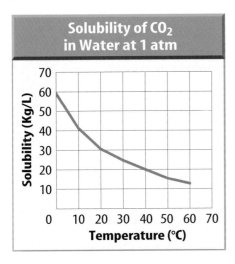

14. Predict Geologists have measured the pH of the water in Mono Lake to be 9.8. What will happen to the pH as water evaporates from the lake? `5.e`

WRITING in Science

15. Design and write a paragraph for an informational sign that could be placed at Mono Lake to explain to visitors how and why tufas form.

Cumulative Review

16. Demonstrate how to balance the equation for the neutralization of sulfuric acid with the base sodium hydroxide:
$$H_2SO_4 + NaOH \longrightarrow Na_2SO_4 + H_2O$$ `5.b`

17. Classify bases as being usually ionic compounds or usually covalent compounds and give evidence for your answer. `7.c`

18. Decide whether neutralization is a chemical change. `5.e`

Applying Math

Use the table below to answer questions 19–21.

Difference in pH	Power of 10	Decimal Form
1	10^1	10
2	10^2	100
3	10^3	1000
4	10^4	10,000
5	10^5	100,000
6	10^6	1,000,000

19. Find the difference in acidity between apple juice that has a pH of 3 and lemon juice that has a pH of 2. `MA8: ALG 2.0`

20. If tomato juice has a pH of 4 and white bread has a pH of 6, find the difference in acidity. `MA8: ALG 2.0`

21. Find the difference in acidity between normal rain that has a pH of 5.7 and acid rain that has a pH of 5.2. `MA8: ALG 2.0`

1 What is the symbol for the hydroxide ion?

A H_3O^+

B OH^-

C H_2O

D H_2O_2 5.e

2 The image below shows a mixture of sand and iron filings being separated.

What physical property is used to separate the sand and iron?

A density

B ductility

C magnetism

D malleability   7.c

3 Which is a property of acidic solutions?

A They taste sour.

B They feel slippery.

C They are in many cleaning products.

D They taste bitter.   5.e

4 When iodine is dissolved in alcohol, what term is used to describe the alcohol?

A alloy

B solvent

C mixture

D solute   7.c

Use the graph below to answer questions 5 and 6.

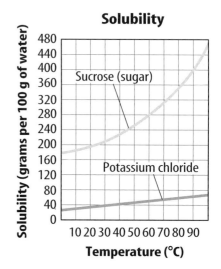

5 How does the solubility of sucrose change as the temperature increases?

A It increases.

B It does not change.

C It decreases.

D It fluctuates randomly.   7.c

6 Which statement is TRUE?

A Potassium chloride is more soluble in water than sucrose.

B As water temperature increases, the solubility of potassium chloride decreases.

C Sucrose is more soluble in water than potassium chloride.

D Water temperature has no effect on the solubility of these two chemicals.   7.c

Science Online Standards Assessment ca8.msscience.com

7 Which type of molecule is water?

A   polar

B   ionic

C   nonpolar

D   precipitate   7.c

8 A change of what property permits certain materials to act as indicators?

A   acidity

B   color

C   concentration

D   basicity   5.e

Use the illustration below to answer questions 9 and 10.

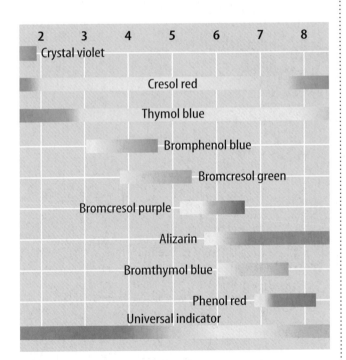

9 What indicator can be used at a pH of 7?

A   bromphenol blue

B   bromcresol green

C   bromcresol purple

D   phenol red   5.e

10 What indicators could be used to produce a color change at both pH 2 and pH 8?

A   cresol red and thymol blue

B   universal indicator and alizarin

C   thymol blue and bromophenol blue

D   phenol red and bromocresol green   5.e

11 What characteristic do aqueous solutions share?

A   They contain more than three solutes.

B   No solids or gases are present as solutes in them.

C   All are extremely concentrated.

D   Water is the solvent in them.   7.c

12 Which is the symbol for a hydronium ion?

A H^+

B H_3O^+

C H_3O^-

D OH^- 5.e

13 A solution is prepared by adding 100 g of solid sodium hydroxide, NaOH, to 1,000 mL of water. What is the solid NaOH called?

A   solution

B   solute

C   solvent

D   mixture   7.c

14 The reaction between an acidic and basic solution is called

A   neutralization.

B   saturated.

C   substance.

D   mixture.   5.e

The BIG Idea

All living things share a common set of chemical elements that make up most cell molecules.

LESSON 1 6.b, 6.c
Chemistry of Life

Main Idea Living organisms are made of molecules formed primarily of carbon, hydrogen, nitrogen, oxygen, phosphorus, and sulfur.

LESSON 2 3.c, 6.a, 6.b
Carbon Compounds

Main Idea Organic molecules of various sizes, shapes, and chemical properties are based on carbon.

LESSON 3 6.c, 9.c
Compounds of Life

Main Idea Large biomolecules include proteins, nucleic acids, carbohydrates, and lipids.

Bear Necessities of Life

The California state animal, the grizzly bear, and human beings are composed of the same type of molecules. In fact, all living things are composed of similar chemical compounds.

Science Journal What molecules do you think bears and humans have in common?

What is a life chemical?

Chemical changes are essential parts of the chemistry of life. Is it possible to observe chemical changes and their products?

Procedure 🔆 👕 🧪

1. Read and complete a lab safety form.

2. Collect a **plain wood splint** and a **burned wood splint,** a **new birthday candle,** and a **burned birthday candle.**

3. Draw a line on a piece of **white paper** with each wood splint and the wicks of each candle.

4. Observe the differences in the lines on the paper with a **hand lens.**

Think About This

Evaluate The black substance that made lines on the paper is composed of carbon. Where was this carbon before it turned black?

 6.b

Visit ca8.msscience.com to:

▶ view **Concepts in Motion**

▶ explore Virtual Labs

▶ access content-related Web links

▶ take the Standards Check

Substituted Hydrocarbons Make the following Foldable to explain the functional groups of substituted hydrocarbons.

STEP 1 **Collect** two sheets of paper and layer them about 2 cm apart vertically. Keep the left edges even.

STEP 2 **Fold** up the bottom edges of the paper to form 3 equal tabs. **Crease** the fold to hold the tabs in place.

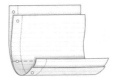

STEP 3 **Staple** along the fold. Label as shown.

Reading Skill

Using What You Know

As you read Lesson 2, explain how each group forms, describe its properties, and give examples for each functional group.

Get Ready to Read

Summarize

1 Learn It! Summarizing helps you organize information, focus on main ideas, and reduce the amount of information to remember. To summarize, restate the important facts in a short sentence or paragraph. Be brief and do not include too many details.

2 Practice It! Read the text on page 422 under the heading *Elements of Life.* Then read the summary below and look at the important facts from that passage.

Important Facts

These elements are carbon, hydrogen, nitrogen, oxygen, phosphorus, and sulfur.

All living organisms obtain these elements from their environment.

These elements go through natural cycles and they are reused over and over.

Many elements that are cycled are cycled as part of a compound.

Summary

Most of Earth's biomass is composed of six elements.

3 Apply It! Practice summarizing as you read this chapter. Stop after each lesson and write a brief summary.

Target Your Reading

Use this to focus on the main ideas as you read the chapter.

Reading Tip

Reread your summary to make sure you didn't change the author's original meaning or ideas.

1 **Before you read** the chapter, respond to the statements below on your worksheet or on a numbered sheet of paper.

- Write an **A** if you **agree** with the statement.
- Write a **D** if you **disagree** with the statement.

2 **After you read** the chapter, look back to this page to see if you've changed your mind about any of the statements.

- If any of your answers changed, explain why.
- Change any false statements into true statements.
- Use your revised statements as a study guide.

Science Online

Print a worksheet of this page at:
ca8.msscience.com.

Before You Read A or D	Statement	After You Read A or D
	1 Living things are primarily made of six elements.	
	2 Carbon is the only element that goes through a cycle between living and nonliving organisms.	
	3 Human blood contains a small percentage of water.	
	4 Ice is more dense than liquid water.	
	5 Water is a polar molecule.	
	6 Carbon molecules have three-dimensional shapes.	
	7 A compound that contains only hydrogen and carbon is called a hydrocarbon.	
	8 The suffix in the name of a hydrocarbon indicates the type of bonds found in the compound.	
	9 Nucleic acids are found only in plants.	
	10 Lipids, proteins, and carbohydrates are examples of biomolecules.	

Reading Guide

What You'll Learn

▶ **List** the six elements that can combine in many different ways to make up most of the molecules in living things.

▶ **Describe** how carbon, nitrogen, and phosphorus go through natural cycles.

▶ **Explain** why water is important to life.

Why It's Important

The basic elements that are needed to keep humans alive are also needed to keep plants and animals alive.

Vocabulary

biomass
polar molecule
nonpolar molecule

Review Vocabulary

element: a substance that cannot be broken down into simpler substances (p. 195)

Chemistry of Life

Main Idea Living organisms are made of molecules formed primarily of carbon, hydrogen, nitrogen, oxygen, phosphorus, and sulfur.

Real-World Reading Connection Think of things you have been doing today: eating, breathing, moving, and reading. All of these activities involve atoms and chemical reactions. Even when you are sitting still, atoms in your body are rearranging into different combinations of molecules.

Elements of Life

The basic elements that you need to live are the same basic elements found in all living things. It may surprise you to learn that the number of elements found in all living things is quite small. More than 96 percent of your body is made of just four elements, as shown in **Figure 1.** These elements are carbon, hydrogen, oxygen, and nitrogen. Sulfur and phosphorus also are found in your body in small amounts. These six elements make up most of Earth's biomass. **Biomass** is the total mass of all living matter. Living matter, which includes all plants and animals, gets these elements from the environment. These elements flow through the environment in natural cycles.

Figure 1 The human body is composed of primarily four elements: oxygen, carbon, hydrogen, and nitrogen.

Composition of the Human Body

Nitrogen 3.3%
Other 3.7%
Hydrogen 9.5%
Carbon 18.5%
Oxygen 65%

Cycles in Life

The flow of matter through a food web is part of the natural cycles of carbon, nitrogen, and phosphorus. Hydrogen, oxygen, and sulfur flow through food webs too. They are included in the molecules that flow through these natural cycles. Notice how often oxygen is attached to molecules containing carbon in the carbon cycle shown in **Figure 2.**

The Carbon Cycle

The carbon **cycle,** shown in **Figure 2,** shows how carbon and oxygen cycle through an ecosystem. Plants obtain carbon in the form of carbon dioxide from the atmosphere to make carbon-based sugar molecules. Plants use sugars to store energy and to provide energy for growth and other cellular processes. When animals eat plants, they obtain carbon that is needed for cellular processes in their bodies. As they digest these foods, they breathe out carbon dioxide as a waste product. Carbon compounds are passed from animal to animal when one animal eats another.

Some carbon also cycles when fossil fuels such as coal and natural gas burn, as shown in **Figure 2.** Fossil fuels are carbon compounds buried deep underground that formed millions of years ago from living organisms. During burning, fossil fuels undergo a chemical reaction and are changed to carbon dioxide and water vapor. The carbon dioxide is released into the atmosphere and absorbed by plants, as shown in **Figure 2.**

Reading Check How is carbon used in the bodies of animals and where is it obtained?

ACADEMIC VOCABULARY
cycle (SI kuhl)
(noun) a recurring sequence of events
In the water cycle, water is moving between Earth and the atmosphere.

Figure 2 Carbon and oxygen are cycled through the environment by natural processes.

Explain what roles humans have in the carbon cycle.

Plant releases oxygen into the atmosphere

Plant takes in carbon dioxide from the atmosphere

Burning fossil fuels release carbon dioxide into the atmosphere.

Plant uses carbon to make sugar molecules

Animal breaks down sugar molecules found in foods.

Animal takes in oxygen

Animal releases carbon dioxide into the atmosphere

Labels within the figure:

Nitrogen in air

Organisms eat nitrogen compounds in plants

Bacteria release some nitrogen back to the air

Decomposers break down wastes and plant remains and return nitrogen compounds into the soil where they can be used by plants

Bacteria found on some plant roots convert nitrogen into nitrogen compounds

Figure 3 The nitrogen cycle continuously cycles nitrogen so that it can be used by living organisms.

Explain what role nitrogen-fixing bacteria have in the nitrogen cycle.

SCIENCE USE V. COMMON USE

process

Science Use a series of actions, changes, or functions bringing about a result. *The carbon cycle is a natural process that results in the reuse of the element carbon.*

Common Use to handle through a routine set of procedures. *The students did not understand the teacher's process for grading research papers.*

The Nitrogen Cycle

Figure 3 shows how nitrogen cycles through living and nonliving parts of the environment. Although the atmosphere is 78 percent nitrogen, most plants cannot use this source of nitrogen. Certain types of bacteria, called nitrogen-fixing bacteria, live in soil and convert nitrogen in the air into nitrogen compounds that plants can use. Plants then absorb the nitrogen compounds as nutrients from the soil. The nitrogen is used to make compounds that are used to form plant cells and for cellular processes. Nitrogen compounds pass through the food web from producers to consumers when consumers eat the plants. Nitrogen also passes through a food web when a consumer eats another consumer. Decomposers also play a role in the nitrogen cycle, as shown in **Figure 3.** Decomposers break down nitrogen compounds found in dead organisms.

The Phosphorus Cycle

Phosphorus (FAHS frus) is another element that cycles through living and nonliving parts of the environment. Natural processes make phosphorus available to living organisms by breaking down rocks that contain phosphorus. The roots of plants absorb small particles of phosphorus from the soil. The plants use phosphorus to make molecules needed by the plants. Consumers get phosphorus by consuming plants or by consuming other organisms that have eaten plants.

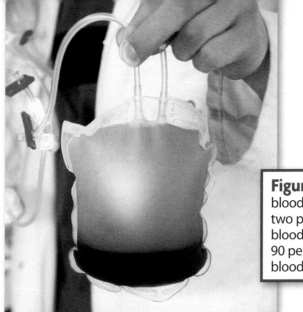

Figure 4 This sample of human blood has been separated into its two primary components—red blood cells and plasma. Plasma is 90 percent water, which gives blood its fluid properties.

Water and Living Organisms

Carbon, nitrogen, and phosphorus are important elements that make up living tissue. However, living organisms cannot survive without water. In fact, an individual cell is about 70 percent water by weight. The human body is 60–75 percent water by weight. Essentially all of life's processes, such as the absorption of nutrients and the elimination of wastes, occur in a water mixture.

The Importance of Water

In organisms, such as humans, the bloodstream carries dissolved nutrients to cells. The bloodstream also carries waste products away from the cells. This is possible because the liquid portion of blood, called plasma, is 90 percent water. **Figure 4** shows the plasma in separated human blood. The fluid properties of water enable blood to flow through the body. Water is also used in plants to transport nutrients. Like blood, plant sap is mostly water. Even tiny, single-celled organisms are dependent upon water for survival. Many single-celled organisms cannot live unless they are in a wet environment. Water is used by these tiny organisms to move nutrients into the cell and move waste out of the cell.

 Reading Check Explain the importance of water to living organisms.

Water and Life on Other Planets

Because water is essential for life on Earth, scientists use the existence of water as an indicator of life on other planets. One of the missions of the *Mars Rover* was to determine whether water was present on Mars. Scientists knew that if water was present on Mars, it was possible for life to exist there. Evidence collected suggests that Mars once had liquid water. However, no evidence of life was found.

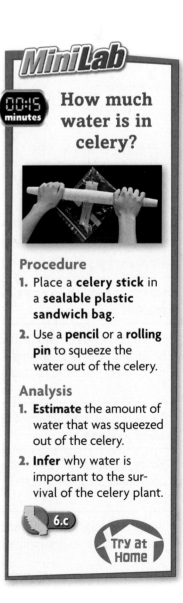

MiniLab

⏱ 00:15 minutes

How much water is in celery?

Procedure
1. Place a **celery stick** in a **sealable plastic sandwich bag**.
2. Use a **pencil** or a **rolling pin** to squeeze the water out of the celery.

Analysis
1. **Estimate** the amount of water that was squeezed out of the celery.
2. **Infer** why water is important to the survival of the celery plant.

6.c

Try at Home

Life-Sustaining Properties of Water

Water has unique properties that make it essential for life. These properties are due to the structure of the water molecule. Water is a polar molecule. A **polar molecule** is a molecule that has a positive end and a negative end because of unequal sharing of electrons. A **nonpolar molecule** is a molecule that shares electrons equally and does not have oppositely charged ends. **Figure 5** shows the molecular structure of a water molecule. Notice that the exposed electrons of the molecule give one side of the water molecule a slightly negative charge. The hydrogen nuclei give the other side of the water molecule a slightly positive charge.

Hydrogen Bonding Individual water molecules act like tiny magnets. The positive end of one molecule attracts the negative end of another polar molecule. And the negative end of one molecule attracts the positive end of another polar molecule. This weak attraction between water molecules is called hydrogen bonding. Hydrogen bonding gives water molecules many unique properties that are essential for life. **Table 1** explains some of these properties.

 Table 1 Choose three properties of water and explain why it benefits living organisms.

Dense Liquid If you have ever seen ice floating on top of a lake, you have seen another characteristic of water. Because ice is less dense than water, it can form a protective layer, protecting organisms from freezing temperatures.

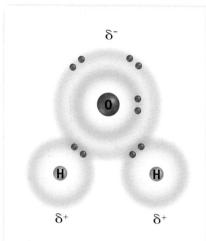

Figure 5 Water is a polar molecule.

Explain how this structure is related to hydrogen bonding.

WORD ORIGIN
polar
from Latin *polus;* means *directly opposite*

Table 1 Properties of Water	
Property of Water	**Example of a Benefit to Life**
Hydrogen bonds hold water molecules together.	Leaves pull water upward from the roots; seeds swell and germinate; small insects can walk on water.
Hydrogen bonds absorb heat when they break and release heat when they form, minimizing temperature changes.	Water stabilizes the temperature of living organisms and the surrounding environment; this keeps the temperature from changing quickly, such as when the Sun sets or when living organisms are exposed to hot or cold temperatures.
Many hydrogen bonds must be broken for water to evaporate.	Evaporation of water, or sweating, cools body surfaces when water pulls heat from the body as the hydrogen bonds break.
Water molecules in ice are spaced farther apart than the molecules in liquid water.	Because ice is less dense than water, ice forms a protective, insulating layer on top of lakes and rivers. The liquid water below the ice keeps fish and other organisms alive.
Water is a polar molecule making ions and other polar molecules soluble in water.	Many kinds of ions and molecules can move freely in and out of cells in a water solution, allowing many chemical processes to occur in living organisms.

What You Have Learned

You have read that most of Earth's biomass is composed primarily of six elements—carbon, hydrogen, nitrogen, oxygen, phosphorus, and sulfur. All living organisms obtain these elements from their environment. These elements go through natural cycles where they are used and reused by organisms. Other elements are cycled because they are found in compounds that are part of natural cycles.

Water's unique properties make it essential for life. All life processes occur in water mixtures. The hydrogen bonding between water molecules causes it to stabilize temperatures of living things. Water's lesser density as a solid than as a liquid allows it to insulate bodies of water.

LESSON 1 Review

Summarize

Create your own lesson summary as you write a script for a **television news report.**

1. **Review** the text after the **red** main headings and write one sentence about each. These are the headlines of your broadcast.

2. **Review** the text and write 2–3 sentences about each **blue** subheading. These sentences should tell *who, what, when, where,* and *why* information about each **red** heading.

3. **Include** descriptive details in your report, such as names of reporters and local places and events.

4. **Present** your news report to other classmates alone or with a team.

 ELA8: LS 2.1

Standards Check

Using Vocabulary

1. Describe a polar molecule. **6.c**

2. Use the term *biomass* in a sentence. **6.b**

Understanding Main Ideas

3. **Organize Information** Copy the graphic organizer below and fill in one fact from the lesson about the element or compound listed. **6.b, 6.c**

Substance	Description
Carbon	
Nitrogen	
Phosphorus	
Water	

4. **Describe** the importance of water to living organisms. **6.c**

5. Which is one of the six elements that make up most of Earth's biomass?

   A. copper
   B. nitrogen
   C. potassium
   D. selenium   **6.b**

Applying Science

6. **Design** an experiment that determines the density of water and the density of ice. **6.c**

7. **Defend** the concept of searching for water on planets to determine whether or not they can support life. **6.c**

Science Online

For more practice, visit **Standards Check** at ca8.msscience.com.

Science Content Standards

3.c Students know atoms and molecules form solids by building up repeating patterns, such as the crystal structure of NaCl or long-chain polymers.

6.a Students know that carbon, because of its ability to combine in many ways with itself and other elements, has a central role in the chemistry of living organisms.

6.b Students know that living organisms are made of molecules consisting largely of carbon, hydrogen, nitrogen, oxygen, phosphorus, and sulfur.

Reading Guide

What You'll Learn

▶ **Explain** why carbon is able to form many compounds.

▶ **Describe** molecular shapes of carbon compounds.

▶ **Identify** functional groups in organic compounds.

Why It's Important

Living organisms are made of carbon compounds.

Vocabulary

organic compound
hydrocarbon
saturated hydrocarbon
unsaturated hydrocarbon
functional group
amino acid

Review Vocabulary

covalent bond: a chemical bond that forms when atoms share electrons (p. 225)

Carbon Compounds

Main Idea Organic molecules of various sizes, shapes, and chemical properties are based on carbon.

Real-World Reading Connection Have you ever read about a comic-book superhero changing a lump of coal into a diamond? Comic-book stories such as this are fictional, but the real-life examples of carbon are just as amazing.

Organic Compounds

Except for water and salts, most compounds in living cells are organic compounds. The skin, hair, horns, and tissues of the bighorn sheep in **Figure 6** also are made of organic compounds. An **organic compound** is a compound that contains the element carbon. There are so many different types of carbon compounds that an entire branch of chemistry is devoted to them—organic chemistry. All organic compounds contain carbon atoms. However, not all compounds that contain carbon are organic. For example, carbon dioxide contains carbon but it is not an organic compound.

Figure 6 Carbon and other elements form many compounds, including the compounds found in the horns, muscles, skin, and hair of these sheep.

Carbon Bonds

Carbon is a unique element because of the type of bonds it can form. Carbon can form four covalent bonds with other elements and with other carbon atoms. Carbon can form short chains, long chains, branched chains, and rings. **Figure 7** shows a few examples of the millions of carbon molecules that exist. Just as the structure of the compounds varies, so do the properties.

Another unique property of carbon is its ability to form double and triple bonds. Notice the double bonds in ethylene and vanillin shown in **Figure 7.** Ethyne, or acetylene, shown in **Figure 7,** is an example of a molecule with a triple bond.

 Figure 7 Identify each compound that contains a single bond, a double bond, and a triple bond.

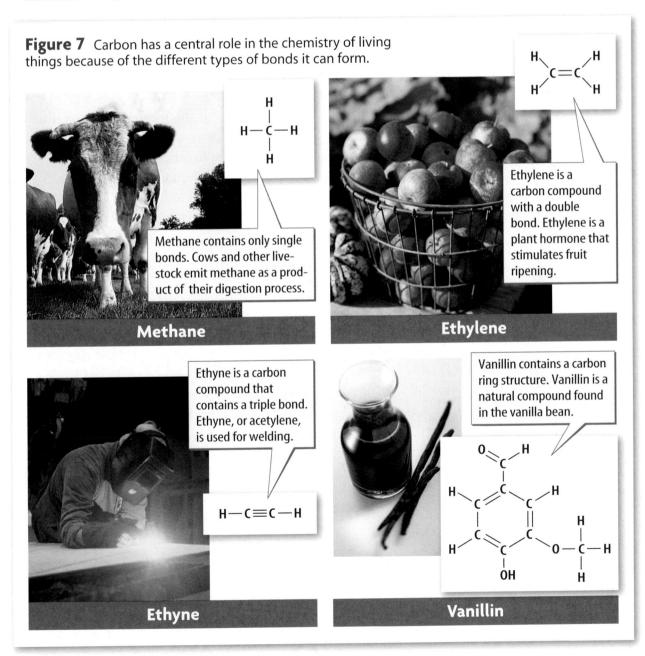

Figure 7 Carbon has a central role in the chemistry of living things because of the different types of bonds it can form.

Methane contains only single bonds. Cows and other livestock emit methane as a product of their digestion process.

Methane

Ethylene is a carbon compound with a double bond. Ethylene is a plant hormone that stimulates fruit ripening.

Ethylene

Ethyne is a carbon compound that contains a triple bond. Ethyne, or acetylene, is used for welding.

Ethyne

Vanillin contains a carbon ring structure. Vanillin is a natural compound found in the vanilla bean.

Vanillin

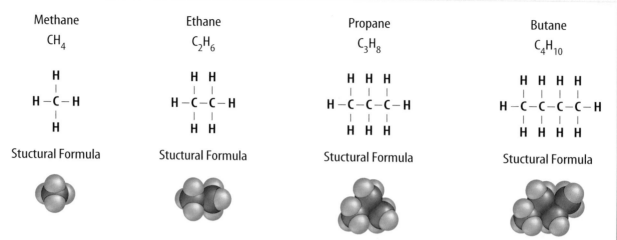

Figure 8 Methane, ethane, propane, and butane are four of the simplest hydrocarbons and organic compounds.

Hydrocarbons

One of the most common elements bonded to carbon is hydrogen. Molecules that contain only carbon and hydrogen atoms are called **hydrocarbons.** The simplest hydrocarbon is methane. Recall that methane contains one carbon atom and four hydrogen atoms. **Figure 8** shows the structure of four simple hydrocarbons—methane, ethane, propane, and butane. Notice the differences in their structures.

 Figure 8 How many carbon atoms are in propane?

Naming hydrocarbons Not all hydrocarbons are as simple as methane, ethane, and propane. Because carbon bonds easily to other atoms, it can form long chains and complicated ring structures. Many of these molecules also contain double and triple bonds. The type of bonds found in a hydrocarbon is one way in which they are classified. A **saturated hydrocarbon** is a compound that contains only single covalent bonds between carbon atoms. An **unsaturated hydrocarbon** is a compound that contains at least one double or triple covalent bond between carbon atoms, such as ethylene or ethyne. The structure of the molecule determines the name of the hydrocarbon. **Figure 9** illustrates how hydrocarbons and other organic compounds are named.

 Figure 9 Explain how the name *cyclopentane* was derived.

WORD ORIGIN
saturate
from Latin *saturatus;* means *to fill, drench*

430 **Chapter 10** • Chemistry of Living Systems

Visualizing Organic Chemistry Nomenclature

Figure 9

More than one million organic compounds have been discovered and created, and thousands of new ones are made in laboratories every year. To keep track of these carbon-containing molecules, the International Union of Pure and Applied Chemistry, or IUPAC, devised a special naming system (a nomenclature) for organic compounds. As shown here, different parts of an organic compound's name—its root, suffix, or prefix—give information about its size and structure.

Carbon Atoms	Name	Molecular Formula
1	Methane	CH_4
2	Ethane	CH_3CH_3
3	Propane	$CH_3CH_2CH_3$
4	Butane	$CH_3CH_2CH_2CH_3$
5	Pentane	$CH_3CH_2CH_2CH_2CH_3$
6	Hexane	$CH_3CH_2CH_2CH_2CH_2CH_3$
7	Heptane	$CH_3CH_2CH_2CH_2CH_2CH_2CH_3$
8	Octane	$CH_3CH_2CH_2CH_2CH_2CH_2CH_2CH_3$
9	Nonane	$CH_3CH_2CH_2CH_2CH_2CH_2CH_2CH_2CH_3$
10	Decane	$CH_3CH_2CH_2CH_2CH_2CH_2CH_2CH_2CH_2CH_3$

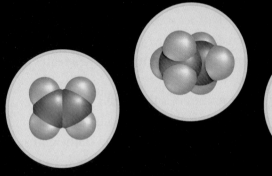

ROOT WORDS The key to every name given to a compound in organic chemistry is its root word. This word tells how many carbon atoms are found in the longest continuous carbon chain in the compound. Except for compounds with one to four carbon atoms, the root word is based on Greek numbers.

SUFFIXES The suffix of the name for an organic compound indicates the kind of covalent bonds joining the compound's carbon atoms. If the atoms are joined by single covalent bonds, the compound's name will end in –*ane*. If there is a double covalent bond in the carbon chain, the compound's name ends in –*ene*. Similarly, if there is a triple bond in the chain, the compound's name will end in –*yne*.

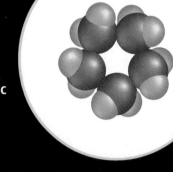

PREFIXES The prefix of the name for an organic compound describes how the carbon atoms in the compound are arranged. Organic molecules that have names with the prefix *cyclo*– contain a ring of carbon atoms. For example, cyclopentane contains five carbon atoms all joined by single bonds in a ring.

Contributed by National Geographic

Substituted Hydrocarbons

Carbon and hydrogen make up the basic structure of most organic compounds. However, organic compounds can contain other elements as well. Oxygen, nitrogen, phosphorus, and sulfur are examples of elements that can form chemical groups called functional groups. A **functional group** is a group of atoms that replaces a hydrogen atom in organic compounds. Organic compounds that contain functional groups are called **substituted** hydrocarbons.

Hydroxyl Group

One common type of functional group is the hydroxyl group. A hydroxyl group contains an oxygen atom and a hydrogen atom covalently bonded to one another, as shown in **Table 2.** A hydrocarbon substituted with a hydroxyl group is called an alcohol. Isopropyl alcohol is propane with the functional group –*OH* added to the center carbon atom in the compound. Isopropyl alcohol, or rubbing alcohol, kills bacteria and other potentially harmful microorganisms.

Functional groups change the properties of the original hydrocarbon, as shown in **Figure 10.** Hydrocarbons do not dissolve in water. Rubbing alcohol is 70 percent isopropyl alcohol and 30 percent water. The addition of the functional group to propane creates a liquid that is soluble in water.

Chemists use suffixes in the names of substituted hydrocarbons to indicate the functional group found in a compound. If the hydroxyl group is present in a compound, the name of the compound usually ends in –*ol* to indicate that it is an alcohol. Isopropyl alcohol also is known as propanol. The –*ol* suffix indicates that it is an alcohol.

ACADEMIC VOCABULARY····

substitute (SUB stuh toot)

(verb) to take the place of another

The mechanic substituted the new tire for the flat tire.

Figure 10 Functional groups change the properties of hydrocarbons.

Explain how the substitution of the hydroxyl group for hydrogen changed the properties of the hydrocarbon.

Propane gas

70% isopropyl alcohol

Isopropyl alcohol

Concepts In Motion
Illustrated Table Organize information about functional groups at ca8.msscience.com.

Table 2 Functional Groups

Suffix	Type of Compound	Functional Group	Examples
–ol	alcohol	–O–H Hydroxyl group	Ethanol
–oic	carboxylic acid	–C–O–H Carboxyl group	Ethanoic acid
–amine	amine	–N–H Amino group	Ethamine

Carboxyl Group

Another functional group found in substituted hydrocarbons is the carboxyl group. A carboxyl group contains a carbon atom, two oxygen atoms, and a hydrogen atom, as shown in **Table 2.** The carbon atom is bonded to one of the oxygen atoms with a double covalent bond.

Acids that have a carboxylic acid functional group are called carboxylic acids. Aspirin, which is used as a pain reliever, is a carboxylic acid. **Figure 11** shows the molecular structure of aspirin.

Other carboxylic acids include many pheromones. Pheromones are chemical compounds used by animals to communicate. When an ant finds food, it leaves behind a pheromone trail that other ants can follow to the food source. The toxin in ant stings is the carboxylic acid *formic acid.*

Carboxylic acids are also found in foods that you eat. Vinegar found in salad dressings contains acetic acid, which forms during the fermentation of many liquids, such as grape juice and apple juice. Citrus fruits, such as lemons, contain citric acid. Cheese, buttermilk, and yogurt contain lactic acid, which is formed during the fermentation of milk products.

 Table 2 Identify the elements in a carboxyl group.

Figure 11 Aspirin is an organic acid. Notice the highlighted carboxylic acid group.

Amino Group

Another common functional group found in living organisms is the amino group. The structure of the amino group is shown in **Table 2.** The amino group contains a nitrogen atom and two hydrogen atoms. The nitrogen atom is attached to a carbon atom to form a substituted hydrocarbon. The two hydrogen atoms are attached to the nitrogen atom.

Compounds that contain the amino group are called amines. Histamine, a hormone that sometimes causes watery eyes and sneezing, is an amine. Several of the B vitamins are amines. These include vitamin B_1 and vitamin B_6. Vitamin B_1 is called thiamine (THI uh mun). Vitamin B_6 is called pyridoxamine (pihr uh DOKS uh meen). Notice that these two vitamins have the suffix –*amine* in their names, which indicates that the compounds contain the amino functional group.

Reading Check What is the chemical structure of an amine?

Amino Acids

Some compounds can contain both an amino group and a carboxylic group. Compounds that contain both of these functional groups are called amino acids. An **amino acid** is a member of a class of organic compounds that are the basic building blocks of proteins. Because they contain both amino groups and carboxyl groups, amino acids are both amines and carboxylic acids. **Figure 12** shows how these functional groups are arranged around a central carbon atom.

Twenty common amino acids can combine in various ways to make different protein molecules, much like the 26 letters in the alphabet can be used to make many different words. Your cells can make 11 of the 20 common amino acids. The other nine amino acids must be obtained from your diet.

Figure 12 Glycine is one of the 20 common amino acids. Look at the chemical formula to identify the amino group and the carboxylic acid group.

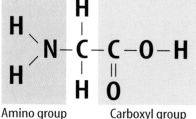

Amino group   Carboxyl group

Amino acid – Glycine

Amino Acids and Proteins

Amino acids make up proteins, which make up living organisms and control many of their functions. There are fiberlike proteins, called collagen, that make up the bone, skin, tendons, and cartilage. Another fiberlike protein, keratin, makes up the outermost layer of skin and hair, scales, hooves, nails, and feathers. The protein, fibrinogen, is a protein found in the blood that aids in the clotting of blood. Hemoglobin is a protein found in the blood that carries oxygen to the cells in the body. Other proteins control cellular processes, contract muscle tissue, and fight viruses and bacteria that invade the body.

Shapes of Molecules

Scientists use models like the ones shown in **Figure 13** to study and explain the shapes of molecules. The best way to learn about the three-dimensional shapes of molecules is to make your own molecular models, like those shown in **Figure 13.** These are just three of the many possible shapes that molecules can have.

Tetrahedral

Methane is an example of a molecule that has a tetrahedral shape, as shown in **Figure 13.** A tetrahedral is shaped like a pyramid. The bonds around each carbon atom all have single bonds that form the molecule.

Planar

Figure 13 shows the arrangement of atoms in a molecule of ethylene. The arrangement of hydrogen atoms around each carbon atom is a flat, triangular arrangement. Because all six atoms lie in the same plane, it is a planar molecule.

Linear

The bottom illustration of **Figure 13** shows ethyne as an example of a linear carbon compound. In ethyne ($HC\equiv CH$), the two carbon atoms are linked by a triple bond. Carbon dioxide ($O=C=O$) is also a linear molecule.

 Describe a tetrahedral shape.

Figure 13 Using models of molecules helps scientists understand the arrangement of atoms and helps scientists understand the chemical and physical properties.

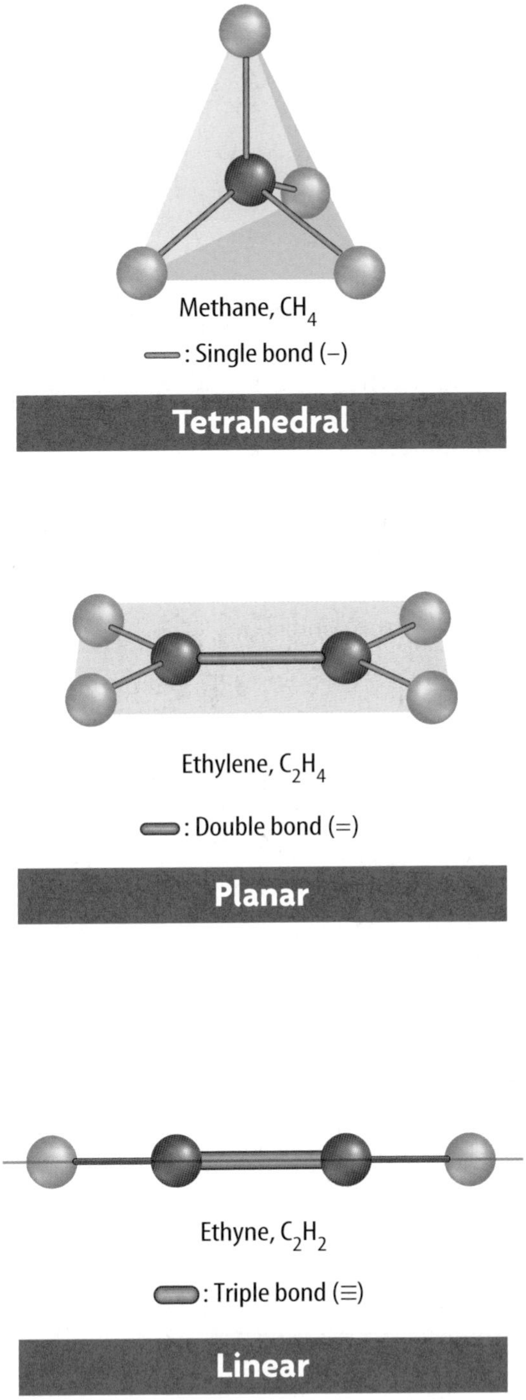

Methane, CH_4

⬤⬤ : Single bond (−)

Tetrahedral

Ethylene, C_2H_4

⬤⬤ : Double bond (=)

Planar

Ethyne, C_2H_2

⬤⬤ : Triple bond (≡)

Linear

What do you know about carbon compounds?

You have read that carbon forms the basis of life because it forms many different organic molecules of various sizes, shapes, and chemical properties. Carbon compounds that contain only carbon and hydrogen are hydrocarbons. Groups of atoms, called functional groups, often replace one or more hydrogen atoms in a hydrocarbon. These substituted hydrocarbons form alcohols, carboxylic acids, amines, and amino acids. Substituted hydrocarbons form many of the molecules that are essential for life.

LESSON 2 Review

Summarize

Create your own lesson summary as you organize an **outline**.

1. **Scan** the lesson. Find and list the first **red** main heading.

2. **Review** the text after the heading and list 2–3 details about the heading.

3. **Find** and list each **blue** subheading that follows the **red** main heading.

4. **List** 2–3 details, key terms, and definitions under each **blue** subheading.

5. **Review** additional **red** main headings and their supporting **blue** subheadings. List 2–3 details about each.

 ELA8: R 2.3

Standards Check

Using Vocabulary

1. Distinguish between a saturated and an unsaturated hydrocarbon. **6.a**

2. Use the terms *organic compound* and *hydrocarbon* in a sentence. **6.a**

Understanding Main Ideas

3. **Organize** Copy and fill in the graphic organizer below to summarize functional groups. **6.a**

Functional Groups	
Group	Structure
Hydroxyl	
Carboxyl	
Amino	

4. **Explain** why carbon is able to form so many compounds. **6.b**

5. Which element is NOT found in the carboxylic acid functional group?

   A. carbon   **6.b**
   B. hydrogen
   C. oxygen
   D. sulfur

6. **Analyze** the shapes of the molecules for methane, ethylene, and ethyne. Explain why these molecules have these molecular shapes. **6.a**

Applying Science

7. **Draw** a diagram of a hydrocarbon that has seven carbons and all single covalent bonds. What is the name of this hydrocarbon? **6.a**

8. **Defend** the concept that eating a variety of foods is important for a healthful diet, using the term *amino acids* in your argument. **6.c**

Science Online

For more practice, visit **Standards Check** at ca8.msscience.com.

Applying Math

Bond Lengths in Organic Compounds

Every organic compound has specific bond lengths and angles between the individual atoms of the molecules. Bond length is the distance between the nuclei of two bonded atoms. The table below shows the distance in picometers (1 pm = 10^{-12} m) between some common bond types.

Common Bond Type	
Bond	**Bond Length (pm)**
H–H	74
C–C	154
C=C	134
C–H	109
H–N	101
C–N	147

A molecule of ethene is shown below.

Example

Ethene is composed of two carbon atoms and four hydrogen atoms. The carbon atoms are joined by a double bond. Each carbon atom is bonded to two hydrogen atoms. What is the bond length of H–C–H?

What you know: the bond length of C–H

What you need to find: the number of C–H bonds

- H–C–H is composed of two C–H bonds.
- The bond length for each C–H is 109 pm.
- 2 × 109 pm = 218 pm

Answer: The bond length of H–C–H is 218 pm.

Practice Problems

1. What is the bond length of the double bond, C=C, in the ethene molecule?
2. What is the bond length of the ethene molecule?

Science nline

For more math practice, visit **Math Practice** at ca8.msscience.com.

Reading Guide

What *You'll Learn*

▶ **Describe** the composition of biomolecules.

▶ **Classify** the major types of large, complex, organic molecules found in cells.

▶ **Explain** the roles of organic and other compounds in the body.

Why *It's Important*

All living organisms contain similar biomolecules.

Vocabulary

polymer
monomer
synthetic polymer
natural polymer
biomolecule
lipid
nucleic acid
carbohydrate

Review Vocabulary

compound: a pure substance that contains two or more elements (p. 218)

Compounds of Life

Main Idea Large biomolecules include proteins, nucleic acids, carbohydrates, and lipids.

Real-World Reading Connection In an automobile assembly line, factory workers build auto parts from smaller components. The parts are then put together to make a car. Like an industrial assembly line, living organisms build cellular molecules from smaller components and then put the molecules together to make cells.

Polymers

If you have ever placed a sandwich in plastic wrap, you have used a polymer by using the plastic wrap. A **polymer** is a large molecule formed from smaller molecules called monomers. A **monomer** is a small molecule that forms a link in a polymer chain and can be made to combine with itself repeatedly. The plastic wrap that you use to wrap your sandwich is a synthetic polymer. **Synthetic polymers** are human-made polymer compounds that are not found in nature. **Natural polymers,** such as those shown in **Figure 14,** are made by living organisms. Natural polymers include proteins, complex carbohydrates, and nucleic acids.

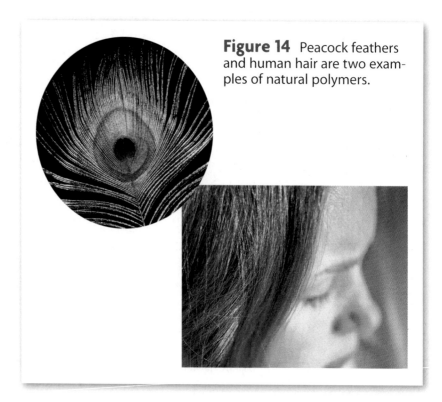

Figure 14 Peacock feathers and human hair are two examples of natural polymers.

Biological Molecules

The human body contains 60–75 percent water. The rest of the human body is composed of carbon and non-carbon compounds. All living organisms share the same few monomers that make up large natural polymers. A large organic molecule found in living organisms is called a **biomolecule.** Examples of biomolecules include lipids, proteins, carbohydrates, and nucleic acids, as shown in **Table 3.** Recall that amino acids are the monomers that make up proteins. Sugars are the monomers that make up complex carbohydrates. Nucleotides are the monomers that make up nucleic acids.

In addition to the three natural polymers—proteins, carbohydrates, and nucleic acids—there is a fourth type of large molecule in living organisms—lipids. A **lipid** is a biological compound, including fats and oils, that is not soluble in water. It contains carbon, hydrogen, and oxygen.

Nucleic Acids

A **nucleic acid** is a biomolecule that is found in all plant and animal cells. RNA and DNA are examples of nucleic acids that store cellular information in cells in the form of a code. Recall that DNA, or deoxyribonucleic acid, is the genetic material of living organisms and is located in each cell. The DNA in your cells determines your eye color, hair color, and every other feature of your body. A single DNA molecule can contain millions of atoms. Recall that RNA, or ribonucleic acid, is a nucleic acid that forms a copy of DNA for use in making proteins.

DNA and RNA are composed of monomers called nucleotides, shown in **Figure 15.** Nucleic acids consist of three parts: a five-carbon sugar, a group called a phosphate group that contains phosphorus, and a base called the nitrogen group that contains nitrogen. All nucleotides contain the same phosphate group, but the sugar- and nitrogen-containing group varies.

 What elements compose nucleic acids?

WORD ORIGIN········
lipid
from Greek *lipos*; means *fat, grease*

Table 3 Biomolecules and Polymer Biomolecules

Biomolecules	Biomolecules that Are Polymers
lipids	proteins
proteins	carbohydrates
carbohydrates	nucleic acids
nucleic acids	

Figure 15 Nucleic acids are polymers formed from nucleotide monomers.

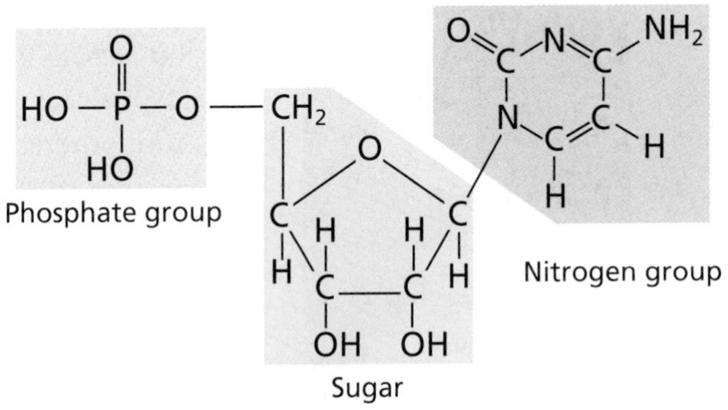

Phosphate group

Nitrogen group

Sugar

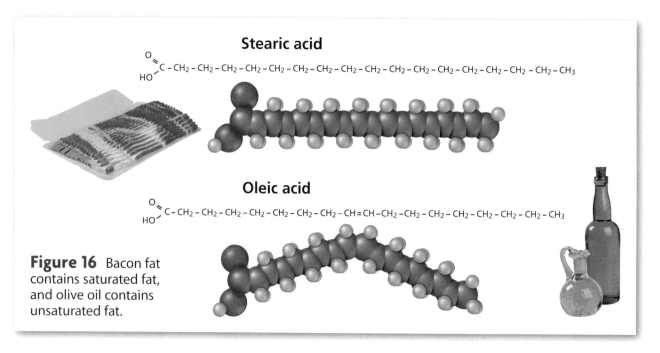

Stearic acid

$$O = C - CH_2 - CH_2 - CH_2 - CH_2 - CH_2 - CH_2 - CH_2 - CH_2 - CH_2 - CH_2 - CH_2 - CH_2 - CH_2 - CH_2 - CH_2 - CH_2 - CH_3$$

Oleic acid

$$O = C - CH_2 - CH_2 - CH_2 - CH_2 - CH_2 - CH_2 - CH_2 - CH = CH - CH_2 - CH_2 - CH_2 - CH_2 - CH_2 - CH_2 - CH_2 - CH_3$$

Figure 16 Bacon fat contains saturated fat, and olive oil contains unsaturated fat.

Lipids

Have you ever shaken a bottle of Italian salad dressing to mix the oil and vinegar? If so, you have seen a lipid. Recall that a lipid is not soluble in water and contains carbon, hydrogen, and oxygen. Like hydrocarbons, lipids are nonpolar molecules. Lipids that contain phosphorus are important components of cell membranes. Lipids are also used to store energy in cells.

Lipids can be saturated or unsaturated. A saturated fat has only single bonds between its carbon atoms. Saturated fats, like the bacon shown in **Figure 16,** are solid at room temperature. An unsaturated fat has at least one double bond between carbon atoms. The olive oil in **Figure 16** is an unsaturated fat. Unsaturated fats are liquid at room temperature. A polyunsaturated fat, such as sunflower oil and corn oil, has several double bonds between carbon atoms.

Carbohydrates

Glucose, sucrose, starch, and cellulose are examples of carbohydrates. A **carbohydrate** is an organic compound used by cells to store and release energy. Carbohydrates contain carbon, hydrogen, and oxygen. About 1–2 percent of the mass of your cells is carbohydrates. Complex carbohydrates are polymers made from sugar monomers. Complex carbohydrates are used to create plant-cell walls and to store energy in all living organisms. Three main complex carbohydrates are cellulose, starch, and glycogen. Cellulose is the fiber in wood and cotton. Starch is used by plants to store energy. It is part of many foods, such as pasta, rice, potatoes, bread, and tortillas, shown in **Figure 17.** Glycogen is a polymer used by animals to store energy.

Figure 17 Tortillas contain carbohydrates in the form of starch.

$$\underset{\text{Amino group}}{H_2N} - \underset{\underset{H}{|}}{\overset{\overset{R}{|}}{C}} - \underset{\underset{O}{\|}}{C} - OH$$

R — Variable side chain
Amino group — H₂N
Carboxyl group
Hydrogen atom — H

Figure 18 Amino acid monomers form proteins.

Proteins

A protein is an organic polymer made of amino acid monomers. **Figure 18** shows the general structure of an amino acid. Notice that amino acids are made of an amino group, a carboxyl group, and another group called a side chain. The side chain is also referred to as an R-group because it is the only group that is different in all the 20 amino acids. The variable side chain, or R-groups, can be single hydrogen atoms or complex double-ring structures.

Proteins are not **random** arrangements of amino acid monomers. The amino acids that make up individual proteins have specific arrangements. The instructions for building proteins from amino acids are stored in the DNA of a cell. The various arrangements of amino acids give proteins specific properties.

 **Reading Check** What functional groups compose proteins?

Other Elements in the Human Body

In addition to carbon molecules, living organisms contain minerals, which are also elements. Living organisms obtain these elements from their diet. **Figure 19** shows the function that sodium, which is found in table salt or NaCl, has in living organisms, including humans. **Figure 19** also shows the source and function of other elements that are required by most living organisms.

 Visual Check **Figure 19** Choose three minerals and describe in your own words the source from your diet and their function in your body.

WORD ORIGIN · · · · · · · · · · ·
protein
from Greek *proteios;* means *the first quality*

ACADEMIC VOCABULARY · · ·
random (RAN dum)
(*adjective*) lacking a definite plan, purpose, or pattern. *The dog ran in a random manner.*

Figure 19 Even though minerals make up only a small percentage of the mass of a human body, they are essential for many functions.

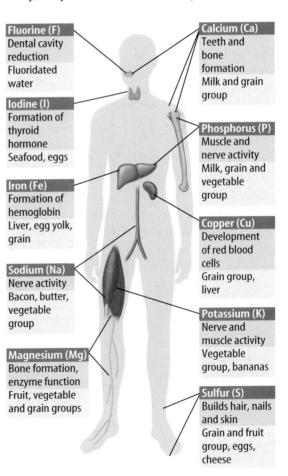

Fluorine (F)
Dental cavity reduction
Fluoridated water

Iodine (I)
Formation of thyroid hormone
Seafood, eggs

Iron (Fe)
Formation of hemoglobin
Liver, egg yolk, grain

Sodium (Na)
Nerve activity
Bacon, butter, vegetable group

Magnesium (Mg)
Bone formation, enzyme function
Fruit, vegetable and grain groups

Calcium (Ca)
Teeth and bone formation
Milk and grain group

Phosphorus (P)
Muscle and nerve activity
Milk, grain and vegetable group

Copper (Cu)
Development of red blood cells
Grain group, liver

Potassium (K)
Nerve and muscle activity
Vegetable group, bananas

Sulfur (S)
Builds hair, nails and skin
Grain and fruit group, eggs, cheese

What have you learned about biomolecules?

You have read that many of the molecules in living cells are large biomolecules. These biomolecules include lipids, proteins, carbohydrates, and nucleic acids. Nucleotides are the building blocks of nucleic acids. Sugars are the building blocks of carbohydrates. Amino acids are the building blocks of proteins.

Lipids are another group of biomolecules that are found in living organisms. Lipids, or fats, can be saturated or unsaturated. An unsaturated fat has at least one double bond in its structure. Saturated fats contain only single bonds between the carbon atoms.

Living organisms also need minerals to support their cellular functions. These minerals are found in the nutrients that organisms eat or absorb.

LESSON 3 Review

Summarize

Create your own lesson summary as you write a **newsletter.**

1. **Write** this lesson title, number, and page numbers at the top of a sheet of paper.

2. **Review** the text after the **red** main headings and write one sentence about each. These will be the headlines of your newsletter.

3. **Review** the text and write 2–3 sentences about each **blue** subheading. These sentences should tell *who, what, when, where,* and *why* information about each headline.

4. **Illustrate** your newsletter with diagrams of important structures and processes next to each headline.

 ELA8: W 2.1

Standards Check

Using Vocabulary

1. Distinguish between a carbohydrate and a protein. **6.c**

2. In your own words, write the definition of *biomolecule*. **6.c**

Understanding Main Ideas

3. **Organize** Copy and fill in the graphic organizer below to summarize one additional fact about each biomolecule. **6.c**

Compounds of Life	
Biomolecule	**Fact**
Lipids	
Carbohydrates	
Proteins	

4. **Explain** What roles do nucleic acids, lipids, carbohydrates, and minerals have in the human body? **6.c**

5. Which is NOT found in a nucleic acid?

   A. amino group **6.c**
   B. carboxylic acid
   C. hydroxyl group
   D. phosphate group

6. **Draw** the following biomolecules and label the functional groups for each: nucleic acids, fats, carbohydrates, and proteins. **6.c**

Applying Science

7. **Evaluate** Many athletes eat carbohydrates several days before a competition to increase the energy storage in their bodies. Discuss the advantages and disadvantages of this practice. **6.c**

Science Online

For more practice, visit **Standards Check** at ca8.msscience.com.

Which fat is healthy for you?

The fats and oils in your diet are lipids. Eating the right kinds of fats and oils makes a difference in your long-term health. A diet rich in saturated fats has been linked to heart disease and stroke. A diet rich that is rich in unsaturated lipids has been linked to people with good health. This data table includes the composition of a few fats and oils that many people eat daily.

Data

The table shows the percentage of saturated and unsaturated fatty acids present in various lipids.

Percent Fatty Acid Present in Lipids					
Lipid	Saturated		Unsaturated		Other fatty acids
	Palmitic fatty acid	Stearic fatty acid	Oleic fatty acid	Linoleic fatty acid	
Butter	27	12	29	2	30
Beef fat	24	19	43	3	11
Soybean oil	11	4	24	54	7
Olive oil	13	3	71	10	3

Source: *Food Fats and Oils, ninth edition.* Institute of Shortening and Edible Oils.

Data Analysis

1. **Calculate** the percentage of saturated fatty acids in each lipid.

2. **Graph** the percentage of saturated fatty acids for each type of lipid.

3. **Identify** the lipid that contains the least percentage of saturated fats.

4. **Select** the lipid that is best for a heart-healthy diet.

 ## Science Content Standards

6.c Students know that living organisms have many different kinds of molecules, including small ones, such as water and salt, and very large ones, such as carbohydrates, fats, proteins, and DNA.
9.e Construct appropriate graphs from data and develop quantitative statements about the relationship between variables.
MA8: ALG 6.0

Polarity and Living Systems

Problem

Living systems are composed of many substances including water, salts, and lipids. Many cellular processes in the body occur because of polarity. Water and salts are polar substances. Lipids are nonpolar. Detergents are large molecules that have a polar end and a nonpolar end. How does the polarity of a molecule affect the processes in a living system?

Collect Data and Make Observations

1. Read and complete a lab safety form.
2. Copy the data table below in your Science Journal.
3. Pour 50 mL of water into one 250-mL beaker. Label the beaker. Pour 50 mL of rubbing alcohol into the other beaker. Label the beaker.
4. Add about 0.3 g of salt to each beaker and gently swirl both beakers for 30 s.
5. Record your observations in the data table.
6. Empty and rinse the beakers with water. Refill them as in step 3.
7. Using a dropper, add ten drops of vegetable oil to each beaker, and record your observations.
8. Add five drops of dish detergent to each beaker and gently swirl for 30 s.
9. Record your observations.

Materials

250-mL beakers (2)
water
rubbing alcohol
table salt
dropper
vegetable oil
liquid dishwashing
  detergent
graduated cylinder
balance

Safety Precautions

WARNING: *Rubbing alcohol is flammable.*

Science Content Standards

6.c Students know that living organisms have many different kinds of molecules, including small ones, such as water and salt, and very large ones, such as carbohydrates, fats, proteins, and DNA.
9.c Distinguish between variable and controlled parameters in a test.

Data Table		
Substance	**Interaction with Water**	**Interaction with Alcohol**
Salt		
Oil		
Detergent/oil		

Analyze and Conclude

1. **Compare and contrast** how salt, oil, and detergent reacted in the water and alcohol.

2. **Explain** why the salt readily dissolved in the water but not in the rubbing alcohol.

3. **Explain** why the oil did not dissolve in or mix with the water.

4. **Distinguish** Which were the variables and which were the controlled parameters in this investigation?

5. **Infer** The plasma membrane surrounding cells is composed of a sandwich of molecules that have a polar end and a nonpolar end. The polar ends form the outside layer of the membrane and the nonpolar ends are on the inside layer of the membrane. Infer how this structure is beneficial to the transport of materials in and out of the cell.

6. **Think Critically** Living systems have detergentlike molecules in them. Based on your observation of the detergentwater-oil mixture, what role(s) might these detergentlike molecules play in a living system?

7. **Think Critically** Blood contains water, salts, lipids, and detergentlike molecules. Determine which of these compounds would be suspended and which would form a solution with the blood.

Communicate

Research the structure of the plasma membrane. Find out the role that polarity plays in transporting materials into and out of the cell. Create visual aids and present a short report to your class.

Real World Science

Science & Career

Something in the Air...

Like the scientist in the photo, Krishna Foster is an atmospheric chemist. Her research on the chemical composition of our atmosphere and sunlight's effects on it took her to the Arctic. She spent many months conducting tests on gases related to the ozone layer. Many atmospheric chemists are currently doing studies trying to determine what is happening with global warming.

Visit **Careers** at ca8.msscience.com to learn more about what atmospheric chemists do. **Write** a 500–700-word essay about how the work that atmospheric chemists do is important to us all.

ELA8: W 2.2

Science & Technology

Now, Spit!

Fast, safe, and cheap saliva tests may soon replace blood tests. Scientists at Oregon Health and Science University of Dentistry are using Multidimensional Protein Identification Technology, a method that uses spectrography and chromatography to identify protein "markers" in saliva that indicate the presence of disease. With this technology, testing for some cancers or diabetes would only require a patient to spit in a cup or lick a swab!

How do you think saliva testing might change our lives? Visit **Technology** at ca8.msscience.com to find out more about this test. Write 200–300-words about how saliva testing might change lives.

What do you mean by that?

What would the world be like if scientists had no common language? For example, if you discovered a new molecule and named it "Fluffy," no one would understand what it was. But if you named it cyclopentane, scientists around the world would know its exact structure and composition. *Cyclo* means ring of carbon atoms. *Pentane* means a five-carbon compound with all single bonds. Thus, cyclopentane is a five-carbon compound joined by single bonds in a ring. Since 1919, scientists have followed rules for naming compounds. This process was determined by a single organization—the IUPAC (The International Union of Pure and Applied Chemistry).

Create alternative, descriptive names for hydrogen, oxygen, and water. Have a classmate suggest something else that your new name might refer to.

Labeling Trans Fat

You probably heard a lot about healthy vs. unhealthy fats. That's when food companies had to start including amounts of trans fat on nutrition labels. The new labeling requirement was partly the result of a 2003 lawsuit brought against a food company asking them to stop selling cookies to California's children. The lawsuit was dropped when the food company voluntarily started making cookies with a healthier kind of fat.

Visit Society at ca8.msscience.com to see the difference in molecular structure between unhealthy *trans* fat and healthier, unsaturated *cis* fat. Draw a diagram of each in your Science Journal.

The BIG Idea All living things share a common set of chemical elements that make up most cell molecules.

Lesson 1 Chemistry of Life 6.b, 6.c

Main Idea Living organisms are made of molecules formed primarily of carbon, hydrogen, nitrogen, oxygen, phosphorus, and sulfur.

- Living organisms are made of molecules consisting largely of carbon, hydrogen, nitrogen, oxygen, phosphorus, and sulfur.

- The elements that make up living things flow through the environment in natural cycles.

- Water is essential for all living organisms because most of life's processes require water.

- **biomass** (p. 422)
- **nonpolar molecule** (p. 426)
- **polar molecule** (p. 426)

Lesson 2 Carbon Compounds 3.c, 6.a, 6.b

Main Idea Organic molecules of various sizes, shapes, and chemical properties are based on carbon.

- Carbon has a central role in the chemistry of living things because of its ability to form bonds with itself and other elements.

- The names of organic compounds are derived from the structure of the compound.

- Many organic molecules in living systems contain functional groups.

- Scientists use models to understand the shape of molecules and their properties.

- **amino acid** (p. 434)
- **functional group** (p. 432)
- **hydrocarbon** (p. 430)
- **organic compound** (p. 428)
- **saturated hydrocarbon** (p. 430)
- **unsaturated hydrocarbon** (p. 430)

Lesson 3 Compounds of Life 6.c, 9.c

Main Idea Large biomolecules include proteins, nucleic acids, carbohydrates, and lipids.

- Living organisms are composed of biomolecules including proteins, carbohydrates, nucleic acids, and lipids.

- DNA and RNA are nucleic acids composed of nucleotides.

- Lipids are classified as saturated or unsaturated.

- The three main complex carbohydrates are cellulose, starch, and glycogen.

- Proteins are made of amino acid monomers.

- The human body contains many elements that support life functions.

- **biomolecule** (p. 439)
- **carbohydrate** (p. 440)
- **lipid** (p. 439)
- **monomer** (p. 438)
- **natural polymer** (p. 438)
- **nucleic acid** (p. 439)
- **polymer** (p. 438)
- **synthetic polymer** (p. 438)

 STUDY TO GO Download quizzes, key terms, and flash cards from ca8.msscience.com.

Linking Vocabulary and Main Ideas

Use vocabulary terms from page 448 to complete this concept map.

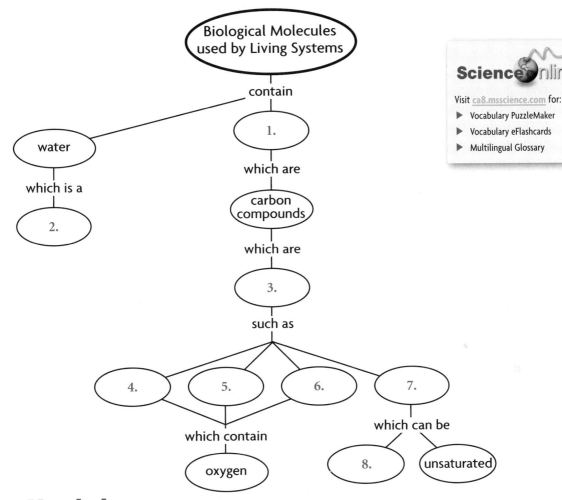

Science online

Visit ca8.msscience.com for:
▶ Vocabulary PuzzleMaker
▶ Vocabulary eFlashcards
▶ Multilingual Glossary

Using Vocabulary

Fill in each blank with the correct vocabulary term.

9. A(n) _____ is a molecule that has a positive end and a negative end because of unequal sharing of electrons.

10. The total mass of all living matter is _____.

11. Molecules that contain only carbon and hydrogen are called _____.

12. A large molecule formed from smaller molecules called monomers is a(n) _____.

13. A(n) _____ is a compound that contains at least one double or triple covalent bond between carbon atoms.

14. A(n) _____ is an organic compound used by cells to store and release energy.

15. A polymer that is humanmade and not found in nature is a(n) _____.

16. A group of atoms that replaces a hydrogen atom in organic compounds is called a(n) _____.

17. The basic building blocks of proteins are _____.

CHAPTER 10

Understanding Main Ideas

Choose the word or phrase that best answers the question.

1. What are the elements that make up most of Earth's biomass?
   A. carbon, calcium, magnesium, hydrogen, and oxygen
   B. oxygen, hydrogen, carbon, nitrogen, phosphorus, and sulfur
   C. carbon, hydrogen, iron, sodium, phosphorus, and potassium
   D. oxygen, nitrogen, hydrogen, phosphorus, and calcium   **6.b**

2. How does carbon move from animals to plants in the carbon cycle?
   A. animals eating plants
   B. decomposition
   C. photosynthesis
   D. respiration   **6.b**

3. Plants obtain carbon, oxygen, and hydrogen from photosynthesis.

   $$6CO_2 + 6H_2O \rightarrow C_6H_{12}O_6 + 6O_2$$

   Which molecule supplies hydrogen to plants?
   A. carbon dioxide
   B. glucose
   C. methane
   D. water   **6.b**

4. What do ethane and ethylene have in common?
   A. They are biomolecules.
   B. They have the same functional group.
   C. They are hydrocarbons.
   D. They are substituted hydrocarbons.   **6.a**

5. Which elements compose bones and teeth?
   A. carbon and magnesium
   B. carbon and phosphorus
   C. sodium and potassium
   D. calcium and phosphorus   **6.c**

6. Which biomolecules are not natural polymers?
   A. complex carbohydrates
   B. lipids
   C. nucleic acids
   D. proteins   **6.c**

7. Which is NOT a characteristic of water?
   A. Hydrogen bonding holds water molecules together.
   B. Water stabilizes the temperature and environment of living organisms.
   C. The solid form of water, ice, is more dense than liquid water.
   D. Water molecules form solutions with many polar molecules and ions.   **6.c**

8. Which molecule contains a triple carbon-to-carbon bond?
   A. methane
   B. ethylene
   C. propene
   D. ethyne   **6.a**

9. This illustration is an organic compound.

   $$\begin{array}{ccc} H & H & O \\ \backslash & | & || \\ N - & C - & C - OH \\ | & | & \\ H & CH_3 & \end{array}$$

   Which type of organic compound is shown above?
   A. alcohol
   B. amine
   C. amino acid
   D. carboxylic acid   **6.c**

10. How many carbon atoms are there in a butane molecule?
    A. 1
    B. 2
    C. 3
    D. 4   **6.a**

Science Online Standards Review ca8.msscience.com

Applying Science

11. Describe two properties of water and explain how each property benefits life. **6.c**

12. Predict what might happen to life on Earth if all the carbon dioxide were removed from the atmosphere. **6.a**

13. Relate the density of water and ice to its importance to living organisms. **6.c**

14. Compare and contrast saturated and unsaturated hydrocarbons. **6.a**

15. Infer why life is based on carbon even though carbon is not the most abundant element on Earth. **6.a**

16. Relate how carbohydrates, proteins, and lipids are important to body functions. **6.c**

17. Explain why proteins are important to your diet. **6.c**

18. Analyze What do complex carbohydrates, proteins, and lipids have in common? **6.c**

19. Explain how hydrogen bonding in water is important to fish living in a large lake in the mountains in northern California. **6.c**

20. Identify the type of organic compound below and explain how you identified it. **6.c**

WRITING in Science

21. Write a news report describing proteins, carbohydrates, and lipids, and their roles in the body. **ELA8: W 1.1**

Cummulative Review

22. Describe three regions of the periodic table that share similar properties. **7.a**

23. Explain why adding sugar to iced tea is a physical change. **7.c**

Applying Math

Use the table below to answer questions 24–26.

Common Bond Type	
Bond	**Bond Length (pm)**
H–N	101
C–C	154
C–H	109
C=C	134

24. Ammonia has the formula NH_3. It has three H–N bonds. What is the bond length for three H–N bonds?

25. Methane has the formula CH_4. It has four C–H bonds. What is the bond length for four C–H bonds?

26. Propene has the formula C_3H_6. The molecule is shown below.

Propene

What is the bond length of the entire molecule?

1 Which chemical formula below represents an amino acid?

A CH₃COOH   **6.b**

B CH₃NH₂

C NH₂CH₂COOH

D CH₄

2 Which molecule stores energy in the cells?

A lipids   **6.c**

B proteins

C nucleic acids

D carbohydrates

3 Ethamine is a substituted hydrocarbon.

$$H-\overset{\overset{\displaystyle H}{|}}{\underset{\underset{\displaystyle H}{|}}{C}}-\overset{\overset{\displaystyle H}{|}}{\underset{\underset{\displaystyle H}{|}}{C}}-\overset{\overset{\displaystyle H}{}}{\underset{\underset{\displaystyle H}{}}{N}}$$

Ethamine

What functional group is on this compound?

A alcohol   **6.a**

B amine

C carboxylic acid

D amino acid

4 Amino acids combine to form large organic polymers known as

A carbohydrates.   **6.c**

B proteins.

C biomolecule.

D nucleotides.

5 Which formula represents an alcohol?

A CH₃COOH   **6.a**

B CH₃OH

C CH₃NH₂

D CH₄

6 Organic compounds such as fats are called

A lipids.   **6.c**

B proteins.

C carbohydrates.

D nucleic acids.

7 A model of methane is shown below.

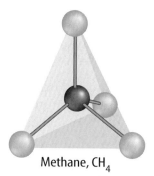

Methane, CH₄

What is the shape of this molecule?

A bent   **6.a**

B planar

C linear

D tetrahedral

8 What are the small units that make up polymers called?

A monomers   **6.c**

B isomers

C plastics

D carbohydrates

Science🖱️nline Standards Assessment ca8.msscience.com

9 Compounds that contain the element carbon are called

A organic compounds.   **6.a**

B polar molecules.

C nonpolar molecules.

D hydrocarbons.

10 Which chemical formula below represents an amine?

A CH_3COOH **6.c**

B CH_3NH_2

C NH_2CH_2COOH

D CH_4

11 Which molecule is NOT a biomolecule?

A lipid   **6.c**

B nucleic acid

C carboxylic acid

D protein

12 Based on its root name and suffix, what is the chemical formula of propyne?

A $H\text{-}C{\equiv}C\text{-}CH_3$ **6.a**

B $CH_3\text{-}CH_2\text{-}CH_3$

C $H_2C{=}CHCH_3$

D $HC{\equiv}CH$

13 Compounds that contain the elements carbon and hydrogen are called

A hydrocarbons.   **6.a**

B polar molecules.

C nonpolar molecules.

D organic compounds.

14 Which elements are important in making up living tissue?

A carbon, nitrogen, calcium   **6.b**

B phosphorus, carbon, calcium

C carbon, nitrogen, phosphorus

D nitrogen, phosphorus, calcium

15 The total mass of all living matter is

A biomass.   **6.b**

B biomolecule.

C monomer.

D organic compound.

Use the figure below to answer questions 16 and 17.

16 What is the name of this compound?

A pentane   **6.a**

B pentene

C cyclopentane

D cyclopentene

17 What is the chemical formula for this compound?

A C_5H_{12} **6.a**

B C_5H_{10}

C C_5H_8

D C_5H_{14}

Reading on Your Own...

From the Recommended Literature for Science and Math

Are you interested in learning more about chemical reactions, principles of chemistry, and the periodic table? If so, check out these great books.

Nonfiction

Oxygen (Sparks of Life: Chemical Elements that Make Life Possible), by Jean Blashfield, is the story of one of Earth's most abundant elements. This book contains discussions of oxidation, ozone, respiration, and photosynthesis. Color photographs and diagrams make the content easier to understand. *The content of this book is related to* Science Standard 8.5.

Nonfiction

The Bone Lady: Life as a Forensic Anthropologist, by Mary Manhein, is a series of truthful accounts of how artifacts from a crime scene can be used to reconstruct the crime. This book introduces forensic science and crime-solving techniques. *The content of this book is related to* Science Standard 8.6.

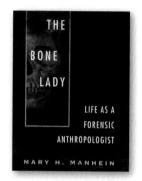

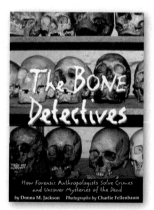

Narrative Nonfiction

The Bone Detectives: How Forensic Anthropologists Solve Crimes and Uncover Mysteries of the Dead, by Donna Jackson, is the story of mapmaker on a routine survey who discovers a human skull. This book introduces the history of forensics and demonstrates how scientists help criminologists solve mysteries. *The content of this book is related to* Science Standard 8.6.

Nonfiction

Hydrogen (Sparks of Life: Chemicals that Make Life Possible), by Jean Blashfield, is the story of the discovery of hydrogen, its importance as the "builder of the universe," its position on the periodic table of elements, its chemical structure, and its common uses. The book includes an overview of some hydrogen uses. *The content of this book is related to* Science Standard 8.7.

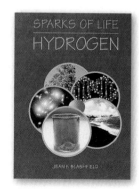

Choose the word or phrase that best answers the question.

1. Which term best describes a chemical reaction that absorbs heat energy?
   A. catalytic
   B. exothermic
   C. endothermic
   D. acidic **5.c**

2. What is the pH of pure water at 25°C?
   A. 0
   B. 5
   C. 7
   D. 10 **5.e**

3. Which type of compound is formed when a $-NH_2$ group replaces a hydrogen in a hydrocarbon?
   A. alcohol
   B. amine
   C. amino acid
   D. carboxylic acid **6.a**

4. The decomposition of water is shown below.

   $$2H_2O + energy \longrightarrow 2H_2 + O_2$$

   What is change in the number of hydrogen atoms during the reaction?
   A. 0
   B. +4
   C. −4
   D. +2 **5.b**

5. Which is a chemical change?
   A. Paper is shredded.
   B. Liquid wax turns solid.
   C. A raw egg is broken.
   D. Soap scum forms. **5.a**

Write your responses on a sheet of paper.

6. **Explain** why Lavoisier considered a chemical reaction similar to a mathematical equation. **5.b**

7. **Describe** how litmus paper is used to determine the pH of a solution. **5.e**

8. The illustration below shows benzene (left) and cyclohexane (right).

   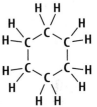

   Compare and contrast the benzene and cyclohexane molecules. **6.a**

9. **Explain** The reaction of magnesium and oxygen gas forms magnesium oxide, MgO. Write the chemical equation for this reaction and explain the process you use to balance the equation. **5.b**

10. **Describe** biomass. Identify the predominant elements in Earth's biomass. **6.b**

11. **Analyze** how a paper chain is a model of a protein. Describe the importance of proteins in the human body. **6.c**

12. **Explain** how the polarity of water molecules makes water effective in dissolving ionic compounds. **7.c**

Earth in Space

Martian Explorer This artist's rendition shows how scientists think the Spirit Mars Exploration Rover looked, situated on "Husband Hill" on Mars.

West Coast Events

13,000 Years Ago–Today
The Chumash people around Santa Barbara and Ventura once made up the largest culture in California; rock art matches legend of the Sun sending out sparks, making stars.

1677
Scientists think some Chumash rock art found in cave represents a solar eclipse that occurred November 24, 1677.

 A.D. 200 **1500** **1600** **1700**   **1800**   **190**

World Events

250–900
The Maya build observatory called El Caracol in the Yucatan Peninsula (Mexico and Guatemala) from which they could observe the Sun, Moon, and Venus.

1530
Nicolas Copernicus of Poland defies the thinking of the time and claims that Earth rotates on its axis once daily and travels around the Sun once yearly.

1610
Galileo Galilei from Italy observes Jupiter and Venus with his telescope; he hypothesizes that Earth is not the center of the universe.

Science Online

To learn more about astronomers and astrophysicists their work, visit ca8.msscience.com.

Concepts In Motion

Interactive Time Line To learn more about these events and others, visit ca8.msscience.com.

1947–1949
Palomar Observatory built northeast of San Diego.

July 2005
Caltech announces scientists at the Palomar Observatory discover a possible tenth planet in our solar system; larger than Pluto, it lies in the outer regions of the solar system.

November 2005
Ashley Stroupe at the Jet Propulsion Lab in Pasadena, California, trains robots to be able to build shelters for people who may explore Mars.

1940   **1960**   **1980**   **2000**   **2020**

July 1969
Neil Armstrong and Edwin Aldrin, Jr, are first to land on the Moon and Armstrong is the first to walk on Moon.

June 1983
Sally Ride is the first woman to travel in space, on *Challenger* mission STS-7.

1990
The *Hubble Space Telescope* is launched by the space shuttle *Discovery* at the Kennedy Space Center at Cape Canaveral, Florida.

2003
US launches rovers *Spirit* and *Opportunity* to explore Mars and look for clues about the existence of water there.

Our Solar System

The BIG Idea

Our solar system includes planets and dwarf planets and their moons, and other objects such as asteroids and comets, all orbiting the Sun.

LESSON 1 (2.g, 4.c, 4.d, 4.e)
Structure of the Solar System

Main Idea Even at great distances, gravity holds objects in our solar system in almost circular orbits around the Sun.

LESSON 2 (4.d)
The Sun-Earth-Moon System

Main Idea Eclipses and lunar phases demonstrate that the Moon reflects sunlight.

LESSON 3 (4.d, 4.e, 9.e)
The Planets and Their Moons

Main Idea The planets vary in appearance, composition, relative position, size, and motion.

LESSON 4 (4.c, 4.e, 9.a)
Asteroids, Comets, and Meteoroids

Main Idea Comets, asteroids, and meteoroids orbit the Sun.

What is a planet?

If you were standing on recently discovered Eris, once known as 2003 UB_{313} or Xena, the Sun might appear as just a bright star in the sky. This is because Eris is more than twice as far from the Sun as Pluto. The discovery of Eris and other objects in our solar system was partly why the International Astronomical Union redefined *planet*. Pluto now is called a dwarf planet because of this new definition.

Science Journal How do you define a planet? Make a list of several criteria you would use to decide which objects would be classified as planets.

How do you measure distance?

People use words such as *far, close, long,* and *short* to describe distance. The meaning of these words depends on your experience and what you are describing. In the following activity, use different units to measure distance.

Procedure

1. Using only your hands as measuring devices, measure the length of this **book.**

2. Using a **metric ruler,** measure the length of a **paperclip,** your hand, your desk, and your classroom.

Think About This

- **List** What are distance units? Give some examples of different distance units.

- **Determine** Why do people use standard distance units?

- **Evaluate** Is one type of standard distance unit more useful than the others? Explain.

FOLDABLES
Study Organizer

Our Solar System Make the following Foldable to compare and contrast the objects in our solar system.

> **STEP 1** **Collect** three sheets of paper and layer them about 2 cm apart vertically. Keep the left edges even.

> **STEP 2** **Fold** up the bottom edges of the paper to form 5 equal tabs. Crease the fold to hold the tabs in place.

> **STEP 3** **Staple** along the fold. **Label** as shown.

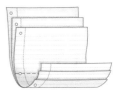

Asteroids–Comets
Inner Planets–Outer Planets
Planets–Moons
Earth–the Moon
The Sun–Planets

Our Solar System

Reading *Skill*

Compare and Contrast
As you read this chapter, draw a Venn diagram on each tab to compare and contrast the solar system objects shown on the tab.

Science nline

Visit ca8.msscience.com to:

▶ view **Concepts in Motion**

▶ explore Virtual Labs

▶ access content-related Web links

▶ take the Standards Check

459

Compare and Contrast

① Learn It! Good readers compare and contrast information as they read. This means they look for similarities and differences to help them to remember important ideas. Look for signal words in the text to let you know when the author is comparing or contrasting.

Compare and Contrast Signal Words	
Compare	**Contrast**
as	but
like	or
likewise	unlike
similarly	however
at the same time	although
in a similar way	on the other hand

② Practice It! Read the excerpt below and notice how the author uses compare and contrast signal words to describe the similarities and differences between Earth and Venus.

> **In some ways,** Venus is **similar** to Earth. The two planets are **similar** in size, mass, composition, and distance from the Sun. **However,** there are also significant differences. Venus has no oceans and is covered by thick clouds....

③ Apply It! Compare and contrast the inner planets and the outer planets in Lesson 3.

Target Your Reading

Use this to focus on the main ideas as you read the chapter.

Reading Tip

As you read, use other skills, such as summarizing and connecting, to help you understand comparisons and contrasts.

1 **Before you read** the chapter, respond to the statements below on your worksheet or on a numbered sheet of paper.
- Write an **A** if you **agree** with the statement.
- Write a **D** if you **disagree** with the statement.

2 **After you read** the chapter, look back to this page to see if you've changed your mind about any of the statements.
- If any of your answers changed, explain why.
- Change any false statements into true statements.
- Use your revised statements as a study guide.

Science Online

Print a worksheet of this page at ca8.msscience.com.

Before You Read A or D	Statement	After You Read A or D
	1 Planets orbit the Sun in circular paths.	
	2 The farther away a planet is from the Sun, the longer it takes to complete one revolution around the Sun.	
	3 Gravity keeps the Moon in orbit around Earth.	
	4 Kilometers are the most useful unit of measure when discussing objects in our solar system.	
	5 Neptune is the most distant planet from the Sun.	
	6 Scientists have found life on other planets.	
	7 Earth is the only planet that rotates as it orbits the Sun.	
	8 Comets always have a tail.	
	9 Earth's atmosphere prevents meteors or asteroids from crashing into its surface.	
	10 A solar eclipse can only occur at new moon.	

Science Content Standards

2.g Students know the role of gravity in forming and maintaining the shapes of planets, stars, and the solar system.
4.c Students know how to use astronomical units and light years as measures of distances between the Sun, stars, and Earth.
4.e Students know the appearance, general composition, relative position and size, and motion of objects in the solar system, including planets, planetary satellites, comets, and asteroids.
Also covers: 4.d

Reading Guide

What *You'll Learn*

▶ **Explain** why the planets can be seen in the night sky.

▶ **Identify** the different objects in the solar system.

▶ **Describe** the size of the solar system.

▶ **Describe** how the planets move around the Sun.

Why *It's Important*

Earth's rotation and revolution form the basis of our measurement of time.

Vocabulary

axis of rotation
period of rotation
period of revolution
ellipse
astronomical unit

Review Vocabulary

balanced forces: a net force of zero (p. 91)

Structure of the Solar System

Main Idea Even at great distances, gravity holds objects in our solar system in almost circular orbits around the Sun.

Real-World Reading Connection Have you ever looked up at a dark sky filled with stars and wondered whether there is life on other planets? How large is our solar system? What and how do we know about other planets in our solar system?

What is the solar system?

For thousands of years, humans have watched the night sky. Ancient sky watchers noticed that, night after night, the positions of the stars didn't change relative to each other. However, they noticed that some objects in the night sky moved relative to the stars. The ancient Greeks called these objects *planets*, their word for wanderers.

The solar system we live in includes planets and dwarf planets and their moons, a star called the Sun, and objects such as asteroids and comets. Planets, dwarf planets, asteroids, and comets move around the Sun in closed paths called orbits. Some orbits around the Sun are shown in **Figure 1.** Planets can be seen at night because they reflect light from the Sun. The stars you see at night are far outside our solar system.

 Figure 1 Are the stars you see at night located inside or outside our solar system?

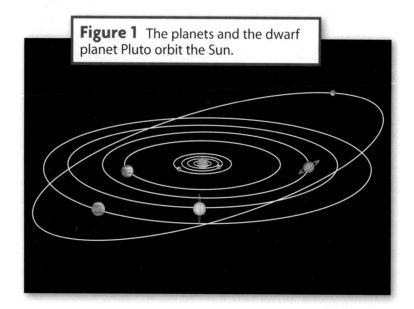

Figure 1 The planets and the dwarf planet Pluto orbit the Sun.

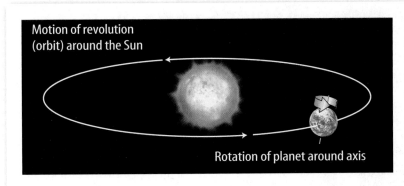

Figure 2 All planets spin around an axis of rotation while orbiting the Sun.

Describe the difference between rotation and revolution.

The Motion of Planets

Have you ever seen a top spinning on the floor? The top has two types of motion. It spins, or rotates, around a rod through its center called the axis. While it is spinning, it also might move along the floor. **Figure 2** shows how a planet in the solar system also moves in two different ways, much like a top. Each planet rotates around its axis of rotation. A planet's **axis of rotation** is an imaginary line through the center of the planet. Planets also orbit the Sun while they are rotating about their axes.

The Period of Rotation

Each day, Earth rotates once around its rotation axis. Earth's rotation axis is an imaginary line that passes through the north pole and the south pole, as shown in **Figure 2.** The time it takes for one rotation is called the **period of rotation.**
The period of rotation for Earth is one day, or about 24 hours. **Table 1** shows the period of rotation for the planets. Six planets complete one rotation in 24 hours or less, which means that the length of a day on these planets is 24 hours or less. Mercury and Venus take much longer to make one rotation.

The Period of Revolution

The time it takes a planet to move completely around the Sun is the planet's **period of revolution.** The difference between the period of revolution and the period of rotation is shown in **Figure 2.** The period of revolution for each of the planets is given in **Table 1.** Earth takes about 365 days, or one year, to orbit the Sun. For the other planets, the period of revolution varies from 88 days for Mercury, the closest planet to the Sun, to 165 years for Neptune, the outermost planet.

WORD ORIGIN

period
from Latin *periodus;* means *recurring portion, cycle;* **peri–** from Greek; means *around;* **–hodos** from Greek; means *a going, way, journey*

Table 1 Revolution and Rotation Periods of the Planets		
Planet	**Period of Rotation**	**Period of Revolution**
Mercury	59 days	88 days
Venus	243 days	225 days
Earth	24 hours	365 days
Mars	24 hours	687 days
Jupiter	10 hours	11.9 years
Saturn	11 hours	29.5 years
Uranus	17 hours	84 years
Neptune	16 hours	165 years

How do planets move?

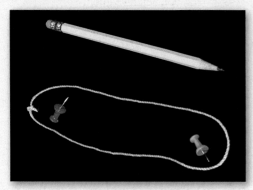

Procedure

1. Read and complete a lab safety form.

2. Place a blank **sheet of paper** on top of a piece of **cardboard**. Press two **thumb tacks** into the paper.

3. Tie the ends of a **string** together.

4. Loop the ends of the string around the tacks.

5. Place your **pencil** inside the loop of string and pull it tight. Hold the string tight and mark a line around the tacks. Make a complete closed curve. This is an ellipse.

6. Move the two tacks and mark another curve. Repeat several times with different tack positions.

Analysis

1. **Describe** Is the ellipse more circular when the tacks are closer together or farther apart?

2. **Explain** If one of your ellipses were a planet's orbit, where would the Sun be on the page?

 4.d

Kepler's Laws of Planetary Motion

In the early seventeenth century, German astronomer Johannes Kepler studied the motions of the planets. Kepler used the observations of the movement of the planets collected by other astronomers to deduce three laws that describe the motions of the planets.

Kepler's First Law: Planets Orbit the Sun in Elliptical Paths

Kepler began studying planetary orbits in the early 1600s. Until this time, it was widely thought that planets moved in circular orbits. Kepler analyzed observations of Mars and soon realized that it did not orbit the Sun in a circular path. He found that Mars's orbit around the Sun is an oval, or **ellipse.** Kepler also noticed that the Sun was not at the center of the ellipse, but slightly off to one side, as illustrated in **Figure 3.** Soon he realized that this fact holds true for all planets in our solar system, not just Mars. Today, scientists realize that all objects in the solar system move around the Sun in elliptical paths. This fact is called Kepler's first law.

Visual Check **Figure 3** At what part of an elliptical orbit is the Sun located?

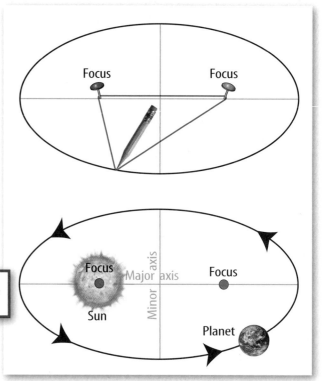

Figure 3 All planets have elliptical, not circular, orbits around the Sun.

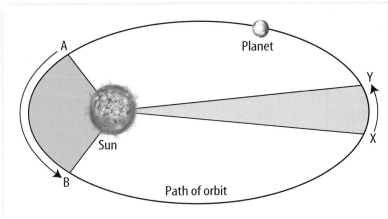

Figure 4 In this figure, the time to go from x to y and from A to B are equal. Then, according to Kepler's second law, the blue area equals the green area. A planet must move faster when it is closer to the Sun.

Kepler's Second Law: Equal Area in Equal Time

Kepler also discovered that planets move faster when they are closer to the Sun. He found that an imaginary line connecting a planet to the Sun sweeps out equal areas in equal amounts of time. This is known as Kepler's second law. In **Figure 4,** the planet takes the same amount of time to move from x to y as it does to move from A to B. For the blue area to equal the green area, the distance from x to y must be less than the distance from A to B. This means the planet moves faster when it is closer to the Sun.

Kepler's Third Law: Orbital Period Increases with Distance from the Sun

If you look at **Table 1** on the previous page and **Table 2** on the next page, you'll notice that a planet's period of revolution increases as it gets farther from the Sun. Kepler found that there was a specific mathematical relationship between a planet's period of revolution and its distance from the Sun. This mathematical relationship is known as Kepler's third law. **Figure 5** shows how the period of revolution becomes shorter for planets that are closer to the Sun.

 What is Kepler's third law?

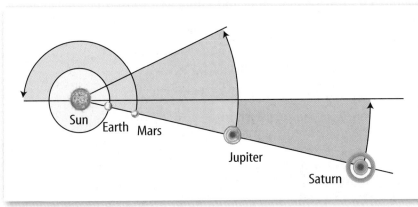

Figure 5 During an Earth orbit, Mars makes approximately one-half an orbit, Jupiter about $\frac{1}{12}$ of an orbit, and Saturn about $\frac{1}{30}$ of an orbit.

Table 2 Average Distances of Planets from the Sun		
Planet	Average Distance from Sun (km)	Average Distance from Sun (AU)
Mercury	57,900,000	0.39
Venus	108,200,000	0.72
Earth	149,600,000	1.00
Mars	227,900,000	1.52
Jupiter	778,300,000	5.20
Saturn	1,427,000,000	9.54
Uranus	2,871,000,000	19.19
Neptune	4,497,000,000	30.06

The Astronomical Unit

To measure the distances on Earth, units such as meters and kilometers are used. However, because the distances between the planets and the Sun are so large, astronomers use a different unit of distance. This unit of distance is the astronomical unit, which is abbreviated AU. The **astronomical unit** is the average distance from Earth to the Sun. One AU equals 149,600,000 km.

Distances of Planets from the Sun

In **Table 2**, the average distance of each planet from the Sun is given both in units of km and AU. Neptune is farthest from the Sun, as shown in **Figure 6.** The average distance from Neptune to the Sun is about 4,497,000,000 km, which equals about 30.06 AU. Neptune is so far from the Sun that light from the Sun takes more than 4 h to reach the planet.

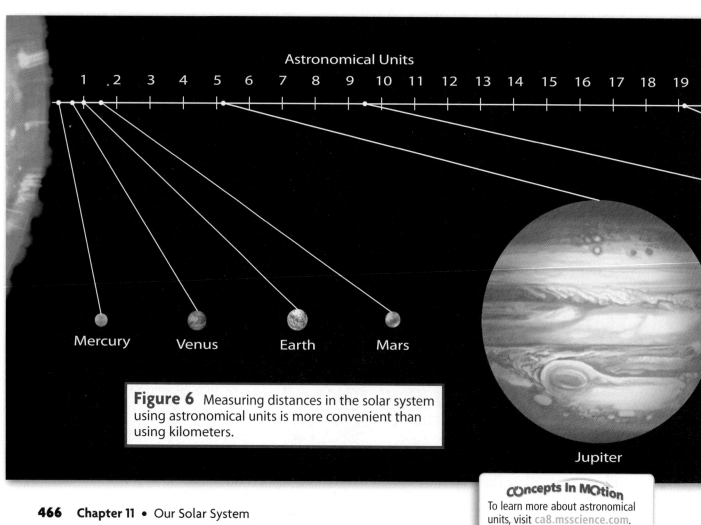

Figure 6 Measuring distances in the solar system using astronomical units is more convenient than using kilometers.

Jupiter

Gravity and the Solar System

Recall from Chapter 2 that every particle of matter in the entire universe exerts an attractive force—gravity—on every other particle of matter. Gravity is what keeps planets in orbit around the Sun. Recall from Chapter 2 that when an object moves in a circle, there must be a force on the object that is always toward the center of the circle. An example is shown in **Figure 7.** In the same way, the gravitational force between a planet and the Sun causes the planet to move in a nearly circular orbit.

 Describe the motion of objects in the solar system if there were no gravity.

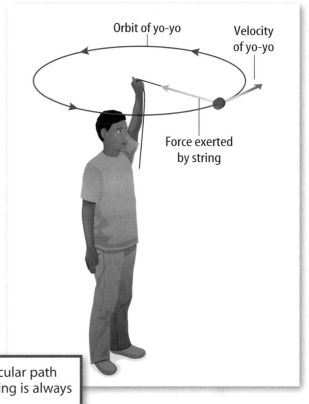

Figure 7 The yo-yo moves in a circular path because the force exerted by the string is always toward the center of the circle.

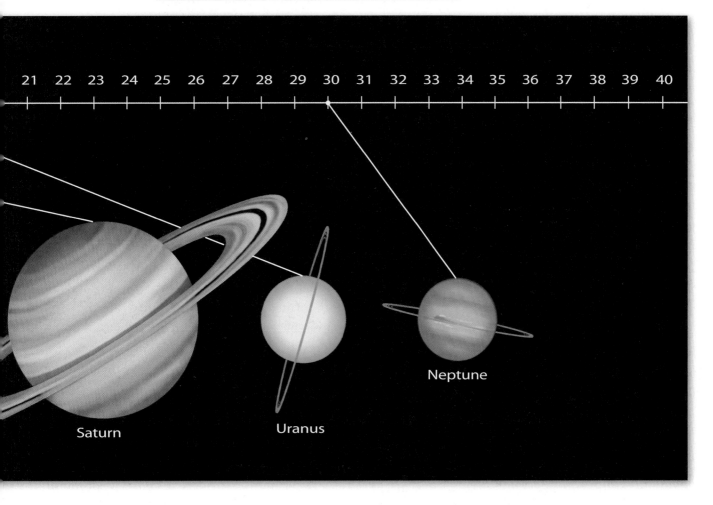

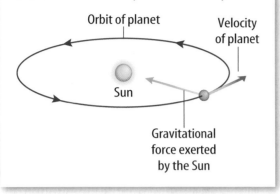

Figure 8 A planet orbits the Sun because the gravitational force changes the direction of the planet's velocity.

Orbit of planet

Velocity of planet

Sun

Gravitational force exerted by the Sun

ACADEMIC VOCABULARY

force (FORS)

(noun) an influence tending to change the motion of an object or produce motion in a stationary object *The force of the bat sent the baseball in the opposite direction.*

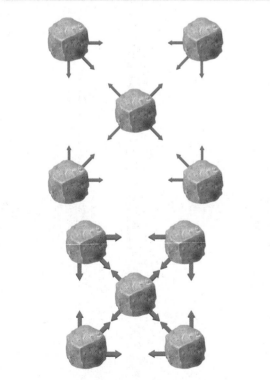

Figure 9 Gravity caused matter in the solar nebula to clump together, forming the objects in our solar system.

The Law of Universal Gravitation

In the late seventeenth century Isaac Newton realized that the same type of force that causes apples to fall from trees also causes the planets to orbit the Sun. This force was the gravitational force. Newton's law of universal gravitation showed how to calculate the gravitational force between any two objects. This force gets stronger as objects get closer together or if the mass of either object increases.

The Orbits of Planets

The Sun exerts an attractive gravitational force on a planet. However, instead of causing the planet to be pulled into the Sun, this force causes the planet to orbit the Sun. **Figure 8** shows that it is the combination of the planet's motion and the force of gravity that causes the planet to orbit the Sun. Gravity causes the velocity of a moving planet to keep changing. The direction of the velocity changes so that the planet continues to move in a curved path around the Sun.

Formation of the Solar System

The solar system formed from a giant cloud of gas and dust in space called a nebula. The matter in this nebula began to contract as gravity pulled the particles closer together, as shown in **Figure 9.** Denser areas had more mass and exerted a stronger gravitational pull on matter in the nebula. This caused matter in these areas to clump together.

As the center of the nebula became more dense its temperature increased. Eventually, it became so hot that nuclear reactions began to occur and the Sun formed. You will read more about the formation of the Sun in Chapter 12.

The rest of the nebula, farther from the center, began to form into a disk. Material in this disk clumped together. As these clumps became larger, they attracted more matter, eventually forming the planets, moons, and other objects in the solar system, as shown in **Figure 10.**

Visualizing the Formation of the Solar System

Figure 10
Through careful observations, astronomers have found clues that help explain how the solar system might have formed. More than 4.6 billion years ago, the solar system was a cloud fragment of gas, ice, and dust. Gradually, this cloud fragment contracted into a large, tightly packed, spinning disk. **A** The disk's center was so hot and dense that nuclear fusion reactions began to occur, and the Sun was born. **B** Eventually, the rest of the material in the disk cooled enough to clump into scattered solids. **C** Finally, these clumps collided and combined to become the planets that make up the solar system today.

Contributed by National Geographic

Understanding the Solar System

Our solar system is comprised of a star (the Sun), planets and dwarf planets, and other objects such as asteroids, meteoroids, and comets. Gravity helped our solar system to form from a nebula and keeps all other objects in elliptical orbits around the Sun. Planets spin around an axis of rotation while they orbit the Sun. To measure the enormous distance between the planets and the Sun, astronomers use the astronomical unit, or AU. One AU is the average distance from Earth to the Sun.

LESSON 1 Review

Summarize

Create your own lesson summary as you design a **visual aid.**

1. **Write** the lesson title, number, and page numbers at the top of your poster.

2. **Scan** the lesson to find the **red** main headings. Organize these headings on your poster, leaving space between each.

3. **Design** an information box beneath each **red** heading. In the box, list 2–3 details, key terms, and definitions from each **blue** subheading.

4. **Illustrate** your poster with diagrams of important structures or processes next to each information box.

 ELA8: R 2.3

Standards Check

Using Vocabulary

1. Distinguish between the terms *period of rotation* and *period of revolution*. **4.e**

2. In your own words, define the term *astronomical unit*. **4.c**

Understanding Main Ideas

3. **Determine** why **Table 2** gives distances between the Sun and each planet as an average distance. What does it imply? **4.c**

4. **Organize Information** Copy and fill in the graphic organizer below to describe Kepler's laws of planetary motion. **4.e**

Laws	Description
1st Law	
2nd Law	
3rd Law	

5. **Describe** the direction a planet would travel if gravity did not affect it. **2.g**

6. What did the ancient Greek term *planet* mean? **4.d**

   A. the leaders
   B. the wanderers
   C. planers of fortune
   D. travelers on the plane

Applying Science

7. **Hypothesize** why a planet farther from the Sun has a longer period of revolution than a planet closer to the Sun. **4.e**

8. **Determine** from **Table 2** how many times farther from the Sun is Neptune compared to Earth. **4.c**

9. **Rank** the planets from shortest to longest periods of rotation. Is there any connection between distance from the Sun and period of rotation? **4.e**

 Science Online

For more practice, visit **Standards Check** at ca8.msscience.com.

Applying Math

Parts of an Elliptical Orbit

2.g, 4.e

ALG: 5.0

Planets orbit the Sun in a mathematically predictable path called an ellipse. An ellipse has three measures—the length of the major axis, 2a, the length of the minor axis, 2b, and the distance between the center of the ellipse and the point called the focus, c. The diagram shows these measures.

Imagine the Sun is at a focus point and the planet is moving around the outer path of the ellipse. The orbits of planets are nearly circular. The eccentricity, e, shows how closely the orbit matches a circle. The eccentricity $e = \frac{c}{a}$. A circle's eccentricity is zero.

Focus | Major axis | b | Minor axis | axis | Focus | a | c

Example

If the eccentricity of Mercury's orbit is 0.206 and half of the major axis, a is 5.79×10^{10} m, find the approximate distance to the focus point where the Sun could be located in the orbit, c. Use the formula $c = e \times a$.

What you know: Eccentricity: $e = 0.206$
Length of half of the major axis: $a = 5.79 \times 10^{10}$ m

What you need to find: Length from the focus to the center of the ellipse: c

Multiply: $e \times a = 0.206 \times 5.79 \times 10^{10}$ or 1.19×10^{10}

Answer: The distance from the center of Mercury's orbit to the location of the Sun is about 1.19×10^{10} m.

Practice Problem

If the eccentricity of Pluto's orbit is 0.25, and half of the major axis, a is 5.90×10^{12} m, find the approximate distance from the center to the focus point where the Sun could be located in the orbit, c.

Science Online

For more math practice, visit Math Practice at ca8.msscience.com.

Science Content Standards

4.d Students know that stars are the source of light for all bright objects in outer space and that the Moon and planets shine by reflected sunlight, not by their own light.

Reading Guide

What *You'll Learn*

▶ **Model** how reflected light from the Sun causes the Moon to shine.

▶ **Explain** why the Moon has phases.

▶ **Compare** an eclipse of the Moon and an eclipse of the Sun.

Why *It's Important*

While lacking scientific knowledge about eclipses, people have been historically deceived and misled.

Vocabulary

satellite
lunar phase
eclipse

Review Vocabulary

gravity: an attractive force between all objects that have mass (p. 96)

The Sun-Earth-Moon System

Main Idea Eclipses and lunar phases demonstrate that the Moon shines by reflected sunlight.

Real-World Reading Connection Even if you live in a city where the sky is too bright at night to see many stars, you might have noticed that the appearance of the Moon is always changing. Sometimes, it isn't visible at all. Other times, only a thin crescent is visible or the entire Moon can be seen. How does the appearance of the Moon depend on Earth and the Sun?

Earth's Motion Around the Sun

The Sun, Earth, and the Moon can be thought of as participating in a complex three-body dance, as shown in **Figure 11.** Their movements are determined by gravitational forces. At the same time that the Moon orbits Earth, the Moon and Earth orbit the Sun together in an elliptical path. Both bodies rotate about their rotational axes as they move through space.

Earth's Orbit

Earth orbits the Sun in a path that is almost circular. The actual path is an ellipse, so the distance between Earth and the Sun is not constant. Earth is closest to the Sun in January and farthest away in July. The difference between the closest and farthest approach to the Sun is about 5 million kilometers. According to Kepler's laws of planetary motion, Earth moves faster when it's closer to the Sun and slower when it's farther away from the Sun.

Figure 11 The Moon orbits Earth, but at the same time, the Earth-Moon system orbits the Sun.
Infer why you always see the same side of the Moon.

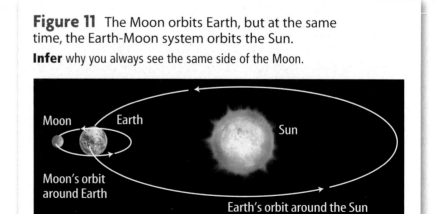

Earth's Rotation

The gravitational force between Earth and the Sun causes Earth to revolve around the Sun. Earth also rotates about its axis as it revolves around the Sun. This 24-hour rotation cycle gives rise to our experience of day and night as one side of Earth turns away from the Sun to the darkness of space. Earth's rotational axis is not perpendicular to the orbital plane, but is tilted at an angle of 23.5°.

The Moon—Earth's Satellite

Earth has one moon revolving around it. All planets, except Mercury and Venus, have moons. Moons are also called satellites. A **satellite** is an object that revolves around a planet. The surface of the Moon has many craters, as shown in **Figure 12.** These craters were formed when chunks of rock struck the Moon's surface.

 What is a satellite?

Formation of the Moon

The Moon is about the same age as Earth, 4.5 billion years old. It has a diameter of about 3,476 km, which is about one-fourth of Earth's diameter. It has no atmosphere, and it has a smaller core than does Earth.

The present theory of the formation of the Moon is the giant impact hypothesis. According to this hypothesis, a collision between Earth and another large object caused a tremendous amount of material to be ejected into space, as shown in **Figure 13.** This material would have gone into orbit around Earth, eventually forming the Moon. The density of the Moon is less than that of Earth, which is consistent with the impact theory. The material in Earth's crust and mantle has a density similar to that of the Moon.

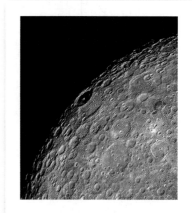

Figure 12 The Moon's surface is covered with many impact craters.

SCIENCE USE v. COMMON USE

satellite

Science Use any celestial body orbiting around a planet or star. *Earth is one of the Sun's satellites.*

Common Use human-made equipment that orbits around Earth. *The* Hubble *telescope is a satellite.*

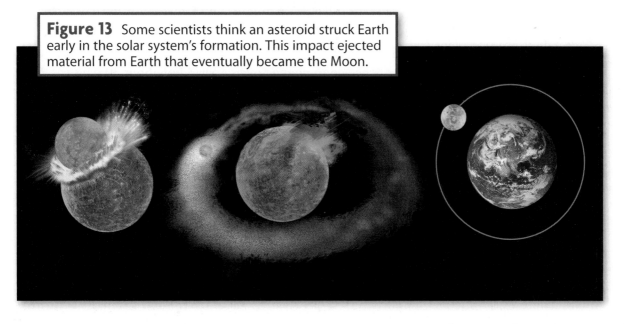

Figure 13 Some scientists think an asteroid struck Earth early in the solar system's formation. This impact ejected material from Earth that eventually became the Moon.

Concepts In Motion
To see an animation of the Moon's path around Earth, visit ca8.msscience.com.

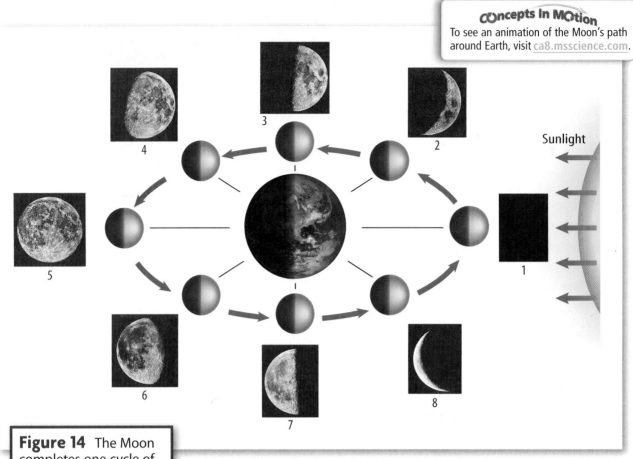

Sunlight

Figure 14 The Moon completes one cycle of phases in about 30 days.

WORD ORIGIN

lunar
from Latin *lunaris;* means *of the moon*

ACADEMIC VOCABULARY

phase (FAYS)
(*noun*) a particular appearance in a recurring cycle of changes
Many people gain most of their height during the adolescent phase of human development.

The Motion of the Moon

The gravitational force between Earth and the Moon causes the Moon to orbit Earth. The Moon also rotates on its axis, completing one rotation in about 28 days. While the Moon rotates and moves around Earth, Earth is moving around the Sun.

Phases of the Moon

We see the Moon because it reflects the Sun's light. As the Moon revolves around Earth, the illuminated portion of the Moon appears to change. The different appearances of the Moon as it orbits Earth are called **lunar phases,** or **phases** of the Moon. The phases of the Moon change over a period of about 30 days.

Figure 14 shows the phases of the Moon. As viewed from Earth, at position 1 you cannot see any of the illuminated portion of the Moon. This is called a new moon. As the Moon moves from position 1 to position 5, you are able to see more of the Moon. At position 5, you see the Moon as being full. Only half of the Moon is illuminated at the full moon phase. In fact, only half of the Moon is illuminated at all phases. As the Moon completes its cycle, moving from position 5 to 8, the portion of the illuminated Moon that you can see decreases, eventually returning to the new moon.

 Figure 14 What lunar phase occurs when the Moon is between Earth and the Sun?

Eclipses

An **eclipse** is a total or partial obscuring of one celestial body by another. For example, when the Moon and Earth move so that they line up with the Sun, an eclipse can occur. A solar eclipse, or eclipse of the Sun, occurs when the Moon moves directly between Earth and the Sun, casting a shadow on Earth's surface. A lunar eclipse occurs when Earth is between the Sun and the Moon, causing Earth to cast its shadow on the Moon.

Lunar Eclipses

A lunar eclipse occurs when a portion of the Moon is shaded from direct sunlight. **Figure 15** illustrates a lunar eclipse. Planets and the Moon do not generate the light that makes them visible, a fact that is demonstrated during eclipses of the Moon. During a lunar eclipse, Earth moves between the Sun and Moon and a portion of the Moon is shaded. A lunar eclipse can occur only when the Moon is full.

Solar Eclipses

In order to have a total solar eclipse on Earth, it is necessary for there to be an exact alignment of the Moon, Earth, and the Sun, as shown in **Figure 16.** Then, the Moon can cast its shadow on a portion of Earth. The Moon's shadow is quite small, so a total solar eclipse can be seen over only a small area on Earth. A total eclipse of the Sun can last from a few seconds to a few minutes.

Figure 15 Eclipses occur only when the Sun, the Moon, and Earth are all perfectly aligned so they can be connected by a straight line.

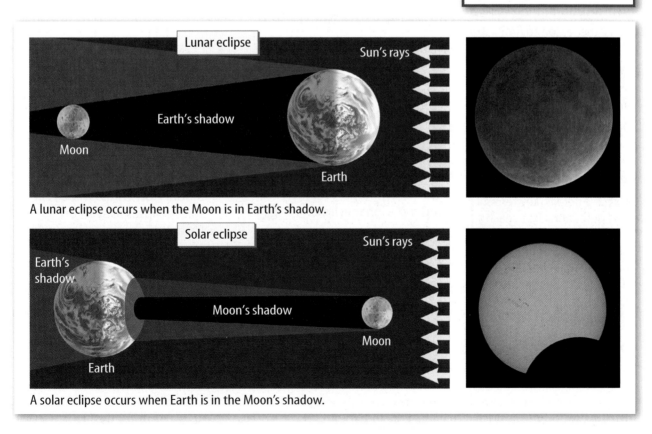

A lunar eclipse occurs when the Moon is in Earth's shadow.

A solar eclipse occurs when Earth is in the Moon's shadow.

Observing the Sun-Earth-Moon System

Gravity keeps the Moon in orbit around Earth and also keeps the Earth-Moon system in orbit around the Sun. The Moon can be seen in the night sky because it reflects light from the Sun. The portion of the Moon's illuminated side that you can see changes appearance as the Moon orbits Earth. These changes are called lunar phases. Sometimes the Sun, Earth, and the Moon align so an eclipse can occur. When Earth casts its shadow on the Moon, a lunar eclipse occurs. When the Moon casts its shadow on Earth, a solar eclipse occurs.

LESSON 2   Review

Summarize

Create your own lesson summary as you design a **study web.**

1. **Write** the lesson title, number, and page numbers at the top of a sheet of paper.

2. **Scan** the lesson to find the **red** main headings.

3. **Organize** these headings clockwise on branches around the lesson title.

4. **Review** the information under each **red** heading to design a branch for each **blue** subheading.

5. **List** 2–3 details, key terms, and definitions from each **blue** subheading on branches extending from the main heading branches.

 ELA8: R 2.3

Standards Check

Using Vocabulary

1. In your own words, define the term *eclipse*. **4.d**

2. An object that revolves around a planet is called a(n) ____. **4.d**

Understanding Main Ideas

3. During which lunar phase can a solar eclipse occur? **4.d**

   A. blue moon

   B. full moon

   C. honeymoon

   D. new moon

4. **Diagram** the positions of Earth, the Moon, and the Sun during a lunar eclipse. **4.d**

5. **Summarize** the giant impact hypothesis—the present theory of the formation of the Moon. **4.d**

6. **Compare and Contrast** Copy and fill in the graphic organizer below to compare and contrast details of solar eclipses and lunar eclipses. **4.d**

Eclipses	Similarities	Differences
Solar		
Lunar		

Applying Science

7. **Think Critically** Imagine an Earth-Moon-Sun system in which the Moon was much smaller than the present Moon. How would this affect solar eclipses as seen on Earth? **4.d**

8. **Explain** why a new moon cannot be seen in the night sky. **4.d**

Science nline

For more practice, visit **Standards Check** at ca8.msscience.com.

MiniLab

How does the Moon change its shape in the sky?

The Moon changes shape as you watch it in the night sky. Why does it do so? You can see all the phases that the Moon goes through in a month by modeling Earth, the Moon, and the Sun with foam balls and a lamp.

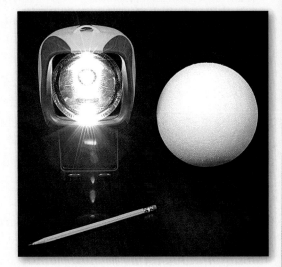

Procedure

1. Read and complete a lab safety form.

2. Stick a **foam ball** onto a **pencil.**

3. Face a **lamp** or **light source** and hold the ball in front of you. Record the positions of the lamp, the ball, and yourself. Draw the appearance of the ball and its shadow.

4. Move yourself and the ball in increments of one-eighth of a circle. At each position, record the positions of the lamp, the ball, and yourself. Draw the appearance of the ball.

Analysis

1. **Model** the positions of Earth and the Moon relative to the Sun to make a:

   - quarter moon
   - full moon
   - half moon
   - solar eclipse

   Record the positions of Earth, the Sun, and the Moon for each phase.

2. **Sequence** the different phases. Make a diagram to show the reason for the order.

Science Content Standards

4.d Students know that stars are the source of light for all bright objects in outer space and that the Moon and planets shine by reflected sunlight, not by their own light.

Science Content Standards

4.d Students know that stars are the source of light for all bright objects in outer space and that the Moon and planets shine by reflected sunlight, not by their own light.

4.e Students know the appearance, general composition, relative position and size, and motion of objects in the solar system, including planets, planetary satellites, comets, and asteroids.

9.e Construct appropriate graphs from data and develop quantitative statements about the relationships between variables.

Reading Guide

What *You'll Learn*

► **Compare and contrast** the inner planets.

► **Compare and contrast** the outer planets.

► **Compare and contrast** these planets' moons.

Why *It's Important*

When considering human population growth, people will need to look to the planets to understand their options and limitations.

Vocabulary

inner planet
outer planet

Review Vocabulary

atmospheric pressure: force exerted per unit area by air particles (p. 144)

The Planets and Their Moons

 The planets vary in appearance, composition, relative position, size, and motion.

Real-World Reading Connection You might have read or heard about the discoveries made by recent spaceflight missions. What do you know about the planets?

The Inner Planets

The four planets closest to the Sun—Mercury, Venus, Earth, and Mars—are often called the **inner planets.** Their orbits are shown in **Figure 16.** They are rocky in composition and all are found within 1.5 AUs from the Sun. Like Earth and the Moon, they have a hard surface on which a space probe can land. All these planets have craters on their surfaces. Meteor impacts created most of those craters. Two of the inner planets, Mercury and Venus, do not have moons. Most of what we know about these planets and their moons has come from robotic spaceflight missions.

Reading Check Name the inner planets.

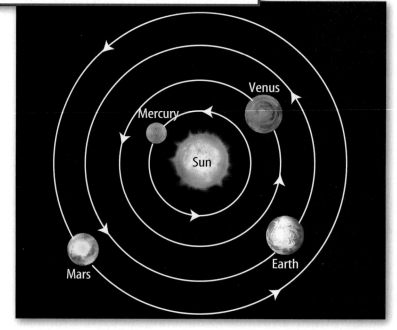

Figure 16 The rocky inner planets include Mercury, Venus, Earth, and Mars.

Table 3 Planetary Data for the Inner Planets

Planet	Diameter (km)	Relative Mass (Earth = 1)	Average Density (g/cm³)	Average Temperature (°C)	Distance from Sun (AU)	Number of Moons
Mercury	4,880	0.06	5.43	170	0.39	0
Venus	12,104	0.82	5.24	450	0.72	0
Earth	12,756	1.00	5.52	10	1.00	1
Mars	6,787	0.11	3.94	−65	1.52	2

Mercury

Mercury is the closest planet to the Sun, and it moves around the Sun in a highly elliptical orbit. Because it is closest to the Sun, it moves faster than any other planet. Mercury's distance from the Sun varies from as close as 47 million km to as far as 70 million km. There has been only one spacecraft, the *Mariner* in 1975, to visit Mercury. *Mariner* took the picture shown in **Figure 17.**

Because Mercury is so close to the Sun, temperatures on its surface can reach as high as 467°C. Essentially lacking an atmosphere, nighttime temperatures can fall to −183°C. Heat absorbed by the surface during the day easily escapes into space during the night without any atmosphere to act like a blanket.

Venus

In some ways, Venus is similar to Earth. The two planets are similar in size, mass, composition, and distance from the Sun. However, there are also significant differences. Venus has no oceans and is covered by thick clouds, as shown in **Figure 18.** It has an atmosphere of mostly carbon dioxide—a greenhouse gas—that keeps heat in just as a greenhouse glass window does. It absorbs infrared radiation emitted by the surface. The clouds reflect so much sunlight that, when visible, Venus is usually the brightest object in the sky. The planet's great atmospheric pressure has crushed spacecraft and its surface temperatures are hot enough to melt lead.

Figure 17 Mercury has almost no atmosphere, and its surface is covered with impact craters.

Figure 18 Venus has an extremely thick atmosphere. Only special probes have been able to "see" beneath Venus's dense clouds.

Figure 19 NASA's *Magellan* space probe used Radar to obtain these pictures of Maat Mons, the highest volcano on Venus.

Figure 20 From space it is easy to see that more than 70 percent of Earth's surface is covered by liquid water.

Identify How is Earth unique among planets in our solar system?

Exploring Venus

Venus has a long period of rotation, taking 243 Earth days to complete one Venusian day. It takes 225 days to orbit the Sun, so Venus's day is longer than its year. Scientists have used radar images of Venus, like the one shown in **Figure 19,** to learn about its surface. They have found volcanic features and impact craters. Venus is believed to have an interior similar to Earth's.

Earth

Earth, shown in **Figure 20,** is the only known body in our solar system to have life on it. Earth's atmosphere—consisting mostly of nitrogen and oxygen—affects Earth's climate and weather; shields us from nearly all harmful radiation coming from the Sun; and also protects us from meteors, most of which burn up before they can strike the surface.

Mars

For many years, people have been interested in Mars, shown in **Figure 21,** as a likely place for life to have existed in the past. Although some astronomers claimed to have seen canals on Mars, there is no solid evidence for life having existed there. Its atmosphere—composed mostly of carbon dioxide, nitrogen, and argon—is so thin that average atmospheric pressure is less than 1 percent of Earth's. Surface temperatures vary greatly from −133°C to 27°C.

Mars has two small moons, Phobos and Deimos. Although no one knows how they formed, they may be asteroids captured by Mars's gravity.

Figure 21 Many of Mars's surface features are similar to Earth's. For example, liquid water once flowed on Mars's surface.

Figure 22 Iron gives Mars's soil its red hue.

Exploring Mars

An essential ingredient for life is water. There is evidence that water might have flowed on Mars in the distant past. In May 2002, the *Mars Odyssey* spacecraft detected large quantities of water ice close to the surface. The ice is believed to be mixed into the soil near the Martian south pole. **Figure 21,** on the previous page, shows the ice cap at one of the poles.

At present, Mars is too cold and its atmosphere is too thin to allow liquid water to exist at the surface for long. More water exists frozen in the polar ice caps, and enough water exists to form ice clouds. Images from NASA's *Mars Global Surveyor* spacecraft suggest that underground reserves of water may break through the surface as springs. In 2004 and 2005, two land **vehicles** collected data and took many pictures, such as the one shown in **Figure 22.** But, the question about life on Mars remains unanswered.

The Outer Planets

The planets beyond the inner planets—Jupiter, Saturn, Neptune, and Uranus—are often called the **outer planets.** They come after the asteroid belt, which is between Mars and Jupiter. Some data for the outer planets are given in **Table 4.**

ACADEMIC VOCABULARY
vehicle (VEE hih kuhl)
(noun) a means of transporting something; a piece of mechanized equipment
Before driving, people acquire a driver's license to operate a vehicle.

WORD ORIGIN
Jupiter
from Greek *Zeus pater;* means *father Zeus*

Table 4 Planetary Data for the Outer Planets						
Planet	**Diameter (km)**	**Relative Mass (Earth = 1)**	**Average Density (g/cm³)**	**Average Temperature (°C)**	**Distance from the Sun (AU)**	**Number of Moons**
Jupiter	139,822	317.8	1.33	−110	5.20	63
Saturn	116,464	95.2	0.69	−140	9.58	47
Uranus	50,724	14.5	1.27	−195	19.20	27
Neptune	49,248	17.1	1.64	−200	30.04	13

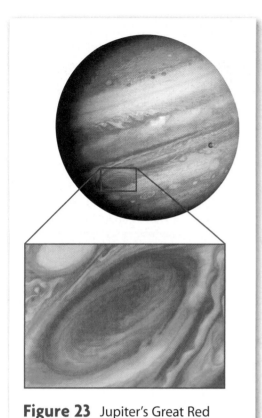

Figure 23 Jupiter's Great Red Spot is a giant storm three times the size of Earth.

Jupiter

The largest planet in our solar system is often thought of as a mini solar system. That is because Jupiter has numerous moons and it resembles a small star in composition. The four largest and most well-known moons are called the Galilean moons. They first were observed by Italian scientist Galileo Galilei in 1610. Jupiter is the first planet out from the Sun to have rings, which are made up of small pieces of icy material that orbit the planet. Jupiter's moons can be seen by looking at Jupiter through a moderate-sized telescope. You also might see the Great Red Spot, shown in **Figure 23,** which is a giant storm system in the atmosphere of Jupiter.

The Moons of Jupiter

The Galilean moons—Io, Europa, Ganymede, and Callisto—are shown in **Figure 24.** Io is the most volcanically active body in our solar system. Ganymede, the largest planetary moon, has its own magnetic field. A liquid ocean might lie beneath the frozen crust of Europa. An icy ocean also might lie beneath the crust of Callisto. Jupiter has more than 60 moons—by far the most in the solar system.

Exploring Jupiter

In 1995, the spacecraft *Galileo* dropped a package of instruments into Jupiter's atmosphere. Tremendous atmospheric pressure caused the instruments to fail after only one hour. Small amounts of water vapor and oxygen are detected in Jupiter's atmosphere, but most of Jupiter is composed of hydrogen and helium. Jupiter's clouds, which are seen when viewing Jupiter through a telescope, are largely made up of ammonia.

Figure 24 Jupiter's four largest moons are called the Galilean moons because they were first observed by Galileo Galilei.

Ganymede　　　Callisto　　　Io　　　Europa

Figure 25 Saturn's rings are mainly composed of ice and rock.

Saturn

Many planetary observers believe that Saturn, shown in **Figure 25,** is the most beautiful object in the night sky. Saturn is the most distant of the planets known to ancient stargazers. It is a gas giant composed of mostly hydrogen and helium. Saturn's ring system is the most extensive and complex in our solar system. Its rings, which are composed of mostly ice and rock, would just fit into the space between Earth and the Moon. Material in the rings ranges in size from grains of salt to houses.

Saturn has more than 30 known moons. The largest, Titan, is similar in size to Mercury. It has a nitrogen-rich atmosphere which might also include the gases methane and ethane.

Exploring Saturn

Several spacecraft have been sent to explore Saturn. In 2004, the *Cassini* spacecraft was the first to explore Saturn's rings from orbit. In 2005, the European Space Agency's *Huygens* spacecraft entered Titan's thick atmosphere. Scientists are interested in studying Titan because of its thick atmosphere shown in **Figure 26.** Also, some areas on Titan contain relatively pure water-ice, while other areas contain organic compounds. Scientists feel they will learn about planetary formation and maybe about the formation of life by studying this moon.

SCIENCE USE V. COMMON USE· ice

Science Use the solid state of a substance usually found as a gas or liquid. *The rings of Saturn contain particles of ammonia ice.*

Common Use frozen water. *They drank refreshing iced tea.*

Figure 26 This image of Titan shows two thin layers of hazy atmosphere that are thought to contain nitrogen and methane.

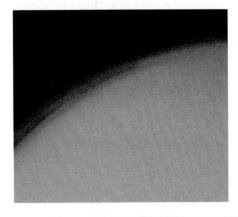

Figure 27 Uranus's axis of rotation is nearly parallel with its orbital plane.

Oribital path

Axis

Figure 28 Uranus has faint cloud bands and a ring system that are visible only in false color.

Figure 29 Methane in Neptune's atmosphere produces its distinct blue color.

Uranus

Uranus (YOOR un us) and Neptune are both gas giants that were discovered with telescopes. Uranus gets its blue-green color from methane gas above the deeper cloud layers. It is so distant from the Sun that it takes 84 years to complete one orbit. Uranus is unusual in that its axis of rotation is nearly parallel to the plane of its orbit around the Sun, as illustrated in **Figure 27.** It rotates on its side as it orbits the Sun. It has 27 known moons and a series of rings shown in **Figure 28.** The atmosphere of Uranus is composed of hydrogen and helium with a liquid core composed of water, methane, and ammonia.

 Figure 27 How does the tilt of Uranus's axis of rotation compare to those of the other planets?

Neptune

Neptune was the first planet located using theoretical predictions rather than through ordinary observations of the sky. The clue to Neptune's existence was that Uranus did not orbit the Sun precisely as expected. Neptune has 13 known moons and several rings. Discovered in 1846, it has not quite finished one orbit of the Sun since its discovery. Neptune's atmosphere is made up of the gases hydrogen, helium, and methane. It is methane that gives the planet its blue color, as shown in **Figure 29.**

Dwarf Planets

The solar system also includes at least three dwarf planets—Ceres, Pluto, and Eris. A dwarf planet differs from a planet because a dwarf planet has not cleared the neighborhood around its orbit. Ceres is one of the many objects in the asteroid belt. Pluto and Eris are part of the Kuiper belt. You will read more about the asteroid belt and the Kuiper belt in the next lesson.

Ceres

Discovered in 1801, Ceres has an average diameter of about 940 km. It is located at an average distance of about 2.7 AU from the Sun. Ceres orbits the Sun in about 4.6 years.

Pluto

From the time of Pluto's discovery in 1930 until 2006, it was known as a planet. Pluto's average distance to the Sun is 39.2 AU and its orbit lasts 248 years. Pluto has a diameter of 2,300 km and three moons. Its largest moon, Charon, as shown in **Figure 30,** has a diameter of about 1,200 km and orbits Pluto at a distance of about 19,500 km.

Eris

Astronomers at the California Institute of Technology discovered Eris in 2005. Eris has a diameter of about 2,400 km and is slightly larger than Pluto is. Its elliptical orbit varies from about 38 AU to 98 AU from the Sun and takes 557 years to complete. It has one moon, Dysnomia.

Figure 30 Pluto's diameter is about two-thirds of the diameter of Earth's Moon.

Charon

Pluto

How large are the planets?

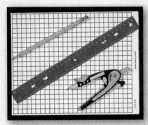

Data Collection

1. Read and complete a lab safety form.

2. Make a data table with three columns. In the first column, write the name of each planet.

3. Copy the data on the diameters of the planets from **Tables 3–4** into the second column.

4. Using a scale of 1 mm = 1,000 km, find the diameters of a scale model of each planet in millimeters by dividing the diameters in **Tables 3–4** by 1,000. Copy the scaled diameter of each planet into the third column.

5. Using a **compass,** draw circles representing each of the planets where the diameter of each circle is the value in the third column of your data table.

Data Analysis

1. **Compare** the planets' diameters by using the scaled diameters from your table and making a bar graph representing the nine planets. How much larger is Jupiter compared to Earth?

2. **Evaluate** Which gave you a better perspective to compare the relative sizes of the planets—the bar graph or the set of circles?

4.e, 9.e

Table 5 Planets

Mercury
- Closest to the Sun
- Second-smallest planet
- Surface has many craters and high cliffs
- No atmosphere
- Temperatures range from 425°C during the day to –170°C at night
- Has no moons

Venus
- Similar to Earth in size and mass
- Thick atmosphere made mostly of carbon dioxide
- Droplets of sulfuric acid in atmosphere give clouds a yellowish color
- Surface has craters, faultlike cracks, and volcanoes
- Greenhouse effect causes surface temperatures of 450°C to 475°C
- Has no moons

Earth
- Atmosphere, with its ozone layer, protects life
- Surface temperatures allow water to exist as a solid, a liquid, and a gas
- Only planet where life is known to exist
- Has one large moon

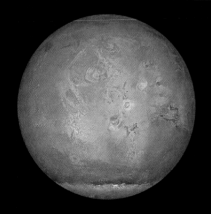

Mars
- Surface appears reddish-yellow because of iron oxide in soil
- Ice caps are made of frozen carbon dioxide and water
- Channels indicate that water had flowed on the surface; has large volcanoes and valleys
- Has a thin atmosphere composed mostly of carbon dioxide
- Surface temperatures range from –125°C to 35°C
- Huge dust storms often blanket the planet
- Has two small moons

Table 5 Planets

Concepts In Motion
Interactive Table To organize information about the planets, visit ca8.msscience.com.

Jupiter
- Largest planet
- Has faint rings
- Atmosphere is mostly hydrogen and helium; continuous storms swirl on the planet—the largest is the Great Red Spot
- Has four large moons and at least 63 smaller moons; one of its moons, Io, has active volcanoes

Saturn
- Second-largest planet
- Has faint rings
- Atmosphere is mostly hydrogen and helium
- Has a complex ring system
- Has at least 47 moons—the largest, Titan, is larger than Mercury

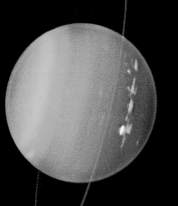

Uranus
- Large, gaseous planet with thin, dark rings
- Atmosphere is hydrogen, helium, and methane
- Axis of rotation is nearly parallel to plane of orbit
- Has at least 27 moons

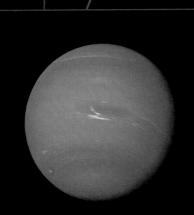

Neptune
- Large, gaseous planet with rings that vary in thickness
- Is sometimes farther from the Sun than Pluto
- Methane atmosphere causes its bluish-green color
- Has dark-colored storms in atmosphere
- Has at least 13 moons

Summing Up the Planets

Our solar system's planets vary greatly in size and appearance. The first four planets from the Sun are relatively small and rocky, whereas the next four are relatively large and gaseous. The dwarf planets are part of the asteroid belt or the Kuiper belt. Planets are only visible from Earth because they reflect sunlight. Much of our knowledge about our solar system's planets has come from various spacecraft that have orbited the planets.

LESSON 3 Review

Summarize

Create your own lesson summary as you write a script for a **television news report.**

1. **Review** the text after the **red** main headings and write one sentence about each. These are the headlines of your broadcast.

2. **Review** the text and write 2–3 sentences about each **blue** subheading. These sentences should tell *who, what, when, where,* and *why* information about each **red** heading.

3. **Include** descriptive details in your report, such as names of reporters and local places and events.

4. **Present** your news report to other classmates alone or with a team.

 ELA8: LS 2.1

Standards Check

Using Vocabulary

1. The rocky planets also are called the _____. **4.e**

2. The _____ are sometimes referred to as the gaseous planets. **4.e**

Understanding Main Ideas

3. **Contrast** Earth with Jupiter. List three differences. **4.e**

4. **Explain** why Jupiter and its moons are sometimes thought of as forming their own "solar" system. **4.e**

5. **Identify** a solar system body that might have harbored life at one time. Why did you make your choice? **4.e**

6. **Compare** Earth to Mars and list three similarities. **4.e**

7. Which planet is shown in the picture below, taken by a land vehicle from a NASA spacecraft? **4.d**

8. **Describe** what was detected by *Mars Odyssey* when it landed on Mars in 2002. **4.d**

9. **Compare and Contrast** Copy and fill in the graphic organizer below to compare and contrast details of the inner planets and the outer planets. **4.e**

Planets	Similarities	Differences
Inner		
Outer		

Applying Science

10. **Make a table** that lists the distance from the Sun in AU, diameter, number of moons, and presence or absence of rings for each planet. **4.e**

11. **Rank** the planets by number of moons. Is there any connection between number of moons and any other characteristics of the planets? **4.e**

Science nline

For more practice, visit **Standards Check** at ca8.msscience.com.

Science Content Standards

4.c Students know how to use astronomical units and light years as measures of distances between the Sun, stars, and Earth.

4.e Students know the appearance, general composition, relative position and size, and motion of objects in the solar system, including planets, planetary satellites, comets, and asteroids.

9.a Plan and conduct a scientific investigation to test a hypothesis.

Reading Guide

What *You'll Learn*

▶ **Compare and contrast** comets, asteroids, and meteoroids.

Why *It's Important*

An asteroid collision with Earth would cause mass devastation.

Vocabulary

asteroid
comet
meteoroid

Review Vocabulary

erosion: the process of wearing away rock or soil (Grade 6)

Asteroids, Comets, and Meteoroids

Main Idea Comets, asteroids, and other objects orbit our Sun.

Real-World Reading Connection Have you seen a meteor streak across the sky? Could an asteroid strike Earth, causing damage? How do comets, asteroids and meteors differ?

Asteroids

Asteroids are rocky objects, smaller than a planet, that are found between the orbits of Mars and Jupiter. Their elliptical orbits around the Sun can sometimes be disturbed. This can cause asteroids to hit Earth or other planets.

Where are asteroids in the solar system?

There are hundreds of thousands of asteroids in the asteroid belt between Mars and Jupiter, as illustrated in **Figure 31.** Asteroids are left over from the formation of the solar system about 4.6 billion years ago. It is thought that they crashed into the inner planets during the early period of our solar system. Asteroids lack enough gravity to have an atmosphere. Consequently, their surfaces have many craters from impacts with other objects.

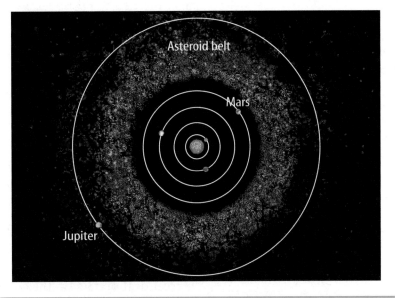

Figure 31 Asteroids range in size from Ceres, which has a diameter of 940 km, to ones that are less than 1 km across.

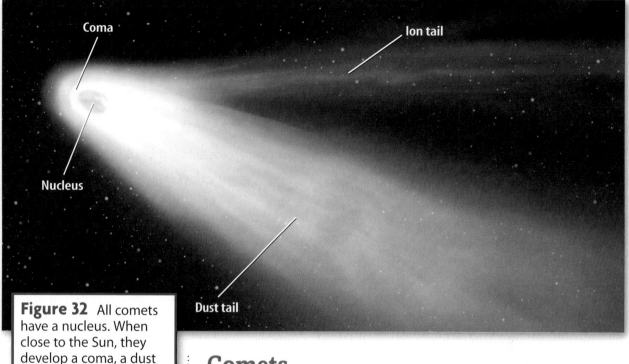

Coma

Ion tail

Nucleus

Dust tail

Figure 32 All comets have a nucleus. When close to the Sun, they develop a coma, a dust tail, and an ion tail.

Figure 33 *Deep Impact* produced the clearest images yet of a comet's nucleus.

Comets

A **comet** is a small, icy body in orbit around the Sun. Some comets have highly elliptical orbits—bringing them close to the Sun and taking them well beyond the orbit of Pluto. Comets may be leftover material from the formation of the solar system.

The Structure of Comets

Each comet has a solid part called a nucleus. The nucleus is a loosely packed lump of icy material that is often only a few kilometers across. Aside from water ice, the nucleus contains frozen gases, dust, and bits of rock and may have a small, rocky core.

Heat vaporizes the frozen gases when the nucleus is close to the Sun. An atmosphere, called the coma, is produced when gases and dust are released by "vents" from the nucleus. This atmosphere can extend tens of thousands of kilometers beyond the nucleus. A tail, illustrated in **Figure 32,** extends from the coma and forms only when a comet is near the Sun. Solar radiation causes gases in the coma to glow, allowing you to see a comet from Earth.

Deep Impact

On July 4, 2005, the *Deep Impact* spacecraft launched a small probe on a collision course with comet Temple-1. The collision is shown in **Figure 33.** Before the probe collided with Temple-1 at a speed of 10 km/s, it recorded extraordinarily clear images of the comet. These images showed that the comet's surface is covered in craters very much like the Moon and Mercury. Since material from inside Temple-1 was ejected by the **impact,** scientists also obtained a great deal of data on the composition of comets.

Short-Period Comets and the Kuiper Belt

Some comets sweep very close to Earth and are seen often. For example, Halley's Comet, last seen in 1986, has a period of 76 years. Short-period comets are more predictable because they take less than 200 years to orbit the Sun. Most short-period comets come from a region of icy bodies beyond the orbit of Neptune. These icy bodies, shown in **Figure 34,** are called Kuiper (KI puhr) belt objects.

The Kuiper belt is an area of the solar system that extends about 50 AU from the Sun toward the orbit of Neptune, which is 30 AU from the Sun. For many years, it was assumed that most short-period comets originated from the Kuiper belt. However, many astronomers now suggest that some short-period comets originate from a region of space that is more distant than the Kuiper belt.

Long-Period Comets and the Oort Cloud

Recall that a comet has an extreme elliptical orbit and travels a great distance from the Sun, which takes a very long time. Long-period comets have orbital periods longer than 200 years. Some long-period comets have orbital periods in the millions or tens of millions of years.

Some scientists have proposed that these comets originated from a spherical, shell-like swarm of comets called the Oort cloud. The Oort cloud surrounds the solar system. It is estimated that the outer edge of the Oort cloud might be as far as 100,000 AU from the Sun—about half of the distance to Proxima Centauri, the star nearest to the Sun.

WORD ORIGIN·············

comet
from Greek *(aster) kometes;*
means *long-haired (star)*

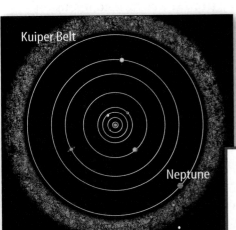

Kuiper Belt

Neptune

Figure 34 Many objects in the Kuiper Belt have very elongated orbits. Most of the time, these orbits carry them farther from the Sun than Neptune.

How do craters appear?

Some objects in the solar system have many craters. The Moon is covered with them. Even Earth has some craters.

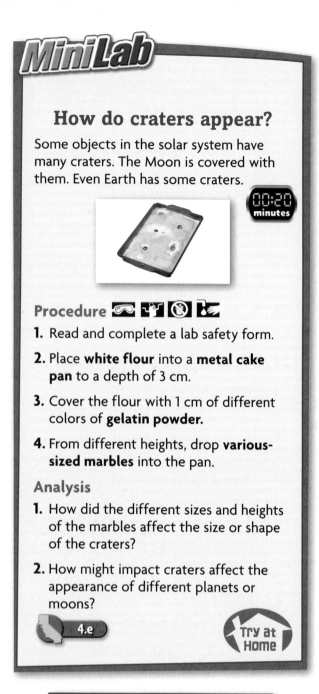

00:20 minutes

Procedure

1. Read and complete a lab safety form.

2. Place **white flour** into a **metal cake pan** to a depth of 3 cm.

3. Cover the flour with 1 cm of different colors of **gelatin powder.**

4. From different heights, drop **various-sized marbles** into the pan.

Analysis

1. How did the different sizes and heights of the marbles affect the size or shape of the craters?

2. How might impact craters affect the appearance of different planets or moons?

4.e

Try at Home

Figure 35 Barringer Crater in Arizona is about 1.2 km in diameter and about 200 m deep.

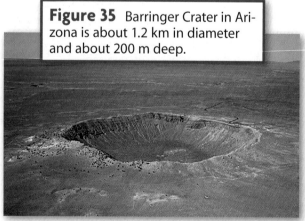

Meteoroids

Have you ever seen shooting stars in the night sky? **Meteoroids** are solid, interplanetary particles passing through Earth's atmosphere. The term *meteor* refers to the streak of light produced by a meteoroid as it moves rapidly through Earth's atmosphere. Friction vaporizes the meteoroid and heats atmospheric gases along the path of the meteoroid, making it look like a shooting star. The term *meteorite* refers to the remaining portion of a meteoroid that reaches Earth's surface.

What are meteoroids made of?

Most meteorites found on Earth are rocky. The composition of rocky meteorites is so similar to Earth's mantle that it suggests a similar origin. Some astronomers think meteorites came from a small planet that broke apart during the formation of the solar system. That planet, like Earth, would have had a small iron-nickel core and a large, rocky mantle.

Impact Craters on Earth

Earth, like other objects in the solar system, is continually bombarded by meteoroids. Most burn up in the atmosphere. Some are large enough to reach Earth's surface. It is estimated that somewhere between 1,000 and 10,000 kilograms of meteoritic material falls to Earth each day.

Large meteoroids can produce impact craters. For example, Barringer Crater in Arizona, shown in **Figure 35,** was formed about 50,000 years ago when a large meteoroid struck Earth. Over time, erosion from wind and water causes impact craters to be filled in. However, Barringer Crater is located in a very dry part of the United States, so it is still visible. Because the Moon has no atmosphere or water, no erosion occurs. Therefore, impact craters don't get filled in. On most moons in the solar system, there is little or no atmosphere to protect the surface from crater-making meteoroids.

Within the Planets' Neighborhood

Comets, asteroids, and meteoroids orbit the Sun. Asteroids are rocky objects, smaller than planets, mostly found between the orbits of Mars and Jupiter. Some asteroids and all comets have highly elliptical orbits, causing them to range great distances from very close to the Sun to well beyond the orbit of Pluto. Meteoroids are rocky objects, smaller than 50 m across, usually not found in the asteroid belt. Meteoroids can collide with planets, sometimes creating large impact craters that alter the appearance to a planet's surface. To impact Earth's surface, a meteoroid must be large enough to pass through Earth's atmosphere without disintegrating.

LESSON 4 Review

Summarize

1. **Find** the main topics in this lesson. Use the **red** headings to help you.

2. **Write** these main topics on a piece of paper, leaving several blank lines between each topic.

3. Each main heading is divided into subheadings. **List** these below each main heading, leaving three blank lines between each. Use the **blue** headings to help you.

4. **Skim** the text below each subheading and select 2–3 supporting details. List these below each subheading.

 ELA8: R 2.4

Standards Check

Using Vocabulary

1. **Compare and contrast** asteroids and comets. `4.e`

2. Before a meteorite strikes Earth, it is called a(n) _____. `4.e`

Understanding Main Ideas

3. Which term refers to the streak of light produced by a rock from space as it moves rapidly through Earth's atmosphere?

    A. asteroid
    B. comet
    C. meteor
    D. meteorite `4.e`

4. **Explain** how life would be different if Earth had an orbit like that of a comet. `4.e`

5. **Explain** why asteroids do not have an atmosphere. `4.e`

6. **Organize** Copy and fill in the graphic organizer below to summarize information about short-period comets and long-period comets. `4.e`

Types of Comets	
Short-Period	**Long-Period**

Applying Science

7. **Explain** how an atmosphere is produced around a comet. `4.e`

8. **Evaluate** Many objects orbit the Sun in the Kuiper belt. Should such an object be called a comet if it does not have a tail? Develop an argument to support your opinion. `4.e`

Science nline

For more practice, visit **Standards Check** at ca8.msscience.com.

Model the Solar System

00:45 minutes

Materials

roll of calculator paper
meterstick or
  measuring tape
colored pencils
calculator

Science Content Standards

4.c Students know how to use astronomical units and light years as measures of distance between the Sun, stars, and Earth.
9.a Plan and conduct a scientific investigation to test a hypothesis.

Problem

The planets of the solar system are very far apart and are different sizes. But, you can visualize their relationships better if you model the distances on a manageable scale. In this lab, you will decide on a scale for the distance of the planets from each other and a scale to compare their diameters. You will model these distances on a ticker tape (calculator paper).

Form a Hypothesis

➤ Review Tables 2, 3, and 4 of this chapter.
➤ **Predict** whether you will be able to use the same scale to model the planets' diameters and their distances from the Sun.

Collect Data and Make Observations

1. Create a data table with five columns.
   - List the names of the planets in column 1.
   - Use **Table 2** from this chapter to record the distances of the planets from the Sun in astronomical units (AU) in column 2.
   - Use **Table 3** and **Table 4** to record the diameters of the planets in column 4.
2. Decide what distance will have a unit of 1 on your scale(s).
3. Convert all of your distances by using your scale(s).
4. Record the scaled distances of the planets from the Sun in column 3 and the scaled diameters of the planets in column 5.
5. Clear an area where you can spread your ticker tape without having to crawl under tables or desks and it will not be a hazard for a major traffic area.
6. **Model** the distances of the planets from the Sun by measuring and marking the distances on one roll of calculator paper. Model the diameters of the planets by measuring and marking the diameters on a second roll of calculator paper.

Analyze and Conclude

1. **Describe** the method you used to calculate the distances of the planets from the Sun and their diameters. Use an example to demonstrate your exact method.

2. **Describe** the locations of the planets in relation to each other and their relative sizes.

3. **Explain** why it is difficult to model both sets of distances on the same ticker tape.

4. **Error Analysis** Explain any mistakes you made in your calculations and why you think you made those mistakes. What precautions can you take to avoid making the same mistakes again?

Communicate

Write an Article Write a newspaper article about distance units. Explain why some distance units are more useful than others for different situations. Give some examples of situations that require different distance units.

Real World Science

Designing the Next Generation of Spacecraft

Thanks to NASA engineers like Dallias Pearson, the next generation of spacecraft will one day travel to the *International Space Station,* the Moon, and Mars. Pearson and other engineers research, design, and test new space transportation systems. Pearson's experience with projects including *Viking I* and *Viking II, Mars Observer,* and *Magellan* is furthering the development of the *Crew Exploration Vehicle,* the spacecraft now being designed to replace the Space Shuttle fleet.

Write a help-wanted ad for a professional to join Pearson's group. Include qualifications and skills needed to create and test the software and systems integral to spacecraft design.

The Search for Extra-Solar Planets

Astronomers have identified more than 150 planets outside our solar system. No one knows what these planets really look like, because the faint light they reflect is overwhelmed by the stars they orbit. Scientists are using the new Keck Interferometer Nuller at the W. M. Keck Observatory to make these stars "disappear." It combines light waves from multiple telescopes to cancel each other out, dramatically reducing stellar glare. This may allow scientists to observe planets orbiting other stars.

NASA's Terrestrial Planet Finder mission will use the technology of the Keck Nuller in orbiting observatories to detect and study planets. Visit **Technology** at ca8.msscience.com to **research** and write a short paper outlining the goals, structure, and timelines for the mission.

ELA8: W 1.1

Johannes Kepler's Revolutionary Laws

What tools are required to make a groundbreaking discovery? As a scientist working in the early 1600s, Kepler did not have the powerful technologies and advanced mathematics used by today's astronomers. His first two laws of motion were published in 1609, only one year after the telescope was discovered! What Kepler did have was volumes of carefully recorded planetary data from years of observation, the ability to apply mathematics to the data, and a vision of the solar system that was revolutionary. With those tools, Kepler changed the scientific world.

Visit **History** at **ca8.msscience.com** to **research** events, discoveries, and inventions made by Kepler and others during the early 1600s. Develop and perform a news show that highlights some of these events. Use the publishing of one or more of Kepler's laws of planetary motion as the lead story.

DEADLY IMPACT

Asteroid 99942 Apophis is a near-Earth asteroid, one of hundreds studied by scientists at NASA's Jet Propulsion Laboratory in Pasadena, California. Following its current path, Apophis will zoom close enough in 2029 to be seen with the unaided eye. In 2036, the asteroid could collide with Earth. Though a collision with Apophis is unlikely, NASA has developed a tentative response strategy, recognizing that an impact could cause significant damage and potential loss of life.

Visit **Society** at **ca8.msscience.com** to gather data about 10 near-Earth objects that will approach Earth within the next 10 years. Organize the data, including date of approach, distance from Earth, and approximate size, in a chart and/or graph. Based on your research, assign an impact threat level from 1–5 for the time period investigated.

The BIG Idea Our solar system includes planets and dwarf planets and their moons, and other objects such as asteroids and comets, all orbiting the Sun.

Lesson 1 The Structure of the Solar System
2.g, 4.c, 4.d, 4.e

Main Idea Even at great distances, gravity holds objects in our solar system in almost circular orbits around the Sun.

- Distances between the planets and the Sun are vast.
- The planets revolve around the Sun in almost-circular orbits called ellipses.
- Planets also rotate about their axes as they travel about the Sun.

- **astronomical unit** (p. 465)
- **axis of rotation** (p. 463)
- **ellipse** (p. 464)
- **period of revolution** (p. 463)
- **period of rotation** (p. 463)

Lesson 2 The Sun-Earth-Moon System
4.d

Main Idea Eclipses and lunar phases demonstrate that the Moon shines by reflected sunlight.

- The Moon revolves around Earth and is seen through reflected sunlight.
- The portions of the Moon that are visible from Earth as the monthly cycle unfolds are called the phases of the Moon.
- Earth rotates on its axis once each day as it revolves around the Sun in one year.
- A lunar eclipse can take place when Earth is between the Sun and the Moon.
- A solar eclipse can take place when the Moon is between Earth and the Sun.

- **eclipse** (p. 475)
- **lunar phase** (p. 474)
- **satellite** (p. 473)

Lesson 3 The Planets and Their Moons
4.d, 4.e, 9.e

Main Idea The planets vary in appearance, composition, relative position, size, and motion.

- The four inner planets (Mercury, Venus, Earth, and Mars) are small and rocky compared to the next four planets.
- The four outer planets (Jupiter, Saturn, Uranus, and Neptune) are more distant from the Sun, very large, and composed of gases.
- Mars and some moons of Jupiter and Saturn show evidence of the presence of water.

- **inner planet** (p. 478)
- **outer planet** (p. 481)

Lesson 4 Asteroids, Comets, and Meteoroids
4.c, 4.e, 9.a

Main Idea Comets, asteroids, and meteoroids orbit our Sun.

- Asteroids are rocky bodies, smaller than planets, orbiting the Sun between Mars and Jupiter.
- Comets are icy bodies orbiting the Sun in often highly elliptical orbits. They sometimes come close to the Sun and develop comas.

- **asteroid** (p. 489)
- **comet** (p. 490)
- **meteoroid** (p. 492)

 Download quizzes, key terms, and flash cards from ca8.msscience.com.

 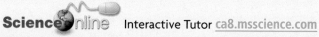

Linking Vocabulary and Main Ideas

Use the vocabulary terms on page 498 to complete the concept map.

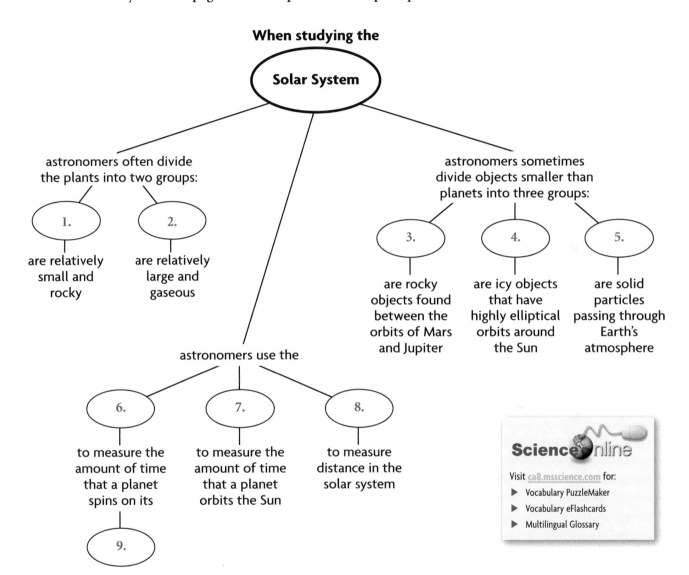

When studying the

Solar System

astronomers often divide the plants into two groups:

1. are relatively small and rocky

2. are relatively large and gaseous

astronomers sometimes divide objects smaller than planets into three groups:

3. are rocky objects found between the orbits of Mars and Jupiter

4. are icy objects that have highly elliptical orbits around the Sun

5. are solid particles passing through Earth's atmosphere

astronomers use the

6. to measure the amount of time that a planet spins on its

7. to measure the amount of time that a planet orbits the Sun

8. to measure distance in the solar system

9.

Using Vocabulary

Fill in the blanks with the correct vocabulary words.

10. _____ are called meteorites when they reach Earth's surface.

11. A different appearance of the Moon as it orbits Earth is called a(n) _____.

12. The shape of each planet's orbit about the Sun is a(n) _____.

13. Earth's _____ is tilted at 23.5° perpendicular to the plane of Earth's orbit about the Sun.

14. A(n) _____ is an object that revolves around a planet.

Understanding Main Ideas

Choose the word or phrase that best answers the question.

1. An illustration of the Sun-Earth-Moon system is shown below.

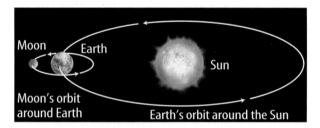

What does the illustration above indicate?
A. The Sun is rotating around Earth.
B. Earth is rotating around the Sun.
C. Earth is revolving around the Moon.
D. The Moon is revolving around Earth. `4.e`

2. What is the definition of an astronomical unit?
A. the average distance from Jupiter to the Sun
B. the average distance from Earth to the Moon
C. the average distance from Earth to the Sun
D. the average distance from the Sun to the next nearest star `4.c`

3. What is the name for a rock orbiting the Sun between the orbits of Mars and Jupiter?
A. a comet
B. an asteroid
C. a planet
D. a moon `4.e`

4. Which planet is farthest from Earth?
A. Mercury
B. Jupiter
C. Neptune
D. Mars `4.e`

5. Which planet is the closest to Earth?
A. Mercury
B. Venus
C. Mars
D. Jupiter `4.e`

6. Which best describes the inner planets?
A. relatively large
B. contain much hydrogen
C. rocky
D. gaseous `4.e`

7. Which planet has a moon with active volcanoes?
A. Mars
B. Venus
C. Jupiter
D. Earth `4.e`

8. The illustration below shows the Sun, Earth, and the Moon in a straight line.

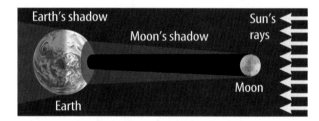

What does the illustration above indicate?
A. a lunar eclipse during full moon
B. a lunar eclipse during new moon
C. a solar eclipse during full moon
D. a solar eclipse during new moon `4.d`

9. Which object comes close to the Sun but is also found far from the Sun in a highly elliptical orbit?
A. planet
B. moon
C. asteroid
D. a comet `4.e`

Science Online Standards Review ca8.msscience.com

Applying Science

10. Infer During what phase of the Moon can a lunar eclipse occur?   `4.d`

11. Infer Use the illustration below to determine where in a planet's orbit the planet moves the fastest.   `4.e`

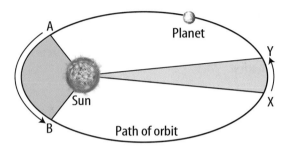

12. Compare and contrast the inner planets with the outer planets.   `4.e`

13. Describe how a comet changes as it travels through space.   `4.e`

14. Infer Why does Venus have higher surface temperatures than Mercury even though Venus is farther from the Sun?   `4.e`

15. Explain why astronomers use the astronomical unit (AU) to measure distances in the solar system.   `4.c`

16. Describe how a full moon produces so much light at night. Also describe where it is located in the Sun-Earth-Moon system during this lunar phase.   `4.d`

17. Explain The term *planet* comes from an ancient Greek word that means "the wanderers." Why did the ancient Greeks refer to the planets as wanderers?   `4.d`

WRITING in Science

18. Write one paragraph that compares and contrasts asteroids, meteors, and comets.

Cumulative Review

19. Explain how gravity keeps planets in orbit around the Sun.   `2.g`

20. Identify the components of our solar system.   `4.e`

Applying Math

Use the illustration below to answer questions 21 through 22.

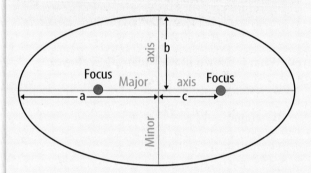

21. If the eccentricity of Venus's orbit is 0.0068, and half the major axis, *a*, is 1.08×10^{11} m, find the approximate distance to the focus point where the Sun could be located in the orbit, *c*. Use the formula $c = e \times a$.   **MA8:** ALG 2.0

22. If the eccentricity of Mars's orbit is 0.0934, and half the major axis, *a*, is 2.28×10^{11} m, find the approximate distance to the focus point where the Sun could be located in the orbit, *c*. Use the formula $c = e \times a$.   **MA8:** ALG 2.0

1 The illustration below is of an object in the solar system.

What is shown in the illustration above?

A asteroid   4.e

B comet

C meteor

D meteorite

2 Which term would you use to describe the spinning of Earth on its axis?

A eclipse   4.e

B ellipse

C revolution

D rotation

3 Which is the sixth planet from the Sun?

A Earth   4.e

B Jupiter

C Mars

D Saturn

4 Which planet has a large, permanent storm in its atmosphere known as the Great Red Spot?

A Jupiter   4.e

B Neptune

C Saturn

D Venus

5 Which object's gravity holds the planets in their orbits?

A Earth   2.g

B Jupiter

C Mercury

D Sun

6 The illustration below is of an eclipse.

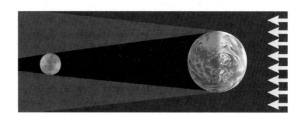

During which phase of the Moon could a lunar eclipse occur?

A crescent moon   4.d

B full moon

C harvest moon

D new moon

Use the photo below to answer questions 7 and 8.

7 Which feature is shown in the photo above?

A coma   `4.e`

B nucleus

C impact crater

D volcanic crater

8 Which object produced this feature?

A asteroid   `4.e`

B comet

C meteor

D meteorite

9 Which unit is most useful for measuring distances in the solar system?

A astronomical unit   `4.c`

B kilometer

C light-year

D meter

10 Which planet is closest to the Sun?

A Earth   `4.e`

B Mercury

C Pluto

D Saturn

11 In what month is Earth closest to the Sun?

A January   `4.d`

B March

C July

D September

12 Which is referred to as an inner planet?

A Neptune   `4.e`

B Saturn

C Uranus

D Venus

13 The illustration below shows the orbit of a planet around the Sun.

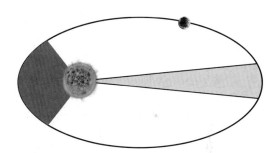

Which law is best represented by this illustration?

A Kepler's first law   `4.e`

B Kepler's second law

C Newton's second law

D Newton's third law

14 Between which two planets' orbits does the asteroid belt occur?

A Earth and Mars   `4.e`

B Mars and Jupiter

C Mercury and Venus

D Uranus and Neptune

Stars and Galaxies

The BIG Idea

The Milky Way galaxy, which is composed of billions of stars, is one of billions of galaxies in the universe.

LESSON 1 4.b, 4.c, 4.d
Stars

Main Idea Although the Sun is considered to be a fairly typical star, analysis of starlight indicates that stars vary greatly in size, temperature, and color and are composed primarily of hydrogen and helium.

LESSON 2 2.g, 4.d
How Stars Shine

Main Idea Stars generate light from energy released in nuclear fusion.

LESSON 3 4.a, 4.b, 4.c, 9.d
Galaxies

Main Idea Gravitational attraction causes stars to group together into galaxies.

Spinning Through Space?

These circles in the night sky are not a new type of fireworks. Instead, this image was formed by pointing a camera at the night sky and keeping the shutter open for several hours. As Earth rotates, the stars seem to move across the sky, forming circular streaks on the camera film.

Science Journal Write a short paragraph describing where you think stars are located relative to the solar system.

Launch Lab

00:20
minutes

How far away are the stars and how many are there?

Humans have asked these questions since time began. Try to model what you know about the stars, galaxies, and the universe.

Think About This

Make a concept map with answers to questions such as these and anything else you know about the universe.

- How old and how big is the universe?
- How did the universe form?
- How do stars shine?
- How far apart are the galaxies?
- How many galaxies are there?

Procedure

After you have thought about the questions, draw the universe as you think it looks.

2.g, 4.a, 4.b, 4.c

Science Online

Visit ca8.msscience.com to:

▶ view Concepts in Motion
▶ explore Virtual Labs
▶ access content-related Web links
▶ take the Standards Check

FOLDABLES™
Study Organizer

Stars and Galaxies Make the following Foldable to help you organize information about stars and galaxies.

▷ **STEP 1 Fold** the bottom of a horizontal sheet of paper up about 2 cm.

▷ **STEP 2 Fold** in half.

▷ **STEP 3 Unfold** once and dot with glue to make two pockets.

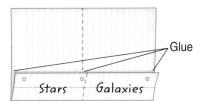

Glue

Stars | Galaxies

Reading Skill

Determining the Main Idea
As you read this chapter, write the main ideas about stars and galaxies on note cards and sort them into their correct pockets.

Get Ready to Read

Make Inferences

1 Learn It! When you make inferences, you draw conclusions that are not directly stated in the text. This means you "read between the lines." You interpret clues and draw upon prior knowledge. Authors rely on a reader's ability to infer because all the details are not always given.

2 Practice It! Read the excerpt below and pay attention to highlighted words as you make inferences. Use this Think-Through chart to help you make inferences.

If the molecules in a nebula block light from stars contained within it, the nebula is called an absorption nebula. If the nebula's molecules become excited by energy from the stars within it, they emit their own light. These are called emission nebulae.

—*from page 520*

Text	Question	Inferences
Molecules in a nebula	What are they?	Dust? Gas?
Become excited	What is this?	Higher energy state?
Emit their own light	How do they do this?	Return to original state releasing energy?

3 Apply It! As you read this chapter, practice your skill at making inferences by making connections and asking questions.

Target Your Reading

Use this to focus on the main ideas as you read the chapter.

1. **Before you read** the chapter, respond to the statements below on your worksheet or on a numbered sheet of paper.
   - Write an **A** if you **agree** with the statement.
   - Write a **D** if you **disagree** with the statement.

2. **After you read** the chapter, look back to this page to see if you've changed your mind about any of the statements.
   - If any of your answers changed, explain why.
   - Change any false statements into true statements.
   - Use your revised statements as a study guide.

Science Online

Print a worksheet of this page at ca8.msscience.com.

Reading Tip

Sometimes you make inferences by using other reading skills, such as questioning and predicting.

Before You Read A or D	Statement	After You Read A or D
	1 The Sun has an atmosphere.	
	2 Gravity helped form our solar system.	
	3 Planets produce their own light.	
	4 Everything you see in the night sky is inside the Milky Way galaxy.	
	5 A star's color is related to its temperature.	
	6 The space between stars is totally empty.	
	7 Gravity causes stars to cluster together.	
	8 Astronomers use kilometers to measure distances between stars.	
	9 The Sun is a supergiant star.	
	10 The light from some galaxies can take over a billion years to reach Earth.	

Science Content Standards

4.b Students know that the Sun is one of many stars in the Milky Way galaxy and that stars may differ in size, temperature, and color.

4.c Students know how to use astronomical units and light years as measures of distance between the Sun, stars, and Earth.

4.d Students know that stars are the source of light for all bright objects in outer space and that the Moon and planets shine by reflected sunlight, not by their own light.

Reading Guide

What *You'll Learn*

▶ **Identify** what stars are made of.

▶ **Explain** how the composition of stars can be determined.

▶ **Describe** how the temperature and the color of a star are related.

Why *It's Important*

Our star, the Sun, is the source of nearly all energy on Earth.

Vocabulary

light-year
luminosity
apparent magnitude
absolute magnitude

Review Vocabulary

spectral line: a single wavelength of light that can be seen when the light from an excited element passes through a prism (p. 190)

Stars

Main Idea Although the Sun is considered to be a fairly typical star, analysis of starlight indicates that stars vary greatly in size, temperature, and color and are composed primarily of hydrogen and helium.

Real-World Reading Connection Have you ever wondered how stars generate the light that allows us to see them in the night sky? You may have noticed that some stars appear blue or red. What are stars and why do stars have different colors?

What are stars?

A star is a large ball of gas that emits energy produced by nuclear reactions in the star's interior. Much of this energy is emitted as electromagnetic radiation, including visible light. Light emitted by stars enables other objects in the universe to be seen by reflection. For example, planets, comets, and asteroids shine by reflecting light from the Sun.

The Structure of Stars

The layered structure of a star is shown in **Figure 1.** Energy is produced at the core, which is denser than the outer layers. The temperature in the core can range from 5,000,000 K to more than 100,000,000 K, causing atoms to separate into their nuclei and electrons, forming plasma. Energy produced in a star's core travels outward to the photosphere, where most light is emitted. The photosphere is the surface of the Sun—the part that we see.

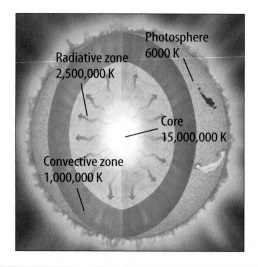

Figure 1 A star's interior includes two distinct zones that surround the core. Most light is emitted by the photosphere at the surface.

Photosphere 6000 K
Radiative zone 2,500,000 K
Core 15,000,000 K
Convective zone 1,000,000 K

Table 1 Properties of Different Types of Stars

Star Type	Diameter (1 = Sun's diameter)	Mass (1 = Sun's Mass)	Surface Temperature (K)
Supergiant	100–1,000	8–17	variable
Red giant	10–100	1–4	3,000–4,000
Main sequence	0.1–15	0.1–60	2,400–50,000
White dwarf	0.01	0.5–1.44	100,000–6,000
Neutron star	0.00	1–4	variable

Types of Stars

Stars come in many different sizes and have various masses and surface temperatures. **Table 1** shows some different types of stars. The Sun is medium sized with a surface temperature of about 5,800 K. Supergiants, the largest stars, are as big as the orbits of our outer planets. Red giant stars began with a mass and a diameter similar to those of our Sun, but later expanded to be 10–100 times larger. Eventually, our Sun will expand into a red giant, too. Neutron stars are only a few kilometers in diameter, but have a mass greater than that of the Sun.

The Distances Between Stars

Recall from the previous chapter that one AU is the average distance between Earth and the Sun or about 150 million km. Distances between stars are so much greater than the distances in the solar system that a larger unit of measure is needed. This unit is a **light-year** (ly), which equals the distance light travels in one year. Because light travels at a speed of 300,000 km/s, a light-year is approximately 9,500,000,000,000 km, or about 63,000 AU. **Figure 2** shows some of the stars nearest to our solar system.

 How many years pass before light from Alpha Centauri reaches Earth?

Figure 2 The nearest star to our solar system, Alpha Centauri, is 4.3 ly or more than 40 trillion km away.

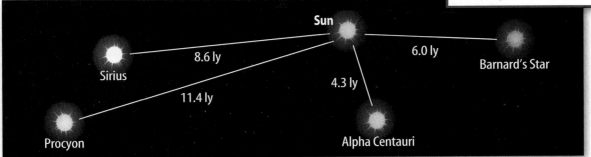

Sirius — 8.6 ly — Sun
Procyon — 11.4 ly
Alpha Centauri — 4.3 ly
Sun — 6.0 ly — Barnard's Star

What are stars made of?

Because stars other than the Sun are so far away, they can only be studied by analyzing the light they emit. By analyzing the light emitted by a star, you can learn about the star's motion, its temperature, and the chemical elements it contains.

Spectroscopes

A spectroscope is an instrument that can be used to study the light that comes from stars. **Figure 3** shows the different parts of a spectroscope. Spectroscopes often contain elements, such as slits, prisms, diffraction gratings, and lenses to distribute and focus light. Using spectroscopes, astronomers can determine what elements are present in stars.

Continuous Spectra

When light from a bright lightbulb passes through a prism, it is spread out in a rainbow of colors. This "rainbow" is called a continuous spectrum. A continuous spectrum is emitted by hot, dense materials, such as the filament of a lightbulb or the hot, dense gas of the Sun's photosphere.

Reading Check What emits a continuous spectrum?

Absorption Spectra

Sometimes when a continuous spectrum is examined in a spectroscope, some dark lines might be seen. This is called an absorption spectrum. Absorption spectra are produced when the light emitted from a hot, dense material passes through a cooler, less dense gas. Atoms in the cooler gas absorb certain wavelengths of light, producing dark lines superimposed on the continuous spectrum. These lines correspond to energy states of atoms in the gas. Each element absorbs only certain wavelengths, as shown in **Figure 4.** Thus, analyzing the pattern of these dark lines tells you what elements are present in the cooler gas.

Light

Figure 3 A simple spectroscope uses a slit and a prism to break light into its component wavelengths or colors.

Figure 4 Dark lines in the continuous spectrum reveal the elements present in the cooler gas. Each element has its own distinctive pattern or fingerprint.

Spectroscope

Continuous spectrum

Hot, dense gas   Cooler, less dense gas   Spectroscope   Absorption spectrum

Light

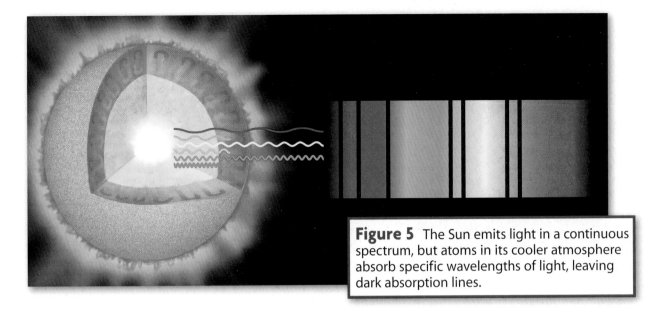

Figure 5 The Sun emits light in a continuous spectrum, but atoms in its cooler atmosphere absorb specific wavelengths of light, leaving dark absorption lines.

Identifying Elements in a Star

When light from a star is passed through a spectroscope, astronomers see dark absorption lines that are produced as light passes through the star's cooler, less dense atmosphere. Each **element** contributes its own set of absorption lines to this absorption spectrum, such as those shown in **Figure 5.** When many elements are present, an absorption spectrum has many lines. However, astronomers know the pattern of lines each element produces. As a result, from an absorption spectrum they can determine which elements are present in a star's outer layers. The pattern of these absorption lines is like a fingerprint that identifies the elements in the star's outer layers.

 **Reading Check** Why do stars produce absorption spectra?

Astronomers have found that most stars are composed mainly of hydrogen and a smaller amount of helium. In fact, helium was first discovered in stars before it was found on Earth. Stars contain much smaller amounts of other chemical elements, such as carbon, nitrogen, and oxygen.

Temperature and Color of Stars

Have you ever watched a piece of metal being heated in a hot fire? As the metal gets hotter, its color changes. First it glows red, then it becomes yellow, and when it is extremely hot it may appear white. Just as the color of the metal depends on its temperature, the color of a star also depends on its temperature. You might be able to see colors in some stars. For example, Sirius [SIHR ee us], one of the brightest stars in the sky, is white. Betelgeuse [BET el jooz], a bright star in the constellation Orion [oh RYE un], is reddish. Some stars have an orange or a yellow tint.

ACADEMIC VOCABULARY
element (EH leh mehnt)
(noun) fundamental substance consisting of only one kind of atom
The element helium is produced by fusion in the Sun's core.

WORD ORIGIN
spectrum, (plural, spectra) spectroscope
spectrum– from Latin *specere;* means *to look at, view*
–scope from Greek *skoion;* meaning *means (or instrument) for viewing*

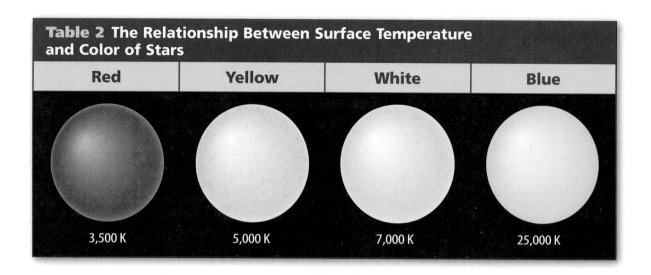

Table 2 The Relationship Between Surface Temperature and Color of Stars

Red	Yellow	White	Blue
3,500 K	5,000 K	7,000 K	25,000 K

Temperature and Wavelengths Emitted

Every object emits energy in the form of electromagnetic radiation. The wavelength of the radiation emitted depends upon the temperature of the object. Objects at human body temperature emit mainly long, infrared waves. As temperature rises, however, the wavelengths of the emitted radiation become shorter. Recall that a heated metal object turns red and then yellow. The reason for this is that the wavelength of yellow light is shorter than that of red light.

Likewise, the wavelengths of light emitted by a star depend on the star's temperature. This means that yellow stars are hotter than red stars. The hottest stars appear bluish because blue light has an even shorter wavelength. **Table 2** gives the surface temperature for different color stars. Note that the Sun's temperature makes it appear yellowish.

The Brightness of Stars

Why are some stars brighter than others? The brightness of a star is due to two things. One is the amount of energy the star emits. The other is the star's distance from Earth. All stars, except the Sun, are so far away that they look like tiny points of light in the night sky.

Brightness and Distance

The headlights of a distant car at night might seem like tiny points of light when the car is far away. But as the car gets closer, the headlights appear brighter. The brightness of a source of light, such as a headlight, depends on how far away it is. As **Figure 6** shows, a light source looks brighter when it is closer to you. The same is true for stars. The closer a star is, the brighter it looks.

Figure 6 All these street lamps are of equal brightness, but those closer appear brighter.

Luminosity

One lightbulb in **Figure 7** appears brighter than the other. This brightness is called luminosity. **Luminosity** is the amount of light energy emitted per second. Energy is expressed in joules. One joule per second is called a watt. The brighter lightbulb in **Figure 7** emits 100 watts of energy, compared to 30 watts for the other bulb. The 100-W bulb has a higher luminosity because it emits more energy each second. Stars have different luminosities too—some emit more energy than others.

Apparent Magnitude

Luminosity is only partly responsible for how bright a star appears from Earth. If a very luminous star is far enough away, it appears dim. **Apparent magnitude** is the observed luminosity of a celestial body, such as a star, as observed from Earth. The apparent magnitude of a star depends on luminosity and distance. The smaller the magnitude number, the brighter the star.

A star of magnitude 1 is brighter than one of magnitude 2 but not just twice as bright. Each unit of magnitude is brighter by a factor of 2.5. A star of magnitude 1.0 appears 2.5 times as bright as a star of magnitude 2.0. Thus, a star of magnitude 1.0 appears about 100 times brighter than a star of magnitude 6.0. The faintest objects visible to the unaided eye have an apparent magnitude of about +6. A bright, full moon has a magnitude of about −12.6.

Absolute Magnitude

A better way to compare the brightness of stars is to calculate their absolute magnitudes. **Absolute magnitude** is the apparent magnitude a star would have if it were 32.6 ly away from Earth. **Table 3** compares the apparent and absolute magnitudes of several stars with those of the Sun.

 Table 3 Based on absolute magnitude, how much brighter than the Sun is Antares?

Figure 7 These bulbs are at the same distance, but one appears brighter because it emits more energy per second. The 100-watt light bulb emits 100 joules per second, compared to 30 joules per second for the other bulb.

Table 3 Apparent and Absolute Magnitudes of Stars			
Star	**Distance (light-years)**	**Apparent Magnitude**	**Absolute Magnitude**
Sun	0.0	−26.7	5.0
Sirius	8.7	−1.5	1.4
Canopus	98.0	−0.7	−0.3
Antares	520	0.9	−5.1

Concepts In Motion
Interactive Table To organize information abou
Orion's stars, visit Tables at ca8.msscience.com

Table 4 Four Major Stars in the Constellation of Orion

Star	Apparent Magnitude	Distance (ly)	Absolute Magnitude
Betelgeuse	0.45	427	−7.2
Bellatrix	1.64	243	−4.2
Saiph	2.07	720	−4.66
Rigel	0.18	773	−8.1

Looking at Stars

Although some stars might appear close or far to the unaided human eye, analysis of starlight might yield different information. **Table 4** lists and shows four major stars that make up the constellation of Orion. Even though the stars might look similar to your eye, they are all very different. What can you learn about these stars from their data? Recall that a smaller magnitude means brighter.

Although Bellatrix is the closest of these stars to Earth, Betelgeuse and Rigel appear brighter. This is because Betelgeuse, a red supergiant, and Rigel, a blue supergiant, have much greater luminosities and therefore, smaller absolute magnitudes.

Classifying Stars—The H-R Diagram

Early in the twentieth century, two astronomers independently developed diagrams of how absolute magnitude, or luminosity, is related to the temperature of stars. Hertzsprung and Russell found that stars fell into certain regions of the diagram. About 90 percent of stars seemed to fall on a roughly diagonal, curved line, called the main sequence. **Figure 8** shows a Hertzsprung-Russell (H-R) diagram.

The Sun, like 90 percent of all stars, is a main sequence star. The rest of the stars seem to fall into three regions of the diagram based on luminosity and temperature. Two of these star groupings lie above the main sequence line. The group closest to the main sequence has large-diameter stars with lower temperatures. They are called red giants. The stars in the group at the top of an H-R diagram are very large and have varying temperatures. They are known as supergiants. The third group, which lies below the main sequence, includes the white dwarfs. These are very hot stars and have small diameters relative to most main sequence stars.

Figure 8 On which end of the y-axis—top or bottom—are stars the brightest? On which end of the x-axis—left or right—are stars the hottest?

SCIENCE USE v. COMMON USE
magnitude
Science Use brightness of a star. *The Sun has a smaller apparent magnitude than Antares and appears brighter.*
Common Use great size or extent. *The magnitude of the incident eventually led to sweeping social changes.*

Figure 8 The H-R diagram indicates the temperature and luminosity of stars, but does not indicate their frequency. In fact, supergiant stars at the top right of the diagram are very rare with fewer than one star in 10,000 fitting this category.

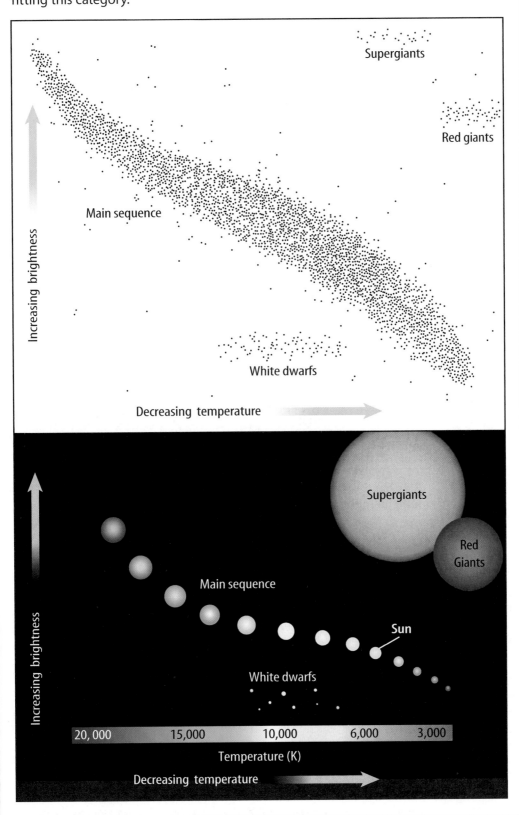

Understanding Variations Among Stars

Stars are the source of all light in the universe. The amount of light a star emits per second is known as its luminosity. This light is emitted as a continuous spectrum, although some wavelengths are absorbed by elements in a star's atmosphere, producing dark lines on its spectrum. The color of a star is related to its temperature; hotter stars tend to be blue while cooler stars are yellow or red. The distance between stars is so great that it is measured by how many years it takes light to travel between them. How bright a star appears in the night sky depends both upon its luminosity and its distance from Earth. Astronomers compare the brightness of stars using a scale, called absolute magnitude, which eliminates differences caused by distance.

LESSON 1 Review

Summarize

Create your own lesson summary as you write a **newsletter.**

1. **Write** this lesson title, number, and page numbers at the top of a sheet of paper.

2. **Review** the text after the **red** main headings and write one sentence about each. These will be the headlines of your newsletter.

3. **Review** the text and write 2–3 sentences about each **blue** subheading. These sentences should tell *who, what, when, where,* and *why* information about each headline.

4. **Illustrate** your newsletter with diagrams of important structures and processes next to each headline.

Standards Check

Using Vocabulary

1. **Distinguish** between apparent magnitude and absolute magnitude. **4.d**

2. In your own words, define *luminosity.* **4.d**

Understanding Main Ideas

3. **Identify** the two most common elements found in stars. **4.b**

4. **Explain** how a spectroscope is used to identify the elements in a star. **4.b**

5. **Recognize** Copy and fill in the graphic organizer below to describe the factors that affect a star's apparent brightness. **4.d**

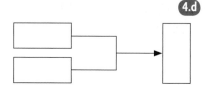

6. **Compare** the surface temperature of a red star with the temperature of a yellow star. **4.b**

7. **Identify** which is brighter, a second-magnitude star or a third-magnitude star. **4.b**

8. **Explain** Which type of stars are found at the bottom left of the H-R diagram? **4.b**

   A. Main sequence stars
   B. Red giants
   C. Supergiants
   D. White dwarfs

Applying Science

9. **Plan** how to determine the composition of a new star that is located outside our solar system and inside our galaxy. **4.b**

10. **Decide** whether a newly observed object that emits visible light is a planet or a star. What information would you like to gather? **4.d**

Science nline

For more practice, visit **Standards Check** at ca8.msscience.com.

00:25 minutes

Try at Home

Can you identify elements in a star?

Astronomers study the composition of stars by observing their absorption spectra. Each element in a star's outer layers produce a set of lines in the star's absorption spectrum. From the pattern of lines, astronomers can determine what elements are in a star. You will examine the spectra patterns of four elements and use the information to interpret the elements present in the Sun and in a mystery star.

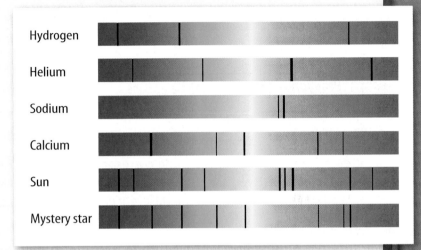

Hydrogen

Helium

Sodium

Calcium

Sun

Mystery star

Procedure

1. Study the spectra for the four elements.

2. Examine the spectra for the Sun and the mystery star.

3. Use a **ruler** to help you line up the spectral lines.

4. Compare the spectral pattern of the known elements to those of the Sun and the mystery star.

Analysis

1. **Identify** Which elements are present in the part of the absorption spectrum shown for the Sun?

2. **Identify** Which elements are present in the absorption spectrum shown for the mystery star?

 ## Science Content Standards

4.d Students know that stars are the source of light for all bright objects in outer space and that the Moon and planets shine by reflected sunlight, not by their own light.

Applying Math

Brightness of Stars

4.b, 4.d, 1.d

MA8: ALG 2.0

The apparent magnitude of a star is a measure of how bright a star appears in the sky. As the stars appear brighter, their magnitudes become smaller. Use the following table of apparent magnitudes of stars to determine how much brighter one star is than another.

Star	Apparent Magnitude
Vega	0.03
Capella	0.08
Procyon	0.38
Achernar	0.46
Acrux	0.76

If each 1-unit change in magnitude corresponds to a brightness change by a factor of 2.5, you can use the expression 2.5^x to find the change in magnitude of the star if x is the difference in the apparent magnitudes.

Example

How much brighter is Vega than Acrux? Recall that the smaller the apparent magnitude, the brighter the star appears.

Use this equation:

Difference in brightness = 2.5^x
Where x = larger apparent magnitude value − smaller apparent magnitude value

Solve for x:

larger apparent magnitude (Acrux) − smaller apparent magnitude (Vega) = $0.76 - 0.03$ or 0.73.

Substitute x Into the Equation:

$2.5^{0.73} = 1.95$
Use your calculator to solve.

Answer: Vega is nearly two times brighter than Acrux.

Practice Problems

1. Which star is brighter, Capella or Acrux? By how many times brighter is one star than the other?

2. How much brighter is Vega than Achernar?

Science nline
For more math practice, visit Math Practice at ca8.msscience.com.

Science Content Standards

2.g Students know the role of gravity in forming and maintaining the shapes of planets, stars, and the solar system.

4.d Students know that stars are the source of light for all bright objects in outer space and that the Moon and planets shine by reflected sunlight, not by their own light.

Reading Guide

What *You'll Learn*

▶ **Describe** how gravity causes a star to form.

▶ **Explain** how stars produce light.

▶ **Describe** what happens to a star when fusion stops.

Why *It's Important*

Learning how stars form, produce energy, and eventually die gives you a sense of the dynamic nature of the universe.

Vocabulary

nebula
nuclear fusion
red giant
white dwarf
supernova
neutron star
black hole

Review Vocabulary

pressure: force exerted per unit area (p. 141)

How Stars Shine

Main Idea Stars generate light from energy released in nuclear fusion.

Real-World Reading Connection Have you ever wondered how the Sun and other stars generate light? Perhaps you have heard of exploding stars, known as supernovas. How are stars formed? What determines a star's lifetime?

How Stars Form

Initially, the universe consisted of light elements such as hydrogen, helium, and a smaller amount of lithium. These elements were produced in the big bang, or origin of the universe. Stars are formed in a **nebula,** which is a large cloud of gas and dust in space. Nebulae are also known as interstellar clouds and can be millions of light-years across.

Matter in a Nebula

The space between stars is called interstellar space. Interstellar space contains mostly gas and dust. The density of matter is so low in interstellar space that there is only one atom per cubic centimeter. In a nebula, the density of gas and dust is hundreds of times higher. In some regions of a nebula, dust particles are close enough to form dust clouds. These dust clouds can be dense enough to block the light emitted by nearby stars, as shown in **Figure 9.**

Figure 9 Dust and gas in an interstellar cloud completely block the stars in the center of this photo. Because this gas includes high concentrations of molecules, it is called a molecular cloud.

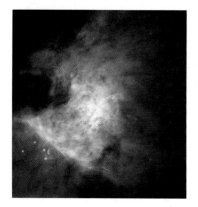
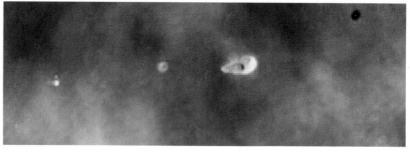

Figure 10 The enlarged blow-out shows a proplyd—an abbreviation for *protoplanetary disk*—found in the Orion Nebula.

MiniLab

00:30 minutes

Modeling the Size of Nebulae

Nebulae can be huge. The Orion Nebula, for example, is 30 LY across. A light-year equals about 63,241 AU. Because Neptune is about 30 AU from the Sun, the diameter of Neptune's orbit is about 1/1,000 of a light-year.

Procedure

1. Use a scale of 1 mm = diameter of Neptune's orbit.

2. Research the sizes of several nebulae.

3. Use a gymnasium or open field to model your nebulae.

Analysis

1. **Describe** Based on your scale, how large was a light year?

2. **Explain** How large would your nebula be if the scale used was 1 cm – the diameter of Neptune's orbit?

4.c

Try at Home

Components of Nebulae

The dust in nebulae is not like house dust. It is made up of much smaller particles, and might include clumps of carbon and silicate molecules. Hydrogen and helium are the most common gases in nebulae. However, some nebulae contain small quantities of gaseous molecules, and so these are called molecular clouds. One of these is shown in **Figure 9** on the previous page.

If the molecules in a nebula block light from stars contained within it, the nebula is called an absorption nebula. If the nebula's molecules become excited by energy from the stars within it, they emit their own light. These are called emission nebulae.

Contraction and Heating

The gravitational force between particles can cause clumps of matter to form in a nebula. Each particle in the clump exerts an attractive force on all the other particles. Even though this force is very weak, it causes the atoms in the clump to move closer together toward the center. As the particles move closer together, they move faster. Because the particles in the clump of matter are moving faster, the temperature of the matter increases. This means that as the clump of matter contracts, it heats up.

Protostars

As the clump contracts, it becomes spherical. When the mass of the clump of matter reaches a few percent of one solar mass, it is called a protostar. As the protostar continues to contract, its temperature continues to increase. Higher temperatures mean that particles move faster and the sphere begins to rotate. Then, it flattens into a disk that is denser and hotter at the center, such as the disk shown in **Figure 10.** After millions of years, the temperature in the center of the protostar becomes hot enough for nuclear fusion to occur. When the central mass reaches 8 percent that of the Sun, fusion begins and a new star is born. **Figure 11** shows the process of star formation.

Visualizing the Formation of Stars

Figure 11

Stars form in clouds of dust and gas where the density of matter is hundreds of times higher than in interstellar space. In some parts of these clouds, dust and gas have clumped together to become even more dense.

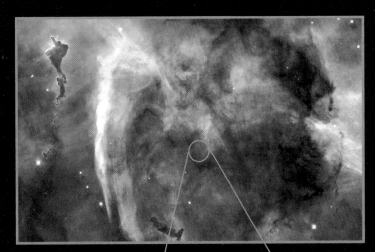

The attractive force of gravity causes the particles in the clump to move closer together. As the particles move closer together, they move faster, and the temperature of the matter increases.

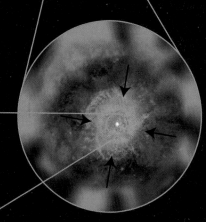

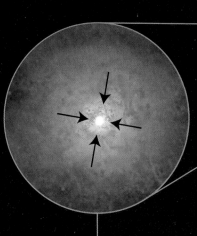

As the clump contracts even more, it begins to take the shape of a sphere. The matter continues to become hotter as the clump continues to contract. The spherical mass begins to spin and becomes a disk that is hottest in the center.

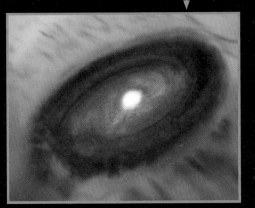

Finally the temperature at the center of the disk becomes hot enough for nuclear fusion to occur. Then a new star begins to glow. The material in the outer part of the disk can contract and possibly form planets, asteroids, and comets.

Contributed by National Geographic

How Stars Produce Light

Stars emit enormous amounts of energy, part of which is seen as visible light. When the temperature in the core of a protostar becomes high enough, a process called nuclear fusion occurs. Energy released during fusion passes through the star and is emitted from its photosphere.

Nuclear Fusion

In a **nuclear fusion** reaction, two atomic nuclei combine to form a larger nucleus with a higher mass. The energy from the Sun and other stars that can be seen as visible light is caused by nuclear fusion reactions that occur deep inside the stars' hot cores. This energy flows from the interior to the exterior of the star, where it is radiated into space. Most of the energy emitted into space by the Sun is in the form of visible light and infrared radiation.

Figure 12 shows the nuclear reactions in a star's core that change hydrogen nuclei into helium nuclei and release energy. Recall that isotopes of an element have the same number of protons, but different numbers of neutrons. The nuclear reactions shown in **Figure 12** involve isotopes of hydrogen and helium.

Figure 12 This three-step fusion reaction is one way energy is produced in the cores of stars.

Infer In what form is most of the energy released during fusion in the Sun's core?

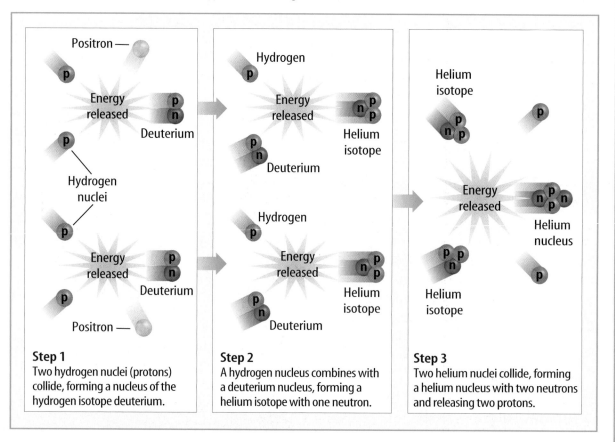

Step 1
Two hydrogen nuclei (protons) collide, forming a nucleus of the hydrogen isotope deuterium.

Step 2
A hydrogen nucleus combines with a deuterium nucleus, forming a helium isotope with one neutron.

Step 3
Two helium nuclei collide, forming a helium nucleus with two neutrons and releasing two protons.

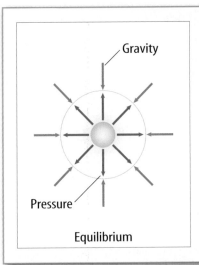

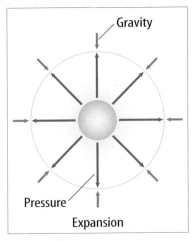

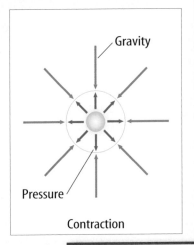

Equilibrium

Expansion

Contraction

Figure 13 As long as the inward pressure from gravity is balanced by the outward pressure of fusion, a star remains stable.

The Balance Between Pressure and Gravity

There are two major forces at play in stars. Fusion reactions produce an outward pressure, which tends to push the matter in a star outward. However, the attractive gravitational force between all particles in a star pulls these particles inward toward each other. The force of gravity tends to make the star contract. As the fusion reactions occur, the outward pressure becomes large enough to balance the inward pull of gravity. When these two opposing forces balance each other, the star stops contracting.

 **Reading Check** State what forces determine whether a star expands or contracts.

Expansion and Contraction

As seen in **Figure 13,** a star will begin to expand if its rate of fusion increases. This is because the force produced by nuclear fusion within the star is greater than the force of gravity. **Figure 13** also shows how a star contracts if its rate of fusion decreases. As the rate of fusion decreases, the force exerted by fusion from within the star also decreases. This means gravity can begin to pull matter back toward the star's core.

How Stars Come to an End

As fusion continues in a star's core, the star eventually converts all its hydrogen into helium. In stars with masses about the same or greater than that of the Sun, nuclear fusion will convert helium into carbon, nitrogen, and oxygen. In very massive stars, fusion reactions involving these elements form even heavier elements. When fusion stops, there is no longer any force balancing the inward pull of gravity and a star will continue to contract. Depending on the initial mass of the star, the result could be a white dwarf, a supernova, a neutron star, or a black hole.

ACADEMIC VOCABULARY

contract (kahn TRAKT)
(verb) to draw together, to reduce to a smaller size. *The engineers calculated how much the metal would contract when cooled.*

The Life Cycle of Low-Mass Stars

When a low-mass star runs out of hydrogen to fuse into helium, gravity can make its core **contract** rapidly. This is followed by an expansion to a red giant stage. Finally, the star contracts again to a white dwarf stage. This process is illustrated in **Figure 14** below.

Red Giants When Sun-sized (about one to eight solar masses) stars use up their fuel, they become **red giants.** When the hydrogen in the core is converted to helium, the core contracts rapidly. This rapid contraction is often called a collapse. The temperature rises and hydrogen fusion begins outside the core. Carbon, oxygen, and other elements may be produced in the helium core during this next fusion stage. Fusion causes expansion, and this results in cooling. The cooler star emits reddish light—it is now a red giant.

White Dwarfs Red-giant stars lose mass from their surfaces, until eventually only the core remains. Because fusion in the core has ceased, gravity causes it to contract until it is about the size of Earth. Such stars are known as white dwarfs. A **white dwarf** is the small, dense core of a giant star that remains after the star has lost its exterior matter. Some are so hot that they emit blue light. The Sun will become a dwarf star in billions of years.

The Life Cycle of High-Mass Stars

High-mass stars begin the end of their life cycle much like low-mass stars do. Their greater mass, however, means that the collapsed core can continue to fuse nuclei into heavier and heavier elements until the element iron is formed.

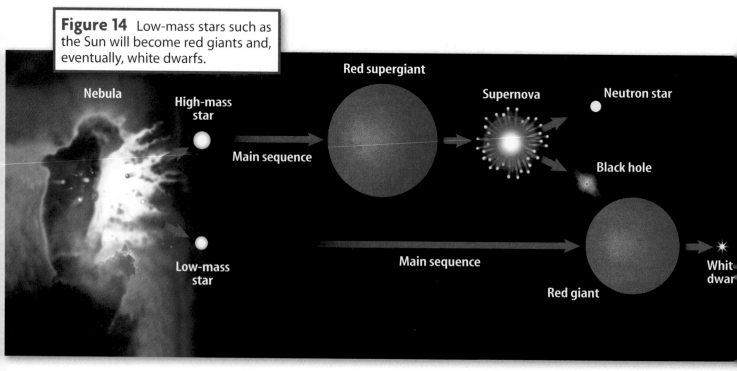

Figure 14 Low-mass stars such as the Sun will become red giants and, eventually, white dwarfs.

Supernova

A supergiant star can explode before it dies. When a supergiant star explodes before dying, it is called a **supernova.** The debris of a great supernova explosion still is visible as an interstellar cloud, known as the Crab Nebula, shown in **Figure 15.** Chinese astronomers observed this explosion in 1054. Supergiants are stars with initial masses greater than ten solar masses. They develop like red giants at first. However, fusion reactions continue to make elements heavier than oxygen.

Fusion Rates Increase The formation of each heavier element involves a cycle of expansion and contraction, and these cycles take place at an ever increasing rate. For example, a very massive star might burn carbon for 1,000 years, oxygen for one year, and silicon for a week. When iron is made, the star has less than a day to live.

Fusion Stops At this point, the fusion process stops, because the iron nucleus does not undergo nuclear fusion reactions. Iron accumulates in the star's core and gravity compresses it producing temperatures of several billion K. Finally, as shown in **Figure 16,** the core collapses in on itself, releasing a huge amount of energy. This explosive collapse is called a supernova. So much energy is released in this explosion that the star brightens greatly, making it suddenly visible from Earth. It appears to be a new star.

An important feature of this supernova explosion is that its force blasts apart the star's outer layers dispersing all the heavy elements in its outer layers throughout space. Eventually, these elements become part of new stars, like our Sun. This is how the heavier elements found on Earth and in our bodies were created.

 Distinguish between a star and a supernova.

Figure 15 The crab nebula was produced by a supernova explosion in A.D. 1054.

Figure 16 The formation of iron in the core of a star triggers a supernova explosion.

Core collapses

Infalling material

Core (neutron star)

Infalling material rebounds.

Shockwaves

Core

Material explodes outward.

Neutron Stars

A **neutron star** is a star composed mainly of neutrons. Neutron stars are what remain of stars after supernova explosions. A neutron star is very small. It is about as large as a city. Because so much matter is packed into a small volume, it is very dense—so dense that one teaspoon would weigh billions of kilograms. Neutron stars form from the cores of supergiant stars after the iron core stage. The pressures in these massive stars is great enough to fuse protons and electrons, forming neutrons.

The term *neutron star* is misleading, however, because these objects are not stars, according to the definition you have learned. They do not shine as stars do. However, they can be detected. Two properties make this possible: they rotate rapidly and have strong magnetic fields. This results in pulses of radiation, usually in the radio portion of the electromagnetic spectrum. Some pulsars radiate in the visible, X-ray, and gamma-ray regions too. Such pulsating neutron stars are termed pulsars.

Black Holes

If a neutron star has an original mass between 10 and 1,000,000 times that of the Sun, contraction will continue. The neutron star contracts until its mass is concentrated into a single point called a black hole. A **black hole** is a region of space from which no matter or radiation can escape.

Because light cannot escape from black holes, they usually cannot be seen directly. However, black holes can be detected when they are located near some other object in space. Often a black hole passes through a cloud of interstellar matter, or is located close to another "normal" star. This allows the black hole to draw matter from such objects into itself, as illustrated in **Figure 17.**

Reading Check How can you "see" black holes if they do not emit light?

Figure 17 Matter falling into a black hole emits high-energy radiation. The black hole itself often emits jets of matter and energy at nearly light speed.

Companion star

Radiation

Black hole

Star Evolution

Stars form when gravity causes matter in a nebula or an interstellar cloud to clump together. Then it contracts, causing temperature and pressure at the center to increase, and the clump becomes spherical and begins to rotate. Once enough matter accumulates, the temperature becomes high enough to trigger nuclear fusion, and becomes a star. Stars release much of their energy in the form of light. Eventually, stars run out of elements to fuel the fusion reaction. Smaller stars, like the Sun, become red giant stars and then white dwarfs. More massive stars undergo periods of expansion and contraction until iron accumulates in their cores. Iron resists further fusion, and these stars collapse in supernova explosions. The core remaining after such an explosion may form a neutron star or a black hole. Supernova explosions release sufficient energy to produce heavier elements, which are dispersed throughout space and can be incorporated in new stars.

LESSON 2 Review

Summarize

Create your own lesson summary as you write a script for a **television news report.**

1. **Review** the text after the **red** main headings and write one sentence about each. These are the headlines of your broadcast.

2. **Review** the text and write 2–3 sentences about each **blue** subheading. These sentences should tell *who, what, when, where,* and *why* information about each **red** heading.

3. **Include** descriptive details in your report, such as names of reporters and local places and events.

4. **Present** your news report to other classmates alone or with a team.

 ELA8: LS 2.1

Standards Check

Using Vocabulary

1. In your own words, define *nebula.* **4.a**

Complete the sentences using the correct term.

2. The Sun will eventually become a(n) _____. **4.a**

3. Protons and electrons are compressed in a(n) _____. **4.a**

Understanding Main Ideas

4. **Compare and contrast** neutron stars and black holes. **4.a**

5. **Explain** how elements heavier than iron are formed. **4.a**

6. **Describe** what a supernova explosion might look like if visible from Earth. **4.a**

7. **Describe** what happens to a star when it uses up its fuel. **4.a**

8. **Sequence** Draw a diagram showing how a star forms within a nebula. **2.g**

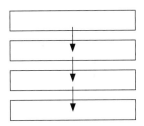

Applying Science

9. **Predict** the fate of a star that has used up its fuel and has a mass twice that of the Sun. **4.a**

10. **Compare** how gravity and nuclear fusion affect a star's size. **4.a, 2.g**

For more practice, visit **Standards Check** at ca8.msscience.com.

Science Content Standards

4.a Students know galaxies are clusters of billions of stars and may have different shapes.
4.b Students know that the Sun is one of many stars in the Milky Way galaxy and that stars may differ in size, temperature, and color.
4.c Students know how to use astronomical units and light years as measures of distance between the Sun, stars, and Earth.
9.d Recognize the slope of the linear graph as the constant in the relationship $y = kx$ and apply this principle in interpreting graphs constructed from data.

Reading Guide

What *You'll Learn*

▶ **Describe** how gravity causes stars to form galaxies.

▶ **Compare** the different types of galaxies.

▶ **Determine** the Sun's location in the Milky Way galaxy.

Why *It's Important*

Studying galaxies allows us to comprehend the size of the universe and our place in it.

Vocabulary

galaxy
big bang theory

Review Vocabulary

ellipse: an oval

Galaxies

Main Idea Gravitational attraction causes stars to group together into galaxies.

Real-World Reading Connection Maybe you have seen a picture of a galaxy. If you have seen the bright band of stars that span a dark sky, then you have seen part of a galaxy. It is the Milky Way galaxy, where our solar system is.

Stars Cluster in Galaxies

Some of the fuzzy points of light in the sky that originally were thought to be stars or nebulae now are known to be distant galaxies. Stars are not uniformly distributed throughout the universe but are unevenly clustered into groups. Massive systems of stars, dust, and gas held together by gravity are called **galaxies.** Within galaxies are smaller groups of stars known as star clusters. One of these star clusters is shown in **Figure 18.**

Gravity is the fundamental force responsible for the formation and motion of stars. It also causes stars to group together into galaxies. Some galaxies contain billions of stars. The gravitational forces between stars and other types of matter hold the enormous numbers of stars together in a galaxy.

Figure 18 This cluster, known as M13, is within our galaxy and can be viewed using binoculars. Although it appears to the unaided eye as one fuzzy star, it is over 100,000 stars.
Infer What force caused these stars to cluster into a sphere?

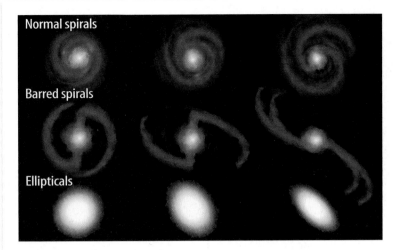

Normal spirals

Barred spirals

Ellipticals

Figure 19 Barred spiral galaxies differ from spiral galaxies only by the barred pattern of dust, gas, and stars over their centers. Elliptical galaxies are completely different in structure and range from spheres to ellipsoids.

Types of Galaxies

Galaxies can have different sizes and different shapes. The most common shapes are spiral, elliptical, and irregular, as shown in **Figure 19.** Spiral galaxies tend to be more luminous than elliptical galaxies.

Spiral Galaxies

There are two kinds of spiral galaxies: regular and barred. For both types, when seen from a top view, spiral arms can be seen. They have three components, as shown in **Figure 20.** These are the nucleus (or central bulge), the spiral arms, and the halo. The spiral arms contain star-forming regions. They are outlined by young blue stars. The halo is relatively free of dust and gas, and contains mostly old star clusters. Viewed on edge, spiral galaxies are relatively flat with a central bulge. Some spiral galaxies contain a bar of stars, dust, and gas that passes through the center of the galaxy. These are called barred spirals.

WORD ORIGIN

galaxy

galax– from Greek *galaxis;* means *milky.* (The first known galaxy was the Milky Way.)

Figure 20 Viewed edge-on, a spiral galaxy like the Sombrero reveals the nuclear bulge of stars at its center, but the disk appears as straight lines to the sides. To see the spiral structure, you must view such a galaxy from above.

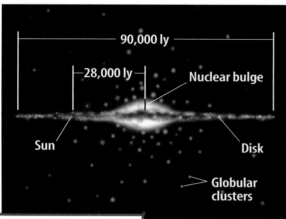

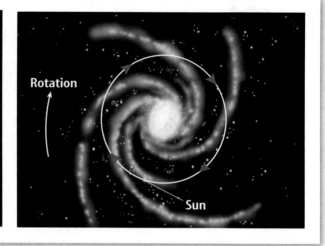

Figure 21 Our solar system is located 28,000 ly from the center of the Milky Way and takes about 240 million years to complete one orbit. From above you can see that it lies within one of the spiral arms.

The Milky Way Galaxy—Our Sun's Home

The Sun is one of billions of stars in the Milky Way galaxy—a typical spiral galaxy. The Milky Way is 90,000 light-years in diameter. All the stars we can see from Earth without a telescope are located in the Milky Way. The bright band of stars cutting across the night sky is the Milky Way as seen from Earth. **Figure 21** shows the location of the solar system in the Milky Way galaxy. Earth lies within the disk of the galaxy. The Sun is located about mid way from the center of the Milky Way and orbits the galactic center. In similar spiral galaxies, this galactic center appears as a bulge of stars in the heart of the disk.

Elliptical and Irregular Galaxies

Elliptical galaxies have an oval shape. They vary greatly in size and numbers of stars. Old, reddish stars tend to populate elliptical galaxies. They contain little interstellar gas or dust. There are no spiral arms. Irregular galaxies include all those that are neither elliptical nor spiral. They have a patchy appearance and are difficult to classify. Examples of elliptical and irregular galaxies are shown in **Figure 22.**

 How do the three types of galaxies differ?

Figure 22 The elliptical galaxy shown on the left has a strongly defined spherical shape compared to that of the irregular galaxy shown on the right.

Elliptical Galaxy

Irregular Galaxy

Figure 23 The Andromeda galaxy shown here resembles the Milky Way galaxy both in size and shape.

The Distances Between Galaxies

Galaxies are so far away that, to the unaided eye, even the closest ones appear as faint, fuzzy patches of light. Recall that the distance between stars usually is expressed in terms of light-years. One light year is 9.5 trillion km, which is the distance light travels in one year. The closest galaxy to Earth is about one million light-years away. The Andromeda galaxy in **Figure 23** is about two million light-years away. This means that light from the Andromeda galaxy takes two million years to reach Earth. When you look at **Figure 23,** you are seeing the Andromeda galaxy as it was two million years ago.

The Local Group

Galaxies are not scattered **randomly** throughout the universe. They group together in clusters, which are parts of larger groupings called superclusters. Gravity causes galactic clusters to form. There is a lot of almost empty space between those clusters called voids. Our galaxy is part of a cluster of galaxies called the Local Group. **Figure 24** shows the galaxies that are part of the Local Group.

ACADEMIC VOCABULARY
randomly (RAN dom lee)
(*adverb*) lacking a definite plan or pattern
The data points were distributed randomly over the graph, so no trend was obvious.

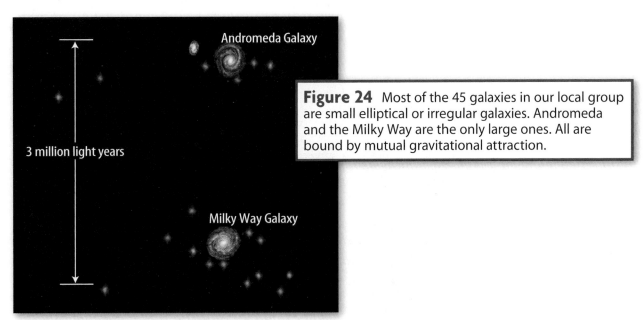

3 million light years

Andromeda Galaxy

Milky Way Galaxy

Figure 24 Most of the 45 galaxies in our local group are small elliptical or irregular galaxies. Andromeda and the Milky Way are the only large ones. All are bound by mutual gravitational attraction.

Figure 25 The Milky Way galaxy is moving toward the Virgo cluster shown here.

Superclusters

Looking beyond our Local Group, there are other groups of galaxies, some very large and in the shape of ribbons or clumps. We belong to the Virgo supercluster with thousands of galaxies spread across 100 million light-years. Part of the Virgo supercluster is shown in **Figure 25.**

The farthest galaxies from Earth are about 14 billion light-years away. Looking at those galaxies shows the universe as it was 14 billion years ago. **Figure 26** gives some idea of the large number of galaxies that are seen in a small region of the sky.

 In what supercluster is the Milky Way located?

The Big Bang Theory

In the late 1920s, the astronomer Edwin Hubble discovered that most of the galaxies he observed were moving away from Earth. He found that the farther away a galaxy was from Earth, the faster it was moving. Hubble's discovery could be explained only if the entire universe was expanding. Then galaxies would be moving away from each other with a speed that increased as they got farther apart.

Figure 26 This *Hubble* telescope image of a tiny area of the sky shows at least 1,500 galaxies in various stages of evolution. Some appear as they were about 10 billion years ago.

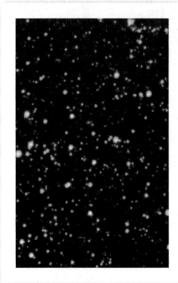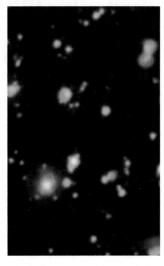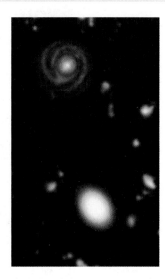

Figure 27 Milestones in galaxy formation after the big bang: at one second, formation of protons, electrons, and neutrons; after three minutes, formation of nuclei of He, Li, D, Be; at 300,000 years, atoms form.

The Expanding Universe and the Big Bang

According to the **big bang theory,** this expansion of the universe began about 14 billion years ago. At that time, the universe was the size of a tiny point. This point contained all the matter and energy in the universe and was extremely hot. Then the universe began to expand rapidly, and as it grew, it began to cool.

For several hundred thousand years, the universe was too hot for elements to form from subatomic particles. So the universe consisted of a mix of radiation and subatomic particles. As the universe continued to expand, it cooled, and hydrogen and helium atoms began to form.

The Formation of Galaxies

Galaxies began forming several hundred million years after the big bang. Astronomers do not completely understand how galaxies formed. One hypothesis is that as space expanded, clouds of hydrogen and helium in some regions of space became more dense than in other regions. The matter in these denser regions began to clump together due to the pull of gravity. In these regions stars began to form. As more stars continued to form, gravity gradually pulled them together to form galaxies, as illustrated in **Figure 27.**

Dark Matter and Dark Energy

Based on the way galaxies rotate and move through space, astronomers can calculate how much mass it should contain. However, when they add up all the matter they can detect, they find that it does not equal the needed amount. They call this missing matter *dark matter.*

Similarly, additional energy is needed to explain the fact that the expansion of the universe is accelerating. They call this missing energy *dark energy.*

Evolution of the Universe

Stars are not distributed evenly through space, but grouped in large units called galaxies that are millions of light-years apart and contain billions of stars. Within galaxies are clumps of stars known as star clusters that contain from a dozen to a million stars. Galaxies themselves are grouped in clusters. Galaxies are divided into three types: spiral, elliptical, and irregular. The Milky Way galaxy is a spiral type and our solar system is about halfway between the center and the edge on one arm of the spiral. Galaxies are moving apart from each other, and those farthest from us are moving the fastest. According to the big bang theory, all the matter and energy in the universe was the size of a tiny point about 14 billion years ago. Then it expanded rapidly and cooled. Radiation and subatomic particles formed as it expanded followed by atoms, and eventually stars and galaxies.

LESSON 3 Review

Summarize

Create your own lesson summary as you design a **study web**.

1. **Write** the lesson title, number, and page numbers at the top of a sheet of paper.

2. **Scan** the lesson to find the **red** main headings.

3. **Organize** these headings clockwise on branches around the lesson title.

4. **Review** the information under each **red** heading to design a branch for each **blue** subheading.

5. **List** 2–3 details, key terms, and definitions from each **blue** subheading on branches extending from the main heading branches.

ELA8: R 2.3

Standards Check

Using Vocabulary

1. **Distinguish** between the terms *spiral galaxy* and *irregular galaxy*. `4.a`

2. **Describe** what is meant by the term *big bang theory*. `4.a`

Understanding Main Ideas

3. **Organize** Copy and complete the diagram below with steps describing the formation of the universe, starting with the big bang. Add steps as needed. `2.g, 4.a`

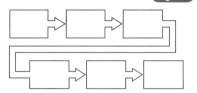

4. **Infer** why only a few galaxies can be seen without a telescope. `4.a`

5. **Show** in a drawing where stars are likely to form in a spiral galaxy. `4.b`

6. **Compare** the rates at which distant galaxies move away from Earth with the rates at which closer galaxies move away. `4.a`

Applying Science

7. **Evaluate** how long it would take a light beam to go across a galaxy 50,000 light-years in diameter and return. `4.c`

8. **Predict** which galaxy a star is in if it is 100 light-years from our Sun. `4.c`

Science Online

For more practice, visit **Standards Check** at ca8.msscience.com.

DataLab

00:45 minutes

How fast is the universe expanding?

The distances between galaxies are large and are measured in megaparsecs. A megaparsec (Mpc) is about 3,260,000 light-years or 9.5 trillion km. Scientists measure how fast galaxies are moving away from Earth by measuring the light they emit. Similar to how the sound of a train changes when it is moving toward or away from you, the wavelength of light gets shorter or longer when it is moving toward or away from Earth. The table shows the speeds and distances from Earth of 12 galaxies.

Analysis

1. Plot distance on the *x*-axis and speed on the *y*-axis.

2. Draw a line of best fit through the graphed points.

3. Find the slope of the line. The slope is *Hubble's* constant. It tells you how fast the space between the galaxies is expanding.

Data Analysis

1. **Compare** your result expressed in km/s/Mpc with the known value of *Hubble's* Constant.

2. **Combine** your result with those obtained by other students and find the average value. How does this compare with the known value? Why is it better or worse than your original value?

Data

Distance and Speed of 12 Galaxies		
Galaxy	Distance (Mpc)	Doppler Speed (km/s)
NGC 598	0	0
NGC 5055	5	610
NGC 4594	16	991
NGC 5236	5	305
NGC 3031	3	76
NGC 3351	12	686
NGC 7331	21	1067
NGC 5457	4	381
NGC 5194	5	610
NGC 4826	6	381
NGC 4321	28	1525
NGC 4486	21	1220

 Science Content Standards

4.c Students know how to use astronomical units and light years as measures of distance between the Sun, stars, and Earth.

9.d Recognize the slope of the linear graph as the constant in the relationship $y = kx$ and apply this principle in interpreting graphs constructed from data.

Model and Invent:
A Star is Born

Materials

field guides
   about stars and
   galaxies
star chart of
   constellations
pair of binoculars
   or small telescope
computer with
   internet access

Science Content Standards

4.b Students know that the Sun is one of many stars in the Milky Way galaxy and that stars may differ in size, temperature, and color.

4.d Students know that stars are the source of light for all bright objects in outer space and that the Moon and planets shine by reflected sunlight, not by their own light.

Problem

The universe is made up of matter and energy. You have learned that stars are different colors and sizes because of their distance, the amount of energy, and the type of matter they contain. Many questions remain about the universe, however. For example, how was it formed? The most popular theory right now is that the universe formed in a massive expansion from a single point called the "big bang." Use this Design-Your-Own Lab to learn more about a topic involving energy and matter. You might want to learn more about what stars are made of, how they are born, or their life cycles. You might want to study the big bang, black holes, neutron stars, or the next-nearest galaxy to Earth.

Form a Hypothesis

➤ First, brainstorm a list of topics that interest you. You must choose a topic that involves stars, matter, and energy.

➤ Create a large concept web of topics.

➤ Then, narrow down your interest to one topic. Decide what you want to research.

➤ Write a question and predict what the answer to your question will be by writing a hypothesis.

Collect Data and Make Observations

1. Decide how you will research the answer to your question.

2. Make a list of possible resources.

3. Make a list of search terms that you will use to research. List at least ten search terms. Remember that the more specific your terms, the better information you will find. Put stars beside the terms you think will work best.

4. Make sure your teacher has approved your experiment before you proceed further.

5. When you have gathered enough data to answer your question, create a poster, diorama, or computer presentation to share your findings.

Analyze and Conclude

1. **State** the answer to your question.

2. **Evaluate** How much matter and energy does your object of study have compared to other celestial objects?

3. **Describe** How do scientists measure the energy given off by your star or other object?

4. **Explain** What have scientists learned about the universe from their studies of these objects?

5. **Identify** When did scientists start to study these objects? What technology did they need to develop to do these studies?

6. **Recognize** What basic science principles are behind the behavior of these objects?

7. **Error Analysis** Explain difficulties you had answering your question. Would you change your question or hypothesis? Could you improve your research methods? Explain.

Communicate

WRITING in Science

Make a Presentation Display the poster that answers your question on a bulletin board, or give your presentation to the class. After you have listened to or read your classmates' questions and answers, write two paragraphs about what you learned from others' projects.

Real World Science

Stephen Hawking: An Extraordinary Mind

Stephen Hawking is widely regarded as the greatest mind in physics since Albert Einstein. A mathematics professor at Cambridge University, he is best known for discovering that black holes emit subatomic particles, called Hawking Radiation. His work allows astronomers to study black holes in detail. Hawking's book *A Brief History of Time: From the Big Bang to Black Holes* explains complicated concepts in language nonscientists can understand.

Visit **Careers** at  **ca8.msscience.com** to learn more about Stephen Hawking. **Write** a newspaper article focusing on an aspect of Hawking's life, such as his research, books he has published, or his family history.

ELA8: W 2.1

Adaptive Optics

Powerful Earth-based telescopes must view the sky through Earth's atmosphere. The problem? The atmosphere distorts light, blurring the image of faraway stars and galaxies. Today, some telescopes obtain crisp images using "rubber mirrors." These deformable mirrors can be manipulated faster than the atmosphere can change. The technology, called adaptive optics, removes the atmosphere's blurring effect. These two images of binary star IW Tau show a blurry mass taken without adaptive optics and a clearer image using adaptive optics.

Visit **Technology** at **ca8.msscience.com** to view objects photographed with adaptive optics. **Create** a catalog of images with brief captions. **Present** your photo gallery to the class.

Kepler's Supernova

On October 9, 1604, observers in Europe and Asia saw a bright object appear on the horizon. Though they did not know it, the men were witnessing the death of a star. Within days, the object became the brightest object in the sky. Johannes Kepler studied the object for over a year until it was no longer visible. While the unusual object remained a mystery to Kepler, astronomers ultimately rewarded his perseverance by naming the supernova after him. Kepler's supernova is one of only six stellar explosions seen in our galaxy in the past 1,000 years.

Visit **History** at ca8.msscience.com to learn about these six supernovae. Create a time line of these events which includes details about the historical record supporting each.

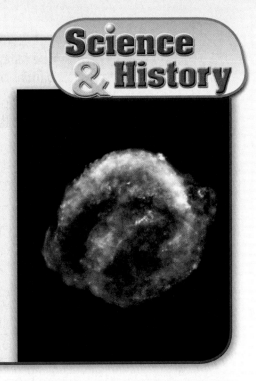

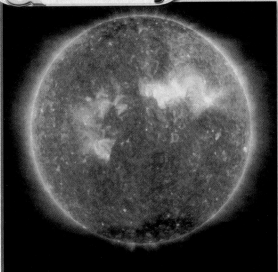

Watching the Heat

Since 1996, the Solar and Heliospheric Observatory (SOHO) has stood watch between Earth and the Sun. From its vantage point 930,000 miles from Earth, SOHO stares at the Sun 24 hours a day, sending back a steady stream of solar data. While helping astronomers uncover the Sun's mysteries, SOHO also acts as an early warning system, alerting Earth engineers to periodic, high-energy shockwaves produced by the Sun that affect astronauts and satellites in space and communication systems on Earth. Thanks to SOHO, space weather forecasters have up to three days to prepare for incoming disturbances caused by unusual solar activity.

Visit **Society** at ca8.msscience.com to view solar data. Use the information provided to create a "space weather forecast" for astronauts on the *International Space Station*. Include charts and graphs in your forecast.

The BIG Idea The Milky Way galaxy, which is composed of billions of stars, is one of the billions of galaxies in the universe.

Lesson 1 Stars
4.b, 4.c, 4.d

Main Idea Although the Sun is considered to be a fairly typical star, analysis of starlight indicates that stars vary greatly in size, temperature, and color and are composed primarily of hydrogen and helium.

- Stars are large balls of mostly hydrogen gas that emit energy.
- Large distances between stars are measured in light-years.
- A spectroscope is used to identify the elements in stars.
- The color of a star depends on its temperature.
- Luminosity measures the intrinsic brightness of stars.
- Both luminosity and distance affect how bright stars appear.
- The H-R diagram relates temperature to luminosity of stars.

- **absolute magnitude** (p. 513)
- **apparent magnitude** (p. 513)
- **light-year** (p. 509)
- **luminosity** (p. 513)

Lesson 2 How Stars Shine
2.g, 4.d

Main Idea Stars generate light from energy released in nuclear fusion.

- Stars form as matter in interstellar clouds is drawn together by gravity and is heated enough to start nuclear fusion.
- Energy produced at a star's core is emitted at its surface as light.
- The fate of a star depends on its initial mass.
- Stars having an initial mass similar to that of the Sun become red giants and then white dwarfs.
- More massive stars may undergo supernova explosions and become neutron stars or black holes.

- **black hole** (p. 526)
- **nebula** (p. 519)
- **neutron star** (p. 526)
- **nuclear fusion** (p. 522)
- **red giant** (p. 524)
- **supernova** (p. 525)
- **white dwarf** (p. 524)

Lesson 3 Galaxies
4.a, 4.b, 4.c, 9.d

Main Idea Gravitational attraction causes stars to group together into galaxies.

- Galaxies are star groups containing billions of stars held together by gravitational attraction.
- Galaxies are divided into three types: spiral, elliptical, and irregular.
- The Sun is located in one arm of the spiral galaxy called the Milky Way.
- The big bang theory states that the universe began about 14 billion years ago when all matter and energy was concentrated at a single, tiny point.

- **big bang theory** (p. 533)
- **galaxy** (p. 528)

STUDY TO GO Download quizzes, key terms, and flash cards from ca8.msscience.com.

Linking Vocabulary and Main Ideas

Use vocabulary terms from page 540 to complete this concept map.

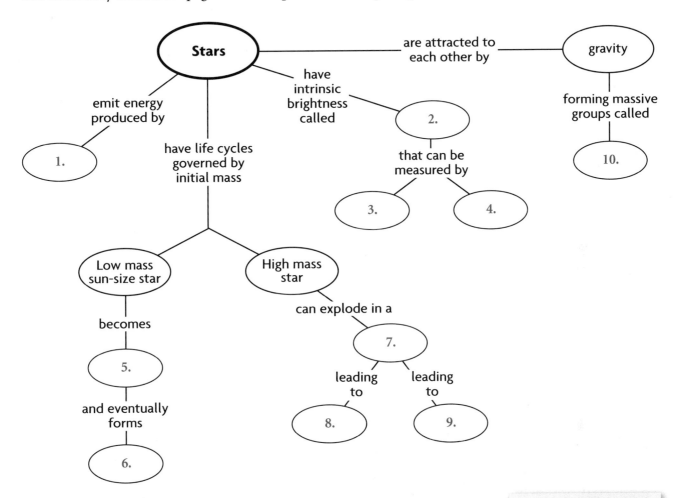

Using Vocabulary

Fill in the blanks with the correct vocabulary terms. Then read the paragraph to a partner.

According to the _____11._____, all matter and all energy in the universe originated from a single point. First, matter was spread evenly, but soon clumps of dust and gas began to form stars. A large group of stars numbering in the billions is called a(n) _____12._____. The space between stars contains clouds of gas and dust. Such a cloud is called a(n)_____13._____. The distances between stars and galaxies are so great that astronomers measure them using a unit called a(n) _____14._____.

Understanding Main Ideas

Choose the word or phrase that best answers the question.

1. What color star has the highest surface temperature?
   A. blue
   B. red
   C. white
   D. yellow   **4.b**

2. Which means the same as luminosity?
   A. apparent brightness
   B. absolute brightness
   C. brightness
   D. intrinsic brightness   **4.d**

3. Which is not part of a spiral galaxy?
   A. halo
   B. supercluster
   C. nuclueus
   D. spiral arms   **4.a**

4. The photograph below is of the Sombrero galaxy.

   Which unit of measurement is most appropriate for measuring distances within the group of stars shown above?
   A. astronomical unit
   B. kilometer
   C. light-year
   D. mile   **4.c**

5. What is the most important factor that causes matter in a nebula to form clumps?
   A. gravitational attraction
   B. heating
   C. molecular motion
   D. rotation   **2.g**

Use the figure below to answer questions 6–8.

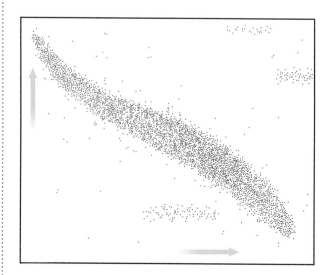

6. What is measured on the *y*-axis?
   A. diameter
   B. color
   C. luminosity
   D. temperature   **4.b**

7. Which type of star is located in the bottom center of the diagram?
   A. giant
   B. supergiant
   C. white dwarf
   D. main sequence star   **4.b**

8. What type of star is topmost in the diagram?
   A. giant
   B. Sun-like
   C. supergiant
   D. white dwarf   **4.b**

9. Which magnitude describes the brightest star?
   A. 2.5
   B. 1.3
   C. −0.5
   D. −2.5   **4.b**

Applying Science

10. **Explain** why a low-mass star contracts to form a white dwarf. **4.b**

11. **Describe** how absorption spectra are formed. **4.d**

12. **Examine** the nuclear fusion reaction that begins star formation. Include the number and type of particles that take part, the particles formed, and the type of energy released. **4.d**

13. **Identify** the layers of the Sun-like star shown in the illustration below and indicate where light energy is emitted. **4.d**

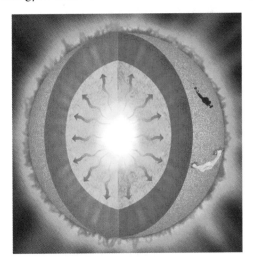

14. **Hypothesize** A new galaxy has just been discovered using a powerful new telescope. Astronomers report that it is composed mostly of older reddish stars and that it has little interstellar dust or gas. What type of galaxy is it most likely to be? **4.a**

15. **Explain** how the wavelengths of light emitted by a star depend on the star's temperature. **4.b**

WRITING in Science

16. **Write** a brief biography of a star about the size of the Sun. Describe the role of gravity in its formation and in maintaining its stable existence while on the main sequence. **ELA8: W 2.1**

Cumulative Review

17. **Explain** why astronomers measure distances of planets and their moons using astronomical units instead of kilometers or light-years.

18. **Compare** a total lunar eclipse with a total solar eclipse.

19. **Infer** Based on what you have learned about the asteroids, what type of planet might have formed in the orbit occupied by the asteroid belt? Would it be more like the inner or outer planets?

Applying Math

Use the table below to answer questions 20–24.

Star	Apparent Magnitude
Vega	0.03
Capella	0.08
Procyon	0.38
Achernar	0.46
Acrux	0.76

20. How much brighter is Procyon than Capella? **MA8: ALG 2.0**

21. How much brighter is Procyon than Vega? **MA8: ALG 2.0**

22. How much brighter is Acrux than Achernar? **MA8: ALG 2.0**

23. How much brighter is Acrux than Capella? **MA8: ALG 2.0**

24. How much brighter is Acrux than Vega? **MA8: ALG 2.0**

1 The illustration below shows part of the Sun.

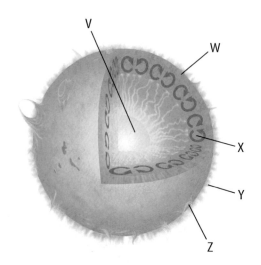

In which layer of the Sun is energy produced?

A V

B X

C Y

D Z 4.d

2 About how long does it take light from the Sun to reach Earth?

A 8 seconds

B 8 minutes

C 8 hours

D 8 days 4.c

3 The most massive stars end their lives as which type of object?

A black hole

B white dwarf

C neutron star

D black dwarf 4.b

4 Which is a group of stars, gas, and dust held together by gravity?

A constellation

B supergiant

C black hole

D galaxy 4.b

Use the graph below to answer questions 5 and 6.

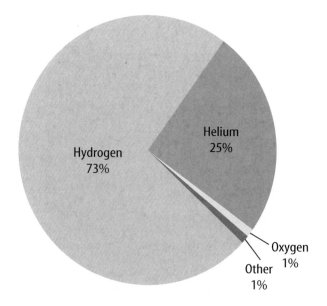

5 Which is the most abundant element in the Sun?

A helium

B hydrogen

C oxygen

D carbon 4.d

6 How will this circle graph change as the Sun ages?

A The hydrogen slice will get smaller.

B The hydrogen slice will get larger.

C The helium slice will get smaller.

D The circle graph will not change. 4.d

Science Online Standards Assessment ca8.msscience.com

7 Which do astronomers use to determine what elements are present in stars?

A gyroscope

B microscope

C spectroscope

D telescope   **4.d**

8 Which is produced in the nuclear fusion reaction between four hydrogen nuclei?

A carbon

B helium

C oxygen

D neutrons

9 In which of the following choices are the objects ordered from smallest to largest?

A stars, galaxies, galaxy clusters, universe

B galaxy clusters, galaxies, stars, universe

C universe, galaxy clusters, galaxies, stars

D universe, stars, galaxies, galaxy clusters   **4.a**

10 The illustration below shows a side view of the Milky Way galaxy.

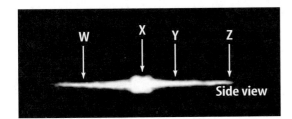

Where is the Sun located?

A W

B X

C Y

D Z   **4.b**

11 The Milky Way is an example of which stellar object?

A an elliptical galaxy

B a spiral galaxy

C an irregular galaxy

D a star cluster   **4.a**

12 The illustration below shows the distance between Earth and the nearest star other than the Sun, Proxima Centauri.

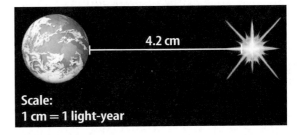

How far away from Earth is Proxima Centauri?

A 8.4 AUs

B 8.4 light-years

C 4.2 AUs

D 4.2 light-years   **4.c**

13 Why do stars and other large celestial objects have a spherical shape?

A All objects become spherical when they melt.

B Atomic and molecular forces cause all objects to become spherical.

C Gravity attracts matter within these objects toward a central point.

D Multiple collisions cause these objects to become rounded.   **2.g**

Are you interested in stars, galaxies, and the universe? If so, check out these great books.

Nonfiction

The Universe, by Seymour Simon, is a study of the vastness of the universe. Full-color photographs show nebulas and galaxies and support the topics discussed, including the big bang and theories about the future of the universe. *The content of this book is related to* Science Standard 8.4.

Nonfiction

Sun, by Steve Tomecek, introduces readers to the physics of the Sun. This book gives readers an in-depth look at our closest star, explaining the Sun's size, distance from Earth, composition, temperature, sunspots, and solar flares. *The content of this book is related to* Science Standard 8.4.

Nonfiction

Big Bang: The Story of the Universe, by Heather Couper, begins with hydrogen atoms and explains the origins and formation of the elements that are now commonplace in the universe. This book gives clear explanations of a complicated subject. *The content of this book is related to* Science Standard 8.4.

Nonfiction

Gems of Hubble: Superb Images from the Hubble Space Telescope, by Jacqueline Mitton, features images made with the Hubble Space Telescope. Planets, moons, star birth, galaxies, and black holes are explained in easy-to-understand language. *The content of this book is related to* Science Standard 8.4.

Choose the word or phrase that best answers the question.

Use the figure below to answer questions 1–3.

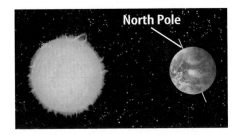

North Pole

1. Which season is it in the southern hemisphere when Earth is in this position?
   A. spring
   B. summer
   C. autumn
   D. winter   4.e

2. Which part of Earth receives the greatest total amount of solar radiation when Earth is in this position?
   A. northern hemisphere
   B. south pole
   C. southern hemisphere
   D. equator   4.e

3. In what month is Earth closest to the Sun?
   A. March
   B. September
   C. July
   D. January   4.e

4. Which is the closest star to Earth?
   A. Sirius
   B. the Sun
   C. Betelgeuse
   D. the Moon   4.e

5. What unit is often used to measure distances between stars and galaxies?
   A. kilometer
   B. astronomical unit
   C. light-year
   D. meter   4.e

Write your responses on a sheet of paper.

6. **Compare and contrast** the different types of galaxies.   4.a

7. **Discuss** what an astronomical unit is and why it is useful.   4.c

8. **Explain** how a moon remains in orbit around a planet.   2.g

9. **Sequence** the phases of the Moon starting and ending with a new moon. Explain why we can see only these lighted portions of the Moon. Consider the fact that the Sun lights one half of the Moon at all times.   4.d

10. **Explain** how eclipses of the Sun occur only occasionally despite the fact that the Moon's rotation causes it to pass between Earth and the Sun every month.   4.d

11. **Define** *constellation* and give three examples of a constellation.   4.b

The figure below shows Earth and the star Proxima Centauri. Use the figure below to answer questions 12 and 13.

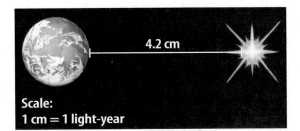

4.2 cm

Scale:
1 cm = 1 light-year

12. **Identify** How many light-years from Earth is the star Proxima Centauri?   4.c

13. **Infer** how many years it would take for light from Proxima Centauri to reach Earth.   4.c

14. **Sketch and label** the Sun and the four parts of a comet as it moves away from the Sun.   4.e

To Students and Their Families,

Welcome to eighth-grade physical science. You will begin your journey by learning about the tools that physicists and chemists use. Then you will continue with interactions between objects and the structure of matter. You will also learn about our solar system and galaxies.

Take a few moments each day to review what you have learned about physical science. Test your knowledge of each Standard by answering the questions.

Remember, the knowledge and skills you will gain this year will be important beyond the classroom. They will help you to become environmentally aware and to better understand the planet on which you live.

Table of Contents

Standard Set 1 Motion 550

Standard Set 2 Forces 552

Standard Set 3 Structure of Matter 554

Standard Set 4 Earth in the Solar System
(Earth Science) 556

Standard Set 5 Reactions 558

Standard Set 6 Chemistry of Living Systems
(Life Science) 560

Standard Set 7 Periodic Table 562

Standard Set 8 Density and Buoyancy 564

Standard Set 9 Investigation and Experimentation 566

Answers 568

Standard Set 1: Motion

Directions: Select the best answer for each of the following questions.

1 Koto walks 3 blocks north, 4 blocks west, then 3 blocks south. If her starting place is the reference point, how far away is her final position?

A 4 blocks west
B 7 blocks northwest
C 10 blocks west
D 10 blocks northwest

2
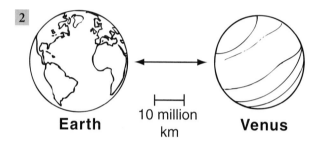
Earth   10 million km   **Venus**

Earth is the reference point for Venus' position in the diagram above. How could you express the position of Venus?

A 30 million km apart
B 30 million km to the left
C 30 million km to the right
D 30 million km from the Sun

3 Earth orbits the Sun in one year. Which is the *best* object to use as a point of reference to describe Earth's orbit?

A the Moon
B the Sun
C other planets
D other stars

4 Which units would be appropriate for measuring the speed of a space shuttle orbiting Earth?

A cm/s
B km/h
C km/s
D m/h

5 A hiking trail is 10 km long. If it takes you 2 h to walk the trail, which is your average speed?

A 0.2 km/h
B 2 km/h
C 5 km/h
D 10 km/h

6 In an experiment, you find that a ball takes 3 s to roll down a ramp. Its average speed is 18 cm/s. Which is the length of the ramp?

A 3 cm
B 9 cm
C 18 cm
D 54 cm

7 During a flight, the pilot announces that the plane can travel at a maximum speed of 1,500 km/h, but including takeoff and landing, the average speed for the trip is 1,000 km/h. If the flight takes 2 h, what is the distance traveled?

A 500 km
B 750 km
C 2,000 km
D 3,000 km

8 It takes you about 5 min to walk 2 city blocks. You have to walk 25 blocks to get to your friend's house. Which equation could you use to calculate the amount of time this walk will take?

A $t = 5 \times 2 \times 25$
B $t = (5 \div 2) \times 25$
C $t = 25 \div 2.5$
D $t = 25 \div 5$

9 Why would it be more useful for an air traffic controller to know the velocity of an airplane than its speed?

A Speed can be expressed only in m/s.
B Speed refers to objects traveling only on the ground.
C Velocity gives the speed and the direction.
D Velocity is a more accurate measurement than speed.

10 An airplane flies west at 500 km/h for 2 h, then flies north at 500 km/h for 2 h. Which is its average velocity for the trip?

A 250 km/h
B 500 km/h
C 500 km/h northwest
D 1,000 km/h northwest

Standard Set 1: Motion

Directions: Select the best answer for each of the following questions.

11 Ana drives her car from a parking lot at 15 km/h. She moves onto the highway, where she drives at 100 km/h. Then she gets off the highway onto a city street, where she drives at 70 km/h. At which point is the car's acceleration greatest?

A driving on the highway

B driving in the parking lot

C moving from the highway to a city street

D moving from the parking lot to the highway

12 How could a pitcher throw a baseball and cause it to accelerate in flight?

A throw the baseball at a faster speed than usual

B throw the baseball from a spot higher above the ground

C throw the baseball in an absolutely straight line

D throw the baseball so that its path curves

13 Which is the *best* definition of acceleration?

A a change in an object's direction

B a change in an object's speed

C a change in an object's velocity

D an increase in an object's speed

14 Suppose a person's walking speed increases from 10 m/s to 15 m/s in a period of 5 s. Which is the acceleration?

A 1 m/s

B 1 m/s^2

C 5 m/s

D 5 m/s^2

15 A graph shows distance (km) v. time (h) for a car trip. If two points on the graph are (1, 40) and (3, 130), which is the average speed during this interval of time?

A 45 km/h

B 65 km/h

C 90 km/h

D 130 km/h

Use the graph below to answer questions 16 and 17.

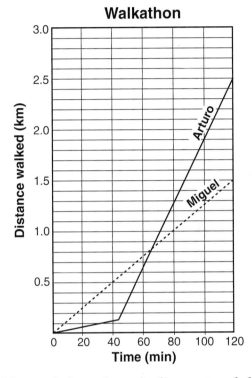

Walkathon

16 The graph above shows the distance traveled by two different walkers during a 2-h walkathon. Which statement expresses the walkers' speeds?

A After 65 min, Miguel and Arturo were walking at the same speed.

B Miguel's average speed was greater than Arturo's.

C Arturo's average speed was greater than Miguel's.

D The two walkers had the same average speed throughout.

17 Based on the graph, which time period represents a change in speed?

A Miguel, between 0 and 20 min

B Miguel, at 65 min

C Arturo, at 45 min

D Arturo, between 60 and 80 min

Standard Set 2: Forces

Directions: Select the best answer for each of the following questions.

1 Before you draw a vector diagram representing forces, you need to know *only* the

A direction of the forces and the scale used to represent force and magnitude.

B magnitude and direction of the forces and the resultant of adding the forces.

C magnitude and direction of the forces and the scale used to represent force magnitude.

D magnitude of the forces and the scale used to represent force magnitude.

2 Two groups of students are engaged in a tug-of-war. The rope has a knot in the middle. The group on the right pulls with a force of 2,000 N, and the group on the left pulls with a force of 1,000 N. Which scale diagram best represents the forces acting on the knot (shown as a • in the diagram)?

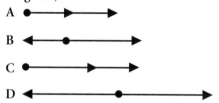

3 Which can cause a moving object to come to rest?

A electricity

B friction

C gravity

D power

4 The net force on a piece of paper as it falls through the air is 1 N. If the force from air resistance acting on the paper is 2 N, what is the downward force on the paper?

A 1 N

B 2 N

C 3 N

D 4 N

5

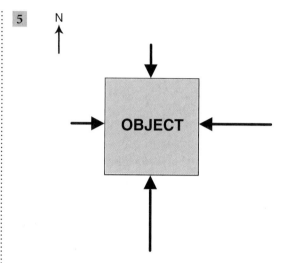

In the illustration above, the length of each arrow indicates the magnitude of each force acting on the object. How will these forces affect the object?

A The object will move east.

B The object will move northwest.

C The object will not be affected by friction.

D The object will not move at all.

6 Four forces act on an airplane. Lift is the upward force, and weight is the downward force. Thrust is the force in a forward direction, and drag is a force that acts against thrust. As an airplane moves forward at a constant altitude, which is true?

A Lift and drag are equal.

B Lift is less than weight.

C Thrust and drag are equal.

D Thrust is greater than drag.

7 An object in motion tends to continue in the same motion if the net force on that object is zero. Which rule is this?

A conservation of energy

B conservation of momentum

C Newton's first law

D Newton's third law

Science Online Standards Practice ca8.msscience.com

Standard Set 2: Forces

Directions: Select the best answer for each of the following questions.

8 A book with a weight of 3 N is resting on a table. The force of friction acting on the book is 2 N. Which is the least amount of force you could apply to move the book across the table?

A 1 N

B 2 N

C 3 N

D 5 N

9 After you push a toy car, it rolls across the floor and comes to a stop. Which is the *best* explanation for the motion of the car?

A The car would have continued at a constant velocity if it had a larger mass.

B The car would have continued at a constant velocity if it had a smaller mass.

C The forces on the car were balanced; therefore, its velocity changed.

D The forces on the car were unbalanced; therefore, its velocity changed.

10 Which is not an example of an action-reaction pair of forces, according to Newton's third law?

A When a car pushes on the road, the road pushes on the car.

B When a soccer ball pushes on a wall, the wall pushes on the soccer ball.

C When you hit a ball with a bat, you push on the bat and the bat pushes on the ball.

D When you pull on a rope to start a lawn mower, the rope pulls on you.

11 Objects have weight on Earth because of the gravitational force of

A Earth.

B the Milky Way.

C the Moon.

D the Sun.

12 The weights of astronauts are much less when they walk on the Moon than when they walk on Earth. This is because of the

A depth of the Moon's craters.

B force of the solar winds.

C light coming from the Sun.

D strength of the Moon's gravity.

13 Two objects of the same mass are dropped from the same height. Object A has a higher velocity than object B when it reaches the ground. Which causes this difference?

A Object A has a greater weight.

B The force of friction on object A is less.

C The force of gravity on object B is less.

D The forces of gravity and friction acting on object B are balanced.

14 A force of 2 N is needed to overcome the force of friction acting on an object. If the mass of the object doubled, how would this affect the force needed to move it?

A The force would remain the same.

B A greater force would be needed.

C The necessary force would be less than 2 N.

D It is impossible to determine without knowing the force of friction.

15

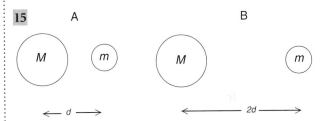

In Figure A, two masses, *M* and *m*, are at a distance *d* apart. If the masses were moved to a distance 2*d* apart, as shown in Figure B, the gravitational force between them would be

A one-fourth as much.

B half as much.

C two times larger.

D four times larger.

16 Two satellites, each with a mass of about 50 kg, orbit Earth. They follow paths close to each other. Between these two satellites,

A there is no gravitational pull.

B there is a strong gravitational pull.

C the gravitational pull is about equal to the pull between one satellite and Earth.

D the gravitational pull is weaker than the pull between one satellite and Earth.

Standard Set 3: Structure of Matter

Directions: Select the best answer for each of the following questions.

1 The way scientists view the atom has changed dramatically over the last 150 years. New discoveries have led to new models of the atom that have resulted in advances in chemistry and technology. Four of the models are shown below. Which is the correct order of their development?

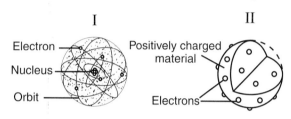

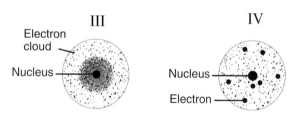

A I, II, III, IV

B III, II, IV, I

C II, IV, I, III

D IV, I, II, III

2 The mass of a proton is

A about the same as the mass of an electron.

B about the same as the mass of a helium nucleus.

C about 1,000 times greater that the mass of a neutron.

D about 2,000 times greater than the mass of an electron.

3 Sometimes two elements combine to make a new substance with its own special properties. This new substance is an example of a

A compound.

B conglomerate.

C heterogeneous mixture.

D homogeneous mixture.

4 Which is a compound?

A carbon

B hydrogen

C oxygen

D salt

5

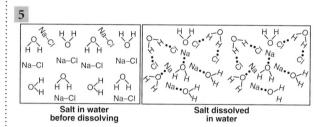

Salt in water before dissolving   Salt dissolved in water

According to the diagram, which statement *best* describes what happens to ionic compounds when they are dissolved?

A They get larger in size.

B They increase in density.

C They become a new compound.

D They are pulled apart by water molecules.

6 Carlos set a container of a warm saltwater solution on the table to cool. One hour later, he returned to find some white crystals forming at the bottom of the container. The crystals *most* likely

A crystallized out of the cooling solution.

B fell into the container from the ceiling.

C were already formed but invisible.

D were ice forming as the water cooled.

7 Which explains how stalactites form in some caves?

A A fungus grows in this shape.

B Groundwater evaporates from solar heat.

C Sediment erodes by rainwater.

D Solids crystallize from a solution.

8 Which substance does *not* form crystals in its solid form?

A glass

B sugar

C Epsom salts

D table salt

 Science online Standards Practice ca8.msscience.com

Standard Set 3: Structure of Matter

Directions: Select the best answer for each of the following questions.

9 Which is *not* a state of matter?

A gas

B liquid

C solid

D substance

10 Atmospheric pressure decreases as altitude increases above sea level. Which is the effect of decreased air pressure on the boiling point of water?

A The boiling point does not change because of changes in air pressure.

B The boiling point is higher when air pressure is lower.

C The boiling point is lower when air pressure is lower.

D Changes in boiling point depend on the amount of water.

11 In which type of substance would you expect the collisions between molecules to be most frequent?

A gas

B liquid

C solid

D solution

12 Which phase change occurs when the molecules in a substance lose energy and no longer slide past each other easily?

A gas → liquid

B liquid → gas

C liquid → solid

D solid → gas

13 If a substance gains energy and becomes less dense, which phase change is probably happening?

A gas → liquid

B gas → solid

C liquid → gas

D liquid → solid

14 Element X appears on the periodic table as $X^{10}_{22.076}$. How many electrons would you expect to find in one atom of this element?

A 10

B 12

C 22

D 32

15 In the periodic table, what do elements in the same group have in common?

A They bond most easily with one another.

B They have the same atomic number.

C They have the same atomic weight.

D They have the same number of electrons available for bonding.

16 KCl is a naturally occurring compound. Chlorine is in the same group as fluorine and bromine and in the same period as sulfur and argon. Which compound would be *most* likely to form with potassium?

A KAr

B KBr

C KCl_2

D KS

At-Home Standards Practice

Standard Set 4: Earth in the Solar System (Earth Science)

Directions: Select the best answer for each of the following questions.

1 According to a simple definition, a comet is a collection of dust, gas, and rocks. Which is one other characteristic of a comet?
A A comet forms large rings around a planet.
C A comet consists of widely scattered chunks of matter.
C A comet is a bright ball of gases at the center of a solar system.
D A comet has a glowing tail.

2 Approximately how many stars are found in a galaxy?
A hundreds
B thousands
C millions
D billions

3 Why do some people predict that, somewhere in the universe, there could be life on another planet like Earth?
A Other galaxies are similar to the Milky Way galaxy.
B Other galaxies form into clusters with one another.
C Other planets exist in this solar system.
D Other stars are similar to the Sun.

4 Which *best* represents the composition of the universe, from smallest to largest parts?
A planet → solar system → star
B solar system → star → galaxy
C star → galaxy → cluster of galaxies
D star → galaxy → empty space

5 Which characteristic helps scientists estimate the temperature of a star?
A color
B shape
C distance from Earth
D number of planets

6 Our solar system is located in the
A Andromeda galaxy.
B Earth-Sun galaxy.
C Milky Way galaxy.
D Whirlpool galaxy.

7 The diagram below shows the Milky Way galaxy, as viewed from the side.

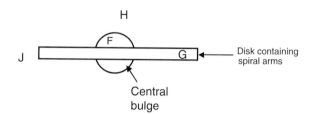

Which letter best represents the position of Earth?
A F
B G
C H
D J

8 Our solar system's nine planets orbit a star that is part of
A the Andromeda galaxy.
B the big bang.
C the Crab nebula.
D the Milky Way galaxy.

9

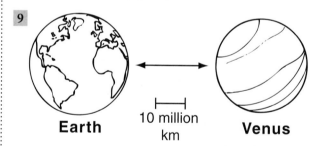

One astronomical unit (AU) is equivalent to 1.496×10^8 km. Which would be the distance between Earth and Venus, expressed in AU?
A approximately 1 AU
B approximately 2 AU
C It is impossible to express this distance in AU.
D much less than 1 AU

10 The unit *light-year* is used for measuring
A distance.
B speed.
C speed and distance.
D time.

Science Online Standards Practice ca8.msscience.com

Standard Set 4: Earth in the Solar System (Earth Science)

Directions: Select the best answer for each of the following questions.

11 The astronomical unit is useful because
- **A** distances in space are too large to be measured in other units.
- **B** distances in space often need to be estimated.
- **C** it is helpful to measure distances in comparison to the speed of light.
- **D** it relates all distances to the average distance between Earth and the Moon.

12 An amateur astronomer measured the distance to a new asteroid located near Pluto. The distance she recorded was *most* likely recorded in
- **A** centimeters.
- **B** miles.
- **C** kilometers.
- **D** astronomical units.

13 The reaction thought to be the *most* important energy source of the Sun is
- **A** helium nuclei combining to make hydrogen nuclei.
- **B** helium nuclei splitting to form hydrogen nuclei.
- **C** hydrogen nuclei combining to form helium nuclei.
- **D** hydrogen nuclei splitting to form protons.

14 Which contributes *most* to making half the Moon bright?
- **A** light from distant stars
- **B** light from cities on Earth
- **C** light from other planets
- **D** light from the Sun

15 Sometimes people see figures, such as animals, in the arrangements of stars in the sky. These figures are called
- **A** constellations.
- **B** galaxies.
- **C** supergiants.
- **D** supernovas.

16 Occasionally, a full moon seems to temporarily darken as Earth passes between it and the Sun. This event is called
- **A** an Earth eclipse.
- **B** a lunar eclipse.
- **C** a planetary eclipse.
- **D** a solar eclipse.

17 The diameter of Earth is 12,756 km. The diameter of the Moon is 3,476 km. Which pair of circles *best* represents the relative sizes of Earth and the Moon?

A

B

C
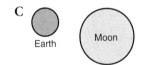

D

18 Two of the inner, rocky planets are
- **A** Earth and Pluto.
- **B** Mars and Venus.
- **C** Mercury and Jupiter.
- **D** Venus and Saturn.

19 Which *best* describes the shape of Earth?
- **A** pear-shaped
- **B** perfectly spherical
- **C** spherical, with a slight bulge at the poles
- **D** spherical, with a slight bulge at the equator

Standard Set 5: Reactions

Directions: Select the best answer for each of the following questions.

1 Chemical reactions occur when
A electrons are rearranged.
B nuclear changes occur.
C physical changes occur.
D protons are rearranged.

2 Several grams of table salt are dissolved in a beaker of water. How would this change be classified?
A Chemical reaction; heat is usually required to make salt dissolve.
B Chemical reaction; the salt changed form as it dissolved.
C Physical change; no heat was released during the change.
D Physical change; the salt and water did not form new substances.

3 In the reaction below, which are the products?

$$FeCl_2 + 2NaOH \rightarrow Fe(OH)_2 + 2NaCl$$

A $FeCl_2$ and $Fe(OH)_2$
B $FeCl_2$ and NaOH
C $Fe(OH)_2$ and NaCl
D NaOH and NaCl

4 After Koko added some vinegar to a test powder in a beaker, the mixture started to fizzle and changed color. Considering this result, which statement *most* likely applies?
A A chemical change did not occur.
B A chemical change produced new substances.
C A physical change produced new substances.
D A physical change usually gives off heat.

5 In a balanced chemical equation, which is true about the number of atoms of each element in the products and in the reactants?
A They are equal.
B They are not equal.
C It depends on the reaction.
D It is impossible to determine.

6 What should the coefficient for H_2O be for the equation to be balanced?

$$CH_4 + 2O_2 \rightarrow CO_2 + H_2O$$

A 1
B 2
C 3
D 4

7 A student observes a combustion reaction in which 5 g of oil is burned. She finds that the mass of the solid product is 1 g. She concludes that the total mass decreases in a combustion reaction. Which is the problem with her conclusion?
A The oil was a liquid, so it is a problem to measure the solid products.
B She should also find the mass of the gases released during combustion.
C She should have measured the oil in milliliters instead of grams.
D There is no problem with her conclusion.

8 In order to balance an incomplete chemical equation, such as $H_2 + N_2 \rightarrow NH_3$, which must be done?
A Coefficients must be added.
B New reactants must be added.
C Products must be changed.
D Subscripts must be changed.

9

Chemical Reaction	Energy Change
I $H_2O \longrightarrow H_2 + \frac{1}{2}O_2$	Absorbs energy
II glucose + oxygen $\longrightarrow$ carbon dioxide + water	Releases energy
III $CH_4 + 2O_2 \longrightarrow CO_2 + 2H_2O$	Releases energy
IV $2C + H_2 \longrightarrow C_2H_2$	Absorbs energy

The table above shows the results of four different chemical reactions. Which are exothermic reactions?
A I only
B II only
C I and IV
D II and III

Standard Set 5: Reactions

Directions: Select the best answer for each of the following questions.

10 When potassium metal is placed in water, it bursts into flames. This reaction is identified as
A endothermic.
B exothermic.
C neutralizing.
D reactant favored.

11 A certain chemical reaction involves breaking many of the bonds in the reactants. This reaction would probably be
A a catalyzed reaction.
B an endothermic reaction.
C an exothermic reaction.
D a slow reaction.

12 You are observing a reaction occurring in a beaker. Which would be the *best* method for determining whether the reaction is exothermic or endothermic?
A Find the difference between the mass of the reactants and the products.
B Hold the beaker in your hand while the reaction takes place.
C Put a thermometer in the beaker and observe any temperature change.
D Record the total time required for the reaction to take place.

13 Some thermometers are mercury-filled glass tubes sealed at both ends. The mercury indicates the temperature through
A catalytic reactions.
B chemical exchanges.
C exothermic reactions.
D physical changes.

14 Wood is a complex material made of many substances. Which does *not* occur as a result of a physical change in wood?
A It floats in water.
B It is broken into pieces.
C It is sculpted into art.
D It is turned into ash.

15

Which process is occurring in all three pictures?
A condensation
B conduction
C conservation
D vaporization

16 Condensation happens when a gas changes into a liquid. Which is an example of condensation?
A a pond freezing in the winter
B a pond melting in the spring
C water vapor turning to rain
D water vapor turning to snow

17 Which liquids are *most* likely to chemically neutralize each other when mixed?
A ammonia and water
B orange juice and lemonade
C orange juice and oven cleaner
D vinegar and lemonade

18 A solution of citric acid has a pH of 5.7. If you add water to the solution, what would happen to its pH?
A The pH would decrease.
B The pH would increase.
C The pH would stay the same.
D It depends on the amount of water added.

At-Home Standards Practice

Directions: Select the best answer for each of the following questions.

1 Two carbon-containing molecules are CH_4 and CH_3CH_3. The structure of these two molecules shows that
 A carbon bonds better with hydrogen atoms than with other carbon atoms.
 B carbon can bond only with hydrogen and carbon.
 C carbon is found only in small molecules.
 D one carbon atom tends to bond with four other atoms at once.

2 Which is a carbon-based molecule?
 A oxygen
 B salt
 C sugar
 D water

3

Nutrition Facts
Serving Size 1/2 Cup (124g)
Servings Per Container about 4.2

Amount Per Serving	
Calories 115	Calories from Fat 40

	% Daily Value**
Total Fat 5g	8%
Saturated Fat 3g	15%
Cholesterol 25mg	8%
Sodium 380mg	16%
Total Carbohydrate 3g	1%
Dietary Fiber 0g	0%
Sugars 4g	
Protein 15g	30%

Which of the items listed on the Nutrition Facts label is *not* a carbon-containing compound?
 A cholesterol
 B fat
 C protein
 D sodium

4 Which is *not* a common shape in carbon-based molecules?
 A linear
 B planar
 C tetrahedral
 D triangular

5 Which is an organic compound?
 A CH_4
 B HCl
 C NaCl
 D O_2

6 The naming of carbon-based molecules is based *mainly* on which characteristic?
 A the number of carbon atoms in the molecule
 B the number of oxygen atoms in the molecule
 C the shape of the molecule
 D the type of bonding in the molecule

7 Which element would you find in a DNA molecule, but not in a carbohydrate molecule?
 A carbon
 B nitrogen
 C oxygen
 D phosphorus

8 Which element is *not* usually found in molecules that make up living organisms?
 A C
 B N
 C O
 D Pb

9 Which could you do to determine whether a substance is an organic compound?
 A Determine the products of its combustion.
 B Observe its reaction with an acid.
 C Test whether it is fat-soluble.
 D Test whether it is water-soluble.

Directions: Select the best answer for each of the following questions.

10 The black material that remains when organic matter is burned is evidence of the presence of

A carbon.

B hydrogen.

C oxygen.

D sulfur.

11 The molecules that make up living things consist mostly of carbon, hydrogen, nitrogen, oxygen, phosphorus, and sulfur. Which type of compound is *not* made up of these elements?

A DNA

B lipids

C proteins

D salts

12 Which element would you find in a protein molecule, but not in a starch molecule?

A carbon

B nitrogen

C oxygen

D zinc

13 Which is the name of the monomers that make up a molecule of protein?

A amino acids

B citric acids

C nucleic acids

D protein acids

14 Which *non-organic* compound is necessary for cellular processes such as photosynthesis and respiration?

A carbon dioxide

B citric acid

C pyruvic acid

D water

15 A large DNA molecule is made of which small unit molecules?

A nucleotides

B peptides

C protein acids

D citric acids

16 Which is *not* a function of large carbohydrate molecules in living things?

A providing an energy source for offspring

B providing structure or support for the organism

C storing energy for the organism

D storing the organism's genetic information

17 Large RNA molecules are made up of smaller parts known as

A biotides.

B nucleotides.

C peptides.

D sugars.

18 Which is *not* an example of a large organic molecule made from many smaller parts?

A amino acid

B DNA

C protein

D starch

19 Which property of water makes it a good solvent, allowing many chemical processes to occur in living organisms?

A Its molecules are held together by hydrogen bonds.

B Its molecules are polar.

C Water can evaporate.

D Its density is higher in the solid state than in the liquid state.

20 Which of the following biomolecules is *not* a polymer?

A carbohydrates

B nucleic acids

C proteins

D lipids

Standard Set 7: Periodic Table

Directions: Select the best answer for each of the following questions.

1 The portion of the periodic table shown below has five elements in various locations noted by letters, not by their symbols.

Periodic Table
Group Number

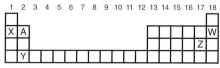

Which element would be expected to have chemical properties similar to those of element A?

A W
B X
C Y
D Z

Use the periodic table to answer questions 2 and 3.

2 Which element would be the *most* reactive?

A Al
B Cl
C P
D Na

3 From its position on the periodic table, which of these elements should exhibit the most metallic character?

A Bi
B P
C Sb
D Se

4 Which is a characteristic you would associate with an element that is a metal?

A conductivity
B fluorescence
C radioactivity
D unreactivity

5 In the periodic table of elements, the most reactive metals are found

A at the bottom of the group of elements on the far left side of the table.
B at the bottom of the group of elements on the far right side of the table.
C at the top of the group of elements on the far left side of the table.
D at the top of the group of elements on the far right side of the table.

6 Which property of metals is the main reason they are used to make pots and pans for cooking?

A high density
B reaction with nonmetals
C good heat conduction
D good electrical conduction

7

Elements

Element	Number of Protons	Number of Neutrons
Hydrogen	1	0
Carbon	6	6
Oxygen	8	8
Uranium	92	142

The mass number of an atom is equal to the number of protons and neutrons in its nucleus. Which of the elements in the table has the highest mass number?

A hydrogen
B carbon
C oxygen
D uranium

Science Online Standards Practice ca8.msscience.com

Standard Set 7: Periodic Table

Directions: Select the best answer for each of the following questions.

8 Which statement is correct?

A All isotopes of hydrogen have one neutron in the nucleus.

B All isotopes of hydrogen have one proton in the nucleus.

C Isotopes of hydrogen have different numbers of electrons.

D Isotopes of hydrogen have the same number of protons and neutrons.

9 An isotope of uranium emits a particle composed of two protons and two neutrons. Which remains after the isotope emits the particle?

A a new element with a greater mass than the uranium mass

B a new element with a smaller mass than the uranium mass

C a new isotope of uranium with a greater mass than the starting mass.

D a new isotope of uranium with a smaller mass than the starting mass

10 Which explains why the atomic mass of an element is usually greater than the atomic number of the element?

A Electrons have more energy levels in atoms with larger atomic numbers.

B Neutrons in the nucleus give more mass to the element.

C The atomic mass depends only on the number of protons in the nucleus.

D The number of electrons is greater than the number of protons.

11 Which is a property of a nonmetal?

A It can be bent into different shapes.

B It has a hard and shiny surface.

C It is a good conductor of heat.

D It is a poor conductor of electricity.

Use the periodic table of elements below to answer questions 12 through 14.

12 Which nonmetal is *most* reactive?

A Cl

B F

C O

D S

13 Which would be *best* to use for electrical wiring?

A Cl

B I

C In

D S

14 Predict which would be most reactive with water.

A Ba

B Ca

C Mg

D Sr

15 Which would *best* conduct electricity?

A copper

B oxygen

C paper

D wood

16 A column of elements is labeled as *U, V, X, Y,* and *Z. U* and *V* are metals, *X* is a metalloid, and *Y* and *Z* are nonmetals. Which is the expected order of these elements in a column on the periodic table?

A U, V, X, Y, Z

B X, U, V, Y, Z

C Y, X, U, V, X

D Y, Z, X, U, V

Standard Set 8: Density and Buoyancy

Directions: Select the best answer for each of the following questions.

1 You calculate the density of a 10-g piece of clay to be 5 g/cm³. Which is the density of a 5-g piece of the same clay?

A 2.5 g/cm³

B 5 g/cm³

C 10 g/cm³

D It is impossible to know without finding the volume.

2 Density is a measurement of a substance's mass per unit volume. The density of gold is

A 19.28 cm/g³.

B 19.28 g/cm³.

C 19.28 L/cm³.

D 19.8 m/s³.

3 To determine the density of lead, you need to determine

A mass only.

B shape only.

C mass and volume.

D mass and viscosity.

4 Which units would you use to express the density of a liquid?

A g/mL

B m/s

C kg/cm³

D N/cm³

5 A piece of metal has a density of 12 g/cm³. What is the mass of a piece of metal with a volume of 3 cm³?

A 4 g

B 12 g

C 36 g

D 40 g

6

The graph above shows five different measurements of mass and volume taken from samples of the same substance. Which is the density of this substance?

A about 1 g/cm³

B about 3.5 g/cm³

C about 12 g/cm³

D It depends on the mass.

7 A ruler could be used to find the volume of which?

A 10 g of a particular gas

B a container of oil

C a cube-shaped piece of metal

D a piece of rock with an irregular shape

8 A piece of plastic has a mass of 15 g, and it displaces 30 mL of water. What is its density?

A 0.5 g/cm³

B 0.5 cm³/g

C 2 g/cm³

D 2 cm³/g

Science Online Standards Practice ca8.msscience.com

Standard Set 8: Density and Buoyancy

Directions: Select the best answer for each of the following questions.

9

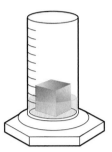

The illustration above shows one step in the method a student used to calculate the density of a piece of metal. Which is *not* a necessary step in this method for calculating density?

A adding enough water to cover the piece of metal

B finding the mass of the piece of metal, using a balance

C finding the volume of water in the cylinder with and without the metal

D using the lines on the graduated cylinder to estimate the metal's volume

10 A boulder in a river has a weight of 65 N. It displaces a volume of water with a weight of 10 N. Which is the net force on this rock?

A 55 N down

B 65 N down

C 75 N up

D 75 N down

11 My Lien makes a small boat out of aluminum foil. When she places it in water, the boat sinks. How could she change the boat to make it float?

A make the boat deeper, so it displaces more water

B make the boat heavier, using thicker foil

C make the boat lighter, using less foil

D make the boat smaller, so it displaces less water

12 Measurements of Objects

Object	Mass (g)	Volume (cm³)	Density (g/cm³)
Ball	100	50	2
Box	40	40	1
Toy Car	50	10	5
Book	90	30	3

If the four objects were placed in identical containers of water and all objects sank to the bottom, which one would displace the *most* water?

A ball

B book

C box

D toy car

13 An object has a weight of 5 N. This object sinks when placed in 10 L of water. Which statement describes how this object could float?

A It is impossible for the object to float.

B The object would float if placed in a larger volume of water.

C The object would float in a liquid with a density less than that of water.

D The object would float in a liquid with a density greater than the object.

14

Liquid Measurement Data					
Liquid	Mass of cup (g)	Mass of liquid and cup (g)	Mass of liquid (g)	Volume of liquid (mL)	Density (g/mL)
Tap water	7.0	106.0	99.0	100.0	0.99
Saltwater	6.0	110.0	104.0	100.0	1.04
Oil	6.0	98.0	92.0	100.0	0.92

A small object is placed in each of the liquids in the table above. Which would exert the greatest buoyant force on the object?

A oil

B salt water

C tap water

D The buoyant force depends only on the weight of the object.

Standard Set 9: Investigation and Experimentation

Directions: Select the best answer for each of the following questions.

1 Alberto and George suspected that lawn fertilizer from their neighborhood was causing excessive algae to grow in the pond at the end of their street. Which would be the *best* test of their hypothesis?

A Compare the growth of algae in ponds near fertilized lawns and other ponds near unfertilized lawns.

B Compare the growth of algae in ponds near fertilized lawns in spring, summer, fall, and winter.

C Conduct a neighborhood survey to find out what kind of fertilizers everyone uses.

D Suggest that the neighborhood use more fertilizer to see if this results in an increase in algae.

2

Annual Rainfall

City	Average Annual Rainfall (cm)	Years Rainfall Measured
Cairo, Egypt	25	1903–1990
London, England	62	1697–1978
Moscow, Russia	60	1820–1989
New York, USA	113	1944–1990

The table above shows average annual rainfall for four cities. The data from which city is *most* reliable for predicting future rainfall?

A Cairo

B London

C Moscow

D New York

3 Sometimes you can see that a measurement is incorrect because its value is unreasonable. Which of these measured values is unreasonable?

A The average speed of the winning race car was 2.4 km/h.

B The diameter of the basketball was 24 cm.

C The temperature of the ice water was 0.2°C.

D The time for a stone to fall 20 m was 2.0 s.

4 Alexis wants to determine which of her rubber balls can bounce the highest. She takes the first ball and drops it onto the cement sidewalk. She then drops the second ball from the same height onto the sidewalk. She records how high each ball bounced. The accuracy of her experiment could be improved by

A bouncing each ball a different number of times.

B doing the experiment multiple times.

C dropping the second ball from a higher place.

D measuring the time it takes for each ball to reach its maximum height.

5

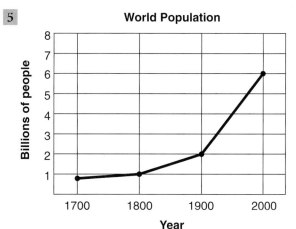

World Population

Suppose the pattern of population change shown in the graph continues for another 100 years. Students should assume that the population in 2100 would be

A exactly 6 billion.

B impossible to predict.

C less than 6 billion.

D more than 6 billion.

Standard Set 9: Investigation and Experimentation

Directions: Select the best answer for each of the following questions.

6 A line graph shows the size of the largest particles carried by a river (cm) v. the speed of the river (m/s). Why could it be useful to find the slope of this graph?

A You could predict the speed of a river based on the particles carried in the river.

B You could use the information to classify the different types of rivers.

C You could use the information to predict flooding of rivers.

D You could use the slope to find the largest particle carried by a stream.

7 Keshia collects data about the percentage of students in school who are allergic to milk. Which form would be *best* for presenting this data?

A a bar graph of milk allergies in different classes

B a line graph of students v. milk allergy

C a list of the students with milk allergies

D a pie graph showing the percentages of students with milk allergies

8

Velocity v. Time for a 500-kg Race Car

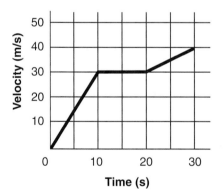

Force can be calculated by the equation $F = ma$. Which is the force on the race car from 0 s to 10 s?

A 0.06 kg m/s^2

B 600 kg m/s^2

C $1,500 \text{ kg m/s}^2$

D $15,000 \text{ kg m/s}^2$

9 Rivers and streams carry sediment from one location to another. Which graph shows that the faster a river follows, the larger the particles the river can carry?

A

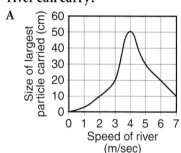

B

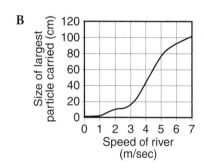

C

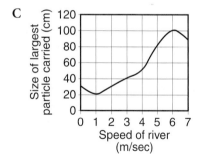

D

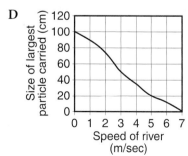

At-Home Standards Practice

The answers for the At-Home Standards Practice presented on the previous pages are listed below. Use this answer key to check your understanding of the Standards. If you need help with a question, use the chapter and lesson reference to go back and review.

Standard Set 1:
Pages 550–551

1. A Chap. 1, Lesson 1
2. C Chap. 1, Lesson 1
3. B Chap. 1, Lesson 1
4. B Chap. 1, Lesson 2
5. C Chap. 1, Lesson 2
6. D Chap. 1, Lesson 2
7. C Chap. 1, Lesson 2
8. B Chap. 1, Lesson 2
9. C Chap. 1, Lesson 2
10. C Chap. 1, Lesson 2
11. D Chap. 1, Lesson 2
12. D Chap. 1, Lesson 2
13. C Chap. 1, Lesson 2
14. B Chap. 1, Lesson 2
15. A Chap. 1, Lesson 3
16. C Chap. 1, Lesson 3
17. C Chap. 1, Lesson 3

Standard Set 2:
Pages 552–553

1. C Chap. 2, Lesson 1
2. B Chap. 2, Lesson 1
3. B Chap. 2, Lesson 2
4. C Chap. 2, Lesson 1
5. B Chap. 2, Lesson 1
6. D Chap. 2, Lesson 2
7. C Chap. 2, Lesson 1
8. C Chap. 2, Lesson 1
9. D Chap. 2, Lesson 3
10. C Chap. 2, Lesson 3
11. A Chap. 2, Lesson 2
12. D Chap. 2, Lesson 2
13. B Chap. 2, Lesson 3
14. B Chap. 2, Lesson 3
15. A Chap. 2, Lesson 3
16. D Chap. 2, Lesson 3

Standard Set 3:
Pages 554–555

1. C Chap. 4, Lesson 2
2. D Chap. 4, Lesson 2
3. A Chap. 5, Lesson 1
4. D Chap. 5, Lesson 1
5. D Chap. 5, Lesson 1
6. A Chap. 5, Lesson 1
7. C Chap. 5, Lesson 2
8. A Chap. 5, Lesson 2
9. D Chap. 6, Lesson 1
10. C Chap. 6, Lesson 2
11. A Chap. 6, Lesson 1
12. C Chap. 6, Lesson 2
13. C Chap. 6, Lesson 2
14. A Chap. 7, Lesson 1
15. B Chap. 7, Lesson 1
16. B Chap. 7, Lesson 1

Standard Set 4:
Pages 556–557

1. D Chap. 11, Lesson 4
2. D Chap. 12, Lesson 3
3. D Chap. 12, Lesson 1
4. C Chap. 12, Lesson 3
5. A Chap. 12, Lesson 2
6. C Chap. 12, Lesson 3
7. B Chap. 12, Lesson 3
8. D Chap. 12, Lesson 3
9. D Chap. 11, Lesson 1
10. A Chap. 11, Lesson 1
11. A Chap. 11, Lesson 1
12. D Chap. 11, Lesson 1
13. C Chap. 12, Lesson 2
14. D Chap. 11, Lesson 1
15. A Chap. 12, Lesson 1
16. B Chap. 12, Lesson 2
17. D Chap. 12, Lesson 2

18. B Chap. 12, Lesson 3
19. D Chap. 12, Lesson 3

Standard Set 5:
Pages 558–559

1. A Chap. 8, Lesson 1
2. D Chap. 7, Lesson 3
3. C Chap. 8, Lesson 2
4. B Chap. 8, Lesson 1
5. A Chap. 8, Lesson 2
6. B Chap. 8, Lesson 2
7. B Chap. 8, Lesson 2
8. A Chap. 8, Lesson 2
9. D Chap. 8, Lesson 3
10. B Chap. 8, Lesson 3
11. B Chap. 8, Lesson 3
12. C Chap. 8, Lesson 3
13. D Chap. 7, Lesson 3
14. D Chap. 7, Lesson 3
15. D Chap. 7, Lesson 3
16. C Chap. 7, Lesson 3
17. C Chap. 9, Lesson 2
18. B Chap. 9, Lesson 2

Standard Set 6:
Pages 560–561

1. D Chap. 10, Lesson 2
2. C Chap. 10, Lesson 2
3. D Chap. 10, Lesson 3
4. D Chap. 10, Lesson 2
5. A Chap. 10, Lesson 3
6. A Chap. 10, Lesson 2
7. D Chap. 10, Lesson 3
8. D Chap. 10, Lesson 3
9. A Chap. 10, Lesson 3
10. A Chap. 10, Lesson 3
11. D Chap. 10, Lesson 3
12. B Chap. 10, Lesson 3

13 A Chap. 10, Lesson 3
14 D Chap. 10, Lesson 3
15 A Chap. 10, Lesson 3
16 D Chap. 10, Lesson 3
17 B Chap. 10, Lesson 3
18 A Chap. 10, Lesson 3
19 B Chap. 10, Lesson 1
20 D Chap. 10, Lesson 3

Standard Set 7:
Pages 562–563

1   C Chap. 7, Lesson 1
2   A Chap. 7, Lesson 3
3   B Chap. 7, Lesson 1
4   A Chap. 7, Lesson 3
5   A Chap. 7, Lesson 1
6   C Chap. 7, Lesson 3
7   D Chap. 7, Lesson 1
8   B Chap. 7, Lesson 2
9   B Chap. 7, Lesson 2
10 B Chap. 7, Lesson 1
11 D Chap. 7, Lesson 3
12 B Chap. 7, Lesson 1
13 C Chap. 7, Lesson 1
14 A Chap. 7, Lesson 1
15 A Chap. 7, Lesson 1
16 D Chap. 7, Lesson 1

Standard Set 8:
Pages 564–565

1   B Chap. 3, Lesson 1
2   B Chap. 3, Lesson 1
3   C Chap. 3, Lesson 1
4   A Chap. 3, Lesson 1
5   C Chap. 3, Lesson 1
6   B Chap. 3, Lesson 1
7   C Chap. 3, Lesson 1

8   A Chap. 3, Lesson 1
9   D Chap. 3, Lesson 1
10 A Chap. 3, Lesson 2
11 A Chap. 3, Lesson 3
12 A Chap. 3, Lesson 3
13 D Chap. 3, Lesson 3
14 B Chap. 3, Lesson 2

Standard Set 9:
Pages 566–567

1   A Tools of the Scientist
2   B Tools of the Scientist
3   A Tools of the Scientist
4   B Tools of the Scientist
5   D Tools of the Scientist
6   A Tools of the Scientist
7   D Tools of the Scientist
8   C Tools of the Scientist
9   B Tools of the Scientist

Student Resources

For Students and Parents/Guardians

These resources are designed to help you achieve in science. You will find useful information on laboratory safety, technology skills, and math skills. In addition, some physical science reference materials are found in the Reference Handbook. You'll find the information you need to learn and sharpen your skills in these resources.

Student Resources Table of Contents

Science Safety Skill Handbook

Safety Symbols..572
Safety in the Science Laboratory.......................................573
   General Safety Rules..573
   Prevent Accidents..573
   Laboratory Work..573
   Laboratory Cleanup...574
   Emergencies..574

Technology Skill Handbook

   Hardware Basics..575
   Storing Your Data...575
   Getting Started with Word Processing Programs.................576
   Getting Started with Spreadsheet Programs........................576
   Getting Started with Presentation Programs.......................577
   Doing Research with the World Wide Web..........................578

Math Skill Handbook

Math Review
   Use Fractions..579
   Use Ratios...582
   Use Decimals...582
   Use Proportions..583
   Use Percentages..584
   Solve One-Step Equations...584
   Use Statistics..585
   Use Geometry...586
Science Application
   Measure in SI..589
   Dimensional Analysis...589
   Precision and Significant Digits..591
   Scientific Notation...591
   Make and Use Graphs..592

Reference Handbook

   Using a Calculator..594
   Understanding Scientific Terms..595
   Science Reference Guide..597
   Physical Science Reference Tables...598
   Periodic Table of Elements..600

Science Safety Skill Handbook

These safety symbols are used in laboratory and field investigations in this book to indicate possible hazards. Learn the meaning of each symbol and refer to this page often. *Remember to wash your hands thoroughly after completing lab procedures.*

SAFETY SYMBOLS	HAZARD	EXAMPLES	PRECAUTION	REMEDY
DISPOSAL	Special disposal procedures need to be followed.	certain chemicals, living organisms	Do not dispose of these materials in the sink or trash can.	Dispose of wastes as directed by your teacher.
BIOLOGICAL	Organisms or other biological materials that might be harmful to humans	bacteria, fungi, blood, unpreserved tissues, plant materials	Avoid skin contact with these materials. Wear mask or gloves.	Notify your teacher if you suspect contact with material. Wash hands thoroughly.
EXTREME TEMPERATURE	Objects that can burn skin by being too cold or too hot	boiling liquids, hot plates, dry ice, liquid nitrogen	Use proper protection when handling.	Go to your teacher for first aid.
SHARP OBJECT	Use of tools or glassware that can easily puncture or slice skin	razor blades, pins, scalpels, pointed tools, dissecting probes, broken glass	Practice common-sense behavior and follow guidelines for use of the tool.	Go to your teacher for first aid.
FUME	Possible danger to respiratory tract from fumes	ammonia, acetone, nail polish remover, heated sulfur, moth balls	Make sure there is good ventilation. Never smell fumes directly. Wear a mask.	Leave foul area and notify your teacher immediately.
ELECTRICAL	Possible danger from electrical shock or burn	improper grounding, liquid spills, short circuits, exposed wires	Double-check setup with teacher. Check condition of wires and apparatus. Use GFI-protected outlets.	Do not attempt to fix electrical problems. Notify your teacher immediately.
IRRITANT	Substances that can irritate the skin or mucous membranes of the respiratory tract	pollen, moth balls, steel wool, fiberglass, potassium permanganate	Wear dust mask and gloves. Practice extra care when handling these materials.	Go to your teacher for first aid.
CHEMICAL	Chemicals that can react with and destroy tissue and other materials	bleaches such as hydrogen peroxide; acids such as sulfuric acid, hydrochloric acid; bases such as ammonia, sodium hydroxide	Wear goggles, gloves, and an apron.	Immediately flush the affected area with water and notify your teacher.
TOXIC	Substance may be poisonous if touched, inhaled, or swallowed.	mercury, many metal compounds, iodine, poinsettia plant parts	Follow your teacher's instructions.	Always wash hands thoroughly after use. Go to your teacher for first aid.
FLAMMABLE	Open flame may ignite flammable chemicals, loose clothing, or hair.	alcohol, kerosene, potassium permanganate, hair, clothing	Avoid open flames and heat when using flammable chemicals.	Notify your teacher immediately. Use fire safety equipment if applicable.
OPEN FLAME	Open flame in use, may cause fire.	hair, clothing, paper, synthetic materials	Tie back hair and loose clothing. Follow teacher's instructions on lighting and extinguishing flames.	Always wash hands thoroughly after use. Go to your teacher for first aid.

 Eye Safety
Proper eye protection must be worn at all times by anyone performing or observing science activities.

 Clothing Protection
This symbol appears when substances could stain or burn clothing.

 Animal Safety
This symbol appears when safety of animals and students must be ensured.

 Handwashing
After the lab, wash hands with soap and water before removing goggles

Safety in the Science Laboratory

Introduction to Science Safety

The science laboratory is a safe place to work if you follow standard safety procedures. Being responsible for your own safety helps to make the entire laboratory a safer place for everyone. When performing any lab, read and apply the caution statements and safety symbol listed at the beginning of the lab.

General Safety Rules

1. Complete the *Lab Safety Form* or other safety contract BEFORE starting any science lab.

2. Study the procedure. Ask your teacher any questions. Be sure you understand safety symbols shown on the page.

3. Notify your teacher about allergies or other health conditions which can affect your participation in a lab.

4. Learn and follow use and safety procedures for your equipment. If unsure, ask your teacher.

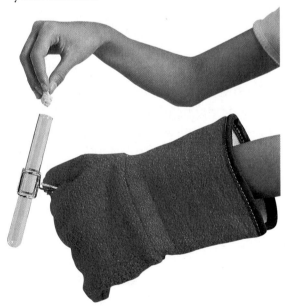

5. Never eat, drink, chew gum, apply cosmetics, or do any personal grooming in the lab. Never use lab glassware as food or drink containers. Keep your hands away from your face and mouth.

6. Know the location and proper use of the safety shower, eye wash, fire blanket, and fire alarm.

Prevent Accidents

1. Use the safety equipment provided to you. Goggles and a safety apron should be worn during investigations.

2. Do NOT use hair spray, mousse, or other flammable hair products. Tie back long hair and tie down loose clothing.

3. Do NOT wear sandals or other open-toed shoes in the lab.

4. Remove jewelry on hands and wrists. Loose jewelry, such as chains and long necklaces, should be removed to prevent them from getting caught in equipment.

5. Do not taste any substances or draw any material into a tube with your mouth.

6. Proper behavior is expected in the lab. Practical jokes and fooling around can lead to accidents and injury.

7. Keep your work area uncluttered.

Laboratory Work

1. Collect and carry all equipment and materials to your work area before beginning a lab.

2. Remain in your own work area unless given permission by your teacher to leave it.

Science Safety Skill Handbook

3. Always slant test tubes away from yourself and others when heating them, adding substances to them, or rinsing them.

4. If instructed to smell a substance in a container, hold the container a short distance away and fan vapors towards your nose.

5. Do NOT substitute other chemicals/substances for those in the materials list unless instructed to do so by your teacher.

6. Do NOT take any materials or chemicals outside of the laboratory.

7. Stay out of storage areas unless instructed to be there and supervised by your teacher.

Laboratory Cleanup

1. Turn off all burners, water, and gas, and disconnect all electrical devices.

2. Clean all pieces of equipment and return all materials to their proper places.

3. Dispose of chemicals and other materials as directed by your teacher. Place broken glass and solid substances in the proper containers. Never discard materials in the sink.

4. Clean your work area.

5. Wash your hands with soap and water thoroughly BEFORE removing your goggles.

Emergencies

1. Report any fire, electrical shock, glassware breakage, spill, or injury, no matter how small, to your teacher immediately. Follow his or her instructions.

2. If your clothing should catch fire, STOP, DROP, and ROLL. If possible, smother it with the fire blanket or get under a safety shower. NEVER RUN.

3. If a fire should occur, turn off all gas and leave the room according to established procedures.

4. In most instances, your teacher will clean up spills. Do NOT attempt to clean up spills unless you are given permission and instructions to do so.

5. If chemicals come into contact with your eyes or skin, notify your teacher immediately. Use the eyewash, or flush your skin or eyes with large quantities of water.

6. The fire extinguisher and first-aid kit should only be used by your teacher unless it is an extreme emergency and you have been given permission.

7. If someone is injured or becomes ill, only a professional medical provider or someone certified in first aid should perform first-aid procedures.

Computer Skills

People who study science rely on computer technology to do research, record experimental data, analyze results from investigations, and communicate with other scientists. Whether you work in a laboratory or just need to write a lab report, good computer skills are necessary.

Figure 1 Students and scientists rely on computers to gather data and communicate ideas.

Hardware Basics

Your personal computer is a system consisting of many components. The parts you can see and touch are called hardware.

Figure 2 Most desktop computers consist of the components shown above. Notebook computers have the same components in a compact unit.

Desktop systems, like the one shown in **Figure 2**, typically have most of these components. Notebook and tablet computers have most of the same components as a desktop computer, but the components are integrated into a single, book-sized portable unit.

Storing Your Data

When you save documents created on computers at your school, they probably are stored in a directory on your school's network. However, if you want to take the documents you have created home, you need to save them on something portable. Removable media, like those shown in **Figure 3**, are disks and drives that are designed to be moved from one computer to another.

Figure 3 Removable data storage is a convenient way to carry your documents from place to place.

Removable media vary from floppy disks and recordable CDs and DVDs to small solid-state storage. Tiny USB "keychain" drives have become popular because they can store large amounts of data and plug into any computer with a USB port. Each of these types of media stores different amounts of data. Be sure that you save your data to a medium that is compatible with your computer.

Getting Started with Word Processing Programs

A word processor is used for the composition, editing, and formatting of written material. Word processors vary from program to program, but most have the basic functions shown in **Figure 4**. Most word processors also can be used to make simple tables and graphics.

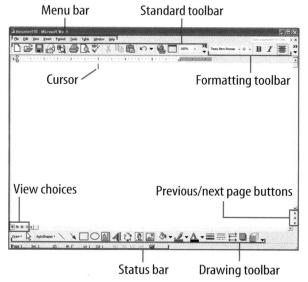

Figure 4 Word processors have functions that easily allow you to edit, format, view, and save text, tables, and images, making them useful for writing lab reports and research papers.

Word Processor Tips

■ As you type, text will automatically wrap to the next line. Press *Enter* on your keyboard if you wish to start a new paragraph.

■ You can move multiple lines of text around by using the *cut* and *paste* functions on the toolbar.

■ If you make a typing or formatting error, use the *undo* function on the toolbar.

■ Be sure to save your document early and often. This will prevent you from losing your work if your computer turns off unexpectedly.

■ Use the *spell-check* function to check your spelling and grammar. Remember that *spell-check* will not catch words that are misspelled to look like other words, such as *cold* instead of *gold*. Reread your document to look for spelling and grammar mistakes.

■ Graphics and spreadsheets can be added to your document by copying them from other programs and pasting them into your document.

■ If you have questions about using your word processor, ask your teacher or use the program's *help* menu.

Getting Started with Spreadsheet Programs

A spreadsheet, like the one shown in **Figure 5**, helps you organize information into columns and rows. Spreadsheets are particularly useful for making data tables. Spreadsheets also can be used to perform mathematical calculations with your data. Then, you can use the spreadsheet to generate graphs and charts displaying your results.

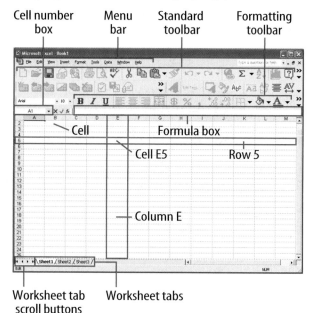

Figure 5 With formulas and graphs, spreadsheets help you organize and analyze your data.

Spreadsheet Tips

■ Think about how to organize your data before you begin entering data.

■ Each column (vertical) is assigned a letter and each row (horizontal) is assigned a number. Each point where a row and column intersect is called a cell, and is labeled according to where it is located. For example: column A, row 1 is cell A1.

■ To edit the information in a cell, you must first activate the cell by clicking on it.

■ When using a spreadsheet to generate a graph, make sure you use the type of graph that best represents the data. Review the *Science Skill Handbook* in this book for help with graphs.

■ To learn more about using your spreadsheet program ask your teacher or use the program's Help menu.

Getting Started with Presentation Programs

There are many programs that help you orally communicate results of your research in an organized and interesting way. Many of these are slideshow programs, which allow you to organize text, graphs, digital photographs, sound, animations, and digital video into one multimedia presentation. Presentations can be printed onto paper or displayed on-screen. Slideshow programs are particularly effective when used with video projectors and interactive whiteboards, like the one shown in **Figure 6**. Although presentation programs are not the only way to communicate information publicly, they are an effective way to organize your presentation and remind your audience of major points.

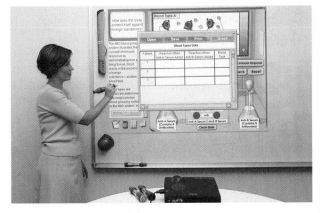

Figure 6 Video projectors and interactive whiteboards allow you to present information stored on a computer to an entire classroom. They are becoming increasingly common in the classrooms.

Presentation Program Tips

■ Often, color and strong images will convey a point better than words alone. But, be sure to organize your presentation clearly. Don't let the graphics confuse the message.

■ Most presentation programs will let you copy and paste text, spreadsheets, art and graphs from other programs.

■ Most presentation programs have built-in templates that help you organize text and graphics.

■ As with any kind of presentation, familiarize yourself with the equipment and practice your presentation before you present it to an audience.

■ Most presentation programs will allow you to save your document in html format so that you can publish your document on a Web site.

■ If you have questions about using your presentation software or hardware, ask your teacher or use the program's Help menu.

Doing Research with the World Wide Web

The Internet is a global network of computers where information can be stored and shared by anyone with an internet connection. One of the easiest ways to find information on the internet is by using the World Wide Web, a vast graphical system of documents written in the computer language, html (hypertext markup language). Web pages are arranged in collections of related material called "Web sites." The content on a Web site is viewed using a program called a Web browser. Web browsers, like the one shown in **Figure 7,** allow you to browse or surf the Web by clicking on highlighted hyperlinks, which move you from Web page to Web page. Web content can be searched by topic using a search engine. Search engines are located on Web sites which catalog key words on Web pages all over the World Wide Web.

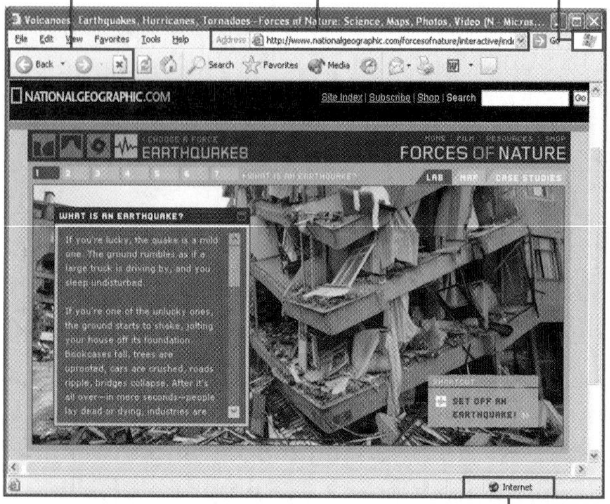

Navigation buttons   Address bar   Loading indicator

Link indicator

Figure 7 Web browsers have all the tools you need to navigate and view information on the Web.

World Wide Web Tips

■ Search the Web using specific keywords. For example, if you want to research the element gold don't type *elements* into the search engine.

■ When performing a Web search, enclose multiple keywords with quotes to narrow your results to the most relevant pages.

■ The first hit your Web search results in is not always the best. Search results are arranged by popularity, not by relevance to your topic. Be patient and look at many links in your search results to find the best information.

■ Think critically when you do science research on the Web. Compared to a traditional library, finding accurate information on the Web is not always easy because anyone can create a Web site. Some of the best places to start your research are websites for major newspapers and magazines, as well as U.S. government (*.gov*) and university (*.edu*) Web sites.

■ Security is a major concern when browsing the Web. Your computer can be exposed to advertising software and computer viruses, which can hurt your computer's data and performance. *Do not download software at your school unless your teacher tells you to do so.*

■ Cite information you find on the Web just as you would books and journals. An example of proper Web citation is the following:
Menk, Amy J. (2004). *Urban Ecology.* Retrieved January 21, 2005, from McGraw-Hill Web site: http://www.mcgraw-hill.com/papers/urban.html

■ The World Wide Web is a great resource for information, but don't forget to utilize local libraries, including your school library.

Math Review

Use Fractions ALG: 1.0

A fraction compares a part to a whole. In the fraction $\frac{2}{3}$, the 2 represents the part and is the numerator. The 3 represents the whole and is the denominator.

Reduce Fractions To reduce a fraction, you must find the largest factor that is common to both the numerator and the denominator, the greatest common factor (GCF). Divide both numbers by the GCF. The fraction has then been reduced, or it is in its simplest form.

Example Twelve of the 20 chemicals in the science lab are in powder form. What fraction of the chemicals used in the lab are in powder form?

Step 1 Write the fraction.
$$\frac{\text{part}}{\text{whole}} = \frac{12}{20}$$

Step 2 To find the GCF of the numerator and denominator, list all of the factors of each number.
Factors of 12: 1, 2, 3, 4, 6, 12
(the numbers that divide evenly into 12)
Factors of 20: 1, 2, 4, 5, 10, 20
(the numbers that divide evenly into 20)

Step 3 List the common factors.
1, 2, 4

Step 4 Choose the greatest factor in the list. The GCF of 12 and 20 is 4.

Step 5 Divide the numerator and denominator by the GCF.
$$\frac{12 \div 4}{20 \div 4} = \frac{3}{5}$$

In the lab, $\frac{3}{5}$ of the chemicals are in powder form.

Practice Problem At an amusement park, 66 of 90 rides have a height restriction. What fraction of the rides, in its simplest form, has a height restriction?

Add and Subtract Fractions with Like Denominators To add or subtract fractions with the same denominator, add or subtract the numerators and write the sum or difference over the denominator. After finding the sum or difference, find the simplest form for your fraction.

Example 1 In the forest outside your house, $\frac{1}{8}$ of the animals are rabbits, $\frac{3}{8}$ are squirrels, and the remainder are birds and insects. How many are mammals?

Step 1 Add the numerators.
$$\frac{1}{8} + \frac{3}{8} = \frac{(1 + 3)}{8} = \frac{4}{8}$$

Step 2 Find the GCF.
$$\frac{4}{8} \text{ (GCF, 4)}$$

Step 3 Divide the numerator and denominator by the GCF.
$$\frac{4 \div 4}{8 \div 4} = \frac{1}{2}$$

$\frac{1}{2}$ of the animals are mammals.

Example 2 If $\frac{7}{16}$ of the Earth is covered by freshwater, and $\frac{1}{16}$ of that is in glaciers, how much freshwater is not frozen?

Step 1 Subtract the numerators.
$$\frac{7}{16} - \frac{1}{16} = \frac{(7 - 1)}{16} = \frac{6}{16}$$

Step 2 Find the GCF.
$$\frac{6}{16} \text{ (GCF, 2)}$$

Step 3 Divide the numerator and denominator by the GCF.
$$\frac{6 \div 2}{16 \div 2} = \frac{3}{8}$$

$\frac{3}{8}$ of the freshwater is not frozen.

Practice Problem A bicycle rider is riding at a rate of 15 km/h for $\frac{4}{9}$ of his ride, 10 km/h for $\frac{2}{9}$ of his ride, and 8 km/h for the remainder of the ride. How much of his ride is he riding at a rate greater than 8 km/h?

Math Skill Handbook

Add and Subtract Fractions with Unlike Denominators To add or subtract fractions with unlike denominators, first find the least common denominator (LCD). This is the smallest number that is a common multiple of both denominators. Rename each fraction with the LCD, and then add or subtract. Find the simplest form if necessary.

Example 1 A chemist makes a paste that is $\frac{1}{2}$ table salt (NaCl), $\frac{1}{3}$ sugar ($C_6H_{12}O_6$), and the remainder is water (H_2O). How much of the paste is a solid?

Step 1 Find the LCD of the fractions.

$$\frac{1}{2} + \frac{1}{3} \text{ (LCD, 6)}$$

Step 2 Rename each numerator and each denominator with the LCD.

Step 3 Add the numerators.

$$\frac{3}{6} + \frac{2}{6} = \frac{(3 + 2)}{6} = \frac{5}{6}$$

$\frac{5}{6}$ of the paste is a solid.

Example 2 The average precipitation in Grand Junction, CO, is $\frac{7}{10}$ inch in November, and $\frac{3}{5}$ inch in December. What is the total average precipitation?

Step 1 Find the LCD of the fractions.

$$\frac{7}{10} + \frac{3}{5} \text{ (LCD, 10)}$$

Step 2 Rename each numerator and each denominator with the LCD.

Step 3 Add the numerators.

$$\frac{7}{10} + \frac{6}{10} = \frac{(7 + 6)}{10} = \frac{13}{10}$$

$\frac{13}{10}$ inches total precipitation, or $1\frac{3}{10}$ inches.

Practice Problem On an electric bill, about $\frac{1}{8}$ of the energy is from solar energy and about $\frac{1}{10}$ is from wind power. How much of the total bill is from solar energy and wind power combined?

Example 3 In your body, $\frac{7}{10}$ of your muscle contractions are involuntary (cardiac and smooth muscle tissue). Smooth muscle makes $\frac{3}{15}$ of your muscle contractions. How many of your muscle contractions are made by cardiac muscle?

Step 1 Find the LCD of the fractions.

$$\frac{7}{10} - \frac{3}{15} \text{ (LCD, 30)}$$

Step 2 Rename each numerator and each denominator with the LCD.

$$\frac{7 \times 3}{10 \times 3} = \frac{21}{30}$$

$$\frac{3 \times 2}{15 \times 2} = \frac{6}{30}$$

Step 3 Subtract the numerators.

$$\frac{21}{30} - \frac{6}{30} = \frac{(21 - 6)}{30} = \frac{15}{30}$$

Step 4 Find the GCF.

$$\frac{15}{30} \text{ (GCF, 15)}$$

$$\frac{1}{2}$$

$\frac{1}{2}$ of all muscle contractions are cardiac muscle.

Example 4 Tony wants to make cookies that call for $\frac{3}{4}$ of a cup of flour, but he only has $\frac{1}{3}$ of a cup. How much more flour does he need?

Step 1 Find the LCD of the fractions.

$$\frac{3}{4} - \frac{1}{3} \text{ (LCD, 12)}$$

Step 2 Rename each numerator and each denominator with the LCD.

$$\frac{3 \times 3}{4 \times 3} = \frac{9}{12}$$

$$\frac{1 \times 4}{3 \times 4} = \frac{4}{12}$$

Step 3 Subtract the numerators.

$$\frac{9}{12} - \frac{4}{12} = \frac{(9 - 4)}{12} = \frac{5}{12}$$

$\frac{5}{12}$ of a cup of flour

Practice Problem Using the information provided to you in Example 3 above, determine how many muscle contractions are voluntary (skeletal muscle).

Multiply Fractions To multiply with fractions, multiply the numerators and multiply the denominators. Find the simplest form if necessary.

Example Multiply $\frac{3}{5}$ by $\frac{1}{3}$.

Step 1 Multiply the numerators and denominators.

$$\frac{3}{5} \times \frac{1}{3} = \frac{(3 \times 1)}{(5 \times 3)} = \frac{3}{15}$$

Step 2 Find the GCF.

$$\frac{3}{15} \text{ (GCF, 3)}$$

Step 3 Divide the numerator and denominator by the GCF.

$$\frac{3 \div 3}{15 \div 3} = \frac{1}{5}$$

$\frac{3}{5}$ multiplied by $\frac{1}{3}$ is $\frac{1}{5}$.

Practice Problem Multiply $\frac{3}{14}$ by $\frac{5}{16}$.

Find a Reciprocal Two numbers whose product is 1 are called multiplicative inverses, or reciprocals.

Example Find the reciprocal of $\frac{3}{8}$.

Step 1 Inverse the fraction by putting the denominator on top and the numerator on the bottom.

$$\frac{8}{3}$$

The reciprocal of $\frac{3}{8}$ is $\frac{8}{3}$.

Practice Problem Find the reciprocal of $\frac{4}{9}$.

Divide Fractions To divide one fraction by another fraction, multiply the dividend by the reciprocal of the divisor. Find the simplest form if necessary.

Example 1 Divide $\frac{1}{9}$ by $\frac{1}{3}$.

Step 1 Find the reciprocal of the divisor.

The reciprocal of $\frac{1}{3}$ is $\frac{3}{1}$.

Step 2 Multiply the dividend by the reciprocal of the divisor.

$$\frac{\frac{1}{9}}{\frac{1}{3}} = \frac{1}{9} \times \frac{3}{1} = \frac{(1 \times 3)}{(9 \times 1)} = \frac{3}{9}$$

Step 3 Find the GCF.

$$\frac{3}{9} \text{ (GCF, 3)}$$

Step 4 Divide the numerator and denominator by the GCF.

$$\frac{3 \div 3}{9 \div 3} = \frac{1}{3}$$

$\frac{1}{9}$ divided by $\frac{1}{3}$ is $\frac{1}{3}$.

Example 2 Divide $\frac{3}{5}$ by $\frac{1}{4}$.

Step 1 Find the reciprocal of the divisor.

The reciprocal of $\frac{1}{4}$ is $\frac{4}{1}$.

Step 2 Multiply the dividend by the reciprocal of the divisor.

$$\frac{\frac{3}{5}}{\frac{1}{4}} = \frac{3}{5} \times \frac{4}{1} = \frac{(3 \times 4)}{(5 \times 1)} = \frac{12}{5}$$

$\frac{3}{5}$ divided by $\frac{1}{4}$ is $\frac{12}{5}$ or $2\frac{2}{5}$.

Practice Problem Divide $\frac{3}{11}$ by $\frac{7}{10}$.

Math Skill Handbook

Use Ratios ALG: 1.0

When you compare two numbers by division, you are using a ratio. Ratios can be written 3 to 5, 3:5, or $\frac{3}{5}$. Ratios, like fractions, also can be written in simplest form.

Ratios can represent one type of probability, called odds. This is a ratio that compares the number of ways a certain outcome occurs to the number of possible outcomes. For example, if you flip a coin 100 times, what are the odds that it will come up heads? There are two possible outcomes, heads or tails, so the odds of coming up heads are 50:100. Another way to say this is that 50 out of 100 times the coin will come up heads. In its simplest form, the ratio is 1:2.

Example 1 A chemical solution contains 40 g of salt and 64 g of baking soda. What is the ratio of salt to baking soda as a fraction in simplest form?

Step 1 Write the ratio as a fraction.
$$\frac{\text{salt}}{\text{baking soda}} = \frac{40}{64}$$

Step 2 Express the fraction in simplest form. The GCF of 40 and 64 is 8.
$$\frac{40}{64} = \frac{40 \div 8}{64 \div 8} = \frac{5}{8}$$

The ratio of salt to baking soda in the sample is 5:8.

Example 2 Sean rolls a 6-sided die 6 times. What are the odds that the side with a 3 will show?

Step 1 Write the ratio as a fraction.
$$\frac{\text{number of sides with a 3}}{\text{number of possible sides}} = \frac{1}{6}$$

Step 2 Multiply by the number of attempts.
$$\frac{1}{6} \times 6 \text{ attempts} = \frac{6}{6} \text{ attempts} = 1 \text{ attempt}$$

1 attempt out of 6 will show a 3.

Practice Problem Two metal rods measure 100 cm and 144 cm in length. What is the ratio of their lengths in simplest form?

Use Decimals ALG: 1.0

A fraction with a denominator that is a power of ten can be written as a decimal. For example, 0.27 means $\frac{27}{100}$. The decimal point separates the ones place from the tenths place.

Any fraction can be written as a decimal using division. For example, the fraction $\frac{5}{8}$ can be written as a decimal by dividing 5 by 8. Written as a decimal, it is 0.625.

Add or Subtract Decimals When adding and subtracting decimals, line up the decimal points before carrying out the operation.

Example 1 Find the sum of 47.68 and 7.80.

Step 1 Line up the decimal places when you write the numbers.
$$\begin{array}{r} 47.68 \\ + \ 7.80 \end{array}$$

Step 2 Add the decimals.
$$\begin{array}{r} {}^{1\ 1} \\ 47.68 \\ + \ 7.80 \\ \hline 55.48 \end{array}$$

The sum of 47.68 and 7.80 is 55.48.

Example 2 Find the difference of 42.17 and 15.85.

Step 1 Line up the decimal places when you write the number.
$$\begin{array}{r} 42.17 \\ -15.85 \end{array}$$

Step 2 Subtract the decimals.
$$\begin{array}{r} {}^{3\,11}{}_{1} \\ 42.17 \\ -15.85 \\ \hline 26.32 \end{array}$$

The difference of 42.17 and 15.85 is 26.32.

Practice Problem Find the sum of 1.245 and 3.842.

Multiply Decimals To multiply decimals, multiply the numbers like numbers without decimal points. Count the decimal places in each factor. The product will have the same number of decimal places as the sum of the decimal places in the factors.

Example Multiply 2.4 by 5.9.

Step 1 Multiply the factors like two whole numbers.
$24 \times 59 = 1416$

Step 2 Find the sum of the number of decimal places in the factors. Each factor has one decimal place, for a sum of two decimal places.

Step 3 The product will have two decimal places.
14.16

The product of 2.4 and 5.9 is 14.16.

Practice Problem Multiply 4.6 by 2.2.

Divide Decimals When dividing decimals, change the divisor to a whole number. To do this, multiply both the divisor and the dividend by the same power of ten. Then place the decimal point in the quotient directly above the decimal point in the dividend. Then divide as you do with whole numbers.

Example Divide 8.84 by 3.4.

Step 1 Multiply both factors by 10.
$3.4 \times 10 = 34, 8.84 \times 10 = 88.4$

Step 2 Divide 88.4 by 34.

```
        2.6
   34)88.4
     -68
      204
     -204
        0
```

8.84 divided by 3.4 is 2.6.

Practice Problem Divide 75.6 by 3.6.

Use Proportions ALG: 5.0

An equation that shows that two ratios are equivalent is a proportion. The ratios $\frac{2}{4}$ and $\frac{5}{10}$ are equivalent, so they can be written as $\frac{2}{4} = \frac{5}{10}$. This equation is a proportion.

When two ratios form a proportion, the cross products are equal. To find the cross products in the proportion $\frac{2}{4} = \frac{5}{10}$, multiply the 2 and the 10, and the 4 and the 5. Therefore $2 \times 10 = 4 \times 5$, or $20 = 20$.

Because you know that both ratios are equal, you can use cross products to find a missing term in a proportion. This is known as solving the proportion.

Example The heights of a tree and a pole are proportional to the lengths of their shadows. The tree casts a shadow of 24 m when a 6-m pole casts a shadow of 4 m. What is the height of the tree?

Step 1 Write a proportion.
$$\frac{\text{height of tree}}{\text{height of pole}} = \frac{\text{length of tree's shadow}}{\text{length of pole's shadow}}$$

Step 2 Substitute the known values into the proportion. Let h represent the unknown value, the height of the tree.
$$\frac{h}{6} = \frac{24}{4}$$

Step 3 Find the cross products.
$h \times 4 = 6 \times 24$

Step 4 Simplify the equation.
$4h = 144$

Step 5 Divide each side by 4.
$$\frac{4h}{4} = \frac{144}{4}$$
$$h = 36$$

The height of the tree is 36 m.

Practice Problem The ratios of the weights of two objects on the Moon and on Earth are in proportion. A rock weighing 3 N on the Moon weighs 18 N on Earth. How much would a rock that weighs 5 N on the Moon weigh on Earth?

Use Percentages ALG: 1.0

The word *percent* means "out of one hundred." It is a ratio that compares a number to 100. Suppose you read that 77 percent of the Earth's surface is covered by water. That is the same as reading that the fraction of the Earth's surface covered by water is $\frac{77}{100}$. To express a fraction as a percent, first find the equivalent decimal for the fraction. Then, multiply the decimal by 100 and add the percent symbol.

Example 1 Express $\frac{13}{20}$ as a percent.

Step 1 Find the equivalent decimal for the fraction.

$$
\begin{array}{r}
0.65 \\
20\overline{)13.00} \\
\underline{12\ 0} \\
1\ 00 \\
\underline{1\ 00} \\
0
\end{array}
$$

Step 2 Rewrite the fraction $\frac{13}{20}$ as 0.65.

Step 3 Multiply 0.65 by 100 and add the % symbol.

$0.65 \times 100 = 65 = 65\%$

So, $\frac{13}{20} = 65\%$.

This also can be solved as a proportion.

Example 2 Express $\frac{13}{20}$ as a percent.

Step 1 Write a proportion.

$\frac{13}{20} = \frac{x}{100}$

Step 2 Find the cross products.

$1300 = 20x$

Step 3 Divide each side by 20.

$\frac{1300}{20} = \frac{20x}{20}$

$65\% = x$

Practice Problem In one year, 73 of 365 days were rainy in one city. What percent of the days in that city were rainy?

Solve One-Step Equations ALG: 5.0

A statement that two expressions are equal is an equation. For example, $A = B$ is an equation that states that A is equal to B.

An equation is solved when a variable is replaced with a value that makes both sides of the equation equal. To make both sides equal the inverse operation is used. Addition and subtraction are inverses, and multiplication and division are inverses.

Example 1 Solve the equation $x - 10 = 35$.

Step 1 Find the solution by adding 10 to each side of the equation.

$$x - 10 = 35$$
$$x - 10 + 10 = 35 + 10$$
$$x = 45$$

Step 2 Check the solution.

$$x - 10 = 35$$
$$45 - 10 = 35$$
$$35 = 35$$

Both sides of the equation are equal, so $x = 45$.

Example 2 In the formula $a = bc$, find the value of c if $a = 20$ and $b = 2$.

Step 1 Rearrange the formula so the unknown value is by itself on one side of the equation by dividing both sides by b.

$$a = bc$$
$$\frac{a}{b} = \frac{bc}{b}$$
$$\frac{a}{b} = c$$

Step 2 Replace the variables a and b with the values that are given.

$$\frac{a}{b} = c$$
$$\frac{20}{2} = c$$
$$10 = c$$

Step 3 Check the solution.

$$a = bc$$
$$20 = 2 \times 10$$
$$20 = 20$$

Both sides of the equation are equal, so $c = 10$ is the solution when $a = 20$ and $b = 2$.

Practice Problem In the formula $h = gd$, find the value of d if $g = 12.3$ and $h = 17.4$.

Use Statistics

The branch of mathematics that deals with collecting, analyzing, and presenting data is statistics. In statistics, there are three common ways to summarize data with a single number—the mean, the median, and the mode.

The **mean** of a set of data is the arithmetic average. It is found by adding the numbers in the data set and dividing by the number of items in the set.

The **median** is the middle number in a set of data when the data are arranged in numerical order. If there were an even number of data points, the median would be the mean of the two middle numbers.

The **mode** of a set of data is the number or item that appears most often.

Another number that often is used to describe a set of data is the range. The **range** is the difference between the largest number and the smallest number in a set of data.

Example The speeds (in m/s) for a race car during five different time trials are 39, 37, 44, 36, and 44.

To find the mean:

Step 1 Find the sum of the numbers.
$$39 + 37 + 44 + 36 + 44 = 200$$

Step 2 Divide the sum by the number of items, which is 5.
$$200 \div 5 = 40$$

The mean is 40 m/s.

To find the median:

Step 1 Arrange the measures from least to greatest.
36, 37, 39, 44, 44

Step 2 Determine the middle measure.
36, 37, <u>39</u>, 44, 44

The median is 39 m/s.

To find the mode:

Step 1 Group the numbers that are the same together.
44, 44, 36, 37, 39

Step 2 Determine the number that occurs most in the set.
<u>44, 44</u>, 36, 37, 39

The mode is 44 m/s.

To find the range:

Step 1 Arrange the measures from greatest to least.
44, 44, 39, 37, 36

Step 2 Determine the greatest and least measures in the set.
<u>44</u>, 44, 39, 37, <u>36</u>

Step 3 Find the difference between the greatest and least measures.
$$44 - 36 = 8$$

The range is 8 m/s.

Practice Problem Find the mean, median, mode, and range for the data set 8, 4, 12, 8, 11, 14, 16.

A **frequency table** shows how many times each piece of data occurs, usually in a survey. **Table 1** below shows the results of a student survey on favorite color.

Table 1 Student Color Choice

Color	Tally	Frequency
red	IIII	4
blue	IHH	5
black	II	2
green	III	3
purple	IHH II	7
yellow	IHH I	6

Based on the frequency table data, which color is the favorite?

Math Skill Handbook

Use Geometry

The branch of mathematics that deals with the measurement, properties, and relationships of points, lines, angles, surfaces, and solids is called geometry.

Perimeter The **perimeter** (P) is the distance around a geometric figure. To find the perimeter of a rectangle, add the length and width and multiply that sum by two, or $2(l + w)$. To find perimeters of irregular figures, add the length of the sides.

Example 1 Find the perimeter of a rectangle that is 3 m long and 5 m wide.

Step 1 You know that the perimeter is 2 times the sum of the width and length.
$$P = 2(3\text{ m} + 5\text{ m})$$

Step 2 Find the sum of the width and length.
$$P = 2(8\text{ m})$$

Step 3 Multiply by 2.
$$P = 16\text{ m}$$

The perimeter is 16 m.

Example 2 Find the perimeter of a shape with sides measuring 2 cm, 5 cm, 6 cm, 3 cm.

Step 1 You know that the perimeter is the sum of all the sides.
$$P = 2 + 5 + 6 + 3$$

Step 2 Find the sum of the sides.
$$P = 2 + 5 + 6 + 3$$
$$P = 16$$

The perimeter is 16 cm.

Practice Problem 1 Find the perimeter of a rectangle with a length of 18 m and a width of 7 m.

Practice Problem 2 Find the perimeter of a triangle measuring 1.6 cm by 2.4 cm by 2.4 cm.

Area of a Rectangle The **area** (A) is the number of square units needed to cover a surface. To find the area of a rectangle, multiply the length times the width, or $l \times w$. When finding area, the units also are multiplied. Area is given in square units.

Example Find the area of a rectangle with a length of 1 cm and a width of 10 cm.

Step 1 You know that the area is the length multiplied by the width.
$$A = (1\text{ cm} \times 10\text{ cm})$$

Step 2 Multiply the length by the width. Also multiply the units.
$$A = 10\text{ cm}^2$$

The area is 10 cm².

Practice Problem Find the area of a square whose sides measure 4 m.

Area of a Triangle To find the area of a triangle, use the formula:
$$A = \frac{1}{2}(\text{base} \times \text{height})$$

The base of a triangle can be any of its sides. The height is the perpendicular distance from a base to the opposite endpoint, or vertex.

Example Find the area of a triangle with a base of 18 m and a height of 7 m.

Step 1 You know that the area is $\frac{1}{2}$ the base times the height.
$$A = \frac{1}{2}(18\text{ m} \times 7\text{ m})$$

Step 2 Multiply $\frac{1}{2}$ by the product of 18×7. Multiply the units.
$$A = \frac{1}{2}(126\text{ m}^2)$$
$$A = 63\text{ m}^2$$

The area is 63 m².

Practice Problem Find the area of a triangle with a base of 27 cm and a height of 17 cm.

Circumference of a Circle The **diameter** (d) of a circle is the distance across the circle through its center, and the **radius** (r) is the distance from the center to any point on the circle. The radius is half of the diameter. The distance around the circle is called the **circumference** (C). The formula for finding the circumference is:

$C = 2\pi r$ or $C = \pi d$

The circumference divided by the diameter is always equal to 3.1415926… This nonterminating and nonrepeating number is represented by the Greek letter π (pi). An approximation often used for π is 3.14.

Example 1 Find the circumference of a circle with a radius of 3 m.

Step 1 You know the formula for the circumference is 2 times the radius times π.
$C = 2\pi(3)$

Step 2 Multiply 2 times the radius.
$C = 6\pi$

Step 3 Multiply by π.
$C \approx 19$ m

The circumference is about 19 m.

Example 2 Find the circumference of a circle with a diameter of 24.0 cm.

Step 1 You know the formula for the circumference is the diameter times π.
$C = \pi(24.0)$

Step 2 Multiply the diameter by π.
$C \approx 75.4$ cm

The circumference is about 75.4 cm.

Practice Problem Find the circumference of a circle with a radius of 19 cm.

Area of a Circle The formula for the area of a circle is:
$A = \pi r^2$

Example 1 Find the area of a circle with a radius of 4.0 cm.

Step 1 $A = \pi(4.0)^2$

Step 2 Find the square of the radius.
$A = 16\pi$

Step 3 Multiply the square of the radius by π.
$A \approx 50$ cm^2

The area of the circle is about 50 cm^2.

Example 2 Find the area of a circle with a radius of 225 m.

Step 1 $A = \pi(225)^2$

Step 2 Find the square of the radius.
$A = 50625\pi$

Step 3 Multiply the square of the radius by π.
$A \approx 159043.1$

The area of the circle is about 159043.1 m^2.

Example 3 Find the area of a circle whose diameter is 20.0 mm.

Step 1 You know the formula for the area of a circle is the square of the radius times π, and that the radius is half of the diameter.
$A = \pi\left(\dfrac{20.0}{2}\right)^2$

Step 2 Find the radius.
$A = \pi(10.0)^2$

Step 3 Find the square of the radius.
$A = 100\pi$

Step 4 Multiply the square of the radius by π.
$A \approx 314$ mm^2

The area of is about 314 mm^2.

Practice Problem Find the area of a circle with a radius of 16 m.

Volume The measure of space occupied by a solid is the **volume** (V). To find the volume of a rectangular solid multiply the length times width times height, or $V = l \times w \times h$. It is measured in cubic units, such as cubic centimeters (cm^3).

Example Find the volume of a rectangular solid with a length of 2.0 m, a width of 4.0 m, and a height of 3.0 m.

Step 1 You know the formula for volume is the length times the width times the height.

$$V = 2.0 \text{ m} \times 4.0 \text{ m} \times 3.0 \text{ m}$$

Step 2 Multiply the length times the width times the height.

$$V = 24 \text{ m}^3$$

The volume is 24 m³.

Practice Problem Find the volume of a rectangular solid that is 8 m long, 4 m wide, and 4 m high.

To find the volume of other solids, multiply the area of the base times the height.

Example 1 Find the volume of a solid that has a triangular base with a length of 8.0 m and a height of 7.0 m. The height of the entire solid is 15.0 m.

Step 1 You know that the base is a triangle, and the area of a triangle is $\frac{1}{2}$ the base times the height, and the volume is the area of the base times the height.

$$V = \left[\frac{1}{2}(b \times h)\right] \times 15$$

Step 2 Find the area of the base.

$$V = \left[\frac{1}{2}(8 \times 7)\right] \times 15$$

$$V = \left(\frac{1}{2} \times 56\right) \times 15$$

Step 3 Multiply the area of the base by the height of the solid.

$$V = 28 \times 15$$

$$V = 420 \text{ m}^3$$

The volume is 420 m³.

Example 2 Find the volume of a cylinder that has a base with a radius of 12.0 cm, and a height of 21.0 cm.

Step 1 You know that the base is a circle, and the area of a circle is the square of the radius times π, and the volume is the area of the base times the height.

$$V = (\pi r^2) \times 21$$

$$V = (\pi 12^2) \times 21$$

Step 2 Find the area of the base.

$$V = 144\pi \times 21$$

$$V = 452 \times 21$$

Step 3 Multiply the area of the base by the height of the solid.

$$V \approx 9{,}500 \text{ cm}^3$$

The volume is about 9,500 cm³.

Example 3 Find the volume of a cylinder that has a diameter of 15 mm and a height of 4.8 mm.

Step 1 You know that the base is a circle with an area equal to the square of the radius times π. The radius is one-half the diameter. The volume is the area of the base times the height.

$$V = (\pi r^2) \times 4.8$$

$$V = \left[\pi\left(\frac{1}{2} \times 15\right)^2\right] \times 4.8$$

$$V = (\pi 7.5^2) \times 4.8$$

Step 2 Find the area of the base.

$$V = 56.25\pi \times 4.8$$

$$V \approx 176.71 \times 4.8$$

Step 3 Multiply the area of the base by the height of the solid.

$$V \approx 848.2$$

The volume is about 848.2 mm³.

Practice Problem Find the volume of a cylinder with a diameter of 7 cm in the base and a height of 16 cm.

Science Applications

Measure in SI

The metric system of measurement was developed in 1795. A modern form of the metric system, called the International System (SI), was adopted in 1960 and provides the standard measurements that all scientists around the world can understand.

The SI system is convenient because unit sizes vary by powers of 10. Prefixes are used to name units. Look at **Table 2** for some common SI prefixes and their meanings.

Table 2 Common SI Prefixes			
Prefix	**Symbol**	**Meaning**	
kilo-	k	1,000	thousandth
hecto-	h	100	hundred
deka-	da	10	ten
deci-	d	0.1	tenth
centi-	c	0.01	hundreth
milli-	m	0.001	thousandth

Example How many grams equal one kilogram?

Step 1 Find the prefix *kilo-* in **Table 2.**

Step 2 Using **Table 2,** determine the meaning of *kilo-*. According to the table, it means 1,000. When the prefix *kilo-* is added to a unit, it means that there are 1,000 of the units in a "kilounit."

Step 3 Apply the prefix to the units in the question. The units in the question are grams. There are 1,000 grams in a kilogram.

Practice Problem Is a milligram larger or smaller than a gram? How many of the smaller units equal one larger unit? What fraction of the larger unit does one smaller unit represent?

Dimensional Analysis

Convert SI Units In science, quantities such as length, mass, and time sometimes are measured using different units. A process called dimensional analysis can be used to change one unit of measure to another. This process involves multiplying your starting quantity and units by one or more conversion factors. A conversion factor is a ratio equal to one and can be made from any two equal quantities with different units. If 1,000 mL equal 1 L then two ratios can be made.

$$\frac{1{,}000 \text{ mL}}{1 \text{ L}} = \frac{1 \text{ L}}{1{,}000 \text{ mL}} = 1$$

One can convert between units in the SI system by using the equivalents in **Table 2** to make conversion factors.

Example How many cm are in 4 m?

Step 1 Write conversion factors for the units given. From **Table 2,** you know that 100 cm = 1 m. The conversion factors are
$$\frac{100 \text{ cm}}{1 \text{ m}} \text{ and } \frac{1 \text{ m}}{100 \text{ cm}}$$

Step 2 Decide which conversion factor to use. Select the factor that has the units you are converting from (m) in the denominator and the units you are converting to (cm) in the numerator.
$$\frac{100 \text{ cm}}{1 \text{ m}}$$

Step 3 Multiply the starting quantity and units by the conversion factor. Cancel the starting units with the units in the denominator. There are 400 cm in 4 m.
$$4 \text{ m} = \frac{100 \text{ cm}}{1 \text{ m}} = 400 \text{ cm}$$

Practice Problem How many milligrams are in one kilogram? (Hint: You will need to use two conversion factors from **Table 2.**)

Math Skill Handbook

Table 3 Unit System Equivalents

Type of Measurement	Equivalent
Length	1 in = 2.54 cm 1 yd = 0.91 m 1 mi = 1.61 km
Mass and weight*	1 oz = 28.35 g 1 lb = 0.45 kg 1 ton (short) = 0.91 tonnes (metric tons) 1 lb = 4.45 N
Volume	$1 \text{ in}^3 = 16.39 \text{ cm}^3$ 1 qt = 0.95 L 1 gal = 3.78 L
Area	$1 \text{ in}^2 = 6.45 \text{ cm}^2$ $1 \text{ yd}^2 = 0.83 \text{ m}^2$ $1 \text{ mi}^2 = 2.59 \text{ km}^2$ 1 acre = 0.40 hectares
Temperature	$°C = \frac{(°F - 32)}{1.8}$ $K = °C + 273$

*Weight is measured in standard Earth gravity.

Convert Between Unit Systems **Table 3** gives a list of equivalents that can be used to convert between English and SI units.

Example If a meterstick has a length of 100 cm, how long is the meterstick in inches?

Step 1 Write the conversion factors for the units given. From **Table 3,** 1 in = 2.54 cm.

$$\frac{1 \text{ in}}{2.54 \text{ cm}} \quad and \quad \frac{2.54 \text{ cm}}{1 \text{ in}}$$

Step 2 Determine which conversion factor to use. You are converting from cm to in. Use the conversion factor with cm on the bottom.

$$\frac{1 \text{ in}}{2.54 \text{ cm}}$$

Step 3 Multiply the starting quantity and units by the conversion factor. Cancel the starting units with the units in the denominator. Round your answer to the nearest tenth.

$$100 \text{ cm} \times \frac{1 \text{ in}}{2.54 \text{ cm}} = 39.37 \text{ in}$$

The meterstick is about 39.4 in long.

Practice Problem 1 A book has a mass of 5 lb. What is the mass of the book in kg?

Practice Problem 2 Use the equivalent for in and cm (1 in = 2.54 cm) to show how $1 \text{ in}^3 \approx 16.39 \text{ cm}^3$.

Precision and Significant Digits

When you make a measurement, the value you record depends on the precision of the measuring instrument. This precision is represented by the number of significant digits recorded in the measurement. When counting the number of significant digits, all digits are counted except zeros at the end of a number with no decimal point such as 2,050, and zeros at the beginning of a decimal such as 0.03020. When adding or subtracting numbers with different precision, round the answer to the smallest number of decimal places of any number in the sum or difference. When multiplying or dividing, the answer is rounded to the smallest number of significant digits of any number being multiplied or divided.

Example The lengths 5.28 and 5.2 are measured in meters. Find the sum of these lengths and record your answer using the correct number of significant digits.

Step 1 Find the sum.

5.28 m	2 digits after the decimal
+ 5.2 m	1 digit after the decimal
10.48 m	

Step 2 Round to one digit after the decimal because the least number of digits after the decimal of the numbers being added is 1.

The sum is 10.5 m.

Practice Problem 1 How many significant digits are in the measurement 7,071,301 m? How many significant digits are in the measurement 0.003010 g?

Practice Problem 2 Multiply 5.28 and 5.2 using the rule for multiplying and dividing. Record the answer using the correct number of significant digits.

Scientific Notation ALG: 1.0

Many times numbers used in science are very small or very large. Because these numbers are difficult to work with scientists use scientific notation. To write numbers in scientific notation, move the decimal point until only one non-zero digit remains on the left. Then count the number of places you moved the decimal point and use that number as a power of ten. For example, the average distance from the Sun to Mars is 227,800,000,000 m. In scientific notation, this distance is 2.278×10^{11} m. Because you moved the decimal point to the left, the number is a positive power of ten.

The mass of an electron is about 0.000 000 000 000 000 000 000 000 000 000 911 kg. Expressed in scientific notation, this mass is 9.11×10^{-31} kg. Because the decimal point was moved to the right, the number is a negative power of ten.

Example Earth is 149,600,000 km from the Sun. Express this in scientific notation.

Step 1 Move the decimal point until one non-zero digit remains on the left.
1.496 000 00

Step 2 Count the number of decimal places you have moved. In this case, eight.

Step 2 Show that number as a power of ten, 10^8.

Earth is 1.496×10^8 km from the Sun.

Practice Problem 1 How many significant digits are in 149,600,000 km? How many significant digits are in 1.496×10^8 km?

Practice Problem 2 Parts used in a high performance car must be measured to 7×10^{-6} m. Express this number as a decimal.

Practice Problem 3 A CD is spinning at 539 revolutions per minute. Express this number in scientific notation.

Math Skill Handbook

Math Skill Handbook

Make and Use Graphs `ALG: 6.0`

Data in tables can be displayed in a graph—a visual representation of data. Common graph types include line graphs, bar graphs, and circle graphs.

Line Graph A line graph shows a relationship between two variables that change continuously. The independent variable is changed and is plotted on the *x*-axis. The dependent variable is observed, and is plotted on the *y*-axis.

Example Draw a line graph of the data below from a cyclist in a long-distance race.

Table 4 Bicycle Race Data	
Time (h)	Distance (km)
0	0
1	8
2	16
3	24
4	32
5	40

Step 1 Determine the *x*-axis and *y*-axis variables. Time varies independently of distance and is plotted on the *x*-axis. Distance is dependent on time and is plotted on the *y*-axis.

Step 2 Determine the scale of each axis. The *x*-axis data ranges from 0 to 5. The *y*-axis data ranges from 0 to 50.

Step 3 Using graph paper, draw and label the axes. Include units in the labels.

Step 4 Draw a point at the intersection of the time value on the *x*-axis and corresponding distance value on the *y*-axis. Connect the points and label the graph with a title, as shown in **Figure 8.**

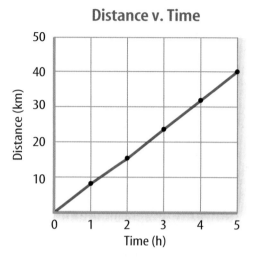

Distance v. Time

Figure 8 This line graph shows the relationship between distance and time during a bicycle ride.

Practice Problem A puppy's shoulder height is measured during the first year of her life. The following measurements were collected: (3 mo, 52 cm), (6 mo, 72 cm), (9 mo, 83 cm), (12 mo, 86 cm). Graph this data.

Find a Slope The slope of a straight line is the ratio of the vertical change, rise, to the horizontal change, run.

$$\text{Slope} = \frac{\text{vertical change (rise)}}{\text{horizontal change (run)}} = \frac{\text{change in } y}{\text{change in } x}$$

Example Find the slope of the graph in **Figure 8.**

Step 1 You know that the slope is the change in *y* divided by the change in *x*.

$$\text{Slope} = \frac{\text{change in } y}{\text{change in } x}$$

Step 2 Determine the data points you will be using. For a straight line, choose the two sets of points that are the farthest apart.

$$\text{Slope} = \frac{(40 - 0) \text{ km}}{(5 - 0) \text{ h}}$$

Step 3 Find the change in *y* and *x*.

$$\text{Slope} = \frac{40 \text{ km}}{5 \text{ h}}$$

Step 4 Divide the change in *y* by the change in *x*.

$$\text{Slope} = \frac{8 \text{ km}}{\text{h}}$$

The slope of the graph is 8 km/h.

Bar Graph To compare data that does not change continuously you might choose a bar graph. A bar graph uses bars to show the relationships between variables. The *x*-axis variable is divided into parts. The parts can be numbers such as years, or a category such as a type of animal. The *y*-axis is a number and increases continuously along the axis.

Example A recycling center collects 4.0 kg of aluminum on Monday, 1.0 kg on Wednesday, and 2.0 kg on Friday. Create a bar graph of this data.

Step 1 Select the *x*-axis and *y*-axis variables. The measured numbers (the masses of aluminum) should be placed on the *y*-axis. The variable divided into parts (collection days) is placed on the *x*-axis.

Step 2 Create a graph grid like you would for a line graph. Include labels and units.

Step 3 For each measured number, draw a vertical bar above the *x*-axis value up to the *y*-axis value. For the first data point, draw a vertical bar above Monday up to 4.0 kg.

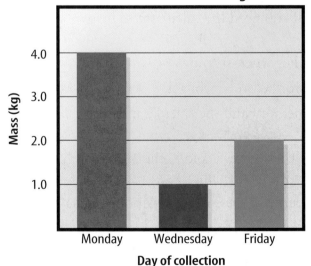

Aluminum Collected During Week

Mass (kg) vs *Day of collection* (Monday, Wednesday, Friday)

Practice Problem Draw a bar graph of the gases in air: 78% nitrogen, 21% oxygen, 1% other gases.

Circle Graph To display data as parts of a whole, you might use a circle graph. A circle graph is a circle divided into sections that represent the relative size of each piece of data. The entire circle represents 100%, half represents 50%, and so on.

Example Air is made up of 78% nitrogen, 21% oxygen, and 1% other gases. Display the composition of air in a circle graph.

Step 1 Multiply each percent by 360° and divide by 100 to find the angle of each section in the circle.

$$78\% \times \frac{360°}{100} = 280.8°$$

$$21\% \times \frac{360°}{100} = 75.6°$$

$$1\% \times \frac{360°}{100} = 3.6°$$

Step 2 Use a compass to draw a circle and to mark the center of the circle. Draw a straight line from the center to the edge of the circle.

Step 3 Use a protractor and the angles you calculated to divide the circle into parts. Place the center of the protractor over the center of the circle and line the base of the protractor over the straight line.

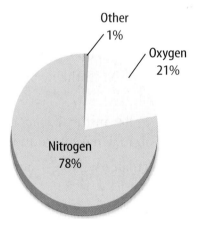

Other 1%
Oxygen 21%
Nitrogen 78%

Practice Problem Draw a circle graph to represent the amount of aluminum collected during the week shown in the bar graph to the left.

Using a Calculator

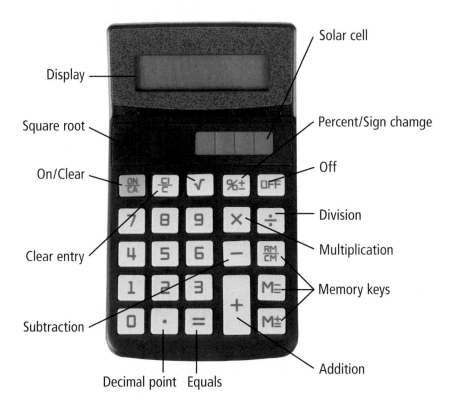

Display

Square root

On/Clear

Clear entry

Subtraction

Decimal point   Equals

Solar cell

Percent/Sign chamge

Off

Division

Multiplication

Memory keys

Addition

- Read the problem very carefully. Decide if you need the calculator to help you solve the problem.

- Clear the calculator by pressing the clear key when starting a new problem.

- If you see an E in the display, clear the error before you begin.

- If you see an M in the display, clear the memory and the calculator before you begin.

- If the number in the display is not one of the answer choices, check your work. You may have to round the number in the display.

- Your calculator will NOT automatically perform the correct order of operations.

- When working with calculators, use careful and deliberate keystrokes, and always remember to check your answer to make sure that it is reasonable. Calculators might display an incorrect answer if you press the keys too quickly.

- Check your answer to make sure that you have completed all of the necessary steps.

Understanding Scientific Terms

This list of prefixes, suffixes, and roots is provided to help you understand science terms used throughout this textbook. The list identifies whether the prefix, suffix, or root is of Greek *(G)* or Latin *(L)* origin. Also listed is the meaning of the prefix, suffix, or root and a science word in which it is used.

ORIGIN	MEANING	EXAMPLE
A		
ad (L)	to, toward	adaxial
aero (G)	air	aerobic
an (G)	without	anaerobic
ana (G)	up	anaphase
andro (G)	male	androecium
angio (G)	vessel	angiosperm
anth/o (G)	flower	anthophyte
anti (G)	against	antibody
aqu/a (L)	of water	aquatic
archae (G)	ancient	archaebacteria
arthro, artio (G)	jointed	arthropod
askos (G)	bag	ascospore
aster (G)	star	Asteroidea
autos (G)	self	autoimmune
B		
bi (L)	two	bipedal
bio (G)	life	biosphere
C		
carn (L)	flesh	carnivore
cephalo (G)	head	cephalopod
chlor (G)	light green	chlorophyll
chroma (G)	pigmented	chromosome
cide (L)	to kill	insecticide
circ (L)	circular	circadian
cocc/coccus (G)	small and round	streptococcus
con (L)	together	convergent
cyte (G)	cell	cytoplasm
D		
de (L)	remove	decompose
dendron (G)	tree	dendrite
dent (L)	tooth	edentate
derm (G)	skin	epidermis
di (G)	two	disaccharide

ORIGIN	MEANING	EXAMPLE
dia (G)	apart	diaphragm
dorm (L)	sleep	dormancy
E		
echino (G)	spiny	echinoderm
ec (G)	outer	ecosystem
endo (G)	within	endosperm
epi (G)	upon	epidermis
eu (G)	true	eukaryote
exo (G)	outside	exoskeleton
F		
fer (L)	to carry	conifer
G		
gastro (G)	stomach	gastropod
gen/(e)(o) (G)	kind	genotype
genesis (G)	to originate	oogenesis
gon (G)	reproductive	archegonium
gravi (L)	heavy	gravitropism
gymn/o (G)	naked	gymnosperm
gyn/e (G)	female	gynoecium
H		
hal(o) (G)	salt	halophyte
hapl(o) (G)	single	haploid
hemi (G)	half	hemisphere
hem(o) (G)	blood	hemoglobin
herb/a(i) (L)	vegetation	herbivore
heter/o (G)	different	heterotrophic
hom(e)/o (G)	same	homeostasis
hom (L)	human	hominid
hydr/o (G)	water	hydrolysis
I		
inter (L)	between	internode
intra (L)	within	intracellular
is/o (G)	equal	isotonic

Reference Handbook

ORIGIN	MEANING	EXAMPLE
K		
kary (G)	nucleus	eukaryote
kera (G)	hornlike	keratin
L		
leuc/o (G)	white	leukocyte
logy (G)	study of	biology
lymph/o (L)	water	lymphocyte
lysis (G)	break up	dialysis
M		
macr/o (G)	large	macromolecule
meg/a (G)	great	megaspore
meso (L)	in the middle	mesophyll
meta (G)	after	metaphase
micr/o (G)	small	microscope
mon/o (G)	only one	monocotyledon
morph/o (G)	form	morphology
N		
nema (G)	a thread	nematode
neuro (G)	nerve	neuron
nod (L)	knot	nodule
nomy(e) (G)	system of laws	taxonomy
O		
olig/o (G)	small, few	oligochaete
omni (L)	all	omnivore
orni(s) (G)	bird	ornithology
oste/o (G)	bone formation	osteocyte
ov (L)	an egg	oviduct
P		
pal(a)e/o (G)	ancient	paleontology
para (G)	beside	parathyroid
path/o (G)	suffering	pathogen
ped (L)	foot	centipede
per (L)	through	permeable
peri (G)	around, about	peristalsis
phag/o (G)	eating	phagocyte
phot/o (G)	light	photosynthesis
phyl (G)	race, class	phylogeny
phyll (G)	leaf	chlorophyll
phyte (G)	plant	epiphyte
pinna (L)	feather	pinnate

ORIGIN	MEANING	EXAMPLE
plasm/o (G)	to form	plasmodium
pod (G)	foot	gastropod
poly (G)	many	polymer
post (L)	after	posterior
pro (G) (L)	before	prokaryote
prot/o (G)	first	protocells
pseud/o (G)	false	pseudopodium
R		
re (L)	back to original	reproduce
rhiz/o (G)	root	rhizoid
S		
scope (G)	to look	microscope
some (G)	body	lysosome
sperm (G)	seed	gymnosperm
stasis (G)	remain constant	homeostasis
stom (G)	mouthlike opening	stomata
syn (G)	together	synapse
T		
tel/o (G)	end	telophase
terr (L)	of Earth	terrestrial
therm (G)	heat	endotherm
thylak (G)	sack	thylakoid
trans (L)	across	transpiration
trich (G)	hair	trichome
trop/o (G)	a change	gravitropism
trophic (G)	nourishment	heterotrophic
U		
uni (L)	one	unicellular
V		
vacc/a (L)	cow	vaccine
vore (L)	eat greedily	omnivore
X		
xer/o (G)	dry	xerophyte
Z		
zo/o (G)	living being	zoology
zygous (G)	two joined	homozygous

Science Reference Guide

Equations

Average speed (v) $\quad = \dfrac{\text{distance}}{\text{time}}$ $\qquad\qquad\qquad v \;=\; \dfrac{d}{t}$

Density (D) $\quad = \dfrac{\text{mass (g)}}{\text{Volume (cm}^3)}$ $\qquad\qquad D \;=\; \dfrac{m}{V}$

Force in newtons (F) $\quad = \text{mass (kg)} \times \text{acceleration (m/s}^2)$ $\qquad F \;=\; ma$

Pressure (P) $\quad = \dfrac{\text{force (N)}}{\text{area (m}^2)}$ $\qquad\qquad P \;=\; \dfrac{f}{A}$

Volume (cm^3) = length (cm) $\times$ width (cm) $\times$ height (cm) $\qquad V \;=\; \ell \times w \times h$

Units of Measure

cm = centimeter $\qquad$ m = meter
g = gram $\qquad\qquad$ N = newton
kg = kilogram $\qquad$ s = second

Physical Science Reference Tables

Standard Units

Symbol	Name	Quantity
m	meter	length
kg	kilogram	mass
Pa	pascal	pressure
K	kelvin	temperature
mol	mole	amount of a substance
J	joule	energy, work, quantity of heat
s	second	time
C	coulomb	electric charge
V	volt	electric potential
A	ampere	electric current
V	ohm	resistance

Physical Constants and Conversion Factors

Acceleration due to gravity	g	9.8 m/s/s or m/s^2
Avogadro's Number	N_A	6.02 3 10^{23} particles per mole
Electron charge	e	1.6 3 10^{219} C
Electron rest mass	m_e	9.11 3 10^{231} kg
Gravitation constant	G	6.67 3 10^{211} N 3 m^2/kg^2
Mass-energy relationship		1 u (amu) 5 9.3 3 10^2 MeV
Speed of light in a vacuum	c	3.00 3 108 m/s
Speed of sound at STP		331 m/s
Standard Pressure		1 atmosphere
		101.3 kPa
		760 Torr or mmHg
		14.7 lb/in.^{2}

Heat Constants

	Specific Heat (average) (kJ/kg 3 °C) (J/g 3 °C)	Melting Point (°C)	Boiling Point (°C)	Heat of Fusion (kJ/kg) (J/g)	Heat of Vaporization (kJ/kg) (J/g)
Alcohol (ethyl)	2.43 (liq.)	2117	79	109	855
Aluminum	0.90 (sol.)	660	2467	396	10500
Ammonia	4.71 (liq.)	278	233	332	1370
Copper	0.39 (sol.)	1083	2567	205	4790
Iron	0.45 (sol.)	1535	2750	267	6290
Lead	0.13 (sol.)	328	1740	25	866
Mercury	0.14 (liq.)	239	357	11	295
Platinum	0.13 (sol.)	1772	3827	101	229
Silver	0.24 (sol.)	962	2212	105	2370
Tungsten	0.13 (sol.)	3410	5660	192	4350
Water (solid)	2.05 (sol.)	0	–	334	–
Water (liquid)	4.18 (liq.)	–	100	–	–
Water (vapor)	2.01 (gas)	–	–	–	2260
Zinc	0.39 (sol.)	420	907	113	1770

Standard Units

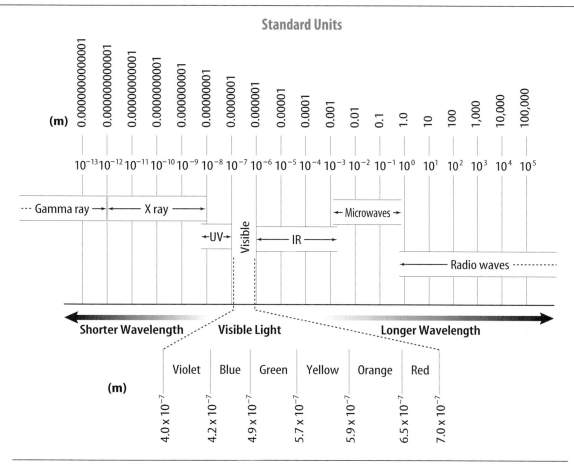

Uranium Decay Series

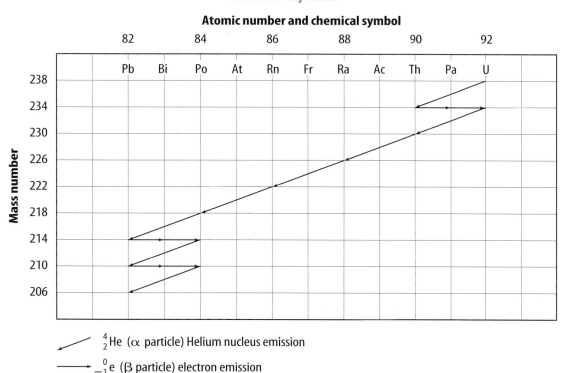

Reference Handbook

PERIODIC TABLE OF THE ELEMENTS

Columns of elements are called groups. Elements in the same group have similar chemical properties.

Gas
Liquid
Solid
Synthetic

Element — Hydrogen
Atomic number — 1
Symbol — H
Atomic mass — 1.008

State of matter

The first three symbols tell you the state of matter of the element at room temperature. The fourth symbol identifies elements that are not present in significant amounts on Earth. Useful amounts are made synthetically.

1

1	Hydrogen 1 **H** 1.008

2

2	Lithium 3 **Li** 6.941	Beryllium 4 **Be** 9.012

3	Sodium 11 **Na** 22.990	Magnesium 12 **Mg** 24.305

	3	**4**	**5**	**6**	**7**	**8**	**9**
4 Potassium 19 **K** 39.098 / Calcium 20 **Ca** 40.078	Scandium 21 **Sc** 44.956	Titanium 22 **Ti** 47.867	Vanadium 23 **V** 50.942	Chromium 24 **Cr** 51.996	Manganese 25 **Mn** 54.938	Iron 26 **Fe** 55.845	Cobalt 27 **Co** 58.933
5 Rubidium 37 **Rb** 85.468 / Strontium 38 **Sr** 87.62	Yttrium 39 **Y** 88.906	Zirconium 40 **Zr** 91.224	Niobium 41 **Nb** 92.906	Molybdenum 42 **Mo** 95.94	Technetium 43 **Tc** (98)	Ruthenium 44 **Ru** 101.07	Rhodium 45 **Rh** 102.906
6 Cesium 55 **Cs** 132.905 / Barium 56 **Ba** 137.327 / Lanthanum 57 **La** 138.906		Hafnium 72 **Hf** 178.49	Tantalum 73 **Ta** 180.948	Tungsten 74 **W** 183.84	Rhenium 75 **Re** 186.207	Osmium 76 **Os** 190.23	Iridium 77 **Ir** 192.217
7 Francium 87 **Fr** (223) / Radium 88 **Ra** (226) / Actinium 89 **Ac** (227)		Rutherfordium 104 **Rf** (261)	Dubnium 105 **Db** (262)	Seaborgium 106 **Sg** (266)	Bohrium 107 **Bh** (264)	Hassium 108 **Hs** (277)	Meitnerium 109 **Mt** (268)

The number in parentheses is the mass number of the longest-lived isotope for that element.

Rows of elements are called periods. Atomic number increases across a period.

The arrow shows where these elements would fit into the periodic table. They are moved to the bottom of the table to save space.

Lanthanide series

Cerium 58 **Ce** 140.116	Praseodymium 59 **Pr** 140.908	Neodymium 60 **Nd** 144.24	Promethium 61 **Pm** (145)	Samarium 62 **Sm** 150.36

Actinide series

Thorium 90 **Th** 232.038	Protactinium 91 **Pa** 231.036	Uranium 92 **U** 238.029	Neptunium 93 **Np** (237)	Plutonium 94 **Pu** (244)

Metal

Metalloid

Nonmetal

The color of an element's block tells you if the element is a metal, nonmetal, or metalloid.

Science Online

Visit ca8.msscience.com for updates to the periodic table.

18

Helium
2
He
4.003

13	**14**	**15**	**16**	**17**

Boron	Carbon	Nitrogen	Oxygen	Fluorine	Neon
5	6	7	8	9	10
B	**C**	**N**	**O**	**F**	**Ne**
10.811	12.011	14.007	15.999	18.998	20.180

Aluminum	Silicon	Phosphorus	Sulfur	Chlorine	Argon
13	14	15	16	17	18
Al	**Si**	**P**	**S**	**Cl**	**Ar**
26.982	28.086	30.974	32.065	35.453	39.948

10	**11**	**12**					

Nickel	Copper	Zinc	Gallium	Germanium	Arsenic	Selenium	Bromine	Krypton
28	29	30	31	32	33	34	35	36
Ni	**Cu**	**Zn**	**Ga**	**Ge**	**As**	**Se**	**Br**	**Kr**
58.693	63.546	65.409	69.723	72.64	74.922	78.96	79.904	83.798

Palladium	Silver	Cadmium	Indium	Tin	Antimony	Tellurium	Iodine	Xenon
46	47	48	49	50	51	52	53	54
Pd	**Ag**	**Cd**	**In**	**Sn**	**Sb**	**Te**	**I**	**Xe**
106.42	107.868	112.411	114.818	118.710	121.760	127.60	126.904	131.293

Platinum	Gold	Mercury	Thallium	Lead	Bismuth	Polonium	Astatine	Radon
78	79	80	81	82	83	84	85	86
Pt	**Au**	**Hg**	**Tl**	**Pb**	**Bi**	**Po**	**At**	**Rn**
195.078	196.967	200.59	204.383	207.2	208.980	(209)	(210)	(222)

Darmstadtium	Roentgenium	Ununbium		Ununquadium				
110	111	* 112		* 114				
Ds	**Rg**	**Uub**		**Uuq**				
(281)	(272)	(285)		(289)				

* The names and symbols for elements 112–114 are temporary. Final names will be selected when the elements' discoveries are verified.

Europium	Gadolinium	Terbium	Dysprosium	Holmium	Erbium	Thulium	Ytterbium	Lutetium
63	64	65	66	67	68	69	70	71
Eu	**Gd**	**Tb**	**Dy**	**Ho**	**Er**	**Tm**	**Yb**	**Lu**
151.964	157.25	158.925	162.500	164.930	167.259	168.934	173.04	174.967

Americium	Curium	Berkelium	Californium	Einsteinium	Fermium	Mendelevium	Nobelium	Lawrencium
95	96	97	98	99	100	101	102	103
Am	**Cm**	**Bk**	**Cf**	**Es**	**Fm**	**Md**	**No**	**Lr**
(243)	(247)	(247)	(251)	(252)	(257)	(258)	(259)	(262)

Glossary/Glosario

Cómo usar el glosario en español:
1. Busca el término en inglés que desees encontrar.
2. El término en español, junto con la definición, se encuentran en la columna de la derecha.

Pronunciation Key
Use the following key to help you sound out words in the glossary.

a . . . . back (BAK)			ew . . . . foo**d** (FEWD)	
ay . . . . d**ay** (DAY)			yoo . . . . p**u**re (PYOOR)	
ah . . . . f**a**ther (FAH thur)			yew . . . . f**ew** (FYEW)	
ow . . . . fl**ow**er (FLOW ur)			uh . . . . comm**a** (CAH muh)	
ar . . . . c**ar** (CAR)			u (+ con) . . . . r**u**b (RUB)	
e . . . . l**e**ss (LES)			sh . . . . **sh**elf (SHELF)	
ee . . . . l**ea**f (LEEF)			ch . . . . na**t**ure (NAY chur)	
ih . . . . tr**i**p (TRIHP)			g . . . . **g**ift (GIHFT)	
i (i + com + e) . . . . **i**dea (i DEE uh)			j . . . . **g**em (JEM)	
oh . . . . **go** (GOH)			ing . . . . s**ing** (SING)	
aw . . . . s**o**ft (SAWFT)			zh . . . . vi**s**ion (VIH zhun)	
or . . . . **or**bit (OR buht)			k . . . . ca**k**e (KAYK)	
oy . . . . c**oi**n (COYN)			s . . . . **s**eed, **c**ent (SEED, SENT)	
oo . . . . f**oo**t (FOOT)			z . . . . **z**one, rai**s**e (ZOHN, RAYZ)	

✳ Academic Vocabulary

English — A — Español

absolute magnitude/apparent magnitude | **magnitud absoluta/magnitud aparente**

absolute magnitude: the apparent magnitude a star would have if it were 32.6 light-years away from Earth (p. 513)

acceleration (ik seh leh RAY shun): rate of change of velocity with time (p. 60)

acid: a substance that contains a hydrogen atom and produces hydronium ions when dissolved in water (p. 395)

accuracy: a description of how close a measurement is to an accepted value (p. 17)

✳ **accurate:** free from error (p. 176)

✳ **affect:** to cause a change in (p. 108)

✳ **alternate:** to perform by turns or in succession (p. 233)

amino acid: a member of a class of organic compounds that are the basic building blocks of proteins (p. 434)

apparent magnitude: the observed luminosity of a celestial body (as a star) as observed from Earth (p. 513)

magnitud absoluta: la magnitud aparente que tendría una estrella si estuviese a 32.6 años luz de distancia de La Tierra (p. 513)

aceleración: tasa de cambio de la velocidad en función del tiempo (p. 60)

ácido: sustancia que contiene un átomo de hidrógeno y produce iones hidronio al disolverse en agua (p. 395)

exactitud: descripción de la aproximación de una medida a un valor aceptado (p. 17)

exacto: libre de errores (p. 176)

afectar: producir un cambio en algo (p. 108)

alternar: realizar por turnos o en sucesión (p. 233)

aminoácido: miembro de una clase de compuestos orgánicos que son los elementos esenciales de las proteínas (p. 434)

magnitud aparente: luminosidad de un cuerpo celeste (como una estrella) según se observa desde La Tierra (p. 513)

Glossary/Glosario

❋ **approximate:** nearly correct or exact (p. 403)

Archimedes' principle: principle stating that the buoyant force exerted on an object by a fluid is equal to the weight of the fluid displaced by the object (p. 147)

❋ **area:** the number of unit squares that fit onto a surface (p. 141)

asteroid: a rocky object, smaller than a planet that is found between the orbits of Mars and Jupiter (p. 489)

astronomical unit: the average distance from Earth to the Sun (p. 465)

atmospheric pressure: force exerted per unit area by air (p. 144)

atom: very small particle that makes up all matter (p. 174)

atomic number: the number of protons an atom has in its nucleus (p. 195)

average atomic mass: weighted-average mass of the mixture of an element's isotopes (p. 198)

average speed: total distance traveled divided by total time taken (p. 58)

axis of rotation: an imaginary line through the center of a planet around which the planet rotates (p. 463)

aproximado: casi correcto o exacto (p. 403)

principio de Arquímedes: principio que afirma que la fuerza de empuje que un líquido ejerce sobre un objeto es igual al peso del líquido desplazado por el objeto (p. 147)

área: número de unidades cuadradas que caben en una superficie (p. 141)

asteroide: objeto rocoso, más pequeño que un planeta, que se halla entre las órbitas de Marte y Júpiter (p. 489)

unidad astronómica: distancia promedio de La Tierra al Sol (p. 465)

presión atmosférica: fuerza que ejerce el aire por unidad de superficie (p. 144)

átomo: partícula muy pequeña que forma la materia (p. 174)

número atómico: número de protones que posee un átomo en su núcleo (p. 195)

masa atómica promedio: promedio ponderado de la masa de la mezcla de los isótopos de un elemento (p. 198)

rapidez promedio: distancia total recorrida dividida entre el tiempo total que ha tardado el recorrido (p. 58)

eje de rotación: línea imaginaria que cruza el centro de un planeta y alrededor de la cual éste gira (p. 463)

B

balanced forces: forces that combine to form a net force of zero (p. 91)

base: a substance that can combine with hydrogen ions and produces hydroxide ions when dissolved in water (p. 396)

bias: an intentional or unintentional preference for one outcome over another in a scientific investigation (p. 20)

big bang theory: states that about 14 billion years ago, the universe began with a huge, fiery explosion (p. 533)

biomass: the total mass of all living matter (p. 422)

biomolecule: a large organic molecule found in living organisms, which includes lipids, proteins, carbohydrates, and nucleic acids (p. 439)

black hole: a region of space from which no matter or radiation can escape (p. 526)

blinding: a procedure that reduces bias by making the subject, investigator or both unaware of which treatment they are testing (p. 20)

boiling: vaporization that occurs within a liquid (p. 267)

boiling point: the temperature at which boiling occurs in a liquid (pp. 267, 314)

buoyant (BOY unt) force: the upward force exerted on an object by the surrounding fluid (p. 146)

fuerzas en equilibrio: fuerzas que se combinan para producir una fuerza neta de cero (p. 91)

base: sustancia que puede combinarse con los iones de hidrógeno y que produce iones de hidróxido al disolverse en agua (p. 396)

predisposición: preferencia intencional o involuntaria por un resultado en lugar de otro en una investigación científica (p. 20)

teoría de la gran explosión: teoría que afirma que el universo comenzó a partir de una inmensa explosión hace alrededor de 14 mil millones de años (p. 533)

biomasa: masa total de toda la materia viviente (p. 422)

biomolécula: molécula grande orgánica que se halla en los seres vivos, la cual incluye los lípidos, las proteínas, los carbohidratos y los ácidos nucleicos. (p. 439)

hoyo negro: región del espacio de la cual no puede escapar materia o radiación alguna (p. 526)

estudio ciego: procedimiento que reduce la predisposición al ocultar al sujeto, al investigador, o a ambos, el tratamiento que se está poniendo a prueba (p. 20)

ebullición: vaporización que ocurre en un líquido (p. 267)

punto de ebullición: temperatura a la cual hierve un líquido (pp. 267, 314)

fuerza de empuje: fuerza ascendente que ejerce el líquido que rodea a un objeto (p. 146)

Glossary/Glosario

C

carbohydrate: an organic compound used by cells to store and release energy (p. 440)

centripetal (sen TRIH puht uhl) force: in circular motion a force that acts perpendicular to the direction of motion toward the center of the circle (p. 108)

chemical bond: a force that holds atoms together in a compound (p. 220)

chemical change: a change of one or more substances into other substances (p. 341)

chemical formula: a shorthand expression that uses atomic symbols and subscripts to show the elements and the number of atoms of each element that combine to form a compound (p. 219)

chemical property: the ability or inability of a substance to combine with or change into one or more new substances (p. 338)

coefficient: a number placed in front of a symbol or a formula in a chemical equation (p. 352)

comet: a small, icy body in orbit around the Sun, often having a highly elliptical orbit (p. 490)

＊ **component:** one of a number of parts that make up a whole (p. 386)

＊ **compound:** (1) a pure substance that contains two or more elements (p. 218); (2) something that is formed by a union of elements, ingredients, or parts (p. 341)

compression force: a squeezing force applied to an object that can make an object shrink (p. 101)

condensation: the change of matter from a gas to a liquid state (p. 269)

＊ **conduct:** to lead from a position of command (p. 297)

conductivity: the ability of a material to transfer heat or electricity (p. 295)

＊ **consist:** to be composed or made up (p. 236)

＊ **constant:** (1) factors in an experiment that remain the same (p. 29); (2) not changing (p. 57)

constant speed: rate of change of position in which the same distance is traveled each second (p. 57)

contact force: a force that is exerted only when objects are touching (p. 88)

＊ **contract:** to draw together, to reduce to a smaller size (p. 524)

＊ **contrast:** to show differences when compared (p. 198)

control group: the part of controlled experiment that contains all of the same variables and constants as the experimental group but the independent variable is not changed (p. 29)

conversion factor: a ratio that describes how much of one unit is in another (p. 16)

carbohidrato: compuesto orgánico que utilizan las células para almacenar y liberar energía (p. 440)

fuerza centrípeta: en el movimiento circular, fuerza que actúa en dirección perpendicular a la del movimiento hacia el centro del círculo (p. 108)

enlace químico: fuerza que sostiene a los átomos unidos en un compuesto (p. 220)

cambio químico: transformación de una o más sustancias en otras sustancias (p. 341)

fórmula química: expresión corta que usa símbolos atómicos y subíndices para indicar los elementos y el número de átomos de cada elemento que se combina para formar un compuesto (p. 219)

propiedad química: capacidad o incapacidad de una sustancia de combinarse con una o más sustancias, o de transformarse en una o más sustancias (p. 338)

coeficiente: número que se coloca delante de un símbolo o de una fórmula en una ecuación química (p. 352)

cometa: cuerpo pequeño, helado, en órbita alrededor del Sol, que a menudo describe una órbita altamente elíptica (p. 490)

componente: una de las partes que forma un todo (p. 386)

compuesto: (1) sustancia pura que contiene dos o más elementos (p. 218); (2) algo que se forma por la unión de elementos, ingredientes o partes (p. 341)

fuerza de compresión: fuerza que comprime un cuerpo y puede hacer que éste se encoja (p. 101)

condensación: cambio de la materia de estado gaseoso a líquido (p. 269)

conducir: dirigir desde una posición de mando (p. 297)

conductividad: capacidad de un material de transferir calor o electricidad (p. 295)

consistir: estar compuesto o formado por algo (p. 236)

constante: (1) factor que permanece invariable en un experimento (p. 29); (2) que no cambia (p. 57)

rapidez constante: tasa de cambio de posición en la cual se recorre la misma distancia en cada segundo (p. 57)

fuerza de contacto: fuerza que se ejerce únicamente cuando los objetos se tocan (p. 88)

contraer: unirse, reducir a un tamaño más pequeño (p. 524)

contrastar: exhibir diferencias en una comparación (p. 198)

grupo de control: parte de un experimento controlado que contiene las mismas variables y constantes que el grupo experimental, pero en el que la variable independiente no se cambia (p. 29)

factor de conversión: proporción que describe la cantidad de una unidad que se halla en otra (p. 16)

covalent bond: a chemical bond that forms when atoms share electrons (p. 225)

critical thinking: comparing what you already know with the explanation you are given in order to decide if you agree with it or not (p. 20)

crystal: a regular, repeating arrangement of atoms, ions, or molecules (p. 232)

✳ **cycle:** a recurring sequence of events (p. 423)

enlace covalente: enlace químico que se forma cuando los átomos comparten electrones (p. 225)

pensamiento crítico: comparación de lo que sabemos con la explicación que recibimos para decidir si estamos de acuerdo o no con ella (p. 20)

cristal: disposición regular y repetitiva de átomos, iones o moléculas (p. 232)

ciclo: secuencia recurrente de eventos (p. 423)

D

data: factual information used as a basis for reading, discussion, or calculation (p. 8)

density: mass per unit volume of a material (p. 130)

dependent variable: the factor that you measure or observe during an experiment (p. 29)

deposition: the change of matter from a gaseous state to a solid state without going through the liquid state (p. 272)

diatomic molecule: a particle consisting of two atoms (p. 350)

✳ **dimension:** measure in one direction (p. 52)

displacement: a vector that is the difference between the initial and final position of an object (p. 53)

dissolving: a process in which substances mix uniformly with one another (p. 343)

✳ **distribute:** to spread out to cover something (p. 259)

ductility: the ability of a substance to be pulled into wires (p. 232)

datos: información factual que se usa como base para la lectura, discusión o cálculo (p. 8)

densidad: masa por unidad de volumen de un material (p. 130)

variable dependiente: factor que se mide u observa durante un experimento (p. 29)

deposición: cambio de la materia del estado gaseoso al estado sólido sin pasar por el estado líquido (p. 272)

molécula diatómica: partícula formada por dos átomos (p. 350)

dimensión: medida en una sola dirección (p. 52)

desplazamiento: vector que representa la diferencia entre la posición inicial y la posición final de un objeto (p. 53)

disolución: proceso mediante el cual las sustancias se mezclan uniformemente unas con otras (p. 343)

distribuir: dispersar para cubrir algo (p. 259)

ductibilidad: capacidad de una sustancia para formar alambres o hilos (p. 232)

E

eclipse: a total or partial obscuring of one celestial body by another (p. 475)

elastic force: force exerted by a material when it is stretched or compressed (p. 101)

electrical conductivity: the ability of a material to transfer electric charges through a material (p. 316)

electron: a negatively charged particle that occupies the space in the atom outside the nucleus (p. 175)

electron cloud: the region surrounding an atomic nucleus where an electron is most likely to be found (p. 190)

✳ **element:** (1) pure substance made from atoms that all have the same number of protons (p. 195); (2) fundamental substance consisting of only one kind of atom (p. 511)

ellipse (ih LIPS): an oval (p. 464)

eclipse: ocultación total o parcial de un cuerpo celeste a causa de otro (p. 475)

fuerza elástica: fuerza que ejerce un material al alargarse o comprimirse (p. 101)

conductividad eléctrica: capacidad de un material de transferir calor o electricidad (p. 316)

electrón: partícula con carga negativa que ocupa el espacio del átomo en el exterior del núcleo (p. 175)

nube de electrones: región que rodea al núcleo atómico donde hay más probabilidad de encontrar un electrón (p. 190)

elemento: (1) sustancia pura formada por átomos que poseen el mismo número de protones (p. 195); (2) sustancia fundamental formada por una sola clase de átomos (p. 511)

elipse: óvalo (p. 464)

Glossary/Glosario

endothermic process: a process that absorbs energy as heat (p. 362)

energy level: regions of space in which electrons can move about the nucleus of an atom (p. 190)

evaporation: vaporization that occurs at the surface of a liquid (p. 268)

exothermic process: a process that releases energy as heat (p. 360)

experimental group: the part of a controlled experiment used to study relationships between variables you are interested in knowing more about (p. 29)

proceso endotérmico: proceso que absorbe energía en forma de calor (p. 362)

nivel energético: región del espacio en la cual los electrones pueden moverse alrededor del núcleo de un átomo (p. 190)

evaporación: vaporización que ocurre en la superficie de un líquido (p. 268)

proceso exotérmico: proceso que libera energía en forma de calor (p. 360)

grupo experimental: parte de un experimento controlado que se usa para estudiar las relaciones entre las variables que se desea investigar (p. 29)

fluid: a material that can flow and has no definite shape (p. 140)

✳ **force:** an influence tending to change the motion of an object or produce motion in a stationary object (pp. 88, 468)

freezing point: the temperature at which a liquid changes to a solid (p. 266)

friction: a contact force that opposes the movement between two surfaces in contact (p. 99)

✳ **function:** to be in action, to serve or operate (p. 360)

functional group: a group of atoms that replaces a hydrogen atom in organic compounds (p. 432)

líquido: material que puede fluir y que no tiene forma definida (p. 140)

fuerza: influencia que tiende a cambiar el movimiento de un objeto, o a producir movimiento en un objeto estacionario (pp. 88, 468)

punto de congelación: temperatura a la cual un líquido se transforma en sólido (p. 266)

fricción: fuerza de contacto que se opone al movimiento entre dos superficies que están en contacto (p. 99)

funcionar: estar en acción, servir u operar (p. 360)

grupo funcional: grupo de átomos que reemplaza a un átomo de hidrógeno en los compuestos orgánicos (p. 432)

galaxy: massive system of stars, dust, and gas held together by gravity (p. 528)

gas: a state of matter that has no fixed shape or volume (p. 258)

gravity: an attractive force between all objects that have mass (p. 96)

group: a vertical column of elements on the periodic table (p. 291)

galaxia: sistema masivo de estrellas, polvo y gas que se mantiene unido por la gravedad (p. 528)

gas: estado de la materia que no tiene forma ni volumen fijo (p. 258)

gravedad: fuerza de atracción entre todos los objetos que poseen masa (p. 96)

grupo: columna vertical de elementos en la tabla periódica (p. 291)

H

half-life: the time needed for one-half the mass of a sample of a radioactive isotope to decay (p. 306)

halogen (HA luh jen): an element in Group 17 of the periodic table (p. 296)

heterogeneous (he tuh ruh JEE nee us) mixture: a mixture in which substances are not evenly mixed (p. 382)

vida media: tiempo que tarda la mitad de la masa de una muestra de un isótopo radiactivo en desintegrarse (p. 306)

halógeno: elemento del grupo 17 de la tabla periódica (p. 296)

mezcla heterogénea: mezcla en la cual las sustancias no se mezclan uniformemente (p. 382)

Glossary/Glosario

homogeneous (hoh muh JEE nee us) mixture: two or more substances that are evenly mixed on the atomic level, but are not bonded together (p. 382)

hydrocarbons: molecules that contain only carbon and hydrogen atoms (p. 430)

hydrometer: an instrument that measures the density of a fluid (p. 152)

hydronium ion: the combination of a hydrogen ion and a water molecule to form H_3O^+ (p. 395)

hypothesis: a tentative explanation that can be tested with a scientific investigation (pp. 19, 28)

mezcla homogénea: mezcla en la cual dos o más sustancias están mezcladas uniformemente a nivel atómico, pero no están enlazadas (p. 382)

hidrocarburos: moléculas que contienen únicamente átomos de carbono y de hidrógeno (p. 430)

hidrómetro: instrumento que mide la densidad de un líquido (p. 152)

ion hidronio: combinación de un ion de hidrógeno y una molécula de agua para formar H_3O^+ (p. 395)

hipótesis: explicación tentativa que puede ponerse a prueba mediante una investigación científica (pp. 19, 28)

✳ **impact:** a forceful contact or collision (p. 490)

independent variable: a factor in an experiment that is manipulated or changed by the investigator to observe how it affects a dependent variable (p. 29)

indicator: a compound that changes from one color to another within a particular pH range (p. 403)

✳ **individual:** distinctly associated with a person or thing (p. 383)

inner planet: one of the four planets closest to the Sun— Mercury, Venus, Earth, and Mars (p. 478)

instantaneous speed: speed at a specific instant in time (p. 57)

✳ **involve:** to have within or as part of itself (p. 98)

ion: an atom that is no longer neutral because it has gained or lost electrons (p. 200)

ionic bond: an electrical attraction between positively and negatively charged ions in an ionic compound (p. 220)

isotope: one of two or more atoms of an element having the same number of protons in their nuclei, but a different number of neutrons (p. 198)

impacto: contacto forzoso o choque (p. 490)

variable independiente: factor que el investigador manipula o cambia en un experimento para observar cómo afecta a una variable dependiente (p. 29)

indicador: compuesto que cambia de color en un rango determinado de pH (p. 403)

individual: distintamente asociado con una persona o cosa (p. 383)

planeta interior: cada uno de los cuatro planetas más cercanos al Sol: Mercurio, Venus, La Tierra y Marte (p. 478)

rapidez instantánea: rapidez en un instante específico de tiempo (p. 57)

involucrar: poseer algo como parte de sí mismo (p. 98)

ion: átomo que ha dejado de ser neutro debido a que ha ganado o perdido electrones (p. 200)

enlace iónico: atracción eléctrica entre iones con carga positiva y negativa en un compuesto iónico (p. 220)

isótopo: uno de dos o más átomos de un elemento con el mismo número de protones en el núcleo, pero con un número diferente de neutrones (p. 198)

law of conservation of energy: energy is neither created nor destroyed in chemical reactions (p. 359)

law of conservation of mass: the total mass before a chemical reaction is the same as the total mass after reaction (p. 347)

law of universal gravitation: all objects are attracted to each other with a force that depends on their masses and the distance between the objects (p. 97)

light-year: the distance light travels in one year (p. 509)

ley de la conservación de la energía: la energía no se crea ni se destruye en las reacciones químicas (p. 359)

ley de la conservación de la masa: la masa total antes de una reacción química es la misma que la masa total después de la reacción (p. 347)

ley de la gravitación universal: ley que afirma que todos los objetos son atraídos unos a otros con una fuerza que depende de la masa de dichos objetos y de la distancia que los separa (p. 97)

año luz: distancia que recorre la luz en un año (p. 509)

Glossary/Glosario

linear relationship: a mathematical relationship between variables that results in a straight line on a graph (p. 23)

lipid (LIH pihd): a biological compound, including fats and oils that is not soluble in water and contains carbon, hydrogen, and oxygen (p. 439)

liquid: a state of matter with a fixed volume but not a fixed shape (p. 257)

luminosity (loo muh NAH suh tee): the quantity of energy in joules a light source emits per second (p. 513)

lunar phase: different appearance of the Moon as it orbits Earth (p. 474)

luster: shine; a property of metals (p. 295)

relación lineal: relación matemática entre variables que se describe con una línea recta en una gráfica (p. 23)

lípido: compuesto biológico, incluyendo las grasas y los aceites, que no es soluble en agua y que contiene carbono, hidrógeno y oxígeno (p. 439)

líquido: estado de la materia que posee un volumen fijo, pero no una forma fija (p. 257)

luminosidad: cantidad de energía en julios que emite una fuente luminosa por segundo (p. 513)

fase lunar: apariencia diferente de La Luna en su órbita alrededor de La Tierra (p. 474)

brillo: lustre, propiedad de los metales (p. 295)

malleability (ma lee uh BIH luh tee): the ability of a substance to be hammered or rolled into sheets (p. 232)

mass number: the sum of the number of protons and neutrons in an atom (p. 197)

matter: anything that has mass and takes up space (p. 174)

mean: the sum of the numbers in a set of data divided by the number of items in the set (p. 24)

median: the middle number in a data set when the data are arranged in numerical order (p. 24)

metal: elements that are usually shiny, good conductors of heat and electricity, and are solids at room temperature (p. 230)

metallic: collective properties of common metals (p. 295)

metallic bond: a bond formed when many metal atoms share their pooled electrons (p. 231)

meteoroid: solid, interplanetary particle passing through Earth's atmosphere (p. 492)

mixture: a combination of two or more substances that can be separated by physical means (p. 382)

mode: the number or item that appears most frequently in a set of data (p. 24)

molecule: neutral particle that forms as a result of electron sharing (p. 219)

monomer (MAH nuh muhr): a small molecule that forms a link in a polymer chain (pp. 235, 438)

maleabilidad: capacidad de una sustancia de ser martillada o enrollada en láminas (p. 232)

número de masa: suma del número de protones y neutrones de un átomo (p. 197)

materia: todo lo que tiene masa y ocupa espacio (p. 174)

media: suma de los números de un conjunto de datos dividida entre el número de unidades u objetos del conjunto (p. 24)

mediana: número central de un conjunto de datos cuando éstos se disponen en orden numérico (p. 24)

metal: elemento normalmente brilloso, buen conductor de calor y electricidad, y sólido a temperatura ambiente (p. 230)

metálicas: propiedades colectivas de los metales comunes (p. 295)

enlace metálico: enlace que se forma cuando muchos átomos de metal comparten sus electrones (p. 231)

meteoroide: partícula sólida, interplanetaria que pasa a través de la atmósfera terrestre (p. 492)

mezcla: combinación de dos o más sustancias que pueden separarse por medios físicos (p. 382)

moda: número o unidad que aparece con más frecuencia en un conjunto de datos (p. 24)

molécula: partícula neutra que se forma como resultado de compartir electrones (p. 219)

monómero: molécula pequeña que forma una conexión en una cadena de polímeros (pp. 235, 438)

natural polymer: polymers made by living organisms, such as proteins, complex carbohydrates, and nucleic acids (p. 438)

polímero natural: polímero elaborado por los seres vivos, como las proteínas, los carbohidratos complejos y los ácidos nucleicos (p. 438)

Glossary/Glosario

nebula: a large cloud of gas and dust in space (p. 519)

net force: the combination of all the forces acting on an object (p. 90)

neutron: a neutral particle located in the nucleus of an atom (p. 175)

neutron star: a star composed primarily of neutrons (p. 526)

Newton's first law of motion: if the net force on an object is zero, an object at rest remains at rest, or, if the object is moving, it continues to move in a straight line with constant speed (p. 93)

Newton's second law of motion: the acceleration of an object is equal to the net force exerted on the object divided by the object's mass (p. 109)

Newton's third law of motion: when one object exerts a force on a second object, the second object exerts an equal force in the opposite direction on the first object (p. 111)

noble gas: an element in Group 18 of the periodic table (p. 297)

noncontact force: a force exerted when objects are not touching (p. 89)

nonlinear relationship: a mathematical relationship between variables that results in a curved line on a graph (p. 23)

nonpolar molecule: a molecule that shares electrons equally and does not have oppositely charged ends (p. 426)

normal force: a force exerted by an object perpendicular to the surface of the object (p. 102)

nuclear fusion: reaction in which two atomic nuclei combine to form a nucleus with a higher mass (p. 522)

nucleic acid: a biomolecule, such as RNA or DNA, that stores cellular information in cells in all plants and animals (p. 439)

nucleus: a region located at the center of an atom that contains most of the mass of the atom (p. 175)

nebulosa: gran nube de gases y polvo en el espacio (p. 519)

fuerza neta: combinación de todas las fuerzas que actúan sobre un objeto (p. 90)

neutrón: partícula neutra ubicada en el núcleo de un átomo (p. 175)

estrella neutrón: estrella formada principalmente por neutrones (p. 526)

primera ley del movimiento de Newton: ley que establece que si la fuerza neta que actúa sobre un objeto es cero, un objeto que está en reposo permanecerá en reposo, o si un objeto está en movimiento, éste continuará moviéndose en línea recta a una rapidez constante (p. 93)

segunda ley del movimiento de Newton: ley que establece que la aceleración de un objeto es igual a la fuerza neta que se ejerce sobre éste dividida entre su masa (p. 109)

tercera ley del movimiento de Newton: ley que establece que cuando un objeto ejerce una fuerza sobre un segundo objeto, éste último ejerce una fuerza igual en magnitud, pero opuesta en dirección con respecto al primer objeto (p. 111)

gas noble: elemento del grupo 18 de la tabla periódica (p. 297)

fuerza sin contacto: fuerza que se ejerce cuando los objetos no se tocan (p. 89)

relación no lineal: relación matemática entre variables que se describe con una línea curva en una gráfica (p. 23)

molécula apolar: molécula que comparte electrones por igual y no posee extremos con cargas opuestas (p. 426)

fuerza normal: fuerza ejercida por un objeto perpendicular a la superficie del mismo (p. 102)

fusión nuclear: reacción en la cual dos núcleos atómicos se combinan para formar un núcleo de mayor masa (p. 522)

ácido nucleico: biomolécula como el ARN o el ADN que almacena información celular en las células de todas las plantas y animales (p. 439)

núcleo: región en el centro del átomo que contiene la mayoría de la masa de éste (p. 175)

O

organic compound: a large number of compounds that contain the element carbon (p. 428)

outer planet: one of four planets—Jupiter, Saturn, Uranus, and Neptune—beyond the inner planets (p. 481)

compuestos orgánicos: gran número de compuestos que contienen el elemento carbono (p. 428)

planeta exterior: cada uno de los cuatro planetas—Júpiter, Saturno, Urano y Neptuno—más lejanos que los planetas interiores (p. 481)

P

particle accelerator: a large machine that is capable of making particles move very fast (p. 307)

acelerador de partículas: máquina grande capaz de hacer que las partículas se muevan con mucha rapidez (p. 307)

Glossary/Glosario

period: a horizontal row of elements on the periodic table (p. 291)

period of revolution: the time it takes a planet to move completely around the Sun (p. 463)

period of rotation: the time it takes for a planet to rotate once around its rotational axis (p. 463)

pH: a numerical scale used to indicate how acidic or basic a solution is (p. 399)

✳ **phase:** a particular appearance in a recurring cycle of changes (p. 474)

pH meter: an electronic instrument with an electrode that is sensitive to the hydronium ions in a solution (p. 404)

physical change: any change in size, shape, or state of matter in which the identity of the substance remains the same (p. 317)

physical property: any characteristic of a material that can be observed without changing the identity of the material itself (p. 313)

physical science: the study of what things are made of and how things change (p. 2)

polar molecule: a molecule that has a positive end and a negative end that comes from unequal sharing of electrons (p. 426)

polymer (PAH luh muhr): a covalent compound made up of many small, repeating units linked together in a chain (pp. 235, 438)

✳ **preceding:** coming just before (p. 132)

✳ **precise:** exact (p. 347)

precision: a description of how similar or close measurements are to each other (p. 17)

prediction: to say in advance what will happen next in a sequence of events (pp. 19, 28)

pressure: force exerted per unit area of a surface (p. 141)

procedure: a sequence of instructions that you use systematically to gather data in a scientific investigation (p. 31)

✳ **process:** a series of actions or operations taken to achieve an end (p. 307)

products: the new substances that result from a chemical reaction (p. 349)

✳ **proportion:** the relation of one part to another or to the whole (p. 177)

proton: neutral particle that has no charge (p. 175)

período: fila horizontal de elementos en la tabla periódica (p. 291)

período de revolución: tiempo que tarda un planeta en dar una vuelta completa alrededor del Sol (p. 463)

período de rotación: tiempo que tarda un planeta en dar una vuelta completa alrededor de su eje de rotación (p. 463)

pH: escala numérica que se usa para indicar cuán ácida o básica es una solución (p. 399)

fase: apariencia determinada en un ciclo recurrente de cambios (p. 474)

metro de pH: instrumento electrónico con un electrodo sensible a los iones hidronio de una solución (p. 404)

cambio físico: cualquier cambio de tamaño, forma o estado de la materia en el cual la identidad de la sustancia permanece invariable (p. 317)

propiedad física: cualquier característica de un material que puede observarse sin cambiar la identidad de éste (p. 313)

ciencias físicas: estudio de la composición de los objetos y de cómo éstos cambian (p. 2)

molécula polar: molécula que posee un extremo positivo y uno negativo como resultado de compartir electrones de manera desigual (p. 426)

polímero: compuesto covalente formado por numerosas unidades pequeñas y recurrentes, enlazadas en una cadena (pp. 235, 438)

precedente: que está inmediatamente antes (p. 132)

preciso: exacto (p. 347)

precisión: descripción de la similitud o cercanía de unas medidas con otras (p. 17)

predicción: establecimiento de lo que va a suceder próximamente en una secuencia de eventos (pp. 19, 28)

presión: fuerza que se ejerce por unidad de superficie (p. 141)

procedimiento: secuencia de instrucciones que se usa sistemáticamente para recabar datos en una investigación científica (p. 31)

proceso: serie de acciones u operaciones que se toman para lograr un fin (p. 307)

productos: nuevas sustancias que resultan de una reacción química (p. 349)

proporción: relación que existe entre las partes o entre una parte y el todo (p. 177)

protón: partícula neutra que no posee carga (p. 175)

Q

qualitative data: descriptions of the natural world using words (p. 30)

quantitative data: descriptions of the natural world using numbers (p. 30)

datos cualitativos: descripción del mundo natural mediante palabras (p. 30)

datos cuantitativos: descripción del mundo natural mediante números (p. 30)

R

radioactive: describes an unstable nucleus that can release nuclear particles and energy (p. 303)

radioactive decay: an unstable atomic nucleus changes into another nucleus by emitting one or more particles and energy (p. 303)

radioactive element: an element that has only radioactive isotopes (p. 305)

✳ **random:** lacking a definite plan, purpose, or pattern (pp. 441, 531)

random motion: the movement of particles in matter in which the particles move in all directions at different speeds (p. 255)

✳ **ratio:** the relation between two numbers expressed by dividing one by the other (p. 152)

reactants: the starting materials in a chemical reaction (p. 349)

rectangular solid: a six-faced block in which all faces are rectangular (p. 135)

red giant: a star whose radius is much larger than the Sun's and appears red because of its relatively cool surface temperature (p. 524)

reference point: a starting point used to describe the position of an object (p. 48)

✳ **remove:** to get rid of (p. 264)

✳ **research:** the collecting of information about a particular subject (p. 184)

rise: the change in the value of the vertical coordinate between two points on a graph (p. 67)

run: the change in the value of the horizontal coordinate between two points on a graph (p. 67)

radiactivo: cualidad que describe un núcleo inestable que puede liberar partículas nucleares y energía (p. 303)

desintegración radiactiva: fenómeno que ocurre cuando un núcleo atómico inestable se transforma en otro núcleo al emitir una o más partículas y energía (p. 303)

elemento radiactivo: elemento que posee únicamente isótopos radiactivos (p. 305)

aleatorio: que carece de un plan, propósito o patrón definido (pp. 441, 531)

movimiento aleatorio: movimiento de las partículas de la materia en todas direcciones y a velocidades diferentes (p. 255)

proporción: relación entre dos números que se expresa dividiendo uno entre el otro (p. 152)

reactores: materiales iniciales en una reacción química (p. 349)

sólido rectangular: bloque de seis caras, todas rectangulares (p. 135)

gigante roja: estrella cuyo radio es mucho mayor que el del Sol y que parece roja debido a la temperatura relativamente fría de su superficie (p. 524)

punto de referencia: punto inicial que se usa para describir la posición de un objeto (p. 48)

eliminar: deshacerse de algo (p. 264)

investigación: recopilación de información sobre un tema determinado (p. 184)

elevación: cambio de valor de la coordenada vertical entre dos puntos de una gráfica (p. 67)

recorrido: cambio de valor de la coordenada horizontal entre dos puntos de una gráfica (p. 67)

S

sampling: a method of data collection that involves studying small amounts of something in order to learn something about the larger whole or group (p. 20)

satellite: an object that revolves around a planet (p. 473)

saturated hydrocarbon: a compound, such as propane or methane that contains only single covalent bonds between carbon atoms (p. 430)

science: the process of studying nature at all levels and the collection of information that is created through this process (p. 2)

scientific law: a rule that describes a pattern in nature (p. 6)

scientific notation: a shorthand way of writing very small or large numbers that involves expressing numbers as a decimal number between 1 and 10 multiplied by a power of 10 (p. 16)

muestreo: método de recopilación de datos que involucra el estudio de pequeñas cantidades de algo para aprender acerca de un aspecto del todo o grupo mayor (p. 20)

satélite: objeto que gira alrededor de un planeta (p. 473)

hidrocarburo saturado: compuesto, como el propano o el metano, que contiene únicamente enlaces individuales covalentes entre los átomos de carbono (p. 430)

ciencia: proceso mediante el cual se estudia la naturaleza a todos niveles, y la recopilación de información que se crea en este proceso (p. 2)

ley científica: regla que describe un patrón de la naturaleza (p. 6)

notación científica: forma corta de escribir números muy pequeños o muy grandes, en la cual éstos se expresan como un decimal entre 1 y 10 multiplicado por una potencia de 10 (p. 16)

Glossary/Glosario

scientific theory: an explanation of things or events that is based on knowledge gained from many observations and investigations (p. 6)

significant figures: the number of digits in a measurement that you know with a certain degree of reliability (p. 18)

✳ **similar:** having characteristics in common (p. 68)

slope: a number describing how steep a plotted line on a graph is; equal to the rise divided by the run (pp. 23, 66)

solid: a state of matter with a fixed shape and a fixed volume (p. 256)

solute: the dissolved substance in a solution (p. 384)

solution: a homogeneous mixture (p. 383)

solvent: substance that is used to dissolve the solute in a solution (p. 384)

✳ **specify:** to name or state in detail (p. 90)

spectral lines: a single wavelength of light that can be seen when the light from an excited element passes through a prism (p. 191)

speed: rate of change of position with time (p. 56)

sublimation: the change of matter from a solid state to a gaseous state without going through the liquid state (p. 272)

substance: a form of matter that has the same composition and properties throughout the sample (p. 381)

✳ **substitute:** to take the place of another (p. 432)

supernova: a supergiant star that explodes before dying (p. 525)

✳ **symbol:** something that stands for or suggests something else (p. 221)

synthetic element: an element that is made in a laboratory or by nuclear reactions (p. 306)

synthetic polymer: human-made polymer compounds that are not found in nature (p. 438)

teoría científica: explicación de circunstancias o eventos basada en el conocimiento obtenido a través de muchas observaciones e investigaciones (p. 6)

cifras significativas: número de dígitos de una medida que se conocen con cierto grado de confiabilidad (p. 18)

similar: que tiene características en común (p. 68)

pendiente: número que describe la inclinación de una línea trazada en una gráfica; es igual al recorrido dividido entre la elevación (pp. 23, 66)

sólido: estado de la materia que posee forma y volumen fijos (p. 256)

soluto: la sustancia disuelta en una solución (p. 384)

solución: mezcla homogénea (p. 383)

solvente: sustancia que se usa para disolver el soluto en una solución (p. 384)

especificar: nombrar o enunciar en detalle (p. 90)

líneas espectrales: longitud de onda individual de la luz que puede verse cuando la luz de un elemento excitado pasa a través de un prisma (p. 191)

rapidez: tasa de cambio de posición en función del tiempo (p. 56)

sublimación: cambio de la materia del estado sólido al estado gaseoso sin pasar por el estado líquido (p. 272)

sustancia: forma de materia que tiene la misma composición y propiedades en toda la muestra (p. 381)

sustituir: tomar el lugar de otro (p. 432)

supernova: estrella supergigante que explota antes de morir (p. 525)

símbolo: algo que representa o sugiere otra cosa (p. 221)

elemento sintético: elemento que se produce en un laboratorio o por medio de reacciones nucleares (p. 306)

polímero sintético: compuestos de polímeros elaborados por el hombre y que no se hallan en la naturaleza (p. 438)

T

---

temperature: a measure of the average kinetic energy of all the particles in an object (p. 262)

tension force: pulling force applied to an object that can make an object stretch (p. 101)

thermal conductivity: the ability of a material to transfer heat by collisions between its particles (p. 316)

thermal energy: the sum of the kinetic energy and potential energy of the particles in a material (p. 263)

✳ **transfer:** to pass from one to another (p. 316)

transmutation: the change of one atom into another through nuclear decay (p. 304)

temperatura: medida de la energía cinética promedio de todas las partículas de un objeto (p. 262)

fuerza de tensión: fuerza tirante que se le aplica a un cuerpo y puede hacer que éste se estire (p. 101)

conductividad térmica: capacidad de un material de transferir calor por medio de choques entre sus partículas (p. 316)

energía térmica: suma de la energía cinética y de la energía potencial de las partículas de un material (p. 263)

transferir: pasar de uno a otro (p. 316)

transmutación: transformación de un átomo en otro mediante desintegración nuclear (p. 304)

Glossary/Glosario

unbalanced forces: forces that combine to form a net force that is not zero (p. 91)

unit cell: the smallest repeating pattern that shows how the atoms, ions, or molecules are arranged in a crystal (p. 233)

unsaturated hydrocarbon: a compound that contains at least one double or triple covalent bond between carbon atoms, such as ethene and ethyne (p. 430)

fuerzas no equilibradas: fuerzas que se combinan para producir una fuerza neta diferente a cero (p. 91)

célula unitaria: patrón recurrente más pequeño que indica cómo los átomos, los iones o las moléculas se disponen en un cristal (p. 233)

hidrocarburo insaturado: compuesto que contiene al menos un enlace covalente doble o triple entre los átomos de carbono, como el eteno y el etino (p. 430)

valence (VAY lunts): the number of electrons in the outermost energy level of the atoms of an element (p. 223)

vaporization: the change of matter from the liquid state to the gaseous state (p. 267)

variable: any factor in a scientific investigation that can have more than one value (p. 29)

vector: a quantity with both size and direction (p. 51)

✷ **vehicle:** a means of transporting something; a piece of mechanized equipment (p. 481)

velocity: a vector that represents an object's speed and direction (p. 59)

✷ **visible:** capable of being seen with the eye (p. 189)

valencia: número de electrones del nivel exterior de energía de los átomos de un elemento (p. 223)

vaporización: cambio de la materia del estado líquido al gaseoso (p. 267)

variable: factor de una investigación científica que puede tener más de un valor (p. 29)

vector: cantidad que tiene magnitud y dirección (p. 51)

vehículo: medio para transportar algo; parte de un equipo mecanizado (p. 481)

velocidad: vector que representa la rapidez y la dirección de un objeto (p. 59)

visible: capaz de ser visto con el ojo (p. 189)

weight: the gravitational force exerted on an object (p. 98)

white dwarf: the small, dense, core of a giant star that remains after the star has lost its exterior matter (p. 524)

peso: fuerza gravitacional que se ejerce sobre un objeto (p. 98)

enana blanca: núcleo pequeño y denso de una estrella gigante que permanece después que ésta ha perdido su materia exterior (p. 524)

Index

Italic numbers = illustration/photo   **Bold numbers** = **vocabulary term**
lab = indicates a page on which the entry is used in a lab
act = indicates a page on which the entry is used in an activity

A

Absolute magnitude, 513
Absorption spectrum, 510, *511*, 511
Acceleration, 60, 106, 462; calculating, 109*act*; Word Origin, 61
Accelerator, particle, **307,** *307*, 308
Accident, Three Mile Island, 207
Accurate, 176
Acetic acid, 349, 433. *See* vinegar
Acetylene, 429, *429*
Acetylsalicylic acid, 411
Acid, 394, *394*, **395;** property of, 395; reacting to metal, *395;* type(s) of, 433; using, 396
Acidic solution, 395, 399
Acidity, pH level, 399
Acid rain, 397; pH level, 397; preventing, 410
Actinide, series on periodic table, *294,* 294
Action force, force pair, 111
Activities, 290; Applying Math, 61, 72, 81, 114, 123, 163, 180, 211, 247, 275, 283, 327, 407, 415, 437, 451, 501, 543; Applying Science, 54, 81, 94, 104, 123, 148, 154, 179, 194, 202, 211, 228, 237, 247, 260, 273, 283, 299, 310, 318, 327, 344, 356, 363, 392, 405, 415, 427, 436, 442, 451, 470, 476, 488, 493, 516, 527, 534, 543; Science Online, 45, 47, 54, 61, 72, 78, 79, 85, 87, 94, 104, 114, 115, 121, 127, 129, 137, 148, 154, 160, 161, 171, 173, 179, 180, 194, 202, 208, 209, 215, 217, 228, 237, 238, 244, 245, 251, 260, 273, 275, 280, 281, 289, 299, 310, 318, 325, 337, 344, 356, 363, 365, 370, 371, 377, 379, 392, 405, 407, 413, 419, 421, 427, 436, 437, 442, 448, 449, 459, 461, 470, 476, 488, 493, 498, 499, 507, 516, 518*act*, 527, 534, 540, 541; Writing in Science, 75*lab*, 81, 117*lab*, 123, 157*lab*, 163, 205*lab*, 211, 247, 277, 283, 321*lab*, 327, 367*lab*, 373, 409*lab*, 415, 445*lab*, 495, 501, 537*lab*, 543
Adaptive optics, 538
Affect, 108
Air, density, 130, *130*
Air pressure, 145, *145*
Alcohol, hydroxyl group, 432
Alloy, solid solution, 385, *385*
Alpha Centauri, nearest star to Earth, *509*

Alpha particle, 303; bouncing backward, 186; gold foil experiment, 186*tab*; pathway, *184,* 184, *185*, 185
Alternate, 233
Aluminum, physical property, 340, *340*
Amine, amino group, 434
Amino acid, 434; making up protein, 434, 435; monomer, *236*, 236; protein, 441
Amino group, functional group, **434**
Ammonia, base, *394*
Analyze and Communicate, 537*lab*
Analyze and Conclude, 75*lab*, 117*lab*, 157*lab*, 205*lab*, 241*lab*, 277*lab*, 321*lab*, 367*lab*, 409*lab*, 445*lab*, 495*lab*
Andromeda galaxy, 531, *531*
Ant sting, formic acid, 433
Apparent magnitude, 513
Appendix. *See* Glossary; Index; Math Skill Handbook; Credits; Reference Handbooks; Science Skill Handbook; Technology Skill Handbook
Applying Math, 58, 61, 72, 81, 114, 115, 123, 131, 135, 137, 142, 163, 180, 211, 238, 247, 275, 283, 311, 327, 365, 373, 407, 415, 437, 451, 471, 501, 518, 543
Applying Science, 54, 81, 94, 104, 123, 148, 154, 163, 179, 194, 202, 211, 228, 237, 247, 260, 273, 283, 299, 310, 318, 327, 344, 356, 363, 392, 405, 415, 427, 436, 442, 451, 470, 476, 488, 493, 501, 516, 527, 534, 543
Approximate, 403
Archimedes principle, 147
Area, 141
Argon, electron structure, 224, *224*
Arizona, meteor crater, 492, *492*
Artificial, transmutation, 307
Aspirin, as organic acid, 433, *433*
Asteroid, 489; Ceres, *489;* deadly impact, 497; moving around sun, 462
Astronomical unit, 466, 472
Atmosphere, buoyant force, 153; chemical composition, 446; nitrogen cycling, *424*, 424
Atmospheric pressure, 144, 314; relating to boiling point, 274*lab*
Atom, 174, 394; arranging, 435, *435*; atomic number, *195*; attractive force, 255; building, 204–205*lab*; conserving in chemical reaction, 346, *346*; counting, 352, 352*tab*; Democritus,

176, 176; hydrogen, 188; joining with bond, 431; metallic, 231; outer energy level, 224; part(s) of, 175; size, 175; size of particle, 181*lab*
Atomic bomb, dropping, 207
Atomic-force microscope, 174, *174*
Atomic model, Bohr, Niels, 191, *191*, 192; changing, 194; Dalton, John, *178*, 178; developing, *193;* Rutherford, Ernest, 186, 187; Thomson, J. J., 183, *183*
Atomic number, 195, *195*, 290, *294*, 294; periodic table, 196
Atomic particles, property of, 175*tab*
Atomic structure, 175; diamond and graphite, 315*tab*
Atomic symbol, 178, *178*
Atomic weight, *See* Average atomic mass
Attractive force, 96, 255, 314; liquid, 256; solid, 256
Automobile, burning fossil fuel, 397
Average atomic mass, 198
Average speed, 58; calculating, 63*lab*, 73*lab*, 75*lab*; equation, 58; of train, 123*act*
Axis, Earth rotating on, 472; moon rotating on, 474
Axis of rotation, 463

B

Bacon, saturated fat, 440, *440*
Baking soda, 340, 349, 355, 394; chemical change, *341,* 341
Balanced equation, 354, 356; writing, 353
Balanced force, 91, *92,* 92, 102, *102*; Newton's second law of motion, 110
Ball, finding average speed, 63*lab*
Barred spiral, 529, *529*
Base, 394, *394*, **396;** property of, 398; sodium hydroxide, *398;* using, 399
Basic, pH level, 399
Basic Solution, 399
Bellatrix, closest star to Earth, 514
Beta particle, transmutation, 304
Betelgeuse, star in constellation in constellation Orion, 511
Big bang theory, 532, **533**
Big Idea, 44, 78, 84, 120, 126, 160, 170, 208, 214, 244, 250, 280, 286, 324, 334, 370, 376, 412, 418, 448, 458, 498, 504, 540

Binary ionic compound, 221, 222
Biodiesel, 158
Biomass, 361, **422**
Biomolecule, 439; as polymer, 439*tab*
Black hole, *526*, **526**, 538
Blood, primary component(s), 425; water percentage, 425, *425*
Body, element in, 422, *422*; water percentage, *425*, 439
Bohr, Niels, atomic model, *191*, 191, 192, *193;* atomic spectrum, 190; hydrogen atom, 188
Boiling, 267; vaporization and, 267
Boiling point, 267, 314; evaporation, 268; physical property, 313; relating to atmospheric pressure, 274*lab*; water, *262*, 262, 271
Bomb, dropping atomic, 207
Bond, 231, covalent bond; ionic bond; metallic bond; carbon forming, 429, *429;* hydrogen, 430; joining by atom, 431; Science Use v. Common Use, 220; sharing electron, 227. *See also* chemical bond
Bonding, hydrogen, 426
Buoyant force, 146; on balloons, *153*, 153; cause of, *146;* depth, 147; feeling, 149*lab;* floating and sinking, 150–151, *150;* volume, *147*
Butane, as hydrocarbon, *430*, 430

C

Calcium carbonate, tufas, 380
Calcium chloride, 364
Calculating, acceleration, 109*act;* average speed, 58; average speed of airplane, 61*act;* average speed of spacecraft, 61*act;* average speed of train, 123*act;* brightness of Vega v. Acrux, 518*act;* changing speed of train, *68*, 68; density, 131, 139*lab;* density of limestone, 137*act;* density of unknown liquid, 157*lab;* distance and time, 59; half-life of uranium, 310; mass and volume, 132; mass of water, 181*lab;* neutron number, 310; percentage of saturated fatty acid in lipid, 443*lab;* pressure, 142; slope of a position-time graph, 67, *67;* slope of line on position-time graph, 72*act;* volume of irregular solid, 136*act;* volume of regular sold, 137*act*
Calculator, using, 594
California Standards Assessment, *See* Standards Assessment
Callisto, Jupiter moon, *482*, 482

Cannery Row, 159
Car, burning fossil fuel, 397; changing speed, 69, *69;* hybrid, 361
Carbohydrate, 440; monomer, 236; storing and releasing energy, 440
Carbon, cycling through environment, *423*, 423; element in human body, *422*, 422; forming bond, 429; forming compound, 225; forming organic compound, 236, 428; losing electron, *225*, 225; mass number, 302
Carbon atom, lipid, 440
Carbon bond, 429, 430
Carbon-based molecules, *See* organic compound
Carbon dioxide, burning, *349*, 349; as linear shape, 435; releasing in the environment, *423*, 423
Carboxyl group, functional group, 433
Carboxylic acid, 433
Career. *See* Real World Science
Cathode ray, *182*, 182, *183*, 183
Celery, water level, 425*lab*
Cell, unit, **233**
Cellulose, complex carbohydrate, 440
Celsius scale, *262*, 262
Central bulge (nucleus), spiral galaxy, *529*, 529
Centripetal, Word Origin, 108
Centripetal force, 108, *110;* Newton's second law of motion, 110
Ceres, *489*
Chadwick, James, discovering neutron, 187
Chain, carbon forming, 429
Changing, in state, 317
Charcoal, equation for, 353
Charge, Science Use v. Common Use, 183
Charon, Pluto companion moon, 485, *485*
Chemical bond, 220, 358; holding molecule together, 236; storing energy, 360
Chemical change, 341
Chemical energy, 361
Chemical equation, balancing, 351, *351;* writing, 349, 351
Chemical formula, 219
Chemical property, 338; observing change, 339, 339*tab*
Chemical reaction, breaking bond, 360; energy, 358, 363; jewelry, 366–367*lab;* light from, 359, *359*
Chemistry, Lavoisier, Antoine, *347*, 347; Nobel Prize, 305, *305*
Chip, computer, 297, *297*
Chlorine, electron structure, *224*, 224

Circular motion, 108
Citric acid, *394;* fruit, 433
Coefficient, 352, 352*tab*
Collagen, 435
Color, physical property, 313; star, 511, 512*tab*
Color strip, testing pH, *404*, 404
Column, of element, *292*
Comet, *490*, **490;** moving around sun, 462; structure, 490
Complex carbohydrate, type(s) of, 440
Component, 386
Compound, *218*, **218**, 218, 438; amino group, 434; carbon forming, organic, 428; chemical formula, 219; covalent, 225; and element, 220; human body, 439; hydroxyl group, 432; ionic, 221, 222; molecule as, 350, *350;* naming, *431*, 431; nitrogen cycle, 424
Compression force, 101, 102
Computer chip, global communication, 297, *297*
Concentration, solute v. solvent, 388
Concept map, 79, 121, 161, 209, 245, 281, 325, 371, 413, 449, 499, 541
Concepts in Motion, 112, 200*tab*, 223, 233, 259*tab*, 384, 433, 474, 514
Condensation, 269, *269*
Conduct, 297; Word Origin, 340
Conductivity, *295*, **295.** *See also* electrical conductivity, thermal conductivity
Conservation of atoms, 346–347
Conservation of mass, law of, 177
Conservation of matter, 346–347
Consist, 236
Constant, 57
Constant speed, 57
Contact force, 88
Continuous spectrum, *510*, 510; sun emitting, *511*
Contract, 524
Contrast, 198
Cooling curve, water, 271, *271*
Copper, electrical conductivity, *316*, 316; physical property, *340*, 340
Corn oil, polyunsaturated fat, 440
Covalent bond, 225, 226–227, 229*lab*, 428
Covalent compound, properties, *225*, 226; salt, 225
Crater, on Earth, 492
Crystal, 232; growing, 240–241*lab;* ionic, 232; pattern, 233; sodium chloride, *233*, 234; structure, 234, *234;* table salt, *233*, 234
Cubic structure, 233
Curie, Marie, *305*, 305
Curium, 309

Index

D

Dalton, John, atomic symbol, *178,* 178; developing atomic model, *193*

Dark energy, 533

Dark matter, 533

DataLab, Can you add vertical forces?, 95; Can you calculate density?, 139; Can You Identify Elements in a Star?, 517; Drawing a Scale Model of the Planets, 485; How are ionic radii and lattice energies of salts related?, 239; How are the boiling point and atmospheric pressure related?, 274; How can a graph show relative positions?, 55; How can you show a visual explanation of half-life?, 312; How do atoms differ?, 203; How does temperature change as chemicals react?, 364; How fast is the universe expanding?, 535*lab;* What can you learn from a graph?, 73; Where does the tablet go?, 348; Which fat is healthy for you?, 443

Decomposer, nitrogen cycle, 424

Deep Impact, 490

Definite Proportion, law of, *177,* 177

Deimos, Mars moon, 480

Democritus, atom, *176,* 176

Density, 130, 313; buoyant force, 151, *151;* calculating, 131, 132, 139*lab;* common material, 133, 133*tab;* measuring, 134; measuring with hydrometer, 152, *152;* physical property, 136, 313, 315

Deoxyribonucleic acid (DNA). *See* DNA

Deposition, *272,* 272

Depth, buoyant force, 147; pressure, *143,* 143

Design Your Own, Comparing Mass and Weight, 116–117; Forensics, Dirty Jewelry, 366–367; Graphing Motion, 74–75; Investigation Lab, 156–157; Investigation Lab, A Homemade Hydrometer, 150–151; Model and Invent, A Star is Born, 536–537; Model and Invent, Build an Atom, 204–205; Solubility and pH, 408–409

Deuterium, 200, 305, *522*

Diamond, atomic structure, 315*tab*

Diatomic Elements, 350*tab*

Diatomic molecule, 350

Dimension, 52; two, 51, 52

Discovering, element, 306

Displacement, 53; distance, *53,* 53

Displacement method, measuring volume, 136

Dissolving, 343; physical change, 317

Distance, 48; calculating, 59, 62; displacement, *53,* 53; equation, 62; measuring, 459*lab*

Distribute, 259

DNA (deoxyribonucleic acid), discovering structure of, 243; monomer, 236, storing cellular information, 439

Doorknob, homogeneous mixture, 382, *382*

Double bonds, 227

Ductile metal, 295

Ductility, 232

E

Earth, *480,* 486–487*tab;* atmosphere, 480; crater, 492; distance to sun, 466; inner planet, 478; motion, 50; orbiting sun, 472, *472;* period of revolution, 463, 463*tab;* period of rotation, 463, 463*tab;* rare earth element, *294;* rotating about axis, 473

Eclipse, 475

Ecosystem, element cycling, 423

Effervescent tablet, dissolving, 348*lab*

Einsteinium, 309

Elastic force, *101,* **101,** 102*lab*

Electrical conductivity, 316, *316*

Electrical energy, decomposing water, *342,* 342

Electrolyte, 391, *391*

Electromagnetic spectrum, 182

Electron, *175,* **175;** diagramming, 223; discovering, 182, *182;* energy level, 191, *191;* in Thomson's atomic model, 183, *183;* moving, 186*lab;* pathway around nucleus, 188; releasing energy, *190,* 190; sharing, 225, 226, 227; transferring, 220

Electron cloud, 192; developing, *193*

Electron-pair theory, 411

Electron structure, *224,* 224

Element, 195, *218,* 218, 230, 290, 422, 511; arranging, 290, *290;* chemical property, 192; for compound, 220; diatomic, 350*tab;* discovering, 309; energy level, *192,* 192; explaining colored light, *187;* explaining different behavior, 187; grouping, 291, *291;* guessing, 300*lab;* in human body, *422,* 422; metal, 230; naming, 306, 309, 309*tab;* periodic table, *292,* 600; proton number, 195; rare Earth, 294, *294;* synthetic, 306, 307, 308

Elevation, varying, 145

Ellipse, 464, *464,* 528

Elliptical galaxy, *530,* 530

Endothermic, Word Origin, 362

Endothermic process, *362,* 362

Energy, ball twirling, 188, *188;* changing during melting, 265; cold-pack process, *362,* 362; electrical, 342, *342;* electron filling, 191, *191;* electron releasing, *190,* 190; exothermic process, *360;* kinetic, 261; law of conservation, **359;** moving gas particle, *261;* nuclear fusion, 522, *522;* potential, 263, *263;* releasing, 358, *358,* 360. *See also* Chemical energy; Energy levels; Thermal energy

Energy levels, 190, 191, 192

Environment, element in, 422

Environmental Standards, correlations to, acid rain, 397, 410; biogeochemical cycles, 423–425; emissions, 397, 410; human practices alter cycles, 397, 423; nutrient cycling, 423–425; oxygen production, 423

Equation, balancing, 353, 354, 356; chemical, 349, 351, *351;* density, 131; Newton's second law of motion, 109; volume of atoms, 275; word, *351,* 355

Ethane, as hydrocarbon, 430, *430*

Ethanol, as solvent, *390,* 390

Ethylene, *429,* 429; as planar shape, *435,* 435

Ethyne, *429,* 429; as linear shape, *435,* 435

Europa, Jupiter moon, *482,* 482

Evaporation, 268; sensing, 268*lab*

Exothermic, Word Origin, 360

Exothermic process, 360; reactant, *360*

Experiment, gold foil, 184; gold-foil, 303; gold foil experiment, 185, *185,* 186*tab*

Extended table, 294, *294*

F

Fahrenheit scale, 262, *262*

Fat, healthy, 443*lab;* trans, 447

Fatty acid, present in lipid, 443*lab*

Fermenting, lactic acid, 433

Fibrinogen, 435

Flammability, 338

Floating, buoyant force, 150, *150,* 151, *151;* ice cube, 155*lab*

Fluid, 140; height and pressure, 143

Fluid motion, observing, 255*lab*

Fluorite, crystal structure, *234,* 234

Foldables, 45, 85, 127, 171, 215, 251, 287, 335, 377, 419, 459, 505

Folic acid, *394*

Food web, nitrogen cycle, 424
Force, 88, 140; adding vertical, 95*lab*; attractive, 96, 255, 314; balanced, 91; balancing, *92, 92, 95lab, 96;* centripetal, 108; combining, 90–91; compression, 101, 102; elastic, *101,* 101, 102*lab*; exerting, *88,* 108, *108,* 140, *140;* gravitational, 97*tab*; measuring friction, 105*lab*; net, 90, 107; sliding friction, 100; static friction, 99, *99;* tension, 101, *101;* type(s) of, 102*tab*; unbalanced, 91, 92, 96; as vector, 89; vertical, *103,* 103; water exerting, 110*lab*. *See also* buoyant force
Force pair, 111, *111*
Formic acid, ant sting, 433
Formula, atom number, 352, *352;* for compound, 219; representing molecule and ionic compound, 350, *350;* using parenthesis, 355
Fossil fuel, burning, *397,* 423
Freezing point, 262, *262,* **266**
Friction, 99; measuring, 105*lab*; sliding, *100,* 100; static, *99;* Word Origin, 99
Fruit, citric acid, 433
Fruit drink, homogeneous mixture, 383, *383*
Fuel cell, 361
Function, 360
Functional group, 432, 433*tab*; changing hydrocarbon property, *432,* 432
Fusion, in star, 523, *523;* in supernova, 525

G

Galactic clusters, *See* supercluster
Galaxy, 528, *528;* distance and velocity, 535*lab*; distance between, 531; evolution of, *532,* 532; forming, *533,* 533; Milky Way, *530,* 531; type(s) of, 529–530; Word Origin, 529
Gallium, melting, *317,* 317
Ganymede, Jupiter moon, *482, 482*
Gas, 258; changing state, 264–269, 272, *272;* nebula, 468; motion of particles in, 259; spreading out, *258,* 258; state of matter, *254,* 254, 259*tab*; thermal conductivity, *316,* 316
Glycine, amino acid, 434
Glycogen, complex carbohydrate, 440
Gold, element substance, *381*
Gold-foil experiment, 184, 185, *185,* 186*tab*; radioactive decay, 303
Granite, heterogeneous mixture, *382, 382*
Graph, atomic mass v. atomic number, 203*lab*; changing state of liquids,

277*lab*; distance between atom, 239*lab*; finding solubility, 387*act;* force v. length, 95*lab*; learning from, 73*lab*; measuring weight and mass, 117*lab*; motion, 74–75*lab*; percentage of saturated fatty acid in lipid, 443*lab*; plotting pennies on an axis, 312*lab*; position-time, 64–68, 70–71, 73*lab*, 74–75; showing relative position, 55*lab*; solubility, 393*lab*; speed-time, 69, 70–71; temperature and time, 64, *64;* temperature v. time, 364*lab*; two-dimensional map, *52, 52*
Graphite, atomic structure, 315*tab*
Gravitional Compression, 468, 523
Gravitational force, mass, *97;* in nebula, 520; on a person, 97*tab*; weight, *98*
Gravity, 96, 150; forming galactic cluster, 531; holding and moving star, 528; law of, 468; solar system, 467
Great Red Spot, Jupiter storm system, *482*
Group, 291
Guinness Book of World Records, 278

H

Hair, natural polymer, *438*
Half-life, 306, 306; explaining, 312*lab*
Halo, spiral galaxy, 529
Halogen, *296,* **296**
Handbook(s). *See* Glossary; Index; Math Skill Handbook; Credits; Reference Handbook; Science Skill Handbook; Technology Skill Handbook
Hardness, physical property, 315
Hawking, Stephen, black hole, 538
Heating curve, *270,* 270
Helium balloon, buoyant force, *153,* 153
Hemoglobin, 435
Heterogeneous mixture, *382,* **382**
High-mass star, life cycle, 524
History. *See* Real World Science
Homogenous mixture, *382,* **382,** 383, *383*
Horizontal force, 103, *103*
Horizontal period, *291,* 291
Hot-Air balloon, buoyant force, *153,* 153
H-R Diagram, *515;* classifying star(s), 514
Hubble, Edwin, 532
Human body, carbon and non-carbon compound, 439; element in, *422, 422;* element in human body, 441; mineral, *441;* water percentage, *425,* 439
Human genome project, 243

Human hair, natural polymer, *438*
Hybrid car, 361
Hydrocarbon, 430; functional group changing property, 432, *432;* naming, 430; substituted, 432
Hydrogen, bonding, 426; element in human body, *422, 422;* gas decomposing from water, *342,* 342; giving off light, *189,* 189; isotope, 200, 200*tab*; producing energy, 361; releasing energy, 190; sharing electron, 226; Word Origin, 354
Hydrogen atom, studying, 188
Hydrogen peroxide, compound substance, *381*
Hydrometer, 152, 152; making, 156–157*lab*
Hydronium ion, 395; pH level, 400, *400*
Hydroxide ion, pH level, *400,* 400; producing, *398,* 398
Hydroxyl group, functional group, 432
Hypothesis, changing pH of vinegar, 405; chemical change, 344*act;* forming, 74*lab*, 116*lab*, 156*lab*, 240*lab*, 276*lab*, 320–321*lab*, 366*lab*, 408*lab*, 494*lab*, 536*lab*; parachute dropping first, 319*lab*; writing balanced equation, 356

I

Ice cube, floating, 155*lab*; sinking, 158
Indicator, *403,* **403**
Individual, 383
Inert gas, 297
Inertia, 93, *93*
Inner planet, 478; composition of, 478; planetary data, 479*tab*
Instantaneous speed, 57
International Union of Pure and Applied Chemistry (IUPAC), 431; molecule naming, 447
Interstellar space, 519
Internet. *See* Science Online; Using the Internet
Involve, 98
Io, Jupiter moon, *482, 482*
Ion, 218; conducting electricity, *391,* 391; electron number, 200, 201; forming, 225; metal, 231, *231;* noble gas, 224
Ionic bond, 220, 220, 229*lab*
Ionic compound, 220, 221; mineral, 232, *232;* properties, 222
Ionic crystal, sodium chloride, 232
Ionic radii, relating to lattice energy of salt, 239*lab*

Iron, observing change, *339, 339*
Irregular galaxy, *530, 530*
Isotope, 198; 301; hydrogen, 200, 200*tab*; neutron number, 197; oxygen, *301*; using, 198; Word Origin, 198
IUPAC (International Union of Pure and Applied Chemistry), 431; molecule naming, 447

J

Jewelry, chemical reaction, 366–367*lab*
Jupiter, *482*, 486–487*tab*; composition of, 482; exploring, 482; outer planet, 481

K

Kelvin scale, 262, *262*
Kepler, Johannes, 464, 497, 539
Kepler's first law, planet orbiting sun in elliptical path, *464, 464*
Kepler's laws of motion, 497
Kepler's second law, equal area in equal time, *465, 465*
Kepler's third law, orbiting period increase with distance, 465, *465*
Keratin, 435
Kinetic energy, moving particle, 261; temperature, *262, 262*

L

Lab, A Homemade Hydrometer, 156–157; A Star is Born, 536–537; Build an Atom, 204–205; Comparing Mass and Weight, 116–117; Dirty Jewelry, 366–367; Does change of state take longer for some liquids?, 276–277; Graphing Motion, 74–75; Growing Crystals, 240–241; Investigating Physical Changes, 320–321; Model the Solar System, 494–495; Polarity and Living Systems, 444–445; Solubility and pH, 408–409; DataLab, 55, 73, 95, 139, 203, 239, 274, 312, 348, 364, 393, 443, 485, 535; Launch Lab, 45, 85, 127, 171, 215, 251, 287, 335, 377, 419, 459, 505; MiniLab, 49, 63, 105, 110, 149, 155, 181, 186, 229, 255, 268, 300, 319, 345, 357, 406, 425, 434, 464, 477, 492, 520
Labeling, fat content of food, 447
Lactic acid, fermenting milk product, 433
Lakeshore, rock formation, *380, 380*
Language Arts standards, correlations to, 45, 54, 61, 72, 81, 85, 94, 104, 114,

117*lab*, 128, 137, 148, 154, 163, 179, 194, 202, 211, 228, 237, 241, 242, 243, 247, 260, 273, 277, 299, 310, 318, 327, 336, 344, 356, 363, 373, 377, 392, 409, 410, 411, 415, 427, 436, 442, 446, 460, 470, 476, 488, 493, 501, 516, 527, 534, 538, 543
Lanthanide, series on periodic table, 294, *294, 600*
Lattice energy, relating to ionic radii, 239*lab*
Launch Lab, Can you push the beach ball under water?, 127; Can you see a chemical reaction taking place?, 335; How do you get there from here?, 45; How do your measure distance?, 459; How far away are the stars and how many are there?, 505; model for Particle Movement, 251; What is a life chemical?, 419; What's in the box?, 171; Which element are you?, 287
Lavoisier, Antoine, father of modern chemistry, *347, 347*
Law of conservation of energy, 359
Law of conservation of mass, 177, **347**
Law of definite proportion, 177, *177*, 219
Law of universal gravitation, 97, 468
Laws of motion, Kepler's, 464–465, 497; Newton's, 93, 96, 109, 110, 111, 112*tab*, 113, 115
Lee, Yuan T., 410
Length, physical property, 313
Lesson Review, 54, 61, 72, 94, 104, 114, 137, 148, 154, 179, 194, 202, 228, 237, 260, 273, 299, 310, 318, 344, 356, 363, 392, 405, 427, 436, 442, 470, 476, 488, 493, 516, 527, 534
Lewis, Gilbert N., 223, 411
Lewis dot diagram, 223, 223*tab*; making, 223
Life chemical, 419*lab*
Light, from chemical reaction, *359, 359*
Light-year, 509
Limestone, tufas, 380
Linear, molecule shape, *435*, 435
Lipid, 439; 440; fatty acid in, 443*lab*; Word Origin, 439
Liquid, 257, 380; change of state, 266–269, 276–277*lab*; condensation, 269; evaporation, *268*, 268; motion of particles in, 257, *257*; state of matter, 254, *254*, 259*tab*; vaporization, 267
Lithium, atom of, *175*
Litmus paper, 395, 398
Living organism, 425
Living system, polarity, 444–445*lab*
Local Group, galactic cluster, *531*, 531

Long-period comet, 491, *491*
Los Angeles, smog, 159
Low-mass star, life cycle, 524, *524*
Luminosity, 513
Lunar, 474
Lunar eclipse, 475, *475*
Lunar phase, 474
Luster, 295; Word Origin, 294

M

Magnesium, electron structure, 224
Magnitude, Science Use v. Common Use, 513
Main Idea, 48, 56, 64, 88, 96, 106, 130, 140, 150, 174, 182, 195, 218, 230, 254, 261, 290, 301, 313, 338, 346, 358, 380, 394, 422, 428, 462, 472, 489, 508, 519, 528. *See also* Understanding Main Ideas
Malleability, 232, 295
Map, two-dimensional graph, 52, *52*
Mars, 486–487*tab*; existing life, 480; exploring, 481; inner planet, 478; moon, *480*
Mass, 174; law of conservation of, 177; calculating, 132; changing, *98, 98*; comparing to weight, 116–117*lab*; conserving in chemical reaction, 346, *346*; inertia, 93; law of conservation, 347; measuring, *134, 134*
Mass number, 197
Mathematics. *See* Applying Math
Matter, 130, *130*, **174**, 254; changing state, 261–273, *272*; density, 519; familiar state of, 259, 259*tab*; random motion, 255, *255*; state of, 254, *254*; statistical, 279. *See also* Gas, Liquid, Solid
Measuring, distance, 459*lab*
Melting point, 265, **314**; physical property, 313
Mercury, *479*, 486–487*tab*; inner planet, 478; temperature, 479
Metal, 230; alloy, *385*, 385; ductile, 232, *295*, 295; electrical conductivity, *316*; malleable, 232, *340*; periodic table, *293, 600*; properties, 232
Metallic, 295, **295**
Metallic bond, 231; property, 231
Metalloid, periodic table, *293, 600*
Meteor crater, Arizona, *492*, 492
Meteoroid, 492
Methane, *429*; burning, 357*lab*; chemical reaction, 354; as hydrocarbon, 430, *430*; producing energy, 361; as tetrahedral shape, 435, *435*

Microscope, atomic-force, *174*, 174

Milky Way galaxy, 50, *530*, 530; moving toward Virgo cluster, 532, *532*

Mineral, human body, *441*, 441

MiniLab, Can you feel the buoyant force?, 149; Can you find the ball's average speed?, 63; Can you guess the element?, 300; Can you measure the force of friction?, 105; Can you model the burning of methane?, 357; Do cold things float?, 155; Does Water Exert a Force?, 110; Elastic Force, 102; How big are the particles in an atom?, 181; How can you determine pH?, 406; How can you model molecules?, 229; How can you tell a chemical change from a physical change?, 345; How do electrons move?, 186; How does the Moon change its shape in the sky?, 477; How do planets move?, 464; How much water is in celery?, 425; Modeling Organic Compound, 434; Modeling the Size of Nebulae, 520; Negative Positions, 49; Observing Fluid Motion, 225; Sensing Evaporation, 268; Which parachute will drop first?, 319

Mixing, physical change, 317

Mixture, 219, 382; separating, 386, *386*

Model and Invent, Build an Atom, 204–205; A Star is Born, 536–537

Molecular cloud, *519*

Molecular formula, organic compound, 431, *431*

Molecule, 219, 346; attractive force, 255; diatomic, 350; making covalent compound, 225; modeling, 229*lab*; naming, 447; polar, 390, 426; shape of, 435; stringlike, 235; structure determining hydrocarbon, 430; Word Origin, 219

Molina, Mario J., ozone layer, 242

Mono Lake, rock formation, 380, *380*

Monomer, 235, 438; amino acid, 236, *236*

Monosaccharide, 236

Moon, changing shape in sky, 477*lab*; forming, 468, 473, *473*; phase(s) of, 474; of planet, 478; solar system, 462

Motion, 384, changing direction, 60; Earth, 50; friction, 100; graphing, 74–75*lab*; observing fluid, 255*lab*; particle in solid, *256*, 256; position-time and speed-time graph(s), 70*tab*, 71*tab*. *See also* Concepts in Motion

Mt. Everest, *145*, 145

N

Naming, element, 306, 309, 309*tab*; hydrocarbon, 430; molecule, 447; organic chemistry, 431; organic compound, 430

Natural cycle, element in environment, 422, *423*, 423

Natural polymer, 236, *438*, **438**

Nebula, **468**, 519

Nebulae, component of, 520; modeling, 520*lab*

Negative ion, 221; gaining electron number, 201

Neon gas, exciting, *189*

Neptune, 484, *484*, 486–487*tab*; outer planet, 481

Net force, **90**, 107

Neutral solution, *See* neutralization

Neutralization, pH level, 402

Neutron, 175, *175*; discovering, 187; finding number of, *197*, 197, *302*, 302; and isotopes, 197–198

Neutron star, **526**

Newton, unit of force, 89

Newton, Isaac, 89, 97, 468

Newton's first law of motion, **93**, 96, 112*tab*, 113

Newton's law of universal gravitation, 97, 468

Newton's laws in sports, 113, *113*

Newton's laws of motion, 112*tab*; applying, 112, *112*

Newton's second law of motion, **109**, 112*tab*, 113; equation for, 109, 115; force, 110

Newton's third law of motion, **111**, *111*, 112*tab*, 113

Nitrogen, cycling through environment, 424; element in human body, *422*, 422

Nitrogen oxide, reacting with water vapor, 397

Nobel Prize, chemistry, *305*, 305; Lee, Yuan T., 410

Noble gas, **297**; electron structure, 224

Nomenclature, organic chemistry, 431

Noncontact force, 89

Nonelectrolyte, *391*, 391

Nonmetal, *296*, 296; noble gas, 297; periodic table, *293*, *600*

Nonpolar molecule, **426**

Normal force, 102

Nuclear fusion, **522**, *522*

Nuclear power, 206

Nucleic acid, *439*, **439**; monomer, 236

Nucleus, 175; discovering, 184; surrounded by electron cloud, *192*, 192; Word Origin, 175

Nucleus (central bulge), spiral galaxy, 529, *529*

O

Oil, unsaturated fat, 440

Olive oil, unsaturated fat, *440*, 440

Orbit, gravity, 467–468, 467; inner planet, *478*

Orbital, *See* energy level

Organic acid, aspirin, *433*, 433

Organic chemistry, nomenclature, 431

Organic compound, 225, 236, **428**; containing functional group, 432; modeling, 434*lab*; naming, 430

Organic polymer, 236; protein, 441

Organism, needing water, 425, *425*

Origin, reference point, 48. *See also* Word Origin

Orion, constellation, 511

Outer planet, **481**; planetary data, 481*tab*

Oxygen, atom number, 353, 354; cycling through environment, *423*, 423; element in human body, *422*, 422; gas decomposing from water, 342, *342*; isotope of, 301, *301*

Ozone, chemical composition, 446

Ozone layer, 242

P

Pair, force, 111, *111*

Paper, burning, 338, 339

Parachute, dropping first, 319*lab*

Parenthesis, using with formula, 355

Particle, alpha, 303; attracting, 255; change in motion, 261; density, 133; moving, 255; moving in a solid, *256*, 256; size in atom, 181*lab*; speed, 308; strength of force, 261

Particle accelerator, **307**, *307*, 308

Peacock feather, natural polymer, *438*

Percentage, calculating saturated fatty acid in lipid, 443*lab*; concentration, *388*, 388; water in celery, 425*lab*; water in organism, 425

Period, **291**

Periodic table, 195, *196*, 196, 206, *292*, *293*, 350, *600*; arranging element, *290*, 290; of elements, 744; metal, 295, *295*; nonmetal, 296, *296*, 297; radioactive element, 305; reading, 291, *291*; region, 294; semimetal, 297, *297*; type(s) of, 298, *298*

Index

Period of revolution, 463, 463*tab*
Period of rotation, 463, 463*tab*
pH, 399; comparing value, 407*act*; determining, 406*lab*; hydronium ion, 400, *400;* hydroxide ion, 400, *400;* level at Monterey Bay Aquarium, *399;* measuring, 402; neutralizing, 402; Word Origin, 399
Pheromone, carboxylic acid, 433
pH meter, 404, *404*
Phobos, Mars moon, 480
Phosphorous, 422; cycling through environment, 424
pH scale, *404*
pH strip, 404
pH value, comparing, *401,* 401
Physical, 341
Physical change, 317, 343; investigating, 320–321*lab*
Physical property, 313, *313,* 338; changing, 318; measuring density, 136; observing change, 340*tab*
Physical Science Reference Table, 742
Planar, molecule shape, *435,* 435; three-dimensional figure, 437*act*
Planet, 486–487*tab,* **489;** average distance to sun, *466,* 466*tab;* drawing scale model, 485*lab;* forming, 468; inner, 478–480; moving, 464*lab;* moving around sun, 462; outer, 481–485; revolving and rotating, 463*tab;* rotating, 463; satellite revolving around, 473; searching for extra-solar, 496; solar system, *462;* tenth, *491,* 491
Planetary satellite, *See* planet; satellite revolving around
Plant, absorbing phosphorous, 424; needing water, 425
Plasma, state of matter, 254; water percentage, 425, *425*
Plastic wrap, polymer, 438
Pluto, *485,* 485, 486–487*tab;* composition of, 485; outer planet, 481
Polar, Word Origin, 426
Polarity, living system, 444–445*lab;* of water, *389,* 389
Polar molecule, 390, 426; water level, *426*
Polar solvent, 390
Polyethylene, 235, *235*
Polymer, 235, 438; biomolecule, 439*tab;* naming, *438;* natural, 438, 439; natural, 236; synthetic, 235
Polyunsaturated fat, 440
Pool, testing pH, 403, *403*
Position, changing, 53; graphing, *65,* 65, 65*tab;* negative, 49*lab;* reference point,

48; showing with two directions, 52; two dimensions, 51, 52; vector, 51
Position-Time graph, 64–68, 70*tab,* 71*tab;* changing speed, 67; slope, 66; using, *66,* 66
Positive ion, 221; losing electron number, 201
Potassium, reaction with water, *338,* 338
Potential energy, 261, 263, *263*
Power, nuclear, 206
Power plant, burning fossil fuel, 397
Preceding, 132
Precipitation, acid rain, 397, 410
Precise, 347
Prefix, organic compound naming, 431
Pressure, 141, 519; air, *145,* 145; applying, 141, *141;* atmospheric, 144, 314, *314;* boiling point, 268, 274*lab;* buoyant force, 146, *146;* calculating, 142; depth, 143, *143;* direction of, *144,* 144; fluid, 140; fluid height, 143, *143;* Science Use v. Common Use, 142; water, 145, *145*
Process, 307
Product, 349; formula for, 355
Propane, as hydrocarbon, 430, *430*
Property, changing, 341; determining, 302; measuring density, 136; Science Use v. Common Use, 315. *See also* Chemical property; Physical property
Proplyd, protoplanetary disk, *520,* 520
Proportion, 177
Protein, 441; monomer, 236; Word Origin, 441
Proton, *175,* **175;** atomic number, 197; discovering, 187; Word Origin, 187
Protostar, 520

Q

Quark, *193*
Quartz, crystal structure, 234, *234*

R

Radiation, 199, 303, *303*
Radioactive, 303
Radioactive decay, 303; transmutation, 304, *304*
Radioactive element, 305, *305*
Radioisotope, 199
Radon, *305*
Rain, acid, 397, 410
Rainbow, continuous spectrum, *510,* 510
Random, 441
Randomly, 531
Random motion, 255, *255*

Rare earth elements, 294
Rate, 56; measuring, 56
Ratio, 152; calculating, 157*lab*
Reactant, 349; exothermic process, *360;* formula for, 355
Reaction, Science Use v. Common Use, 349; Word Origin, 353
Reaction force, force pair, 111
Reading Check, 48, 51, 53, 57, 67, 68, 89, 90, 93, 97, 98, 100, 103, 107, 112, 131, 135, 136, 141, 143, 144, 151, 153, 176, 177, 178, 183, 184, 187, 188, 189, 190, 219, 221, 223, 225, 227, 230, 232, 235, 236, 255, 256, 259, 263, 264, 266, 271, 296, 304, 309, 313, 316, 317, 339, 340, 343, 347, 350, 352, 359, 362, 384, 387, 388, 390, 396, 400, 401, 423, 425, 434, 441, 465, 467, 473, 478, 485, 522, 523, 525, 526, 530, 532
Real-World Reading Connection, 48, 56, 64, 88, 96, 106, 130, 140, 150, 174, 182, 195, 218, 230, 254, 261, 290, 301, 313, 338, 346, 358, 380, 394, 422, 428, 462, 472, 489, 508, 519, 528
Real-World Science, 76–77, 118–119, 158–159, 206–207, 242–243, 278–279, 322–323, 368–369, 410–411, 446–447, 496–497, 538–539
Record holder, 278
Red giant, low-mass star, 524, *524*
Reference direction, describing, 49
Reference Handbook, Periodic Table of the Elements, 600; Physical Science Reference Tables, 598; Science Reference Guide, 597; Using a Calculator, 594; Understanding Scientific Terms, 595
Reference point, *48,* **48;** direction, *49,* 49
Region, periodic table, 294, *600*
Regular spiral, 529
Remove, 264
Research, 184
Reversible change, 343
Review. *See* Lesson Review; Standards Review
Ribonucleic acid (RNA), storing cellular information, 439
Ring, carbon forming, 429
RNA (ribonucleic acid), storing cellular information, 439
Rock, formation, *380,* 380
Roentgenium, unununium, 308
Root word, organic compound naming, 431
Row, of element, *292*
Rutherford, Ernest, atomic model, 186–187, *193;* discovering nucleus, 184–185

S

Salt, covalent compound, 225
Satellite, 473; revolving around planet, 473; Science Use v. Common Use, 473
Saturate, Word Origin, 430
Saturated fat, *440,* 440
Saturated hydrocarbon, 430
Saturn, 486–487*tab*; composition of, 483; exploring, 483; outer planet, 481
Scale, of graph, 55; pH, 399, *400*
Science, Writing in, *See* Writing in Science
Science Online, 45, 47, 54, 61, 72, 78, 79, 85, 87, 94, 104, 114, 115, 121, 127, 129, 137, 148, 154, 160, 161, 171, 173, 179, 180, 194, 202, 208, 209, 215, 217, 228, 237, 238, 244, 245, 251, 275, 280, 281, 287, 289, 299, 310, 318, 325, 337, 344, 356, 363, 365, 370, 371, 377, 379, 392, 405, 407, 412, 413, 419, 421, 427, 436, 437, 442, 448, 449, 459, 461, 470, 476, 488, 493, 498, 499, 507, 516, 518*act*, 527, 534, 540, 541
Scientific notation, writing, 180
Science Reference Guide, 597
Scientific Terms, 595
Seaborg, Glenn, discovering element, 309, *309*
Seaborgium, 309
Semiconductor, silicon, 297, *297*
Semimetal, 296, *297*
Shape, physical property, 313
Short-period comet, 491, *491*
Side chain, 441
Silicon, semiconductor, *297*, 297
Similar, 68
Sinking, buoyant force, 150, *150,* 155*lab*
Sirius, brightest star, 511
Sliding friction, *100,* 100
Slope, 66; calculating, 72
Smog, Los Angeles, 159
Society. *See* Real World Science
Sodium chloride, 342, *342;* ionic crystal, 232, 233; unit cell, *233*
Sodium hydroxide, base, *394;* dissolving in water, 398, *398*
SOHO (Solar and Heliospheric Observatory), 539
Solar and Heliospheric Observatory (SOHO), 539
Solar eclipse, *475,* 475
Solar system, 462; asteroid, 489; forming, 468, 469, *469;* gravity, 467; Milky Way galaxy, 530, *530;* modeling, 494–495*lab;* nearest star, 509, *509;* planet orbiting sun, *464,* 464

Solder, changing physical property, 343, *343*
Solid, 256; changing state, 272; motion of particles in, 256, *256;* state of matter, 254, *254,* 259*tab*
Solubility, 387; differing, 393*lab*
Solute, 384
Solution, 383; acidic, 395, 399; basic, 399; common type(s) of, 384, 384*tab;* saturating, 387; Science Use v. Common Use, 384; water as, *389*
Solvent, polar, 390; water as, 389
Sombrero, spiral galaxy, *529*
Spacecraft, designing, 496; to Mercury, 479; to Venus, 480; to Mars, 481; to Jupiter, 482; to Saturn, 483
Specify, 90
Spectral line, 190, 508; hydrogen, 189, *189*
Spectroscope, 510, *510*
Spectrum, absorption, 510; atomic, 189; continuous, *510,* 510; Word Origin, 511
Speed, 56; acceleration, 60; average, 58, 67; average of a train, 123*act;* changing, *57,* 68, 69, *69;* constant, 57; finding average of a ball, 63*lab;* instantaneous, 57; measuring, *56;* slope, 67; velocity, 59
Speed-Time graph, 70–71*tab;* changing, 69
Spiral arm, spiral galaxy, 529
Spiral galaxy, component(s) of, 529, *529*
Standardized Test Practice. *See* Standards Assessment
Standards Assessment, 82–83, 124–125, 164–165, 212–213, 248–249, 284–285, 328–329, 374–375, 416–417, 452–453, 502–503, 544–545, 548–569
Standards Review, 79–81, 121–123, 161–163, 209–211, 245–247, 281–283, 325–327, 371–373, 449–451, 499–501, 541
Standards Study Guide, 78, 120, 160, 208–209, 244, 280, 324, 370, 412, 448, 498, 540
Star, balancing pressure and gravity, 523, *523;* brightness, 512; classifying, 514; coming to an end, 523; of constellation, 514, 514*tab;* core, 508, 522; forming, 519, *521,* 521, 536–537*lab;* how many and how far, 505*lab;* identifying element of, 511, 517*lab;* made of, 510; outside solar system, 462; producing light, *522,* 522; property of, 509*tab;* state of matter, 254; structure of, 508, *508;* temperature and color,

511, 512*tab;* type(s) of, 509; understanding variation, 516
Starch, complex carbohydrate, 440, *440*
Star cluster, 528, *528*
State, 254; changes in, 261–273, 276–277*lab;* Science Use v. Common Use, 256. *See also* Gas, Liquid, Matter, Solid
Static, Science Use v. Common Use, 99
Static friction, 99, *99*
Statistical matter, 279
Study Guide, 78, 120, 160, 208–209, 244, 280, 324, 370, 412, 448, 498, 540
Sublimation, *272,* **272**
Subscript, 352, 352*tab*
Substance, 381, *381;* Word Origin, 381
Substitute, 432
Sucralose, 242
Suffix, organic compound naming, 431
Sugar, 242
Sulfur, 422, 423
Sulfur dioxide, reacting with water vapor, 397
Sun, average distance to planet, *466,* 466*tab;* distance to Earth, 466; Earth orbiting, 472, *472;* elliptical path, *464,* 464; forming, 468; inner planet, 478; Milky Way galaxy, 50; planet circling, 462; state of matter, 254
Sunflower oil, polyunsaturated fat, 440
Supercluster, 532
Supergiant, star, 514
Supernova, 539; explosion, *525,* 525, 526
Swimming pool, testing pH, 403, *403*
Symbol, 221
Synthetic element, 306, 307, 308
Synthetic polymer, 438

T

Table, Apparent and Absolute Magnitude of Stars, 513; Atomic Structure of Diamond and Graphite, 315; Average Distance of Planets from the Sun, 466; Biomolecules and Polymer Biomolecules, 439; brightness of stars, 518*act;* chemical or physical change, 345*lab;* Chemical Properties of Common Substances, 339; chemical reaction with jewelry, 366*lab;* Common Types of Solution, 384; comparing pH value, 407*act;* Comparison of Coefficients and Subscripts, 352; data, 320*lab;* Densities of Some Common Materials, 133; determining pH,

Index

406*lab*; Diatomic Elements, 350; dissolving effervescent tablet, 348*lab*; Distance and Velocity of 12 Galaxies, 535*lab*; distance from sun to planets, 488*act*; Familiar States of Matter, 259; finding acidity level, 415*act*; Force and Length of Rubber Band, 95*lab*; Force of Friction, 105*lab*; Functional Groups, 433; Gravitational Forces on 70-kg Person, 97; Isotopes of Hydrogen, 200; Mass and Weight Data, 117*lab*; Modeling the Planets, 494*lab*; Newton's Laws of Motion, 112; Number of Atoms, 357*lab*; Origin of Element Names, 309; Percent Fatty Acid Present in Lipids, 443*lab*; Periodic table, 600; Physical Properties of Familiar Substances, 340; Planetary Data for the Inner Planets, 479; Planetary Data for the Outer Planets, 481; Planets, 486–487; Polarity and Living Systems, 444–445*lab*; Position-Time and Speed-Time Graphs, 70, 71; Properties of Atomic Particles, 175; Properties of Different Types of Stars, 509; Properties of Water, 426; The Relationship Between Surface Temperature and Color of Stars, 512; Revolution and Rotation Periods of the Planets, 463; scale model of planets, 485*lab*; Solubility Data, 393*lab*; Stars of Constellation, 514; Summary of Rutherford's Conclusions, 186; temperature change as chemicals react, 364*lab*; Turtle's Position and Time, 65; Types of Force, 102; Valence and Lewis Dot Diagrams, 223

Table salt, *See* sodium chloride

Technetium, first synthetic element, 307

Technology. *See* Real World Science

Telescope, adaptive optics, 538

Temperature, 262; changing as thermal energy is added, 265, *265, 267, 267;* gallium melting, *317,* 317; graphing, *64,* 64; increasing in nebula, 468; kinetic energy, *262,* 262; measuring, 262, *262;* melting and boiling points, 274*lab, 314, 314;* solubility, 387, *387;* star, 511, 512*tab*

Tension force, *101,* **101**

Test Practice. *See* Standards Assessment

Tetrahedral, molecule shape, *435,* 435; three-dimensional figure, 437*act*

Thermal, Word Origin, 316, 359

Thermal conductivity, 316, *316*

Thermal energy, 263; adding, *264,* 264, 270, 271; changing state, 264; changing temperature, 265, *265, 267,* 267; removing, *264,* 264, *271,* 271

Thermometer, measuring temperature, 262

Thomson, J. J., atomic model, 183, *183, 193*

Three Mile Island, accident, 207

Time, calculating, 59; graphing, *64,* 64, 65, *65,* 65*tab;* measuring, 63*lab*

Titan, largest Saturn moon, 483

Tortilla, carbohydrate, *440*

Tracer Element, 199

Traditional table, 294, *294*

Trans fat, labeling, 447

Transmutation, 304; artificial, 307

Triple bonds, 227

Trittium, 260, 305

Try at Home DataLab, Can You Identify Elements in a Star?, 517; Drawing a Scale Model of the Planets, 485; How are ionic radii and lattice energies of salts related?, 239; How are the boiling point and atmospheric pressure related?, 274; How can a graph show relative positions?, 55; How can you show a visual explanation of half-life?, 312; How do atoms differ?, 203; How does temperature change as chemicals react?, 364; How do solubilities differ?, 393; What can you learn from a graph?, 73; Where does the tablet go?, 348; Which fat is healthy for you?, 443

Try at Home MiniLab, Can you model the burning of methane?, 357; How big are the particles in an atom?, 181; How can you model molecules?, 229; How does the Moon change its shape in the sky?, 477; How much water is in celery?, 425; Modeling the Size of Nebulae, 520; Observing Fluid Motion, 255

Tufas, *380;* rock formation, 380

356, 363, 372, 392, 405, 414, 427, 436, 442, 450, 470, 476, 488, 493, 500, 516, 527, 534, 542

Understanding Scientific Terms, 595

Unique, 426

Unit cell, 233

Universal gravitation, law of, 468

Universe, evolution of, 534; expanding, 535*lab*

Unsaturated hydrocarbon, 430

Unununium, Roentgenium, 308

Uranium, 305; half-life, 306

Uranus, *484,* 484, 486–487*tab;* composition of, 484; outer planet, 481

Using Vocabulary, 54, 61, 72, 79, 94, 104, 114, 121, 137, 148, 154, 161, 179, 194, 202, 209, 228, 237, 245, 260, 273, 281, 299, 310, 318, 325, 344, 356, 363, 371, 392, 405, 413, 427, 436, 442, 449, 470, 476, 488, 493, 499, 516, 527, 534, 541

V

Valence, Word Origin, **223**

Vanillin, 429, *429*

Vaporization, 267; reversible process, 269, *269;* water, *270,* 270; Word Origin, 267

Vector, 51, 88; acceleration as, 60, 109; displacement as, 53; force as, 89; velocity as, 59; Word Origin, 51

Vehicle, burning fossil fuel, 397

Velocity, 59, 96; changing, 60; of vector, 89, 106–110

Venus, 486–487*tab;* covered by thick clouds, *479,* 479; exploring, 480, *480;* inner planet, 478

Vertical force, 103, *103*

Vertical group, 291, *291*

Vinegar, acetic acid, 349, 433; chemical change, *341,* 341, 355; comparing pH values, 401; properties of, 395; reaction with baking soda, 349, 355

Virgo cluster, *532,* 532

Visible, 189

Visual Check, 52, 56, 64, 65, 66, 69, 90, 100, 106, 133, 134, 136, 147, 151, 182, 196, 197, 200, 222, 225, 233, 265, 291, 298, 306, 341, 346, 349, 360, 362, 383, 389, 396, 426, 429, 430, 433, 439, 441, 462, 464, 474, 484, 509

Visualizing, Acid Precipitation, 397; Chemical Energy, 361; Crystal Structure, 234; Earth's Motion, 50; Formation of Stars, 521;

U

Unbalanced force, 91, 92, *92,* 96, *96;* changing direction of object, *108,* 108; Newton's second law of motion, 110; object in motion, *107,* 107; resting object, *106,* 106

Understanding Main Ideas, 54, 61, 72, 80, 94, 104, 114, 122, 137, 148, 154, 162, 179, 194, 202, 210, 228, 237, 246, 260, 273, 282, 299, 310, 318, 326, 344,

Index

Formation of the Solar System, 469;
The Heating Curve of Water, 270;
Organic Chemistry Nomenclature,
431; Synthetic element, 308; Tracer
Element, 199; Varying Elevations, 145
Vocabulary, 48, 56, 64, 88, 96, 106, 130,
140, 150, 174, 182, 195, 218, 230, 254,
261, 290, 301, 313, 338, 346, 358, 380,
394, 422, 428, 438, 462, 472, 489, 508,
519, 528. *See also* Using Vocabulary
Void, space between galactic clusters,
531
Volume, 130, 315, *315;* of atoms, 275;
block of iron, 131; buoyant force, 147,
147, 151; calculating, 132, 157*lab;*
measuring irregular solid, 136, *136,*
139*lab;* measuring liquid, 134, *134,*
139*lab;* measuring rectangular solid,
135, *135;* percent by, 388, *388*

W

Water, celery, 425*lab;* changing state,
270, *270,* 271; decomposing into
hydrogen gas and oxygen gas, 342,
342; density, 130, *130;* exerting force,
110*lab;* human body, 439; hydrocarbon dissolving, 432; polarity, 389, *389;*
polar molecule, *426,* 426; pressure,
145, *145;* property of, 426*tab;* reaction
with potassium, 338, *338;* as solvent,
389, *389*
Water vapor, 266, 271
Wavelength, spectral line, 190; visible
light, 189
Weight, 98, comparing to mass, 98,
116–117*lab*
West-Coast Events, 42–43, 168–169,
332–333, 456–457
White dwarf, low-mass star, *524,* 524
Word equation, *351,* 355
Word Origin, acceleration, 60; centripetal, 108; conduct, 340; endothermic,
362; exothermic, 360; friction, 99;
galaxy, 529; hydrogen, 354; isotope,
198; lipid, 439; luster, 294; molecule,
219; Nucleus, 175; pH, 399; polar, 426;
protein, 441; proton, 187; reaction,
353; saturate, 430; spectrum, 511; substance, 381; thermal, 316, 359; valence,
223; vaporization, 267; vector, 51
Writing in Science, 75*lab,* 81, 117*lab,*
123, 157*lab,* 163, 205*lab,* 211, 241*lab,*
247, 277*lab,* 283, 321*lab,* 327, 367*lab,*
373, 409*lab,* 415, 445*lab,* 495*lab,* 501,
537*lab,* 543
Wu, Chien-Shiung, 206

Y

Year, Earth orbiting sun, 463

Credits

Magnification Key: Magnifications listed are the magnifications at which images were originally photographed.

LM–Light Microscope

SEM–Scanning Electron Microscope

TEM–Transmission Electron Microscope

Acknowledgments: Glencoe would like to acknowledge the artists and agencies who participated in illustrating this program: Argosy Publishing; Articulate Graphics; Craig Attebery represented by Frank and Jeff Lavaty; Emily Damstra; Gary Hincks; Precision Graphics; Michael Rothman; Zoobotanica.

Photo Credits

List of Abbreviations:

AA=Animals Animals; CBS=Carolina Biological Supply; CB=Corbis-Bettmann; CP=Color-Pic; CMSP=Custom Medical Stock Photo; DRK=DRK Photo; ES=Earth Scenes; FPG=FPG International; GH=Grant Heilman Photography; LI=Liaison International; MP=Minden Pictures; OSF=Oxford Scientific Films; PA=Peter Arnold, Inc.; PR=Photo Researchers; PT=Phototake, NYC; SPL=Science Photo Library; SS=Science Source; TSM=The Stock Market; TSA=Tom Stack & Associates; TSI=Tony Stone Images; VU=Visuals Unlimited

Cover Roger Ressmeyer/CORBIS; vii Aqua Image/Alamy Images; viii Digital Instruments/Veeco/Photo Researchers; ix Charles D. Winters/Photo Researchers; x European Space Agency/Photo Researchers; xi Marshall Space Flight Center/NASA; xii Michael Dunning/Photo Researchers; xv Laura Sifferlin; xix CORBIS; **2** (t)Getty Images, (c)Jim Olive/Peter Arnold, Inc., (b)Getty Images; **4** (t)Science VU/USGS/Visuals Unlimited, (c)CORBIS, (b)Lawrence Migdale/SPL/Photo Researchers; **7** (t)Matt Meadows, (b)Amos Morgan/Getty Images; **8** (t)Steve Cole/Getty Images, (b)Andrew Lambert Photography/Photo Researchers; **9** Matt Meadows; **10** Horizons Companies; **11** Matt Meadows; **12** (t)Horizons Companies, (b) Mark Burnett/First Image; **13** (t)Comstock Images/Alamy Images, (b)Hemera Technologies/Alamy Images; **18** Matt Meadows; **21** (t)Fabrizio Cacciatore/Index Stock Imagery, (b)Michael Newman/PhotoEdit; **28** (l)Chuck Savage/CORBIS, (r)Getty Images; **31 32** Matt Meadows; **34** Kevin Schafer/CORBIS; **36** Stephen Street/Alamy Images; **38** (t)Peter Szekely/Alamy Images, (b)Martin Bond/Photo Researchers; **41** Visions of America, LLC/Alamy Images; **42** Joel W. Rogers/CORBIS; **42-43** (bkgd)Keith Lawson/Bettmann/CORBIS; **43** (t)Bettmann/CORBIS, (b)Keith Kent/Photo Researchers; **44** Mike Chew/CORBIS; **45** Matt Meadows; **48** Aerial Photos of New Jersey; **49** Matt Meadows; **50** Stephen R. Wagner; **63** Matt Meadows; **65** Gray Hardel/CORBIS; **68** Michael Dunning/Photo Researchers; **70** (t)Robert Holmes/CORBIS, (b)Adam Pretty/Getty Images; **71** (t)Eyecon Images/Alamy Images, (b)H. Armstrong Roberts; **74** Matt Meadows; **76** (t)George Steinmetz/CORBIS, (b)CORBIS; **77** (t)CORBIS, (b)Zuma/CORBIS; **84** Bobby Modell/National Geographic/Getty Images; **85** Horizons Companies; **88** (l)Altrendo Images/Getty Images, (r)Michael Newman/PhotoEdit; **89** (t)Joe McBride/CORBIS, (bl)Ed Bock/CORBIS, (br)E Braverman/Taxi/Getty Images; **90 91** Bob Daemmrich; **92** (t)David Young-Wolff/PhotoEdit, (b)Keith Kent/Peter Arnold, Inc.; **93** TRL Ltd./Photo Researchers; **95** Matt Meadows; **96** Doug Menuez/Getty Images; **98** NASA; **99** Horizons Companies; **100** (t)Horizons Companies, (b)Rhoda Sidney/Stock Boston/PictureQuest; **101** (t)Stockbyte, (b)CORBIS; **102** (l)Matt Meadows, (r)Lili K./Zefa/CORBIS; **103** Matt Meadows; **105** Horizons Companies; **107** (l)Tim Garcha/CORBIS, (r)Myrleen Cate/PhotoEdit; **111** Matt Meadows; **112** (t)Richard Hutchings, (b)Stephen Simpson/Getty Images; **113** Scott Cunningham; **114** (l)Denis Boulanger/Allsport, (r)Icon SMI/CORBIS, (b)Tony Freeman/PhotoEdit/PictureQuest; **117** Matt Meadows; **119** (t)James King-Holmes/Photo Researchers, (b) Lester Lefkowitz/Getty Images; **120** (t)Bettmann/CORBIS, (b)Larry Lee Photography/CORBIS; **126** Craig Aurness/CORBIS; **127** Horizons Companies; **130** (l)Horizons Companies, (r)Matt Meadows; **132** Laura Sifferlin; **134 136** Horizons Companies; **140** Peter Poby/CORBIS; **141** David Young-Wolff/PhotoEdit; **143** (t)Horizons Companies, (b)Matt Meadows; **144** Stephen Frink/Zefa/CORBIS; **145** (t)Bobby Model/National Geographic Image Collection, (cl)Richard Nowitz/National Geographic Image Collection, (cr)George Grall/National Geographic Image Collection, (bl)Ralph White/CORBIS, (br)CORBIS, (bkgd)Janet Dell Russell Johnson; **146** (t)Richard Bickel/CORBIS, (b)Aqua Image/Alamy Images; **148** Richard Bickel/CORBIS; **149 150** Horizons Companies; **151** Ryan McVay/Getty Images; **153** (t)Matt Meadows, (b)CORBIS; **155 156 157** Horizons Companies; **158** (t)CORBIS, (b)Tom Pantages; **159** (t)Ralph A. Clevenger/CORBIS, (b)Mark S. Wexler/Getty Images; **162** Horizons Companies; **164** (l)Getty Images, (r)Mark Burnett; **165** Vince Streano/Getty Images; **166** (tl bl)StudiOhio, (tr)Eclipse Studios, (br)Doug Martin; **168** Bettmann/CORBIS; **168-169** (bkgd)Ian M. Butterfield/Alamy Images; **169** (t)Susan Ragan/AP/Wide World Photos, (b)CORBIS; **170** ArSciMd/Photo Researchers; **171** Horizons Companies; **174** Digital Instruments/Veeco/Photo Researchers; **176** Horizons Companies; **177** (l)Tek Image/Photo Researchers, (r)AP Photo/NASA; **181 186** Horizons Companies; **187** Andrew Lambert Photography/Photo Researchers; **189** Douglas Mesney/CORBIS; **193** Laguna Design/SPL/Photo Researchers; **195** (tl)David Lees/CORBIS, (tr)Charles D. Winters/Photo Researchers, (b)Andrew Lambert Photography/Photo Researchers; **199** (tl)Lester Lefkowitz/CORBIS, (tr)Look GMBH/eStock Photo, (bl)David Parker/SPL/Photo Researchers, (br)Roger Ressmeyer/CORBIS; **204 205** Horizons Companies; **206** (t)Segre Collection/AIP/Photo Researchers, (b)Yann Arthus-Bertrand/Photo Researchers; **207** (t)Dale O'Dell/Omni-Photo Communications, (b)CORBIS; **214** Alfred Pasieka/Photo Researchers; **215** Horizons Companies; **218** (tl)Barry Runk/Grant Heilman Photography, (tcl)Fotopic/Omni-Photo Communications, (tcr)Index Stock Imagery, (tr)David Parket/Omni-Photo Communications, (bl)Sinclair Stammers/Photo Researchers, (br)Arnold Fisher/Photo Researchers; **221 227** Matt Meadows; **230** (tl)Creatas/Picture Quest, (r)Tony Freeman/PhotoEdit, (bl)David Wrobel/Visuals Unlimited; **231** Ken Lucas/Visuals Unlimited; **232** (tl)A. & F. Michler/Peter Arnold, Inc., (bl bc)Paul Silverman/Fundamental Photographs, (br)Roberto De Gugliemo/Photo Researchers; **233** Arnold Fisher/Photo Researchers; **234** (tl)Albert J. Copley/Visuals Unlimited, (tc tr)Kenneth Libbrecht/Caltech, (bl)Arnold Fisher/Photo Researchers, (br)file photo; **235** Matt Meadows; **240 241** Horizons Companies; **242** (t)Bettman/CORBIS, (b)IFA Bilderteam/eStock Photo; **243** (t)Dr. Tim Evans/Photo Researchers, (b)Anna Clopet/CORBIS; **250** Fabrik Studios/Index

Credits

PERIODIC TABLE OF THE ELEMENTS

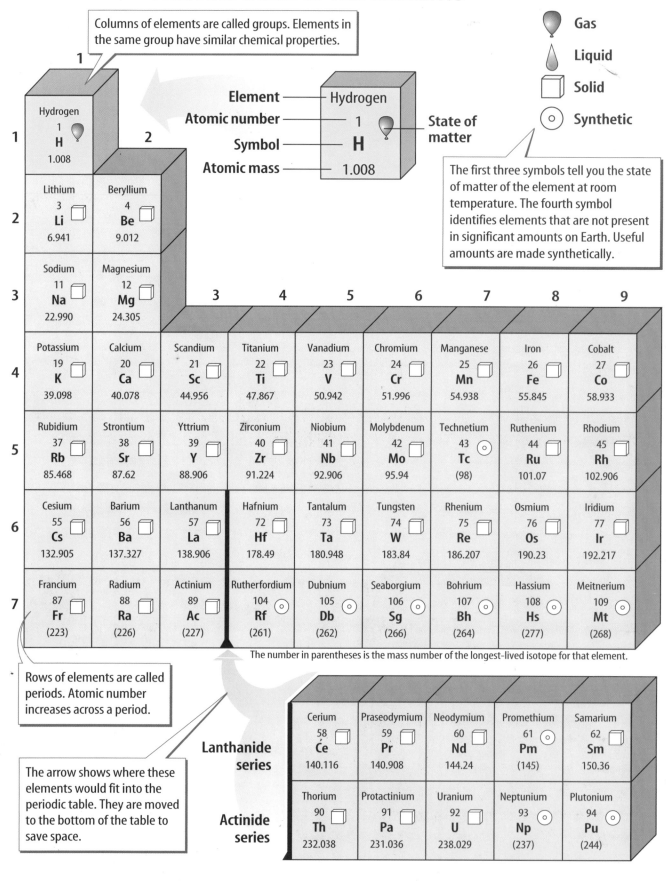

Columns of elements are called groups. Elements in the same group have similar chemical properties.

Gas
Liquid
Solid
Synthetic

Element — Hydrogen
Atomic number — 1
Symbol — H
Atomic mass — 1.008
State of matter

The first three symbols tell you the state of matter of the element at room temperature. The fourth symbol identifies elements that are not present in significant amounts on Earth. Useful amounts are made synthetically.

1	2	3	4	5	6	7	8	9
Hydrogen 1 **H** 1.008								
Lithium 3 **Li** 6.941	Beryllium 4 **Be** 9.012							
Sodium 11 **Na** 22.990	Magnesium 12 **Mg** 24.305							
Potassium 19 **K** 39.098	Calcium 20 **Ca** 40.078	Scandium 21 **Sc** 44.956	Titanium 22 **Ti** 47.867	Vanadium 23 **V** 50.942	Chromium 24 **Cr** 51.996	Manganese 25 **Mn** 54.938	Iron 26 **Fe** 55.845	Cobalt 27 **Co** 58.933
Rubidium 37 **Rb** 85.468	Strontium 38 **Sr** 87.62	Yttrium 39 **Y** 88.906	Zirconium 40 **Zr** 91.224	Niobium 41 **Nb** 92.906	Molybdenum 42 **Mo** 95.94	Technetium 43 **Tc** (98)	Ruthenium 44 **Ru** 101.07	Rhodium 45 **Rh** 102.906
Cesium 55 **Cs** 132.905	Barium 56 **Ba** 137.327	Lanthanum 57 **La** 138.906	Hafnium 72 **Hf** 178.49	Tantalum 73 **Ta** 180.948	Tungsten 74 **W** 183.84	Rhenium 75 **Re** 186.207	Osmium 76 **Os** 190.23	Iridium 77 **Ir** 192.217
Francium 87 **Fr** (223)	Radium 88 **Ra** (226)	Actinium 89 **Ac** (227)	Rutherfordium 104 **Rf** (261)	Dubnium 105 **Db** (262)	Seaborgium 106 **Sg** (266)	Bohrium 107 **Bh** (264)	Hassium 108 **Hs** (277)	Meitnerium 109 **Mt** (268)

The number in parentheses is the mass number of the longest-lived isotope for that element.

Rows of elements are called periods. Atomic number increases across a period.

The arrow shows where these elements would fit into the periodic table. They are moved to the bottom of the table to save space.

Lanthanide series

Cerium 58 **Ce** 140.116	Praseodymium 59 **Pr** 140.908	Neodymium 60 **Nd** 144.24	Promethium 61 **Pm** (145)	Samarium 62 **Sm** 150.36

Actinide series

Thorium 90 **Th** 232.038	Protactinium 91 **Pa** 231.036	Uranium 92 **U** 238.029	Neptunium 93 **Np** (237)	Plutonium 94 **Pu** (244)